Learning SOLIDWORKS 2018: A Project Based Approach

Sham Tickoo
Professor
Purdue University Northwest
Hammond, Indiana, USA

Contributing Authors
Tickoo Institute of Emerging Technologies (TIET)
Gurgaon, India

CADCIM Technologies
Indiana, USA

BPB PUBLICATIONS

ISBN: 978-93-88176-32-3
13th Revised and Updated Edition
(For Distribution in SAARC countries only)

Limits of Liability and Disclaimer of Warranty

Distributors

COMPUTER BOOK CENTRE
12, Shrungar Shopping Centre
M.G. Road
BENGALURU–560001
Ph: 25587923/25584641

BPB BOOK CENTRE
376 Old Lajpat Rai Market
DELHI-110006
Ph: 23861747

DECCAN AGENCIES
4-3-329, Bank Street
HYDERABAD-500195
Ph: 24756967/24756400

INFOTECH
G-2, Sidhartha Building, 96 Nehru Place
NEW DELHI-110019
Ph: 26438245

MICRO MEDIA
Shop No. 5, Mahendra Chambers
150 DN Rd. Next to Capital Cinema
V.T (C.S.T.) Station
MUMBAI-400001

BPB PUBLICATIONS
20, Ansari Road, Darya Ganj
New Delhi-110002
Ph: 23254990/23254991

Published by Manish Jain for BPB Publications, 20 Ansari Road, Darya Ganj
New Delhi-110002 and Printed Repro India Pvt. Ltd, Mumbai

DEDICATION

To teachers, who make it possible to disseminate knowledge to enlighten the young and curious minds of our future generations

To students, who are dedicated to learning new technologies and making the world a better place to live in

THANKS

To employees at CADCIM Technologies and Tickoo Institute of Emerging Technologies (TIET) for their valuable help

Note

If you are a faculty member, you can register by clicking on the following link to access the teaching resources: ***https://www.cadcim.com/Registration.aspx***. The student resources are available at ***https://www.cadcim.com***. We also provide **Live Virtual Online Training** on various software packages. For more information, write us at ***sales@cadcim.com***.

Table of Contents

This page is intentionally left blank

Preface

SOLIDWORKS 2018

SOLIDWORKS, originally developed by the SOLIDWORKS Corporation, USA, was acquired by Dassault Systemes, France, in 1997. Dassault Systemes is world's leading developer of product life cycle management (PLM) solutions. It is one of the fastest growing solid modeling software. It is a parametric, feature-based solid modeling tool that not only unites the three-dimensional (3D) parametric features with two-dimensional (2D) tools, but also addresses every design-through-manufacturing needs. SOLIDWORKS 2018 includes a number of customer requested enhancements, substantiating that it is completely tailored to address customers needs. Based mainly on the user feedback, this solid modeling tool is remarkably user-friendly and allows you to be productive from day one.

In SOLIDWORKS, you can easily generate the 2D drawing views of the components. The drawing views that can be generated include detailed, orthographic, isometric, auxiliary, section, and other views. You can use any predefined standard drawing document to generate the drawing views. Besides displaying the model dimensions in the drawing views or adding reference dimensions and other annotations, you can also add the parametric Bill of Materials (BOM) and balloons in the drawing view. If a component in the assembly is replaced, removed, or a new component is assembled, the modification will automatically reflect in the BOM placed in the drawing document. The bidirectional associative nature of this software ensures that any modification made in the model is automatically reflected in the drawing views and any modification made in the dimensions in the drawing views automatically updates the model.

In addition to creating solid models, assembly features, and drawing views, SOLIDWORKS enables you to effectively and easily create complex sheet metal components using a number of tools. Apart from modeling and detailing, you can print your solid models directly through 3D printers. You can also define position, orientation and other parameters of the model for 3D printing in SOLIDWORKS.

Learning SOLIDWORKS 2018: A Project Based Approach textbook has been written to help the users who are interested in learning 3D design. Real-world mechanical engineering industry examples and tutorials have been used to ensure that the users can relate the knowledge of this textbook with the actual mechanical industry designs. In this edition, one chapter has been added on mold design. Some of the main features of the textbook are as follows:

- **Project-based Approach**
  In this textbook, the author has used the project-based approach to explain the tools of SOLIDWORKS and their functioning. This approach guides users in understanding the usage of the tools as well as the procedure to design real world models.

- **Coverage of Major SOLIDWORKS Modes**
  All major modes of SOLIDWORKS are covered in this textbook. These include the **Part** mode, the **Assembly** mode, and the **Drawing** mode.

- **Tips and Notes**
  Additional information related to various topics is provided to the users in the form of tips and notes.

- **Learning Objectives**
  The first page of every chapter summarizes the topics that are covered in the chapter.

- **Self-Evaluation Test, Review Questions, and Exercises**
  Each chapter ends with Self-Evaluation Test that enables the users to assess their knowledge of the chapter. The answers to Self-Evaluation Test are given at the end of the chapter. Also, the Review Questions and Exercises are given at the end of the chapters and they can be used by the instructors as test questions and exercises.

Symbols Used in the Textbook

Note

The author has provided additional information to the users about the topic being discussed in the form of Notes.

Tip

Special information on various techniques is provided in the form of Tips that will increase the efficiency of the users.

Formatting Conventions Used in the Textbook

Please refer to the following list for the formatting conventions used in this textbook.

- Names of tools, buttons, options, toolbars, and are written in boldface. Example: The **Extrude Boss/Base** tool, the **Mid-Plane** option, the **OK** button, the **Features** toolbar, and so on.

- Names of CommandManager, PropertyManager, rollouts, dialog box, drop-down lists, spinners, selection boxes, areas, edit boxes, check boxes, and radio buttons are written in boldface. Example: The **Features CommandManager**, the **Boss-Extrude PropertyManager**, the **Open** dialog box, the **End Condition** drop-down list, the **Depth** spinner, the **Direction of Extrusion** selection box, the **Draft outward** check box, and so on.

- Values entered in edit boxes are written in boldface. Example: Enter **5** in the **Radius** edit box.

- Names and paths of the files are written in italics. Example: *C:\Documents\SOLIDWORKS\c08\c08_tut01*

Naming Conventions Used in the Textbook

Tool

If you click on an item in a toolbar and a command is invoked to create/edit an object or perform some action, then that item is termed as tool.

For example:
To Create: **Line** tool, **Smart Dimension** tool, **Extruded Boss/Base** tool
To Modify: **Fillet** tool, **Draft** tool, **Trim Surface** tool
Action: **Zoom to Fit** tool, **Pan** tool, **Copy** tool

If you click on an item in a toolbar and a dialog box is invoked wherein you can set the properties to create/edit an object, then that item is also termed as tool, refer to Figure 1.

For example:
To Create: Extruded Boss/Base tool, **Mirror** tool, **Rib** tool
To Modify: Flex tool, **Deform** tool

Flyout

A flyout is the one in which a set of tools are grouped together. You can identify a flyout with a down arrow on it. A flyout is given a name based on the types of tools grouped in it. For example, **Line** flyout, **View Settings** flyout, **Fillet** flyout, and so on; refer to Figure 1.

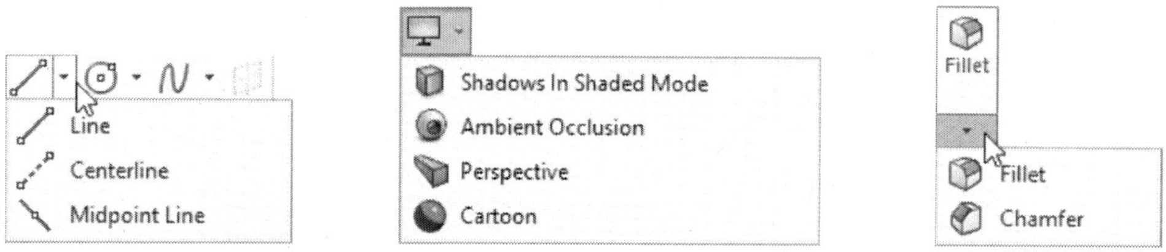

Figure 1 The ***Line, View Settings****, and* ***Fillet*** *flyouts*

PropertyManager

The naming conventions for the components in a PropertyManager are mentioned in Figure 2.

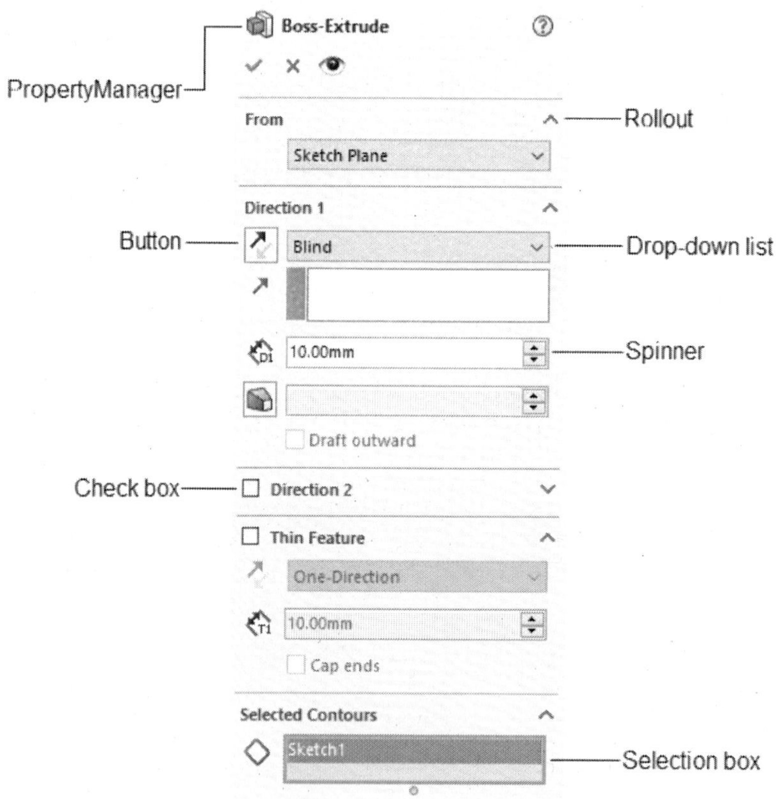

Figure 2 The ***Boss-Extrude PropertyManager***

Button

The items in a dialog box that has a 3D shape like a button is termed as **Button**. For example, **OK** button, **Cancel** button, and so on.

Free Companion Website

It has been our constant endeavor to provide you the best textbooks and services at affordable price. In this endeavor, we have come out with a Free Companion website that will facilitate the process of teaching and learning of SOLIDWORKS 2018. If you purchase this textbook, you will get access to the files on the Companion website.

To access the files, you need to register by visiting the **Resources** section at ***www.cadcim.com***. The following resources are available for the faculty and students in this website:

Faculty Resources

- **Technical Support**
  You can get online technical support by contacting ***techsupport@cadcim.com***.

- **Instructor Guide**
  Solutions to all review questions and exercises in the textbook are provided in the Instructor guide to help the faculty members test the skills of the students.

- **Part Files**
  The part files used in illustrations, examples, and exercises are available for free download.

Student Resources

- **Technical Support**
  You can get online technical support by contacting ***techsupport@cadcim.com***.

- **Part Files**
  The part files used in illustrations and examples are available for free download.

If you face any problem in accessing these files, please contact the publisher at ***sales@cadcim.com*** or the author at ***Stickoo@pnw.edu*** or ***tickoo525@gmail.com***.

Stay Connected

You can now stay connected with us through Facebook and Twitter to get the latest information about our textbooks, videos, and teaching/learning resources. To stay informed of such updates, follow us on Facebook ***(www.facebook.com/cadcim)*** and Twitter (***@cadcimtech***). You can also subscribe to our YouTube channel ***(www.youtube.com/cadcimtech)*** to get the information about our latest video tutorials.

This page is intentionally left blank

Chapter 1

Introduction to SOLIDWORKS 2018

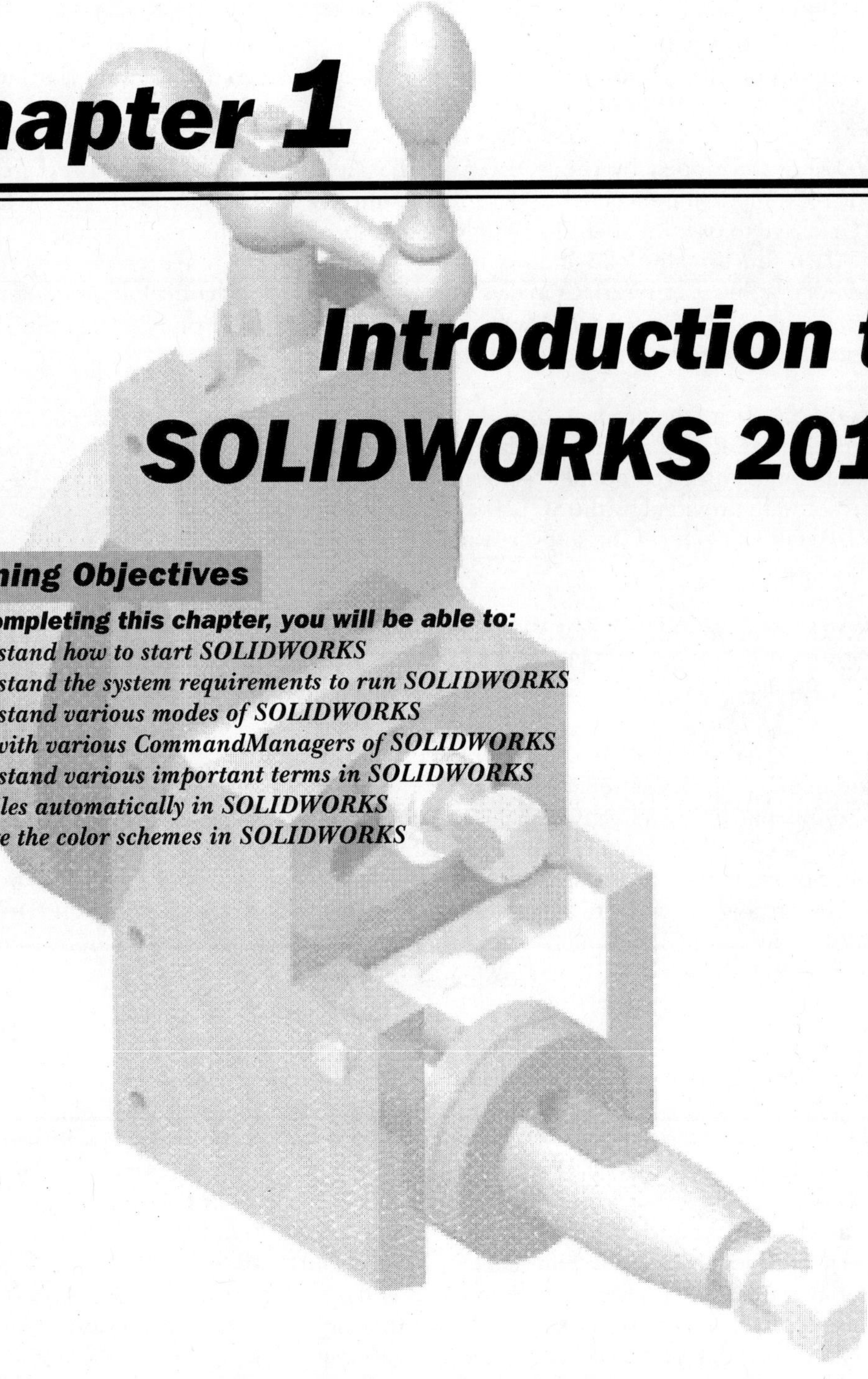

Learning Objectives

After completing this chapter, you will be able to:

- *Understand how to start SOLIDWORKS*
- *Understand the system requirements to run SOLIDWORKS*
- *Understand various modes of SOLIDWORKS*
- *Work with various CommandManagers of SOLIDWORKS*
- *Understand various important terms in SOLIDWORKS*
- *Save files automatically in SOLIDWORKS*
- *Change the color schemes in SOLIDWORKS*

INTRODUCTION TO SOLIDWORKS 2018

Welcome to the world of Computer Aided Design (CAD) with SOLIDWORKS. If you are a new user of this software package, you will be joining hands with thousands of users of this parametric, feature-based, and one of the most user-friendly software packages. If you are familiar with the previous releases of this software, you will be able to upgrade your designing skills with this improved release of SOLIDWORKS.

SOLIDWORKS, developed by the SOLIDWORKS Corporation, USA, is a feature-based, parametric solid-modeling mechanical design and automation software. SOLIDWORKS is the first CAD package to use the Microsoft Windows graphical user interface. The use of the drag and drop (DD) functionality of Windows makes this CAD package extremely easy to learn. The Windows graphic user interface makes it possible for the mechanical design engineers to innovate their ideas and implement them in the form of virtual prototypes or solid models, large assemblies, subassemblies, and detailing and drafting.

SOLIDWORKS is one of the products of SOLIDWORKS Corporation, which is a part of Dassault Systemes. SOLIDWORKS also works as platform software for a number of software. This implies that you can also use other compatible software within the SOLIDWORKS window. There are a number of software provided by the SOLIDWORKS Corporation, which can be used as add-ins with SOLIDWORKS. Some of the software that can be used on SOLIDWORKS's work platform are listed below:

SOLIDWORKS Motion	SOLIDWORKS Routing	ScanTo3D	eDrawings
SOLIDWORKS Simulation	SOLIDWORKS Toolbox	PhotoView 360	CircuitWorks
SOLIDWORKS Plastics	SOLIDWORKS Inspection	TolAnalyst	

As mentioned earlier, SOLIDWORKS is a parametric, feature-based, and easy-to-use mechanical design automation software. It enables you to convert the basic 2D sketch into a solid model by using simple but highly effective modeling tools. It also enables you to create the virtual prototype of a sheet metal component and the flat pattern of the component. This helps you in the complete process planning for designing and creating a press tool. SOLIDWORKS helps you to extract the core and the cavity of a model that has to be molded or cast. With SOLIDWORKS, you can also create complex parametric shapes in the form of surfaces. Some of the important modes of SOLIDWORKS are discussed next.

Part Mode

The **Part** mode of SOLIDWORKS is a feature-based parametric environment in which you can create solid models. In this mode, you are provided with three default planes named as **Front Plane**, **Top Plane**, and **Right Plane**. First, you need to select a sketching plane to create a sketch for the base feature. On selecting a sketching plane, you enter the sketching environment. The sketches for the model are drawn in the sketching environment using easy-to-use tools. After drawing the sketches, you can dimension them and apply the required relations in the same sketching environment. The design intent is captured easily by adding relations and equations and using the design table in the design. You are provided with the standard hole library known as the **Hole Wizard** in the **Part** mode. You can create simple holes, tapped holes, counterbore holes, countersink holes, and so on by using this wizard. The holes can be of any standard such as ISO, ANSI, JIS, and so on. You can also create complicated surfaces by using the surface modeling tools available in the **Part** mode. Annotations such as weld symbols, geometric tolerance, datum references, and surface finish symbols can be added to the model within the **Part** mode. The standard features that are used frequently can be saved as library features and retrieved when needed. The palette feature library of SOLIDWORKS contains a number of standard mechanical parts and features. You can also create the sheet metal components in this mode of SOLIDWORKS by using the related tools. Besides this, you can also analyze the part model for various stresses applied to it in the real physical conditions by using an easy and user-friendly tool called SimulationXpress. It helps you reduce the cost and time in physically testing your design in real testing conditions (destructive tests). You can also analyze the component during modeling in the SOLIDWORKS windows. In addition, you can work with the weld modeling within the **Part** mode of SOLIDWORKS by creating steel structures and adding weld beads. All standard weld types and welding conditions are available for your reference. You can extract the core and the cavity in the **Part** mode by using the mold design tools.

Assembly Mode

In the **Assembly** mode, you can assemble components of the assembly with the help of the required tools. There are two methods of assembling the components:

1. Bottom-up assembly
2. Top-down assembly

In the bottom-up assembly method, the assembly is created by assembling the components created earlier and maintaining their design intent. In the top-down method, the components are created in the assembly mode. You may begin with some ready-made parts and then create other components in the context of the assembly. You can refer to the features of some components of the assembly to drive the dimensions of other components. You can assemble all components of an assembly by using a single tool, the **Mate** tool. While assembling the components of an assembly, you can also animate the assembly by dragging. Besides this, you can also check the working of your assembly. Collision detection is one of the important features in this mode. Using this feature, you can rotate and move components as well as detect the interference and collision between the assembled components. You can see the realistic motion of the assembly by using physical dynamics. Physical simulation is used to simulate the assembly with the effects of motors, springs, and gravity on the assemblies.

Drawing Mode

The **Drawing** mode is used for the documentation of the parts or the assemblies created earlier in the form of drawing views. The procedure for creating drawing views is called drafting. There are two types of drafting done in SOLIDWORKS:

1. Generative drafting
2. Interactive drafting

Generative drafting is a process of generating drawing views of a part or an assembly created earlier. The parametric dimensions and the annotations added to the component in the **Part** mode can be generated in the drawing views. Generative drafting is bidirectionally associative in nature. Automatic BOMs and balloons can be added to an assembly while generating the drawing views of it.

In interactive drafting, you have to create the drawing views by sketching them using normal sketching tools and then add dimensions to them.

SYSTEM REQUIREMENTS

The system requirements to ensure the smooth functioning of SOLIDWORKS on your system are as follows:

- Microsoft Windows 10, Windows 8.1 or Windows 8 (64 bit only) or Windows 7 (SP1 required).
- Intel or AMD Processor with SSE2 support.
- 2 GB RAM minimum (8 GB recommended).
- Hard disk space 5 GB minimum (10 GB recommended).
- A certified graphics card and driver.
- Microsoft Office 2007 or later.
- Adobe Acrobat higher than 8.0.7.
- DVD drive and Mouse or any other compatible pointing device.
- Internet Explorer version 8 or higher.

GETTING STARTED WITH SOLIDWORKS

Install SOLIDWORKS 2018 on your system; the shortcut icon of SOLIDWORKS 2018 will automatically be created on the desktop. Double-click on this icon; the system will prepare to start SOLIDWORKS and after sometime, the SOLIDWORKS window will be displayed on the screen. On opening SOLIDWORKS for the first time, the **SOLIDWORKS License Agreement** dialog box will be displayed, as shown in Figure 1-1. Choose the **Accept** button in this dialog box; the **SOLIDWORKS 2018** window will open and the **SOLIDWORKS Resources** task pane will be displayed on the right. Also, the **Welcome - SOLIDWORKS 2018** dialog box is invoked simultaneously, as shown in Figure 1-2. This window can be used to open a new file or an existing file.

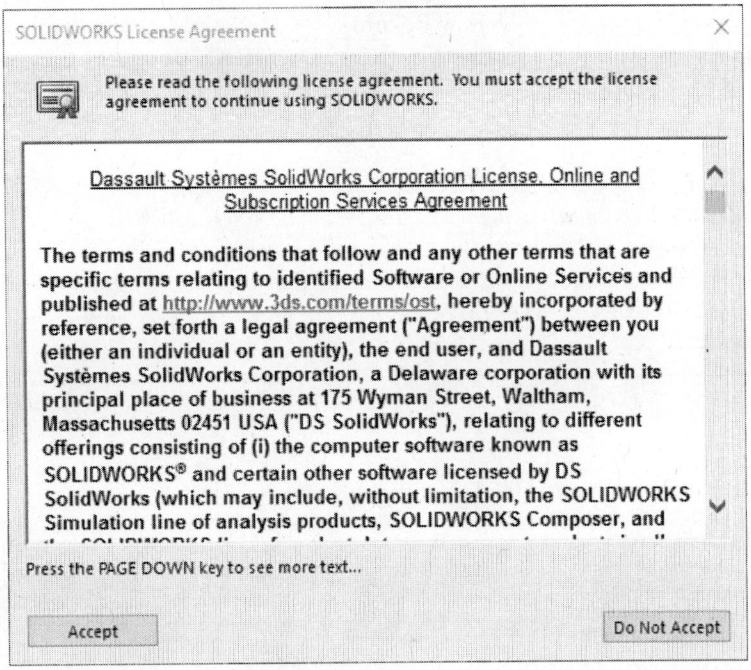

***Figure 1-1** The **SOLIDWORKS License Agreement** dialog box*

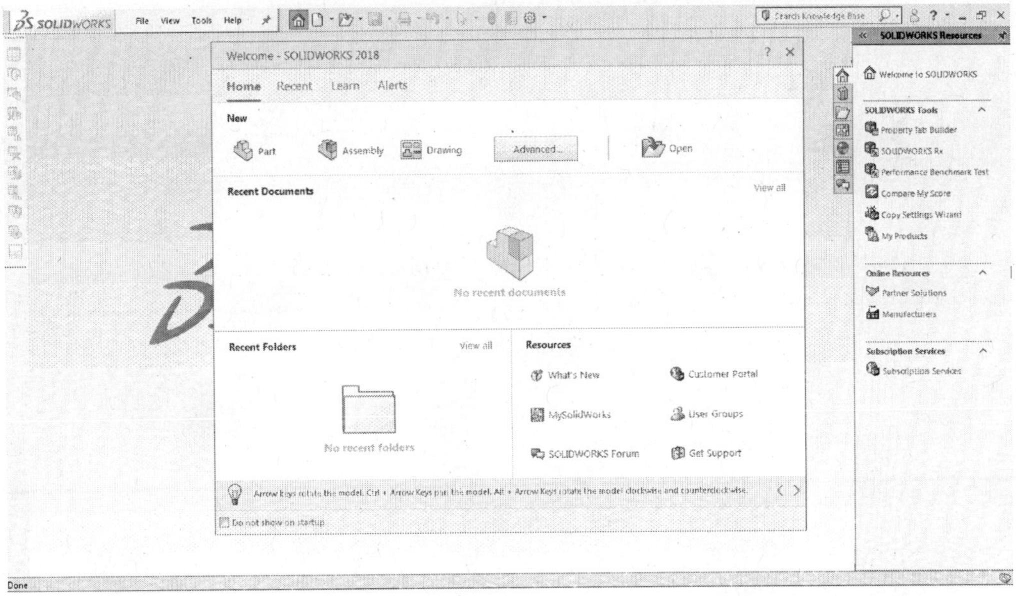

***Figure 1-2** The SOLIDWORKS 2018 window and the **SOLIDWORKS Resources** task pane*

If the **SOLIDWORKS Resources** task pane is not displayed or expanded, choose the **SOLIDWORKS Resources** button located on the right side of the window to display it. This task pane can be used to open online tutorials and to visit the website of SOLIDWORKS partners. Choose the **Part** button from the **Welcome - SOLIDWORKS 2018** dialog box or the **New** button from the Menu Bar to create a new document. If you start a new document using the **New** button from the Menu Bar then the **New SOLIDWORKS Document** dialog box will be displayed, as shown in Figure 1-3.

Note

If you are starting SOLIDWORKS 2018 for the first time, then on invoking the ***New SOLIDWORKS Document*** *dialog box or the* ***Welcome - SOLIDWORKS 2018*** *dialog box, the* ***Units and Dimension Standard*** *dialog box will be displayed, as shown in Figure 1-4. Using this dialog box, you can specify the default units and dimension standards for SOLIDWORKS. In this book, the unit system used is MMGS (millimeter, gram, second) and the dimension standard used is ISO.*

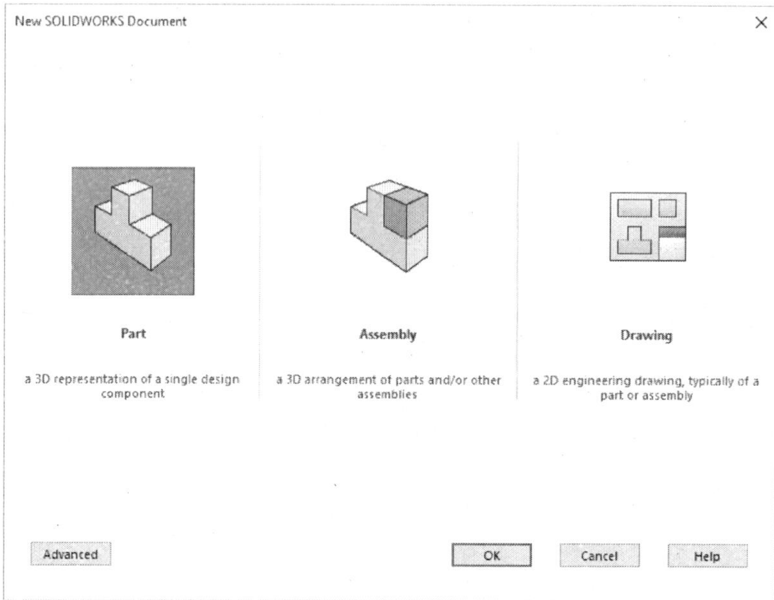

Figure 1-3 *The* ***New SOLIDWORKS Document*** *dialog box*

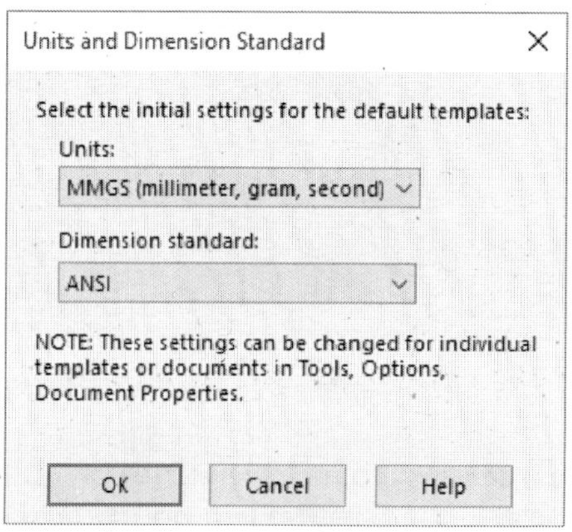

Figure 1-4 *The* ***Units and Dimension Standard*** *dialog box*

Choose the **Part** button to create a part model and then choose **OK** from the **New SOLIDWORKS Document** dialog box to enter the **Part** mode of SOLIDWORKS. Hover the cursor over the SOLIDWORKS logo; the SOLIDWORKS Menus will be displayed on the right of the logo. Note that the task pane is automatically closed once you start a new file and click in the drawing area. The initial screen display on starting a new part file of SOLIDWORKS using the **New** button in the Menu Bar is shown in Figure 1-5.

Tip

*In SOLIDWORKS, the tip of the day will be displayed at the bottom of the **Welcome - SOLIDWORKS 2018** dialog box. You can click on the arrows to view additional tips. These tips help you use SOLIDWORKS efficiently. It is recommended that you view at least 2 or 3 tips every time you start a new session of SOLIDWORKS 2018.*

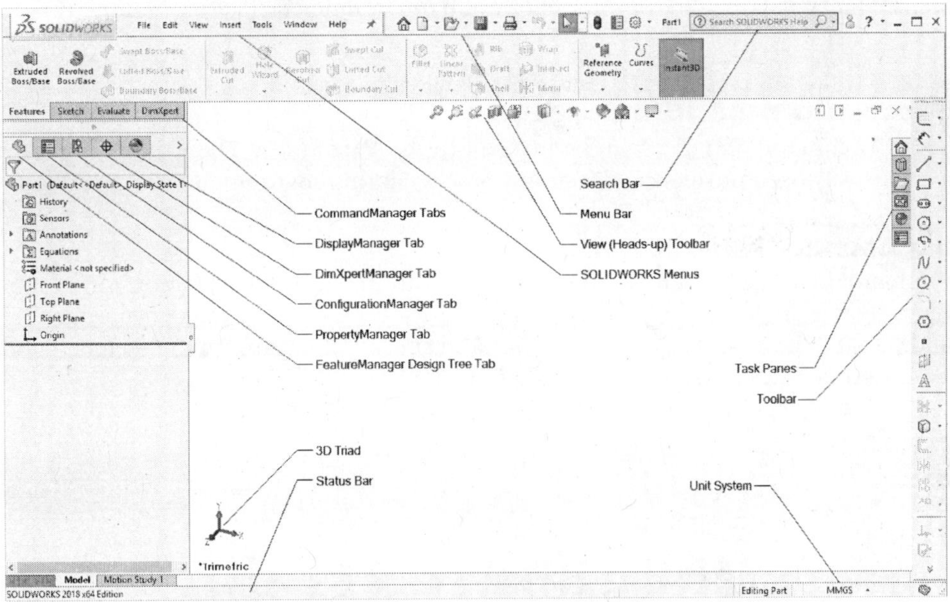

***Figure 1-5** The components of a new part document*

It is evident from the screen that SOLIDWORKS is a very user-friendly solid modeling software. Apart from the default CommandManager shown in Figure 1-5, you can also invoke other CommandManagers. To do so, move the cursor on a CommandManager tab and right-click; a shortcut menu will be displayed. Choose the required CommandManager from the shortcut menu; it will be added. Besides the existing CommandManager, you can also create a new CommandManager.

MENU BAR AND SOLIDWORKS MENUS

In SOLIDWORKS, the display area of the screen has been increased by grouping the tools that have similar functions or purposes. The tools that are in the **Standard** toolbar are also available in the Menu Bar, as shown in Figure 1-6. This toolbar is available above the drawing area. When you move the cursor to the arrow on the right of the SOLIDWORKS logo, the SOLIDWORKS menus will be displayed, as shown in Figure 1-7. You can also fix them by choosing the push-pin button.

Figure 1-6 The Menu Bar

Figure 1-7 The SOLIDWORKS menus

CommandManager

You can invoke a tool in SOLIDWORKS from four locations, CommandManager, SOLIDWORKS menus on top of the screen, toolbar, and shortcut menu. The CommandManagers are docked above the drawing area. While working with CommandManager, you will realize that invoking a tool from the CommandManager is the most convenient method to invoke a tool. Different types of CommandManagers are used for different design environments. These CommandManagers are discussed next.

Part Mode CommandManagers

A number of CommandManagers can be invoked in the **Part** mode. The CommandManagers that are extensively used during the designing process in this environment are described next.

Sketch CommandManager

This CommandManager is used to enter and exit the 2D and 3D sketching environments. The tools available in this CommandManager are used to draw sketches for features. This CommandManager is also used to add relations and smart dimensions to the sketched entities. The **Sketch CommandManager** is shown in Figure 1-8.

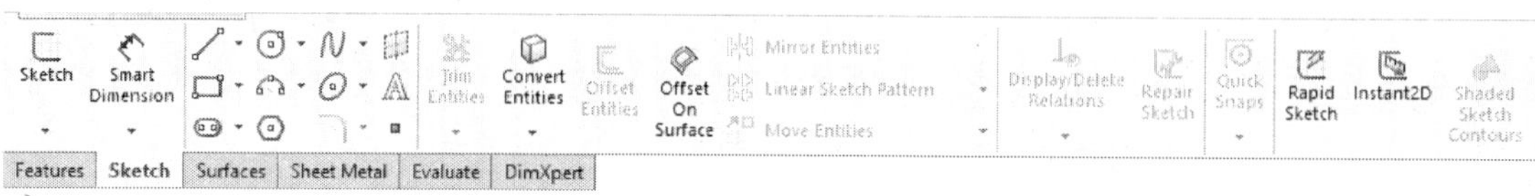

*Figure 1-8 The **Sketch CommandManager***

Features CommandManager

This is one of the most important CommandManagers provided in the **Part** mode. Once the sketch has been drawn, you need to convert the sketch into a feature by using the modeling tools. This CommandManager contains all the modeling tools that are used for feature-based solid modeling. The **Features CommandManager** is shown in Figure 1-9.

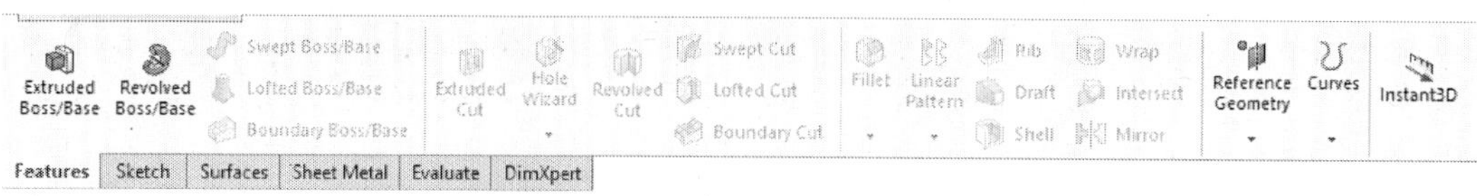

*Figure 1-9 The **Features CommandManager***

DimXpert CommandManager

This CommandManager is used to add dimensions and tolerances to the features of a part. The **DimXpert CommandManager** is shown in Figure 1-10.

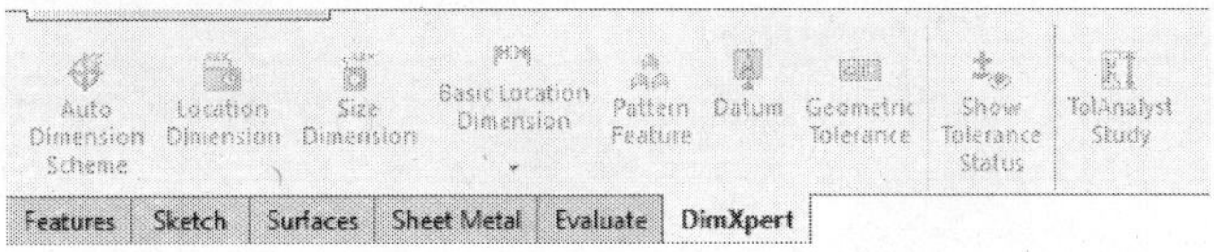

*Figure 1-10 The **DimXpert CommandManager***

Sheet Metal CommandManager

This CommandManager provides you the tools that are used to create the sheet metal parts. In SOLIDWORKS, you can also create sheet metal parts while working in the **Part** mode. This is done with the help of the **Sheet Metal CommandManager** shown in Figure 1-11.

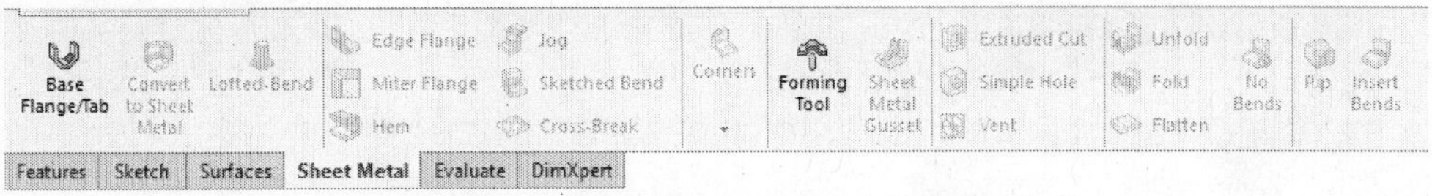

*Figure 1-11 The **Sheet Metal CommandManager***

Mold Tools CommandManager

The tools in this CommandManager are used to design a mold and to extract its core and cavity. The **Mold Tools CommandManager** is shown in Figure 1-12.

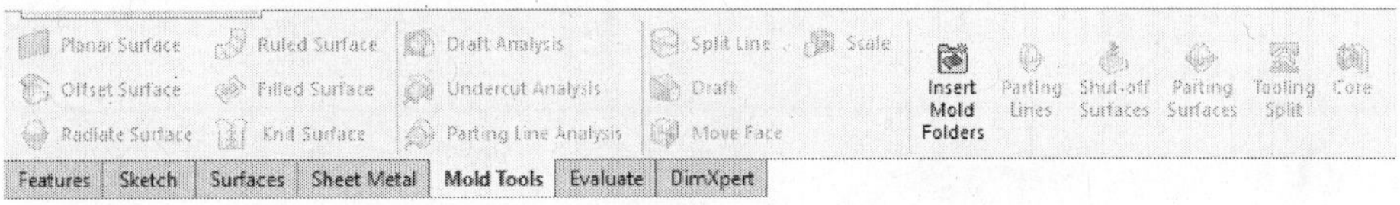

*Figure 1-12 The **Mold Tools CommandManager***

Evaluate CommandManager

This CommandManager is used to measure the distance between two entities, add equations in the design, calculate the mass properties of a solid model, and so on. The **Evaluate CommandManager** is shown in Figure 1-13.

*Figure 1-13 The **Evaluate CommandManager***

Surfaces CommandManager

This CommandManager is used to create complicated surface features. These surface features can be converted into solid features. The **Surfaces CommandManager** is shown in Figure 1-14.

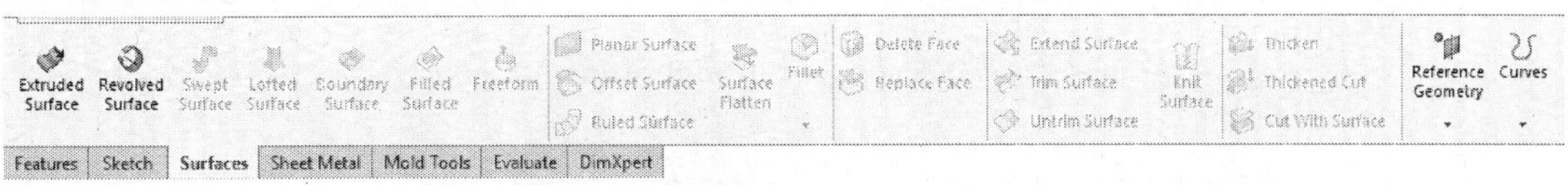

*Figure 1-14 The **Surfaces CommandManager***

Direct Editing CommandManager

This CommandManager consists of tools (Figure 1-15) that are used for editing a feature.

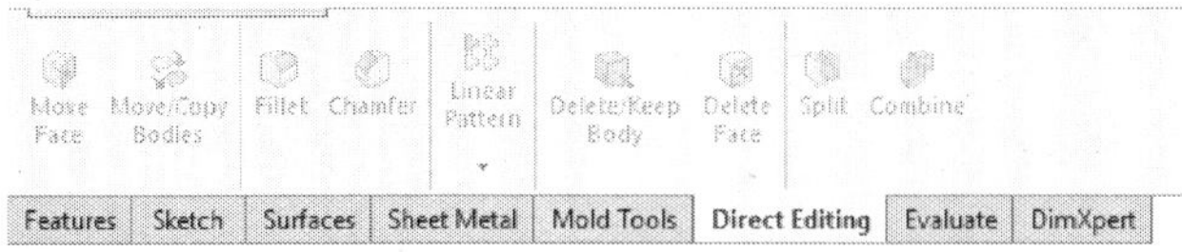

Figure 1-15 The ***Direct Editing CommandManager***

Data Migration CommandManager

This CommandManager consist of tools (Figure 1-16) that are used to work with the models created in other packages or in different environments.

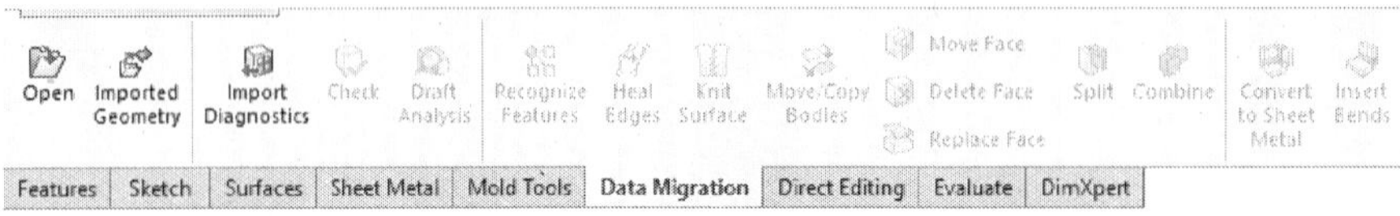

Figure 1-16 The ***Data Migration CommandManager***

Assembly Mode CommandManagers

The CommandManagers in the **Assembly** mode are used to assemble the components, create an explode line sketch, and simulate the assembly. The CommandManagers in the **Assembly** mode are discussed next.

Assembly CommandManager

This CommandManager is used to insert a component and apply various types of mates to the assembly. Mates are the constraints that can be applied to components to restrict their degrees of freedom. You can also move and rotate a component in the assembly, change the hidden and suppression states of the assembly and individual components, edit the component of an assembly, and so on. The **Assembly CommandManager** is shown in Figure 1-17.

Figure 1-17 The ***Assembly CommandManager***

Layout CommandManager

The tools in this CommandManager (Figure 1-18) are used to create and edit blocks.

Figure 1-18 The ***Layout CommandManager***

Drawing Mode CommandManagers

You can invoke a number of CommandManagers in the **Drawing** mode. The CommandManagers that are extensively used during the designing process in this mode are discussed next.

View Layout CommandManager

This CommandManager is used to generate the drawing views of an existing model or an assembly. The views that can be generated using this CommandManager are model view, three standard views, projected view, section view, aligned section view, detail view, crop view, relative view, auxiliary view, and so on. The **View Layout CommandManager** is shown in Figure 1-19.

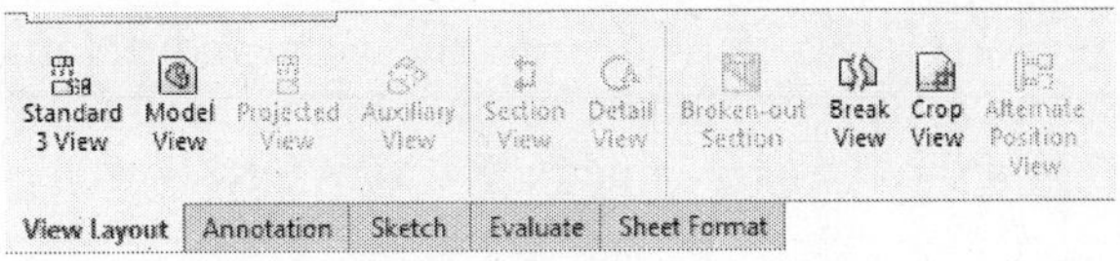

***Figure 1-19** The View Layout CommandManager*

Annotation CommandManager

The **Annotation CommandManager** is used to generate the model items and to add notes, balloons, geometric tolerance, surface finish symbols, and so on to the drawing views. The **Annotation CommandManager** is shown in Figure 1-20.

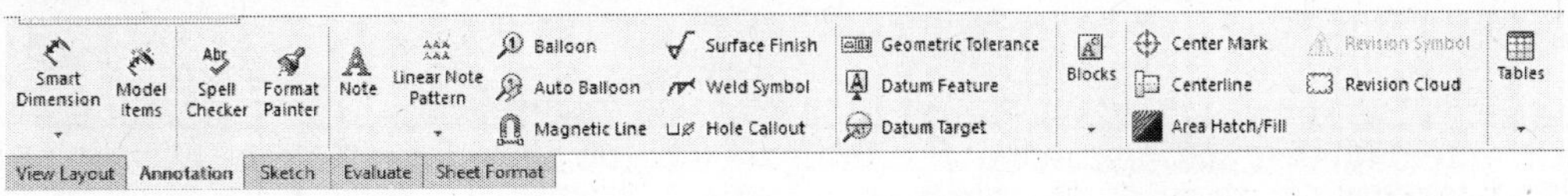

***Figure 1-20** The Annotation CommandManager*

Customized CommandManager

If you often work on a particular set of tools, you can create a customized CommandManager to cater to your needs. To do so, right-click on a tab in the CommandManager; a shortcut menu will be displayed. Choose the **Customize CommandManager** option from the shortcut menu; the **Customize** dialog box will be displayed. Also, a new tab will be added to the CommandManager. Click on this tab; a flyout will be displayed with **Empty Tab** as the first option and followed by the list of toolbars. Choose the **Empty Tab** option; another tab named **New Tab** will be added to the CommandManager. Rename the new tab. Next, choose the **Commands** tab from the **Customize** dialog box. Select a category from the **Categories** list box; the tools under the selected category will be displayed in the **Buttons** area. Select a tool, press and hold the left mouse button, and drag the tool to the customized CommandManager; the tool will be added to the customized CommandManager. Choose **OK** from the **Customize** dialog box.

To add all the tools of a toolbar to the new CommandManager, invoke the **Customize** dialog box and click on the new tab; a flyout will be displayed with **Empty Tab** as the first option followed by the list of toolbars. Choose a toolbar from the flyout; all tools in the toolbar will be added to the **New Tab** and its name will be changed to that of the toolbar.

To delete a customized CommandManager, invoke the **Customize** dialog box as discussed earlier. Next, choose the CommandManager tab to be deleted and right-click; a shortcut menu will be displayed. Choose the **Delete** option from the shortcut menu; the CommandManager will be deleted.

Note
You cannot delete the default CommandManagers.

TOOLBAR

In SOLIDWORKS, you can choose most of the tools from the CommandManager or from the SOLIDWORKS menus. However, if you hide the CommandManager to increase the drawing area, you can use the toolbars to invoke a tool. To display a toolbar, right-click on the CommandManager; the list of toolbars available in SOLIDWORKS will be displayed. Select the required toolbar.

Pop-up Toolbar

A pop-up toolbar will be displayed when you select a feature or an entity and do not move the mouse. Figure 1-21 shows a pop-up toolbar displayed on selecting a feature. Remember that this toolbar will disappear if you move the cursor away from the selected feature or entity.

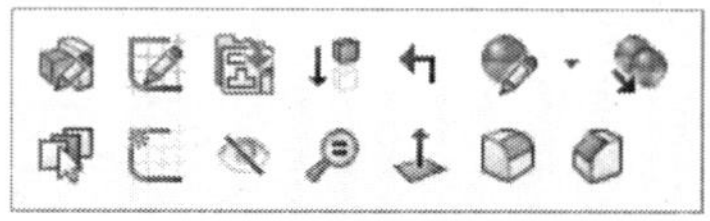

Figure 1-21 *The pop-up toolbar*

You can switch off the display of the pop-up toolbar. To do so, invoke the **Customize** dialog box. In the **Context toolbar settings** area of the **Toolbars** tab, the **Show on selection** check box will be selected by default. It means that the display of the pop-up toolbar is on, by default. To turn off the display of the pop-up toolbar, clear this check box and choose the **OK** button.

View (Heads-Up) Toolbar

In SOLIDWORKS, some of the display tools have been grouped together and are displayed in the drawing area in a toolbar, as shown in Figure 1-22. This toolbar is known as **View (Heads-Up)** toolbar.

Figure 1-22 *The* ***View (Heads-Up)*** *toolbar*

Customizing the CommandManagers and Toolbars

In SOLIDWORKS, all buttons are not displayed by default in toolbars or CommandManagers. You need to customize and add buttons to them according to your need and specifications. Follow the procedure given below to customize the CommandManagers and toolbars:

1. Choose **Tools > Customize** from the SOLIDWORKS menus or right-click on a CommandManager and choose the **Customize** option to display the **Customize** dialog box.
2. Choose the **Commands** tab from the **Customize** dialog box.
3. Select a category from the **Categories** area of the **Customize** dialog box; the tools available in the selected category will be displayed in the **Buttons** area.
4. Click on a button in the **Buttons** area; the description of the selected button will be displayed in the **Description** area.
5. Press and hold the left mouse button on a button in the **Buttons** area of the **Customize** dialog box.

6. Drag the mouse to a CommandManager or a toolbar and then release the left mouse button to place the button on that CommandManager or toolbar. Next, choose **OK**.

To remove a tool from the CommandManager or toolbar, invoke the **Customize** dialog box and drag the tool that you need to remove from the CommandManager to the graphics area.

Shortcut Bar

On pressing the S key on the keyboard, some of the tools that can be used in the current mode will be displayed near the cursor. This is called as shortcut bar. To customize the tools in the shortcut bar, right-click on it, and choose the **Customize** option. Then, follow the procedure discussed earlier.

Mouse Gestures

In SOLIDWORKS, when you press the right mouse button and drag the cursor in any direction, a set of tools that are arranged radially will be displayed. This is called as Mouse Gesture. After displaying the tools by using the Mouse Gesture, move the cursor over a particular tool to invoke it. By default, four tools will be displayed in a Mouse Gesture. However, you can customize the Mouse Gesture and display 2, 3, 4, 8 or 12 tools. To customize a Mouse Gesture, invoke the **Customize** dialog box. Next, choose the **Mouse Gestures** tab; the **Mouse Gesture Guide** window will be displayed, showing various tools that are used in different environments, refer to Figure 1-23. Now you can drag and drop the required tools to this window. Next, specify the options in the appropriate field and choose the **OK** button.

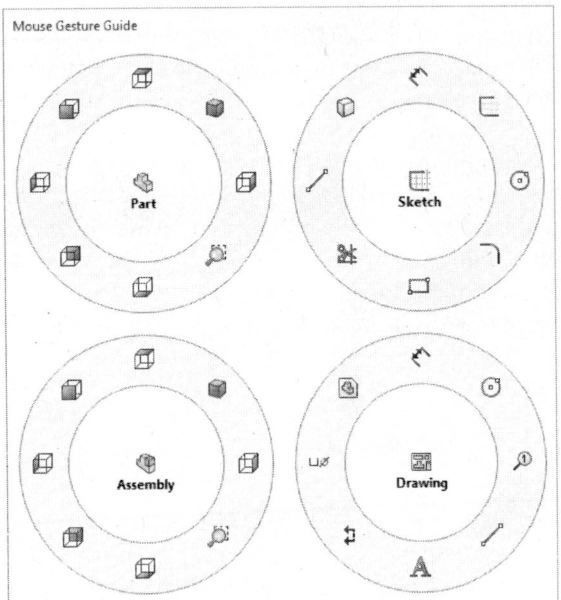

Figure 1-23 *Tools displayed in the* ***Mouse Gesture Guide*** *window in different environments*

Tip

You can display some of the tools by pressing a key on the keyboard. To assign a shortcut key to a tool, invoke the ***Customize*** *toolbar and choose the* ***Keyboard*** *tab. Enter the key in the* ***Shortcut*** *column for the corresponding tool and choose* ***OK****.*

DIMENSIONING STANDARDS AND UNITS

While installing SOLIDWORKS on your system, you can specify the units and dimensioning standards for dimensioning the model. There are various dimensioning standards such as ANSI, ISO, DIN, JIS, BSI, and GOST that can be specified for dimensioning a model and units such as millimeters, centimeters, inches, and so on. This book follows millimeters as the unit for dimensioning and ISO as the dimension standard. Therefore, it is recommended that you install SOLIDWORKS with ISO as the dimensioning standard and millimeter as units.

IMPORTANT TERMS AND THEIR DEFINITIONS

Before you proceed, it is very important to understand the following terms as they have been widely used in this book.

Feature-based Modeling

A feature is defined as the smallest building block that can be modified individually. In SOLIDWORKS, the solid models are created by integrating a number of these building blocks. A model created in SOLIDWORKS is a combination of a number of individual features that are related to one another, directly or indirectly. These features understand their fits and functions properly and therefore can be modified at any time during the design process. If proper design intent is maintained while creating the model, these features automatically adjust their values to any change in their surrounding. This provides greater flexibility to the design.

Parametric Modeling

The parametric nature of a software package is defined as its ability to use the standard properties or parameters in defining the shape and size of a geometry. The main function of this property is to drive the selected geometry to a new size or shape without considering its original dimensions. You can change or modify the shape and size of any feature at any stage of the design process. This property makes the designing process very easy.

For example, consider the design of the body of a pipe housing shown in Figure 1-24. In order to change the design by modifying the diameter of the holes and the number of holes on the front, top, and bottom faces, you need to select the feature and change the diameter and the number of instances in the pattern. The modified design is shown in Figure 1-25.

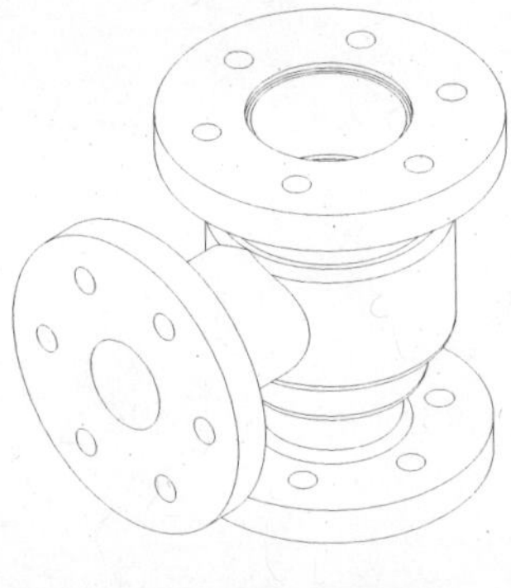

Figure 1-24 Body of pipe housing

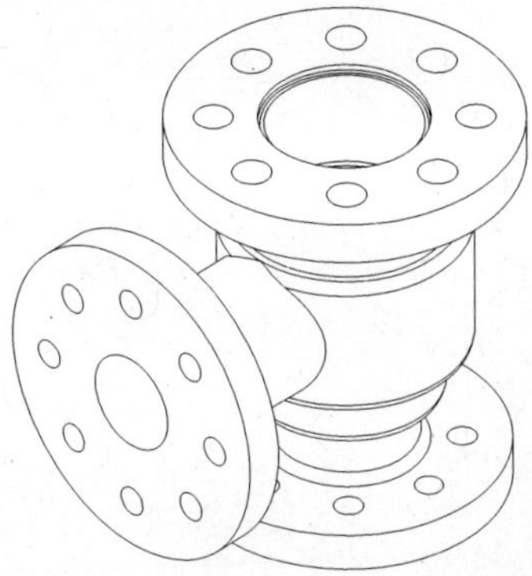

Figure 1-25 Design after modifications

Bidirectional Associativity

As mentioned earlier, SOLIDWORKS has different modes such as **Part**, **Assembly**, and **Drawing**. There exists bidirectional associativity among all these modes. This associativity ensures that any modification made in the model in any one of these modes of SOLIDWORKS is automatically reflected in the other modes immediately. For example, if you modify the dimension of a part in the **Part** mode, the change will reflect in the **Assembly** and **Drawing** modes as well. Similarly, if you modify the dimensions of a part in the drawing views generated in the **Drawing** mode, the changes will reflect in the **Part** and **Assembly** modes. Consider the drawing views shown in Figure 1-26 of the body of the pipe housing shown in Figure 1-24. Now, when you modify the model of the body of the pipe housing in the **Part** mode, the changes will reflect in the **Drawing** mode automatically. Figure 1-27 shows the drawing views of the pipe housing after increasing the diameter and the number of holes.

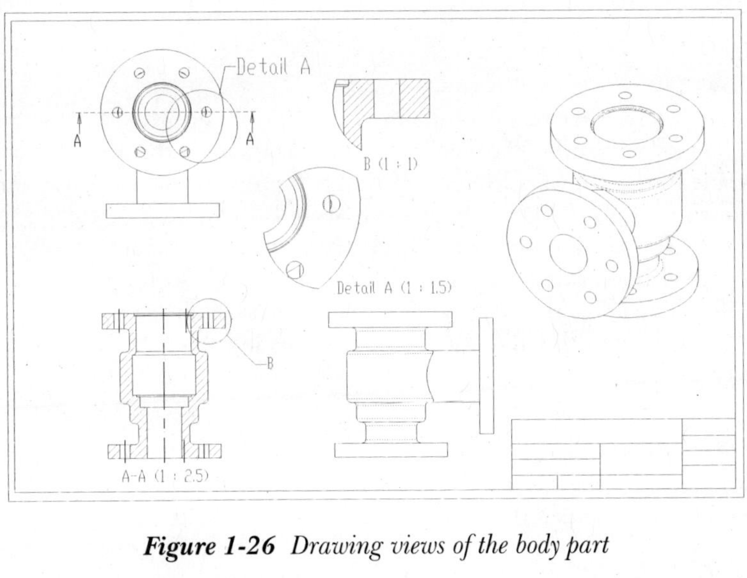

Figure 1-26 Drawing views of the body part

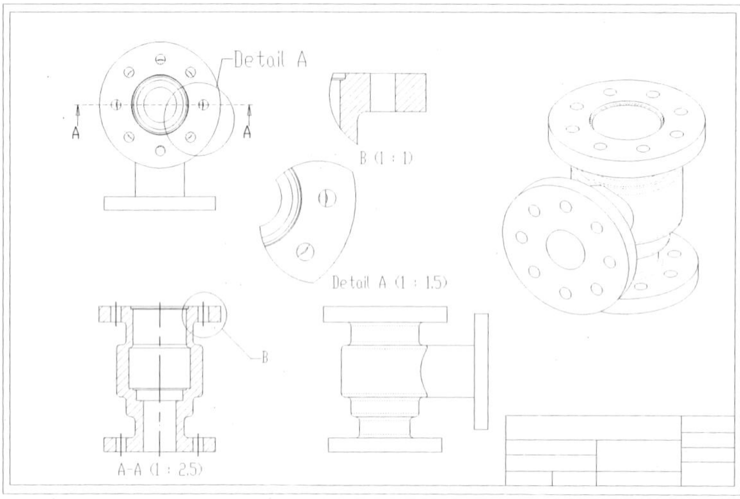

Figure 1-27 Drawing views after modifications

Windows Functionality

SOLIDWORKS is a Windows-based 3D CAD package. It uses Window's graphical user interface and the functionalities such as drag and drop, copy paste, and so on. For example, consider that you have created a hole feature on the front planar surface of a model. Now, to create another hole feature on the top planar surface of the same model, select the hole feature and press CTRL+C (copy) on the keyboard. Next, select the top planar surface of the base feature and press CTRL+V (paste); the copied hole feature will be pasted on the selected face. You can also drag and drop the standard features from the **Design Library** task pane to the face of the model on which the feature is to be added.

SWIFT Technology

SWIFT is the acronym for SOLIDWORKS Intelligent Feature Technology. This technology makes SOLIDWORKS more user-friendly. This technology helps the user think more about the design rather than the tools in the software. Therefore, even the novice users find it very easy to use SOLIDWORKS for their design. The tools that use SWIFT Technology are called as *Xperts*. The different *Xperts* in SOLIDWORKS are **SketchXpert, FeatureXpert, DimXpert, AssemblyXpert, FilletXpert, DraftXpert,** and **MateXpert**. The **SketchXpert** in the sketching environment is used to resolve the conflicts that arise while applying relations to a sketch. Similarly, the **FeatureXpert** in the Part mode is used when the fillet and draft features fail. You will learn about these tools in the later chapters.

Geometric Relations

Geometric relations are the logical operations that are performed to add a relationship (like tangent or perpendicular) between the sketched entities, planes, axes, edges, or vertices. When adding relations, one entity can be a sketched entity and the other entity can be a sketched entity, or an edge, face, vertex, origin, plane, and so on. There are two methods to create the geometric relations: Automatic Relations and Add Relations.

Automatic Relations

The sketching environment of SOLIDWORKS has been provided with the facility of applying auto relations. This facility ensures that the geometric relations are applied to the sketch automatically while creating it. Automatic relations are also applied in the **Drawing** mode while working with interactive drafting.

Add Relations

Add relations is used to add geometric relations manually to the sketch. The sixteen types of geometric relations that can be manually applied to the sketch are as follows:

Horizontal

This relation forces the selected line segment to become a horizontal line. You can also select two points and force them to be aligned horizontally.

Vertical

This relation forces the selected line segment to become a vertical line. You can also select two points and force them to be aligned vertically.

Collinear

This relation forces the two selected entities to be placed in the same line.

Coradial

This relation is applied to any two selected arcs, two circles, or an arc and a circle to force them to become equi-radius and also to share the same center point.

Perpendicular

This relation is used to make selected line segment perpendicular to another selected segment.

Parallel

This relation is used to make the selected line segment parallel to another selected segment.

Tangent

This relation is used to make the selected line segment, arc, spline, circle, or ellipse tangent to another arc, circle, spline, or ellipse.

Note

In case of splines, relations are applied to their control points.

Concentric

This relation forces two selected arcs, circles, a point and an arc, a point and a circle, or an arc and a circle to share the same center point.

Midpoint

This relation forces a selected point to be placed on the mid point of a selected line.

Intersection

This relation forces a selected point to be placed at the intersection of two selected entities.

Coincident
This relation is used to make two points, a point and a line, or a point and an arc coincident.

Equal
The equal relation forces the two selected lines to become equal in length. This relation is also used to force two arcs, two circles, or an arc and a circle to have equal radii.

Symmetric
The symmetric relation is used to force the selected entities to become symmetrical about a selected center line, so that they remain equidistant from the center line.

Fix
This relation is used to fix the selected entity to a particular location with respect to the coordinate system. The endpoints of the fixed line, arc, spline, or elliptical segment are free to move along the line.

Pierce
This relation forces the sketched point to be coincident to the selected axis, edge, or curve where it pierces the sketch plane. The sketched point in this relation can be the end point of the sketched entity.

Merge
This relation is used to merge two sketched points or end points of entities.

Blocks
A block is a set of entities grouped together to act as a single entity. Blocks are used to create complex mechanisms as sketches and check their functioning before developing them into complex 3D models.

Library Feature
Generally, in a mechanical design, some features are used frequently. In most of the other solid modeling tools, you need to create these features whenever you need them. However, SOLIDWORKS allows you to save these features in a library so that you can retrieve them whenever you want. This saves a lot of designing time and effort of a designer.

Design Table
Design tables are used to create a multi-instance parametric component. For example, some components in your organization may have the same geometry but different dimensions. Instead of creating each component of the same geometry with a different size, you can create one component and then using the design table, create different instances of the component by changing the dimension as per your requirement. You can access all these components in a single part file.

Equations

Equations are the analytical and numerical formulae applied to the dimensions during the sketching of the feature sketch or after sketching the feature sketch. The equations can also be applied to the placed features.

Collision Detection

Collision detection is used to detect interference and collision between the parts of an assembly when the assembly is in motion. While creating the assembly in SOLIDWORKS, you can detect collision between parts by moving and rotating them.

What's Wrong Functionality

While creating a feature of the model or after editing a feature, if the geometry of the feature is not compatible and the system is not able to construct that feature, then the **What's Wrong** functionality is used to detect the possible error that may have occurred while creating the feature.

SimulationXpress

In SOLIDWORKS, you are provided with an analysis tool named as SimulationXpress, which is used to execute the static or stress analysis. In SimulationXpress, you can only execute the linear static analysis. Using the linear static analysis, you can calculate the displacement, strain, and stresses applied on a component with the effect of material, various loading conditions, and restraint conditions applied on a model. A component fails when the stress applied on it reaches beyond a certain permissible limit. The Static Nodal stress plot of the crane hook designed in SOLIDWORKS and analyzed using SimulationXpress is shown in Figure 1-28.

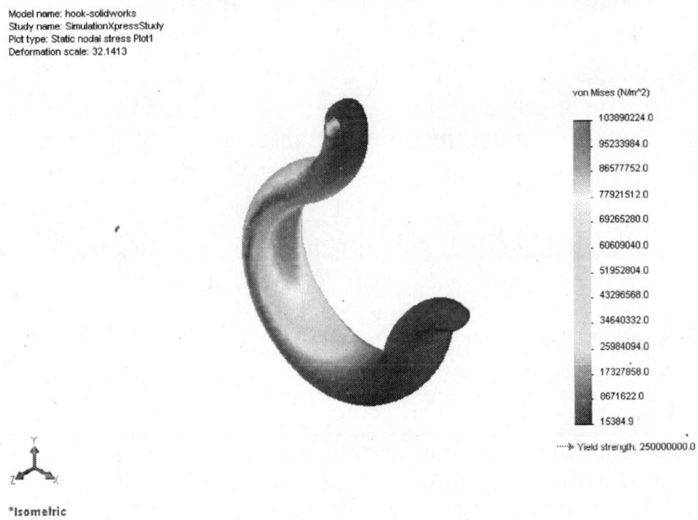

Figure 1-28 The crane hook analyzed using SimulationXpress

Physical Dynamics

The Physical Dynamics is used to observe the motion of the assembly. With this option selected, the component dragged in the assembly applies a force to the component that it touches. As a result, the other component moves or rotates within its allowable degrees of freedom.

Physical Simulation

The Physical Simulation is used to simulate the assemblies created in the assembly environment of SOLIDWORKS. You can assign and simulate the effect of different simulation elements such as linear, rotary motors, and gravity to the assemblies. After creating a simulating assembly, you can record and replay the simulation.

Seed Feature

The original feature that is used as the parent feature to create any type of pattern or mirror feature is known as the seed feature. You can edit or modify only a seed feature. You cannot edit the instances of the pattern feature.

FeatureManager Design Tree

The **FeatureManager Design Tree** is one the most important components of SOLIDWORKS screen. It contains information about default planes, materials, lights, and all the features that are added to the model. When you add features to the model using various modeling tools, the same are also displayed in the **FeatureManager Design Tree**. You can easily select and edit the features using the **FeatureManager Design Tree**. When you invoke any tool to create a feature, the **FeatureManager Design Tree** is replaced by the respective PropertyManager. At this stage, the **FeatureManager Design Tree** is displayed in the drawing area.

Absorbed Features

Features that are directly involved in creating other features are known as absorbed features. For example, the sketch of an extruded feature is an absorbed feature of the extruded feature.

Child Features

The features that are dependent on their parent feature and cannot exist without their parent features are known as child features. For example, consider a model with extrude feature and filleted edges. If you delete the extrude feature, the fillet feature will also get deleted because its existence is not possible without its parent feature.

Dependent Features

Dependent features are those features that depend on their parent feature but can still exist without the parent feature with some minor modifications. If the parent feature is deleted, then by specifying other references and modifying the feature, you can retain the dependent features.

AUTO-BACKUP OPTION

SOLIDWORKS also allows you to set the option to save the SOLIDWORKS document automatically after a regular interval of time. While working on a design project, if the system crashes, you may lose the unsaved design data. If the auto-backup option is turned on, your data will be saved automatically after regular intervals. To turn this option on, choose **Tools > Options** from the SOLIDWORKS menus; the **System Options - General** dialog box will be displayed. Select the **Backup/Recover** option from the display area provided on the left of this dialog box. Next, choose the **Save auto-recover information every** check box in the **Auto-recover** area, if it is not chosen by default. On doing so, the spinner and the drop-down list provided on the right of the check box will be enabled. Use the spinner and the drop-down list to set the number of changes or minutes after which the document will be saved automatically. By default, the backup files are saved at the location *X:\Users\<name of your machine>AppData\Local\TempSWBackupDirectory\swxauto* (where *X* is the drive in which you have installed SOLIDWORKS 2018 and the *AppData* folder is a hidden folder). You can also change the path of this location. To change this path, choose the button provided on the right of the edit box; the **Browse For Folder** dialog box will be displayed. You can specify the location of the folder to save the backup files using this dialog box. If you need to save the backup files in the current folder, select the **Number of backup copies per document** check box and then select the **Save backup files in the same location as the original** radio button. You can set the number of backup files that you need to save using the **Number of backup copies per document** spinner. After setting all options, choose the **OK** button from the **System Options - Backup/Recover** dialog box.

SELECTING HIDDEN ENTITIES

Sometimes, while working on a model, you need to select an entity that is either hidden behind another entity or is not displayed in the current orientation of the view. SOLIDWORKS allows you to select these entities using the **Select Other** option. For example, consider that you need to select the back face of a model, which is not displayed in the current orientation. In such a case, you need to move the cursor over the visible face such that the cursor is also in line with the back face of the model. Now, click on the front face and choose the **Select Other** button from the pop-up toolbar; the cursor changes to the select other cursor and the **Select Other** list box will be displayed. This list box displays all entities that can be selected. The item on which you move the cursor in the list box will be highlighted in the drawing area. You can select the hidden face using this box.

HOT KEYS

SOLIDWORKS is more popularly known for its mouse gesture functionality. However, you can also use the keys of the keyboard to invoke some tools, windows, dialog boxes, and so on. These keys are known as hot keys. Some hot keys along with their functions are given next.

Hot Key	Function
F11	Full screen
S	Invokes the shortcut bar
R	Invokes the recent documents
F	Fits the object in the drawing over the screen
Z	Zooms out

SPACE BAR	Invokes the **Orientation** menu
CTRL+1	Changes the current view to the Front View
CTRL+2	Changes the current view to the Back View
CTRL+3	Changes the current view to the Left View
CTRL+4	Changes the current view to the Right View
CTRL+5	Changes the current view to the Top View
CTRL+6	Changes the current view to the Bottom View
CTRL+7	Changes the current view to the Isometric View
CTRL+8	Changes the current view to the Normal View
CTRL+SHIFT+Z	Changes the current view to the Previous View
CTRL+Arrows	Moves the feature along the arrows direction
SHIFT+Arrows	Rotates the feature along the arrows direction
CTRL+B	Rebuilds the model
CTRL+Z	Invokes the **Undo** tool
CTRL+N	Invokes the **New SOLIDWORKS Document** dialog box
CTRL+O	Invokes the **Open** window
CTRL+S	Saves the document
CTRL+P	Prints the document
CTRL+A	Selects all the parts in the document
CTRL+C	Copies the selected feature
CTRL+V	Pastes the selected feature
CTRL+X	Cuts the selected feature
ALT+F	Opens the **File** menu
ALT+E	Opens the **Edit** menu

ALT+V	Opens the **View** menu
ALT+I	Opens the **Insert** menu
ALT+T	Opens the **Tool** menu
ALT+W	Opens the **Window** menu
ALT+H	Opens the **Help** menu
CTRL+W	Closes the current document

COLOR SCHEME

SOLIDWORKS allows you to use various color schemes as the background color of the screen, color and display style of **FeatureManager Design Tree**, and for displaying the entities on the screen. Note that the color scheme used in this book is neither the default color scheme nor the predefined color scheme. To set the color scheme, choose **Tools > Options** from the SOLIDWORKS menus; the **System Options - General** dialog box will be displayed. Select the **Colors** option from the left of this dialog box; the option related to the color scheme will be displayed in the dialog box and the name of the dialog box will change to **System Options - Colors**. In the list box available in the **Color scheme settings** area, the **Viewport Background** option is available. Select this option and choose the **Edit** button from the preview area on the right. Select white color from the **Color** dialog box and choose the **OK** button. After setting the color scheme, you need to save it so that next time if you need to set this color scheme, you do not need to configure all the settings. You just need to select the name of the saved color scheme from the **Current color scheme** drop-down list. To save the color scheme, choose the **Save As Scheme** button; the **Color Scheme Name** dialog box will be displayed. Enter the name of the color scheme as **SOLIDWORKS 2018** in the edit box in the **Color Scheme Name** dialog box and choose the **OK** button. Now, choose the **OK** button from the **System Options - Colors** dialog box.

Note

In this book, the description of the color has been given considering Window 10/Windows 8 as the operating system. So if you are working on a system with operating system other than Window 10/Windows 8, the color of the entities may be different.

Self-Evaluation Test

Answer the following questions and then compare them to those given at the end of this chapter:

1. The __________ property ensures that any modification made in a model in any of the modes of SOLIDWORKS is also reflected in the other modes immediately.

2. The __________ relation forces two selected arcs, two circles, a point and an arc, a point and a circle, or an arc and a circle share the same centerpoint.

3. The __________ relation is used to make two points, a point and a line, or a point and an arc coincident.

4. The __________ relation forces two selected lines to become equal in length.

5. The __________ is used to detect interference and collision between the parts of an assembly when the assembly is in motion.

6. __________ are the analytical and numerical formulae applied to the dimensions during or after sketching of the feature sketch.

7. The **Part** mode of SOLIDWORKS is a feature-based parametric environment in which you can create solid models. (T/F)

8. Generative drafting is the process of generating drawing views of a part or an assembly created earlier. (T/F)

9. The tip of the day is displayed at the bottom of the task pane. (T/F)

10. In SOLIDWORKS, solid models are created by integrating a number of building blocks called features. (T/F)

Answers to Self-Evaluation Test

1. bidirectional associativity, **2.** concentric, **3.** coincident, **4.** equal, **5.** collision detection, **6.** Equations, **7.** T, **8.** T, **9.** T, **10.** T

Chapter 2

Creating Axle and Disc Plate

Learning Objectives

After completing this chapter, you will be able to:

- *Start a New Session of SOLIDWORKS 2018*
- *Start a New Document in SOLIDWORKS 2018*
- *Understand the concept of Base feature*
- *Understand about the Extruded Boss/Base tool*
- *Understand about the Extruded Cut tool*
- *Understand the concept of Default planes*
- *Invoke Sketching environment*
- *Crate a circle by using the Circle tool*
- *Apply diameter dimensions by using the Smart Dimension tool*
- *Apply cosmetic threads with shaded display*
- *Create Polygon using the Polygon tool*
- *Understand about Convert Entities tool*
- *Understand about the Offset Entities tool*
- *Create centerlines using the Centerline tool*
- *Create a line using the Line tool*
- *Create mirror image of the sketch entities*
- *Trim unwanted entities of the sketch*
- *Create a circular pattern*
- *Create a fill pattern*

CREATING FRONT AXLE

Part Description

In this section, you will create a front axle, as shown in Figure 2-1. The features of this axle will be created by using the **Extruded Boss/Base** tool. The cosmetic threads with shaded display to be created are ANSI Metric of Machine Threads type. The views and dimensions of the axle are given in the Figure 2-2. Note that all the dimensions are in millimeters.

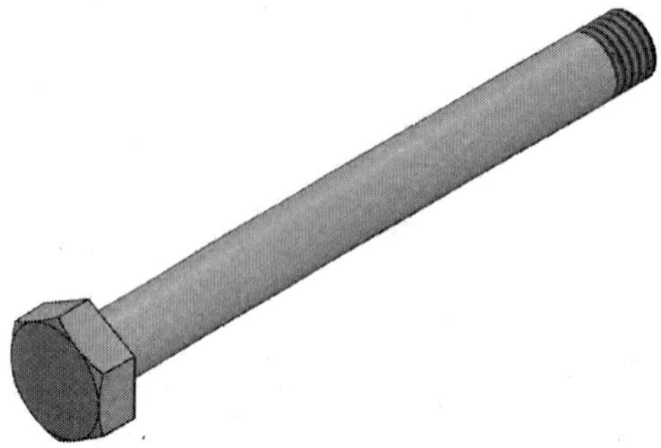

Figure 2-1 *Front axle*

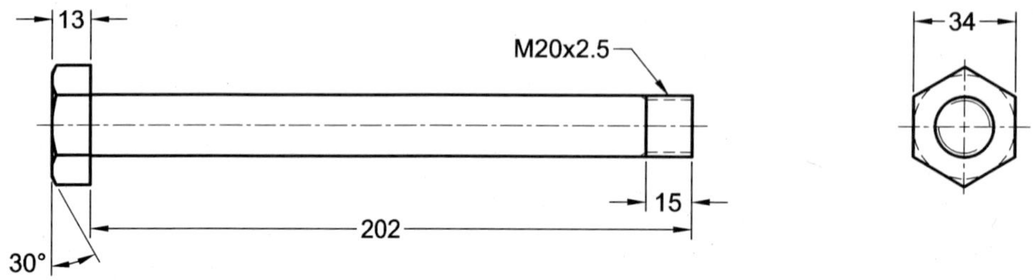

Figure 2-2 *Views and dimensions of the front axle*

Starting SOLIDWORKS and a New Part Document

Once you have installed SOLIDWORKS, an icon is displayed on the Windows desktop and a folder is added to the **Start** menu.

1. Start SOLIDWORKS by choosing **Start > All Programs > SOLIDWORKS 2018 > SOLIDWORKS 2018** or by double-clicking on the shortcut icon of SOLIDWORKS 2018 available on the desktop of your computer; the SOLIDWORKS window is displayed on the screen.

When you start SOLIDWORKS for the first time, the **SOLIDWORKS License Agreement** dialog box is displayed, as shown in Figure 2-3. Choose the **Accept** button from this dialog box; the **SOLIDWORKS** interface window along with the **Welcome - SOLIDWORKS 2018** dialog box will be displayed, as shown in Figure 2-4. This window can be used to open a new file or an existing file.

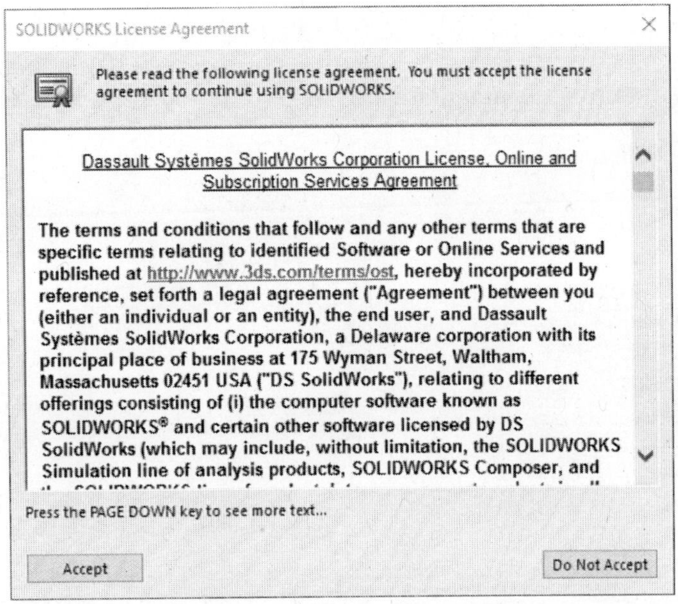

Figure 2-3 *The* ***SOLIDWORKS License Agreement*** *dialog box*

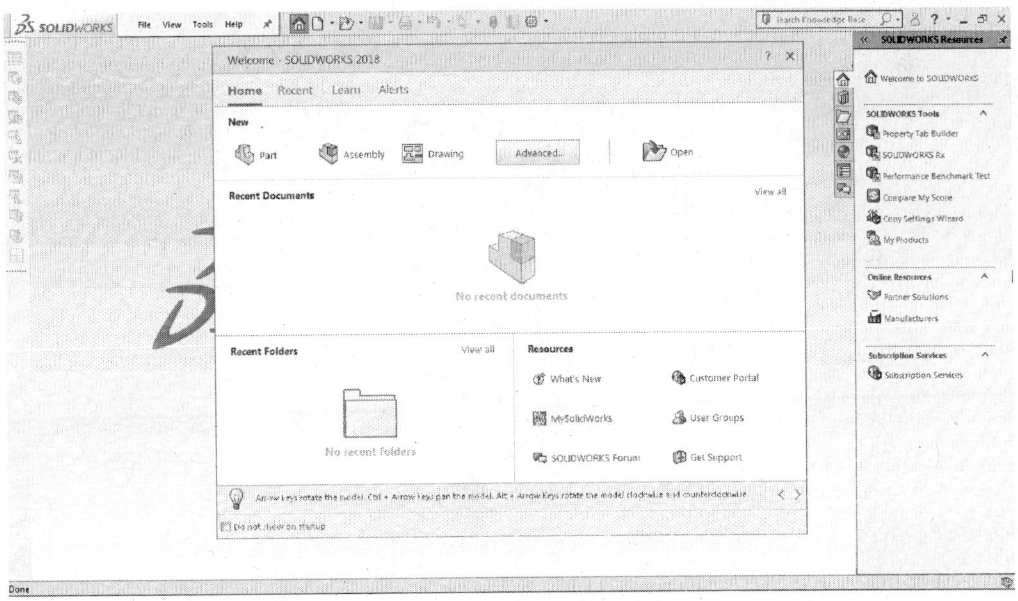

Figure 2-4 *The* ***SOLIDWORKS 2018*** *window*

If the **Welcome - SOLIDWORKS 2018** dialog box is not displayed by default, choose the **SOLIDWORKS Resources** button to display the **SOLIDWORKS Resources** task pane and then choose the **Welcome to SOLIDWORKS** button, the dialog box will be displayed. The **Welcome - SOLIDWORKS 2018** dialog box can be used to open online tutorials and also to visit the website of the SOLIDWORKS partners.

2. From the **Home** tab in the **Welcome - SOLIDWORKS 2018** dialog box, choose the **Part** button to open a new file. Alternatively, you can choose the **New** button from the Menu Bar; the **New SOLIDWORKS Document** dialog box is displayed, as shown in Figure 2-5.

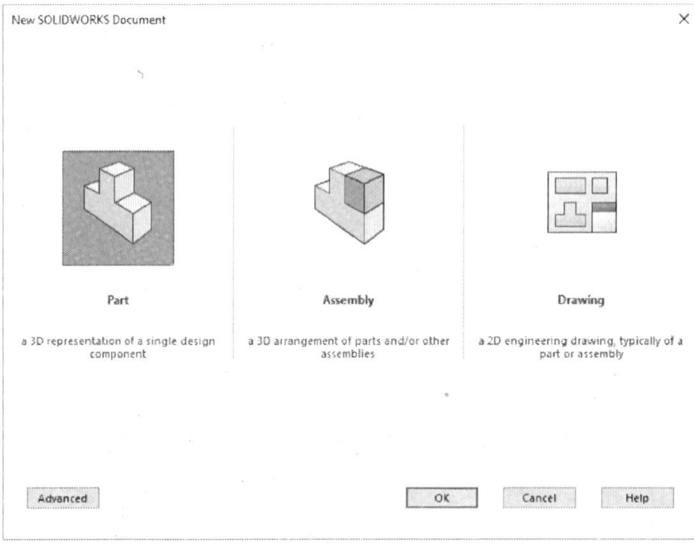

Figure 2-5 *The* ***New SOLIDWORKS Document*** *dialog box*

3. In the **New SOLIDWORKS Document** dialog box, the **Part** button is chosen by default. Choose the **OK** button; a new SOLIDWORKS part document is started, as shown in Figure 2-6. Modify the unit of the current document to millimeters if not set by default.

Note

As mentioned in the part description, all the dimensions are in millimeters ,therefore, you may need to modify the units of the current session to millimeters. To do so, choose the ***Options*** *button from the Menu Bar; the* ***System Options*** *dialog box is displayed and then choose the* ***Document Properties*** *tab. In this tab, select the* ***Units*** *option from the area that is available on the left in the dialog box. The default unit system that was selected while installing SOLIDWORKS is selected in the* ***Unit system*** *area of the dialog box. Select the* ***MMGS (millimeter, gram, second)*** *radio button from the* ***Unit system*** *area and then choose the* ***OK*** *button from the dialog box.*

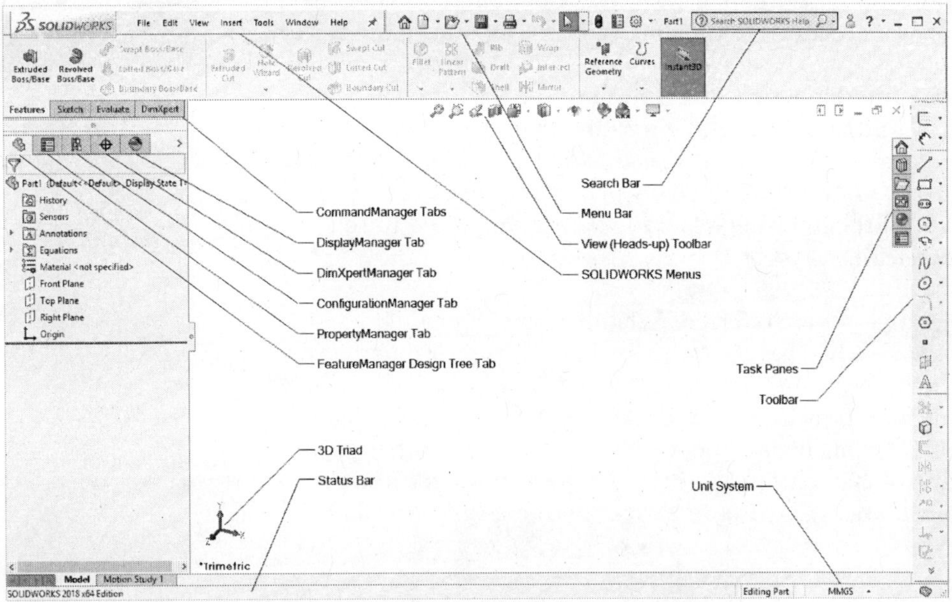

Figure 2-6 *Initial screen of the SOLIDWORKS*

It is evident from the screen that SOLIDWORKS is a very user-friendly solid modeling tool. In addition to the default **CommandManager** shown in Figure 2-6, you can also invoke other **CommandManagers**. To do so, move the cursor on a **CommandManager** tab and right-click; a shortcut menu is displayed. Select the required **CommandManager** from the shortcut menu; the selected **CommandManager** will be added.

Once a new SOLIDWORKS part document is started, you can create a model of the Axle using the different feature creation tools of the SOLIDWORKS.

Creating the Base Feature of the Axle

Most of the products designed by using SOLIDWORKS are a combination of sketched, placed, and derived features. The placed and derived features are created without drawing sketch, but the sketched features required a sketch to be drawn first. Generally, the base feature of any design is a sketched feature and is created using a sketch. Therefore, while creating any design, the first and foremost point is to draw a sketch for the base feature. Once you have drawn the sketch, you can convert it into a base feature and then add other sketched, placed, and derived features to complete the design.

Base feature is the first feature created while creating a model in the Part environment. In this section, the base feature is created by extruding the sketch using the **Extruded Boss/Base** tool available in the **Features CommandManager**. To create a base feature, first you need to draw a sketch of the base feature in the sketching environment using the tools available in the **Sketch CommandManager**. After drawing the sketch of the base feature, you can extrude it using the **Extruded Boss/Base** tool.

1. Choose the **Features** tab from the **CommandManager** to display the **Features CommandManager**, refer to Figure 2-7.

2. Choose the **Extruded Boss/Base** button from the **Features CommandManager**; the **Extrude PropertyManager** is displayed on the left of the drawing area, as shown in Figure 2-8. Also, three default planes are displayed at the center of the drawing area and you are prompted to select the sketching plane.

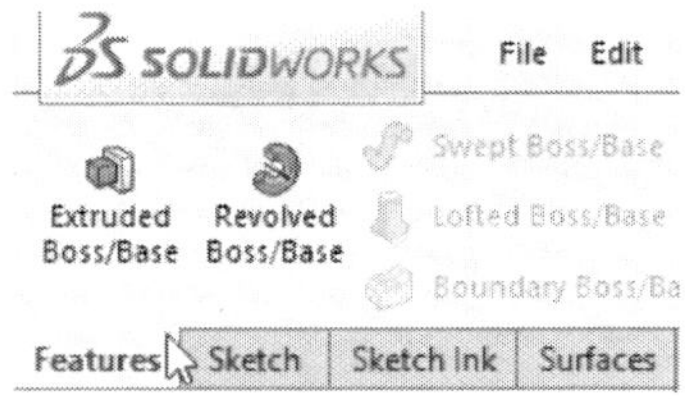

Figure 2-7 The ***Features CommandManager***

The default planes are referred as datum planes and are used to draw a 2D sketch. The 2D sketch is then converted into a 3D model by extruding. These default planes are mutually perpendicular to each other. You can select any of these default planes as sketching plane. You can also create a plane other than the default planes by using the **Plane PropertyManager**. You will learn more about the **Plane PropertyManager** in the later chapters.

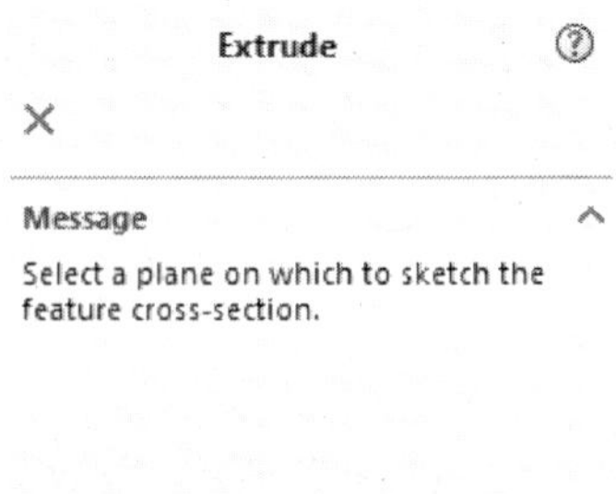

Figure 2-8 The ***Extrude PropertyManager***

3. Next, from the drawing area, select the **Front Plane** as a sketching plane; the sketching environment is invoked and the selected plane is oriented normal to the view. By default, there are two arrows at the origin displaying the X and Y axes directions of the current sketching plane. Also, confirmation corner is displayed with the **Exit Sketch** and **Delete Sketch** options on the upper right corner of the drawing area, refer to Figure 2-9.

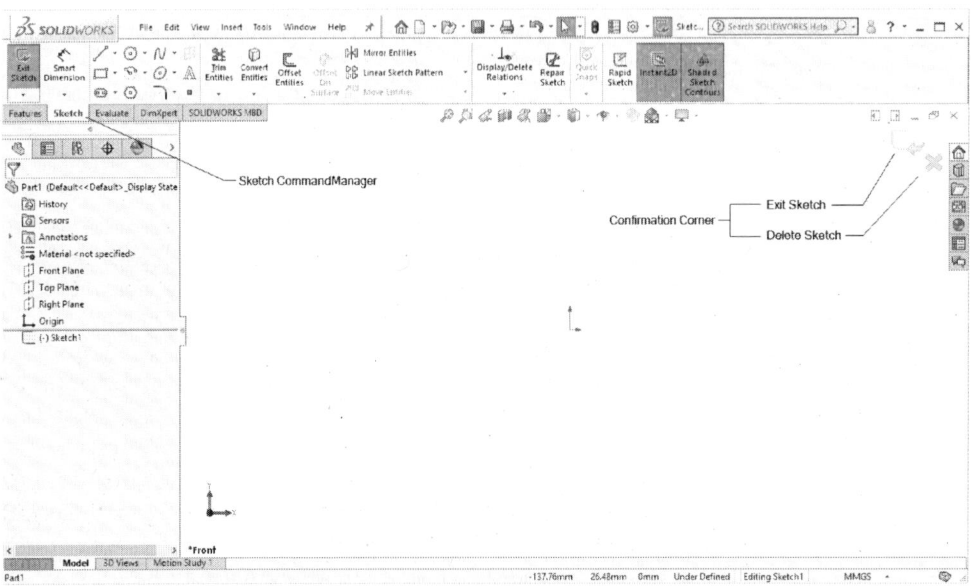

Figure 2-9 *The screen display in the sketching environment*

4. Next, from the **Sketch CommandManager**, choose the **Circle** button; the **Circle PropertyManager** is displayed on the left side of the drawing area, as shown in Figure 2-10. Also, the cursor gets modified. 

The **Circle** button is chosen by default in the **Circle Type** rollout of the **Circle PropertyManager**. This button enables you to draw a circle by specifying its center and radius.

5. Move the circle cursor toward the origin and specify the center point of the circle by pressing the left mouse button when an orange circle and a symbol of coincident relation are displayed. You will learn more about relations later in this chapter. As soon as, you specify center point of the circle, preview of the circle is attached to the circle cursor.

The origin is represented by a red colored point displayed at the center of the sketching environment screen. The coordinates of this point are 0,0. You can hide or display the origin by choosing the **View Origins** button from the **Hide/Show Items** flyout in the **View (Heads-up)** toolbar, refer to Figure 2-11.

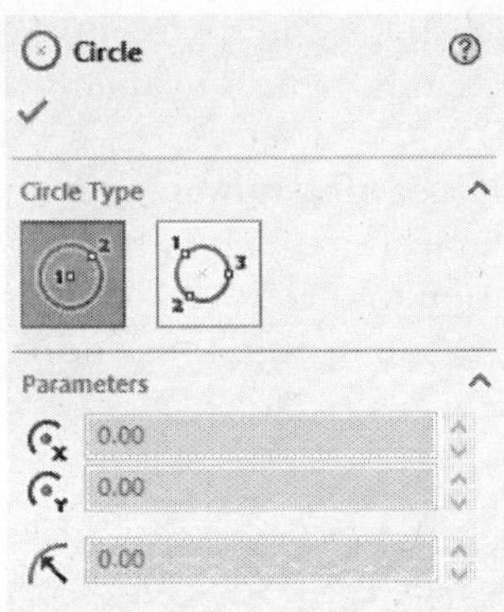

*Figure 2-10 The **Circle PropertyManager***

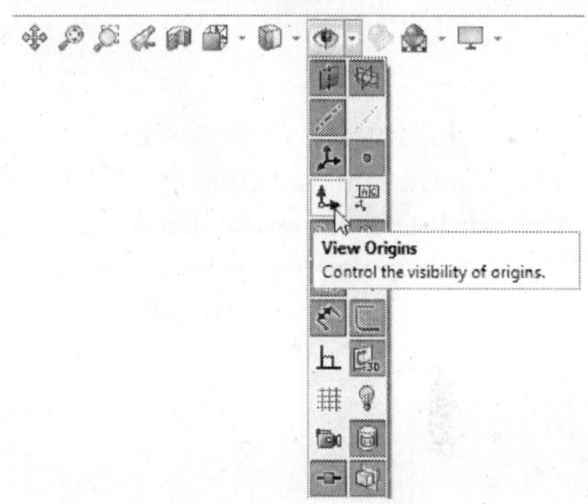

*Figure 2-11 Partial view **Hide/Show** Items flyout*

After specifying the center point of the circle if you move the cursor to define its radius. The current radius of the circle will be displayed above the circle cursor. This radius will change as you move the circle cursor. To specify the radius of the circle, you need to click in the drawing area.

6. Move the circle cursor toward left and press the left mouse button when the value of radius of the circle above the circle cursor is displayed almost 10.

Tip

*After specifying the center point and radius of the circle, you can modify their parameters in the **Parameters** rollout of the **Circle PropertyManager**.*

Note

The sketch is shown in blue color, suggesting that the sketch is underdefined. An underdefined sketch is the one in which some of the dimensions or relations are not defined and the degree of freedom of the sketch is not fully constrained. In these types of sketches, the entities may move or change their size unexpectedly. As a result, the sketched entities of the underdefined sketch are displayed in blue color. In SOLIDWORKS, there are six states in which the sketch may exist named as fully defined, overdefined, underdefined, dangling, no solution found, and invalid solution found.

Tip

*The Sketch Definition area of the status bar that is located at the bottom of the drawing area always display the status of the sketch, dimension, and relation. If the sketch is underdefined, the status area will display **Under Defined**; if the sketch is overdefined, the message displayed in the status area will be **Over Defined**; if the sketch is fully defined, the message displayed in the status area will be **Fully Defined**.*

After drawing the sketch, dimensioning is the most important step in creating a design. SOLIDWORKS is a parametric software. This property of the SOLIDWORKS ensures that irrespective of the original size, the selected entity is driven by the dimension value that you specify. Therefore, when you apply and modify the dimension of an entity, the sketch is forced to change its size in accordance with the specified dimension value.

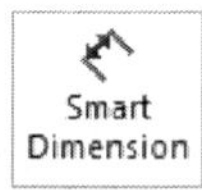

7. Choose the **Smart Dimension** button from the **Sketch CommandManager** to dimension the circle; the cursor is modified. Select the circle; the current diameter of the circle is attached with the cursor. Specify the location to place the diameter of the circle in the drawing area. As soon as, you place the diameter, the **Modify** dialog box is displayed, as shown in Figure 2-12.

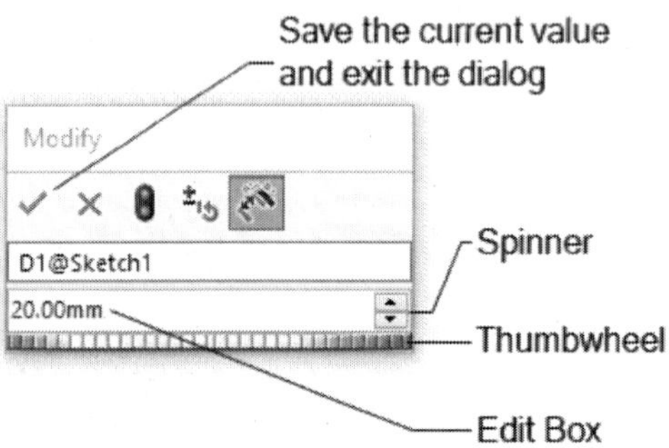

Figure 2-12 *The **Modify** dialog box*

The **Smart Dimension** tool is used to dimension any kind of entity. If you use the **Smart Dimension** tool, the type of dimension that will be applied will depend on the type of entity selected.

The **Modify** dialog box is used to modify the default dimension value using the spinner or by entering a new value in the edit box available in the **Modify** dialog box. You can also drag the thumbwheel provided below the spinner to increase or decrease the value.

8. Enter **20** in the **Modify** dialog box and choose the **Save the current value and exit the dialog** button from this dialog box. Figure 2-13 shows the circle of diameter 20 mm.

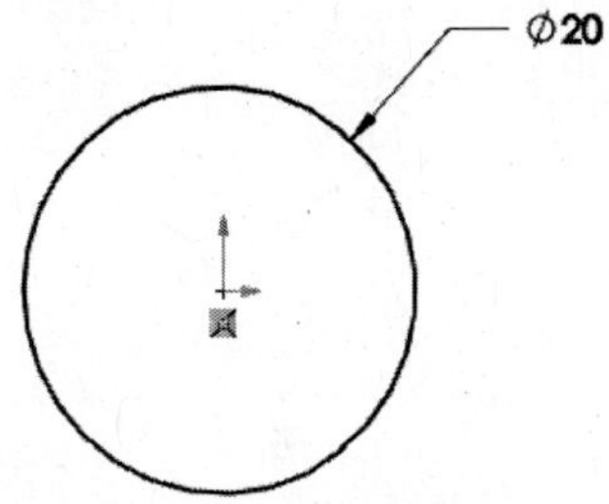

Figure 2-13 Circle of diameter 20

Note
After diameter dimension is applied to the sketch, the color of the sketch changes to black indicating the sketch is fully defined.

A fully defined sketch is the one in which all entities of the sketch and their positions are fully defined by the relations or dimensions, or both. In a fully defined sketch, all degrees of freedom of a sketch are constrained. Therefore, the sketched entities cannot move or change their size and location unexpectedly. If the sketch is not fully defined, it can change its size or position at any time during the design because all degrees of freedom are not constrained. All entities in a fully defined sketch are displayed in black.

9. Next, exit from the sketching environment by clicking on the confirmation corner available on the upper right corner of the drawing area; the **Boss-Extrude PropertyManager** is displayed on the left of the drawing area, refer to Figure 2-14. You will notice that the view is automatically changed to the trimetric view and the preview of the base feature is displayed in the temporary graphics. Also, an arrow will appear in the front of the sketch, as shown in Figure 2-15.

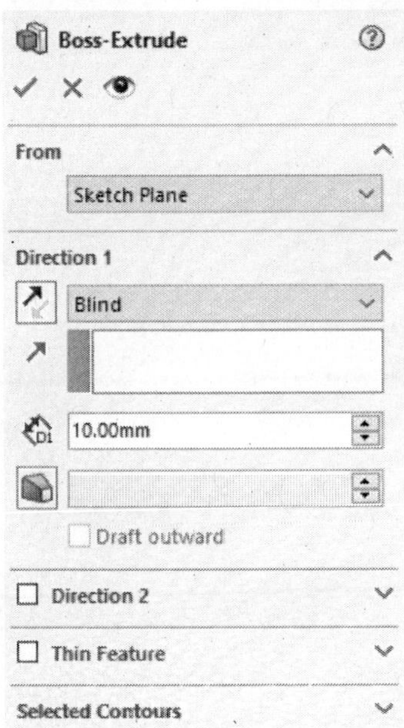

Figure 2-14 *The* ***Boss-Extrude PropertyManager***

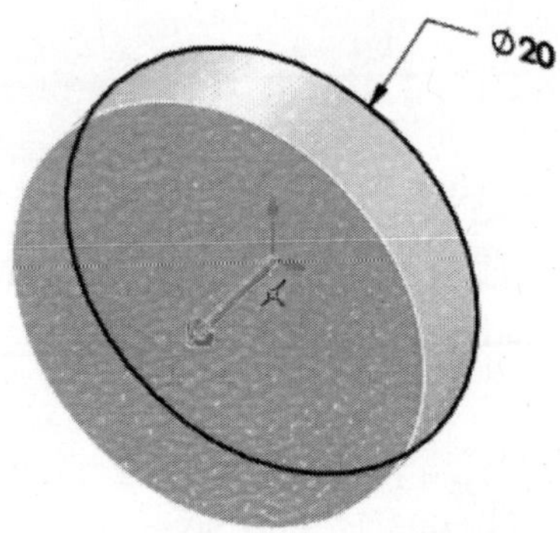

Figure 2-15 *Preview of the base feature with arrow*

The **Direction 1** and **Direction 2** rollouts of the **Boss-Extrude PropertyManager** is used to specify the end conditions for extruding the sketch in first and second directions. The **Direction 1** rollout is expanded by default. However, to expand the **Direction 2** rollout, you need to select the check box available on the title bar of the rollout. The options available in these rollouts are same. You will learn more about these options later.

10. Next, select the **Mid Plane** option from the **End Condition** drop-down list of the **Direction 1** rollout in the **Boss-Extrude PropertyManager**.

Tip
*You can also select the **Mid Plane** option from the shortcut menu that will be displayed by right-clicking in the drawing area when the **Boss-Extrude PropertyManager** is invoked.*

The **End Condition** drop-down list provides the options to define the termination of the extruded feature. The **Mid Plane** option of this drop-down list is used to create the feature by extruding the sketch equally in both directions of the plane on which the sketch is drawn. Note that when you create the first feature, some of the options of this drop-down list will not be available. The other options of this drop-down list will be discussed later.

11. To specify the depth of the extrusion, set the value of the **Depth** spinner to **202mm** in the **Direction 1** rollout.

Tip
You can also specify the depth of extrusion by dragging the arrow provided with the preview of the model.

12. Choose the **OK** button from the **Boss-Extrude PropertyManager** to exit.

13. Choose the **Zoom to Fit** button from the **View (Heads-up)** toolbar to fit the feature on the screen.

The **Zoom to Fit** tool is used to increase or decrease the drawing display area so that all entities are fitted inside the current view. You can also press the F key to invoke this tool. Alternatively, you can double-click the middle mouse button in the drawing area to invoke this tool.

14. Choose the **View Orientation** button from the **View (Heads-up)** toolbar; the **View Orientation** flyout is displayed, refer to Figure 2-16.

15. Choose the **Isometric** button from this flyout; the model is oriented isometric. The model after creating the base feature is shown in Figure 2-17.

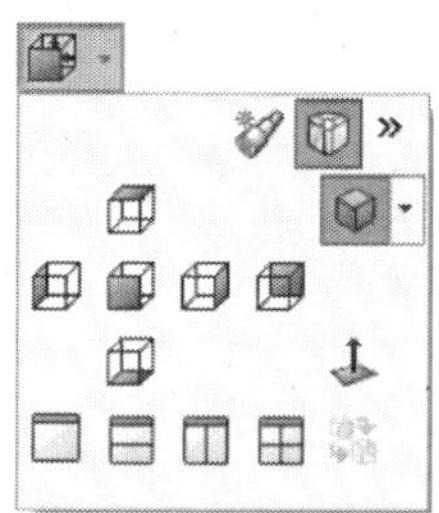

***Figure 2-16** The **View Orientation** flyout*

In SOLIDWORKS, you can manually change the view orientation by using some predefined standard views or user-defined views. The views available in the **View**

Orientation flyout are called as standard views. You will learn more about the user-defined views and the standard views in later chapters.

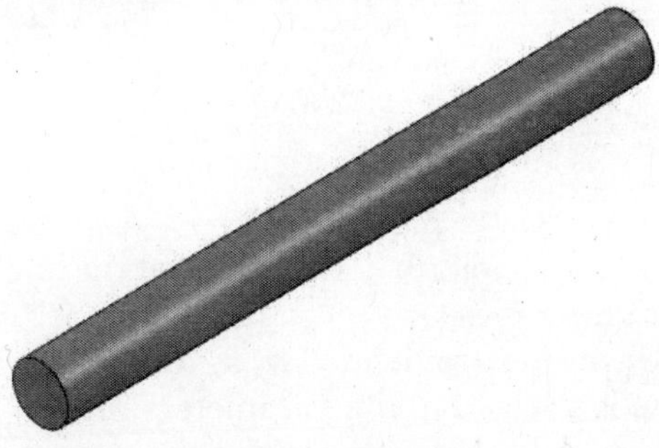

Figure 2-17 Base feature of the Model

Creating the Second Feature

Second feature of the model is an extrude feature. This feature is created by using the **Extruded Boss/Base** tool that is available in the **Features CommandManager**. The sketch of this extrude feature is created on the front planar circular face of the base feature.

1. Choose the **Extruded Boss/Base** button from the **Features CommandManager**; the **Extrude PropertyManager** is displayed on the left side of the drawing area and you are prompted to select the sketching plane.

2. Select the front planar circular face of the base feature as sketching plane, refer to Figure 2-18; the sketching environment is invoked.

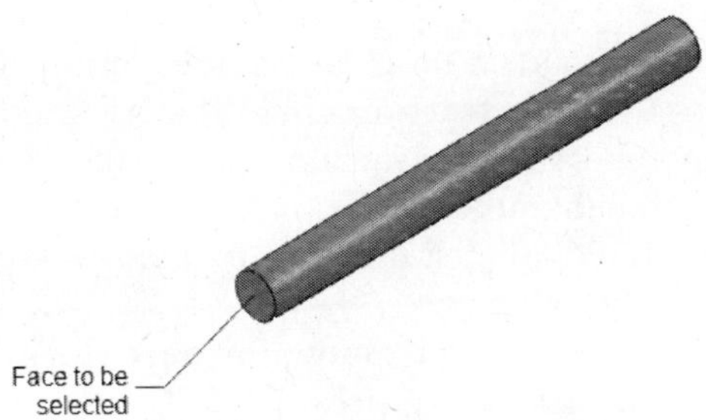

Figure 2-18 Face to be selected

If by default the orientation is not set normal to the screen then you need to change it.

3. Choose the **Normal To** button from the **View Orientation** flyout in the **View (Heads-up)** toolbar; the current orientation is set normal to the screen.

The **Normal To** tool is used to reorient the view normal to a selected face or plane.

4. Choose the **Polygon** button from the **Sketch CommandManager**; the **Polygon PropertyManager** is displayed at the left side of the drawing area and the cursor gets modified. Make sure that the value of the **Number of Sides** spinner is set to 6 and the **Inscribed circle** radio button is selected in the **Parameters** rollout of the **PropertyManager**.

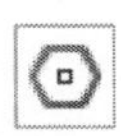

Tip

In SOLIDWORKS 2018, you can set the orientation of sketching plane normal to the viewing direction whenever you start a new sketch or edit an existing sketch. This setting can be toggled by selecting the ***Auto-rotate view normal to sketch plane on sketch creation and sketch edit*** *check box in the* ***Sketch*** *area of the* ***System Options - Sketch*** *dialog box.*

The **Polygon** button is used to draw a regular polygon. A regular polygon is defined as a multisided geometric figure in which length of all sides and the angle between them are same. In SOLIDWORKS, you can draw a regular polygon with number of sides ranging between 3 to 40. The dimensions of the polygon are defined by a circumscribed or inscribed circle. If the **Inscribed circle** radio button is selected in the **Parameters** rollout, the construction circle will be inscribed inside the polygon and the diameters of the construction circle will be taken from the edges of the polygon. However, if the **Circumscribed circle** radio button is selected in the **Parameters** rollout, the construction circle will be circumscribed about the polygon and the diameters of the construction circle will be taken from the vertices of the polygon.

5. Move the polygon cursor towards the center of the circular face of the base feature and specify a point by pressing the left mouse button when the coincident relation symbol is displayed below the polygon cursor, refer to Figure 2-19.

6. Next, move the polygon cursor vertically upward and click when preview of the polygon crosses the circular edge of the base feature. Next, press the ESC key.

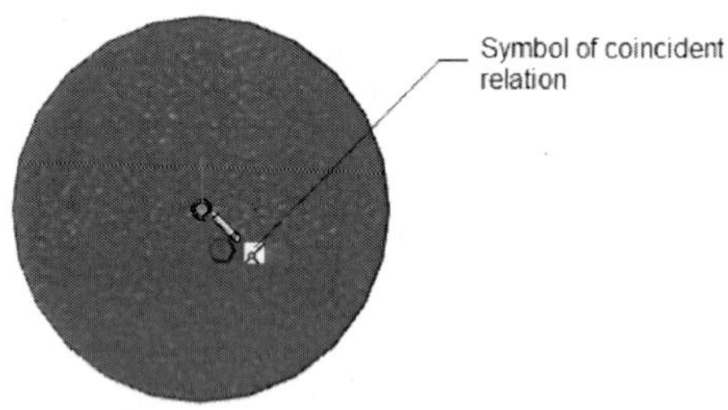

Figure 2-19 *Symbol of coincident relation*

7. Choose the **Smart Dimension** button from the **Sketch CommandManager**; the cursor is modified. Select the construction circle that is inscribed inside the polygon; the current diameter of the construction circle is attached with the cursor. Specify a location to place the diameter of the construction circle in the drawing area. As soon as, you place the diameter, the **Modify** dialog box is displayed.

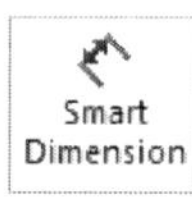

8. Enter **34** in the **Modify** dialog box and choose the **Save the current value and exit the dialog** button from this dialog box. Next, press the ESC key to exit the **Smart Dimension** tool.

9. Select a vertical edge of the polygon and do not move the cursor; a pop-up toolbar is displayed, refer to Figure 2-20.

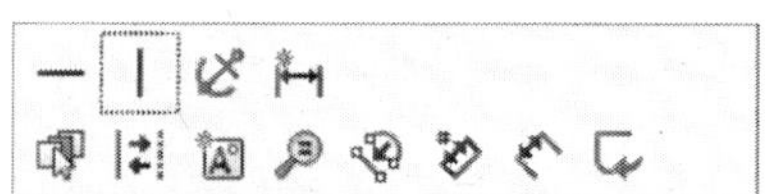

Figure 2-20 *Pop-up toolbar*

Note

The options of the pop-up toolbar will vary as per the entity or feature selected. Also, this toolbar will disappear if you move the cursor away from the selected entity or feature.

10. Select the **Make Vertical** option from the pop-up toolbar, refer to Figure 2-20; the vertical relation is applied to the selected entity and the color of the sketch changes to black, indicating that now the sketch is fully-defined, refer to Figure 2-21.

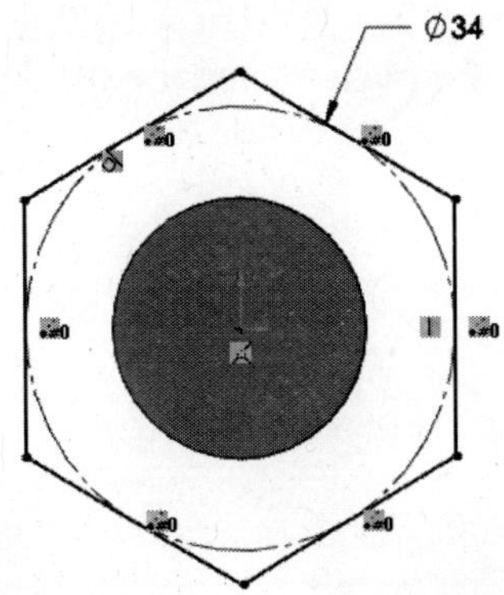

Figure 2-21 *Fully-defined sketch*

The vertical relation forces one or more selected lines or centerlines to become vertical. You can also force two or more points to become vertical using this relation.

> **Note**
> *Figure 2-21 shows all the relations applied to the sketch. You can hide these relations. To do so, choose the* ***View Sketch Relations*** *button from the* ***Hide/Show Items*** *flyout in the* ***View (Heads-up)*** *toolbar. This is a toggle button.*

11. Exit from the sketch environment by clicking on the confirmation corner available at the upper right side of the drawing area; the **Boss-Extrude PropertyManager** is displayed. 

12. In the **Direction 1** rollout of the **Boss-Extrude PropertyManager**, set the value of the **Depth** spinner to **13mm**. Note that, in the **End Condition** drop-down list, the **Blind** option is selected by default.

The **Blind** option is used to define the termination of the extruded base feature by specifying the depth of extrusion in the **Depth** spinner.

13. Choose the **OK** button from the **Boss-Extrude PropertyManager**; the extrude feature is created. Next, set the current orientation of the model to isometric by choosing the **Isometric** button from the **View Orientation** flyout. Figure 2-22 shows the isometric view of the model.

Figure 2-22 *Isometric view of the model*

Creating Chamfer

It is evident from the Figures 2-1 and 2-2 that a chamfer is required in the model. The chamfer will be created using the **Cut-Extrude PropertyManager**. It is generally conical and the angle of chamfer is 15^0 to 30^0 with respect to the base of the head. The sketch of this cut feature is created on the front planar face of the second feature.

1. Choose the **Extruded Cut** tool from the **Features CommandManager**; the **Extrude PropertyManager** is displayed on the left of the drawing area and you are prompted to select the sketching plane.

2. Select the front planar face of the second feature as a sketching plane, refer to Figure 2-23; the sketching environment is invoked.

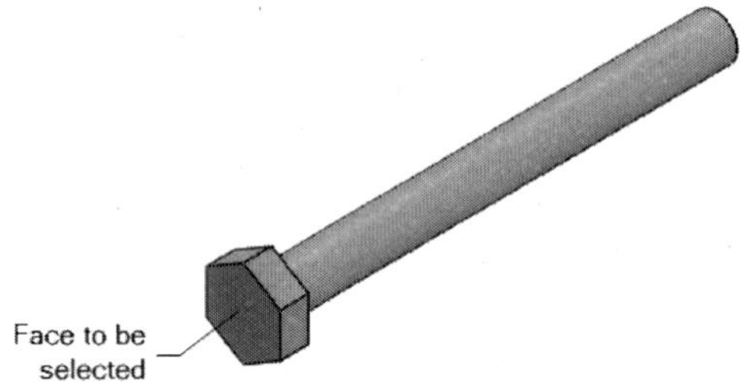

Figure 2-23 *Face to be selected*

3. Choose the **Circle** tool from the **Sketch CommandManager**; the **Circle PropertyManager** is displayed on the left side of the drawing area and the cursor gets modified.

4. Move the cursor towards the center of the face of the second feature and specify a point when coincident relation symbol is displayed below the cursor.

5. Next, move the circle cursor to create a circle. Now, apply tangent relation between the circle and one of the edges of the second feature, refer to Figure 2-24.

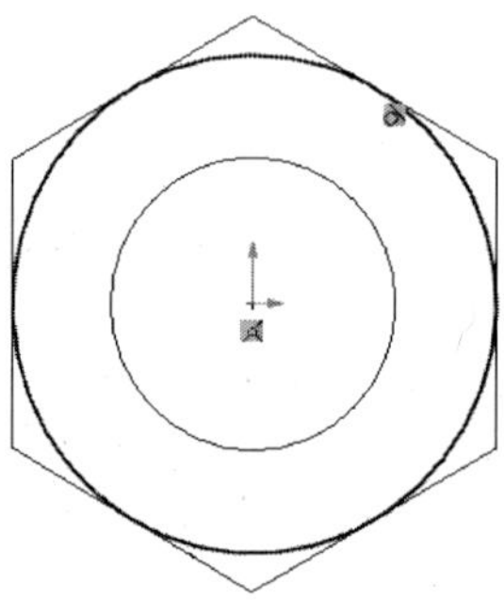

Figure 2-24 *Fully-defined sketch for the chamfer feature*

6. Exit the sketch environment by clicking on the confirmation corner available at the upper right corner of the drawing area; the **Cut-Extrude PropertyManager** is displayed.

7. In the **Direction 1** rollout of the **Cut-Extrude PropertyManager**, select the **Through All** option in the **End Condition** drop-down list and also select the **Flip side to cut** check box.

The **Through All** option is used to define the termination of the cut feature through all the available bodies.

8. Next, click on the **Draft On/Off** button in the **Direction 1** rollout; preview of the cut feature gets modified. Set 60 as the value in the **Angle** spinner and then select the **Draft outward** check box.

The **Draft On/Off** option is used to add draft to the feature. The draft can be set inward and outward using the **Draft outward** check box.

9. Choose the **OK** button from the **Cut-Extrude PropertyManager**; the cut feature is created. Next, set the current orientation of the model to isometric by choosing the **Isometric** button from the **View Orientation** flyout. Figure 2-25 shows isometric view of the model.

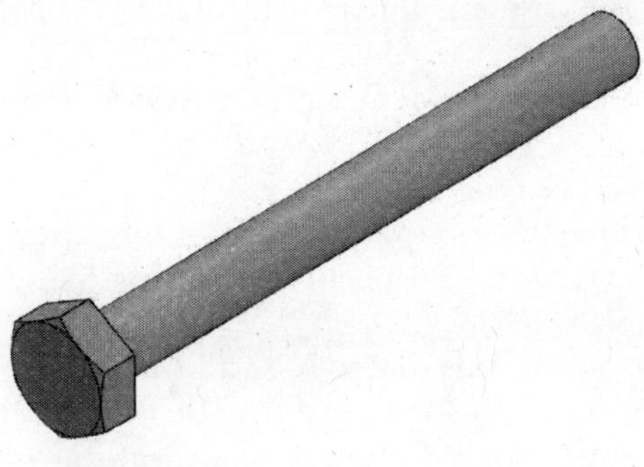

Figure 2-25 *Isometric view of the model*

Applying the Cosmetic Threads

It is evident from the Figures 2-1 and 2-2 that cosmetic threads are required in the model. The cosmetic threads are applied by using the **Cosmetic Thread PropertyManager**. The cosmetic threads are used to display the schematic representation of the threads.

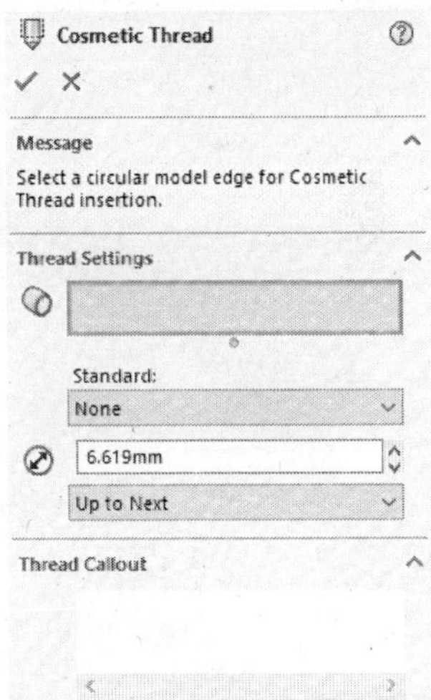

Figure 2-26 Cosmetic Thread PropertyManager

1. Choose **Insert > Annotations > Cosmetic Thread** from the SOLIDWORKS menus; the **Cosmetic Thread PropertyManager** is displayed, as shown in Figure 2-26. Also, you are prompted to select the edges and set the parameters.

2. Select circular edge of the model, refer to Figure 2-27. The name of the selected edge is displayed in the **Circular Edges** selection box of the **Thread Settings** rollout. Also, schematic representation of the threads is displayed in the drawing area.

3. Select the **ANSI Metric** option from the **Standard** drop-down list of the **Thread Settings** rollout.

The **Standard** drop-down list of the **Cosmetic Thread PropertyManager** is used to specify the industrial thread standards. The **None** option of this drop-down list is selected by default and is used to specify user-define specification of the thread. The thread standards available in this drop-down list are **ANSI Inch, ANSI Metric, AS, BSI, DIN, GB, IS, ISO, JIS, KS**.

4. Select the **Machine Threads** and **M20x2.5** options from the **Type** and **Size** drop-down lists, respectively in the **Thread Settings** rollout.

5. Select the **Blind** option from the **End Condition** drop-down list in the **Thread Settings** rollout of the **Cosmetic Thread PropertyManager**.

6. Set the value of the **Depth** spinner to 15.

7. Choose the **OK** button from the **Cosmetic Thread PropertyManager**; the cosmetic thread is added to the model.

   Now you need to display the cosmetic thread with shaded thread pattern on the surface.

8. Choose the **Options** button from the Menu Bar; the **System Options - General** dialog box is displayed.

9. Choose the **Document Properties** tab from this dialog box; the **System Options - General** dialog box is changed to **Document Properties - Drafting Standard** dialog box.

10. Select the **Detailing** option from this dialog box; all the related options are displayed on the right in the dialog box. Select the **Shaded cosmetic threads** check box and then choose the **OK** button; the cosmetic thread is displayed in the drawing area with the shaded thread. Figures 2-28 shows the final model after adding the shaded cosmetic threads.

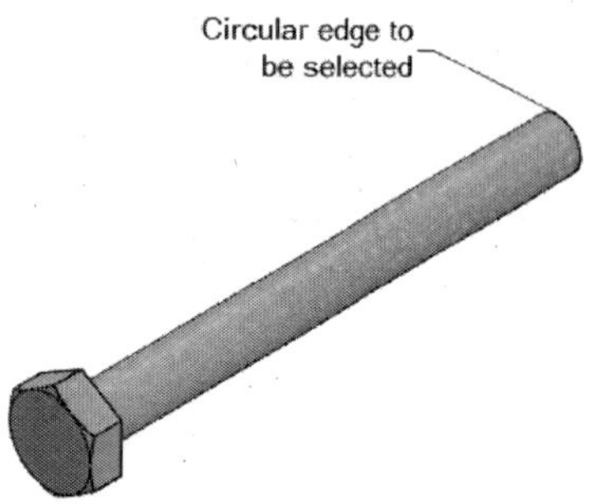

Figure 2-27 *Circular edge to be selected*

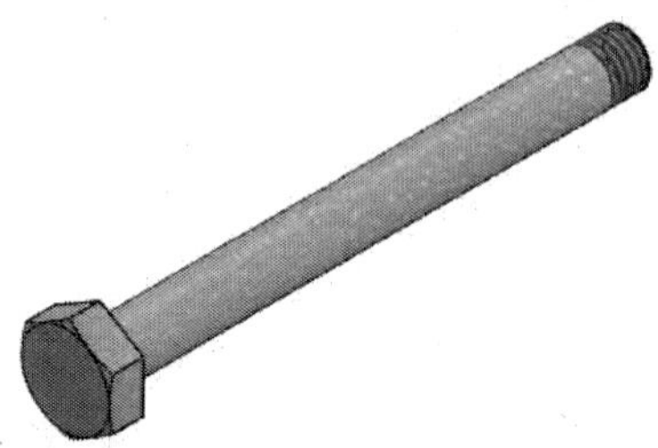

Figure 2-28 *Final model of Axle*

Saving the Model

After creating the model, you need to save it. It is recommended that you create a separate folder for saving all parts that you will create using this text book. When you invoke the option to save a document, the default *Documents* folder will be displayed. You will create a folder with the name *Motor Cycle Project* in the *Documents* folder. Now save all the parts in this folder.

1. Choose the **Save** button from the Menu Bar; the **Save As** dialog box is displayed. Browse to the *Documents* folder and create a new folder with the name *Motor Cycle Project* inside it.

2. Double-click on the newly created folder and then enter the name of the part as **Front Axle** in the **File name** edit box. Next, choose the **Save** button. The document will be saved in the *\Documents\Motor Cycle Project\Front Axle*.

3. Close the document by choosing **File > Close** from the SOLIDWORKS menus.

CREATING THE DISC PLATE

Part Description

In this section, you will create the Disc Plate, as shown in Figure 2-29. It will be created by using feature creation tools of the SOLIDWORKS. First feature of the Disc Plate will be created by using the **Extruded Boss/Base** tool. Then, other features of the Disc Plate will be created by using the **Extruded Cut**, **Circular Pattern**, and **Fill Pattern** tools. The dimensions of the Disc Plate are shown in the Figure 2-30. **(Expected time: 25 min)**

Figure 2-29 *Sketch of the base feature*

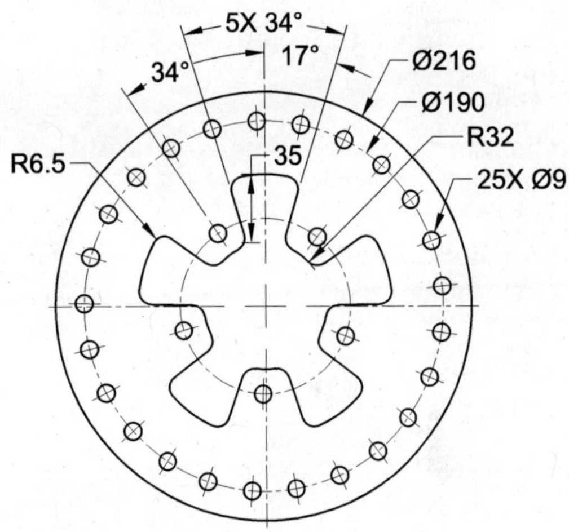

Figure 2-30 *Sketch of the base feature*

Starting a New Part Document

1. Choose the **New** button from the Menu Bar; the **New SOLIDWORKS Document** dialog box is displayed. The **Part** button is chosen by default in this dialog box. Choose the **OK** button; a new part document is started.

Creating the Base Feature of the Disc Plate

The base feature of the model is a extrude feature.

1. Choose the **Extruded Boss/Base** button from the **Features CommandManager**; the **Extrude PropertyManager** is displayed and you are prompted to select the sketching plane.

2. Select the Front Plane as the sketching plane from the drawing area; the sketch environment is invoked and the selected plane is oriented normal to the view.

3. Choose the **Circle** tool from the **Sketch CommandManager**; the **Circle PropertyManager** is displayed. Also, the cursor is changed to circle cursor.

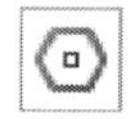

4. Move the cursor close to the origin and press the left mouse button when the coincident symbol is displayed.

5. Next, move the cursor toward the left and when the radius of the circle above the circle cursor shows a value near by 32 mm, press the left mouse button.

6. Similarly, draw the circles of radius 108 mm. Note that the center point of both the circles are at the origin. The sketch after drawing the circles is shown similar to the one given in Figure 2-31.

   After drawing the circles, you need to apply the diameter dimensions using the **Smart Dimension** tool.

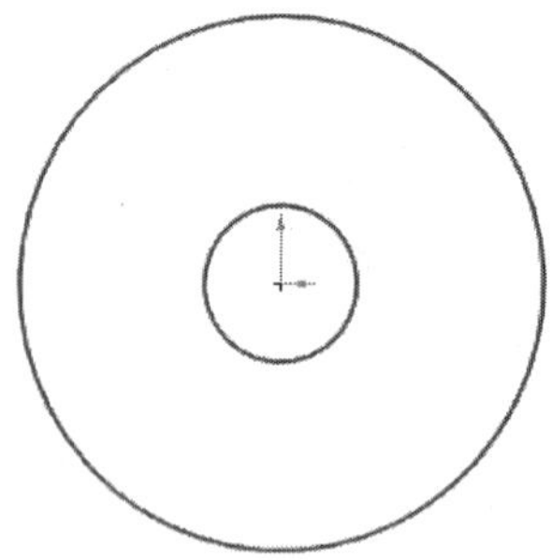

Figure 2-31 *Sketch after drawing the circles*

7. Choose the **Smart Dimension** tool from the **Sketch CommandManager**; the cursor is modified.

8. Move the dimension cursor to the inner circle; the circle is highlighted. Select the highlighted circle; a diameter dimension is attached to the cursor.

9. Move the cursor toward left and click to place the diameter dimension; the **Modify** dialog box is displayed.

Note

*The **Modify** dialog box will display automatically only when the **Input dimension value** check box is selected in the **System Options - General** dialog box. To select this check box, invoke the **System Options - General** dialog box by choosing the **Options** button from the Menu Bar and then select the **Input dimension value** check box.*

10. Enter the diameter value **64** mm in the **Modify** dialog box and then press ENTER, the dimensionis placed and the diameter of the circle is modified to **64** mm.

11. Similarly, apply the diameter dimension to the outer circle, refer to Figure 2-32.

12. Click on the confirmation corner available at the upper right corner of the drawing area; the **Boss-Extrude PropertyManager** is displayed. You will notice that the view is automatically set to trimetric view and preview of the base feature is displayed in the drawing area. Also, an arrow will appear in front of the sketch, refer to Figure 2-33.

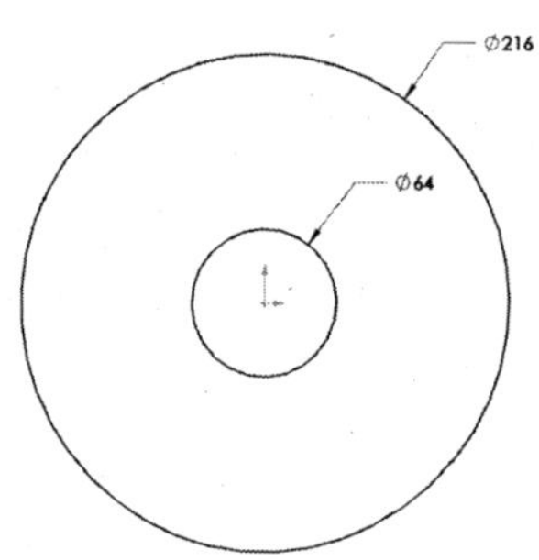

Figure 2-32 *Sketch after applying the diameter dimensions*

13. Select the **Mid Plane** option from the **End Condition** drop-down list of the **Direction 1** rollout in the **Boss-Extrude PropertyManager**.

As discussed earlier, the **End Condition** drop-down list provides the options to define the termination of the extruded feature. The **Mid Plane** option available in the **End Condition** drop-down list is used to create the feature by extruding the sketch equally in both directions of the plane on which the sketch is drawn.

14. Set the value of the **Depth** spinner to **8** mm in the **Direction 1** rollout of the PropertyManager.

You have selected the **Mid Plane** option as the end condition of the feature. Therefore, the feature will be extruded 4 mm toward the front of the sketching plane and 4 mm toward the back.

15. Choose the **OK** button from the **Boss-Extrude PropertyManager**; the base feature is created, as shown in Figure 2-34.

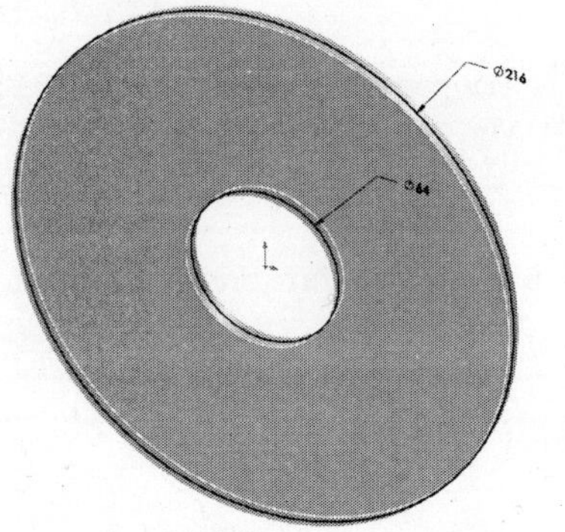

Figure 2-33 *Preview of the base feature*

Figure 2-34 *Base feature of the model*

Creating the Second Feature

Second feature of the model is an extrude cut feature created using the **Extruded Cut** tool.

1. Choose the **Extruded Cut** button from the **Features CommandManager**; the **Extrude PropertyManager** is displayed and you are prompted to select a sketching plane.

2. Select the front planar face of the base feature as the sketching plane; the sketching environment is invoked.

3. Choose the **Normal To** button from the **View Orientation** flyout in the **View (Head-up)** toolbar; the current orientation becomes normal to the screen.

4. Move the cursor over the inner circular edge of the base feature and select it when it is highlighted.

5. Choose the **Convert Entities** button from the **Sketch CommandManager**; the sketch is created by projecting the selected edge into the current sketching plane, refer to Figure 2-35. Next, press the ESC key to exit the tool.

The **Convert Entities** tool is used to create one or more sketch curves by projecting an edge, loop, face, curve, and so on onto the current sketching plane.

Tip
You can select multiple entities to create sketch by projecting them on the current sketching plane. You can also select entities after invoking the ***Convert Entities*** *tool.*

Note
When you create a sketch curve by using the ***Convert Entities*** *tool, the on edge relations is automatically applied to the sketch curve. The on edge relation is applied between the sketch curve created and the selected entity, which causes the sketch curve to update if the entity changes*

6. Choose the **Offset Entities** button from the **Sketch CommandManager**; the **Offset Entities PropertyManager** is displayed.

The **Offset Entities** tool is used to draw parallel lines or concentric arcs and circles. You can offset the selected entities, edges, and loops, and curves. You can also select parabolic curves, ellipse, and elliptical arcs to offset.

7. Set the value of the **Offset Distance** spinner to **35 mm** in the **Parameters** rollout of the PropertyManager.

The **Offset Distance** spinner is used to set the distance through which the selected entity needs to be offset.

Tip
You can also specify the offset distance of the entity by dragging the preview of the offset entity in the drawing area.

8. Accept other default options in the PropertyManager and select the curve from the drawing area; preview of the offset curve is displayed. Also, an arrow is displayed pointing towards the outward direction. If the direction of arrow is pointing towards the inward direction then you need to reverse the direction of arrow by selecting the **Reverse** check box from the **Offset Entities PropertyManager**.

9. Choose the **OK** button from the PropertyManager; a new sketch entity is created at an offset distance of **35** from the selected sketch entity, as shown in Figure 2-35.

10. Choose the **Centerline** button from the **Line** flyout in the **Sketch CommandManager**, refer to Figure 2-36; the **Insert Line PropertyManager** is displayed.

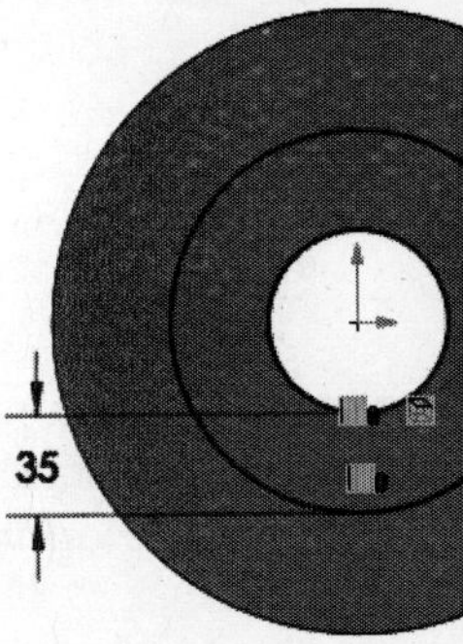

Figure 2-35 *Sketch created by using the* ***Convert Entities*** *and* ***Offset Entities*** *tools*

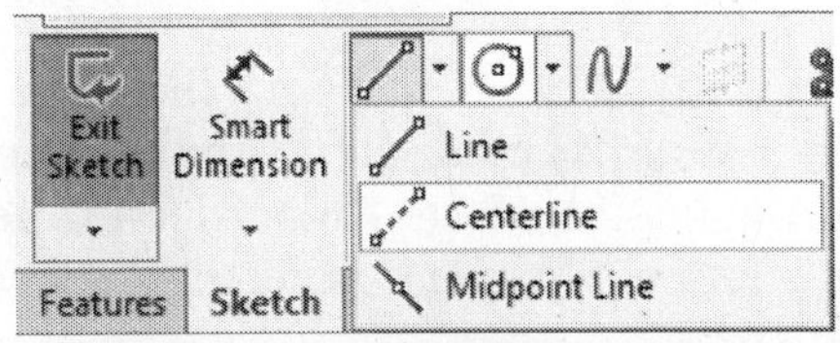

Figure 2-36 *Choosing* ***Centerline*** *button from the* ***Line*** *flyout*

The **Centerline** tool is used to draw construction lines or centerlines lines. These lines are drawn only for the aid of sketching and are not considered while converting the sketches into features.

11. Specify the start point of the centerline at the origin and move the cursor vertically upward. You will notice that the symbol of the vertical relation is displayed next to the cursor.

SOLIDWORKS applies the horizontal and vertical relations automatically to the lines depending upon there direction of movement. These relations ensure that the lines you draw are vertical or horizontal and not inclined.

12. Specify the end point of the centerline by clicking the left mouse button anywhere outside the outer circle, refer to Figure 2-37.

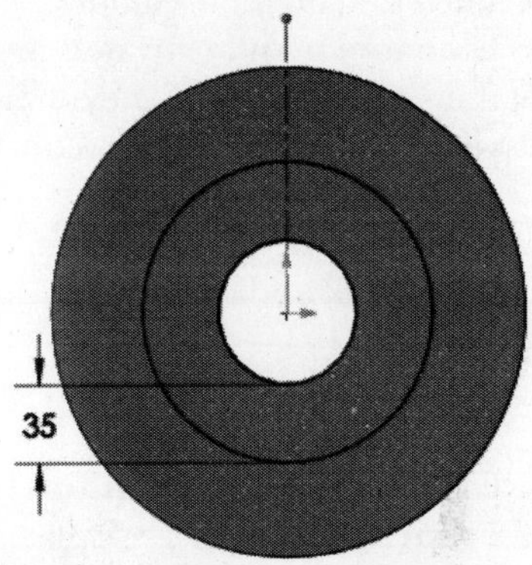

Figure 2-37 *Sketch after drawing the centerline*

Note

In the Figure 2-37, the display of the relations are hidden for the clarity of figure. To hide the relations choose the ***View Sketch Relations*** *button from the* ***Hide/Show Items*** *flyout in the* ***View (Heads-up)*** *toolbar. This is a toggle button.*

13. Choose the **Line** button from the **Sketch CommandManager**; the **Insert Line PropertyManager** is displayed. Also, the cursor is modified. You can also invoke the **Line** tool by pressing the L key.

The **Line** tool is used to draw an individual line or a chain of continuous lines. In SOLIDWORKS, you can also draw tangent or normal arcs originating from the endpoint of the line while drawing continuous lines using the **Line** tool. SOLIDWORKS also allows you to draw lines of infinite length using the **Line** tool.

Tip

You can also draw a line by using the ***Centerline*** *tool. To do so, choose the* ***Centerline*** *tool from the* ***Line*** *flyout; the* ***Insert Line PropertyManager*** *is displayed. In this PropertyManager, clear the* ***For Construction*** *check box in the* ***Options*** *rollout. Similarly, you can draw the centerline by using the* ***Line*** *tool.*

14. Move the line cursor toward the origin and press the left mouse button, when an orange circle is displayed to specify the start point of the line. As soon as you specify the start point of the line, the **Line Properties PropertyManager** is displayed. However, the options of this PropertyManager is not available at this stage.

15. Move the line cursor such that the line drawn subtends an angle of 73-degree with respect to the horizontal axis. Also a symbol of coincident relation is displayed when the line touches the outer circle of the sketch. The angle can be checked from the **Angle** spinner in the **Parameters** rollout of the **Line Properties PropertyManager**.

16. Press the left mouse button at this location to specify the endpoint of the line. Note that the **Line** tool is still activated and the endpoint of the line drawn is automatically selected as the start point of the next line. This is a continuous process and using the left mouse button you can draw a chain of continuous lines by specifying the points on the screen.

17. Press the ESC key to exit the **Line** tool. Alternatively, double-click on the screen or right-click and choose the **End chain** or **Select** option from the shortcut menu displayed.

    After drawing the line, you will mirror it using the **Mirror** tool about the vertical centerline.

18. Choose the **Mirror Entities** button from the **Sketch commandManager**; the **Mirror PropertyManager** is displayed. 

The **Mirror** tool is used to create mirror image of the selected entities. Note that when you create a mirror entity, SOLIDWORKS applies the symmetric relation between the selected entities. Also, if you change the entity, its mirror image will also change.

19. Select the line from the drawing area; the line is highlighted in blue and its name is displayed in the **Entities to mirror** selection box of the **PropertyManager**.

The **Entities to mirror** selection box of the **PropertyManager** displays the name of the entities to be selected for mirror.

20. Click on the **Mirror about** selection box of the **PropertyManager** to activate its selection mode.

The **Mirror about** selection box of the **PropertyManager** allow you to select a entity which is used as a mirroring line.

21. Select the vertical centerline from the drawing area as a mirroring line; the preview of the mirror entity is displayed in the drawing area. Make sure that the **Copy** check box is selected in the PropertyManager.

The **Copy** check box is used to remove or retain the parent selected entities while mirroring them. If you clear this check box, the parent entities will be removed and only the mirror entity will be retained when you mirror the sketched entities.

22. Choose the **OK** button from the **Mirror PropertyManager**; the mirror image of the selected entity is created, as shown in Figure 2-38.

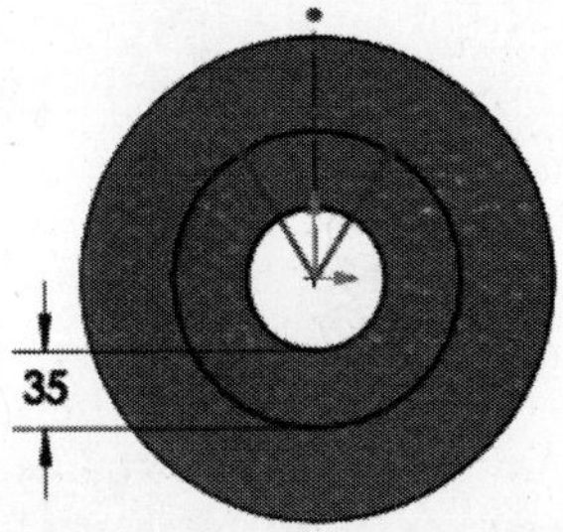

Figure 2-38 *Sketch after mirroring the line*

Now, you need to trim the unwanted entities in a sketch using the **Trim Entities** tool.

23. Choose the **Trim Entities** button from the **Sketch CommandManager**; the **Trim PropertyManager** is displayed.

The **Trim Entities** tool is used to trim the unwanted entities in a sketch. You can use this tool to trim a line, arc, ellipse, parabola, circle, spline, or centerline that is intersecting another line, arc, ellipse, parabola, circle, spline, or centerline.

24. Choose the **Trim to closest** button from the **Options** rollout of the **Trim PropertyManager**; the cursor is modified.

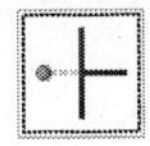

The **Trim Entities** button is used to trim the selected entity to its closest intersection.

25. Move the trim cursor closer to the entity inside the smallest circle of the sketch and click when the entity is highlighted; the entity is trimmed. Next, move the trim cursor to the next entity that is inside the smallest circle of the sketch and click when the entity is highlighted; the entity is trimmed, refer to Figure 2-39.

26. Similarly, trim the other entities of the sketch and press the ESC key to exit from the **Trim Entities** tool. Figure 2-40 shows the resultant sketch after trimming all the unwanted entities of the sketch.

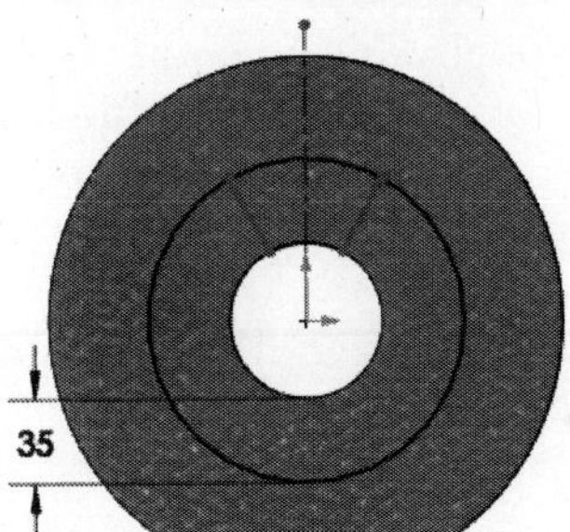

Figure 2-39 *Sketch after trimming the entities*

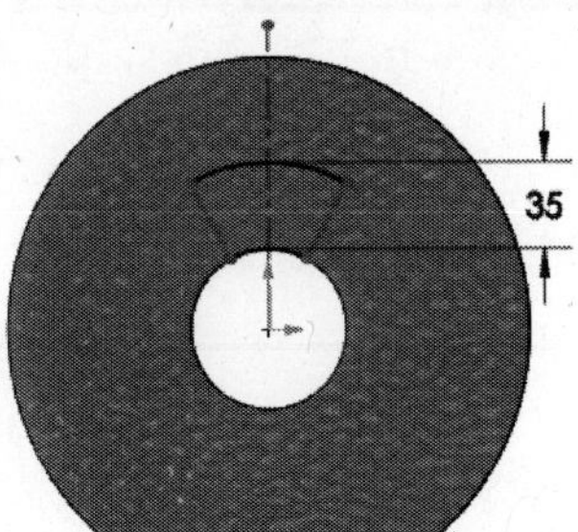

Figure 2-40 *Resultant sketch*

27. Apply angular dimensions between the inclined lines and between the inclined line and the centerline by using the **Smart Dimension** tool, as shown in Figure 2-41. Also, apply a coincident relation between one of the inclined lines and centerpoint of anyone of the arcs.

28. Click on the confirmation corner; the **Cut-Extrude PropertyManager** and preview of the cut feature is displayed.

29. Select the **Up To Next** option from the **End Condition** drop-down list of the **Direction 1** rollout in the **Cut-Extrude PropertyManager**.

As discussed earlier, the **End Condition** drop-down list provides the options to define the termination of the extruded feature. The **Up To Next** option available in this drop-down list is used to extrude the sketch from the sketching plane to the next surface that intersects the feature.

Note
The ***Up To Next*** *option will be available in the* ***End Condition*** *drop-down list only after you create a base feature.*

30. Choose the **OK** button from the **Cut-Extrude PropertyManager**; the cut extruded feature is created. Next, set the current orientation of the model to isometric by choosing the **Isometric** button from the **View Orientation** flyout. Figure 2-42 shows the isometric view of the model after creating the cut extruded feature.

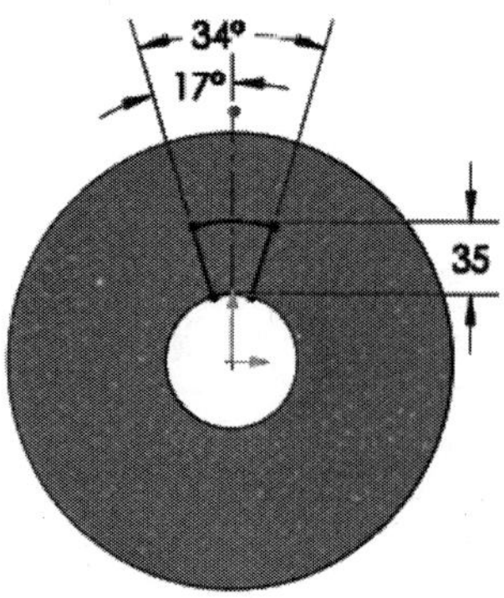

Figure 2-41 *Sketch after applying dimensions*

Figure 2-42 *Isometric view of the model*

Creating the Extrude Cut Feature

Next, you need to create the hole at the base of the model. This hole will be created as an extruded cut feature. First you need to draw a sketch of this feature on the front circular face of the base feature and then convert the sketch drawn to a extruded cut feature using the **Extruded Cut** tool.

1. Select the front circular face of the base feature and do not move the cursor; a pop-up toolbar is displayed. Select the **Sketch** button from the pop-up toolbar; the sketch environment is invoked.

2. Orient the current view normal to the viewing direction by choosing the **Normal To** button from the **View Orientation** flyout.

3. Draw the circle of diameter 90 mm using the **Circle** tool and by specifying its center point at origin. Also, apply the diameter dimension to the circle using the **Smart Dimension** tool. Next, press the ESC key to exit the current tool.

4. Select the circle from the drawing area and do not move the cursor; a pop-up toolbar and **Circle PropertyManager** are displayed.

5. Select the **Construction Geometry** button from the pop-up toolbar; the selected circle is converted into a construction circle, refer to Figure 2-43. Alternatively, you can select the **For construction** check box from the **Options** rollout of the **Circle PropertyManager**.

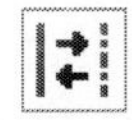

6. Draw the remaining entities of the sketch and apply dimensions to them using the tools available in the **Sketch CommandManager**, refer to Figure 2-44.

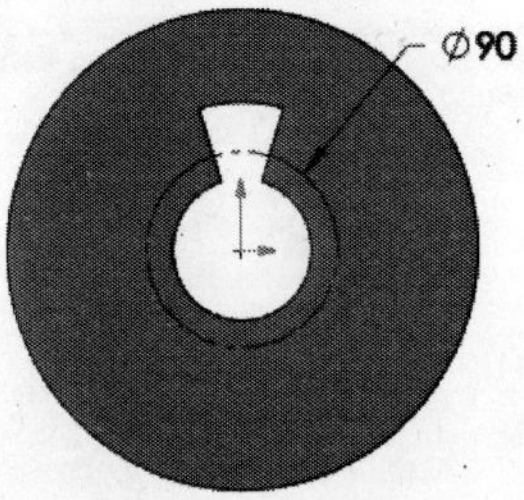

Figure 2-43 Construction circle

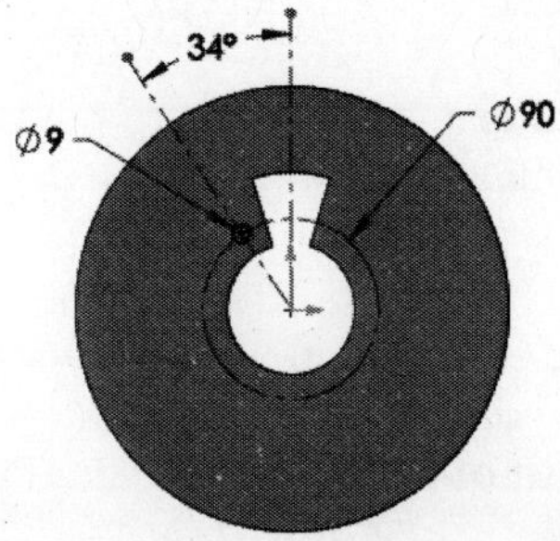

Figure 2-44 Sketch of the cut feature

7. Choose the **Features** tab from the **CommandManager**; the **Features CommandManager** is displayed.

8. Choose the **Extruded Cut** button from the **Features CommandManager**; the **Cut-Extrude PropertyManager** is displayed.

9. Set the current view to isometric view by choosing the **Isometric** button from the **View Orientation** flyout.

10. Select the **Up To Next** option from the **End Condition** drop-down list of the **Direction 1** rollout in the **Cut-Extrude PropertyManager**.

11. Choose the **OK** button from the **Cut-Extrude PropertyManager**. The isometric view of the model after creating the extruded cut feature, as shown in Figure 2-45.

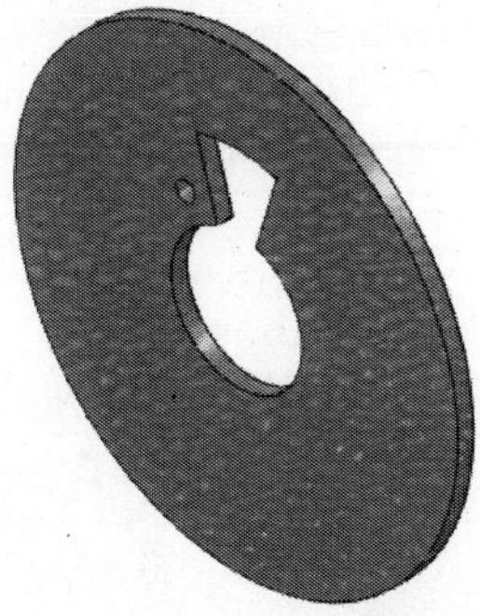

Figure 2-45 Sketch after creating the cut feature

Patterning the Features

After creating the cut features, you need to pattern them using the **Circular pattern** tool.

1. Click on the arrow below the **Linear Pattern** button from the **Feature CommandManager**; the **Linear Pattern** flyout is displayed, refer to Figure 2-46.

2. Choose the **Circular Pattern** tool from the **Linear Pattern** flyout, refer to Figure 2-46; the **CirPattern PropertyManager** is displayed.

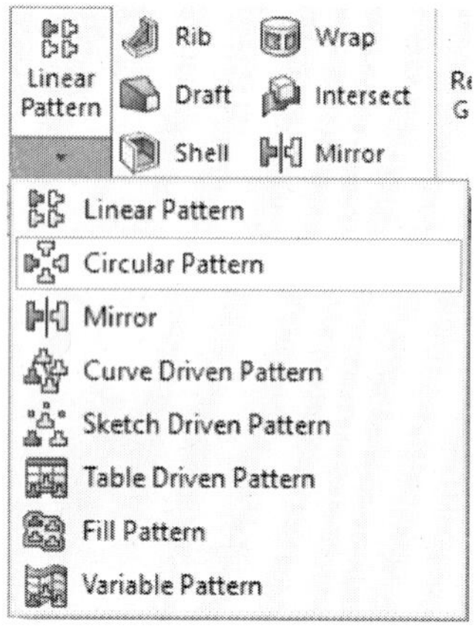

***Figure 2-46 Linear Pattern** flyout*

The **Circular Pattern** tool is used to pattern a feature, face, or body in a circular manner.

3. Click on the (▸) sign on the left of the **FeatureManager Design Tree**, which is now displayed in the left of the drawing area; the **Design Tree** expands. The three default planes and list of the features created in this part file are now visible in this **Design Tree**.

The **FeatureManager Design Tree** stores and displays all the features in a chronicle. You can select any desired feature of a model or an assembly from the **FeatureManager Design Tree** and apply different operations on the selected features.

Note

*In the **Features and Faces** rollout of the **CirPattern PropertyManager**, the **Features to Pattern** selection box is activated by default. Therefore, you can select features from the drawing area or from the **FeatureManager Design Tree** to create a circular pattern.*

4. Select the **Cut-Extrude1** and **Cut-Extrude2** features from the **FeatureManager Design Tree**; the name of the selected features is displayed in the **Features to Pattern** selection box of the PropertyManager.

5. Click once in the **Pattern Axis** selection box of the **Direction 1** rollout in the **CirPattern PropertyManager** to activate it.

The **Pattern Axis** selection box of the **CirPattern PropertyManager** is used to specify the pattern axis. You can select a circular edge or an axis for defining the pattern axis. If you are creating a circular pattern on a circular feature then you can select its circular edge; the center of circular feature will be selected as the pattern axis.

6. Select a circular edge of the base feature; the preview of circular pattern of the selected cut feature with default values is displayed in the drawing area.

7. Set the value of the **Number of Instances** spinner to **5** in the **Direction 1** rollout of the PropertyManager. Also, make sure that the **Equal spacing** radio button is selected and the value of the **Angle** spinner is set to 360-degree in the **Direction 1** rollout of the **CirPattern PropertyManager**.

The **Number of Instances** spinner in the **Parameters** rollout of the PropertyManager is used to specify number of instances in the pattern and the **Equal spacing** check box is used to specify equal or user-defined angular spacing between the instances.

Note

*When you select the **Instance spacing** radio button, you need to set the value of the incremental angle between the instances in the **Angle** spinner and when you select the **Equal spacing** radio button then SOLIDWORKS automatically calculate the angular spacing between the instances.*

8. Choose the **OK** button from the **CirPattern PropertyManager**; the circular pattern of the selected features is created. Next, change the current view of the model to isometric by choosing the **Isometric** button from the **View Orientation** flyout. The isometric view of the model after patterning the cut features is shown in Figure 2-47.

Figure 2-47 *Model after patterning the cut features*

Creating the Fill Pattern of the Predefined Hole

Next, you will create a fill pattern of the predefined holes by using the **Fill Pattern** tool.

1. Choose the **Fill Pattern** button from the **Linear Pattern** flyout in the **Features CommandManager,** refer to Figure 2-48; the **Fill Pattern PropertyManager** is displayed.

The **Fill Pattern** tool is used to fill a defined area with pattern of the features, faces, or predefined holes. The area to be filled with pattern of features or holes can be a sketched entity, face, or a co-planar face.

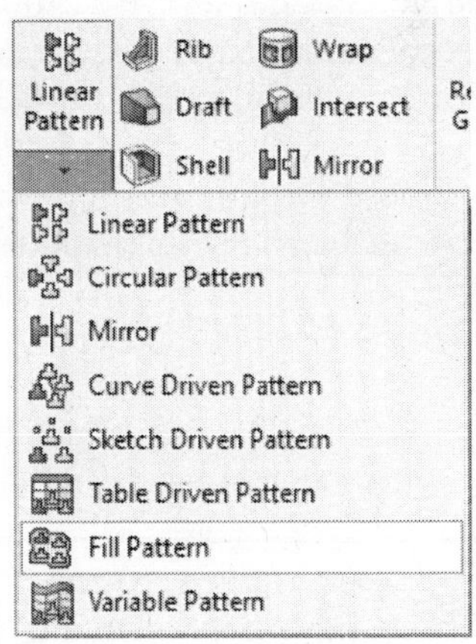

Figure 2-48 ***Linear Pattern*** *flyout*

2. Select the front circular face of the model as the area to be filled from the drawing area; the selected face is highlighted and the name of the selected face is displayed in the selection box of the **Fill Boundary** rollout of the **Fill Pattern PropertyManager**.

3. Expand the **Features and Faces** rollout of the PropertyManager by clicking on the down arrow provided on its right, if not expanded.

The **Features and Faces** rollout of the PropertyManager is used to defined whether you want to create fill pattern of features or predefined holes. By default, the **Selected features** radio button is selected in this rollout therefore you can select features from the drawing area or from the **FeatureManager Design Tree** to create a fill pattern. To create fill pattern of the predefined holes, you need to select the **Create seed cut** radio button from this rollout.

4. Select the **Create seed cut** radio button from the **Features and Faces** rollout of the PropertyManager to create a pattern of the predefined holes. On selecting this radio button, the **Circle**, **Square**, **Diamond**, and **Polygon** buttons get enabled below it. Also, preview of the pattern is displayed in the drawing area.

Note
*By default, the **Circle** button is chosen in the **Features and Faces** rollout therefore preview of the circular hole pattern is displayed in the drawing area.*

Tip
To create the square, diamond, and polygon hole pattern, you need to select there respective button.

5. Set the value of the **Diameter** spinner to **9 mm** in the **Features and Faces** rollout of the PropertyManager.

   Next, you need to specify the parameters of the pattern layout in the **Pattern Layout** rollout of the **Fill Pattern PropertyManager**.

The buttons available in the **Pattern Layout** rollout of the PropertyManager such as **Perforation**, **Circular**, **Square**, and **Polygon** are used to create a perforated style pattern, circular shape pattern, square shape pattern, and polygon style pattern respectively. The **Perforation** button is chosen by default in this rollout.

6. Choose the **Circular** button from the **Pattern Layout** rollout of the **PropertyManager**, to create a circular shape pattern.

7. Set the value of the **Loop Spacing** spinner to **95** mm in the **Pattern Layout** rollout.

8. Choose the **Instances per loop** radio button to define the instances of the loop and then set the value of the **Number of Instances** spinner to **25 mm**.

Note
*In the preview of the fill pattern, the seed feature is located at the center of the fill boundary face and you can accept its position for this tutorial point of view. However, you can specify user-defined position for a seed feature by using the **Vertex or Sketch Point** selection box of the **Features and Faces** rollout in the **Fill Pattern PropertyManager**. To do so, first you need to active this selection area by clicking on it and then by selecting a vertex or sketch point from the drawing box to define the position of the seed feature.*

9. Choose the **OK** button from the **Fill Pattern PropertyManager**; fill pattern of the predefined circular holes is created, as shown in Figure 2-49.

Figure 2-49 Model after creating the fill pattern feature

Creating the Fillet Feature

Now, you need to apply the fillet to the model using the **Fillet** tool. In SOLIDWORKS, fillet is created as a placed feature.

1. Choose the **Fillet** button from the **Features CommandManager**; the **Fillet PropertyManager** is displayed and you are prompted to select edges, faces, features, or loops to create fillet. Note that, if the **FilletXpert PropertyManager** is displayed, you need to choose the **Manual** button from it to display the **Fillet PropertyManager**.

The **Fillet** tool is used to remove sharp corners by adding or removing material from the model. The adding or removing material depends upon the edge references selected. In SOLIDWORKS, you can add fillets as placed features to a model using the **Manual** or the **FilletXpert** options. The **Manual** option is used to fillet an internal or external face or edge of a model. Whereas, **FilletXpert** option is used to create single or multiple fillets and change the existing constant fillets.

2. Make sure that the **Constant Size Fillet** button is selected in the **Fillet Type** rollout of the PropertyManager.

The **Fillet Type** rollout of the PropertyManager provides buttons to create different type of fillets. By default, the **Constant Size Fillet** button is selected and is used to create fillet of constant radius along the selected entity. You can also create variable radius fillet, face fillet, or full round fillet by selecting their respective buttons from the **Fillet Type** rollout of the PropertyManager.

3. Select the required edges of the model to create fillets from the drawing area; preview of the fillet feature with default radius value is displayed in the drawing area, refer to Figure 2-50. Also, a callout is displayed attached to the preview of the fillet with the current radius value of the fillet. The name of the selected edges of the model are displayed in the selection box of the **Items To Fillet** rollout of the **Fillet PropertyManager**.

4. Set the value of the **Radius** spinner to **6.5** mm in the **Items To Fillet** rollout and then choose the **OK** button from the **Fillet PropertyManager**. Final model after applying the fillet feature is shown in Figure 2-51.

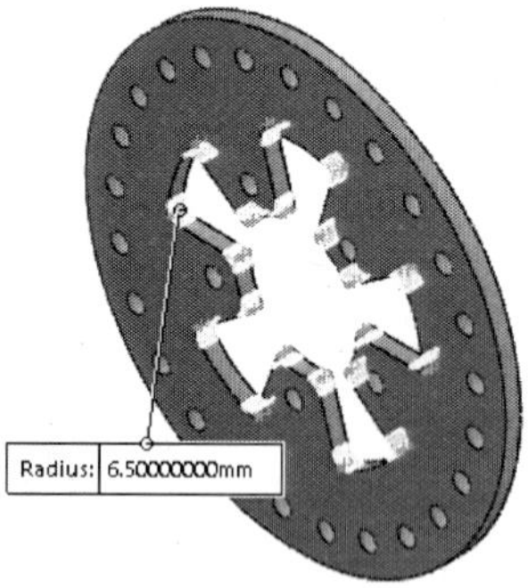

Figure 2-50 Preview of the fillet feature

Figure 2-51 Final model of the Disc plate

Saving the Model

After completing the model, you need to save it in the *Motor Cycle Project* folder.

1. Invoke the **Save As** dialog box by choosing the **Save** button from the Menu Bar and browse to the location of *Motor Cycle Project* folder.

2. Enter the name of the model as Disc Plate in the **File name** edit box and choose the **Save** button from the dialog box. The document will be saved in the *\Documents\Motor Cycle Project\Disc Plate*.

3. Close document by choosing **File > Close** from the SOLIDWORKS menus.

Self-Evaluation Test

Answer the following questions and then compare them to those given at the end of this chapter:

1. Most of the products designed by using SOLIDWORKS are a combination of __________, __________, and __________ features.

2. The __________ feature is the first feature created while creating a model in the Part environment.

3. The __________ planes are called as datum planes.

4. The __________ tool is used to add material defined by a sketch.

5. The __________ drop-down list provides the options to define the termination of the extruded feature.

6. When you create a sketch curve by using the **Convert Entities** tool the __________ and __________ relations are automatically applied to it.

7. Black color of the sketch indicates that it is fully defined sketch. (T/F)

8. You can specify the depth of extrusion by dragging the arrow provided in the preview of the model. (T/F)

9. You can not specify the offset distance of the entity by dragging the preview of the offset entity in the drawing area. (T/F)

10. The **Constant radius** radio button is used to create a fillet of constant radius. (T/F)

Review Questions

Answer the following questions:

1. Which rollout of the **Boss-Extrude PropertyManager** is used to specify the end condition for extruding the sketch in first direction?

   (a) **Direction** (b) **Direction 2**
   (c) **Direction 1** (d) **From**

2. Which of the following radio buttons is used to create fill pattern of the predefined holes?

   (a) **Selected features** (b) **Create seed cut**
   (c) **Instances per loop** (d) None of these

3. The __________ button in the **Hide/Show Items** flyout is used to hide or show the relations applied to the sketch.

4. The __________ tool is used to draw parallel lines or concentric arcs and circles.

5. The __________ tool is used to create the mirror images of the selected entities.

6. The __________ tool is used to pattern a feature, face, or body in a circular manner.

7. The __________ tool is used to fill a defined area with the pattern of the features, faces, or predefined holes.

8. The **Modify** dialog box will display automatically only when the **Input dimension value** check box is selected. (T/F)

9. In SOLIDWORKS, you can draw a regular polygon with infinite number of sides. (T/F)

10. The **Number of Instances** spinner in the **Parameters** rollout of the Circular Pattern PropertyManager is used to specify number of instances in the pattern. (T/F)

EXERCISE

Exercise

In this exercise, you will create a rear axle, as shown in Figure 2-52. The features of this Axle will be created by using the **Extruded Boss/Base** tool. The cosmetic threads with shaded display will be created by using the ANSI Metric of Machine Threads type. The views and dimensions of the axle are given in Figure 2-53. All the dimensions are in millimeters. After completing the model, save it at the location *\Documents\Motor Cycle Project* and named as *Rear Axle.*

(Expected time: 15 min)

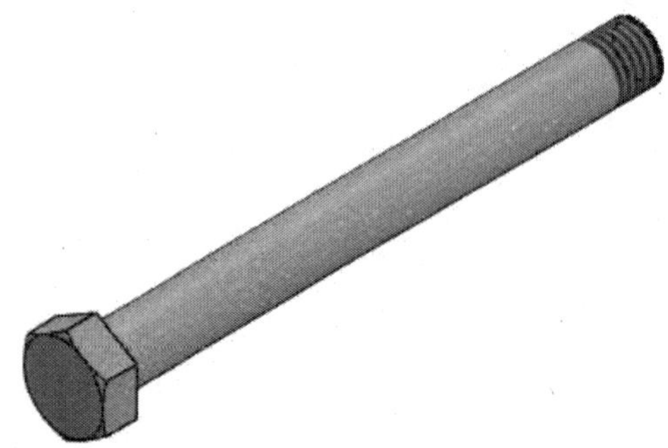

Figure 2-52 *Rear axle*

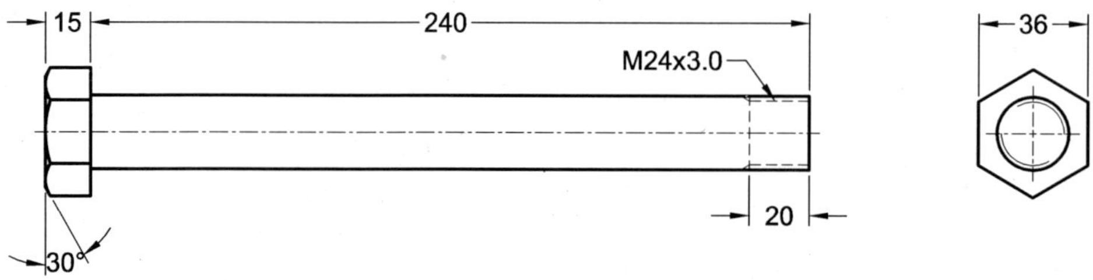

Figure 2-53 *Views and dimensions of the rear axle*

Answers to Self-Evaluation Test

1. sketch, placed, derived, **2.** base, **3.** default, **4. Extruded Boss/Base**, **5. End Condition**, **6. On Edge, Fix**, **7.** T, **8.** T, **9.** F, **10.** T

Chapter 3

Creating Rim and Tire

Learning Objectives

After completing this chapter, you will be able to:

- *Create mirror entities using the Dynamic Mirror tool*
- *Create tangent arcs using the Line tool*
- *Add relations to sketches*
- *Create solid revolved features*
- *Create cut features*
- *Mirror features*
- *Mirror features, faces, and bodies*
- *Customize tools of the View (Heads-up) toolbar*
- *Create the shell features*
- *Create a reference plane at an offset distance*
- *Create wrap features*

CREATING THE RIM

Part Description

In this section, you will create the Rim, as shown in Figure 3-1. It will be created by using different feature creation tools of SOLIDWORKS. The first feature of the Rim will be created by using the **Extruded Boss/Base** tool. Similarly, the other features of the Rim will be created by using the **Revolved Boss/Base**, **Extruded Cut**, **Circular Pattern**, **Mirror**, and **Fillet**. Different views and dimensions of the Rim are given in Figure 3-2. **(Expected time: 55 min)**

Figure 3-1 *The Rim*

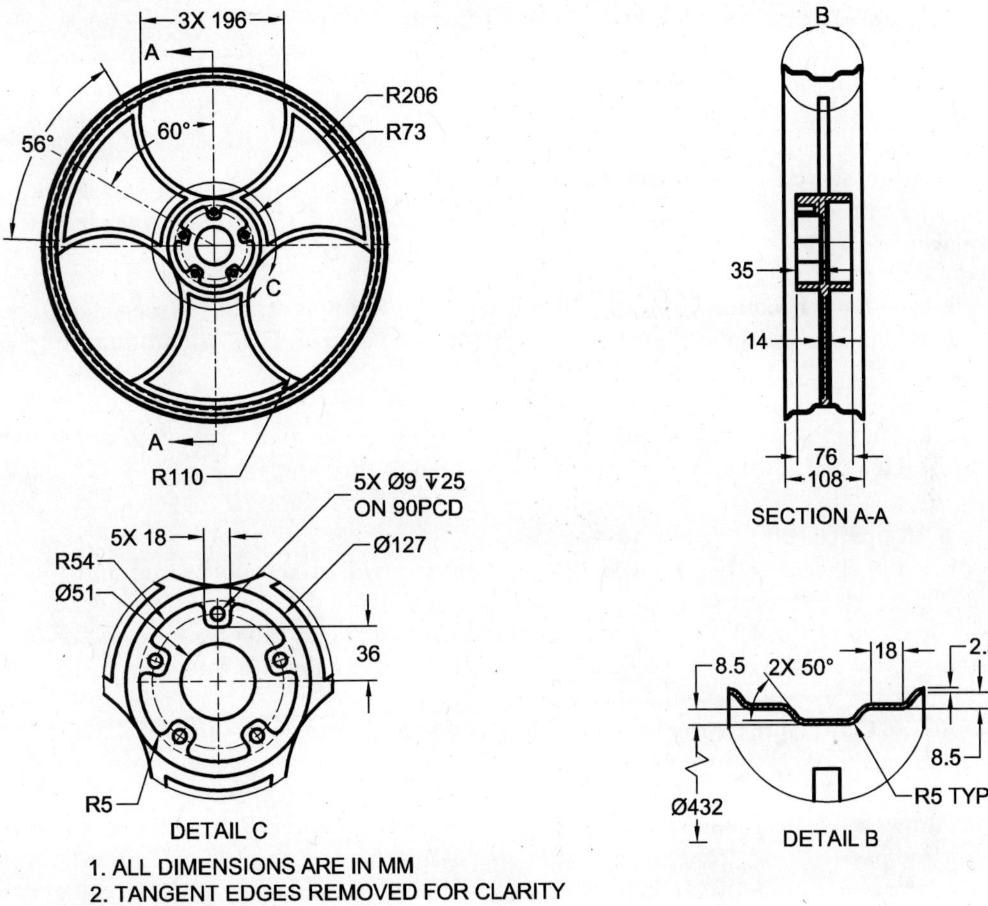

Figure 3-2 Views and Dimensions of the model

Creating the Base Feature

As discussed earlier, the base feature is the first feature created while creating a model in the Part environment. The base feature of the Rim is created by revolving a sketch about a revolution axis using the **Revolved Boss/Base** tool available in the **Features CommandManager**.

Starting a New Part Document

1. Choose the **New** button From the Menu Bar; the **New SOLIDWORKS Document** dialog box is displayed.

2. The **Part** button is chosen by default in this dialog box. Choose the **OK** button; a new SOLIDWORKS part document is started. You can also invoke a new part document by using the **Welcome - SOLIDWORKS 2018** dialog box.

Note

In the last chapter, you learned to invoke sketching environment by first invoking a feature creation tool such as ***Extruded Boss/Base*** *and then selecting a sketching plane. However, in this chapter, you will directly invoke sketching environment by using the* ***Sketch*** *tool.*

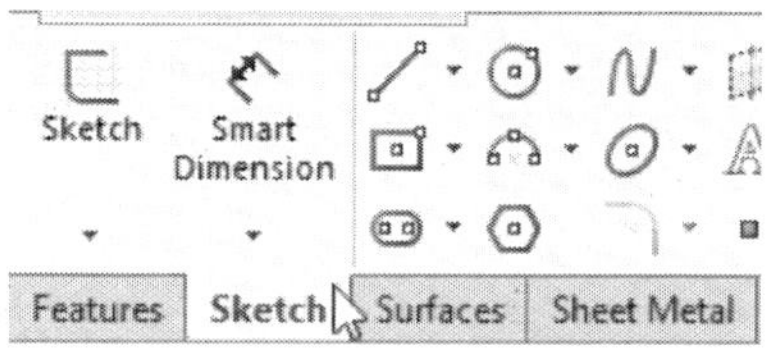

Figure 3-3 *The* ***Sketch*** *tab in the* ***CommandManager***

3. Click on the **Sketch** tab from the **CommandManager**, refer to Figure 3-3; the **Sketch CommandManager** is displayed.

4. Choose the **Sketch** button from the **Sketch CommandManager**; the **Edit Sketch PropertyManager** is displayed at the left of the drawing area and you are prompted to select the sketching plane.

5. Select the **Right Plane** as a sketching plane from the drawing area; the sketching environment is invoked and the selected plane is oriented normal to the view.

Drawing the Sketch

To draw the sketch of the revolved feature, first you will create horizontal and vertical centerlines. The vertical centerline will be used to mirror the sketched entities and the horizontal centerline will be used to apply the linear diameter dimension to the revolved sketch. Also, you will revolve the sketch around the horizontal centerline.

1. Choose the **Centerline** button from the **Line** flyout in the **Sketch CommandManager**; the **Insert Line PropertyManager** is displayed.

2. Next, draw the vertical centerline by specifying its start and end points. Make sure that the centerline passes through the origin. After specifying the end point of the centerline, the **Centerline** tool is still active and the rubber-band line is attached with the cursor suggesting that you can draw a continuous chain of centerlines.

3. Right-click in the drawing area; a shortcut menu is displayed. Choose the **End chain (double-click)** option from it to end the continuous line drawing process. Alternatively, you can double-click in the drawing area.

When you terminate the line/centerline drawing process by double-clicking on the screen or by choosing **End chain** option from the shortcut menu, the current chain is ended but the **Line/Centerline** tool is still active. So, you can draw other lines/centerlines. However, you can exit the **Line/Centerline** tool by choosing **Select** option from the shortcut menu or by pressing the ESC key.

4. Similarly, draw the horizontal centerline passing through the origin and then press the ESC key. The Figure 3-4 shows the sketch after drawing the vertical and horizontal centerlines.

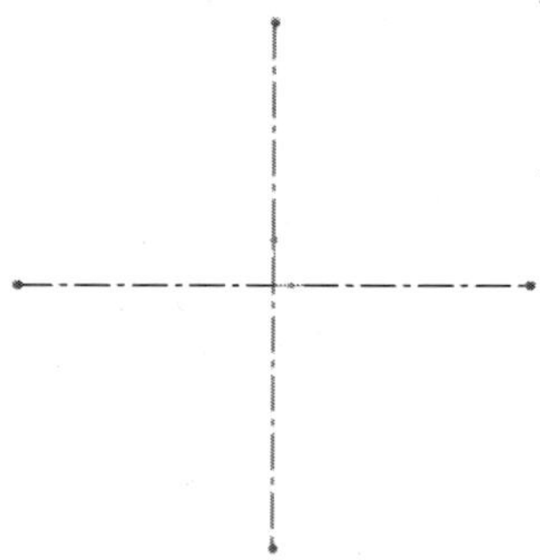

Figure 3-4 *Sketch after drawing the vertical and horizontal centerline*

The centerlines are drawn only for the aid of sketching. These lines are ignored while converting the sketches into features.

Next, you need to draw the sketch of the revolved feature. The sketch of the revolved feature will be drawn using the **Line** and **Dynamic Mirror** tools.

5. From the drawing area, select the vertical centerline.

6. Choose the **Tools > Sketch Tools > Dynamic Mirror** from the SOLIDWORKS menus the vertical centerline is converted to mirror line and the dynamic mirror option is activated.

Tip
You can confirm the creation of the mirror line and the activation of the dynamic mirror option by symmetrical symbol displayed on both ends of the vertical centerline.

The **Dynamic Mirror** tool is used to mirror the entities dynamically about a centerline while sketching.

7. Press the S key; a shortcut toolbar is displayed with set of tools, as shown in Figure 3-5.

On pressing the S key, some of the tools that can be used in the current mode will be displayed near the cursor. This is called as shortcut toolbar. You can customize the tools in the shortcut toolbar by using the **Customize** dialog box. To invoke the **Customize** dialog box, you need to right-click on the shortcut bar and choose the **Customize** option. Once the **Customize** dialog box is displayed, you can drag and drop the required tools from the **Customize** dialog box to the shortcut toolbar.

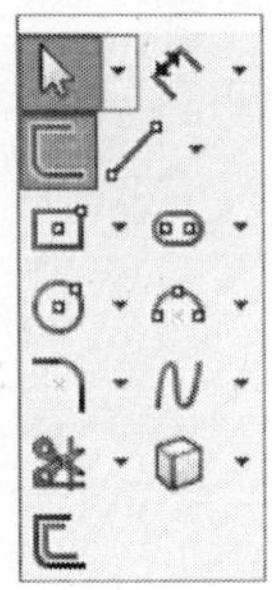

Figure 3-5 *Shortcut toolbar is displayed after pressing the S key*

8. Choose the **Line** button from the shortcut toolbar; the **Line** tool is activated and the cursor is replaced to the line cursor.

Note
As discussed in the last chapter, you can also invoke the ***Line*** *tool from the* ***Sketch CommandManager****.*

9. Move the cursor close to the origin and click when an orange circle is displayed to specify the start point of the line.

10. Move the cursor horizontally toward right and specify the endpoint of the line when its length above the line cursor shows a value close to 38. As soon as you press the left mouse button to specify the endpoint of the line, a line of the same length is drawn automatically on the other side of the mirror line, as shown in Figure 3-6.

Note

1. When you move the cursor horizontally toward right or left, a symbol of horizontal relation is displayed next to the cursor indicating that horizontal relation will be applied if you specify the end point at this stage.

2. The display of the relations in the figures is turned off for clarity. You can also turn on or off the display of relations by choosing the ***View Sketch Relations*** *button from the* ***Hide/Show Items*** *flyout in the* ***View (Heads-up)*** *toolbar.*

Note that the mirrored entity that is automatically created on the left of the mirror line is merged with the line drawn on the right. Therefore, the entire line becomes a single entity. The mirror image of the line will merge with the line you draw only if one of the endpoints of the line is coincident with the mirror line.

11. Move the cursor vertically upward and specify the endpoint of the line when the length of the line on the line cursor displays a value close to 63.5. Figure 3-7 shows the sketch after drawing the vertical line.

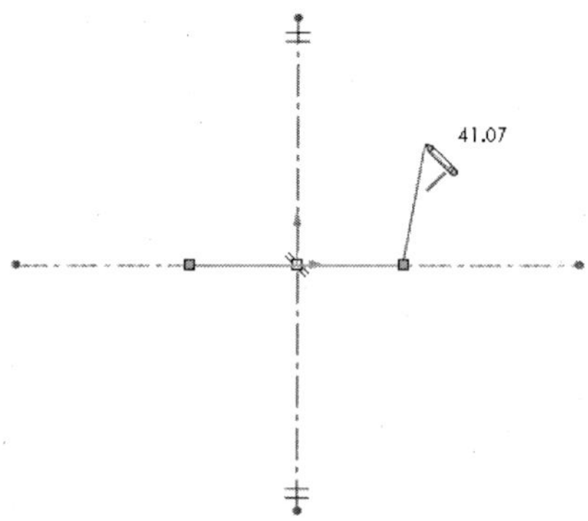

Figure 3-6 *Sketch after drawing the horizontal line*

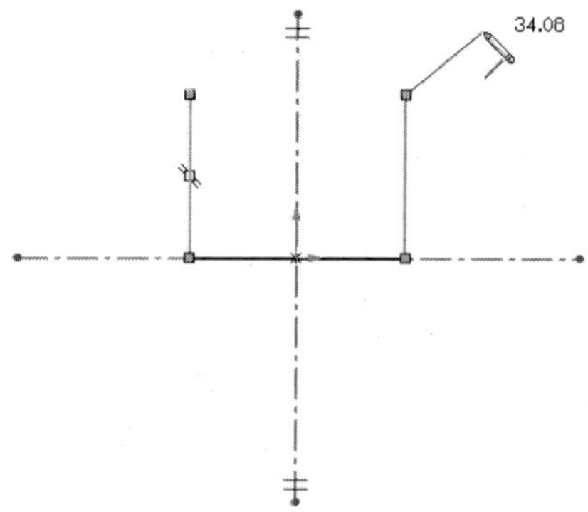

Figure 3-7 *Sketch after drawing the vertical line*

Note

When you move the cursor vertically upward or downward, the symbol of vertical relation is displayed next to the cursor indicating that vertical relation will be applied if you specify the end point at this stage.

12. Move the line cursor horizontally toward left and specify the endpoint of the line when the length above the line cursor shows a value close to 32.

Note that you need to zoom in, zoom out, or pan the drawing display area, while drawing the sketch entities. You can scroll the wheel of mouse to zoom in or zoom out the drawing display area. You can also use the **Zoom In/Out** tool to zoom in or out of the drawing display area. The **Zoom In/Out** tool is used to dynamically zoom in or out of the drawing display area. To invoke this tool, choose **View > Modify > Zoom In/Out** from the SOLIDWORKS menus. When you invoke this tool, the cursor will be replaced by the zoom cursor. To zoom out of a drawing, press and hold the left mouse button and drag the cursor in the downward direction. Similarly, to zoom in a drawing, press and hold the left mouse button and drag the cursor in the upward direction. As you drag the cursor, the drawing display will be modified dynamically. After you get the desired view, exit this tool by pressing the ESC key or you can use the Z key to zoom out of a drawing and SHIFT+Z keys to zoom in the drawing.

You can pan the drawing display area using the **Pan** tool. The **Pan** tool is used to drag the view in the current display. To invoke this tool, choose **View > Modify > Pan** from the SOLIDWORKS menus. You can also pan the drawing display area by pressing the CTRL key and middle mouse button and then drag the cursor to move the entities.

13. Move the cursor vertically upward and specify the endpoint of the line when the length of the line on the line cursor displays a value close to 152.5, refer to Figure 3-8.

14. Zoom in the drawing display area by scrolling the wheel of the mouse and move the cursor horizontal towards the right. Specify the endpoint of the line when its length above the line cursor shows a value close to 7, refer to Figure 3-9.

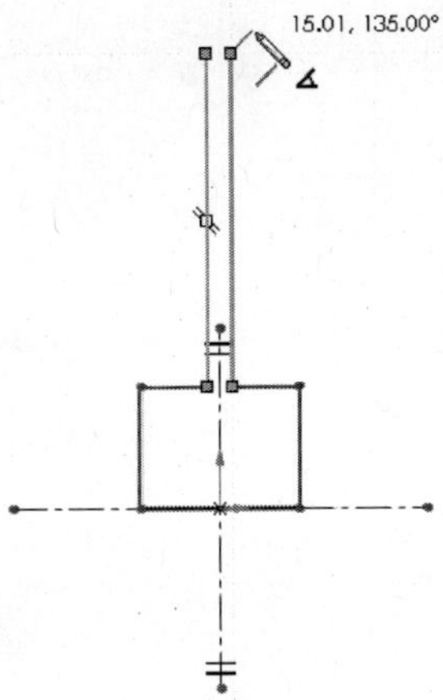

Figure 3-8 *Sketch after drawing the vertical line of length 152.5*

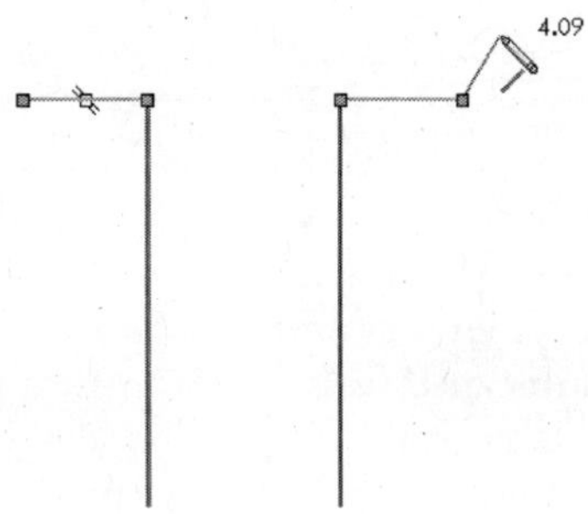

Figure 3-9 *Sketch after drawing the horizontal line of length 7*

It is evident from the DETAIL B of Figure 3-2 that the next entity of the sketch to be drawn is a tangent arc. This arc can be drawn by invoking the **Arc** tool from the **Line** tool. In SOLIDWORKS, you can draw a tangent or normal arcs originating from the endpoint of the line while drawing continuous lines. Note that these arcs can be drawn only if you have drawn at least one line, arc, or spline.

15. Move the line cursor away from the endpoint of the last line and then move it back to the endpoint of the last line. Now, move the cursor through a small distance towards the right along the tangent direction of the line; a dotted line is drawn. Next, move the cursor upward. The arc mode is invoked and the line cursor is replaced by the arc cursor.

    You will notice that a tangent arc is being drawn. The angle of the tangent arc and its radius are displayed above the arc cursor.

16. Press the left mouse button when the angle value above the arc cursor shows 50 and the radius shows a value close to 5 to complete the arc. The tangent arc is drawn, as shown in Figure 3-10. Note that the line mode is automatically invoked after you have drawn the arc using the **Line** tool.

    The next line that you need to draw is an inclined line that makes an angle of 50-degree to the horizontal axis. To draw this line, you need to move the cursor in a direction that makes an angle of 50-degree to the horizontal axis.

17. Move the line cursor such that the line shows the tangent relation with the arc and the length of the line display a value close to 5.1 above the cursor. Specify the end point of the line at this point; the inclined line is created, as shown in Figure 3-11.

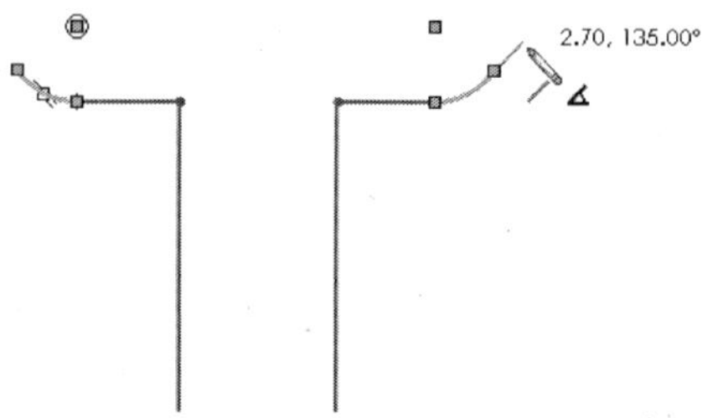

Figure 3-10 *Sketch after drawing the tangent arc*

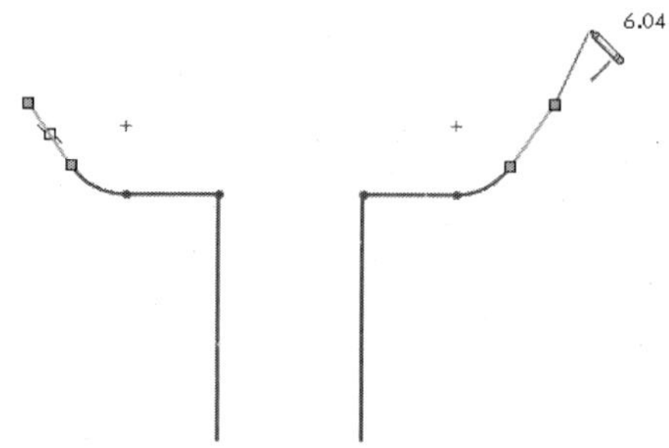

Figure 3-11 *Sketch after drawing the inclined line*

18. Now, the entity that you need to draw is an tangent arc. Zoom In the drawing display area by scrolling the wheel of the mouse and move the line cursor away from the endpoint of the inclined line and then move it back to its endpoint. Next, move the cursor through a small distance vertical upwards; a dotted line is drawn. Now, move the cursor horizontal towards the right, the arc mode is invoked. Also, the angle of the tangent arc and its radius are displayed above the arc cursor.

19. Press the left mouse button when the angle value above the arc cursor shows 50 and the radius shows a value close to 6 to complete the arc. The tangent arc is drawn, as shown in Figure 3-12. Note that the line mode is automatically invoked after you have drawn the arc using the **Line** tool.

20. Next, move the line cursor horizontally toward the right and specify the end point of the line when the length of the line on the line cursor displays a value close to 18, refer to Figure 3-13.

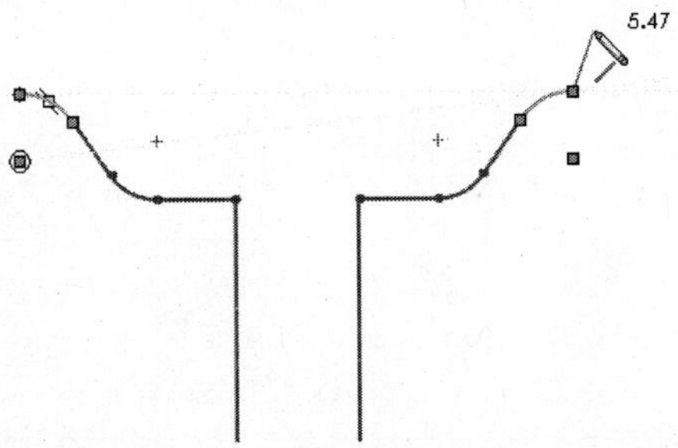

Figure 3-12 Sketch with tangent arc drawn

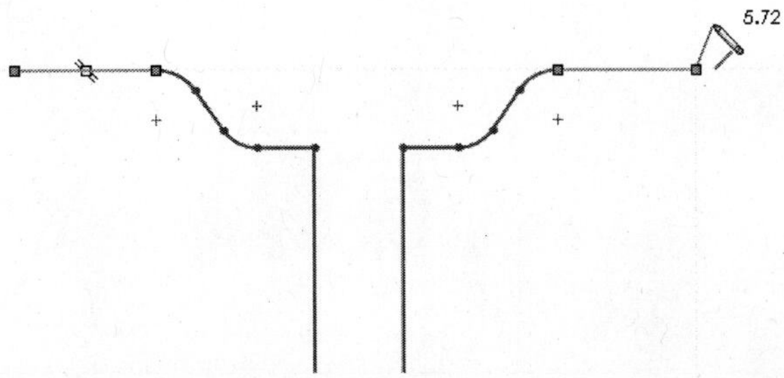

Figure 3-13 Sketch with horizontal line

21. Repeat the steps 15 through 19 and draw the tangent arcs and the inclined line. The sketch after repeating the steps 15 through 19 looks similar to one given in Figure 3-14.

22. Zoom In the drawing display area. Move the line cursor vertical upward and specify the endpoint of the line when the length of the line above the line cursor displays a value close to 2.5, as shown in Figure 3-15.

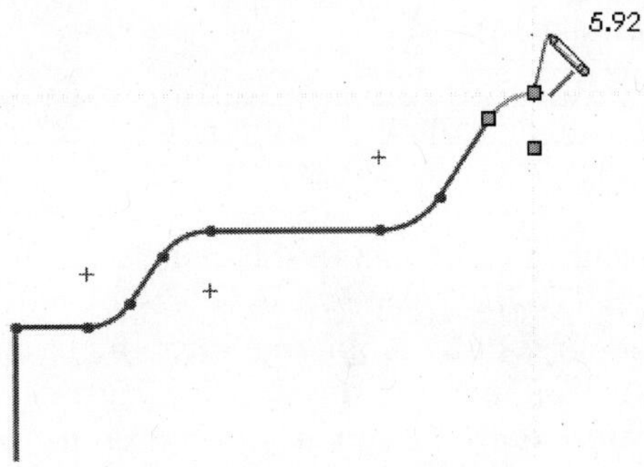

Figure 3-14 Sketch after drawing the tangent arc

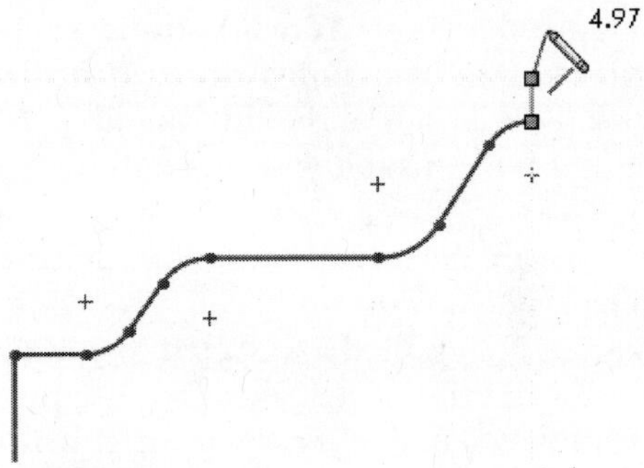

Figure 3-15 Sketch after drawing the vertical line

23. Similarly, draw the other entities of the revolved sketch and then exit from the **Line** and **Dynamic Mirror** tools. You can press the ESC key to exit from the **Line** tool. To exit from the **Dynamic Mirror** tool, you need to right-click in the drawing area and choose the **Recent Commands > Dynamic Mirror Entities** from the shortcut menu. The Figures 3-16 and 3-17 shows partial and complete sketch of the revolved feature after drawing all its entities.

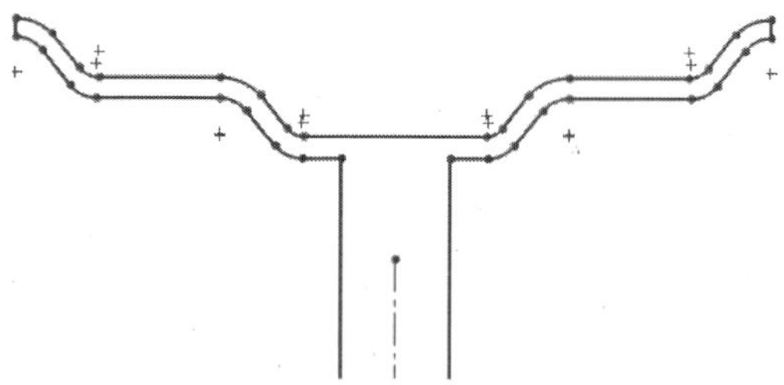

Figure 3-16 Partial view of the sketch

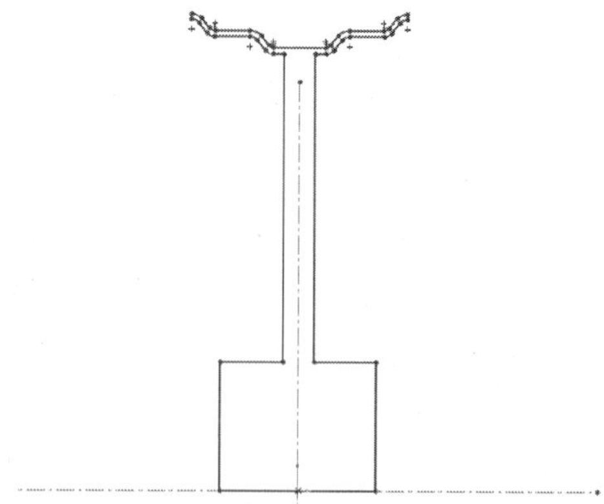

Figure 3-17 Complete view of the sketch

Adding the Required Sketch Relations

After drawing the sketch, you need to add relations to the sketch entities by using the **Add Relation** tool.

1. Choose the **Add Relation** button from the **Display/Delete Relations** flyout in the **Sketch CommandManager**, refer to Figure 3-18; the **Add Relations PropertyManager** is displayed. Also, the confirmation corner is displayed at the upper right corner of the drawing area. Now, you can add required relations to the sketch entities.

*Figure 3-18 The **Display/Delete Relations** flyout*

The relations are the logical operations that are performed to add relationships such as tangent, equal, horizontal, vertical, and so on between the sketched entities, planes, axes, edges, or vertices. The relations are applied to a sketch to constrain its degree of freedom, to reduce the number of dimensions in the sketch, and also to capture the design intent of the sketch. You can apply relations to the sketch entities by using the **Add Relation** tool. This tool is widely used to apply relations to the sketch in the sketching environment.

Note

*In SOLIDWORKS, some of the relations are automatically applied to the sketch entities while drawing them. For example, you will notice that when you specify the start point of a line and move the cursor horizontally towards the right or left, the horizontal line symbol is displayed below the line cursor. This is the symbol of the **Horizontal** relation that is applied to the line while drawing. Similarly, if you move the cursor vertically downward or upwards, the vertical line symbol for the **Vertical** relation will be displayed below the line cursor. The relations that will not applied automatically to the sketch entities, needs to be applied by using the **Add Relations** tool.*

2. Zoom in the drawing area by scrolling the middle mouse button and select the inclined line and arc, refer to Figure 3-19. The name of the selected entities are displayed in the **Selected Entities** rollout of the **Add Relations PropertyManager**.

The relations that can be applied to the two selected entities are displayed in the **Add Relations** rollout of the **Add Relations PropertyManager**. The **Tangent** option is highlighted, suggesting that the tangent relation is the most appropriate relation for the selected entities.

Note

*If the tangent relation is automatically applied between the selected line and the arc while drawing them, the **Tangent** button will not be highlighted in the **Add Relations** rollout of the PropertyManager. Also the name of the tangent relation is displayed in the **Existing Relations** rollout of the PropertyManager, suggesting that the tangent relation is already applied between the selected entities.*

3. Choose the **Tangent** button to apply the tangent relation to the selected entities from the **Add Relations** rollout of the **Add Relations PropertyManager**, if it is not applied already. The tangent relation is applied and the name of the tangent relation is displayed in the selection area of the **Existing Relations** rollout of the PropertyManager.

The tangent relation forces the selected arc, circle, spline, or ellipse to become tangent to the other selected arc, circle, spline, ellipse, line, or edge.

4. Move the cursor to the drawing area and right-click to display the shortcut menu and choose the **Clear Selections** option from it to remove the selected entities from the selection set.

5. Select the line and the arc, refer to Figure 3-20; the relations that can be applied to the selected entities are displayed and the **Tangent** option is highlighted in the **Add Relations** rollout of the PropertyManager.

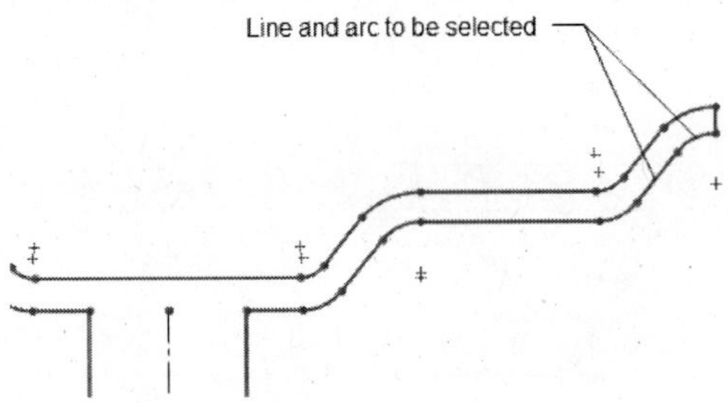

Figure 3-19 *Entities to be selected*

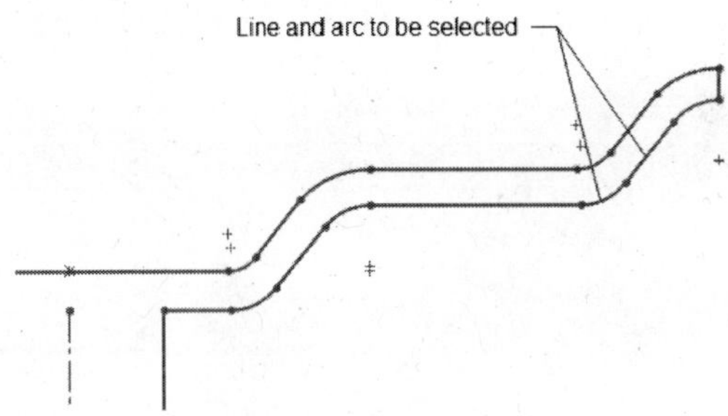

Figure 3-20 *Entities to be selected*

6. Choose the **Tangent** button from the **Add Relations** rollout of the PropertyManager to apply the tangent relation between the selected entities. The tangent relation is applied and the name of the tangent relation is displayed in the selection area of the **Existing Relations** rollout of the PropertyManager.

7. Right-click in the drawing area; a shortcut menu is displayed. Choose the **Clear Selections** option from it to remove the selected entities from the selection set.

8. Similarly, apply the tangent relations between other lines and the arcs of the sketch. The left side sketched entities of the sketch are the mirror images of the right side sketched entities. Therefore, when you apply relation to the entity, the relation will also applied to its mirror image.

   After applying the tangent relations between the lines and arcs of the sketch, you need to apply the concentric relations between the arcs of the sketch.

9. Select the arcs of the sketch from the drawing area, refer to the Figure 3-21; the **Concentric** option is highlighted in the **Add Relations** rollout of the **Add Relations PropertyManager**.

10. Choose the **Concentric** button from the **Add Relations** rollout of the PropertyManager; the concentric relation is applied between the selected arcs. Next, clear the selection set of the **Selected Entities** rollout by selecting the **Clear Selections** option from the shortcut menu displayed on right-clicking in the drawing area.

The concentric relation forces the selected arc or circle to share the same center point with the other arc, circle, point, vertex, or circular edge.

11. Select the arcs, refer to the Figure 3-22 and apply the concentric relation. Next, clear the selection set of the **Selected Entities** rollout in the **Add Relations PropertyManager**.

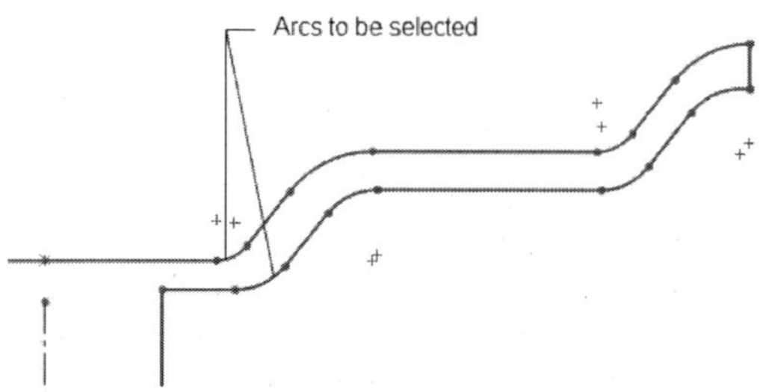

Figure 3-21 *Entities to be selected*

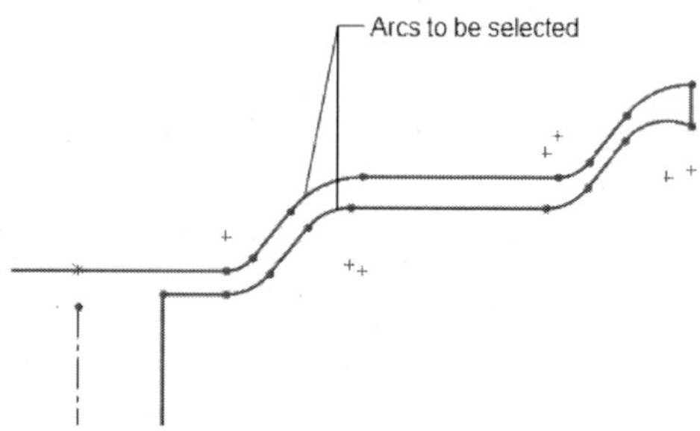

Figure 3-22 *Entities to be selected*

12. Similarly, apply the concentric relation between the other set of arcs, refer to Figure 3-23.

    After applying the concentric relations to the sketch, you need to apply the equal relations between the arcs having equal radii.

13. Select the arcs from the drawing area, refer to the Figure 3-24.

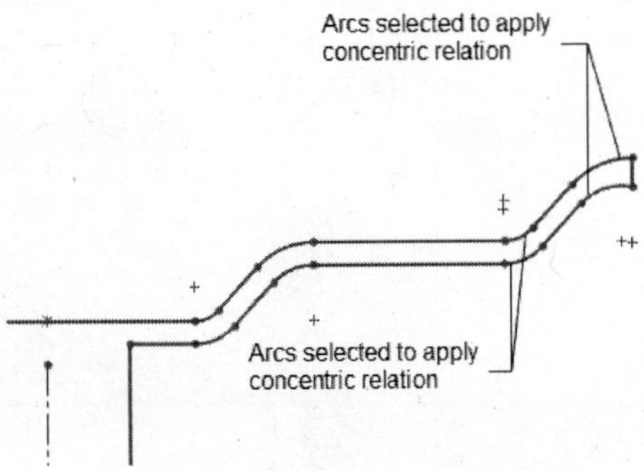

Figure 3-23 Entities to be selected

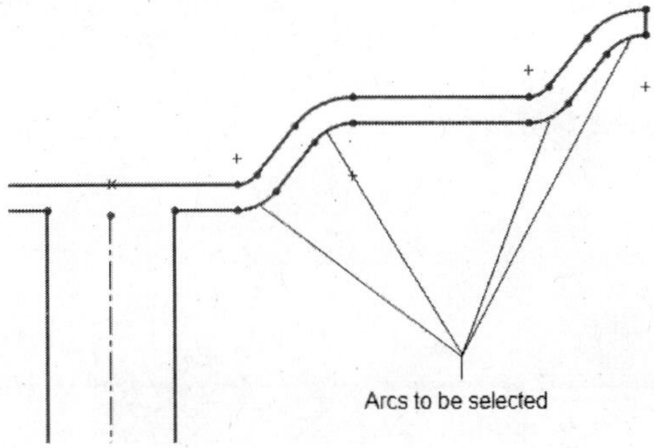

Figure 3-24 Entities to be selected

14. Choose the **Equal** button from the **Add Relations** rollout of the PropertyManager; the equal relation is applied between the selected entities.

The equal relation forces the selected lines to have equal length and the selected arcs, circle, or arc and circle to have equal radii.

Now, you need to apply the equal relations between the lines having equal length.

15. Right-click in the drawing area and select the **Clear Selections** option to remove the selected entities from the selection set.

16. Select the horizontal lines, refer to Figure 3-25; the relations that can be applied to the selected entities are displayed in the **Add Relations** rollout of the **Add Relations PropertyManager**.

17. Choose the **Equal** button from the **Add Relations** rollout of the PropertyManager; the equal relation is applied to the selected entities. Next, clear the selections from the selection set of the **Selected Entities** rollout in the PropertyManager.

18. Select the inclined lines from the drawing area, refer to the Figure 3-26 and apply the equal relation. Next, clear the selections from the selection set of the **Selected Entities** rollout.

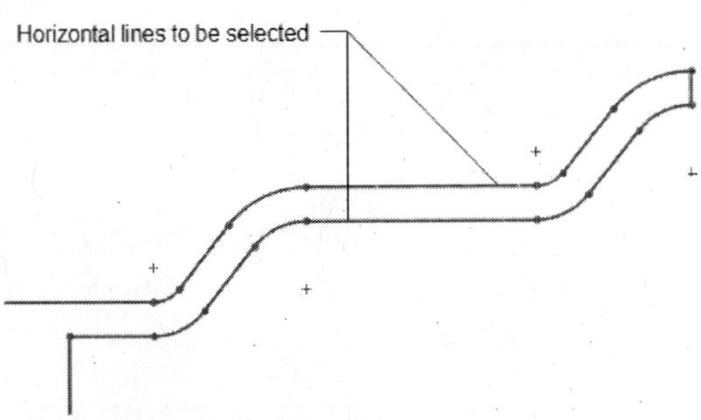

Figure 3-25 Horizontal lines to be selected

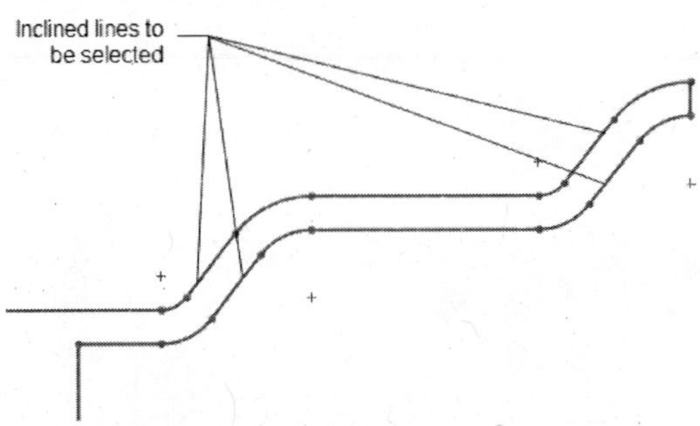

Figure 3-26 Inclined lines to be selected

19. Apply the vertical relations to the vertical lines and the horizontal relations to the horizontal lines, if it is not applied automatically while drawing them.

20. Choose the **OK** button from the **Add Relations PropertyManager** to exit from it. Partial view of the sketch after applying all possible relations looks similar to the one shown in Figure 3-27.

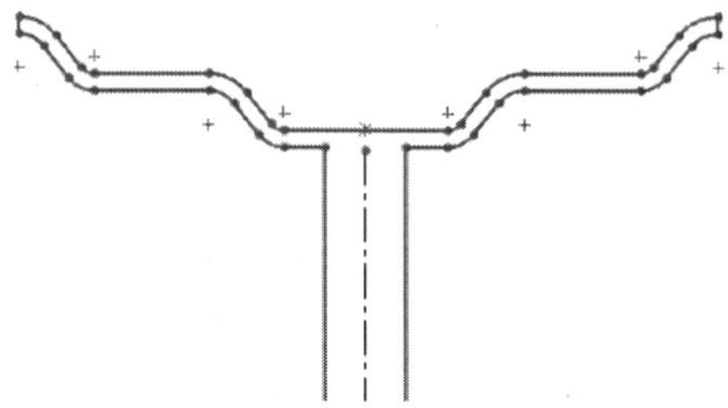

Figure 3-27 *Partial view of the sketch after applying all possible relations*

Applying Dimensions to the Sketch

Next, you need to apply the dimensions to the sketch using the **Smart Dimension** tool and fully defined the sketch. The sketch entities are shown in blue color, suggesting that the sketch is underdefined. It will change to black color after you apply the required dimensions to the sketch.

As discussed in the earlier chapter, a fully defined sketch is the one in which all the entities of the sketch and their positions are filly defined by relations or dimensions, or both. In a fully defined sketch, all the degrees of the freedom of a sketch are constrained. Therefore, the sketched entities cannot move or change their size and location unexpectedly. All the entities of the fully defined sketch are displayed in black color.

1. Choose the **Smart Dimension** button from the **Sketch CommandManager**; the cursor is replaced to dimension cursor.

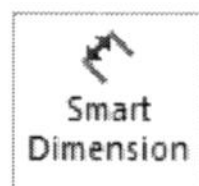

2. Apply all the required dimension to the sketch using the dimension cursor. For dimensions values of the sketch, refer to Figures 3-2 . Figures 3-28 and 3-29 shows partial and complete view of the sketch after applying all the required dimensions.

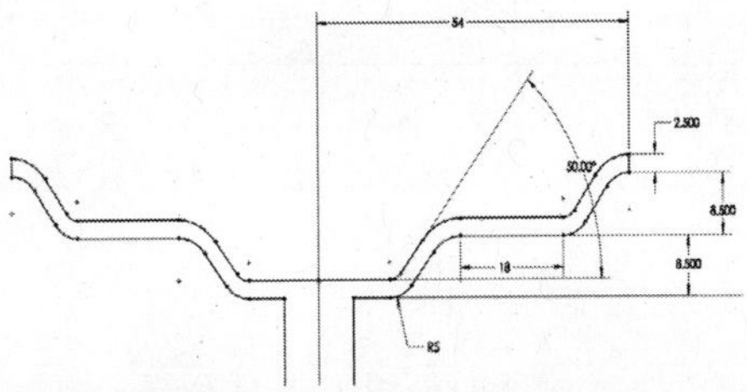

Figure 3-28 Partial view of the sketch after applying the required dimensions

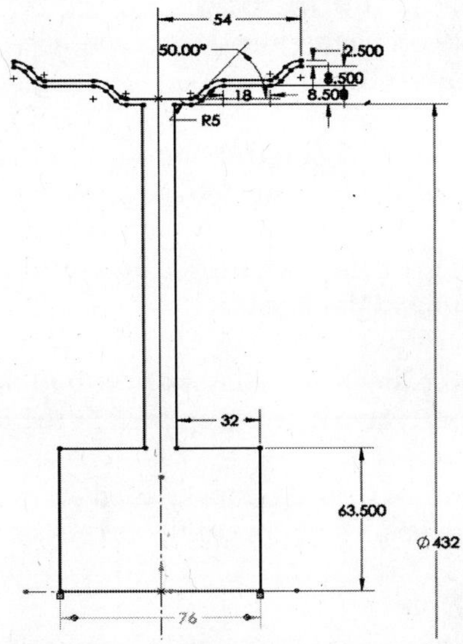

Figure 3-29 Sketch after applying the dimensions

Note

1. The dimension 432 shown in the Figure 3-29 is a linear diameter dimension. The linear diameter dimension is used to dimension the sketch of a revolved component. To apply the linear diameter dimension, choose the **Smart Dimension** *button from the* **Sketch CommandManager**. *Select the entity to be dimensioned and then select the centerline around which the sketch will be revolved. Move the cursor to the other side of the centerline; the linear diameter dimension will be attached with the cursor. Next, click in the drawing area to place the linear diameter dimension.*

2. In the Figure 3-29, the precision value for all the dimensions are not same. To defined the precision value for the individual dimensions, select the required dimension of the sketch; the ***Dimension PropertyManager*** *will be displayed at the left of the drawing area. Next, select the required precision option form the* ***Unit Precision*** *drop-down list of the* ***Tolerance/Precision*** *rollout in the PropertyManager.*

3. To defined the same precision value for all the dimensions in the sketch, invoke the ***System Options-General*** *dialog box by choosing the* ***Options*** *button from the* ***Standard*** *toolbar. Next, from this dialog box, choose the* ***Document Properties*** *tab. In this tab, select the* ***Units*** *option from the area that is available on the left of the dialog box to display the options related to units. Next, click on the cell corresponding to* ***Length*** *and* ***Decimals****; a drop-down list will be displayed. Select the required precision from this drop-down list.*

3. Exit from the sketcher environment by clicking on the conformation corner available on the upper right corner of the drawing area.

Revolving the Sketch

After completing the sketch, you need to revolve it about a horizontal centerline using the **Revolved Boss/Base** tool.

1. Choose the **Isometric** button from the **View Orientation** flyout in the **View (Heads-up)** toolbar; the current view of the sketch is changed to isometric view.

2. Switch to the **Features CommandManager** by choosing the **Features** tab from the **CommandManager**.

3. Choose the **Revolved Boss/Base** button from the **Features CommandManager**; the **Revolve PropertyManager** is displayed at the left side of the drawing area.

The **Revolved Boss/Base** tool is used to revolve the sketch about a revolution axis. The revolution axis could be an axis, an entity of the sketch, or an edge of another feature.

Note
Whether you use a centerline or an edge to revolve the sketch, the sketch should be drawn on one side of the centerline.

4. Select the horizontal centerline as a axis of revolution; preview of the revolved feature is displayed in the drawing area.

Tip
Even though you can revolve the sketch using an entity in the sketch, it is recommended to draw a centerline so that you can create linear diameter dimensions for the revolved features.

5. Make sure that the **Blind** option is selected in the **Revolve Type** drop-down list and value 360 is set in the **Direction 1 Angle** spinner of the **Direction 1** rollout of the **Revolve PropertyManager**, refer to Figure 3-30. Next, choose the **OK** button. The isometric view of the model after creating the revolved feature is shown in Figure 3-31.

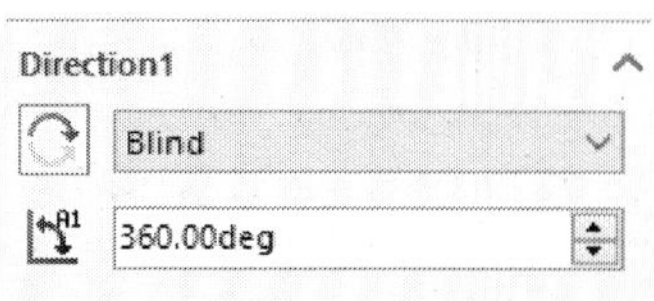

Figure 3-30 Direction1** rollout of the **Revolve PropertyManager

***Figure 3-31** Model after creating the revolve feature*

The **Revolve Type** drop-down list in the **Direction1** rollout of the PropertyManager provides the options to define the termination of the revolved feature. The **Blind** option in this drop-down list is used to define the termination of the revolved feature by specifying the angle of revolution in the **Direction 1 Angle** spinner.

Creating the Cut Feature

The second feature of the model is a extruded cut feature. The extruded cut feature is created by using the **Extruded Cut** tool available in the **Features CommandManager**. To create a extruded cut feature, first you need draw a sketch in the sketcher environment using the tools available in the **Sketch CommandManager**. After drawing the sketch, you can use the **Extruded Cut** tool to remove the material defined by the sketch.

1. Switch to the **Sketch CommandManager** by clicking on the **Sketch** tab in the **CommandManager**.

2. Choose the **Sketch** button from the **Sketch CommandManager**; the **Edit Sketch PropertyManager** is displayed and you are prompted to select a sketching plane.

3. Select the front planar face of the revolved feature as the sketching plane, refer to Figure 3-32; the sketcher environment is invoked.

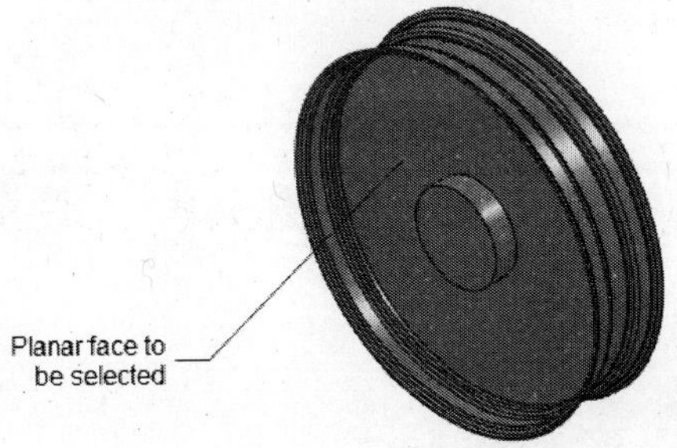

Figure 3-32 *Planar face to be selected*

4. Choose the **Normal To** button from the **View Orientation** flyout in the **View (Heads-up)** toolbar; the current orientation of the model is changed normal to the screen.

5. Choose **Centerline** button from the **Line** flyout in the **Sketch CommandManager** to invoke the **Centerline** tool. Next, move the cursor closer towards the origin and specify the start point of the centerline by pressing the left mouse button when the orange circle and the symbol of coincident relation are displayed.

The coincident relation forces the selected point to be coincident with the selected line, arc, circle, or ellipse. In the above case, if you click the left mouse button to specify the start point of the centerline when the orange circle and the symbol of coincident relation are displayed at the origin, the start point of the centerline will become coincident with the origin.

6. Move the cursor vertical upwards and specify the end point of the centerline when it crosses all the edges of the revolved feature.

7. Choose the **3 Point Arc** button from the **Arc** flyout, refer to Figure 3-33; the cursor is replaced by the three-point arc cursor.

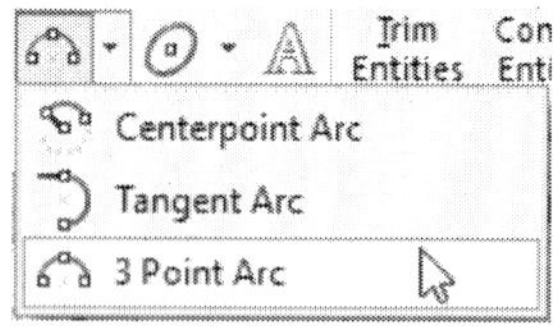

***Figure 3-33** The **3 Point Arc** button in the **Arc** flyout*

In SOLIDWORKS, you can draw arcs by using three tools named as **Centerpoint Arc**, **Tangent Arc**, and **3 Point Arc**. All these tools are grouped together in the **Arc** flyout of the **Sketch CommandManager**. The **3 Point Arc** tool is used to create three point arcs that are drawn by defining the start point and the endpoint of the arc, and a point on the circumference or the periphery of the arc.

8. Zoom in the drawing display area by scrolling the wheel of the mouse and then move the cursor towards a point where the inner most circular edge of the revolve feature and the centerline intersect, refer to Figure 3-34 and click the left mouse button to specify the start point of the arc when symbols of two coincident relation are displayed next to the cursor.

9. Move the cursor upwards toward the right and specify the end point of the arc when the edge of the revolved feature that measures diameter 432 will be highlighted, refer to Figure 3-35. You can specify the end point of the arc anywhere closer to the location of cursor shown in Figure 3-35.

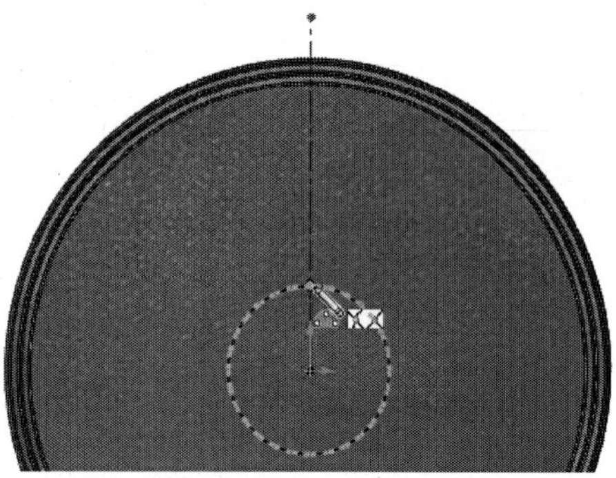

***Figure 3-34** Start point of the arc to be selected*

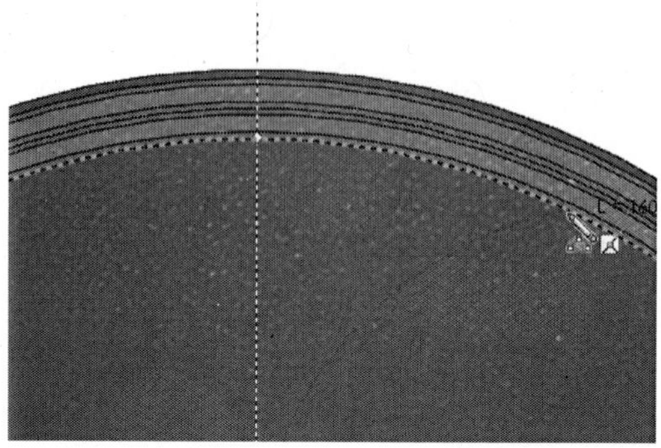

***Figure 3-35** End point of the arc to be selected*

10. Move the cursor downwards toward the right to a small distance and specify a point on the circumference of the arc when radius above the cursor shows a value closer to 110. The Figure 3-36 shows the sketch after creating the first three point arc.

11. Similarly, create a three point arc on the left side of the centerline, refer to Figure 3-37. Note that **3 Point Arc** tool is still activated.

12. Create one more three point arc by specifying its start and end points using the end points of the existing arcs and then point on the circumference when the edge of the revolved feature

that measures diameter 432 will be highlighted. Next, press the ESC Key. Figure 3-37 shows the resultant sketch of the cut feature.

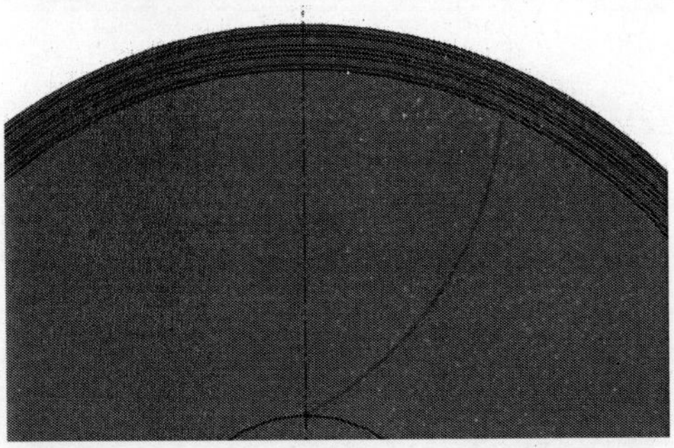

Figure 3-36 Sketch after creating the first three point arc

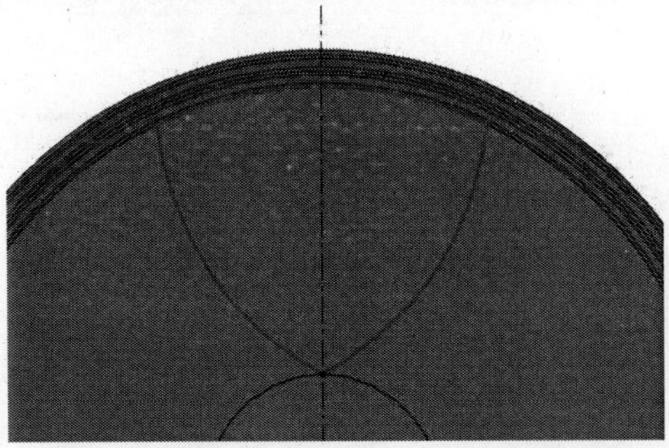

Figure 3-37 Sketch of the cut feature

After creating the sketch for the cut feature, you need to apply relations and dimensions to the sketch to make it fully defined sketch.

13. Invoke the **Add Relations PropertyManager** by choosing the **Add Relation** button from the **Display/Delete Relations** flyout in the **Sketch CommandManager**. 

14. Select end points of the arc and the centerline from the drawing area, refer to Figure 3-38; the names of the selected entities are displayed in the selection box of the **Select Entities** rollout. Also, all the possible relations that can be applied to the selected entities are displayed in the **Add Relations** rollout of the **Add Relations PropertyManager**.

15. Choose the **Symmetric** button from the **Add Relations** rollout of the PropertyManager to apply the symmetric relation. 

The symmetric relation forces two selected lines, arcs, points, and ellipses to remain equidistant from a centerline. This relation also forces the entities to have the same size and orientation.

16. Right-click in the drawing area and select the **Clear Selections** options form the shortcut menu to clear the current selections.

17. Select the Arc 1 and Arc 2 from the drawing area, refer to Figure 3-39 and then choose the **Equal** button form the **Add Relations** rollout of the PropertyManager to apply the equal relation. Next, clear the current selections. 

18. Select the Arc 3 from the drawing area, refer to Figure 3-39 and then select the circular edge of the revolved feature having 432 as the value of diameter. Next, choose the **Coradial** button from the **Add Relations** rollout. Now, press the ESC key. 

The coradial relation forces the selected arcs or circles to share the same radius and the same center point. You can also select an external entity that projects as an arc or a circle in the sketch to apply this relation.

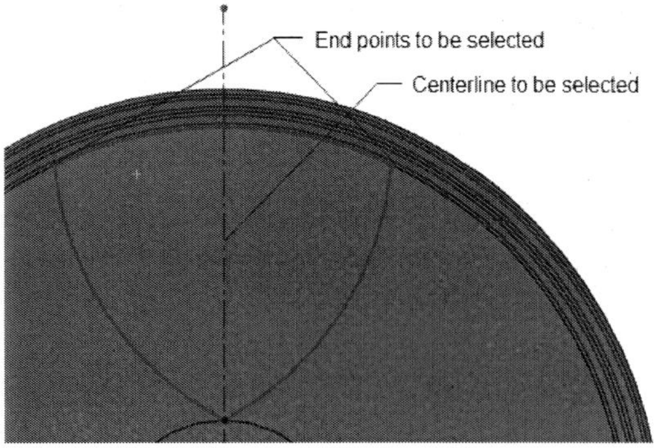

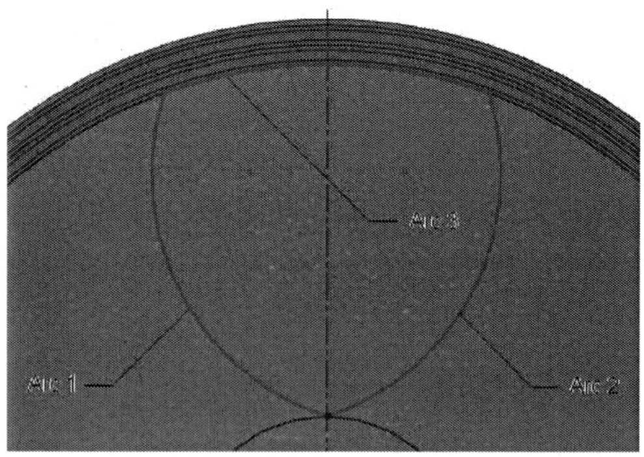

Figure 3-38 *Entities to be selected for applying symmetric relation*

Figure 3-39 *Arc 1, Arc 2, and Arc 3 of the sketch*

Tip

You can also apply relations to the sketched entities by using the pop-up toolbar. To do so, select the required entities from the drawing area by pressing the CTRL key. Once you are done with selections, release the CTRL key and do not move the mouse; a pop-up toolbar with all the possible relations that can apply to the selected entities will be displayed. Now, you can select the required relation from the pop-up toolbar.

After applying all the required relations to the sketch, you need to apply dimension using the **Smart Dimension** tool.

19. Choose the **Smart Dimension** button from the **Sketch CommandManager** and then apply a radius dimension of 110 mm to the Arc 1.

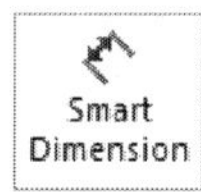

Note

Since you have applied the equal relation between Arc 1 and Arc 2, therefore radius of Arc 2 is automatically modified after applying the radius dimension to Arc 1.

20. Select the end points of the arc, refer to Figure 3-38; the distance value between the selected end points is displayed attached to the cursor.

21. Move the cursor vertical upwards and then click the left mouse button to place the dimension at an appropriate place, refer Figure 3-39; the **Modify** dialog box is displayed.

22. Enter the value **196** in the edit box in the dialog box and press ENTER. All the entities of the sketch turn black indicating that the sketch is fully-defined. Next, press the ESC key. The Figure 3-40 shows the fully-defined sketch.

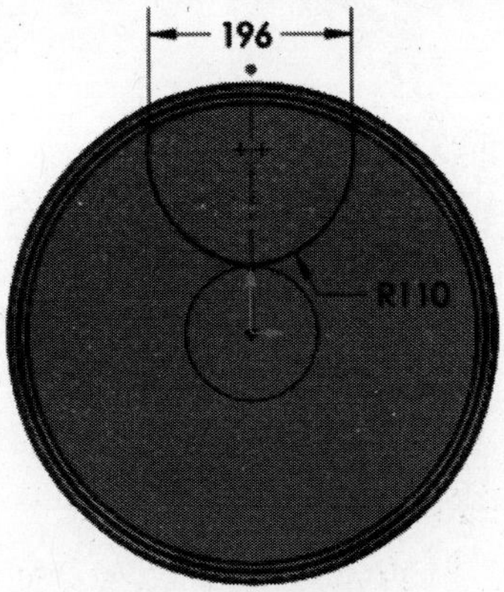

Figure 3-40 Fully defined sketch

23. Exit from the sketching environment by clicking on the confirmation corner or by choosing the **Exit Sketch** button from the **Sketch CommandManager**.

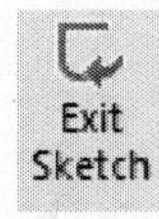

After creating the sketch for the cut feature, you need to invoke the **Extruded Cut** tool.

24. Switch to the **Features CommandManager** by clicking on the **Features** tab in the **CommandManager**.

25. Choose the **Extruded Cut** button from the **Features CommandManager**; the **Extrude PropertyManager** is displayed. Select the sketch from the drawing area; a preview of the cut feature is displayed in the drawing window. Also, the **Extrude PropertyManager** is modified to **Cut-Extrude PropertyManager**.

The **Extruded Cut** tool is used to remove material defined by a sketch drawn on a sketching plane.

Note
If the sketch is selected in the drawing area before choosing the ***Extruded Cut*** *button then the* ***Cut-Extrude PropertyManager*** *will be displayed directly after choosing this button.*

26. Change the current orientation of the model to isometric by choosing the **Isometric** button from the **View Orientation** flyout. You can also press CTRL+7 to change the orientation of the model to isometric.

27. Right-click in the drawing area; a shortcut menu is displayed. Select **Up To Next** from it. Alternatively, you can also select this option from the **End Condition** drop-down list of the **Direction 1** rollout in the **Cut-Extrude PropertyManager**.

28. Choose the **OK** button from the PropertyManager. The isometric view of the model after creating the cut feature is shown in Figure 3-41.

Figure 3-41 Model after creating the cut feature

Patterning the Feature

After creating the cut feature, you need to pattern it using the **Circular pattern** tool. This tool is used to pattern the feature in a circular manner.

1. Choose the **Circular Pattern** button from the **Linear Pattern** flyout in the **Features CommandManager**; the **CirPattern PropertyManager** is displayed.

2. Select the cut feature from the drawing area or from the **FeatureManager Design Tree** displayed on the left of the drawing area.

3. Click once in the **Pattern Axis** selection box in the **Direction 1** rollout of the **CirPattern PropertyManager** to activate its selection mode and then select a circular edge of the revolved feature; a preview of the circular pattern is displayed in the drawing area.

4. Set the value of the **Number of Instances** spinner to **3** and make sure that the **Equal spacing** check box is selected.

When you select the **Instance spacing** radio button, you need to set the value of the incremental angle between the instances in the **Angle** spinner and when you select the **Equal spacing** radio button then SOLIDWORKS automatically calculates the angular spacing between the instances.

5. Choose the **OK** button from the **CirPattern PropertyManager**. The isometric view of the model after patterning the cut feature is shown in Figure 3-42.

Creating the Next Feature

The next feature of the model is also a cut feature. The sketch of this cut feature is drawn on the same planar face on which the sketch of the previously cut feature created. The cut feature is created by using the **Extruded Cut** tool available in the **Features CommandManager**.

1. Choose the **Extruded Cut** button from the **Features CommandManager**; the **Extrude PropertyManager** is displayed on the left of the drawing area and you are prompted to select the sketching plane.

2. Select the front face of the revolved feature as a sketching plane, refer to Figure 3-43; the sketcher environment is invoked.

Figure 3-42 Model after patterning the cut feature

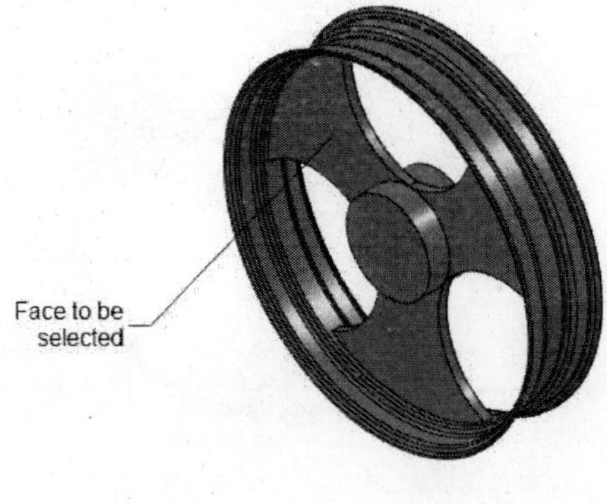

Figure 3-43 Face to be selected

3. Change the current orientation of the model, normal to the screen by choosing the **Normal To** button from the **View Orientation** flyout if not oriented automatically.

4. Draw the sketch of the cut feature using the sketch tools available in the **Sketch CommandManager**. Also, apply the required relations and dimensions, as shown in Figure 3-44.

Note

The sketch shown in Figure 3-44 is fully-defined by applying concentric relations between the arcs of the sketch and the respective edges. Also, the end points of an arc is symmetric along the inclined centerline. The concentric relation forces the selected arc or circle to share the same center point with other arc, circle, point, vertex, or circular edge.

5. Exit from the sketcher environment by clicking on the confirmation corner; the **Cut-Extrude PropertyManager** is displayed. Also, preview of the cut feature is displayed in the drawing area with default value of extrusion.

6. Make sure that the **Blind** option is selected in the **End Condition** drop-down list. Next, set the value of the **Depth** spinner to **4** in the **Direction 1** rollout in the PropertyManager.

7. Change the current orientation of the model to isometric. Next, choose the **OK** button from the PropertyManager. The isometric view of the model after creating the cut feature is shown in Figure 3-45.

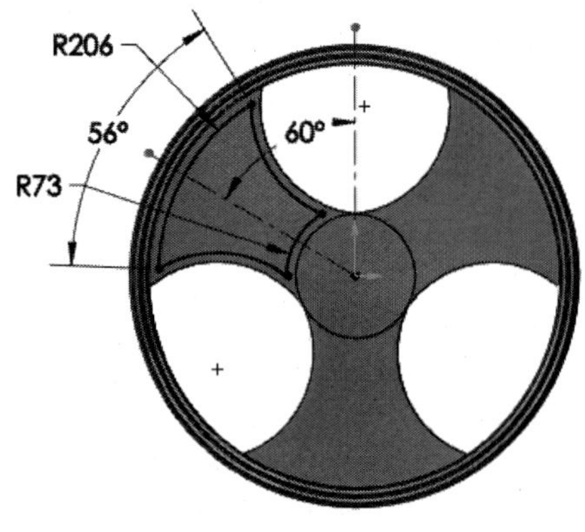

Figure 3-44 Sketch of the cut feature *Figure 3-45 Model after creating the cut feature*

Patterning the Cut Feature

After creating the cut feature, you need to pattern it using the **Circular pattern** tool.

1. Invoke the **Circular Pattern PropertyManager** by choosing the **Circular Pattern** button from the **Linear Pattern** flyout.

2. Create a circular pattern of the previously created cut feature with three instances at equidistant. The model after creating the circular pattern is shown in Figure 3-46.

Figure 3-46 Model after patterning the cut feature

Creating the Mirror Feature

The next feature of the model is a mirror feature. The mirror feature is created by using the **Mirror** tool available in the **Features CommandManager**. To mirror the feature, you need to specify the mirroring plane. The mirroring plane can be a reference plane or a planar face about which you want to mirror the feature. Here you will select the Front Plane as the mirroring plane.

1. Choose the **Mirror** button from the **Features CommandManager**; the **Mirror PropertyManager** is displayed and you are prompted to select a plane or planar face about which the feature is to be mirrored.

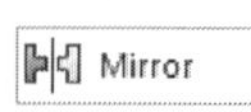

The **Mirror** tool is used to mirror the selected feature, face, or body about a specified mirroring plane, which can be a reference plane or a planar face.

2. Expand the **FeatureManager Design Tree** by clicking on the (▸)sign available on its left and then select the Front Plane from the **FeatureManager Design Tree** as the mirroring plane.

3. Select the previously created circular pattern feature that is **CirPattern2** from the **FeatureManager design tree**; the name of the selected feature is displayed in the **Features to Mirror** selection box in the **Features to Mirror** rollout of the PropertyManager. Also, preview of the mirror feature is displayed in the drawing area.

4. Choose the **OK** button from the **Mirror PropertyManager**; the mirror feature is created. To view the mirrored feature, you need to rotate the model by using the **Rotate View** tool that is available in the **View (Heads-up)** toolbar. You can also press and hold the middle mouse button and then drag the mouse for rotating the model.

Note

*The **Rotate View** tool is not available by default in the **View (Heads-up)** toolbar, you need to customize to add it. To do so, choose **Tools > Customize** from the SOLIDWORKS Menus to display the **Customize** dialog box. Once the dialog box is displayed, choose the **Commands** tab from it. Next, select the **View** option from the **Categories** area of the dialog box; all the tools related to the selected option is displayed in the **Buttons** area. Next, press and hold the left mouse button on the **Rotate View** button from the **Buttons** area of the dialog box and then drag the mouse to the required position in the **View (Heads-up)** toolbar. Next, release the left mouse button to place the button. Similarly, you can drag and drop any required tool from the **Customize** dialog box at some required location. Next, choose the **OK** button from the **Customize** dialog box.*

Creating the Next Feature

The next feature of the model is a cut feature. The sketch of this cut feature is drawn on the front face of the base feature. This sketch is extruded up to the specified surface to create the resultant cut feature.

1. Choose the **Extruded Cut** button from the **Features CommandManager**; the **Extrude PropertyManager** is displayed on the left of the drawing area and you are prompted to select the sketching plane.

2. Select the front planar face of the base feature as the sketching plane, refer to Figure 3-47; the sketcher environment is invoked.

3. Orient the model normal to the screen by choosing the **Normal To** button from the **View Orientation** flyout.

4. Draw a circle of diameter 108 mm by specifying its center point at the origin, refer to Figure 3-48.

5. Exit from the sketch environment; the **Cut-Extrude PropertyManager** is displayed at the left of the drawing area. Change the current orientation to isometric by choosing the **Isometric** button from the **View Orientation flyout**.

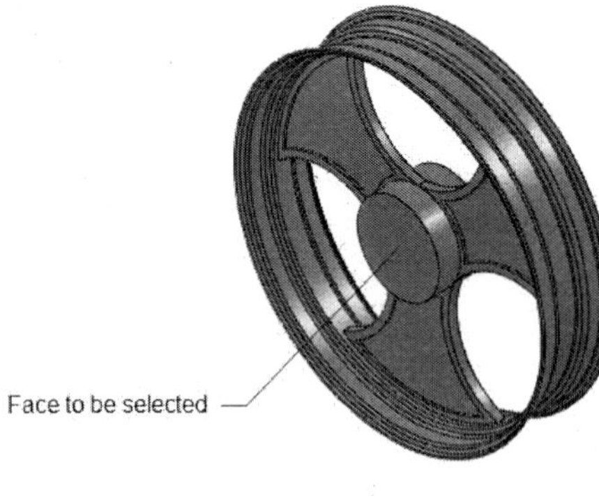

Figure 3-47 Face to be selected

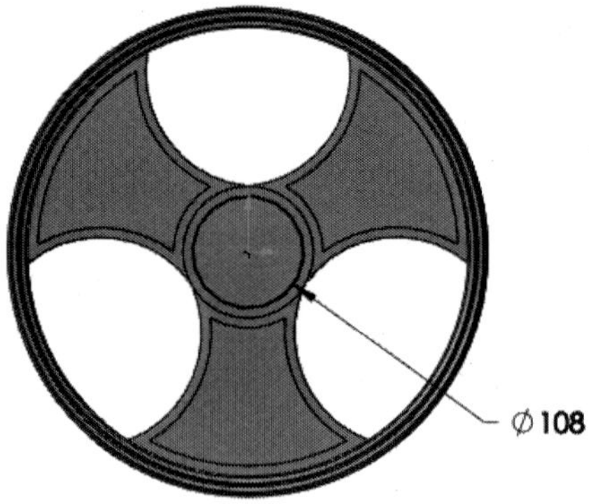

Figure 3-48 Sketch for the cut feature

6. Select the **Up To Surface** option from the **End Condition** drop-down list in the **Cut-Extrude PropertyManager**. As soon as you select the **Up To Surface** option, SOLIDWORKS prompts you to select a face or a surface to complete the specification. Also, the **Face/Plane** selection box is displayed in the **Direction 1** rollout of the PropertyManager.

The **Up To Surface** option is used to define the termination of the extruded feature by selecting a surface or face.

7. Select the inner surface of the cut feature from the drawing area, refer to Figure 3-49.

8. Choose the **OK** button from the **Cut-Extrude PropertyManager**. The isometric view of the model after creating the cut feature is shown in Figure 3-50.

Figure 3-49 Face to be selected

Figure 3-50 Sketch for the cut feature

Mirroring the Feature

The next feature of the model is a mirror feature. This mirror feature will be created by selecting the **Geometric Pattern** check box for the **Mirror PropertyManager**.

1. Invoke the **Mirror PropertyManager** by choosing the **Mirror** button from the **Features CommandManager**.

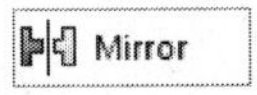

2. Select the Front Plane as the mirroring plane and the previously created cut feature from the **FeatureManager Design Tree**. A preview of the mirror feature is displayed in the drawing area.

3. Select the **Geometric Pattern** check box from the **Options** rollout in the **Mirror PropertyManager**.

On selecting the **Geometric Pattern** check box, the resulting mirror feature will not depend on the relational references. It will create a replica of the selected geometry. On the other hand, if this check box is cleared and you are mirroring a feature that is related to some other entity then the same relationship will be applied to the mirrored feature.

4. Choose the **OK** button from the **Mirror PropertyManager**; the mirror feature is created. You can rotate the model by using the middle mouse button to view the mirrored feature.

Creating the Cut Feature

The next feature of the model is the cut feature.

1. Invoke the sketcher environment by selecting the face, refer to Figure 3-51, as the sketching plane and then create the sketch of the cut feature, as shown in Figure 3-52.

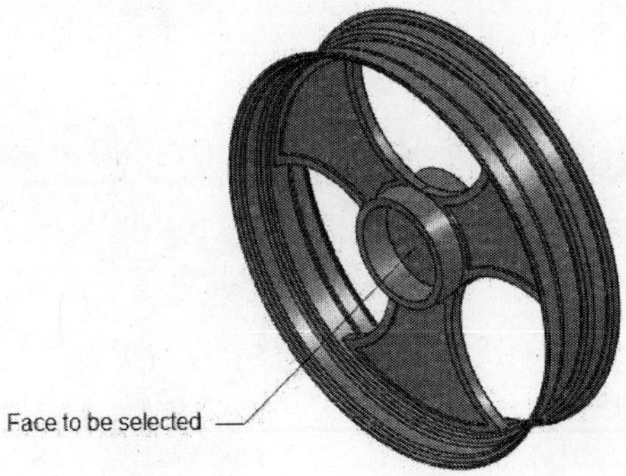

Figure 3-51 *Face to be selected*

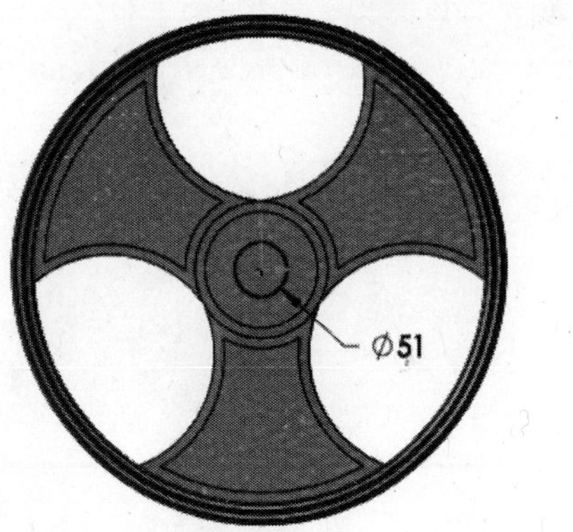

Figure 3-52 *Sketch for the cut feature*

2. Exit from the sketcher environment and create the cut feature by using the **Extruded Cut** tool, as the shown Figure 3-53.

Figure 3-53 *Model after creating the cut feature*

Note

In Figure 3-53, for clarity, the orientation of the model is changed to trimetric by choosing the ***Trimetric*** *button from the* ***View Orientation*** *flyout.*

Creating the Extrude Feature

The next feature of the model is an extrude feature created by using the **Extruded Boss/Base** tool.

1. Choose the **Extruded Boss/Base** button from the **Features CommandManager**; the **Extrude PropertyManager** is displayed at the left of the drawing area and you are prompted to select a sketching plane.

2. Select the sketching plane, refer to Figure 3-54; the sketcher environment is invoked and then orient the model normal to the screen by using the **Normal To** tool.

3. Draw the sketch of the extrude feature, as shown in Figure 3-55.

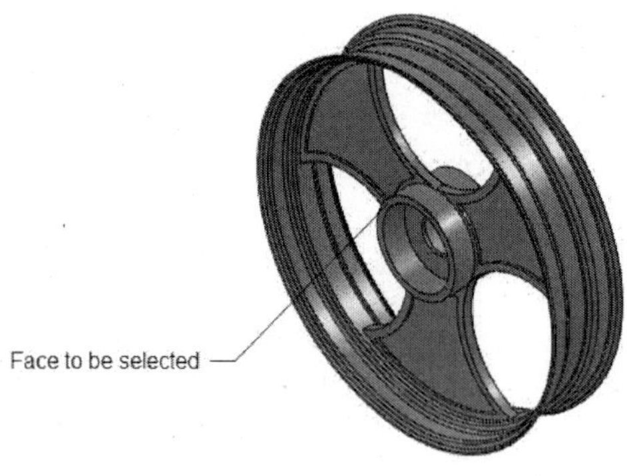

Figure 3-54 *Face to be selected*

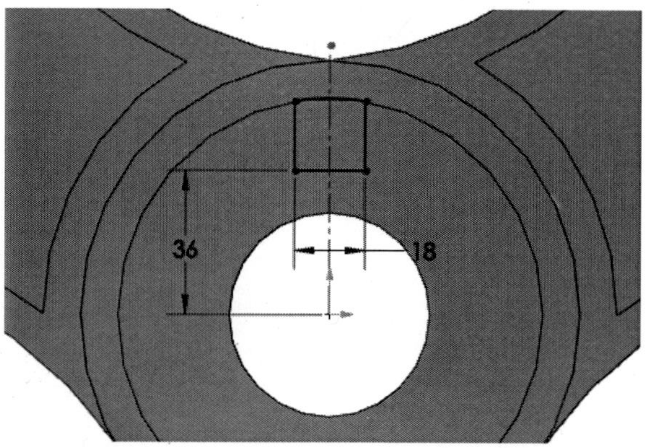

Figure 3-55 *Sketch for the extrude feature*

4. Exit from the sketcher environment; the **Boss-Extrude PropertyManager** is displayed at the

left of the drawing area. Also, preview of the extruded feature is displayed in the drawing area with an arrow pointing in the direction of extrusion.

5. Change the current orientation of the model to isometric view.

6. Choose the **Reverse Direction** button available at the left of the **End Condition** drop-down list in the PropertyManager.

The **Reverse Direction** button is used to reverse the direction of the feature creation.

7. Choose the **Up To Next** option from the **End Condition** drop-down list in the **Direction 1** rollout of the PropertyManager.

As discussed earlier, the **Up To Next** option is used to extrude the sketch from the sketching plane to the next surface that intersects the feature.

8. Choose the **OK** button from the PropertyManager. The model after creating the extruded feature is shown in Figure 3-56.

Figure 3-56 *Model after creating the extrude feature*

Creating the Cut Feature

Next, you need to create the hole on planar face of the previously created extruded feature. This hole will be created as an extruded cut feature. You need to draw the sketch of the cut feature on the front planar face of the previously created extruded feature and then extrude them up to a depth of 25 millimeters.

1. Choose the **Extruded Cut** button; the **Extrude PropertyManager** is displayed on the left of the drawing area and you are prompted to select the sketching plane.

2. Select the front planar face of the previously created extruded feature as the sketching plane; the sketcher environment is invoked. Next, orient the model normal to the screen.

3. Draw a circle of diameter 9 , refer to Figure 3-57. Next, exit the sketcher environment; the **Cut-Extrude PropertyManager** is displayed at the left of the drawing area. Change the current orientation of the model to isometric.

4. Make sure that the **Blind** option is selected in the **End Condition** drop-down list. Next, set the value of the **Depth** spinner to **25** in the **Direction 1** rollout of the PropertyManager.

5. Choose the **OK** button from the PropertyManager. The isometric view of the model after creating the cut feature is shown in Figure 3-58.

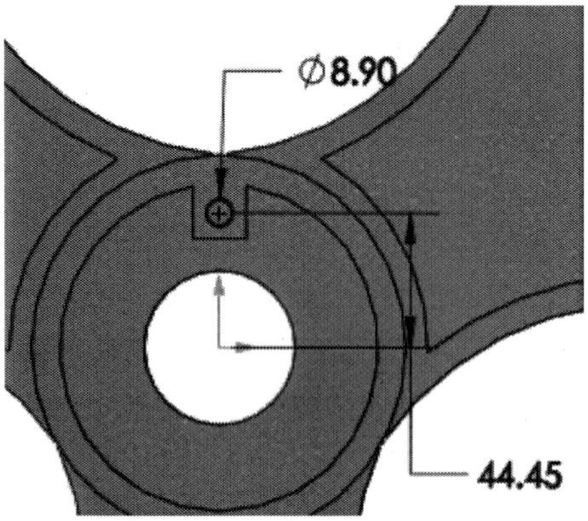

Figure 3-57 *Sketch for the cut feature*

Figure 3-58 *Model after creating the cut feature*

Patterning the Features

After creating the extruded and cut features, you need to pattern them using the **Circular pattern** tool.

1. Choose the **Circular Pattern** button from the **Linear Pattern** flyout in the **Features CommandManager**; the **CirPattern PropertyManager** is displayed. 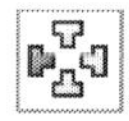

2. Select the last two features, **Boss-Extrude1** and **Cut-Extrude5**, from the **FeatureManager Design Tree**; the name of the selected features are displayed in the **Features to Pattern** selection box of the PropertyManager.

3. Click in the **Pattern Axis** selection area in the **CirPattern PropertyManager** and select a circular edge of the base feature; preview of the circular pattern of the extruded and cut features are displayed in the drawing area.

4. Set the value of the **Number of Instances** spinner to **5** and make sure that the **Equal spacing** check box is selected in the **Parameters** rollout of the PropertyManager.

5. Choose the **OK** button from the **CirPattern PropertyManager**. The isometric view of the model after patterning the extruded and cut features is shown in Figure 3-59.

Figure 3-59 *Model after patterning features*

Applying the Fillet Features

After creating all features of the model, you need to add the fillet feature to the model using the **Fillet** tool.

1. Choose the **Fillet** button from the **Features CommandManager**; the **Fillet PropertyManager** is displayed. You may need to choose the **Manual** button if the **Fillet Xpert PropertyManager** is displayed. 

After invoking the **Fillet PropertyManager**, you are prompted to selected edges, faces, features, or loops to be filleted.

2. Select the required edges of the model to be filleted. For the radius value and the edges to be filleted, refer to Figure 3-2.

3. Choose the **OK** button from the PropertyManager. The isometric view of the final model after creating all features is shown in Figure 3-60.

Figure 3-60 *Final model of the Rim*

Saving the Model

After completing the model, you need to save it in the *Motor Cycle Project* folder.

1. Invoke the **Save As** dialog box by choosing the **Save** button from the Menu Bar and browse to the location of *Motor Cycle Project* folder.

2. Enter the name of the model as Rim in the **File name** edit box and choose the **Save** button from the dialog box. The document will be saved in the *\Documents\Motor Cycle Project\Rim*.

3. Close the document by choosing **File > Close** from the SOLIDWORKS menus.

CREATING THE FRONT TIRE

Part Description

In this section, you will create a Front Tire, as shown in Figure 3-61. First feature of the Front Tire will be created by using the **Revolved Boss/Base** tool and the rest of the features will be created by using the **Shell**, **Wrap**, and **Circular Pattern** tools. Shell thickness of the shell feature will be 16 millimeter. Different views and dimensions of the model are given in the Figure 3-62.

Figure 3-61 Front Tire

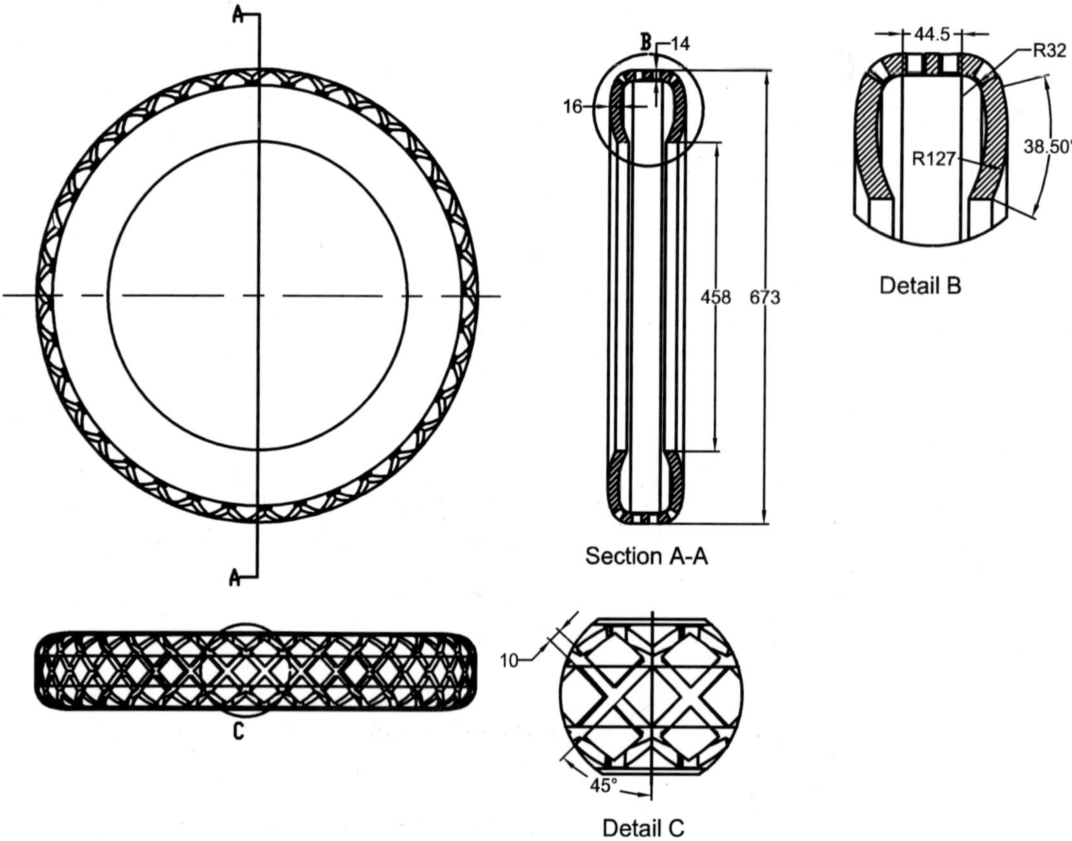

Figure 3-62 *Views and Dimensions of the Front Tire*

Starting a New Part Document

1. Start a new SOLIDWORKS part document using the **New SOLIDWORKS Document** dialog box.

   Once the new part document is invoked, you can create the base feature of the Tire.

Creating the Base Feature

The base feature of the model is a revolve feature.

1. Choose the **Revolved Boss/Base** button from the **Features CommandManager**; the **Revolve PropertyManager** is displayed and you are prompted to select the sketching plane.

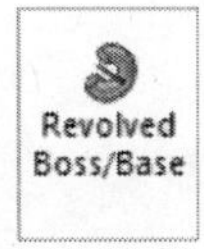

2. Select the Right Plane as the sketching plane; the sketcher environment is invoked and the orientation is changed normal to the view.

3. Draw the sketch of the revolve feature, refer to Figure 3-63.

Note

1. As evident from the Figure 3-63, the sketch of the revolve feature consists of vertical and horizontal centerlines. The vertical centerline is used to apply symmetric relations between the sketch entities and the centerline. However, the horizontal centerline is used to apply linear diameter dimensions to the sketch. Also, you will use the horizontal centerline as the axis of revolution. To make the sketch fully-defined, you also need to apply equal relations between the entities of the sketch having equal length and radius.

2. The dimensions 458 and 673 shown in the Figure 3-63 are linear diameter dimensions. As discussed earlier, linear diameter dimension is used to dimension the sketch of a revolved component. To apply linear diameter dimension, Invoke the ***Smart Dimension*** *tool and then select the entity to be dimensioned and then select the centerline around which the sketch will be revolved. Move the cursor to the other side of the centerline; linear diameter dimension will be attached to the cursor. Next, click in the drawing area to place the linear diameter dimension.*

4. Exit the sketcher environment; the **Revolve PropertyManager** is displayed at the left of the drawing area and you are prompted to select the axis of revolution.

   The above sketch has a two centerlines, therefore SOLIDWORKS cannot determine which one to use as an axis of revolution. This is the reason why you are prompted to select the axis of revolution.

5. Select the horizontal centerline as the axis of revolution. A preview of the complete revolved feature is displayed in the drawing area.

6. Accept the other default values and choose the **OK** button from the **Revolve PropertyManager**. The isometric view of the model after creating the base feature is shown in Figure 3-64.

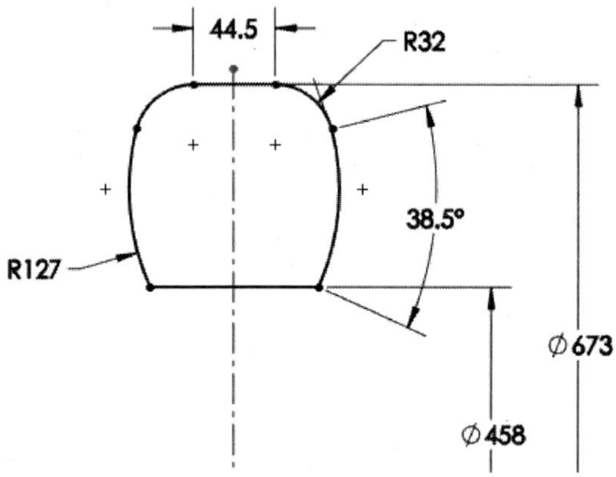

Figure 3-63 Sketch of the revolve feature

Figure 3-64 Model after creating the base feature

Creating the Shell Feature

It is evident from Figure 3-62 that a shell feature is required to create a thin walled structure.

1. Choose the **Shell** button from the **Features CommandManager**; the **Shell Property Manager** is displayed at the left of the drawing area and you are prompted to select the faces to be removed.

The **Shell** tool is used to scoop out material from the model, leaving behind a thin walled hollow part. The selected face or the faces of the model are removed in this operation. If you do not select face to be removed, a closed hollow model will be created.

2. Select the inner circular face of the base feature as a face to be removed from the model; the selected face is highlighted in blue and its name is displayed in the **Faces to Remove** selection box of the **Shell PropertyManager**.

3. Set the value of the **Thickness** spinner to **16** in the **Parameters** rollout of the PropertyManager.

The **Thickness** spinner of the PropertyManager is used to specify the wall thickness of the model.

4. Select the **Show preview** check box from the **Parameters** rollout of the **Shell PropertyManager**; preview of the shell feature is displayed with the specified thickness value. Next, make sure that the **Shell outward** check box is cleared.

The **Show preview** check box from the **Parameters** rollout is used to display the preview of the shell feature and the **Shell Outward** check box is cleared to create the shell feature on the inside of the model.

5. Select the **OK** button from the **Shell PropertyManager**; the shell feature is created, refer to Figure 3-65.

Figure 3-65 *Model after creating the shell feature*

Creating the Wrap Feature

The next feature of the model is a wrap feature created by using the **Wrap** tool. You will create a wrap feature on the outer circular face of the base feature in order to provide the treads on the tire. To create this wrap feature, you first need to create a reference plane at an offset distance from the Top Plane. This reference plane will be used as a sketching plane to create a closed multiloop sketch for the wrap feature.

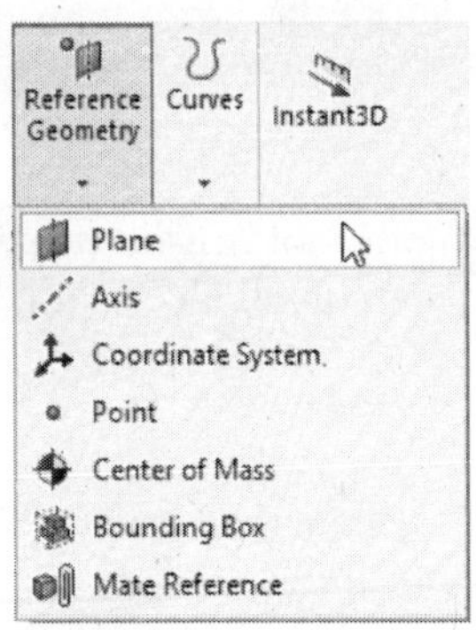

Figure 3-66 *The* ***Plane*** *button in the* ***Reference Geometry*** *flyout*

1. Choose the **Plane** button from the **Reference Geometry** flyout in the **Features CommandManager**, refer to Figure 3-66; the **Plane PropertyManager** is displayed with a selection box activated in the **First Reference** rollout and you are prompted to select first reference to create the plane.

The **Plane** tool is used to create reference planes that are used to draw sketches for the sketch features. Generally, all engineering components or designs are multi-featured models. Therefore, you may need to create planes other than the default planes using the **Plane** tool to complete the model.

2. Click on the (▸) sign located on the left of the **FeatureManager Design Tree**, which is now displayed in the drawing area. The tree view expands and the name of the three default planes along with the features created are visible in the tree view.

3. Select the Top Plane as the first reference from the **FeatureManager Design Tree**; preview of the reference plane is displayed in the drawing area with a default value. As soon as you select the Top Plane; the **First Reference** rollout of the PropertyManager expands and the name of the selected plane is displayed in the selection area of the **First Reference** rollout. Also, the **Offset distance** button is chosen in the **First Reference** rollout of the PropertyManager with the **Flip offset** check box and the **Number of Planes to Create** spinner enabled.

The **Offset distance** button is used to create a reference plane by specifying its offset distance in the **Distance** spinner. You can flip the direction of the reference plane creation by using the **Flip** check box. You can specify number of planes to be created by using the **Number of Planes to Create** spinner.

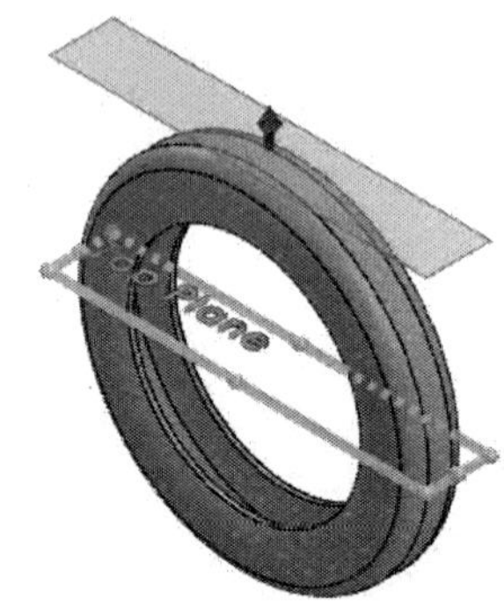

Figure 3-67 *Preview of the reference plane*

4. Set the value of the **Distance** spinner in such a way that the plane should be created outside the outer circular face of the model, refer to Figure 3-67.

5. Choose the **OK** button from the **Plane PropertyManager**; the required plane is created.

   After creating the reference plane, you need to invoke the **Wrap** tool to create the wrap feature.

6. Choose the **Wrap** button from the **Features CommandManager**; the **Message PropertyManager** is displayed and you are prompted to select a plane or a face on which you need to create a closed contour or select an existing sketch.

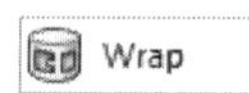

The **Wrap** tool is used to emboss, deboss, and scribe a closed multiloop sketch on a selected planar or curved face that is tangent to the plane on which the selected sketch is created.

Note

If a plane or planar face is selected in the drawing area before invoking the ***Wrap*** *tool then sketcher environment will be invoked directly.*

7. Select the newly created plane as the sketching plane from the drawing area; the sketcher environment is invoked.

8. Change the current orientation normal to the screen by using the **Normal To** tool.

9. Draw the sketch of the wrap feature, refer to Figure 3-68.

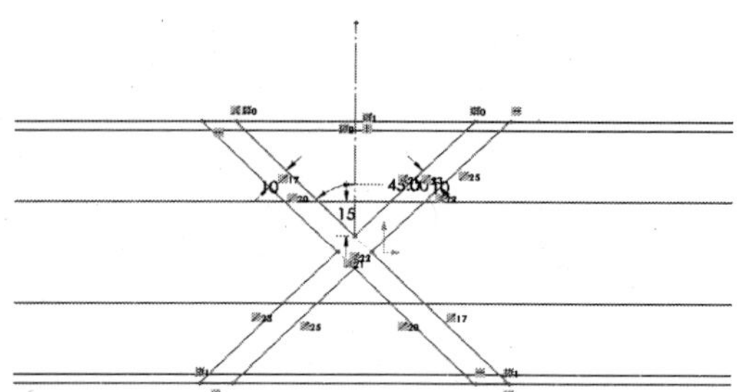

Figure 3-68 *Partial view of the model after creating the sketch for the wrap feature*

Note

The dimensions are not important to create the sketch of this wrap feature. However, make sure that the entities of the sketch should not intersect each other. Also you can create your own design to represent the treads on the tire.

10. Exit from the sketch environment; the **Wrap PropertyManager** is displayed. Also, the name of the sketch created is displayed in the **Source Sketch** selection box of the **Wrap Parameters** rollout of the PropertyManager.

11. Choose the **Deboss** button from the **Wrap Type** rollout of the PropertyManager; the **Depth** spinner is displayed in the **Wrap Parameters** rollout of the **Wrap PropertyManager** to define the depth of the deboss wrap feature. Also, the **Reverse direction** check box is displayed below the **Depth** spinner to reverse the direction of the feature creation.

In the **Wrap Type** rollout of the **Wrap PropertyManager**, you will notice three buttons **Emboss**, **Deboss**, and **Scribe**. The **Emboss** radio button is used to create an emboss wrap feature, the **Deboss** radio button is used to engrave the sketch on a selected planar or curved face, and the **Scribe** radio button is used to project the selected sketch on a planar or a curved face. This projected sketch will split the face on which it is projected.

12. Change the orientation of the model to isometric by choosing the **Isometric** button from the **View Orientation** flyout in the **View (Heads-up)** toolbar.

13. Set the value of the **Depth** spinner to **14** and then select the outer circular face of the base feature; preview of the wrap feature is displayed in the drawing area. Also, the name of the selected face is displayed in the **Face for Wrap Sketch** selection box of the PropertyManager.

14. Choose the **OK** button from the **Wrap PropertyManager**; the wrap feature is created, refer to Figure 3-69.

    Next, hide the reference plane created by using the **Plane** tool.

15. Select the reference plane created by using the **Plane** tool from the drawing area or **FeatureManager design tree** and do not move the cursor; a pop-up toolbar is displayed. Select the **Hide** button from the pop-up toolbar. The selected plane is hidden.

Patterning the Feature

After creating the wrap feature, you need to pattern it using the **Circular pattern** tool. As discussed earlier, this tool is used to pattern the feature in a circular manner.

1. Choose the **Circular Pattern** button from the **Linear Pattern** flyout in the **Features CommandManager**; the **CirPattern PropertyManager** is displayed.

2. Select the wrap feature from the **FeatureManager Design Tree**; the name of the selected feature is displayed in the **Features to Pattern** selection box of the PropertyManager.

3. Click in the **Pattern Axis** selection box and then select a circular edge of the base feature; preview of the circular pattern of the wrap feature is displayed in the drawing area.

4. Set the value of the **Number of Instances** spinner to 36. You can set the value of this spinner, as per your requirement. Make sure that the instances of the feature should not touch each other and the **Equal spacing** check box is selected.

When you select the **Instance spacing** radio button, you need to set the value of the incremental angle between the instances in the **Angle** spinner and when you select the **Equal spacing** radio button then SOLIDWORKS automatically calculates the angular spacing between the instances.

5. Choose the **OK** button from the **CirPattern PropertyManager**; circular pattern feature is created. Final model after creating all the features is displayed similar to one shown in Figure 3-69.

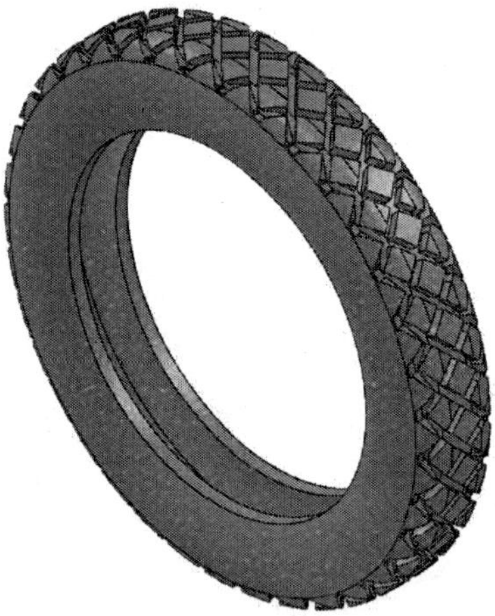

Figure 3-69 *Final model after creating all features*

Saving the Tire

After create all features of the model, you need to save it in the *Motor Cycle Project* folder.

1. Invoke the **Save As** dialog box by choosing the **Save** button and then browse to the location of *Motor Cycle Project* folder.

2. Enter the name of the model as **Front Tire** in the **File name** edit box and choose the **Save** button. The document is saved in the *\Documents\Motor Cycle Project\Front Tire*.

3. Close document by choosing **File > Close** from the SOLIDWORKS menus.

Self-Evaluation Test

Answer the following questions and then compare them to those given at the end of this chapter:

1. The __________ relation forces the selected arc, circle, spline, or ellipse to become tangent to some selected arc, circle, spline, ellipse, line, or edge.

2. The __________ relation forces the selected arc or circle to share same center point with another arc, circle, point, vertex, or circular edge.

3. The __________ drop-down list in the **Direction1** rollout of the **Revolve PropertyManager** provides the options to define the termination of the revolved feature.

4. The __________ tool is used to mirror the selected feature, face, or body about a specified mirroring plane.

5. On selecting the __________ check box, the resulting mirror feature will not depend on the relational references.

6. When you move the cursor horizontal towards the right or left, the symbol of __________ relation will be displayed next to the cursor.

7. In SOLIDWORKS, some of the relations are automatically applied to the sketch entities while drawing them. (T/F)

8. The **3 Point Arc** tool is used to create three point arcs that are drawn by defining the start, center, and end points. (T/F)

9. The **Reverse Direction** button is used to reverse the direction of the feature creation. (T/F)

10. In SOLIDWORKS, you can turn ON or OFF the display of relations in the drawing area. (T/F)

Review Questions

Answer the following questions:

1. Which of the following check boxes in the **Shell PropertyManager** when selected display a preview of the shell feature?

   (a) **Hide** (b) **Show**
   (c) **Show preview** (d) None of these

2. Which of the following keys is used to display the shortcut bar?

   (a) **S** (b) **CTRL + S**
   (c) **K** (d) None of these

3. The __________ tool is used to scoop out material from the model, leaving behind a thin walled hollow part.

4. The __________ tool is used to create reference planes that are used to draw sketches for the sketch features.

5. The __________ tool is used to emboss, deboss, and scribe a closed multiloop sketch on a selected planar or curved face.

6. The _________ relation forces two selected lines, arcs, points, and ellipses to remain equidistant from the centerline.

7. The _________ relation forces the selected lines to have equal _________ and the selected arcs, circles, or arc and circle to have equal _________.

8. The _________ tool is used to remove material defined by a sketch drawn on a sketching plane.

9. You can hide the reference planes by choosing the **Hide** button from the pop-up toolbar that will be displayed on selecting a reference plane. (T/F)

10. In SOLIDWORKS, you can customize the tools of the **View (Heads-up)** toolbar. (T/F)

EXERCISE

Exercise

In this exercise, you will create a Rear Tire, as shown in Figure 3-70. The views and dimensions of the model are given in the Figure 3-71. All the dimensions are in millimeters. After completing the model, save it with name *Rear Tire* at the location *\Documents\Motor Cycle Project.*

(Expected time: 20 min)

Figure 3-70 *Rear Tire*

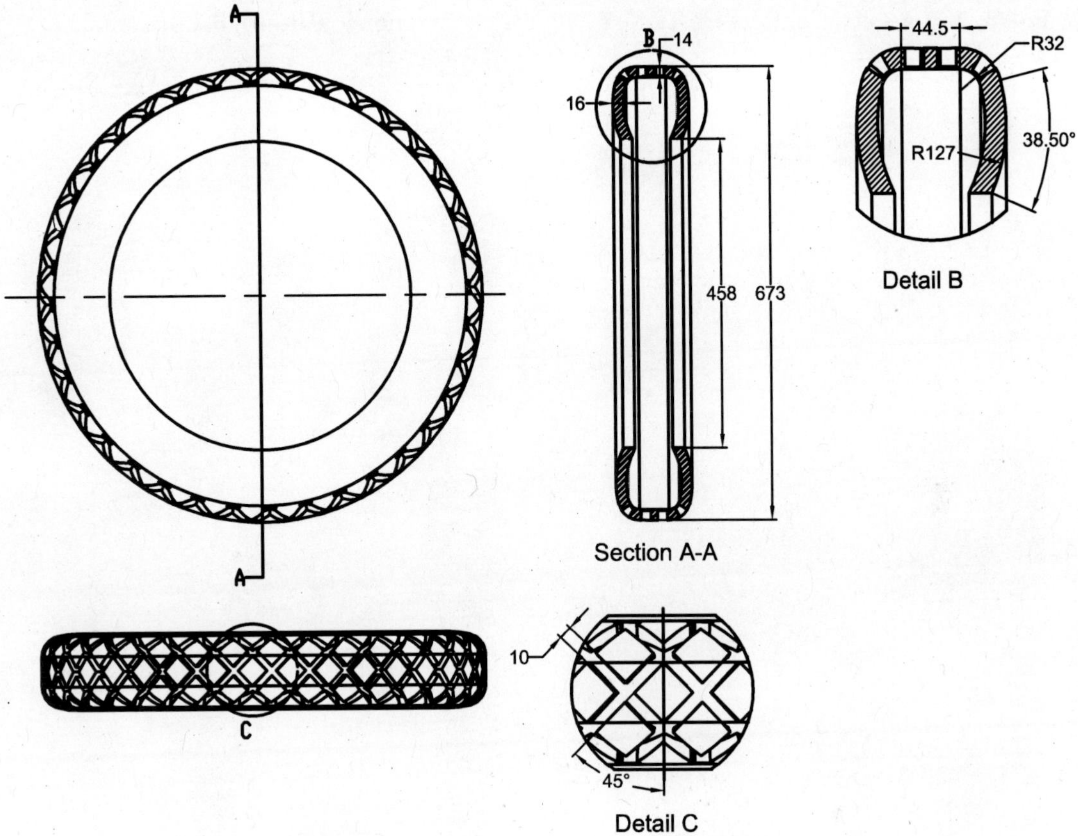

Figure 3-71 *Views and Dimensions of the Rear Tire*

Answers to Self-Evaluation Test

1. tangent, **2.** concentric, **3.** **Revolve Type**, **4.** **Mirror**, **5.** **Geometric Pattern**, **6.** horizontal, **7.** T, **8.** F, **9.** T, **10.** T

Chapter 4

Creating Caliper Piston, Pad, and Body

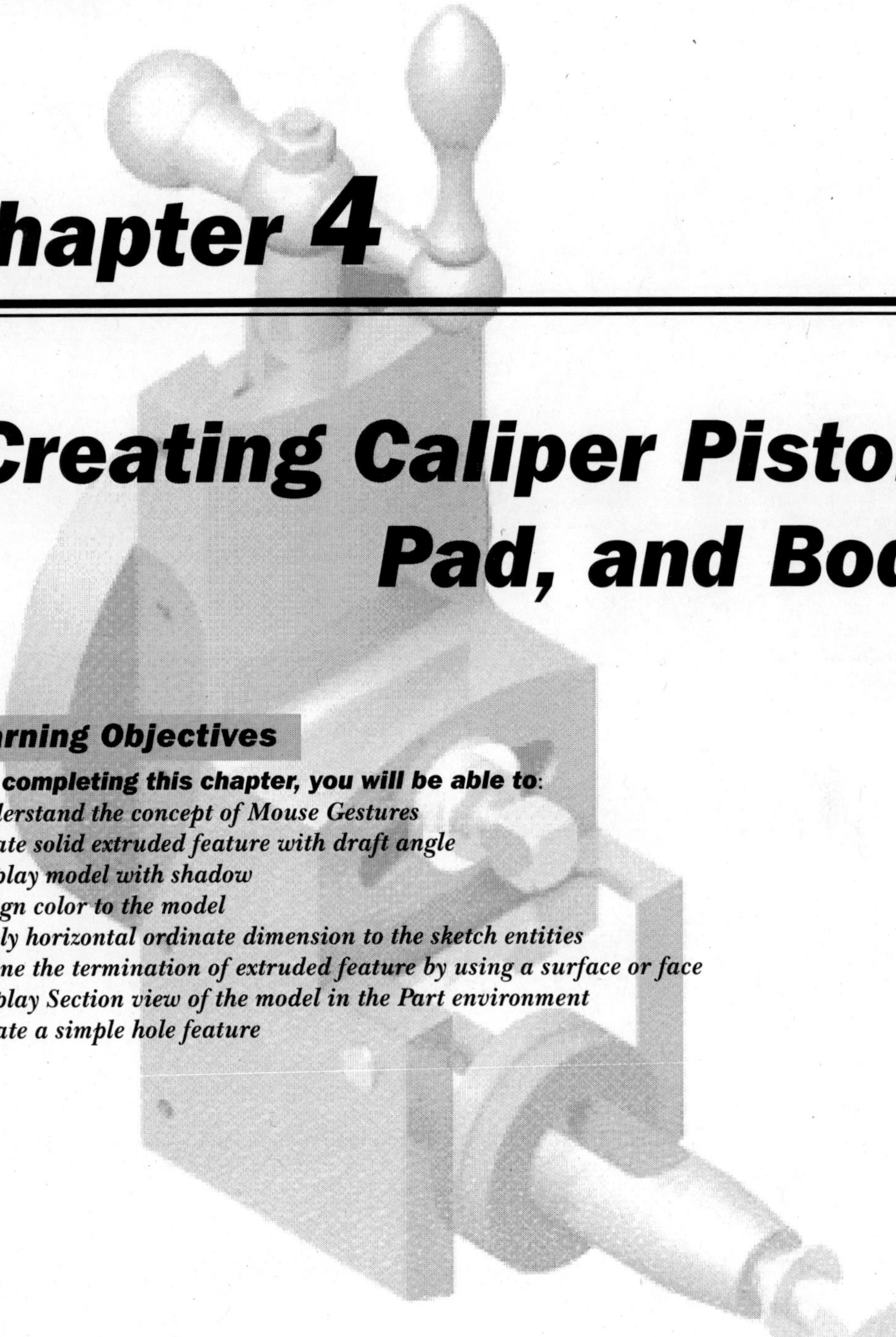

Learning Objectives

After completing this chapter, you will be able to:

- *Understand the concept of Mouse Gestures*
- *Create solid extruded feature with draft angle*
- *Display model with shadow*
- *Assign color to the model*
- *Apply horizontal ordinate dimension to the sketch entities*
- *Define the termination of extruded feature by using a surface or face*
- *Display Section view of the model in the Part environment*
- *Create a simple hole feature*

CREATING THE CALIPER PISTON

Part Description

In this section, you will create a Caliper Piston, as shown in Figure 4-1. It is used to push the Caliper Pad from the back side in the Disc Brake Caliper assembly. The base feature of the Brake Piston is created by using the **Extruded Boss/Base** tool and the second feature is created by using the **Shell** tool. The front and side views of the model with dimensions are shown in Figure 4-2.

Figure 4-1 *The Caliper Piston*

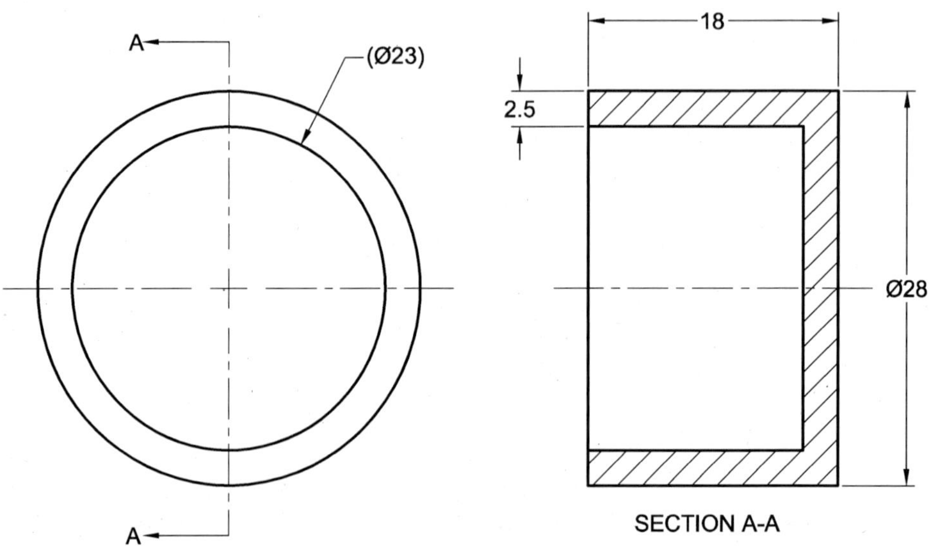

Figure 4-2 *Front and side views of a Caliper Piston*

Starting a New Part Document

Start a new SOLIDWORKS part document using the **New SOLIDWORKS Document** dialog box.

Once the new part document is invoked, you can create the base feature of the Caliper Piston.

Creating the Base Feature

The base feature of the Brake Piston is a extruded feature.

1. Choose the **Extruded Boss/Base** button from the **Features CommandManager**; the **Extrude PropertyManager** is displayed and you are prompted to select a sketching plane.

2. Select Front Plane as the sketching plane from the drawing area; the sketcher environment is invoked and the selected plane is oriented normal to the view.

Note

As discussed in the earlier chapters, you can also create a sketch in the sketcher environment and then invoke a feature creation tool and vice-versa.

3. Press the right mouse button and drag the cursor in any direction, a set of tools that are arranged radially is displayed, refer to Figure 4-3.

In SOLIDWORKS, when you press the right-mouse button and drag the cursor in any direction, a set of tools that are arranged radially will be displayed in the drawing area. This arrangement is known as Mouse Gestures. It is used to invoke a set of tools. The Mouse Gestures works in all the environment of SOLIDWORKS. But, the tools displayed in it will be different in all the environments. By default, only four tools are available in the Mouse Gestures, refer to Figure 4-3. However, you can customize it to add upto twelve tools using the **Customize** dialog box.

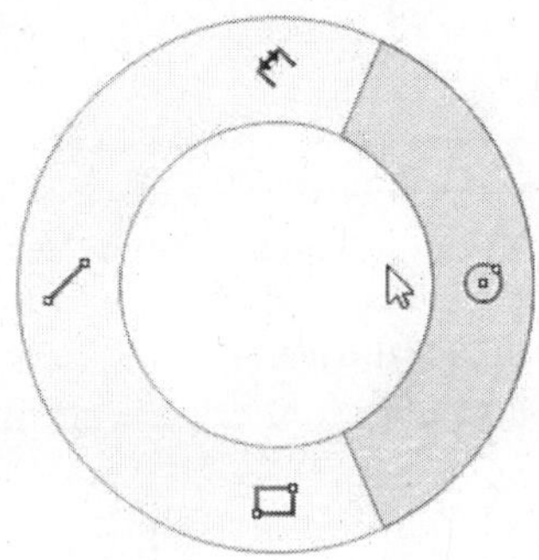

Figure 4-3 *Set of tools displayed after dragging the mouse towards the right side*

To customize the Mouse Gestures, invoke the **Customize** dialog box by choosing the **Tools > Customize** from the SOLIDWORKS menu. Once the **Customize** dialog box is displayed, choose the **Mouse Gestures** tab from it; the **Mouse Gesture Guide** window is displayed. Next, select the required option from the drop-down list available at the upper right corner of the dialog box to display different tools in the Mouse Gestures. You can also display a particular set of tools as per your requirement in the Mouse Gestures. To do so, you need to click on the cell of the required tool row and environment column to display a drop-down list. Next, you can select the required option from the drop-down list to add the tool.

4. Drag the cursor over the **Circle** tool provided in the Mouse Gestures; the **Circle** tool is invoked. The cursor is changed to circle cursor.

5. Move the circle cursor toward the origin and specify the center point of the circle when the orange circle is displayed at the origin.

6. Next, move the circle cursor away from the origin and specify the radius of the circle when the value above the circle cursor displayed closer to 14.

> **Tip**
> *You can specify numeric input while creating lines, rectangles, circles, and arcs. To do so, choose the* ***Options*** *button from the Menu Bar; the* ***System Options: General*** *dialog box will be displayed. Select the* ***Sketch*** *option from the left area of the dialog box; the options related to the sketch are displayed on the right of the dialog box. Select the* ***Enable on screen numeric input on entity creation*** *check box and then choose the* ***OK*** *button to apply the change and then close the dialog box. Now, you can specify the numeric input while creating the lines, rectangles, circles, and arcs.*

7. Press the right mouse button and drag it over the **Smart Dimension** tool in the **Mouse Gestures**; the **Smart Dimension** tool is invoked. Next, apply the diameter dimension of 28 to the circle, refer to Figure 4-4.

8. Exit from the sketch environment by clicking on the confirmation corner; the **Boss-Extrude PropertyManager** is displayed on the left of the drawing area. Also, preview of the extruded feature is displayed with an arrow handle in the drawing area.

The arrow handle displayed with preview of the extruded feature is used to extrude sketch upto a certain depth. To do so, move the mouse to the arrow displayed in the preview; the move cursor will be displayed and the color of the arrow will also be changed. Left-click once on the arrow; a scale will be displayed. Now, you can drag the cursor to specify the depth of the extrusion, the value of the depth of extrusion will change dynamically as you move the cursor.

9. Set the value of the **Depth** spinner to **18** in the **Boss-Extrude PropertyManager**. Make sure that the **Blind** option is selected in the **End Condition** drop-down list of the **Direction 1** rollout.

10. Choose the **OK** button from the PropertyManager; the base feature of the model is created, as shown in Figure 4-5.

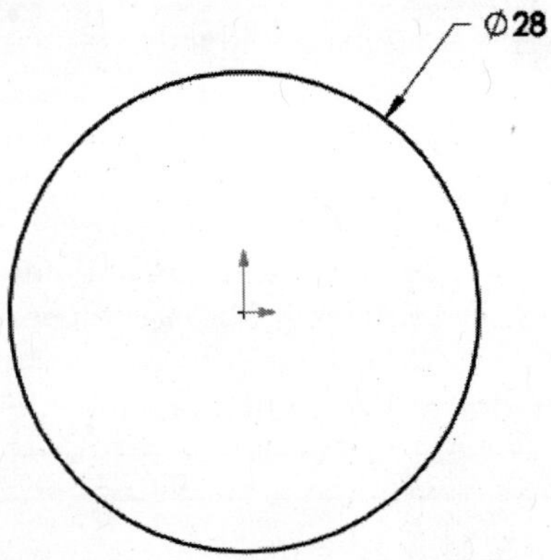

Figure 4-4 *Sketch of the base feature*

Figure 4-5 *Model after creating the base feature*

Creating the Second Feature

It is evident from the Figure 4-1 that a shell feature is required to create a thin walled structure. The shell feature is created by using the **Shell** tool.

1. Choose the **Shell** button from the **Features CommandManager**; the **Shell PropertyManager** is displayed.

2. Set the value of the **Thickness** spinner to **2.5** in the **Shell PropertyManager**.

   Now, you need to select the faces to remove from the model.

3. Select the front face of the base feature to be removed; the name of the selected face is displayed in the **Faces to Remove** selection box of the PropertyManager. Also, the selected face is highlighted in the drawing area. Make sure that the **Shell outward** check box is cleared in the **Parameters** rollout of the PropertyManager.

You can also view the preview of the shell feature by selecting the **Show preview** check box provided in the **Parameters** rollout of the **PropertyManager**.

4. Choose the **OK** button from the **Shell PropertyManager**; the shell feature of the model is created is shown in Figure 4-6.

Figure 4-6 *Final model after creating the shell feature*

Saving the Model

After creating the model, you need to save it in the *Motor Cycle Project* folder.

1. Choose the **Save** button from the Menu Bar to invoke the **Save As** dialog box. Next, browse to the *Motor Cycle Project* folder. 

2. Enter **Caliper Piston** as the name of the model in the **File name** edit box and choose the **Save** button; the model is saved in the *\Documents\Motor Cycle Project\Caliper Piston*.

3. Close the document by choosing **File > Close** from the SOLIDWORKS menus.

CREATING THE CALIPER PAD

Part Description

In this section, you will create a Caliper Pad, as shown in Figure 4-7. It applies the pressure and friction to the circular Disc Plate, created in the chapter 1. The first feature of the Caliper Pad is an extruded feature, the second feature is an extruded feature with a draft angle of 25-degree, the third feature is a cut feature. After creating the model, you will turn on the display of shadow and will also apply black color to the extruded feature having draft angle. The front and side views of the model is shown in Figure 4-8.

Figure 4-7 *The Caliper Pad*

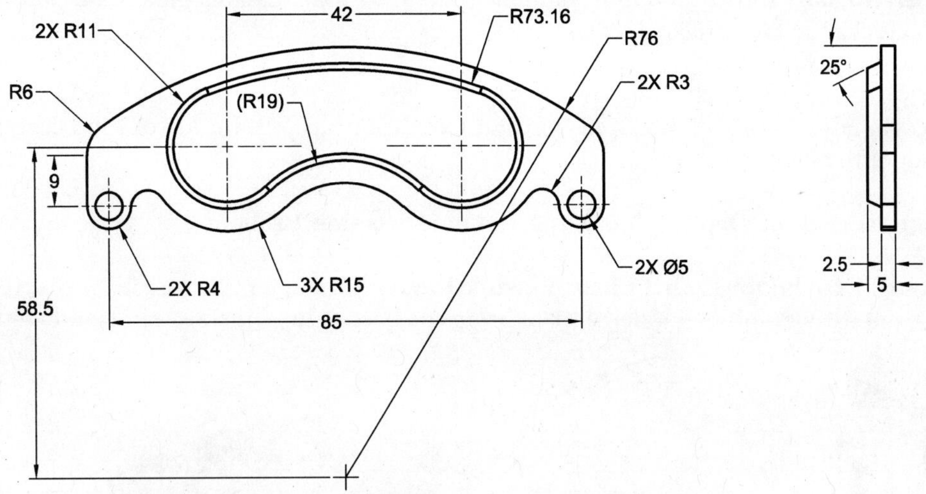

Figure 4-8 Front and side views of a Caliper Pad

Starting a New Part Document

1. Start a new SOLIDWORKS part document using the **New SOLIDWORKS Document** dialog box.

Once the new part document is invoked, you can create the base feature of the model.

Creating the Base Feature

The base feature of the model is an extruded feature created by using **Extruded Boss/Base** tool.

1. Invoke the **Extrude PropertyManager** by choosing the **Extruded Boss/Base** button.

2. Select the Front Plane as the sketching plane; the sketch environment is invoked and the selected plane is oriented normal to the view.

3. Draw the sketch of the base feature using the tools available in the **Sketch CommandManager** and dimension it. The sketch should look similar to the one shown in Figure 4-9. For your reference, the arcs and lines in the sketch are numbered.

Note

In the sketch shown in Figure 4-9, the tangent relation is applied between all entities of the sketch, equal relation is applied between arcs 2 and 12, lines 3 and 11, arcs 4 and 10, arcs 5 and 9, arcs 6 and 8, and arcs 7 and 8. Also, the vertical relation is applied to the line 3 and line 11. The horizontal relation is applied between the center point of arcs 6 and 8 and arcs 4 and 10 to make the sketch fully defined. Make sure that the center point of the arc 1 is at the origin and the center point of the arc 7 is coincident with the centerline.

4. Exit the sketch environment by clicking on the confirmation corner; the **Boss-Extrude PropertyManager** is displayed on the left of the drawing area and the orientation of the model is changed to trimetric orientation. Also, preview of the extrude feature with default value is displayed.

5. Select the **Mid Plane** option from the **End Condition** drop-down list of the **Direction 1** rollout of the PropertyManager.

6. Set the value of the **Depth** spinner to **2.5** in the **Direction 1** rollout.

7. Choose the **OK** button from the **Boss-Extrude PropertyManager**; the base feature is created. The trimetric view of the model after creating the base feature is shown in Figure 4-10.

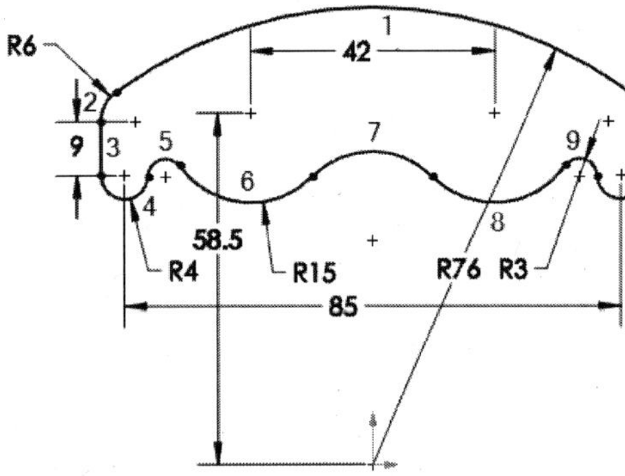

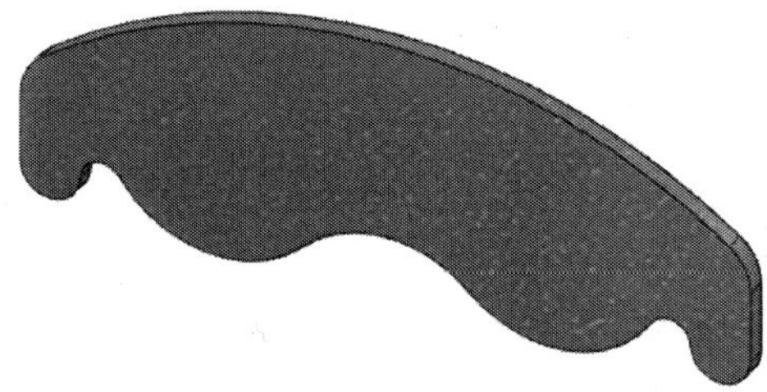

Figure 4-9 *Sketch of the base feature*

Figure 4-10 *Model after creating the base feature*

Creating the Second Feature

The second feature of the model is an extruded feature with a draft angle of 25-degree. The draft angle is used to taper the resulting feature.

1. Invoke the **Extruded Boss/Base** tool and select the front planar face of the base feature as the sketching plane; the sketch environment is invoked.

2. Orient the model normal to the view using the **Normal To** tool.

3. Draw the sketch of the extruded feature using the tools available in the **Sketch CommandManager**. Apply the required relations and dimensions, refer to Figure 4-11.

Note

In the sketch shown in Figure 4-11, the tangent relation is applied between all arcs of the sketch. Also, the concentric relation is applied between edge 1 and arc 1, edge 2 and arc 2, edge 3 and arc 3, and edge 4 and arc 4 to make the sketch fully defined.

4. Exit the sketch environment by clicking on the confirmation corner; the **Boss-Extrude PropertyManager** is displayed on the left of the drawing area. Also, preview of the extruded feature is displayed.

5. Change the current orientation of the model to isometric. Next, set the value of the **Depth** spinner to **2.5** in the **Direction 1** rollout of the PropertyManager.

   It is evident from Figure 4-8 that this extruded feature is created with a draft angle of 25-degree. You can provide the draft angle to the extruded feature using the **Draft On/Off** button provided in the **Boss-Extrude PropertyManager**.

6. Choose the **Draft On/Off** button from the **Direction 1** rollout of the PropertyManager; the **Draft Angle** spinner and the **Draft Outward** check box are enabled in the PropertyManager, refer to Figure 4-12.

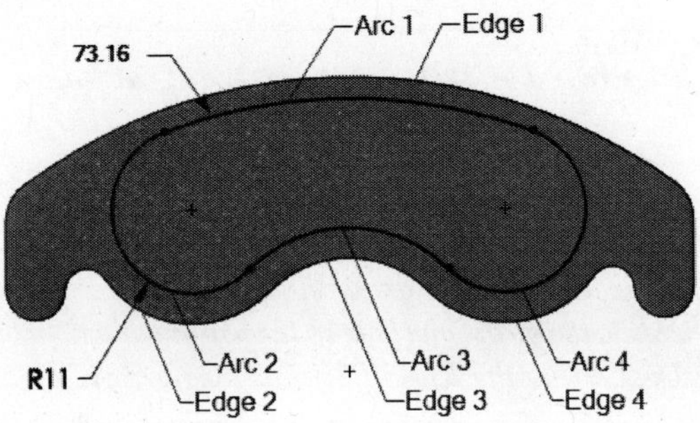

Figure 4-11 Sketch of the second feature

***Figure 4-12** The **Direction 1** rollout of the **Boss-Extrude PropertyManager** with the **Draft On/Off** button chosen*

The **Draft On/Off** button is used to specify a draft angle while extruding the sketch. Apply the draft angle to taper the resulting feature. This button is not chosen by default. Therefore, the resulting base feature will not have any taper. However, if you want to add a draft angle to the feature, you need to choose this button. As soon as you choose this button, the **Draft Angle** spinner and the **Draft outward** check box will be available in the **PropertyManager**. You can enter the draft angle for the feature in the **Draft Angle** spinner. By default, the feature will be tapered inward. If you want to taper the feature outward, select the **Draft outward** check box which is displayed below the **Draft Angle** spinner.

7. Set the value of the **Draft Angle** spinner to **25** and then choose the **OK** button from the **Boss-Extrude PropertyManager**. The model after creating the extruded feature with draft angle of 25-degree is shown in Figure 4-13.

Creating the Third Feature

The third feature of the model is a extruded cut feature.

1. Invoke the **Extruded Cut** tool and select the front planar face of the base feature as the sketching plane; the sketcher environment is invoked.

2. Change the current orientation of the model normal to the view and draw two circles of diameter 5, refer to Figure 4-14.

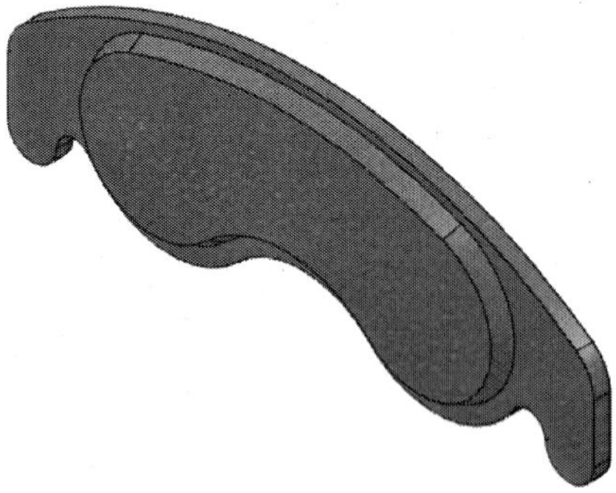

Figure 4-13 Extruded feature with draft angle

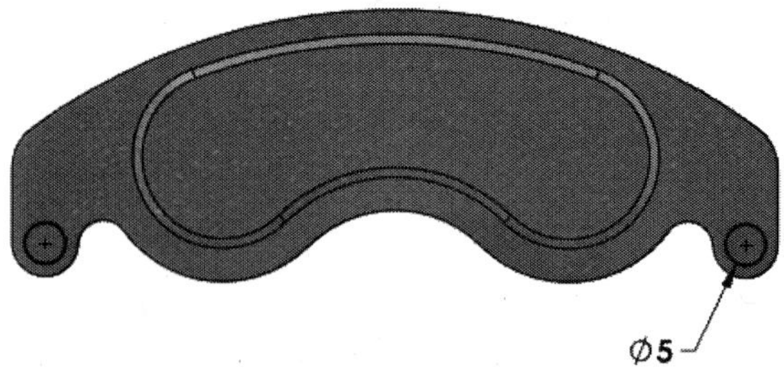

Figure 4-14 Sketch of the extruded cut feature

Note

Both the circles of the sketch are of same diameter 5 therefore you can apply equal relation between them. Also, you can apply concentric relation between one of the circles and respective edge of the model. In the Figure 4-14, the two circles of same diameter are drawn to create an extruded cut feature. You can also draw only one circle in the sketch to create one hole in the feature and then later mirror the feature to create second cut feature by selecting the Right Plane as the mirroring plane.

3. Exit the sketcher environment; the **Cut-Extrude PropertyManager** is displayed. Next, change the current orientation of the model to isometric.

4. Select the **Up-To-Next** option from the **End Condition** drop-down list of the **Direction 1** rollout in the PropertyManager.

5. Choose **OK**; the extruded cut feature is created, as shown in Figure 4-15.

Displaying the Shadow

As mentioned in the part description, you need to display the shadow of the model.

1. Choose **View > Display > Shadows In Shaded Mode** from the SOLIDWORKS menus to display the model with shadow, as shown in Figure 4-16.

The **Shadows In Shadows Mode** option is used to display the shadow of a model. A light appears from the top of the model to display the shadow in the current view. You deactivate this shadow mode by choosing the same button again and vice-versa.

Note

*With the **Shadows In Shaded Mode** option activated, the performance of the system is affected during the dynamic orientation.*

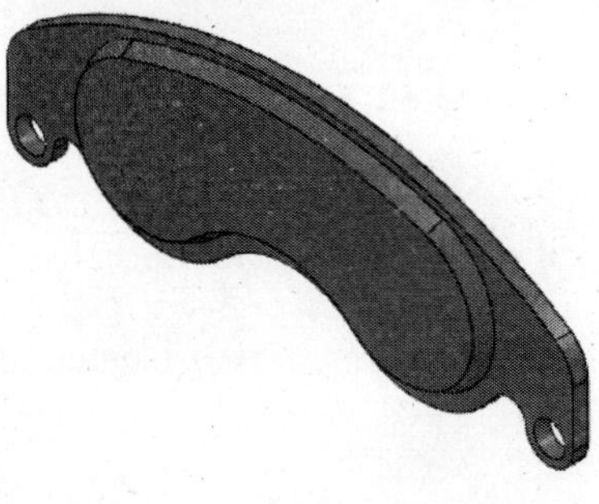

Figure 4-15 *Model after creating the cut feature*

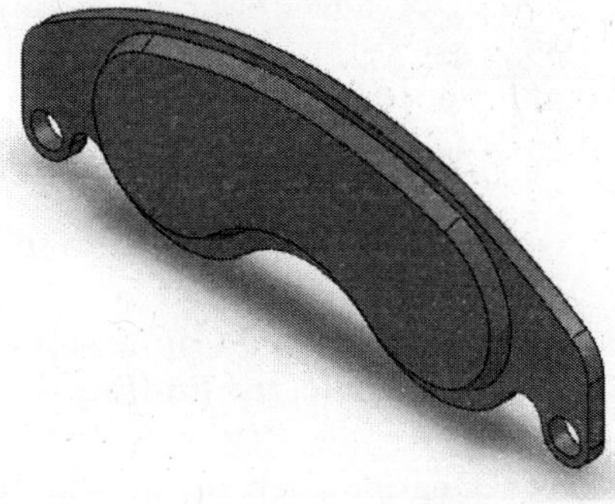

Figure 4-16 *Model with display of shadow*

Assigning Color to the Model

As mentioned in the part description, you need to assign black color to the second feature of the model.

1. Choose the **Edit > Appearance > Appearance** from the SOLIDWORKS Menus; the **color PropertyManager** is displayed. Also, name of the current model is displayed in the selection box of the **Selected Geometry** rollout.

The **color PropertyManager** is used to assign a color to a model, faces, surfaces, bodies, or features.

The **Selected Entities** selection box of the **Selected Geometry** rollout is used to display the name of the selected entities to which color needs to be assigned. Also, it has five buttons on its left, namely, **Select Part**, **Select Faces**, **Select Surfaces**, **Select Bodies**, and **Select Features**. These buttons are used as filters for making a selection to assign color to a model. For example, if you want to assign the color on the face of a model, clear the existing selection from the **Selected Entities** selection box and then choose the **Select Faces** button from the **Selected Geometry** rollout. This allow you to select only a specified face of the model.

Tip

You can also invoke ***color PropertyManager*** *to assign color by using another method. In this method, first you need to select a face; a pop-up toolbar will be displayed. Now, choose the* ***Appearance*** *button from this toolbar; a flyout will be displayed with the name of the face, extrude, body, and part. Select the check box corresponding to the required name; the* ***color PropertyManager*** *will be displayed.*

If you want to assign color to a face, select the check box corresponding to the name of the face from the flyout to display the PropertyManager. Next, select the color; the color will be assign to the selected face only.

2. Right-click in the **Selected Entities** selection box of the **Selected Geometry** rollout and select **Clear Selections** to clear the existing selections.

3. Choose the **Select Features** button from the left of the **Selected Entities** selection box of the **Selected Geometry** rollout.

The **Select Features** button allows you to select only a specified feature of the model.

4. Select the second extruded feature from the drawing area; the name of the selected feature is displayed in the **Selected Entities** selection box.

5. Click on the black swatch in the **Pick to Color** display area of the **Color** rollout in the PropertyManager; the selected color is displayed in the **Dominate Color** display area of the **Color** rollout. You can also use the **Red Component of Color**, **Green Component of Color**, and **Blue Component of Color** spinners to set the color.

6. Choose the **OK** button from the **color PropertyManager**; the color of the second feature is changed to black. The final model after assigning the black color to the second feature is shown in Figure 4-17.

Saving the Model

After creating the model, you need to save it in the *Motor Cycle Project* folder.

1. Choose the **Save** button from the Menu Bar to invoke the **Save As** dialog box. Next, browse to the *Motor Cycle Project* folder. 

2. Enter **Caliper Pad** as the name of the model in the **File name** edit box and choose the **Save** button. The document gets saved in the *\Documents\Motor Cycle Project\Caliper Pad*.

3. Close the document by choosing the **File > Close** from the SOLIDWORKS menu.

Figure 4-17 *Final model after assigning the color*

CREATING THE CALIPER BODY

Part Description

In this section, you will create a Caliper Body, as shown in Figure 4-18. It can be created by using different feature creations tools of SOLIDWORKS. The base feature of the model is created by using the **Extruded Boss/Base** tool. Similarly, the other features of the model can be created by using the **Revolved Cut**, **Mirror**, **Extruded Cut**, **Simple Hole**, and **Fillet** tools. Figure 4-19 shows different views and dimensions of the model.

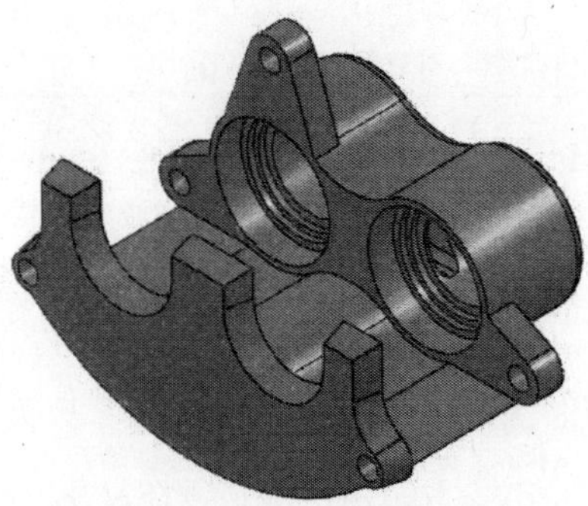

Figure 4-18 *The Caliper Body*

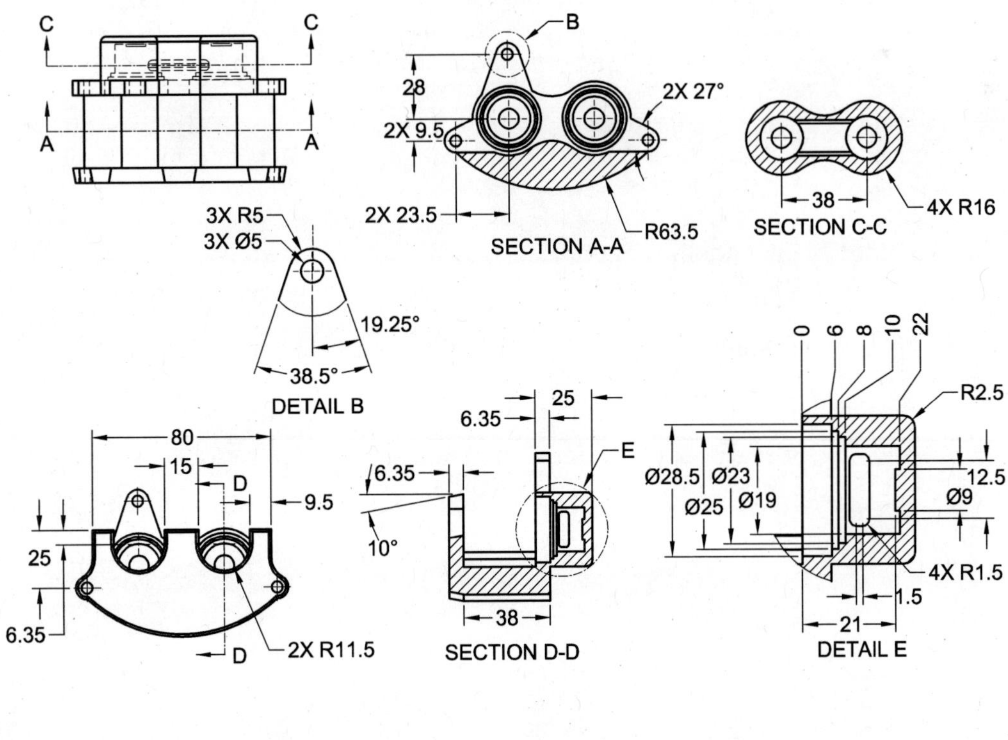

Figure 4-19 *Views and Dimensions of the model*

Starting a New Part Document

1. Start a new SOLIDWORKS part document using the **New SOLIDWORKS Document** dialog box.

Once the new part document is invoked, you can create the base feature of the Caliper Body.

Creating the Base Feature

The base feature of the model is an extruded feature. This extruded feature is created on the Front Plane using the **Mid Plane** option. As discussed in the earlier chapter, the **Mid Plane** option is used to create the base feature by extruding the sketch equally in both the directions of the plane on which the sketch is drawn.

1. Invoke the **Extrude PropertyManager** by choosing the **Extruded Boss/Base** button from the **Features CommandManager**. As soon as you invoke the **Extrude PropertyManager**, you are prompted to select the sketching plane.

2. From the drawing area, select the Front Plane as the sketching plane; the sketcher environment is invoked and the selected plane is oriented normal to the view.

3. Draw the sketch of the extruded feature using the tools available in the **Sketch CommandManager** and dimension it, as shown in Figure 4-20.

Note

In the sketch shown in Figure 4-20, the tangent relation is applied between all arcs of the sketch. Symmetric relations are applied between center points of the arc 1 and arc 3 about the horizontal centerline and center points of the arc 2 and arc 4 about the vertical centerline. Also, the equal relation is applied between all the arcs of the sketch to make the sketch fully defined.

4. Exit the sketcher environment; the **Boss-Extrude PropertyManager** is displayed on the left of the drawing area. Also, preview of the extruded feature with default value is displayed in the drawing area.

5. Select the **Mid Plane** option from the **End Condition** drop-down list of the **Direction 1** rollout in the PropertyManager.

6. Set the value of the **Depth** spinner to **25** in the **Direction 1** rollout.

7. Choose the **OK** button; the base feature is created, as shown in the Figure 4-21.

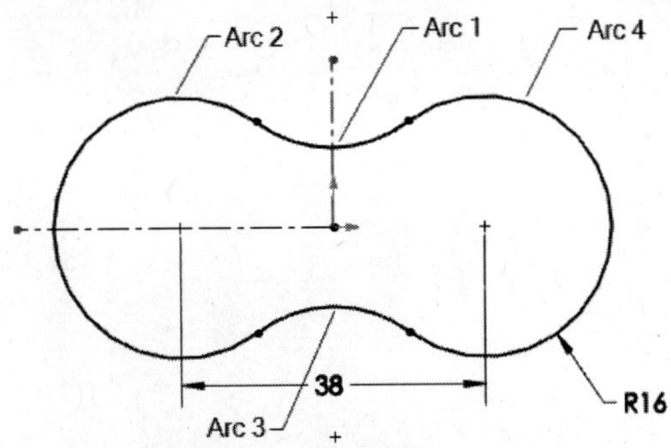

Figure 4-20 Sketch of the base feature

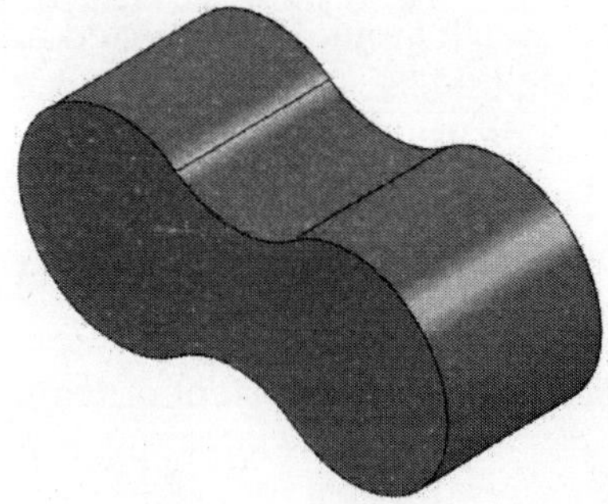

Figure 4-21 Model after creating the base feature

Creating the Second Feature

The second feature of the model is a revolved cut feature. This feature is created by using the **Revolved Cut** tool. To create the revolved cut feature, you need to draw the profile of the revolved cut feature on a reference plane created at an offset distance of 19 mm from the Right Plane.

1. Choose the **Plane** button from the **Reference Geometry** flyout in the **Features CommandManager**; the **Plane PropertyManager** is displayed.

2. Click on the (▸) sign located on the left of the **FeatureManager Design Tree**, which is now displayed in the drawing area; the tree view expands and the three default planes and the name of the base feature are visible in the tree view.

3. Select the Right Plane as the first reference from the **FeatureManager Design Tree**; the **Offset distance** spinner, the **Flip offset** check box, and the **Number of planes to create** spinner are enabled in the **Plane PropertyManager**. Also, preview of the reference plane at default offset distance is displayed in the drawing area.

4. Make sure that the direction of reference plane creation is towards the front side of the Right Plane. If it is not, you need to reverse its direction by selecting the **Flip offset** check box.

5. Set the value of the **Distance** spinner to **19** and then choose the **OK** button from the PropertyManager; the reference plane is created at an offset distance of 19.

   After creating the reference plane at an offset distance of 19 from the Right Plane, you need to draw the sketch for the revolved cut feature by selecting it as the sketching plane.

6. Choose the **Revolved Cut** button from the **Features CommandManager**; the **Revolve PropertyManager** is displayed and you are prompted to select the sketching plane.

Revolved Cut

The **Revolved Cut** tool is used to remove material by revolving a sketch around the selected axis. Similar, to the revolved boss/base features, you need to define the revolution axis using a centerline or an edge in the sketch.

7. Select the newly created plane as the sketching plane from the drawing area; the sketcher environment is invoked. Change the current orientation normal to the view.

8. Draw the sketch of the revolve cut feature using the tools available in the **Sketch CommandManager** and dimension it, refer to Figure 4-22.

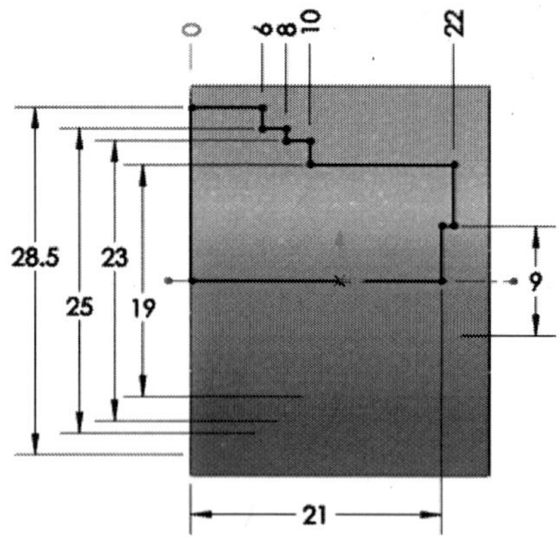

Figure 4-22 *Sketch of the revolve cut feature*

Note

The dimensions 0, 6, 8, 10, and 22 shown in Figure 4-22 are horizontal ordinate dimensions. To apply horizontal ordinate dimension, choose the ***Horizontal Ordinate Dimension*** *button from the* ***Smart Dimension*** *flyout in the* ***Sketch CommandManager****; you will be prompted to select an edge or a vertex. Note that the first entity selected is taken as the datum entity from where the remaining entities will be measured. Select the first entity and place the dimension above or below it. You will notice that the dimension shows the value 0. After placing the first dimension, you will again be prompted to select an edge or a vertex. Select the next entity that you need to dimension with respect to the first selected entity as the datum. As soon as you select the entity, a horizontal dimension between the datum and this entity will be placed. Similarly, you can place the other dimensions.*

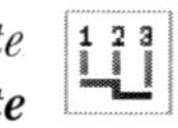

When you apply the ordinate dimensions, the ***Modify*** *dialog box will not be displayed to modify the dimension values. After placing all ordinate dimensions, you need to exit the tool and then double-click on the dimensions to modify their values.*

After drawing the sketch of the revolve cut feature, you need to exit the sketcher environment.

9. Exit the sketch environment by clicking on the confirmation corner; the **Cut-Revolve PropertyManager** is displayed and you are prompted to select the axis of revolution.

10. Change the current orientation of the model to isometric.

11. Select the horizontal centerline from the drawing area as the axis of revolution; preview of the revolve feature with the default angle of revolution is displayed in the drawing area.

12. Make sure that the **Blind** option is selected in the **Revolve Type** drop-down list of the **Direction 1** rollout and the value in the **Direction 1 Angle** spinner is set to 360.

13. Choose the **OK** button from the **Cut-Revolve PropertyManager**; the revolved cut feature is created.

14. Hide the reference plane created for creating the sketch of the revolved cut feature. To hide the reference plane, select it from the drawing area or the **FeatureManager Design**

Tree; a pop-up toolbar is displayed. Choose the **Hide** button from the toolbar; the selected reference plane is hidden. Similarly, you can display the hidden reference plane by choosing the **Show** button from the pop-up toolbar. The model after creating the revolve cut feature and hiding the reference plane is shown in Figure 4-23.

Mirroring the Features

After creating the revolve cut feature, you need to mirror it using the Right Plane as the mirroring plane.

1. Invoke the **Mirror PropertyManager** by choosing the **Mirror** tool and then select the Right Plane as the mirroring plane. After selecting the mirroring plane, the SOLIDWORKS prompted you to select the feature to be mirror.

2. Select revolved cut feature to be mirror from the drawing area or from the FeatureManager Design Tree; the preview of the mirror feature is displayed in the drawing area.

3. Choose the **OK** button. The model after mirroring the revolved cut feature is shown in the Figure 4-24.

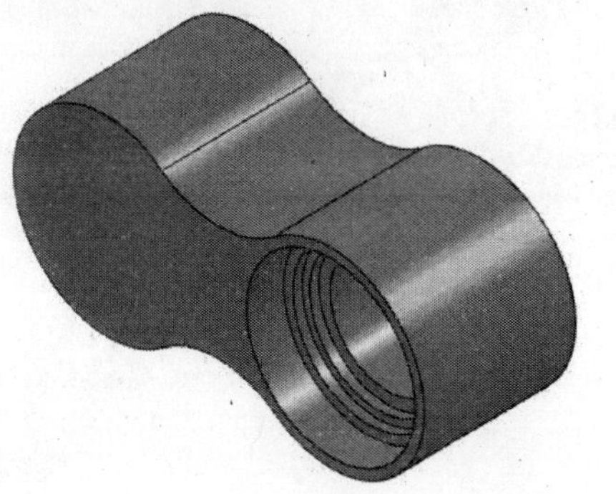

Figure 4-23 *Model after creating the revolve cut feature*

Figure 4-24 *Model after mirroring the revolve cut feature*

Creating the Cut Feature

The next feature of the model is a cut feature. The sketch of this cut feature is created on the Right plane and then extruded using the **Up To Surface** option both in direction 1 and direction 2.

1. Invoke the **Extruded Cut** tool and select the Right Plane from the **FeatureManager Design Tree** as the sketching plane; the sketcher environment is invoked.

2. Change the current orientation normal to the view using the **Normal To** button.

3. Draw the sketch of the cut feature using the tools available in the **Sketch CommandManager**, refer to Figure 4-25.

4. Exit from the sketcher environment; the **Cut-Extrude PropertyManager** is displayed. Next, change the orientation to isometric.

5. Select the **Up To Surface** option from the **End Condition** drop-down list in the **Direction 1** rollout of the PropertyManager; the **Face/Plane** selection box is displayed in the rollout.

The **Up To Surface** option is used to define the termination of the extruded feature using a selected surface or a face.

6. Select the inner most circular face of the mirror feature, refer to Figure 4-26. The name of the selected face is displayed in the **Face/Plane** selection box of the **Direction 1** rollout and preview of the cut feature up to the selected face is displayed in the drawing area.

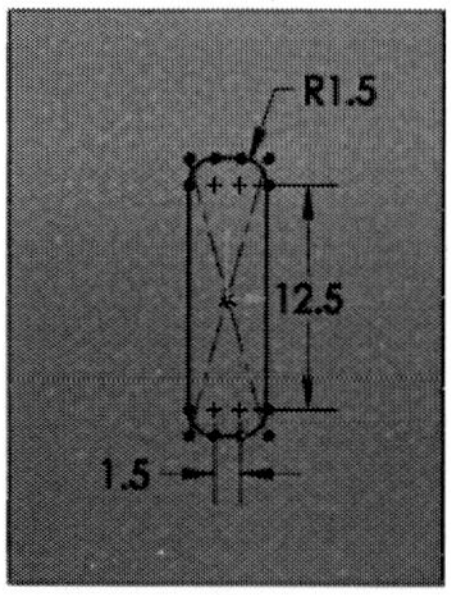

Figure 4-25 *Sketch of the cut feature*

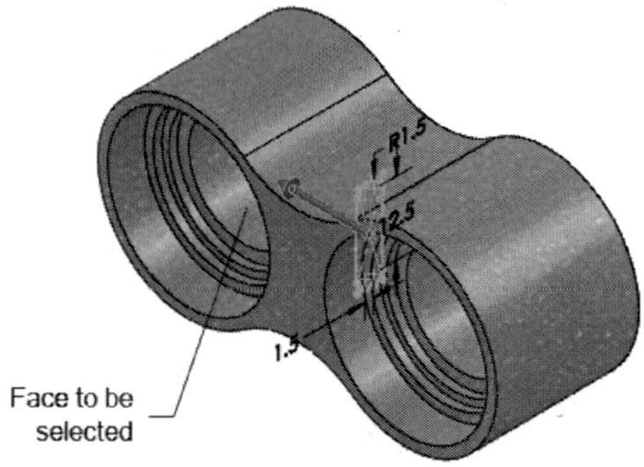

Figure 4-26 *Face to be selected*

7. Select the check box available on the title bar of the **Direction 2** rollout of the **Cut-Extrude PropertyManager** to expand the rollout.

The **Direction 2** rollout is used to extrude the sketch in a direction opposite to the sketching plane. The options in this rollout are similar to those in the **Direction 1** rollout.

Note

The ***Direction 2*** *rollout will not be available in the PropertyManager if you have selected the* ***Mid Plane*** *option from the* ***End Condition*** *drop-down list of the* ***Direction 1*** *rollout of the PropertyManager.*

8. Select the **Up To Surface** option from the **End Condition** drop-down list of the **Direction 2** rollout in the PropertyManager; the **Solid/Surface Body** selection box is displayed below the drop-down list and you are prompted to select the face or the surface.

9. Select the inner most circular face of the revolved cut feature from the drawing area; preview of the cut feature is displayed.

10. Choose the **OK** button from the PropertyManager. The isometric view of the model after creating the cut feature is shown in Figure 4-27.

Figure 4-27 Model after creating the cut feature

Displaying the Section View

Now, you will visualize the section view of the model by using the **Section View** tool.

1. Choose the **Section View** button from the **View (Heads-up)** toolbar; the **Section View PropertyManager** is displayed. Also, preview of the section view of the model created using the Front Plane as the section plane is displayed in the drawing area. 

The **Section View** tool is used to display the section view of the model by cutting it using a plane or a face. You can also save the section view with a name to generate the section view directly on the drawing sheet in the drawing mode.

By default, the Front Plane is automatically selected in the **Section View PropertyManager** and the section view of the model is displayed using the Front Plane as the section plane. You can also select the Right Plane or the Top Plane as the section plane by choosing the corresponding button from the **Section 1** rollout. You can also select a face or a user-defined plane as the section plane. To do so, clear the reference plane selected in the **Reference Section Plane/Face** selection box and select the face or the plane from the drawing area.

You can drag and dynamically adjust the offset distance of the section plane using the drag handle that is provided at the center of the section plane. You can also specify the offset distance using the **Offset Distance** spinner. You will observe that as you modify the offset distance, the preview of the section view is automatically modified. You can also rotate the section plane along the X-axis and the Y-axis using the **X Rotation** and **Y Rotation** spinners, respectively. Alternatively, move the cursor on the edge of the plane; the **Rotate** cursor will be displayed. Left-click and drag the cursor to rotate the section plane dynamically.

2. Choose the **Top Plane** button from the **Section 1** rollout of the PropertyManager; preview of the section view created using the Top Plane is displayed in the drawing area. 

3. Choose the **OK** button from the **Section View PropertyManager** to display the section view of the model shown in Figure 4-28.

4. Choose the **Section View** button from the **View (Heads-up)** toolbar again to return to the full view mode.

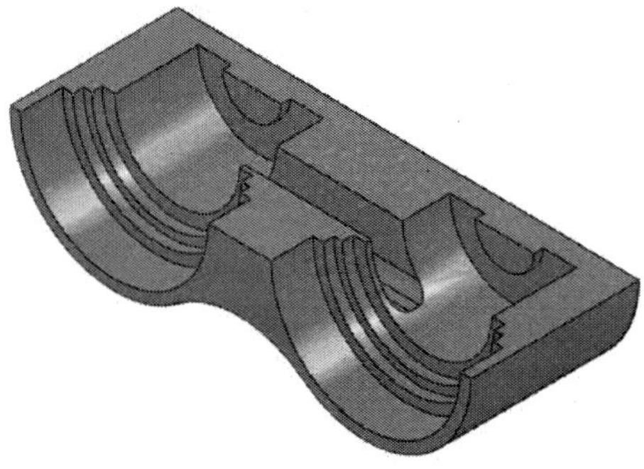

Figure 4-28 Section view of the model

Creating the Extrude Feature

The next feature is an extrude feature. The sketch of this extrude feature is created on the front face of the base feature.

1. Invoke the **Extruded Boss/Base** tool and select the front face of the base feature as the sketching plane, refer to Figure 4-29; the sketcher environment is invoked.

2. Orient the model normal to the screen using the **Normal To** tool.

3. Draw the sketch of the extrude feature using the tools available in the **Sketch CommandManager**, refer to Figure 4-30.

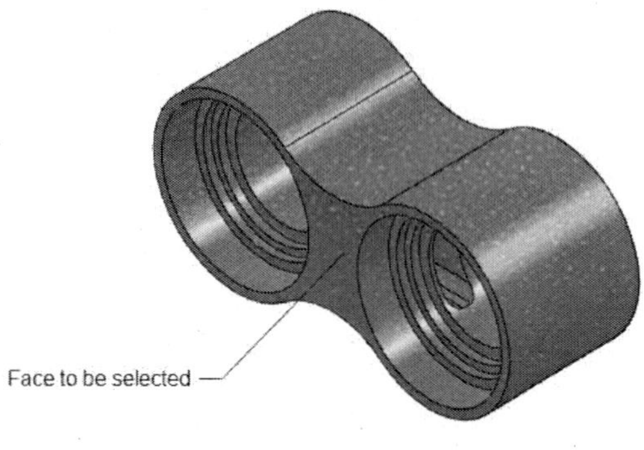

Figure 4-29 Face to be selected

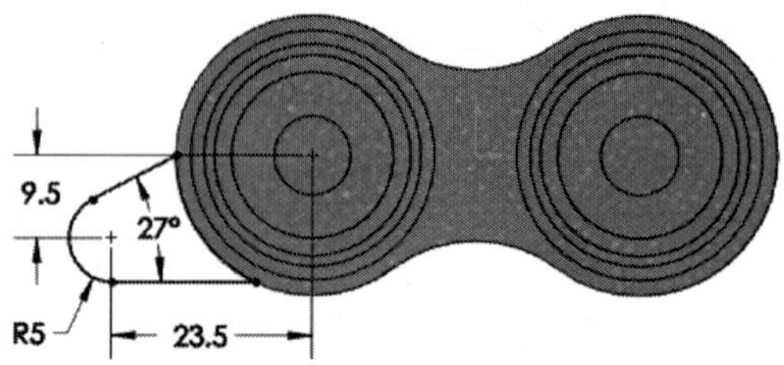

Figure 4-30 Sketch of the extrude feature

4. Exit the sketch environment; the **Boss-Extrude PropertyManager** is displayed. Also, preview of the extruded feature is displayed in the drawing area. Next, change the current orientation to isometric.

5. Choose the **Reverse Direction** button provided on the left of the **End Condition** drop-down list in the PropertyManager to reverse the direction of feature creation. 

6. Make sure that the **Blind** option is selected in the **End Condition** drop-down list. Next, set the value of the **Depth** spinner to **6.35**.

7. Choose the **OK** button from the PropertyManager. The model after creating the extruded feature is shown in Figure 4-31.

Mirroring the Feature

After creating the extruded feature, you need to create its mirror feature. To create this mirror feature, you need to select the Right Plane as the mirroring plane.

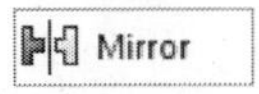

1. Invoke the **Mirror PropertyManager** by choosing the **Mirror** tool and then select the Right Plane as the mirroring plane.

   After selecting the mirroring plane, SOLIDWORKS prompts you to select the feature to be mirrored.

2. Select the previously created extruded feature from the **FeatureManager Design Tree**; preview of the mirror feature is displayed in the drawing area.

3. Choose the **OK** button; the mirror feature is created, as shown in Figure 4-32.

***Figure 4-31** Model after creating the extrude feature*

***Figure 4-32** Model after mirroring the extruded feature*

Creating the Next Extrude Feature

The next feature of the model is also an extrude feature. The sketch of this extrude feature is created on the front face of the base feature.

1. Invoke the **Extruded Boss/Base** tool and select the front face of the base feature as the sketching plane; the sketcher environment is invoked.

2. Orient the model normal to the view and draw sketch of the extrude feature, as shown in Figure 4-33.

3. Exit the sketcher environment and change the orientation of the model to isometric.

4. Choose the **Reverse Direction** button provided on the left of the **End Condition** drop-down list in the **Boss-Extrude PropertyManager** to reverse the direction of the feature creation.

5. Set the value of the **Depth** spinner to **6.35** and then choose **OK**, the extruded feature is created, as shown in Figure 4-34.

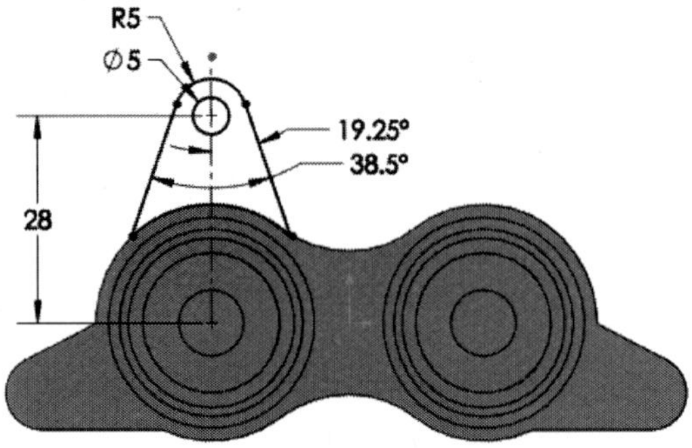

Figure 4-33 *Sketch of the extrude feature*

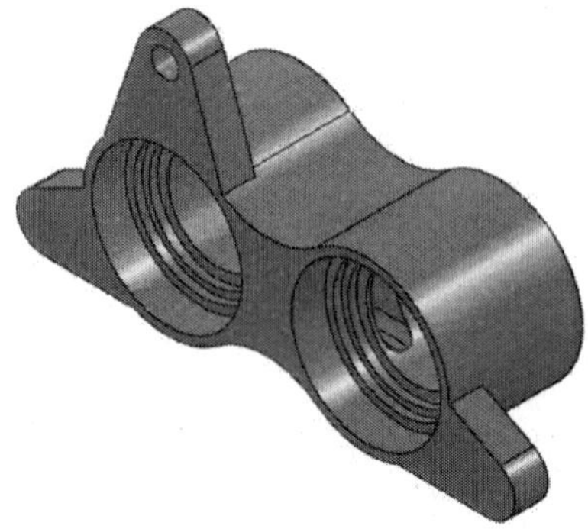

Figure 4-34 *Model after creating the extruded feature*

Creating the Next Feature

The next feature of the model is an extrude feature.

1. Invoke the **Extruded Boss/Base** tool; you are prompted to select the sketching plane.

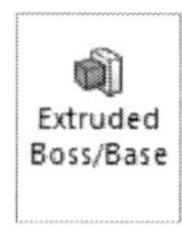

To select the sketching plane, you need to rotate the model in such a way that you can select the back face of the extruded feature that measures 6.35 mm depth.

2. Press and hold the middle mouse button and then drag it; the cursor is replaced to rotate view cursor. Now, rotate the model in such a way that you can easily select the back face of the extruded feature that measures 6.35 mm depth, refer to Figure 4-35.

3. Release the middle mouse button and select the face, refer to the Figure 4-35; the sketcher environment is invoked. Orient the model normal to the view.

4. Draw the sketch of the extruded feature, refer to Figure 4-36.

Note

The sketch shown in Figure 4-36 is created by using the ***Convert Entities****,* ***Trim Entities****, and* ***3 Point Arc*** *tools.*

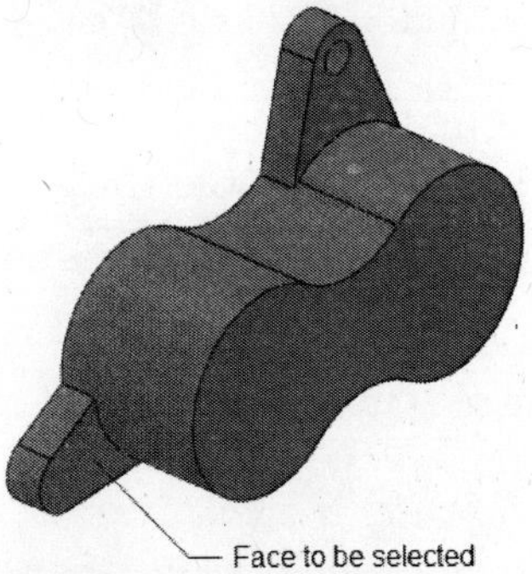

Figure 4-35 Face to be selected

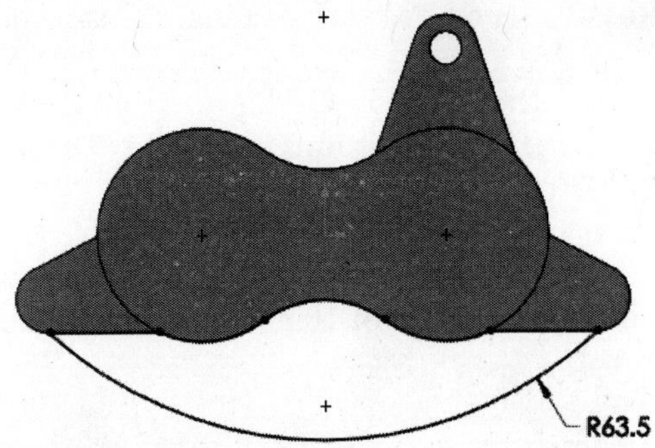

Figure 4-36 Sketch of the extrude feature

As discussed earlier, the **Convert Entities** tool is used to project the selected 2D or 3D entities on the current sketching plane. The 3D entities that you can project are edges, faces, or sketched entities. This is required when you need the reference of existing entities to draw a sketch. To project entities, select the existing entity to be projected on the sketching plane and then choose the **Convert Entities** button from the **Sketch CommandManager**. You can also select a face for projecting. If you do so, all the edges of the selected face will be projected on to the sketching plane.

5. Exit from the sketcher environment and change the orientation to isometric.

6. Choose the **Reverse Direction** button provided on the left of the **End Condition** drop-down list in the **Direction 1** rollout of the **Boss-Extrude PropertyManager** to reverse the direction of the feature creation.

7. Set the value of the **Depth** spinner to **38** and then choose the **OK** button; the extruded feature is created, as shown in Figure 4-37.

Figure 4-37 Model after creating the extruded feature

Creating the Next Feature

The next feature of the model is an extrude feature with a draft angle of 10-degree. This extrude feature is created on the front face of the previously created extruded feature.

1. Invoke the **Extruded Boss/Base** tool and select the front face of the previously created extruded feature as the sketching plane to invoke the sketcher environment. Next, change the orientation normal to the view.

2. Draw the sketch of the extrude feature, as shown in Figure 4-38.

3. Exit the sketcher environment and set the value of the **Depth** spinner to **6.35** in the **Boss-Extrude PropertyManager**. Also, change the orientation to isometric.

4. Choose the **Draft On/Off** button from the **Direction 1** rollout of the PropertyManager; the **Draft Angle** spinner and the **Draft outward** check box are enabled in the PropertyManager. 

5. Set the value of the **Draft Angle** spinner to **10** and then choose the **OK** button; the model with a draft angle of 10 degrees is created as shown in Figure 4-39.

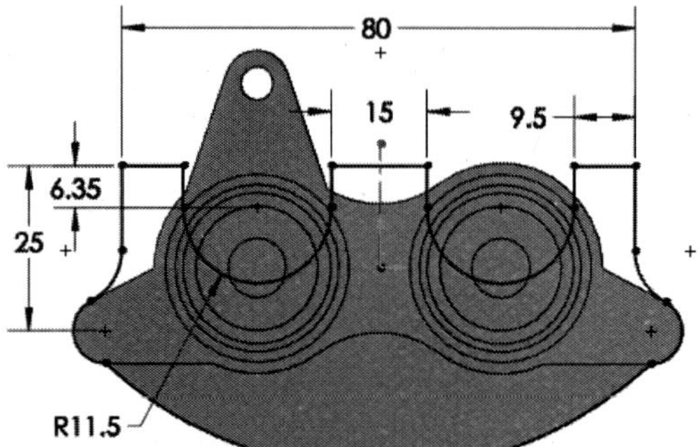

Figure 4-38 Sketch of the extrude feature

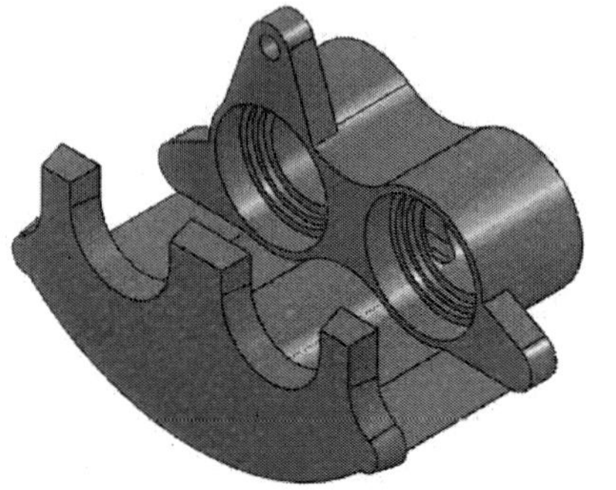

Figure 4-39 Model after creating the feature

Creating the Simple Hole

Up to now you have learned to create holes by extruding a circle using the **Extruded Cut** tool. Now, you will learn to create a hole feature using the **Simple Hole** tool. If you use this tool to create a hole, you do not need to draw a sketch of the hole. The holes created with this tool act as placed features. You will create a hole using the **Simple Hole** tool arbitrarily on the front planar face of the previously created extruded feature and position it later.

1. Choose **Insert > Features > Simple Hole** from the SOLIDWORKS menus; the **Hole PropertyManager** is displayed and you are prompted to select a location on a planar face for the center of the hole.

Tip

*You can customize the **Features CommandManager** and add the **Simple Hole** tool in it. To do so, choose **Tools > Customize** from the SOLIDWORKS menus; the **Customize** dialog box will be displayed. From this dialog box, choose the **Commands** tab. Next, select **Features** from the **Categories** area of the **Customize** dialog box; all tools related to the features will be displayed in the **Buttons** area. Press and hold the left mouse on the **Simple Hole** button in the **Buttons** area of the **Customize** dialog box. Next, drag it to the **Features CommandManager** and release the left mouse button at the required location; the **Simple Hole** tool will be added at the specified location of the **Features CommandManager**. Next, exit from the **Customize** dialog box by choosing the **OK** button from it.*

2. Click anywhere on the front planar face of the previously created extruded feature; the **Hole PropertyManager** is modified and preview of the hole feature with an arrow pointing in the direction of the feature to be created is displayed in the drawing area.

3. Select the **Through All** option from the **End Condition** drop-down list in the **Hole PropertyManager** and then set the value of the **Hole Diameter** spinner to **5**.

The **Through All** option will be available in the **End Condition** drop-down list only after creating the base feature. This option is used to extend a feature from the sketching plane through all existing geometric entities.

4. Choose the **OK** button from the **Hole PropertyManager**; the hole feature is placed on the selected face.

   After placing the hole feature arbitrarily, you need to position it concentric to the left semi-circular edge of the previously created extruded feature.

5. Select the hole feature from the **FeatureManager design tree**; a pop-up toolbar is displayed.

6. Choose the **Edit Sketch** button from the pop-up toolbar; the sketcher environment is invoked. 

7. Select the edge from the drawing area, refer to Figure 4-40 and then press and hold the CTRL key. Next, select the sketch of the hole feature and then release the CTRL key. As soon as, you release the CTRL key, a pop-up toolbar is displayed. Choose the **Make Concentric** button from it

8. Exit from the sketcher environment. The model after creating the hole feature is shown in the Figure 4-41.

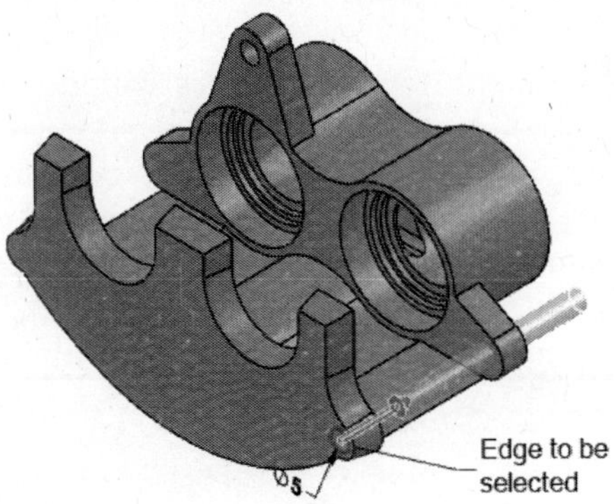

Figure 4-40 *Edge to be selected*

Figure 4-41 *Model after creating the hole feature*

Mirroring the Simple Hole

After creating the hole feature, you need to mirror it using the Right Pane as a mirroring plane.

1. Invoke the **Mirror PropertyManager** and select the Right Plane as the mirroring plane.

2. Next, select the hole feature and choose the **OK** button from the **Mirror PropertyManager**; the mirror feature is created, as shown in Figure 4-42.

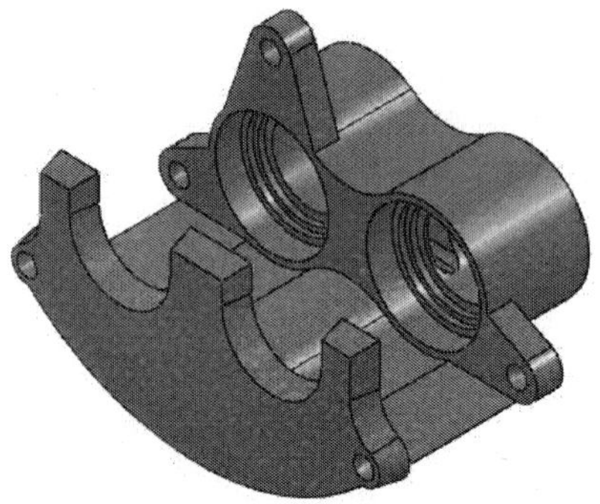

Figure 4-42 *Model after mirroring the hole feature*

Applying the Fillet

After creating all the features of the model, you need to apply fillet using the **Fillet** tool.

1. Choose the **Fillet** button; the **Fillet PropertyManager** is displayed and you are prompted to select the edges, faces, features, or loops to fillet.

2. Select the edge from the drawing area to apply the fillet, refer to Figure 4-43; preview of the fillet is displayed in the drawing area with the default radius value.

3. Set the value of the **Radius** spinner to **2.5** in the **Fillet Parameters** rollout of the PropertyManager.

4. Choose the **OK** button from the PropertyManager; the fillet is applied to the selected edge. Also, the **Fillet1** feature is added to the **FeatureManager Design Tree**. The final model after applying the fillet is shown in Figure 4-44.

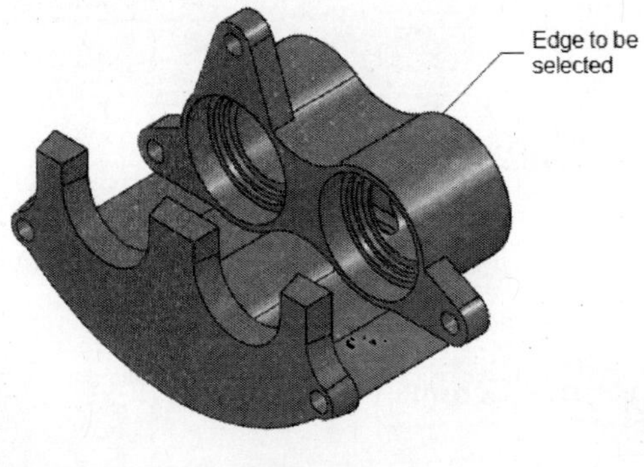

Figure 4-43 Edge to be selected

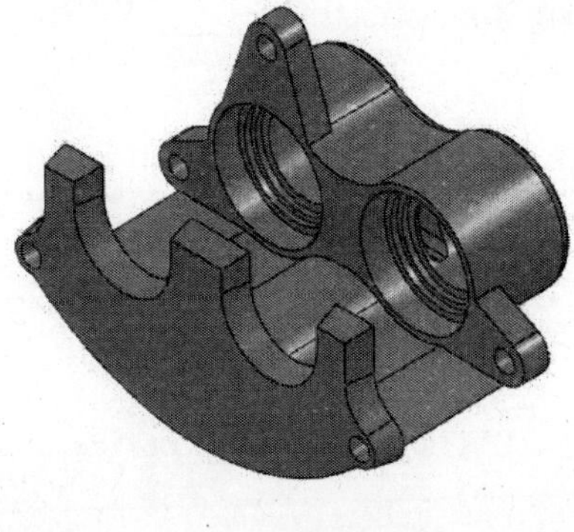

Figure 4-44 Final model after applying the fillet

Saving the Model

After completing the model, you need to save it in the *Motor Cycle Project* folder.

1. Choose the **Save** button from the Menu Bar to invoke the **Save As** dialog box. Next, browse to the *Motor Cycle Project* folder.

2. Enter **Caliper Body** as the name of the model in the **File name** edit box and choose the **Save** button. The model is saved in the *\Documents\Motor Cycle Project\Caliper Body*.

3. Close the document by choosing the **File > Close** from the SOLIDWORKS menu.

Self-Evaluation Test

Answer the following questions and then compare them to those given at the end of this chapter:

1. The _________ option is used to define the termination of the extruded feature using a selected surface or a face.

2. The _________ tool is used to display the section view of a model by cutting the model using a plane or a face.

3. The _________ button is used to specify a draft angle while extruding the sketch.

4. Choose **View > Display > Shadows In Shaded Mode** from the SOLIDWORKS menus to display the model with _________.

5. The _________ **PropertyManager** is used to assign a color to a model, faces, surfaces, bodies, or features.

6. The _________ selection box of the **Selected Geometry** rollout is used to display the name of the selected entities to which color needs to be assigned.

7. When you choose the **Draft On/Off** button from the **Direction 1** rollout of the PropertyManager, the _________ spinner and the _________ check box will be enabled in the PropertyManager.

8. In SOLIDWORKS, when you press the right-mouse button and drag the cursor in any direction, a set of tools that are arranged radially will be displayed in the drawing area. (T/F)

9. When you apply the ordinate dimensions, the **Modify** dialog box will not be displayed to modify the dimension values. (T/F)

10. In SOLIDWORKS, you can not customize the **Features CommandManager**. (T/F)

Review Questions

Answer the following questions:

1. Which of the following PropertyManager will be displayed when you will choose the **Simple Hole** tool from the SOLIDWORKS menus?

   (a) **Hole Spec PropertyManager** (b) **Hole PropertyManager**
   (c) **Shell PropertyManager** (d) **Hole Position PropertyManager**

2. ________ is a radial arrangement of tools.

3. The _________ option will be available in the **End Condition** drop-down list of the PropertyManager only after creating the base feature.

4. The _________ button of the **Color PropertyManager** allows you to select only a specified feature of the model to assign color.

5. The _________ tool is used to remove the material from the model by revolving a sketch around the selected axis.

6. When you choose the _________ button from the **Features CommandManager**, the **Revolve PropertyManager** will be displayed.

7. To apply horizontal ordinate dimension, you need to choose the _________ button from the _________ flyout in the **Sketch CommandManager**.

8. When you select the _________ option from the **End Condition** drop-down list in the **Direction 1** rollout of the PropertyManager, the **Face/Plane** selection area is displayed in the rollout.

9. The **Direction 2** rollout will not be available in the PropertyManager if you have selected the **Mid Plane** option from the **End Condition** drop-down list of the **Direction 1** rollout of the PropertyManager. (T/F)

10. In SOLIDWORKS, once a hole feature is arbitrarily placed, you can not reposition it. (T/F)

Answers to Self-Evaluation Test

1. Up to Surface, 2. Section View, 3. Draft On/Off, 4. shadow, **5. Color, 6. Selected Entities, 7. Draft Angle, Draft Outward, 8.** T, **9.** T, **10.** F

Chapter 5

Creating Fork Tube, Cap, Holder, and Bodies

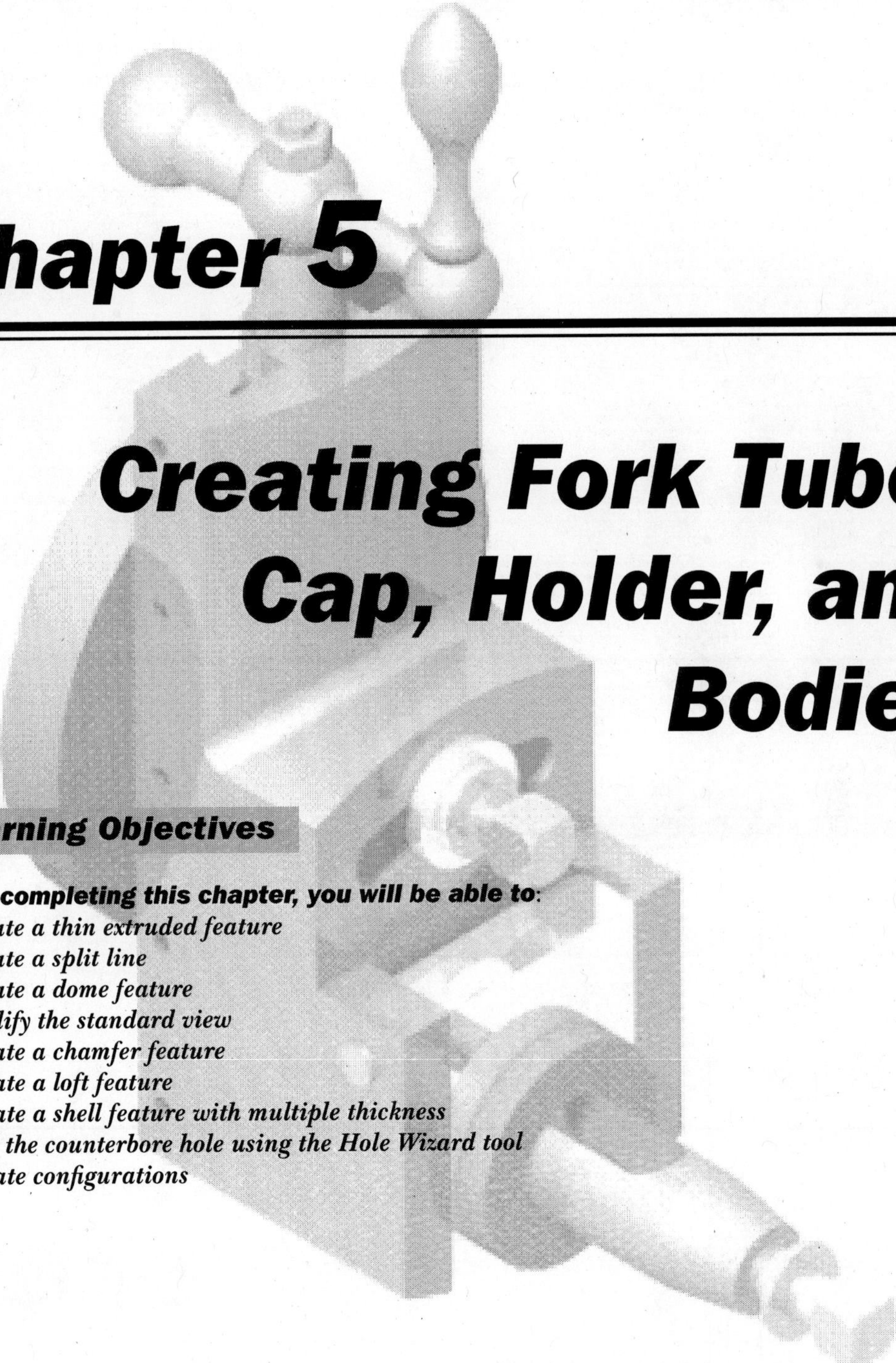

Learning Objectives

After completing this chapter, you will be able to:

- *Create a thin extruded feature*
- *Create a split line*
- *Create a dome feature*
- *Modify the standard view*
- *Create a chamfer feature*
- *Create a loft feature*
- *Create a shell feature with multiple thickness*
- *Add the counterbore hole using the Hole Wizard tool*
- *Create configurations*

CREATING THE FORK TUBE

Part Description

In this section, you will create Fork Tube, as shown in Figure 5-1. The base feature of the model is created as a thin extruded feature. Also, the cosmetic threads with the shaded display is added. The front and detail views, with dimensions are shown in Figure 5-2. **(Expected time: 25 min)**

Figure 5-1 *The Fork Tube*

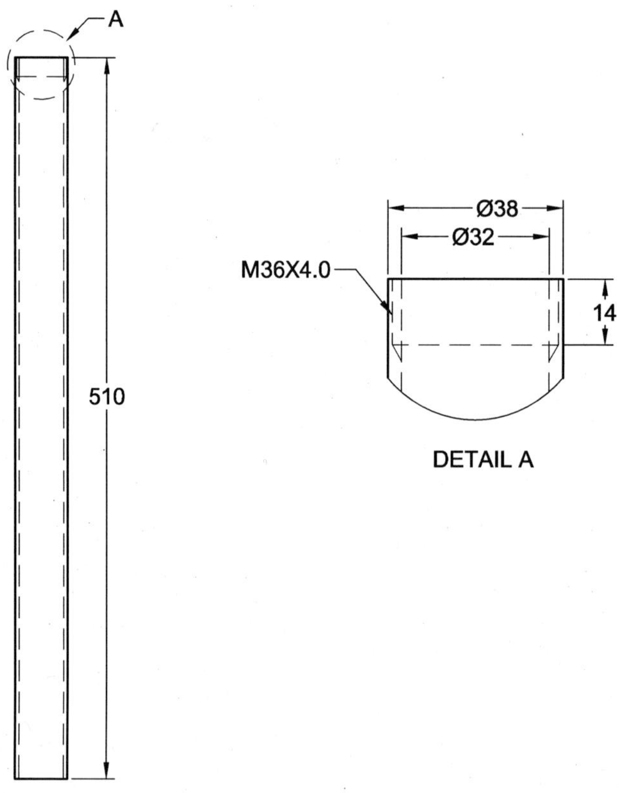

Figure 5-2 *The Front and detail views of the Fork Tube*

Starting a New Part Document

1. Choose the **New** button from the Menu Bar; the **New SOLIDWORKS Document** dialog box is displayed.

2. Choose the **OK** button from the **New SOLIDWORKS Document** dialog box; a new SOLIDWORKS part document is started.

Creating the Base Feature

The base feature of the model is a thin extruded feature created by using the **Extruded Boss/Base** tool.

1. Invoke the **Extrude PropertyManager** by choosing the **Extruded Boss/Base** button from the **Features CommandManager**.

2. Select the Top Plane as the sketching plane; the sketcher environment is invoked and the selected plane is oriented normal to the view.

3. Draw a circle of diameter 38 mm, as shown in Figure 5-3 and then exit from the sketcher environment; the **Boss-Extrude PropertyManager** is displayed. Also, the preview of the solid extruded feature is displayed in the drawing area.

4. Select the **Mid Plane** option from the **End Condition** drop-down list and set the value of the **Depth** spinner to **510 mm** in the **Direction 1** rollout of the PropertyManager.

   As soon as, you specify the depth of the extruded feature, the preview of the feature will be modified accordingly.

5. If the model is not completely displayed in the screen, choose the **Zoom to Fit** button from the **View (Heads-up)** toolbar to fit the model on the screen. Alternatively, press the F key.

6. Expand the **Thin Feature** rollout of the PropertyManager by selecting the check box that is available on the title bar of the **Thin Feature** rollout, refer to Figure 5-4. As the **Thin Feature** rollout is expanded, the preview of the model gets modified.

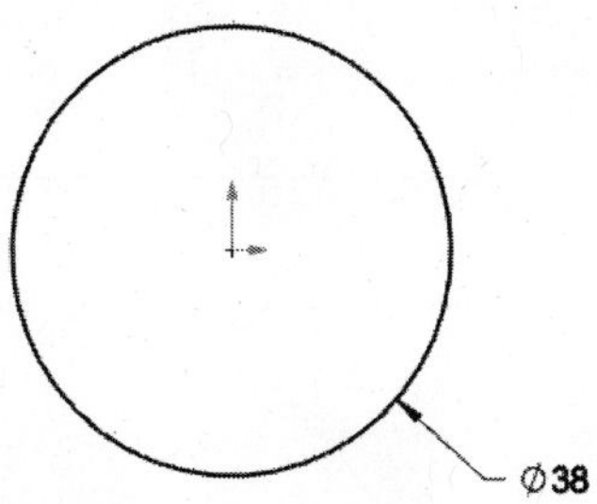

Figure 5-3 *Sketch of the base feature*

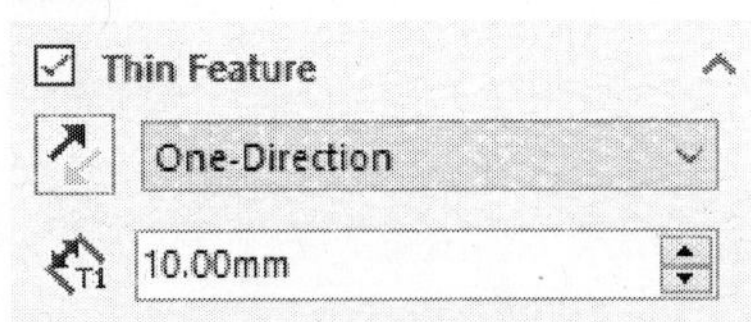

Figure 5-4 *The* ***Thin Feature*** *rollout of the* ***Boss-Extrude PropertyManager***

The **Thin Feature** rollout is used to create thin extruded features. The thin extruded features can be created by using a closed or an open sketch. If the sketch is closed, the thickness will be specified inside or outside the sketch to create a cavity inside the feature. If the sketch to be extruded is open then the **Thin Feature** rollout will be invoked automatically.

7. Make sure the **One-Direction** option is selected in the **Type** drop-down list of the **Thin Feature** rollout.

The options provided in the **Type** drop-down list are used to select the method of defining the thickness of the thin feature. The **One-Direction** option is selected in this drop-down list and it is used to add the thickness on one side of the sketch. The thickness can be specified in the **Thickness** spinner provided below the **Type** drop-down list. Note that for the close sketches, the direction can be inside or outside the sketch. Similarly, for the open sketches, the direction can be below or above the sketch. You can control the direction of thickness using the **Reverse Direction** button available on the left of the **Type** drop-down list. This button will be available only when the **One-Direction** option is selected in the **Type** drop-down list.

The **Mid-Plane** option of the **Type** drop-down list is used to add the thickness equally on both sides of the sketch. Similarly, the **Two-Direction** option of this drop-down list is used to create a thin feature by adding different thicknesses on both sides of the sketch.

8. Choose the **Reverse Direction** button to reverse the direction of thickness inside the sketch and then set the value of the **Thickness** spinner to **3 mm**.

9. Choose the **OK** button from the **Boss-Extrude PropertyManager**. The model after creating the thin extruded feature is shown in Figure 5-5.

Applying the Cosmetic Threads

Cosmetic threads are used to display schematic representation of the threads and are applied using the **Cosmetic Thread PropertyManager**.

1. Choose **Insert > Annotations > Cosmetic Thread** from the SOLIDWORKS menus; the **Cosmetic Thread PropertyManager** is displayed. Also, you are prompted to select the edges and set the parameters.

2. Zoom in the drawing display area by scrolling the wheel of the mouse and select the top inner circular edge of the model, refer to Figure 5-6. The name of the selected edge is displayed in the **Circular Edges** selection box of the **Thread Settings** rollout in the PropertyManager. Also, the schematic representation of the threads is displayed in the drawing area.

Figure 5-5 *Model after creating the thin extruded feature*

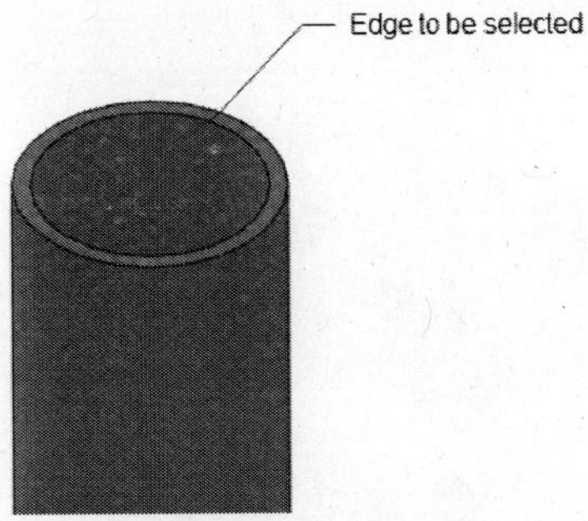

Figure 5-6 *Edge to be selected*

3. Select the **ANSI Metric** option from the **Standard** drop-down list of the PropertyManager, if it is not selected by default.

4. Select the **Blind** option from the **End Condition** drop-down list to specify the depth of the threads. Specify the depth of the threads as 14 in the **Depth** spinner.

5. Select the **M36x4.0** option from the **Size** drop-down list to define the size of the threads.

6. Choose the **OK** button; cosmetic thread is added to the model and is displayed as a dotted circle.

   Now, you need to display the cosmetic thread with shaded thread pattern on the surface.

7. Choose the **Options** button from the Menu Bar; the **System Options - General** dialog box is displayed. 

8. Choose the **Document Properties** tab from this dialog box; the **System Option - General** dialog box is changed to **Document Properties - Drafting Standard** dialog box.

9. Select the **Detailing** option from this dialog box. Next, select the **Shaded cosmetic threads** check box and then choose the **OK** button; the cosmetic thread is displayed in the drawing area with the shaded display. The Figures 5-7 and 5-8 show partial and full views of the final model after adding the cosmetic threads with shaded display.

Figure 5-7 Partial view of the final model

Figure 5-8 Final model after adding the cosmetic threads with shaded display

Expanded view of the **FeatureManager Design Tree** after adding the cosmetic thread is shown in Figure 5-9. To expand the design tree, you need to click on the ▸ sign on the left of the thin extruded feature that is **Extrude-Thin1**.

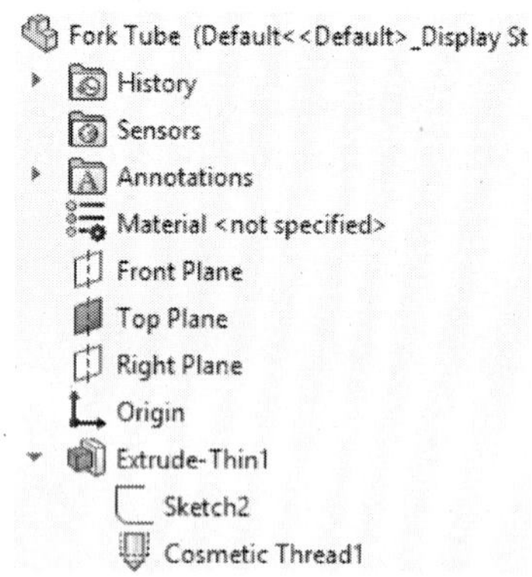

Figure 5-9 FeatureManager Design Tree

Saving the Model

After creating the Fork Tube, you need to save it in the *Motor Cycle Project* folder.

1. Invoke the **Save As** dialog box. Next, browse to the *Motor Cycle Project* folder

2. Enter **Fork Tube** as the name of the model in the **File name** edit box and choose the **Save** button. The model will be saved in the *\Documents\Motor Cycle Project\Fork Tube*.

CREATING THE FORK CAP

Part Description

In this section, you will create Fork Cap, as shown in Figure 5-10. The cosmetic threads with the shaded display is added. The top and front views with dimensions are shown in the same figure. After creating the model, you will modify the standard views such that the front view of the model becomes the top view. **(Expected time: 40 min)**

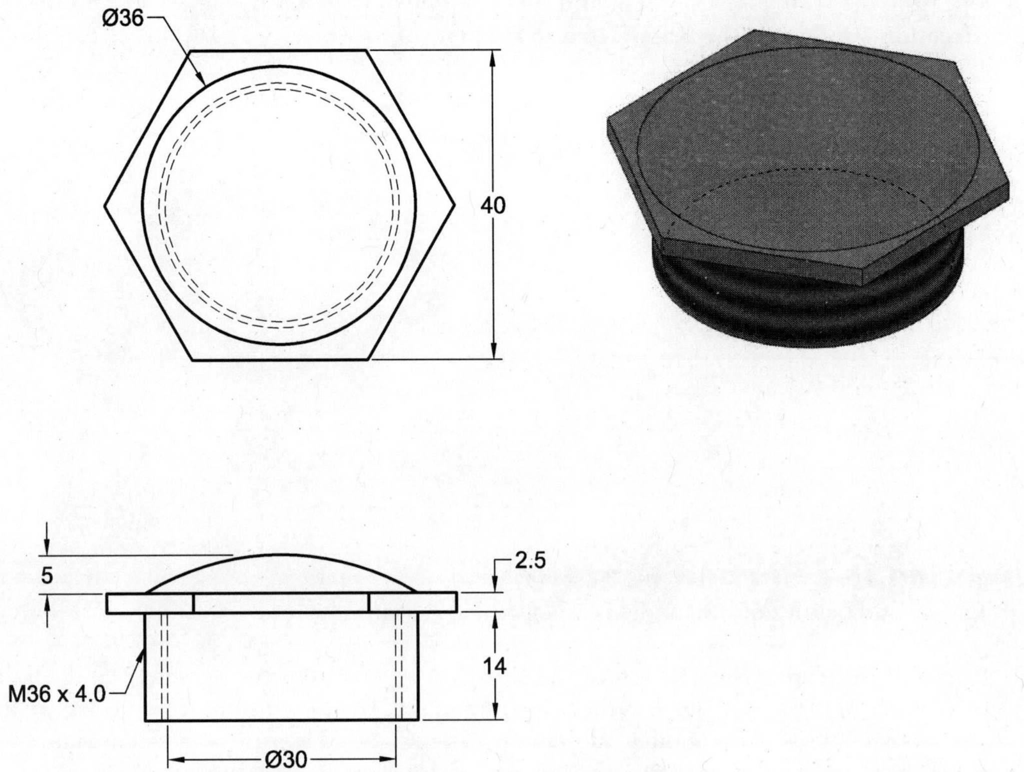

Figure 5-10 The Fork Cap and its Views and Dimensions

Starting a New Part Document

1. Start a new part document using the **New SOLIDWORKS Document** dialog box.

Creating the Base Feature

The base feature of the model is created using the **Extruded Boss/Base** tool.

1. Invoke the **Extruded Boss/Base** tool and then invoke the sketcher environment by selecting the Top Plane as the sketching pane.

2. Draw the six-sided polygon with the construction circle inscribed in the polygon, as shown in Figure 5-11.

Note

To create a six-sided polygon with a construction circle inscribed inside, set the value of the ***Number of Sides*** *spinner to 6 and select the* ***Inscribed circle*** *radio button in the* ***Parameters*** *rollout of the* ***Polygon PropertyManager****.*

3. Exit from the sketch environment and set the value of the **Depth** spinner to **2.5 mm** in the **Direction 1** rollout of the **Boss-Extrude PropertyManager**.

4. Choose the **OK** button. The model after creating the base feature is shown in the Figure 5-12.

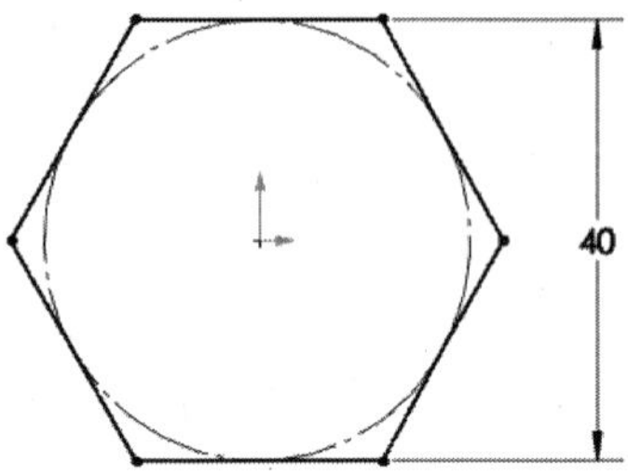

Figure 5-11 Sketch of the base feature

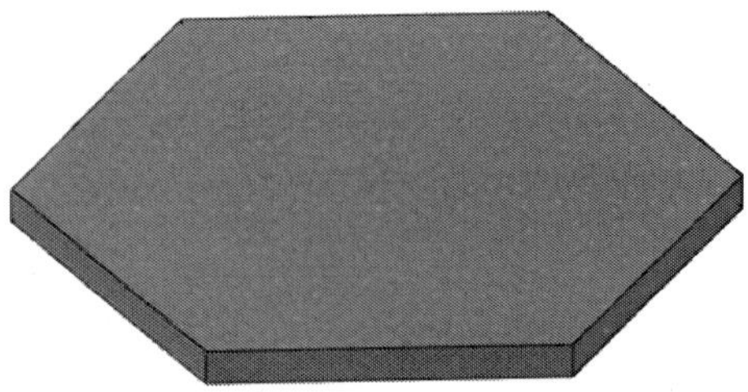

Figure 5-12 Model after creating the base feature

Creating the Second Feature

The second feature of the model is an extruded feature.

1. Invoke the **Extruded Boss/Base** tool and create the extruded feature by selecting the bottom planar face of the base feature as the sketching plane. For dimensions, refer to Figure 5-10. The isometric view of the model after creating the extruded feature is shown in Figure 5-13.

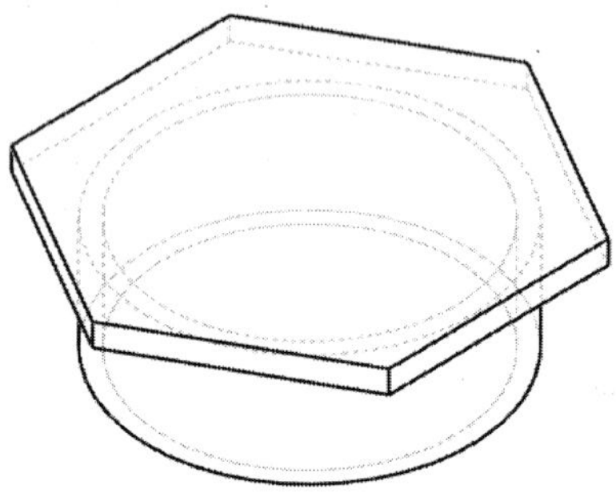

Figure 5-13 Model after creating the extruded feature

Note

*In Figure 5-13, the display of the model is changed to **Hidden Lines Visible** mode for displaying the hidden lines of the model. To change the default display mode of the model to **Hidden Lines Visible** mode, choose the **Display Style** button from the **View (Heads-up)** toolbar; the **Display Style** flyout will be displayed. Next, choose the **Hidden Lines Visible** button from this flyout. In the **Hidden Lines Visible** mode, the model will be displayed in the wireframe and the hidden lines in the model will be displayed as dashed lines.*

Tip

*SOLIDWORKS provides you with various predefined modes to display the model. These display modes: **Wireframe**, **Hidden Lines Visible**, **Hidden Lines Removed**, **Shaded With Edges**, and **Shaded** are grouped together in the **Display Style** flyout.*

*By default, the model is displayed in the **Shaded With Edges** mode. In this display mode, the model is shaded and the edges of the visible faces are displayed. In the **Wireframe** mode, all the hidden lines will be displayed along with the visible lines in the model. In the **Hidden Lines Removed**, the hidden lines will not be displayed in the model. And in the **Shaded** mode, the model will be displayed in shaded and the edges of the visible faces will not be displayed.*

Creating the Split Line

The next feature of the model is a split line. You will divide the top face of the base feature into two faces by using the **Split Line** tool and then create a dome feature on a divided face. To create a split line feature, first you need to create a sketch in the sketcher environment.

1. Invoke the sketcher environment by choosing the **Sketch** button from the **Sketch CommandManager** and selecting the top face of the base feature as the sketching plane.

   Sketch

2. Draw a circle of diameter 36 mm, refer to Figure 5-14 and then exit from the sketcher environment.

3. Choose the **Split Line** button from the **Curves** flyout in the **Features CommandManager**, refer to Figure 5-15; the **Split Line PropertyManager** is displayed.

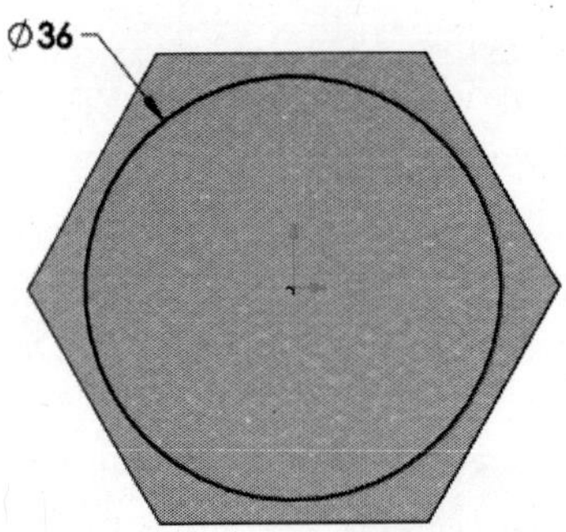

Figure 5-14 Circle of diameter 36 millimeters

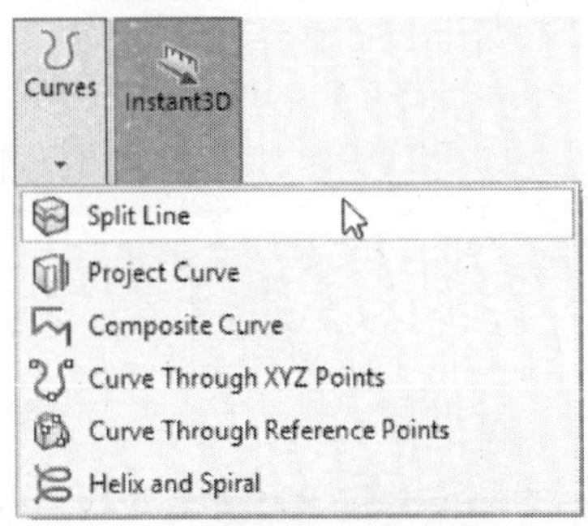

Figure 5-15 *The **Split Line** button in the **Curves** Flyout*

The **Split Line** tool is used to project a sketch on a planar or curved face which in turn splits or divides the single face into two or more than two faces.

4. Select the **Projection** radio button from the **Type of Split** rollout of the **Split Line PropertyManager**.

5. Select the sketch from the drawing area; the name of the selected sketch is displayed in the **Sketch to Project** selection box of the **Selections** rollout in the PropertyManager. Also, the **Faces to Split** selection box is activated and you are prompted to select the faces to be split.

6. Select the top face of the base feature as the face to be split and then choose the **OK** button from the PropertyManager; the selected face splits into two faces. The isometric view of the model with the top face split into two is shown in Figure 5-16.

Figure 5-16 Model after splitting the face

Creating the Dome Feature

The next feature of the model is a dome feature.

1. Choose the **Dome** button from the **Features CommandManager**; the **Dome PropertyManager** is displayed.

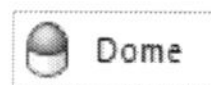

The **Dome** tool is used to create a dome feature on the selected face. Depending on the direction of feature creation, a dome feature can be of convex or concave shape.

2. Select the split face from the drawing area, refer to Figure 5-17; preview of the dome feature is displayed in the drawing area.

3. Set the value of the **Distance** spinner to **5 mm** in the **Parameters** rollout of the **Dome PropertyManager**.

4. Choose the **OK** button from the PropertyManager; the dome feature is created. The front view of the model after creating the dome feature is shown in Figure 5-18. To change the orientation of the model to the front view, choose the **Front** button from the **View Orientation** flyout in the **View (Heads-up)** toolbar.

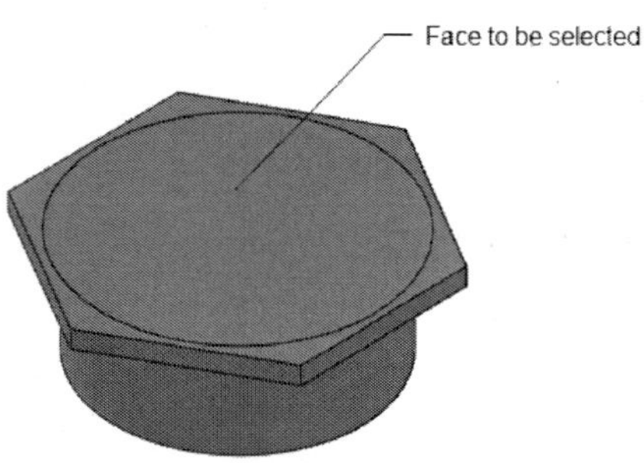

Figure 5-17 Face to be selected

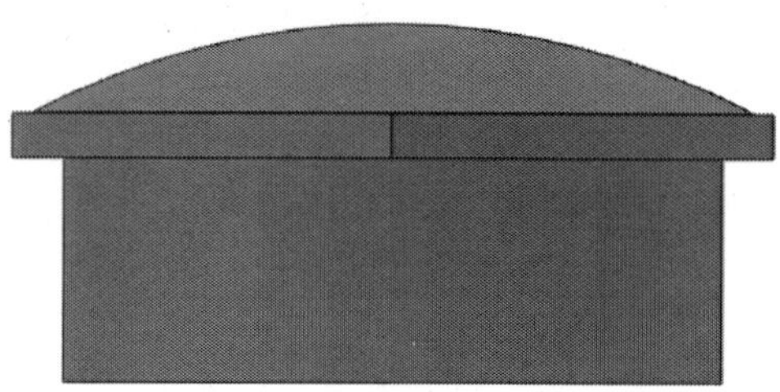

Figure 5-18 Front view of the model

Tip

Instead of creating the dome feature, you can also create a revolve feature by revolving the sketch around the axis of the model to get the required shape of the model. If you will create revolve feature instead of dome feature, you need not to split the top face of the base feature.

Applying the Cosmetic Threads

It is evident from the Figure 5-10 that cosmetic threads are required in the model. The cosmetic threads are applied by using the **Cosmetic Thread PropertyManager**.

1. Choose **Insert > Annotations > Cosmetic Thread** from the SOLIDWORKS menus; the **Cosmetic Thread PropertyManager** is displayed and you are prompted to select the edges and set the parameters.

2. Select the bottom outer circular edge of the model, refer to Figure 5-19.

3. Select the **ANSI Metric** option from the **Standard** drop-down list, if not selected by default.

4. Select the **M36x4.0** option from the **Size** drop-down list and the **Up to Next** option from the **End condition** drop-down list to define the size of the threads.

5. Choosing the **OK** button; the model after adding the cosmetic threads is shown in Figure 5-20.

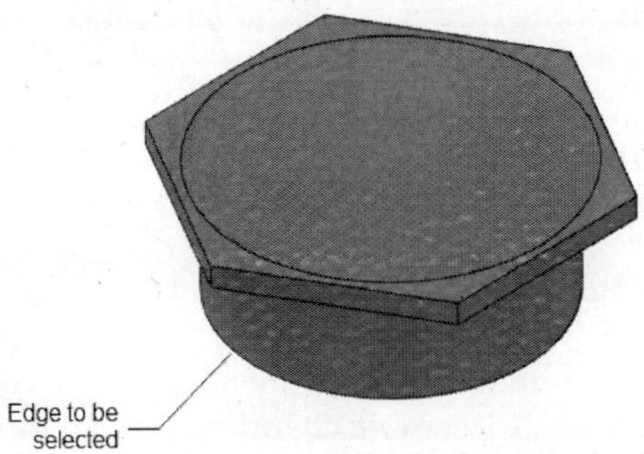

Figure 5-19 *Edge to be selected*

Figure 5-20 *Cosmetic threads with shaded display*

Modifying the Standard View

As mentioned in the Part description, you need to modify the standard views such that the front view of the model becomes the top view. This is done using the Orientation dialog box.

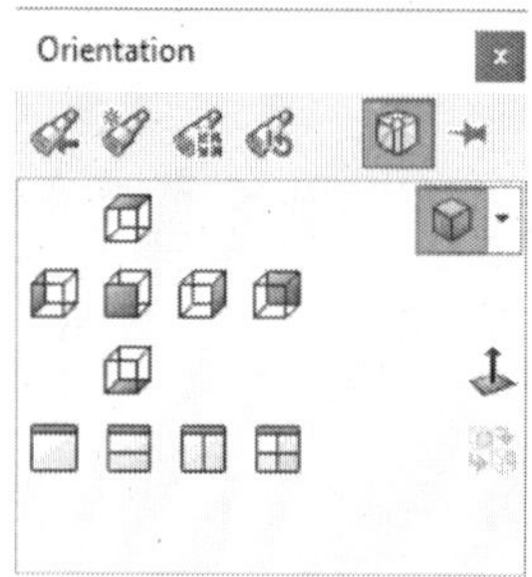

*Figure 5-21 The **Orientation** dialog box*

1. Press the SPACEBAR on the keyboard; the **Orientation** dialog box is displayed, refer to Figure 5-21.

The **Orientation** dialog box is used to change the view orientation of the model using the predefined standard views or user-defined views. You can also modified the orientation of the predefined standard view using this dialog box.

2. Hold the **Orientation** dialog box by selecting it on the title bar of the dialog box and then drag it to the top right corner of the drawing area.

3. Choose the **Pin/Unpin the dialog** button from the **Orientation** dialog box to pin it at the top right corner of the drawing area.

Note

*The **Orientation** dialog box will close automatically if you perform any other operation. Therefore, you need to pin this dialog box.*

4. Click on the **Front (Ctrl + 1)** option in the list box of the **Orientation** dialog box; the current view is automatically changed to the front view and the model is now reoriented and displayed from the front.

   Now, you need to modify the standard views such that the front view of the model becomes the top view. Then, you need to save the model with the current settings.

5. Choose the **Update Standard Views** button to update the standard views; a pop-up box prompts you to select the standard view you would like to assign the current view to.

The **Update Standard Views** button is used to modify the orientation of the standard views.

6. Click on the **Top** option in the list box of the **Orientation** dialog box; the **SOLIDWORKS** message box is displayed stating that modifying the standard view will change the orientation of any view in this document.

7. Choose **Yes** from this message box to modify the standard views. As soon as, you choose Yes from the message box, the front view of the model becomes the top view.

8. Now, double-click on the **Isometric** option in the list box of the **Orientation** dialog box. You will notice that the isometric view is different now.

9. Choose the **Pin/Unpin the dialog** button from the **Orientation** dialog box again and left-click anywhere in the drawing area to close the dialog box.

Tip

After modifying the orientation of the standard view, you can again reset the standard settings of all the standard views in the current document by using the ***Reset Standard Views*** *button from the* ***Orientation*** *dialog box. When you choose this button, the SOLIDWORKS message box will be displayed and you will be prompted to confirm whether you want to reset all standard views to their original settings or not. If you choose* ***Yes****, all the standard views will be reset to their default settings.*

Saving the Model

After completing the model, you need to save it in the *Motor Cycle Project* folder.

1. Invoke the **Save As** dialog box and browse to the location of *Motor Cycle Project* folder.
2. Enter **Fork Cap** as the name of the model in the **File name** edit box and choose the **Save** button. The document is saved in the *\Documents\Motor Cycle Project\Fork Cap*.
3. Choose the **File > Close** from the SOLIDWORKS menus to close the document.

CREATING THE FORK HOLDER

Part Description

In this section, you will create Fork Holder, as shown in Figures 5-22. The views and dimensions of it are shown in Figure 5-23. All fillets dimension is equal to 2.5 mm. For better display of the views hidden lines and some center lines are suppressed. **(Expected time: 40 min)**

Figure 5-22 *The Fork Holder*

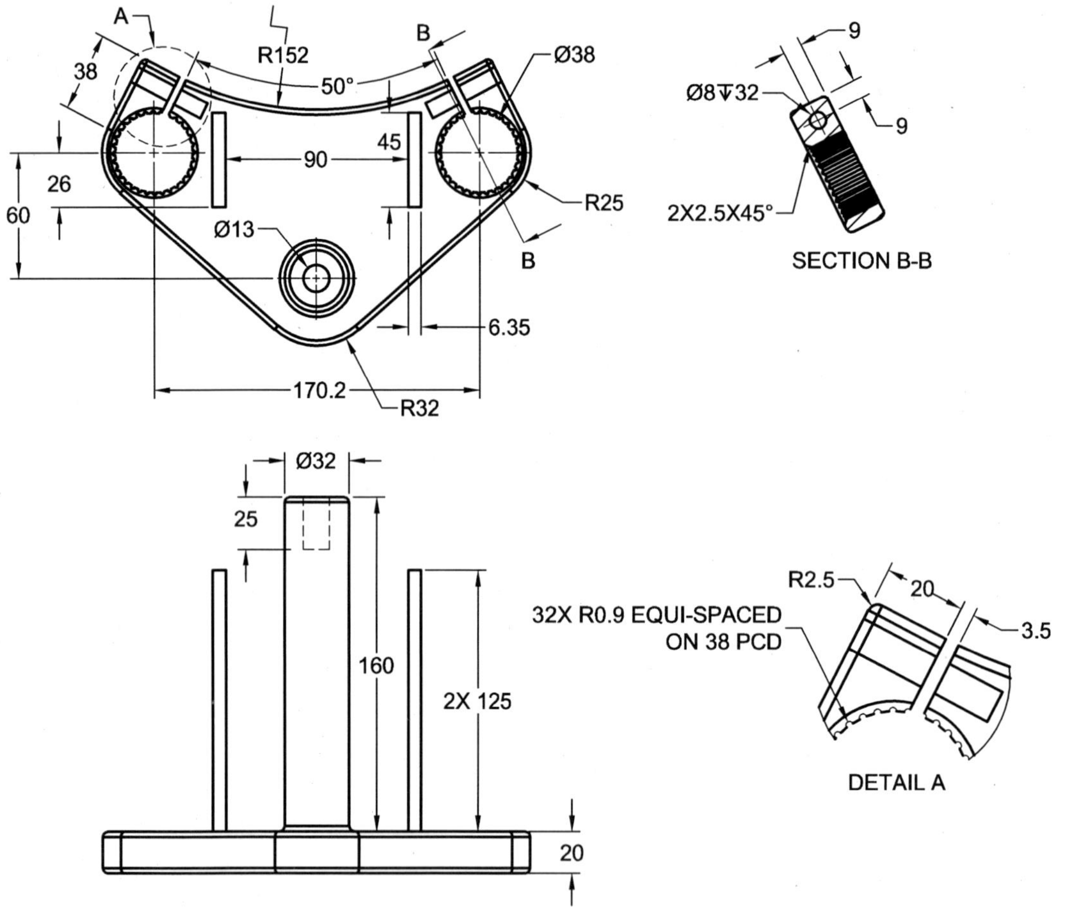

Figure 5-23 *Views and dimensions of the Fork Holder*

Creating the Base Feature

The base feature of the model is an extruded feature. The sketch of the extruded feature will be created on the Top Plane.

1. Start a new SOLIDWORKS part document using the **New SOLIDWORKS Document** dialog box.

2. Choose the **Extruded Boss/Base** button and select the Top Plane as the sketching plane to invoke the sketcher environment.

3. Draw the sketch of the extruded feature using the tools available in the **Sketch CommandManager**, refer to Figure 5-24. For your reference, the arcs and lines in the sketch are numbered.

Note

In the sketch shown in Figure 5-24, the tangent relation is applied between the entities: 1 and 5, 1 and 13, 6 and 7, 7 and 8, 8 and 9, 9 and 10, 10 and 11, and entities 11 and 12. The equal relation is applied between the entities: 5 and 13, 6 and 12, 7 and 11, 8 and 10, and entities 3 and 15. The perpendicular relation is applied between the entities: 5 and 6, 5 and 4, 12 and 13, and entities 13 and 14. Also, the parallel relation is applied between the entities: 2, 4, and 6 and entities 12, 14, and 16 to make the sketch fully defined.

4. Exit from the sketcher environment and extrude the sketch to the depth of 20 mm in an upward direction. The model after creating the base feature is shown in Figure 5-25.

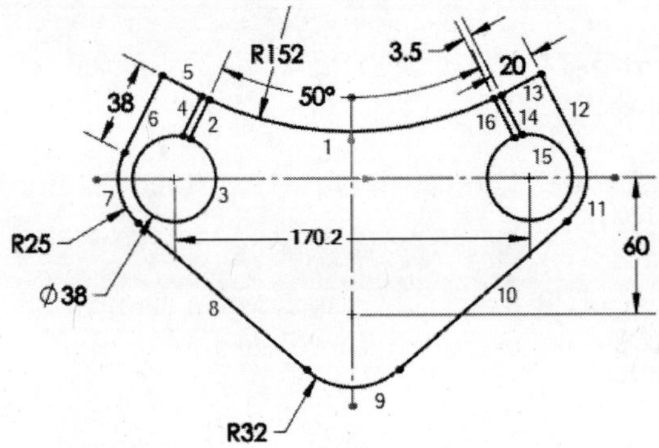

Figure 5-24 Sketch of the base feature

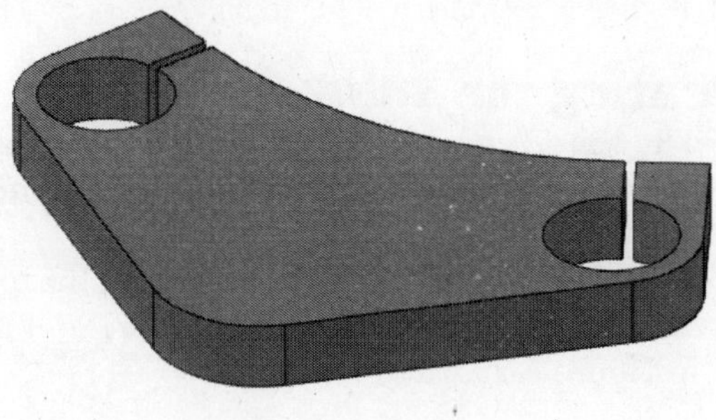

Figure 5-25 Model after creating the base feature

Creating the Second Feature

The second feature of the model is also an extruded feature. The sketch of this extruded feature will be created on the top planar face of the base feature.

1. Choose the **Extruded Boss/Base** button and select the top planar face of the base feature as the sketching plane to invoke the sketcher environment.

2. Draw a circle of diameter 32 mm, refer to Figure 5-26 and then exit the sketcher environment. Note that, to fully define the sketch, concentric relation is applied between the circle of radius 32 mm and the edge of the model.

3. Extrude the sketch to the depth of 160 mm in the upward direction. The model after creating the second feature is shown in Figure 5-27.

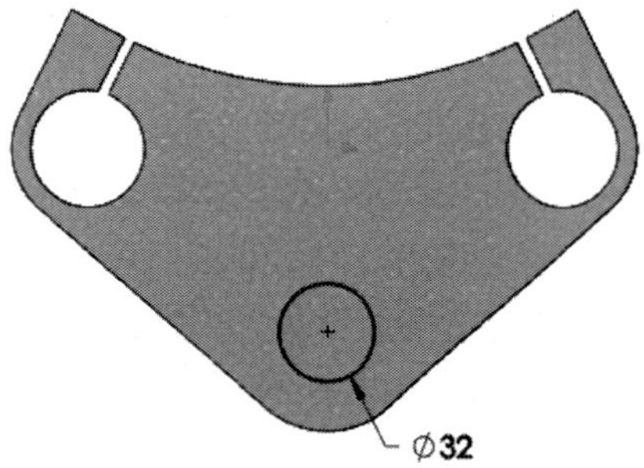

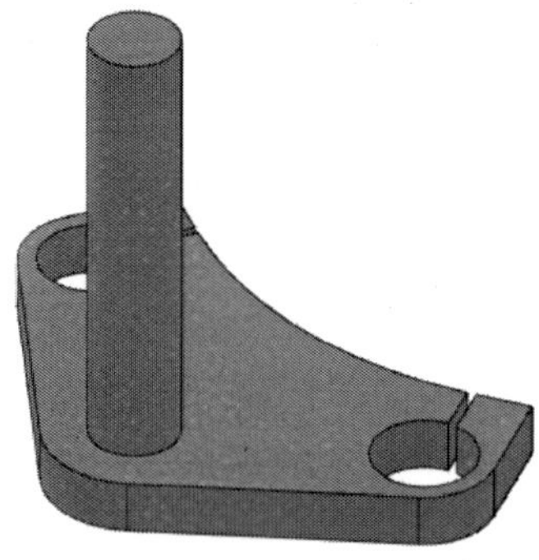

Figure 5-26 *Sketch of the second feature*   *Figure 5-27* *Model after creating the second feature*

Creating the Third Feature

The third feature of the model is an extruded feature. The sketch of this extruded feature will be created on the top planar face of the base feature.

1. Draw sketch of the extruded feature on the top face of the base feature, as shown in Figure 5-28 and then extrude it upto a depth of 125 mm using the **Extruded Boss/Base** tool, as shown in Figure 5-29.

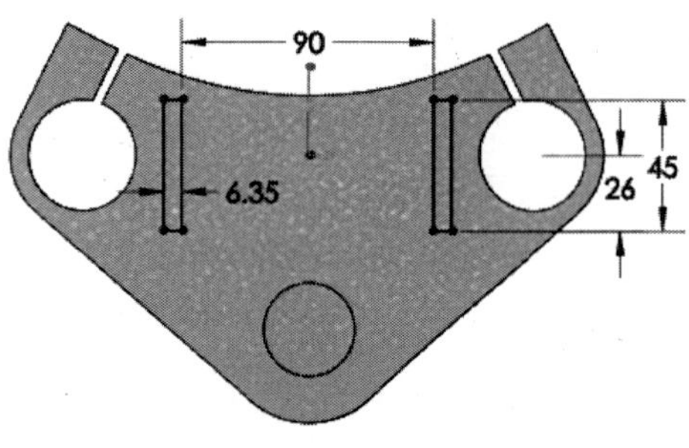

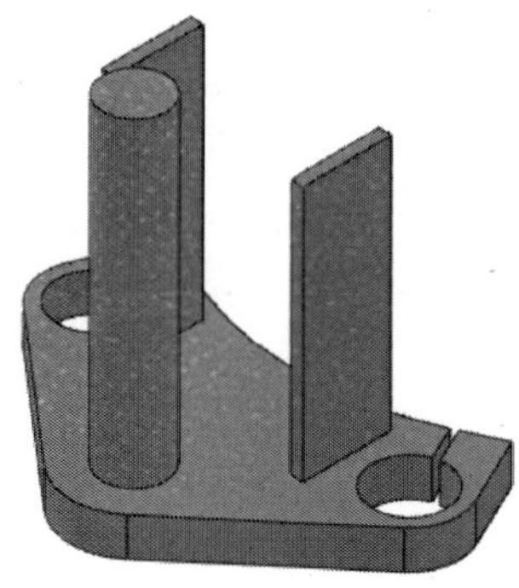

Figure 5-28 *Sketch of the third feature*   *Figure 5-29* *Model after creating the third feature*

Creating the Simple Hole Feature

The next feature of the model is a simple hole feature. In SOLIDWORKS, you can create simple holes and standard holes by using the **Simple Hole** and **Hole Wizard** tools. In this section, using the **Simple Hole** tool, you will create a hole arbitrarily on the top planar face of the second extruded feature and then position the hole.

1. Select the top planar face of the second extruded feature and then choose **Insert > Features > Simple Hole** from the SOLIDWORKS menus; the **Hole PropertyManager** is displayed. Also, preview of the simple hole with default value is displayed in the drawing area.

In the **End Condition** drop-down list of the **Hole PropertyManager**, the **Blind** option is selected by default. Therefore, you need to specify the value of the depth in the **Depth** spinner.

2. Set the value of the **Depth** spinner to **25 mm** and the **Hole Diameter** spinner to **13 mm** in the **Direction 1** rollout of the PropertyManager.

3. Choose the **OK** button; the hole feature is placed arbitrarily on the selected face.

   After creating the hole arbitrarily on the top face of the second feature, you need to position it by applying the concentric relation between the center point of the hole and the circular edge of the second extruded feature.

4. Select the hole feature from the **FeatureManager Design Tree**; a pop-up toolbar is displayed near to the cursor.

5. Choose the **Edit Sketch** button from the pop-up toolbar; the sketcher environment is invoked.

6. Select the center point of the hole. Next, press and hold the CTRL key and then select the circular edge of the second extruded feature; the **Properties PropertyManager** is displayed.

7. Release the CTRL key and then from the **Properties PropertyManager**, choose the **Concentric** button; the concentric relation is applied between the selections.

8. Exit the sketcher environment. The model after creating the hole feature is shown in Figure 5-30.

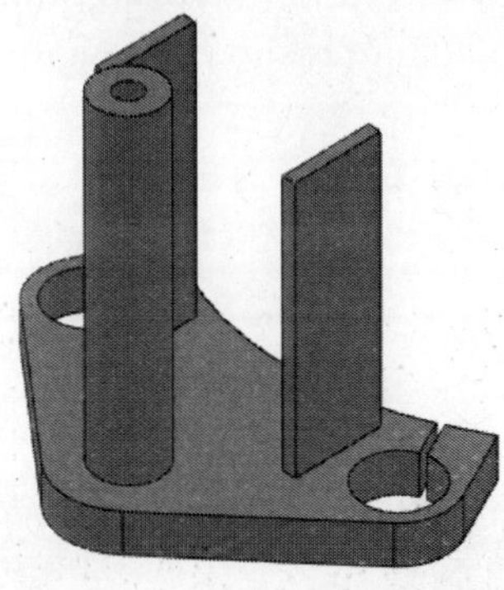

Figure 5-30 *Model after creating the hole feature*

Creating the Fifth Feature

The fifth feature of the model is a hole feature. But, this hole feature will be created as an extruded cut feature. To create a hole feature as an extruded cut feature, you need to draw the sketch of the hole feature on the required plane or planar face.

1. Invoke the **Extruded Cut** tool and select the face, refer to Figure 5-31, as a sketching plane.

2. Change the current orientation of the model normal to the viewing direction and draw a circle of diameter 8 mm, refer to Figure 5-32.

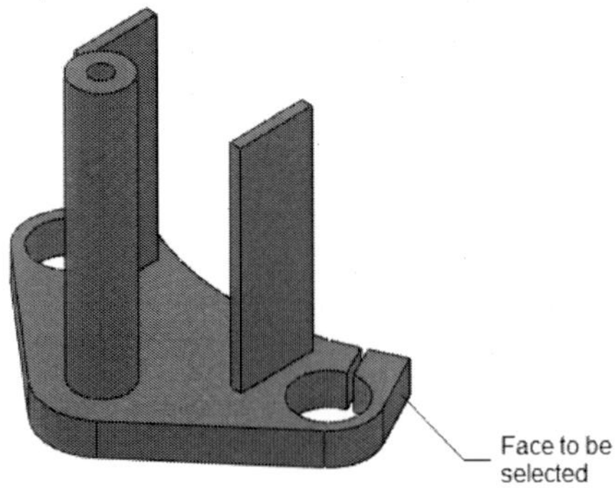

Figure 5-31 *Face to be selected*

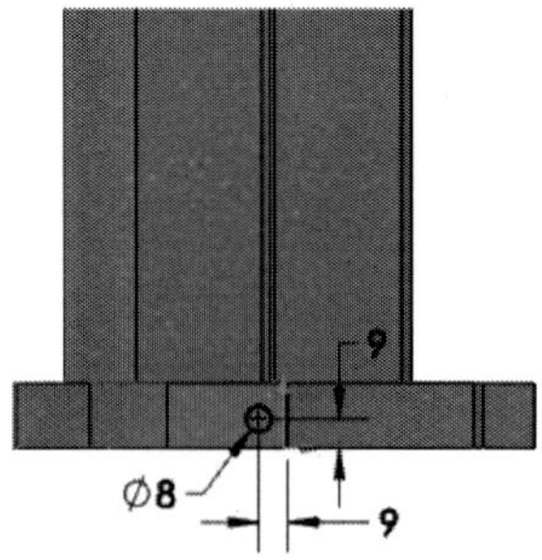

Figure 5-32 *Sketch of the cut feature*

3. Exit the sketcher environment and set the value of the **Depth** spinner to **32 mm** in the **Cut-Extrude PropertyManager**.

4. Choose the **OK** button from PropertyManager. The rotated view of the model after creating the cut feature is shown in Figure 5-33.

Mirroring the Feature

After creating the cut feature, you need to mirror it using the Right Plane as the mirroring plane.

1. Invoke the **Mirror** tool and create the mirror feature of the previously created cut feature using the Right Plane as the mirroring plane. After mirroring the cut feature, the top view of the model with **Hidden Lines Visible** display mode is shown in Figure 5-34.

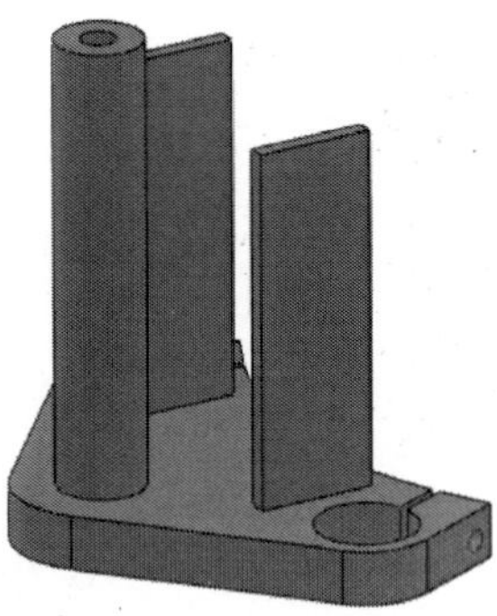

Figure 5-33 *Model after creating the cut feature*

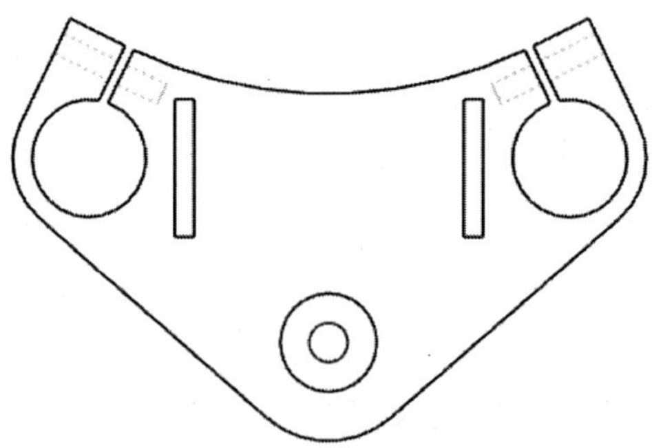

Figure 5-34 *Top view with **Hidden Lines Visible** display mode after mirroring the feature*

Creating the Chamfer

The next feature of the model is a chamfer feature. In SOLIDWORKS, a chamfer is created by using the **Chamfer** tool.

1. Choose the **Chamfer** button from the **Fillet** flyout in the **Features CommandManager**, refer to Figure 5-35; the **Chamfer PropertyManager** is displayed and you are prompted to select the edges/loops/faces to chamfer.

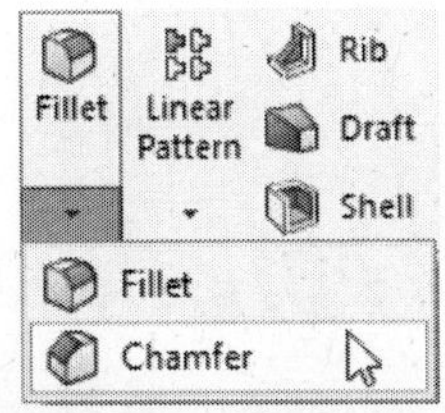

Figure 5-35 *The* ***Chamfer*** *tool in the* ***Fillet*** *flyout*

Chamfering is defined as the process in which sharp edges are beveled in order to reduce the area of stress concentration. This process also eliminates undesirable sharp edges and corners.

2. Select the edges of the model for creating chamfer, refer to Figure 5-36. As soon as you select the edges, preview of the chamfer feature is displayed in the drawing area with default values.

   By default, the **Angle Distance** button is selected in the **Chamfer Type** rollout in the PropertyManager. Therefore, the angle and distance callouts are displayed attached with a selected edge. Also, name of the selected edges are displayed in the selection box of the **Items to Chamfer** rollout in the PropertyManager.

   Next set the value of angle in the **Angle** spinner as 45-degree and value of distance in the **Distance** spinner as 2.5 mm.

3. Set the value of the distance in the **Distance** spinner to **2.5 mm** and then choose the **OK** button. The model after creating the chamfer feature is shown in Figure 5-37.

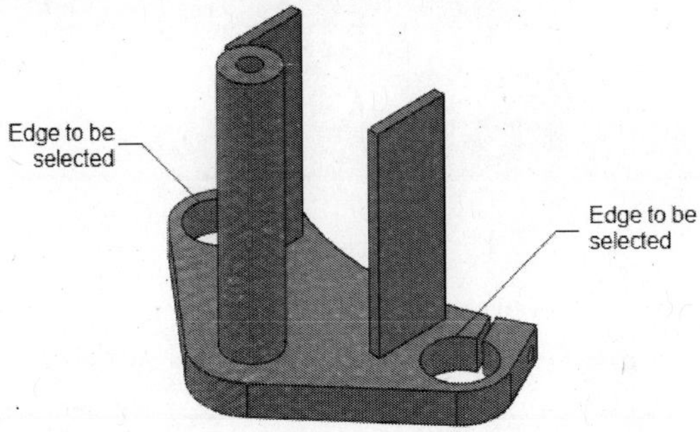

Figure 5-36 *Edges to be selected*

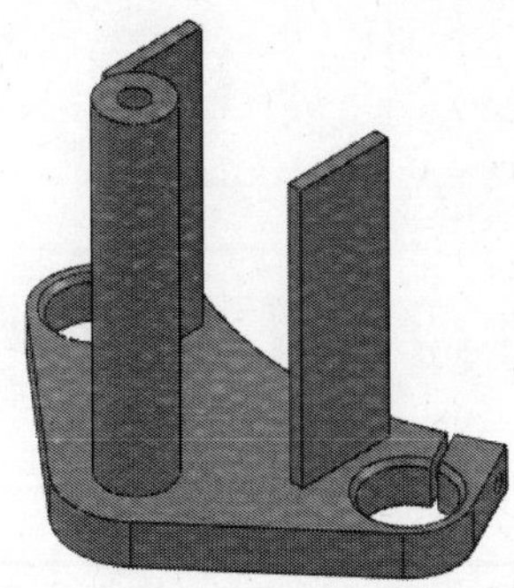

Figure 5-37 *Model after creating the chamfer*

Creating Remaining Features

Now, you need to create the remaining features of the model such as extruded cut, circular pattern, mirror, and fillet features.

1. Invoke the **Extruded Cut** tool and select the top planar face of the base feature as a sketching plane. Next, draw the circle of diameter 1.8 mm, refer to Figure 5-38 and then extrude it using the **Through All** option. Partial view of the model after creating the cut feature is shown in Figure 5-39.

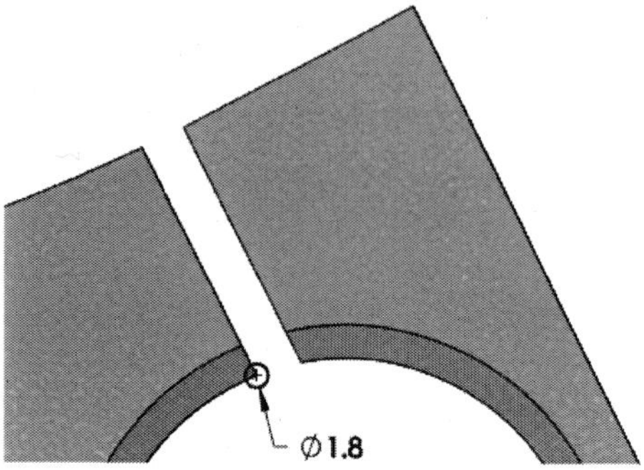

Figure 5-38 *Sketch of the cut feature*

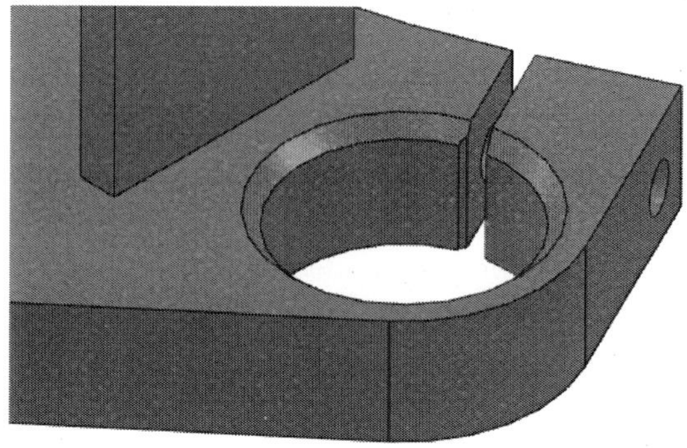

Figure 5-39 *Partial view of the model after creating the cut feature*

2. Select the previously created cut feature and then invoke the **CirPattern PropertyManager**. Select the cylindrical face of the model to define the pattern axis of the circular pattern, refer to Figure 5-40 and set the value of the **Number of Instances** to 32. The model after creating the circular pattern feature is shown in Figure 5-41.

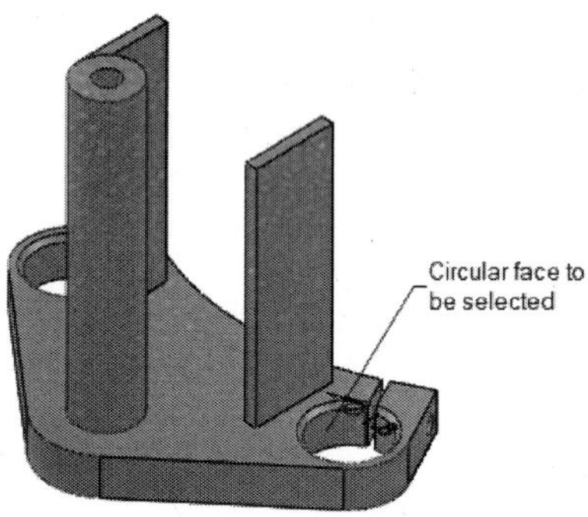

Figure 5-40 *Edges to be selected*

Figure 5-41 *Model after creating the chamfer*

After creating the circular pattern of the cut feature created earlier, you need to mirror it using the Right Plane as the mirroring plane.

3. Invoke the **Mirror PropertyManager** and mirror the previously created circular pattern feature using the Right Plane as the mirroring plane. The model after mirroring the circular pattern feature is shown in Figure 5-42.

   Now, you need to add the fillet feature to the model.

4. Invoke the **Fillet PropertyManager** and select the edges of the model to apply the fillet feature, refer to Figure 5-43. Next, set the value of the **Radius** spinner to **2.5 mm** and then exit the PropertyManager. The final model after applying the fillet is shown in Figure 5-44.

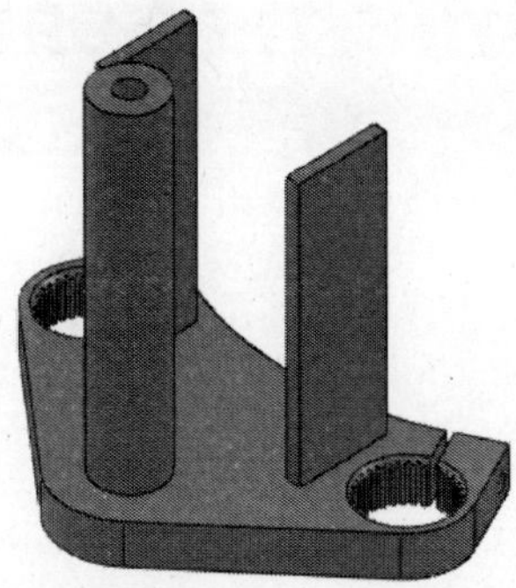

Figure 5-42 *Model after mirroring the feature*

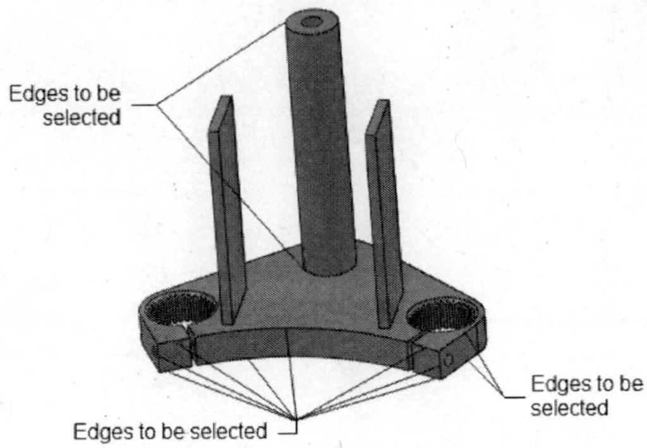

Figure 5-43 *Edges to be selected*

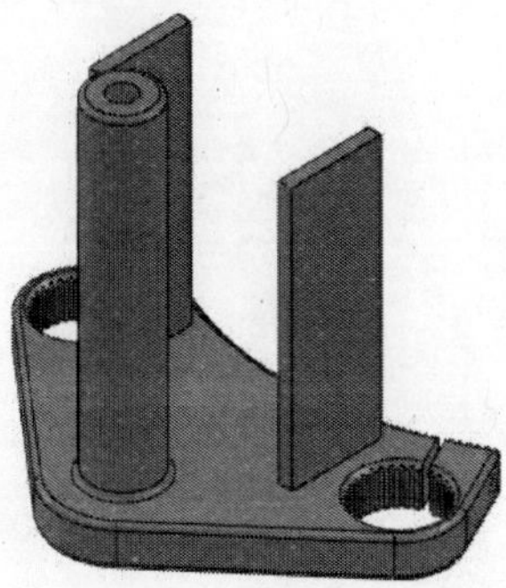

Figure 5-44 *Final model after adding the fillet*

Saving the Model

1. Invoke the **Save As** dialog box and browse to the location of *Motor Cycle Project* folder.

2. Enter **Fork Holder** in the **File name** edit box and choose the **Save** button. The document will be saved in the *\Documents\Motor Cycle Project\Fork Holder*.

3. Close the window.

CREATING THE FORK BODIES

Part Description

In this section, you will create two components, Right Fork Outer Body and Left Fork Outer Body of the Motor Cycle, as shown in Figures 5-45 and 5-46. These components can be created by using different feature creation tools. The base feature will be created by using the **Extruded Boss/Base** tool. Similarly, other features of the components will be created by using the **Lofted Boss/Base**, **Shell**, **Extruded Cut**, **Mirror**, **Hole Wizard**, **Revolved Cut**, and **Fillet** tools. You can create these two components in two different part documents. But, it is recommended to create different configurations of these two components in a single part document. To create them as two configurations, first you will create the Right Fork Outer Body as first configuration and then you will create the Left Fork Outer Body as second configuration by suppressing some of the features of the Right Fork Outer Body. Different views and dimensions of the Right Fork Outer Body are shown in Figure 5-47 . **(Expected time: 40 min)**

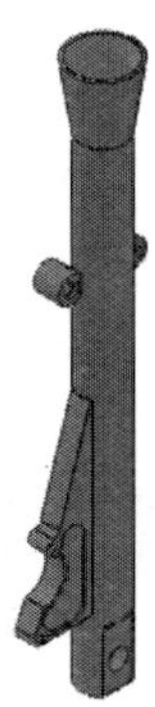

Figure 5-45 *The Right Fork Outer Body*

Figure 5-46 *The Left Fork Outer Body*

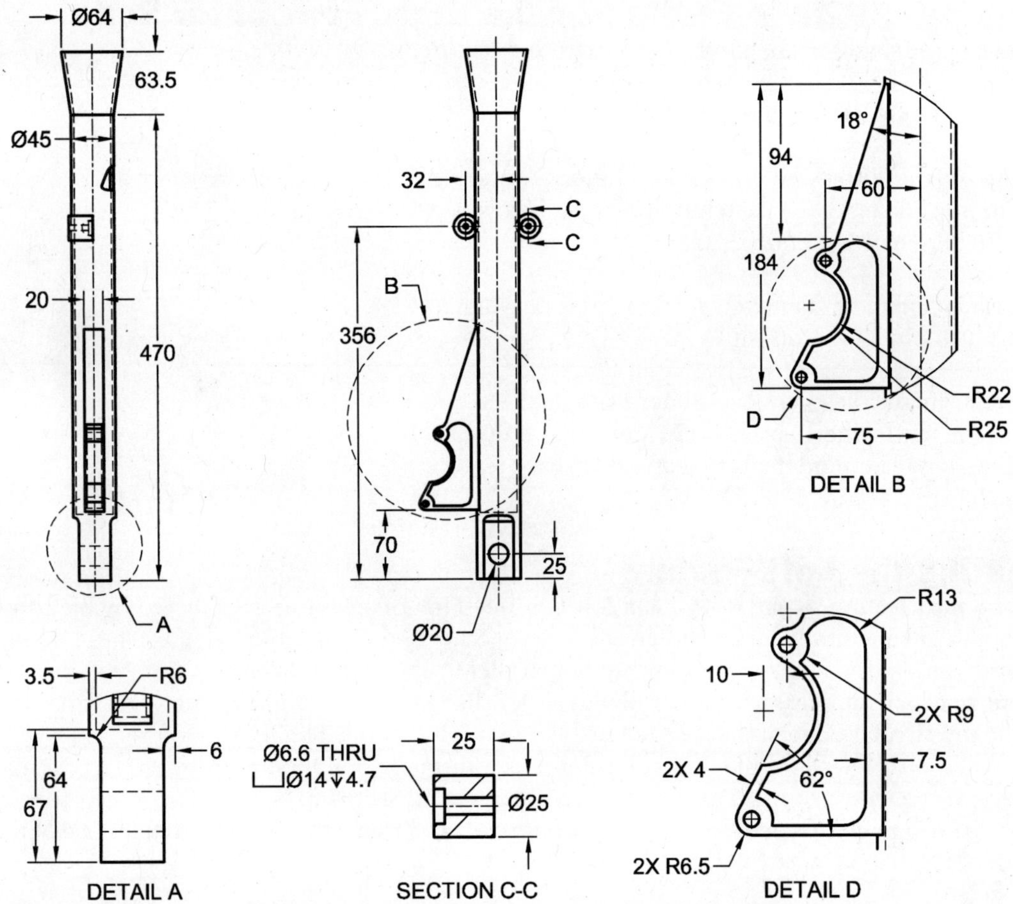

Figure 5-47 Views and dimensions of the model

As mentioned in the Part description, first you will create the Right Fork Outer Body using different feature creation tools of the SOLIDWORKS as first configuration and then you will create the Left Fork Outer Body as second configuration by suppressing some of the features from the Right Fork Outer Body.

Creating the Base Feature of the Right Fork Outer Body

The base feature of the model is an extruded feature.

1. Start a new part document.

2. Invoke the **Extruded Boss/Base** button and select the Top plane as the sketching plane to invoke the sketcher environment.

3. Draw a circle of diameter 45 mm by specifying its center point at the origin.

4. Exit from the sketcher environment and then extrude the sketch to the depth of 470 mm in the upward direction. The model after creating the base feature is shown in Figure 5-48.

Figure 5-48 *Model after creating the base feature*

Creating the Loft Feature

The next feature of the model is a loft feature. The loft features are created by blending more than one similar or dissimilar sections together to get a free form shape. These similar or dissimilar sections may or may not be parallel to each other. In this section, you need to create two dissimilar sections parallel to each other to create the loft feature. You can select the top circular edge of the base feature as a first loft section. The second loft section will be created on a reference plane that is at an offset distance of 63.5 mm from the top circular face of the base feature. Therefore, to create a second sketch of loft feature, first you need to create a reference plane at an offset distance of 63.5 mm from the top circular face of the base feature.

1. Choose **Plane** button from the **Reference Geometry** flyout in the **Features Command Manager**; the **Plane PropertyManager** is displayed.

2. Select the top circular face of the base feature, as a first reference from the drawing area; the preview of the reference plane is displayed in the drawing area with the default offset distance.

3. Set the value of the **Offset distance** spinner to 63.5 mm; the preview of the reference plane is displayed in the drawing area at an offset distance of 63.5 mm.

4. Choose the **OK** button from the PropertyManager; the reference plane is created.

   Once the reference plane is created at an offset distance of 63.5 mm, you can create a second section of the loft feature on it.

5. Switch to the **Sketch CommandManager** and then choose the **Sketch** button; the **Edit Sketch PropertyManager** is displayed and prompted you to select the sketching plane.

Note

*If any plane or planar face is selected in the drawing area before choosing the **Sketch** button from the **Sketch CommandManager**, then SOLIDWORKS consider that selected plane or planar face as a sketching plane and directly invokes the sketcher environment.*

6. Select the newly created plane as the sketching plane to invoke the sketcher environment. Next, change the current orientation normal to the view.

7. Draw a circle of diameter 64 mm as the second loft section by specifying its center point coincident to the center point of the top circular face of the base feature.

8. Exit from the sketcher environment. Change the current orientation to isometric.

9. Switch to the **Features CommandManager** and then choose the **Lofted Boss/Base** button; the **Loft PropertyManager** is displayed. 

10. Select the top outer circular edge of the base feature as the first section of the loft feature and then select the sketch of the second loft section from the drawing area; the preview of the loft feature is displayed in the drawing area and the names of the selection is displayed in the **Profile** selection box of the **Loft PropertyManager**.

11. Choose the **OK** button from the **Loft PropertyManager**. The isometric view of the model after creating the loft feature is shown in Figure 5-49.

Figure 5-49 *The model after creating the loft feature*

Creating the Shell Feature

The next feature of the model is a shell feature. It is evident from the Figure 5-47 that you need to remove the top planar face of the model and specify the multiple thickness using the **Shell** tool.

1. Choose the **Shell** button from the **Features CommandManager**; the **Shell PropertyManager** is displayed and you are prompted to select the faces to be removed.

2. Select the top planar face of the model; the selected face is highlighted in blue and its name is displayed in the **Faces to Remove** selection box of the **Shell PropertyManager**. Set the value of the **Thickness** spinner to 3.5 mm.

3. Select the **Show preview** check box from the **Parameters** rollout of the **Shell PropertyManager**, the preview of the shell feature is displayed with the thickness value 3.5 mm.

   Now, you will apply different thickness value to the selected face of the model using the **Multi-thickness Settings** rollout of the **Shell PropertyManager**.

4. Click on the **Multi-thickness Faces** selection box in the **Multi-thickness Settings** rollout of the **Shell PropertyManager**; you are prompted to select faces to specify multi-thickness.

5. Rotate the model such that you can clearly view the bottom face of the model. Next, select the bottom planar face of the model from the drawing area, the name of the selected face is displayed in the **Multi-thickness Faces** selection box.

6. Set the value of the **Multi-thickness(es)** spinner to 67 mm and then choose the **OK** button from the **Shell PropertyManager**.

   The isometric view of the model after creating the shell feature is shown in Figure 5-50. In this Figure, the display style of the model is changed to wireframe display style by using the **Wireframe** button available in the **Display Style** flyout for better understanding the multiple shell thickness.

Figure 5-50 *Model after creating the shell feature with multiple thickness*

Creating the Cut Feature

The next feature of the model is a cut feature. The sketch of the cut feature will be created on the Front Plane.

1. Invoke the **Extruded Cut** tool and select the Front Plane as a sketching plane to invoke the sketcher environment.

2. Draw the sketch of the cut feature using the tools available in the **Sketch CommandManager**, refer to Figure 5-51.

3. Exit from the sketcher environment; the **Cut-Extrude PropertyManager** is displayed at the left of the drawing area.

4. Select the **Through All-Both** and **Through All** option from the **End Condition** drop-down list in the **Direction 1** and **Direction 2** rollouts of the PropertyManager.

5. Choose **OK** button; the cut feature is created. The isometric view of the model after creating the cut feature is shown in Figure 5-52.

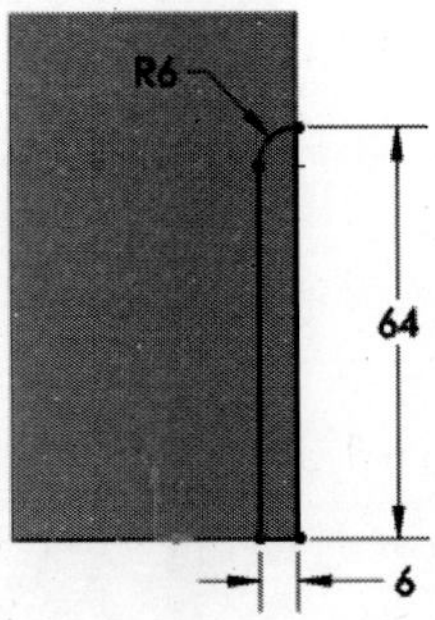

Figure 5-51 Sketch of the cut feature

Figure 5-52 Model after creating the cut feature

Mirroring the Cut Feature

The next feature of the model is a mirror feature.

1. Invoke the **Mirror PropertyManager** and mirror the previously created cut feature by selecting the Right Plane as the mirroring plane.

Creating the Hole Feature

The next feature of the model is a simple hole feature.

1. From the drawing area, select the right planar face of the cut feature and then choose **Insert > Features > Simple Hole** from the SOLIDWORKS menus; the **Hole PropertyManager** is invoked. Also, the preview of the simple hole with the default value is displayed in the drawing area.

2. Select the **Through All** option from the **End Condition** drop-down list and set the value of the **Hole Diameter** spinner to 20 mm as a diameter of the hole in the **Direction 1** rollout of the **Hole PropertyManager**.

3. Choose the **OK** button; the hole feature is placed arbitrarily on the selected face.

   After placing the hole arbitrarily on the selected face, you need to position it by applying dimensions.

4. Select the hole feature from the **FeatureManager Design Tree**; a pop-up toolbar is displayed near to the cursor. Next, choose the **Edit Sketch** button from the pop-up toolbar; the sketcher environment is invoked.

5. Change the current orientation of the model normal to view and apply required dimensions and constraints to the sketch of the hole feature, refer to Figure 5-53.

6. Press CTRL + B on the keyboard to rebuild the model; the hole feature is positioned. The isometric view of the model after creating the hole feature is shown in Figure 5-54.

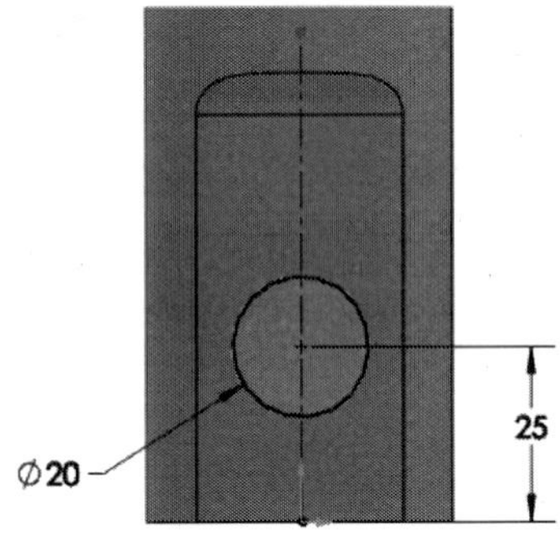

Figure 5-53 *Sketch of the hole feature*

Figure 5-54 *Model after creating the hole feature*

Creating the Extruded Feature

The next feature of the model is a cylindrical extruded feature. This extruded feature will be created on the Right Plane.

1. Invoke the **Extruded Boss/Base** tool and select the Right Plane as the sketching plane to invoke the sketcher environment.

2. Draw the sketch of the cylindrical extruded feature, refer to Figure 5-55 and extrude it to the depth of 25 mm. You may need to reverse the direction of extrusion. The model after creating the extruded feature is shown in Figure 5-56.

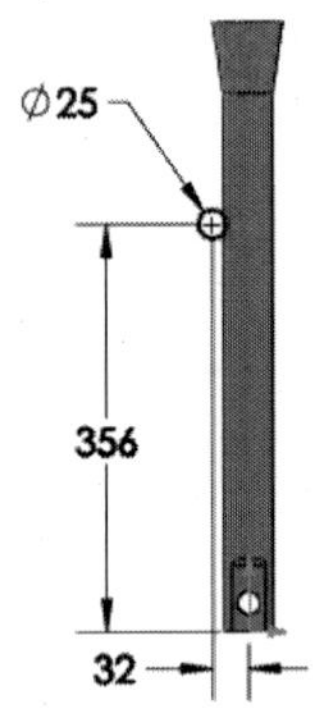

Figure 5-55 *Sketch of the extruded feature*

Figure 5-56 *Model after creating the extruded feature*

Adding the Counterbore Hole Using the Hole Wizard Tool

The next feature of the model is a Counterbore Hole. The Counterbore Hole is created by using the **Hole Wizard** tool.

1. Choose the **Hole Wizard** button from the **Features CommandManager**; the **Hole Specification PropertyManager** is displayed.

The **Hole Wizard** tool is used to add standard holes such as counterbore, countersink, drilled, tapped, and pipe tabbed holes. You can also add a user-defined counterbored drilled hole, simple drilled hole, tapered hole, and so on. You can control all parameters of the holes, including the termination options. You can also modify the holes according to your requirement after placing them.

2. Choose the **Counterbore** button from the **Hole Type** rollout of the PropertyManager, if not chosen by default.

The **Hole Type** rollout of the **Hole Specification PropertyManager** is used to define the type of the standard hole to be created and its parameters. The buttons available in this rollout are used to create a specific type of standard holes. The **Counterbore** button is used to create counterbore holes.

Now, you need to set the parameters to define the counterbore hole.

3. Select the **ANSI Metric** option from the **Standard** drop-down list and the **Hex Screw ANSI B18.6.7M** option from the **Type** drop-down list of the **Hole Type** rollout in the PropertyManager.

4. Select the **M6** option from the **Size** drop-down list and **Normal** option from the **Fit** drop-down list in the **Hole Specifications** rollout.

5. Select the **Through All** option from the **End Condition** drop-down list in the **End Condition** rollout.

   After specifying all the required parameters of the Counterbore hole, you need to define its placement.

6. Choose the **Positions** tab from the **Hole Specification PropertyManager**; you are prompted to select the face where you want to place the hole.

7. Move the cursor toward the right planar face of the previously created extruded feature and select it; the preview of the counterbore hole is displayed in the drawing area.

8. Next, choose the **Add Relation** option from the **Display/Delete Relations** flyout in the Sketch CommandManager; the **Add Relations PropertyManager** is displayed at the left of the drawing area.

9. Select the placement point of the counterbore hole and then select the circular edge of the cylindrical extruded feature from the drawing area.

10. Choose the **Concentric** button from the **Add Relations** rollout of the PropertyManager.

11. Choose the **OK** button from the **Add Relations PropertyManager**; the **Hole Position PropertyManager** is displayed.

12. Choose the **OK** button from the **Hole Position PropertyManager**; the counterbore hole is created, refer to Figure 5-57. This figure shows the partial view of the model after creating the counterbore hole.

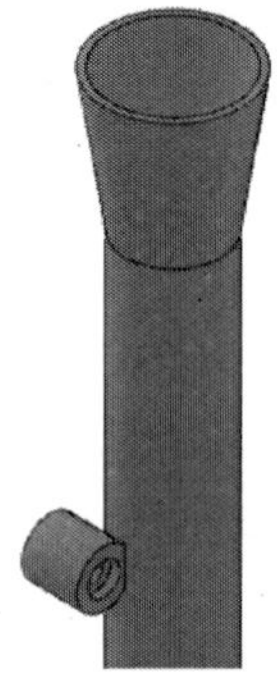

Figure 5-57 *The partial view of the model after creating the counterbore hole*

Mirroring the Last Two Features

The next feature of the model is a mirror feature. You will mirror the last two features of the model named as, **Boss-Extrude2**, and **CBORE for M6 Hex Head Machine Screw1** using the Front Plane as a mirroring plane.

1. Invoke the **Mirror** tool and select the **Front Plane** as the mirroring plane.

   After selecting the mirroring plane, the SOLIDWORKS prompted you to select the feature to be mirror.

2. Select the **Boss-Extrude2**, and **CBORE for M6 Hex Head Machine Screw1** from the **FeatureManager Design Tree** by pressing the CTRL key.

3. Choose the **OK** button from the **Mirror PropertyManager**. The partial view of the model after mirroring the features is shown in the Figure 5-58.

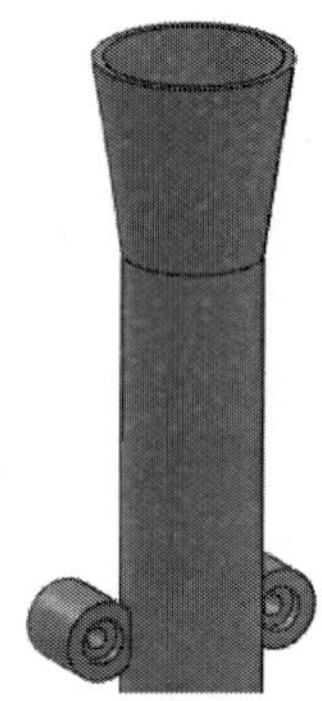

Figure 5-58 *The partial view of the model after mirroring the features*

Creating the Extrude Feature

The next feature of the model is a extrude feature. To create this extrude feature, first you need to create reference plane at an offset distance of 90 mm from the Front Plane. Once the reference plane is created, you will select this plane as the sketching plane for the extrude feature.

1. Choose the **Plane** button from the **Reference Geometry** flyout to invoke the **Plane PropertyManager**.

2. Create a reference plane at a distance of 90 mm from the Front Plane toward the front direction and then exit from the PropertyManager.

3. Invoke the sketcher environment by selecting the newly created reference plane as the sketching plane.

4. Draw the sketch of the extruded feature, refer to Figure 5-59. Next, exit from the sketcher environment.

5. Invoke the **Extruded Boss/Base** tool and extrude the sketch using the **Up To Next** option. You may also need to reverse the direction of feature creation. The model after creating the extruded feature is shown in Figure 5-60.

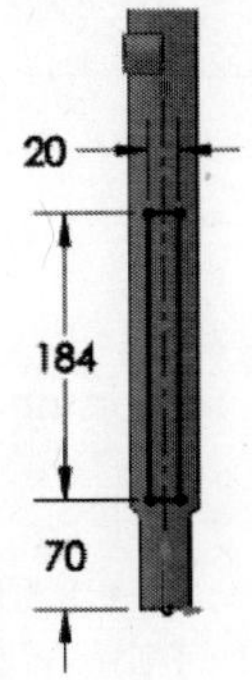

Figure 5-59 Sketch of the extruded feature

Figure 5-60 Model after creating the extruded feature

Creating the Cut Feature

The next feature of the model is the cut feature. To create this feature, you will select the right planar face of the previously created extrude feature as a sketching plane.

1. Invoke the **Extruded Cut** tool and then select the right planar face of the previously created extruded feature as the sketching plane to invoke the sketcher environment.

2. Draw the sketch of the cut feature, refer to Figure 5-61. Next, exit from the sketcher environment and extrude the sketch by using the **Through All** option. The model after creating the cut feature is shown in Figure 5-62.

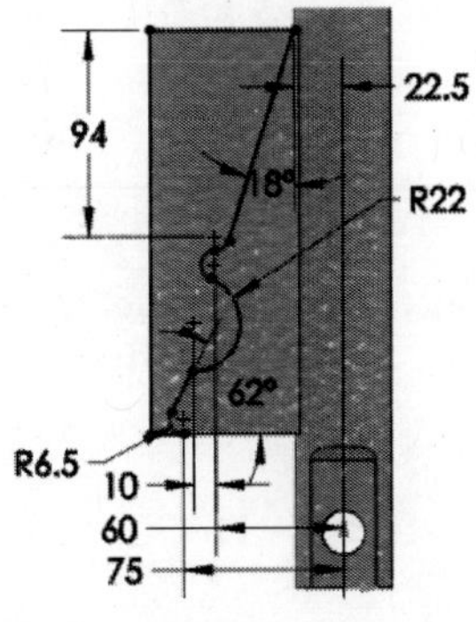

Figure 5-61 Sketch of the cut feature

Figure 5-62 Model after creating the cut feature

Creating the Hole Feature

The next feature of the model is the hole feature.

1. Select the right planar face of the extruded feature, refer to Figure 5-63.

2. Choose the **Insert > Features > Simple Hole** from the SOLIDWORKS menus; the **Hole PropertyManager** is displayed.

3. Select the **Up To Next** option from the **End Condition** drop-down list and set the value of the **Hole Diameter** spinner to **6.5 mm**. Next, choose **OK**; the hole feature is placed arbitrarily on the selected face.

   After placing the hole feature arbitrarily, you need to position it concentric to the upper circular face of the previously created cut feature.

4. Select the hole feature; a pop-up toolbar is displayed. Choose the **Edit Sketch** button from the pop-up toolbar to edit the position of sketch in the sketcher environment.

5. Select the semi-circular edge of the model, refer to Figure 5-64 and then press and hold the CTRL key. Next, select the sketch of the hole feature and then release the CTRL key. As soon as, you release the CTRL key, the pop-up toolbar is displayed. Select the **Make Concentric** button from the pop-up toolbar.

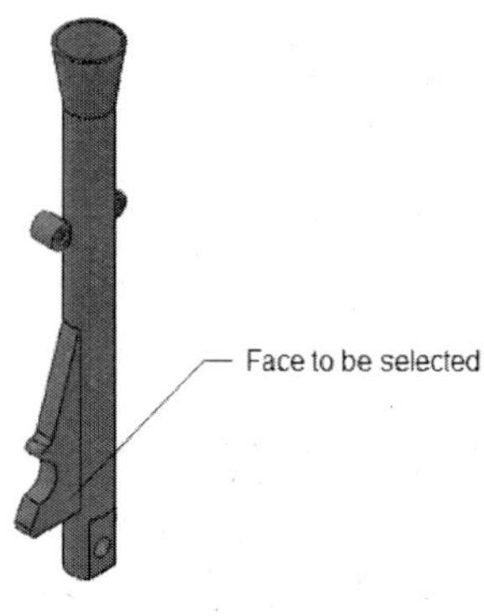

Figure 5-63 *Face to be selected*

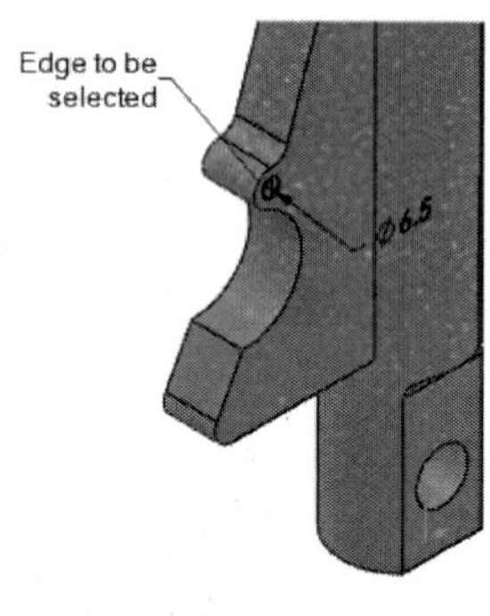

Figure 5-64 *Edge to be selected*

6. Exit from the sketcher environment. The partial view of the model after creating the hole feature is shown in Figure 5-65.

7. Similarly, create the other hole feature using the **Simple Hole** tool of diameter 6.5 mm on the same planar face. Figures 5-66 shows the partial view of the model after creating the both the hole features.

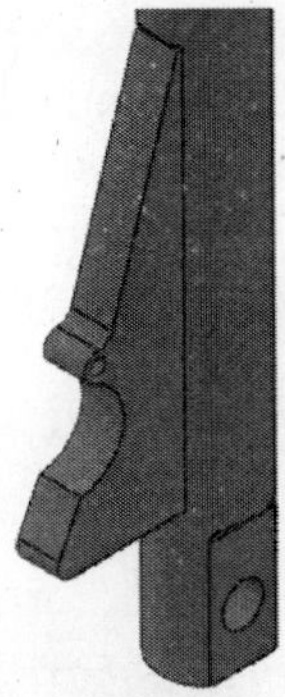

Figure 5-65 Model after creating the hole

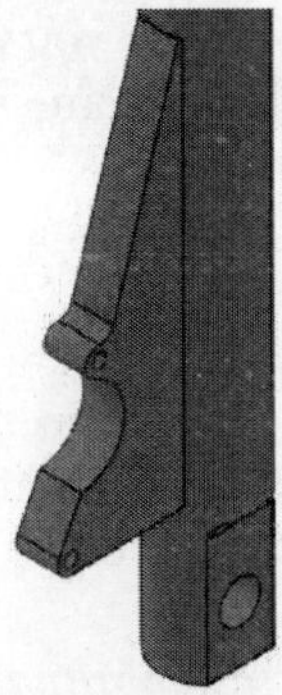

Figure 5-66 Model after creating both the holes

Creating the Next Cut Feature

The next feature of the model is a cut feature.

1. Invoke the **Extruded Cut** tool and select the planar face, refer to Figure 5-63 as the sketching plane to invoke the sketcher environment.

2. Draw the sketch of the cut feature, refer to Figure 5-67. Next, exit from the sketcher environment and extrude the sketch upto the depth of 2.5 mm. The model after creating the cut feature is shown in Figure 5-68.

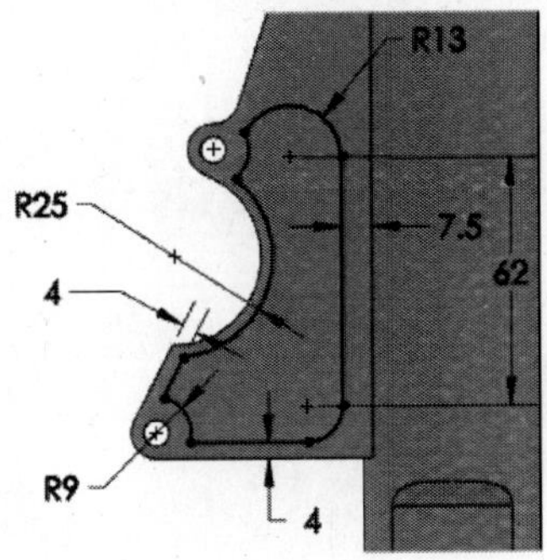

Figure 5-67 Sketch of the cut feature

Figure 5-68 Model after creating the cut feature

Mirroring the Cut Feature

After creating the cut feature, you will mirror it using the **Mirror** tool.

1. Invoke the **Mirror** tool and mirror the previously created cut feature by selecting the Right Plane as the mirroring plane.

Creating Configurations

After creating the model, you will create its configurations using the **ConfigurationManager**. In SOLIDWORKS, you can create multiple configurations of a part or assembly using the **ConfigurationManager**. When you invoke the **ConfigurationManager**, you will observe that the created model is saved as the **Default** configuration and consider as a first configuration of the model.

1. Choose the **ConfigurationManager** tab next to the **PropertyManager** tab below the **CommandManagers** at the left of the drawing area, refer to Figure 5-69.

Note

*In the **ConfigurationManager**, the model is saved as a **Default** configuration and it is activated. The node of the activated configuration is shown in green check mark. The default configuration is the first configuration of the model.*

Now, you need to change the name of the **Default** configuration to **Right Fork Body** configuration to avoid the confusion.

2. Click the left mouse button once on the **Default** configuration and press the F2 key; the name of the configuration is displayed in the text box.

3. Enter the **Right Fork Body** as the name of the default configuration in the text box and press ENTER; the name **Default** is changed to **Right Fork Body**, refer to Figure 5-70.

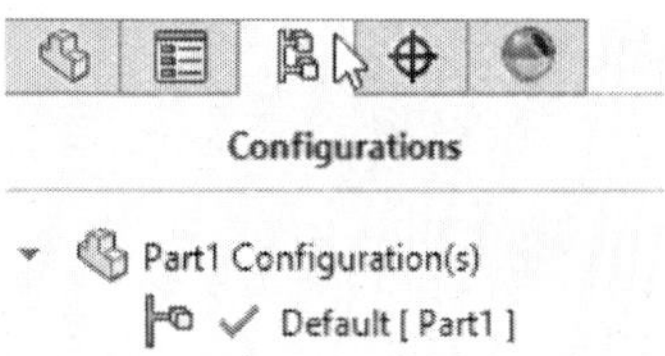

Figure 5-69** The **ConfigurationManager

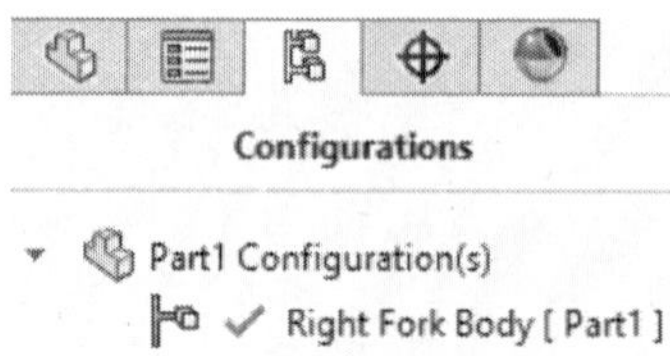

***Figure 5-70** The **ConfigurationManager** after changing the default name*

After changing the name of the **Default** configuration, you will create the second configuration and name it as the Left Fork Body.

4. Select the name of the part file in the **ConfigurationManager** and right-click to invoke the shortcut menu, refer to Figure 5-71.

5. Choose the **Add Configuration** option from the shortcut menu, refer to Figure 5-71; the **Add Configuration PropertyManager** is displayed in the drawing area.

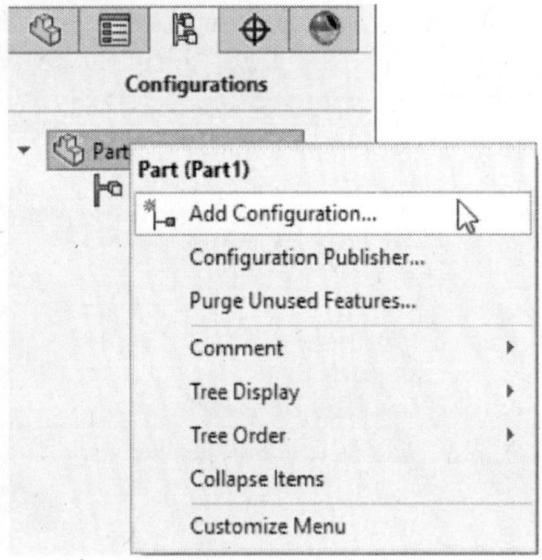

***Figure 5-71** Shortcut menu displayed after right-clicking on the name of the part file*

The **Add Configuration PropertyManager** is used to specify the name and description of the configuration in the respective edit boxes of the **Configuration Properties** rollout. You can also specify the comment about the configuration in the **Comment** edit box of the **Configuration Properties** rollout in the PropertyManager. The **Bill of Materials Options** rollout of the PropertyManager is used to specify the name of the part that has to be displayed in BOM when the drawing views are generated with the selected configuration.

When you expand the **Advanced Options** rollout of the PropertyManager, you will observe that the **Suppress new features and mates** check box is selected, by default. Therefore, the new features and mates added in the some other configuration of the same part will be automatically suppressed in other configurations. You can also specify different colors for the different configurations using the **Use configuration specific color** check box available in the **Advanced Options** rollout of the PropertyManager.

6. Enter **Left Fork Body** as the name of the configuration in the **Configuration name** edit box of the PropertyManager.

   After specifying the required parameters in the **Add Configuration PropertyManager**, you need to exit from it.

7. Choose the **OK** button from the PropertyManager; the **Left Fork Body** configuration is created and it is activated. So, the node of this configuration is displayed with green check mark in the **ConfigurationManager**, as shown in Figure 5-72.

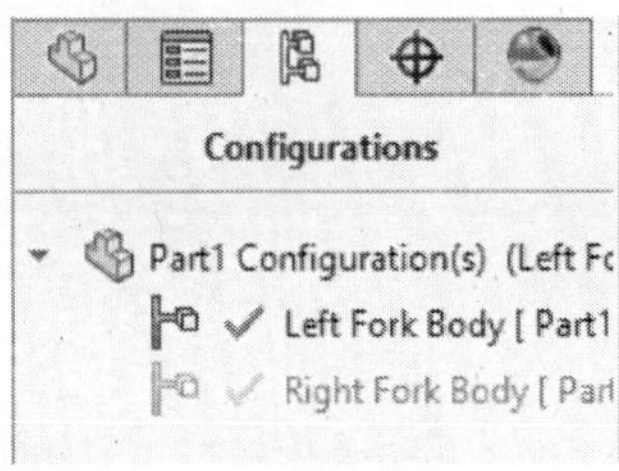

***Figure 5-72** The **Left Fork Body** configuration is created and it is activated*

   It is evident from the Figure 5-46 that the design requirement for the Left Fork Body is that the last six features named as **Boss-Extrude3**, **Cut-Extrude2**, **Hole2**, **Hole3**, **Cut-Extrude3**, and **Mirror3** needs to be removed from the model in the **Left Fork Body** configuration. Therefore, you will suppress these features from the model. Before suppressing the features, make sure that the **Left Fork Body** configuration is activated in the **ConfigurationManager**.

8. Choose the **FeatureManager Design Tree** tab to display the **FeatureManager Design Tree**.

9. Select the **Boss-Extrude3** from the **FeatureManager Design Tree** and then press and hold the SHIFT key. Next, select the **Mirror3** feature. As soon as you select the **Mirror3** feature from the **FeatureManager Design Tree**, all the features in between these two features are also selected. Next, release the SHIFT key; the pop-up toolbar is displayed.

10. Select the **Suppress** button from the pop-up toolbar; all the selected features of the model are suppressed.

Tip

Sometimes, you do not want a feature to be displayed in the model or in its drawing views. Instead of deleting those features, they can be suppressed. When you suppress a feature, it is neither visible in the model nor in the drawing views. Also, if you create an assembly using that model, the suppressed feature will not be displayed. You can resume such suppressed feature at anytime by unsuppressing them.

Now, when you activate the **Right Fork Body** configuration by double-clicking on it in the **ConfigurationManager**, you will observe that the **Boss-Extrude3**, **Cut-Extrude2**, **Hole2**, **Hole3**, **Cut-Extrude3**, and **Mirror3** features of the model are not suppressed in this configuration. On the other hand, when you activate the **Left Fork Body** configuration by double-clicking on it, you will observe that these features are not displayed in the model.

Figure 5-73, shows the model with the **Right Fork Body** configuration and Figure 5-74 shows the isometric view of the model with the **Left Fork Body** after suppressing the features configuration.

Figure 5-73 *Right Fork Body*

Figure 5-74 *Left Fork Body*

Saving the Model

After creating the Right Fork Body and the Left Fork Body configurations, you need to save the model as Forks Bodies.

1. Choose the **Save** button from the Menu Bar to invoke the **Save As** dialog box. Next, browse to the location of *Motor Cycle Project* folder.

2. Enter **Fork Bodies** as the name of the model in the **File name** edit box and choose the **Save** button. The document will be saved in the *\Documents\Motor Cycle Project\Fork Bodies*.

Self-Evaluation Test

Answer the following questions and then compare them to those given at the end of this chapter:

1. The __________ rollout of the **Boss-Extrude PropertyManager** is used to create thin extruded feature.

2. The options provided in the __________ drop-down list are used to select the method of defining the thickness of the thin extruded feature.

3. To change the default display mode to **Hidden Lines Visible** mode, choose the __________ button from the **View (Heads-up)** toolbar.

4. In the __________ display mode, all the hidden lines will be displayed along with the visible lines in the model.

5. The __________ tool is used to project a sketch on a planar or curved face which in turn splits or divides the single face into two or more than two faces.

6. The __________ tool is used to create a dome feature on the selected face.

7. The __________ dialog box is used to change the view orientation of the model using the predefined standard views or user-defined views.

8. The __________ tool is used to add material between more than one similar or dissimilar sections together to get a free form shape. These similar or dissimilar sections may or may not be parallel to each other.

9. The thin extruded features can be created by using a closed or an open sketch. (T/F)

10. After modifying the orientation of the standard view, you can again reset the standard settings of all the standard views in the current document. (T/F)

Review Questions

Answer the following questions:

1. Which one of the following radio buttons is selected by default in the **Chamfer Parameters** rollout of the PropertyManager?

   (a) **Angle** (b) **Angle distance**
   (c) **Distance angle** (d) None of these

2. Which one of the following PropertyManagers is displayed on choosing the **Hole Wizard** button?

   (a) **Hole** (b) **Hole Position**
   (c) **Hole Specification** (d) None of these

3. Choose the __________ button to invoke the **Loft PropertyManager**.

4. The __________ tool is used to add standard holes in the model such as counterbore, countersink, drilled, tapped, and pipe tab holes.

5. The __________ button of the **Orientation** dialog box is used to pin it.

6. The __________ is defined as the process in which the sharp edges are beveled in order to reduce the area of stress concentration.

7. The __________ rollout of the **Hole Specification PropertyManager** is used to define the type of the standard hole to be created and its parameters.

8. The __________ button is used to suppress the selected features from the model.

9. In SOLIDWORKS, you can create multiple configurations of a part or assembly using the **ConfigurationManager**. (T/F)

10. The **Add Configuration PropertyManager** is used to specify the name and description of the configuration in the respective edit boxes of the **Configuration Properties** rollout. (T/F)

nswers to Self-Evaluation Test

1. Thin Feature, 2. Type, 3. Hidden Lines Visible, 4. Wireframe, 5. Split Line, 6. Dome, 7. Lofted Boss/Base, 8. Orientation, 9. T , **10.** T

Chapter 6

Creating Handlebar and Handle Holders

Learning Objectives

After completing this chapter, you will be able to:

- *Create 3D sketch*
- *Create fillet in the sketching environment*
- *Create thin sweep feature*
- *Create a model using the contour selection technique*
- *Create linear patterns of sketched entities*
- *Modified the parameters of the standard holes*
- *Create linear patterns of features*

CREATING THE HANDLEBAR

Part Description

In this section, you will create the Handlebar, as shown in Figure 6-1. It will be created by using the different feature creation tools of the SOLIDWORKS. The base feature of the Handlebar is a sweep feature. This sweep feature is created by sweeping a profile along a 3D path. The other features of the Handlebar are extrude cut, circular pattern, and mirror. The different views and dimensions of the model are given in Figure 6-2.

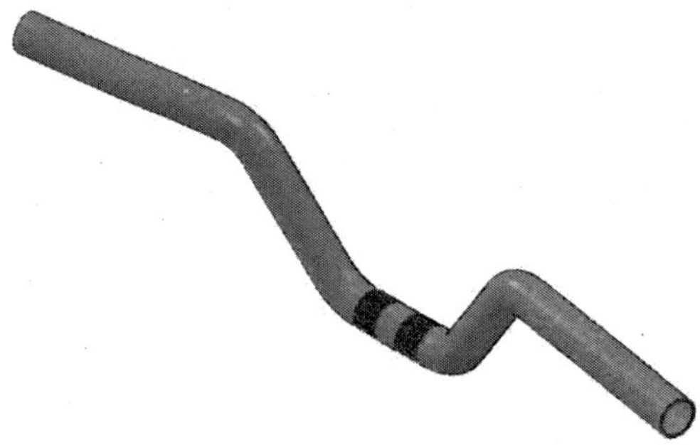

***Figure 6-1** The Handlebar*

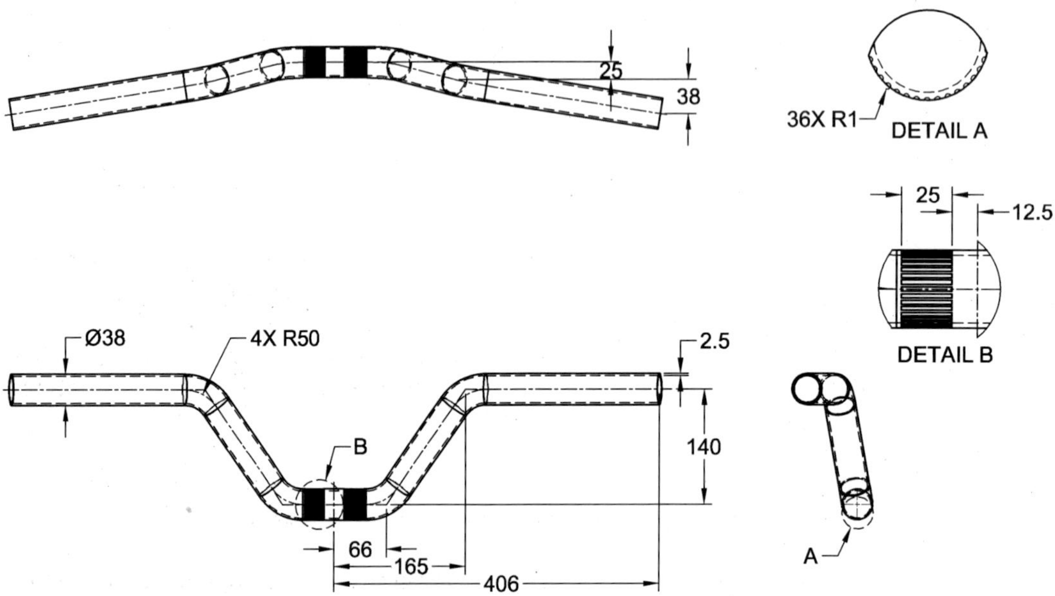

***Figure 6-2** The views and dimensions of the model*

Starting a New Part Document

1. Start a new SOLIDWORKS part document using the **New SOLIDWORKS Document** dialog box or the **Welcome - SOLIDWORKS 2018** dialog box. Next, modify the unit of the current session to mm, if not set by default.

   Once the new part document is invoked, you can create the base feature of the model.

Creating the Base Feature

The base feature of the Handlebar is a sweep feature, created by using **Swept Boss/Base** tool. This tool is one of the most important advanced modeling tools, used to extrude a closed profile along an open or a closed path. Therefore, to create a sweep feature, you need a profile and a path. A profile is a section for the sweep feature and a path is the course taken by the profile while creating the sweep feature. The profile has to be a sketch, but the path can be a 2D sketch, 3D sketch, curve or an edge.

It is evident from Figures 6-1 and 6-2 that the sweep feature is created by sweeping a profile along a 3D path. Therefore, you need to create a path for the sweep feature in the 3D sketching environment. In this section, you will create a 3D sketch using the points. To do so, first you need to create a reference planes at an offset distance from the Front Plane and then points on them.

Creating the Reference Planes

To create a reference plane, you need to invoke the **Plane PropertyManager**.

1. Choose the **Plane** button from the **Reference Geometry** flyout in the **Features CommandManager**; the **Plane PropertyManager** is displayed. 

2. Next, click on the (▸) sign located on the left of the **FeatureManager Design Tree**, which is now displayed in the drawing area. The design tree expands and the three default planes are now visible in the design tree .

3. Select the Front Plane as the first reference; the preview of the reference plane with the default value is displayed in the drawing area and the name of the selected plane is displayed in the **First Reference** selection box of the **First Reference** rollout in the **Plane PropertyManager**. Also, the message **Fully defined** is displayed in the **Message** rollout of the PropertyManager. This indicate that the reference plane to be created is fully defined and no additional references are required.

4. Set the value of the **Distance** spinner to 25 mm and then choose the **OK** button; the reference plane is created at an offset distance of 25 mm from the Front Plane.

5. Similarly, create other reference plane at an offset distance of 38 mm from the newly created plane.

Creating the Points On the Reference Planes

After creating the reference planes, you will create points on them for creating the 3D sketch of the sweep feature.

1. Invoke the sketching environment by selecting the **Plane1** as the sketching plane.

2. Invoke the **Point** tool by choosing the **Point** button from the **Sketch CommandManager** and then place a point on the plane, refer to Figure 6-3. Next, apply dimensions to it using the **Smart Dimension** tool, refer to Figure 6-3.

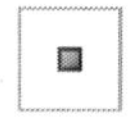

3. Exit the sketching environment; the point is placed on the **Plane1**.

4. Similarly, invoke the sketching environment by selecting the **Plane2** as the sketching plane and place the point using the **Point** tool, refer to Figure 6-4. Next, exit the sketching environment.

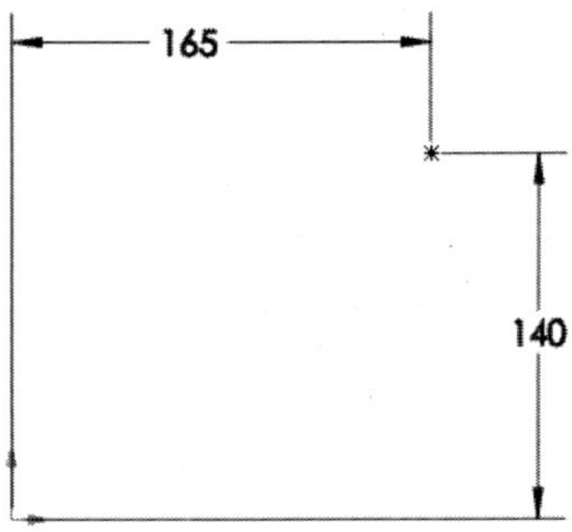

Figure 6-3 *Point on the* ***Plane1***

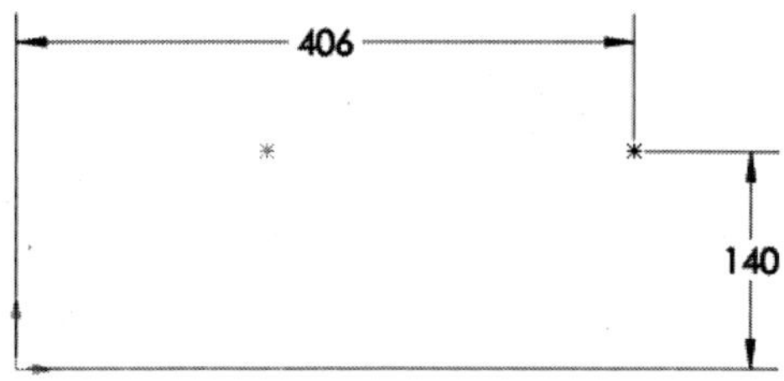

Figure 6-4 *Point on the* ***Plane2***

Creating the Path for the Sweep Feature Using the 3D Sketch Environment

After creating the points, you need to invoke the 3D sketching environment to create the path for the sweep feature. In this section, you will draw only the right half of the sketch as the path of the 3D sketch.

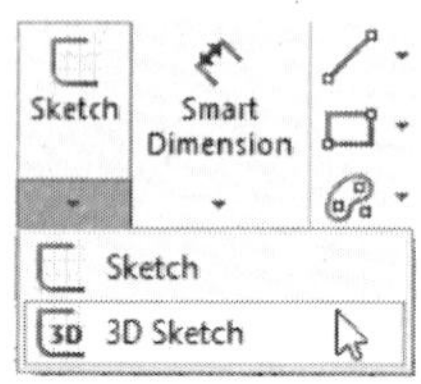

Figure 6-5 *The* ***Sketch*** *flyout*

1. Choose the **3D Sketch** button from the **Sketch** flyout in the **Sketch CommandManager**, refer to Figure 6-5; the 3D sketching environment is invoked and origin is displayed in red color.

Note

1. To invoke the ***Sketch*** *flyout, choose the down arrow provided at the bottom of the* ***Sketch*** *button.*

2. On invoking the 3D sketching environment, some of the sketching tools are activated in the ***Sketch CommandManager*** *and some are not activated. The tools that are activated, can be used to create a 3D sketch in the 3D sketching environment. Also, for creating a 3D sketch, you do not need to select a sketching plane.*

After invoking the 3D sketching environment, you will draw the 3D sketch as the path of the sweep profile.

2. Choose the **Line** button; the **Insert Line PropertyManager** is displayed and the select cursor is replaced by the line cursor. Also, the XY symbol is displayed below the line cursor suggesting that the line will be sketched in the XY plane.

Note

1. You can toggle between the default planes using the TAB key. On doing so, the orientation of the coordinate system will also be modified with respect to the current plane.

2. You can move the cursor to the location from where you want to specify a start point of the sketch. As soon as, you will specify a start point, you will be provided with a space handle. You can also toggle the plane after specifying the start point of the line.

In this 3D sketch, you need to draw the first line in the XY plane. Therefore, no need to toggle the plane.

3. Move the line cursor to the origin. When a red dot is displayed, click to specify the start point of the line.

4. Move the cursor in the positive X direction of the triad; a small triad with X appears below the cursor indicating that you are drawing a line in the X direction. Click when a value above the cursor is displayed close to 66 mm; a rubber-band line is attached to the cursor.

5. Move the cursor toward the point placed in the **Plane1**. When a red dot is displayed, click to specify the endpoint of the line.

6. Similarly, move the cursor toward the point placed in the **Plane2** and specify the endpoint of the line when a red dot is displayed.

7. Right-click in the drawing area to invoke a shortcut menu. Next, choose the **Select** option from the shortcut menu to exit the tool.

8. Apply fillets of radius 50 mm between the intersection of two lines in the 3D sketch using the **Sketch Fillet** tool and then apply the dimensions. The resultant sketch after applying fillets and dimensions is shown in Figure 6-6. Next, exit the sketching environment.

The **Sketch Fillet** tool is used to create a tangent arc at the intersection of two sketched entities. It trims or extends the entities to be filleted, depending on the geometry of the sketched entity. You can also apply a fillet to two nonparallel lines, two arcs, two splines, an arc and a line, a spline and a line, or a spline and an arc.

Creating the Profile of the Sweep Feature

As discussed earlier, the sweep feature is created by sweeping the profile along the path. Therefore, after creating the path, you need to create a profile of the sweep feature. To create the profile of the sweep feature, first you need to create a reference plane normal to the path. In this section, you do not need to create a reference plane normal to the path because the Right Plane already normal to the path created.

9. Invoke the sketching environment by selecting the Right Plane as the sketching plane.

10. Draw a circle of diameter 38 mm and apply dimension, refer to Figure 6-7. Next, exit the sketching environment.

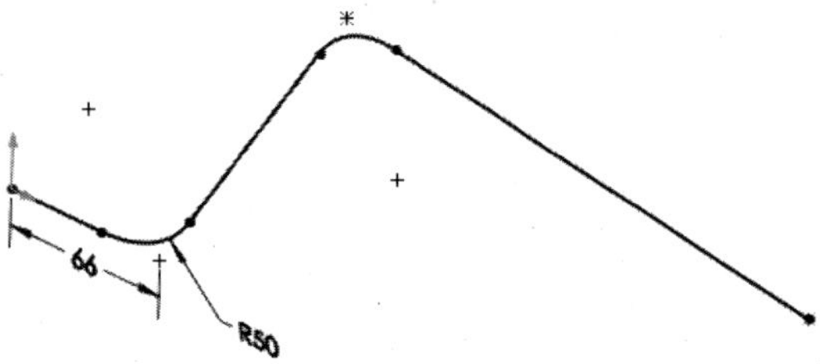

Figure 6-6 3D Sketch of the sweep feature

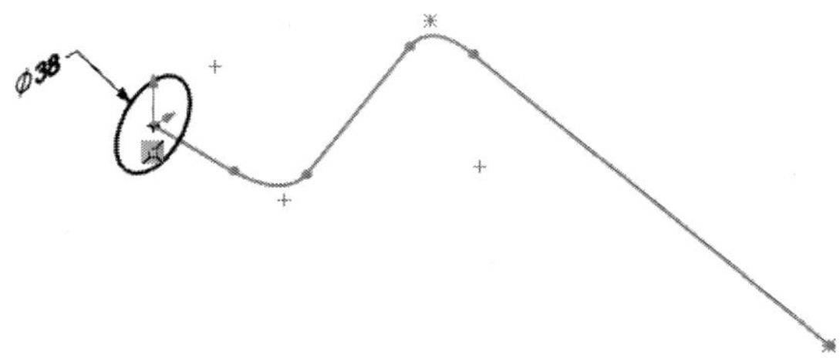

Figure 6-7 Profile of the sweep feature

Sweeping the Profile along the 3D Path

After creating the path and the profile for the sweep feature, you need to sweep the profile along the 3D path using the **Swept Boss/Base** tool. As discussed earlier, this tool is used to extrude a closed profile along an open or a closed path.

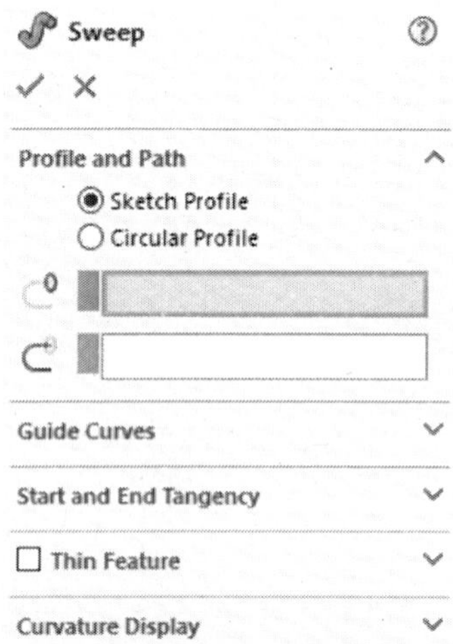

Figure 6-8 Sweep PropertyManager

1. Choose the **Swept Boss/Base** tool from the **Features CommandManager**; the **Sweep PropertyManager** is displayed at the left of the drawing area, as shown in Figure 6-8 and you are prompted to select the sweep profile.

2. Select the circle as the profile of the sweep feature; the name of the selected profile is displayed in the **Profile** selection box of the PropertyManager. Also, the selected sketch is highlighted and the profile callout is displayed attached to the selected circle in the drawing area. Also, you are prompted to select the path of the sweep feature.

You can also select the **Circular Profile** radio button from the **Profile and Path** rollout in the **Sweep PropertyManager** to create a sweep feature using the circular profile along a sketch line, edge, or curve directly on a model. Select the sketch or edge as a path along which the circular profile is to be created from the drawing area and enter the diameter value in the **Diameter** spinner.

3. Select the 3D sketch as the path for the sweep feature; the preview of the sweep feature is displayed in the drawing area and the name of the path is displayed in the **Path** selection box of the PropertyManager. Also, the path callout is displayed attached to the selected path in the drawing area.

It is evident from Figures 6-1 and 6-2, the frame of the model is made up of a hollow pipe. Therefore, you need to create a thin sweep feature to create a hollow Handle frame.

4. Expand the **Thin Feature** rollout of the **Sweep PropertyManager** by selecting the check box available at its left and then set the value of the **Thickness** spinner to **2.5 mm**.

5. Choose the **Reverse Direction** button to reverse the direction of the thin feature creation towards the inside side.

6. Choose the **OK** button from the PropertyManager to end the creation of the feature. The model after creating the sweep feature is shown in Figure 6-9.

   The created sweep feature is only the right half of the Handlebar because you have drawn only the right half of the sketch as the path of the sweep feature. Therefore, for the complete Handlebar, you need to mirror it on the Right Plane.

Mirroring the Sweep Feature

After creating the sweep feature, you will mirror it along the Right Plane.

1. Invoke the **Mirror PropertyManager** by choosing the **Mirror** button from the **Features CommandManager**.

2. Mirror the sweep feature by selecting the Right Plane as the mirroring plane. The model after mirroring the sweep feature is shown in Figure 6-10.

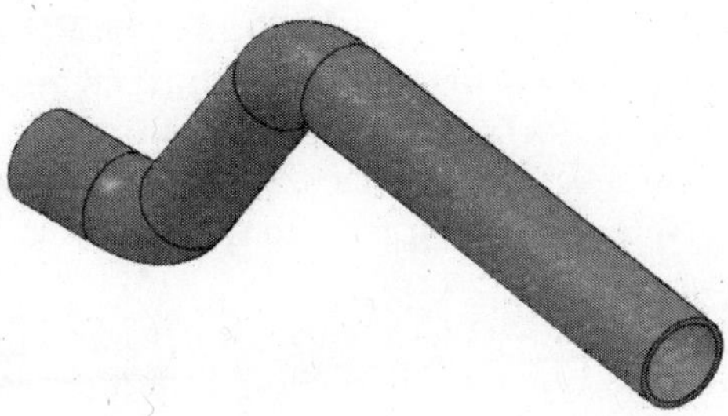

Figure 6-9 *Model after creating the sweep feature*

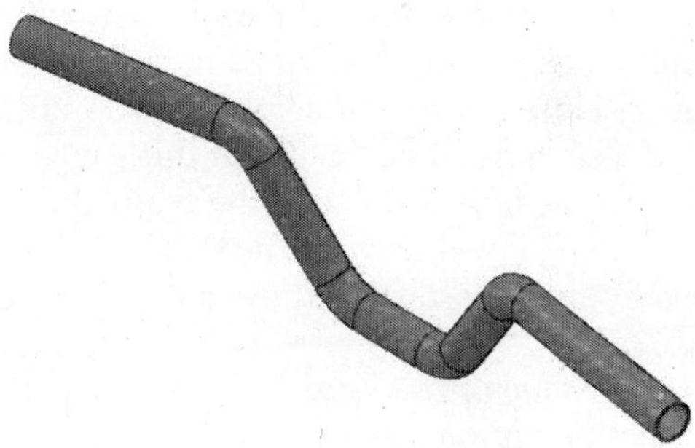

Figure 6-10 *Model after mirroring the feature*

Creating the Cut Feature

The next feature of the model is a cut feature, created at an offset from the plane on which the sketch is drawn.

1. Invoke the **Extruded Cut** tool and select the Right Plane as the sketching plane; the sketching environment is invoked. Next, change the orientation of the model normal to the view if it is not set so by default.

2. Draw the circle of diameter 2 mm, refer to Figure 6-11. Next, exit the sketching environment; the preview of the cut feature is displayed in the drawing area with the default values. Also, the **Cut-Extrude PropertyManager** is displayed at the left of the drawing area.

3. Change the current orientation of the model to isometric.

4. Select the **Offset** option from the **Start Condition** drop-down list of the **From** rollout in the PropertyManager, refer to Figure 6-12; the **Enter Offset Value** spinner is displayed below the drop-down list.

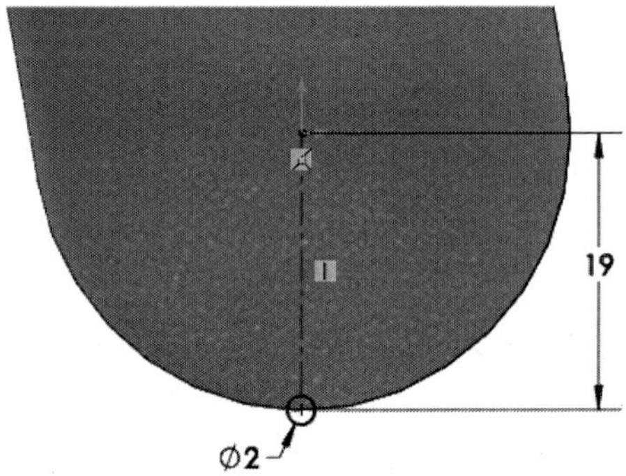

Figure 6-11 *Sketch of the cut feature*

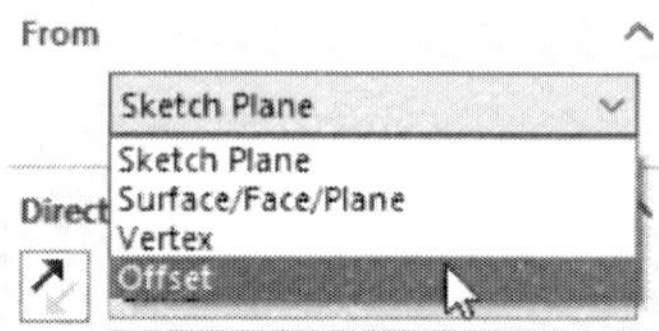

Figure 6-12 *The* ***Start Condition*** *drop-down list*

The **Start Condition** drop-down list of the **From** rollout is used to specify the position from where the sketch will start to extrude. The **Offset** option of this drop-down list is used to start the feature creation at an offset from the plane on which the sketch is drawn. The **Sketch Plane** option is selected by default in this drop-down list and is used to start the feature creation from the sketching plane on which the sketch is drawn. The **Surface/Face/Plane** option of this drop-down list is used to start the feature creation from a selected surface, face, or a plane, instead of the plane on which the sketch is drawn. The **Vertex** option is used to specify a vertex as the reference for starting the extrude feature.

5. Set the value of the **Enter Offset Value** spinner to **12.5 mm** and then choose the **Reverse Direction** button to reverse the direction of the feature creation.

6. Set the value of the **Depth** spinner to **25 mm** in the **Direction 1** rollout of the PropertyManager and then choose the **OK** button; the cut feature is created. The rotated view of the model after creating the cut feature is shown in Figure 6-13.

Creating the Circular Pattern

After creating the cut feature, you need to pattern it in the circular manner using the **Circular Pattern** tool.

1. Invoke the **CirPattern PropertyManager** and select the previously created cut feature as a feature to be pattern.

2. Activate the **Pattern Axis** selection box of the **Direction 1** rollout and select the middle circular face of the sweep feature; the preview of the pattern feature with the default number of instances and angle value is displayed in the drawing area.

3. Set the value of the **Number of Instances** spinner to 36 and the **Angle** spinner to 360-degree. Next, choose the **OK** button; the pattern feature is created, refer to Figure 6-14.

Figure 6-13 *Model after creating cut feature*

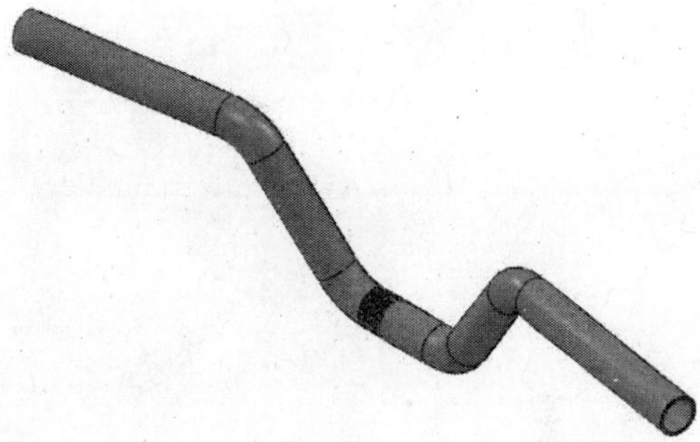

Figure 6-14 *Model after patterning the cut feature*

Mirroring the Circular Pattern Feature

After creating the circular pattern feature, you need to mirror it about the Right Plane.

1. Invoke the **Mirror PropertyManager** and mirror the previously created circular pattern feature by selecting the Right Plane as the mirroring plane. The model after mirroring the circular pattern feature is shown in Figure 6-15.

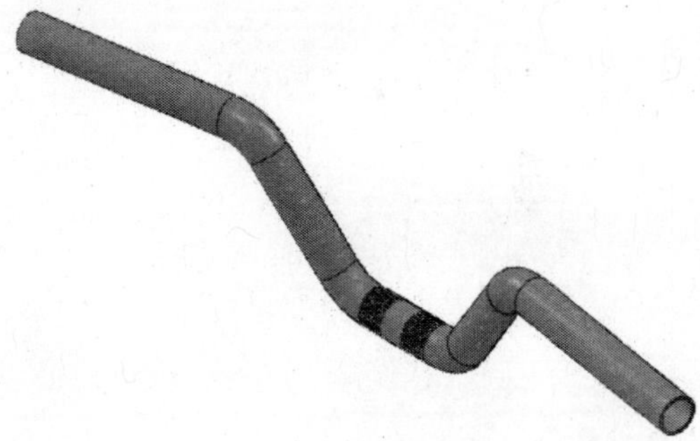

Figure 6-15 *Final model after mirroring the circular pattern feature*

Saving the Model

After create the model, you need to save it in the *Motor Cycle Project* folder.

1. Invoke the **Save As** dialog box and browse to the location of *Motor Cycle Project* folder.

2. Enter **Handlebar** as the name of the model in the **File name** edit box and choose the **Save** button. The document is saved in the *\Documents\Motor Cycle Project\Handlebar.*

3. Close the document by choosing **File > Close** from the SOLIDWORKS menus.

CREATING THE LOWER HANDLEBAR HOLDER

Part Description

In this section, you will create the Lower handlebar holder, as shown in Figure 6-16. The different views and dimensions of the model are given in the Figure 6-17.

Figure 6-16 *The Lower Handlebar Holder*

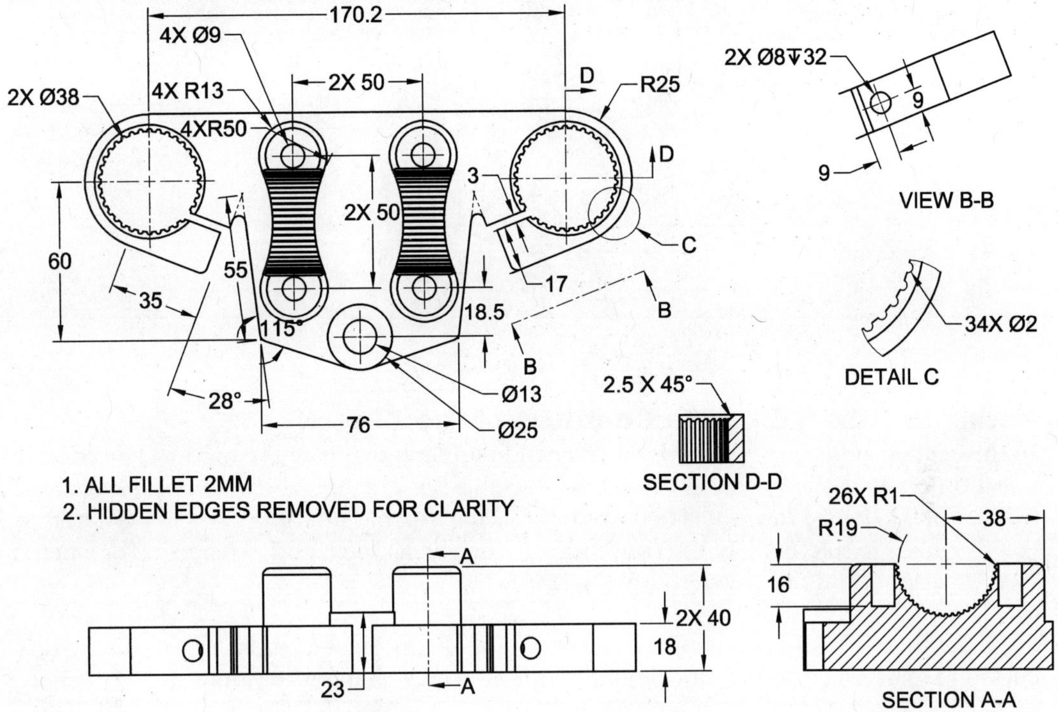

Figure 6-17 Views and dimensions of the model

It is clear from the above figures that the given model is a multi-featured model. It consists of various extruded features. You first need to draw the sketch for each feature and then convert that sketch into a feature. In conventional methods, you create a separate sketch for each sketched feature. But in this section, you will draw a single sketch with multiple contour and then use the contour selection method to create various features from the same sketch.

Creating the Sketch of the Model

1. Start a new SOLIDWORKS part document using the **New SOLIDWORKS Document** dialog box or by using the **Welcome - SOLIDWORKS 2018** dialog box. Next, modify the unit of the current session to millimeters, if not set by default.

2. Invoke the sketching environment by selecting the Top Plane as the sketching plane.

3. Draw the sketch of the top view of the model and apply the required relations and dimensions to the sketch, refer to Figure 6-18. Make sure that you do not exit the sketching environment, after done with the sketch creation.

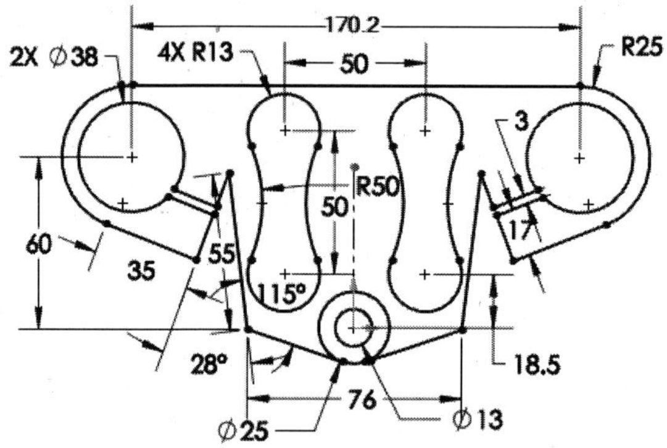

Figure 6-18 Sketch of the model

Selecting and Extruding the Contours of the Sketch

In this section, you will use the contour selection method to create the model. The contour selection method allows you to use partial sketches for creating the features. You can use this method to create the model from a single sketch that has multiple contours. Therefore, you first need to select one of the contour from the given sketch and extrude it. For a better view, you can orient the sketch to isometric view.

1. Press the **SPACEBAR** key; the **Orientation** dialog box is displayed. From this dialog box, click on **Isometric**; the current orientation of the sketch changes to isometric.

2. Right-click in the drawing area to invoke the shortcut menu. Expand the shortcut menu, if required. Choose the **Contour Select Tool** option; the select cursor is replaced by the contour selection cursor and the selection confirmation corner is displayed.

3. Move the cursor towards the outer contour area of the sketch; the outer contour of the sketch is highlighted, refer to Figure 6-19. This indicates that this contour is a closed profile.

4. Click the left mouse button on the highlighted area; the area is selected as a contour.

5. Choose the **Extruded Boss/Base** button from the **Features CommandManager**; the **Boss-Extrude PropertyManager** is displayed and the preview of the base feature is displayed in the drawing area in the temporary graphics.

   The name of the selected contour is displayed in the **Selected Contours** selection box of the **Selected Contours** rollout of the **Boss-Extrude PropertyManager**.

6. Set the value of the **Depth** spinner to **18 mm** and then choose the **OK** button; the selected contour is extruded, refer to Figure 6-20.

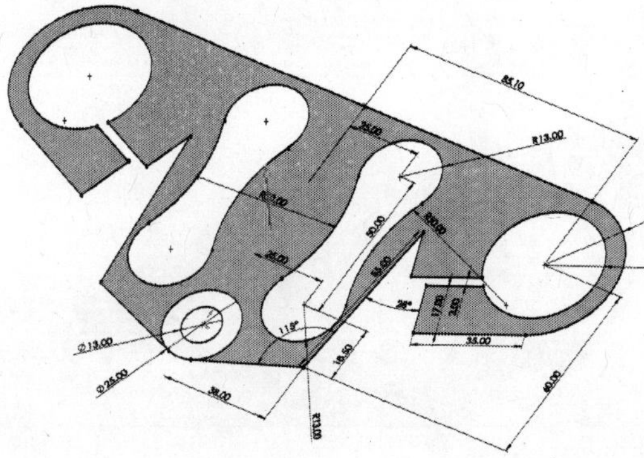

Figure 6-19 *The outer contour area of the sketch is highlighted in the drawing area*

Figure 6-20 *Base feature of the model*

Note

In Figure 6-20, the sketch of the model is hidden for the clarity. To hide the sketch, first select the sketch and then choose the ***Hide*** *button from the pop-up toolbar.*

7. Right-click in the drawing area and choose the **Contour Select Tool** option from the shortcut menu; the select cursor is replaced by the contour selection cursor. You may need to expand the shortcut menu.

8. Select an entity of the sketch using the contour selection cursor to invoke the selection mode of the sketch.

9. Move the cursor towards the closed circular contour of the sketch; the circular contour of the sketch is highlighted, refer to Figure 6-21.

10. Click the left mouse button on the highlighted area; the area is selected as a contour.

11. Invoke the **Boss-Extrude PropertyManager** and set the value of the **Depth** spinner to **23 mm**. Next, choose the **OK** button from the PropertyManager; the selected contour is extruded, as shown in Figure 6-22.

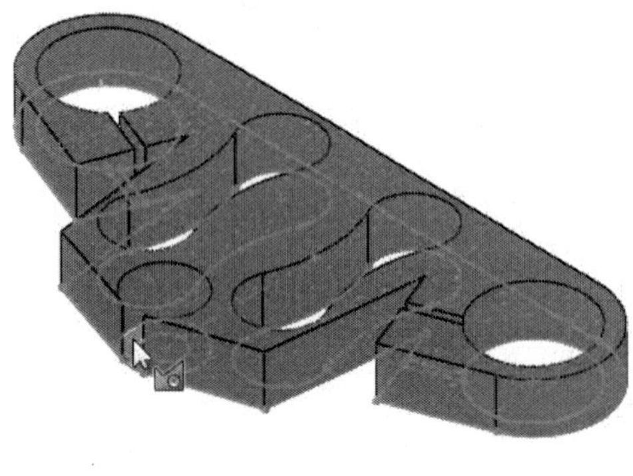

Figure 6-21 The circular contour of the sketch is highlighted in the drawing area

Figure 6-22 Model after extruding the circular contour

12. Again invoke the shortcut menu and choose the **Contour Select Tool** option from it. Next, select a sketched entity of the sketch to invoke the selection mode.

13. Select the contour on the right side. Press and hold the **CTRL** key and then select the contour on the left side, refer to Figure 6-23.

14. Invoke the **Boss-Extrude PropertyManager** and set the value of the **Depth** spinner to **40 mm**.

15. Choose the **OK** button from the PropertyManager; the selected contours are extruded. Next, hide the sketch. The model after hiding the sketch is shown in Figure 6-24.

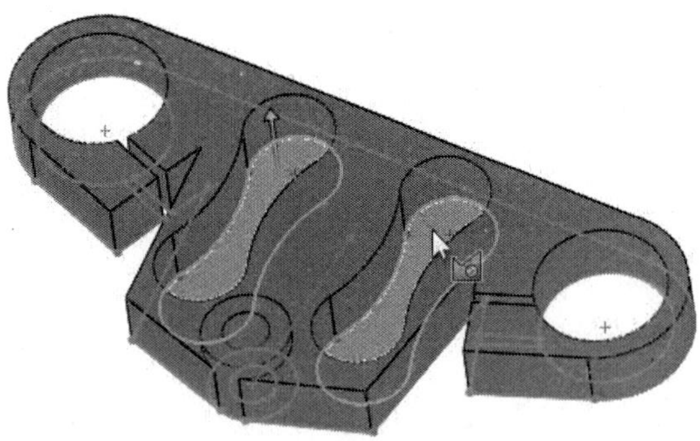

Figure 6-23 The contours of the sketch are highlighted in the drawing area

Figure 6-24 Model after extruding the contours

Creating Holes on the Base Feature

After creating the extruded features of the model, you need to create holes on the base feature of the model. These holes will be created as the extruded cut feature. You will create a hole feature on the right side of the base feature and then mirror it by selecting the Right

Plane as the mirroring plane to create a hole on the other side of the base feature.

1. Select the front planar face of the base feature, refer to Figure 6-25; a pop-up toolbar is displayed.

2. Select the **Sketch** button from the pop-up toolbar to invoke the sketching environment. Next, change the orientation of the model normal to the view if not set by default.

3. Draw a circle of diameter **8 mm**, refer to Figure 6-26.

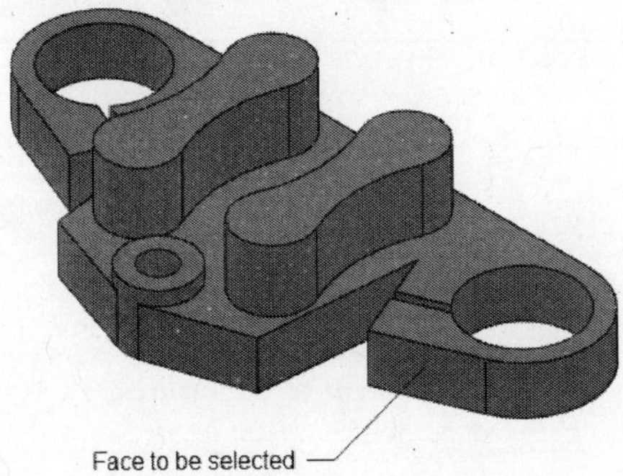

Figure 6-25 *Face to be selected*

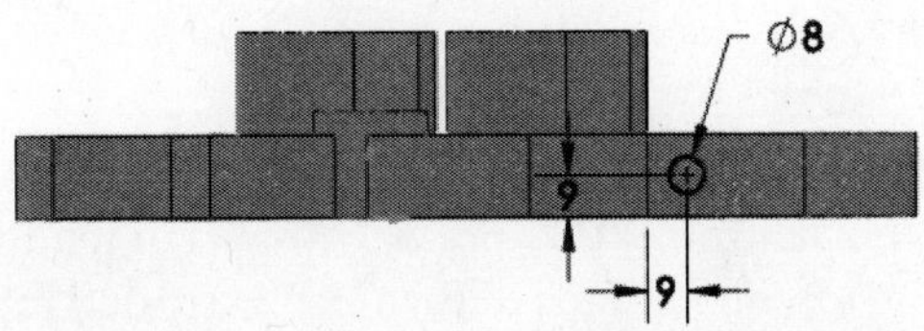

Figure 6-26 *Sketch of the cut feature*

4. Change the current view to the isometric view. Next, invoke the **Extruded Cut** tool and create the cut feature of depth 32 mm. The model after creating the cut feature is shown in Figure 6-27.

   As discussed earlier, after creating the cut feature (hole) on the right side, you need to mirror it by selecting the Right Plane as the mirroring plane.

5. Invoke the **Mirror PropertyManager** by choosing the **Mirror** button from the **Features CommandManager**.

6. Select the Right Plane as a mirroring plane and then select the previously created cut feature; the preview of the mirror feature is displayed in the drawing area.

7. Choose the **OK** button; the mirror feature is created, as shown in Figure 6-28.

Figure 6-27 *Model after creating the cut feature*

Figure 6-28 *Model after mirroring the feature*

Creating the Next Feature

Next feature of the model is also a cut feature. You will draw the sketch of this cut feature on the top planar face of the third extruded feature. To complete the sketch of this feature, you will first draw a circle and then create the pattern of the remaining circles in the sketching environment.

1. Invoke the sketching environment by selecting the top planar face of the third extruded feature named as **Boss-Extrude3**.

2. Draw a circle of diameter **9 mm** and pattern it using the **Linear Sketch Pattern** tool. You may need to apply the horizontal and vertical relations between the center points of the circles to fully define the sketch. The fully defined sketch is shown in Figure 6-29.

In SOLIDWORKS, the **Linear Sketch Pattern** tool is used to create the linear pattern of the sketched entities in the sketching environment. To do so, select the sketched entities from the drawing area. Next, choose the **Linear Sketch Pattern** button from the **Sketch CommandManager**; the **Linear Pattern PropertyManager** and the preview of the linear pattern will be displayed. Also, the arrow cursor will be replaced by linear pattern cursor. Now, you need to specify the required parameters of the linear pattern in the **Direction1** and **Direction2** rollouts of the PropertyManager.

Tip

You can also create a cut feature by creating a circle in the sketching environment and then pattern it using the ***Linear Pattern*** *tool of the* ***Features CommandManager****, instead of creating pattern in the sketching environment.*

3. Exit the sketching environment and change the current orientation to the isometric orientation.

4. Invoke the **Extruded Cut** tool and extrude the sketch upto the depth of 16 mm. The model after creating the cut feature is shown in Figure 6-30.

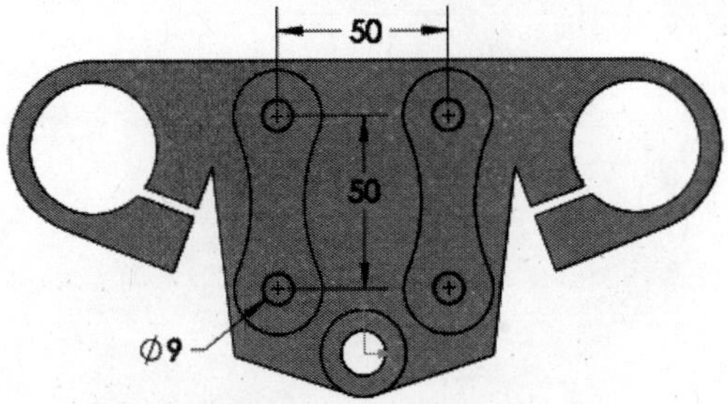

Figure 6-29 Sketch of the cut feature

Figure 6-30 Model after creating the cut feature

Creating Remaining Features

Now, you will create the remaining features of the model.

1. Invoke the sketching environment by selecting the Right Plane as the sketching plane and draw the sketch of the feature, refer to Figure 6-31. Next, invoke the **Extruded Cut** tool and extrude the sketch through all in direction 1 and direction 2, refer to Figure 6-32.

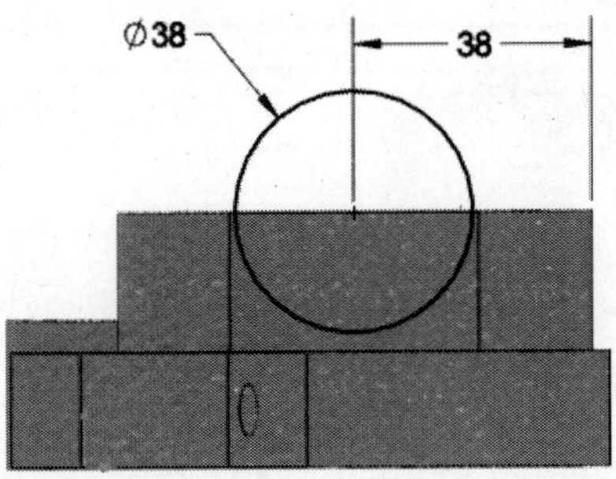

Figure 6-31 Sketch of the cut feature

Figure 6-32 Model after creating the cut feature

2. Invoke the sketching environment by selecting the Right Plane as the sketching plane and draw the sketch of the feature, refer to Figure 6-33. Next, invoke the **Extruded Cut** tool and extrude the sketch through all in direction 1 and direction 2, refer to Figure 6-34.

3. Create the circular pattern feature of the previously created cut feature by specifying the number of instances to 26 and angle of revolution to 180-degree. You may also need to reverse the direction of feature creation. The model after creating the circular pattern feature is shown in Figure 6-35.

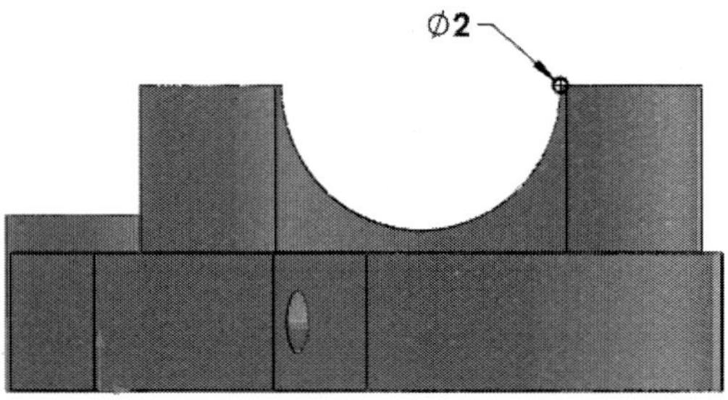

Figure 6-33 *Sketch of the cut feature*

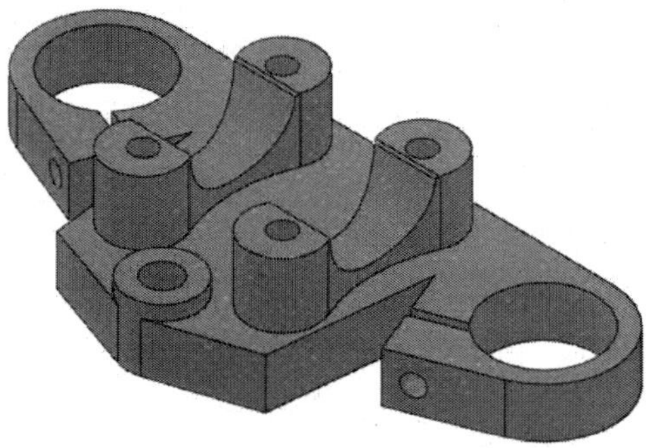

Figure 6-34 *Model after creating the cut feature*

Figure 6-35 *Model after creating the circular pattern feature*

4. Create the chamfer feature on the edges shown in Figure 6-36 by specifying 45-degree as the angle distance and 2.5 mm as the distance value of the chamfer feature. The model after creating the chamfer feature is shown in Figure 6-37.

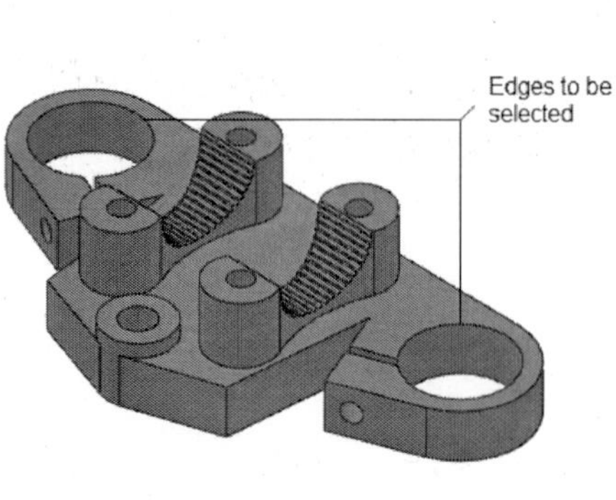

Figure 6-36 *Edges to be selected*

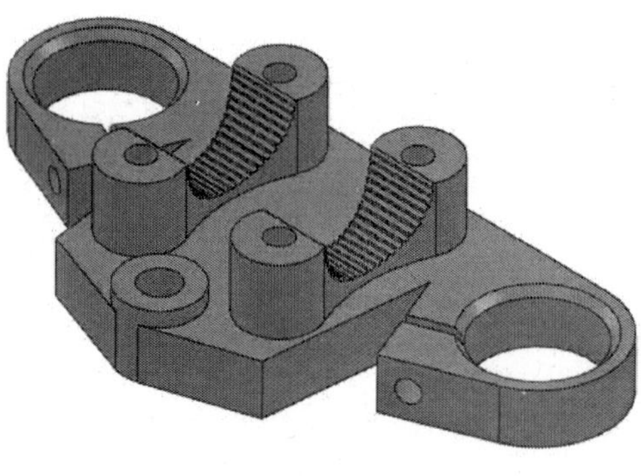

Figure 6-37 *Model after creating the chamfer*

5. Invoke the sketching environment by selecting the top planar face of the base feature as the sketching plane and draw the sketch of the feature, refer to Figure 6-38. Next, invoke the **Extruded Cut** tool and extrude the sketch using the **Through All** option.

6. Create the circular pattern feature of the previously created cut feature by specifying the number of instances to 34 and angle of revolution to 360-degree. The model after creating the circular pattern feature is shown in Figure 6-39.

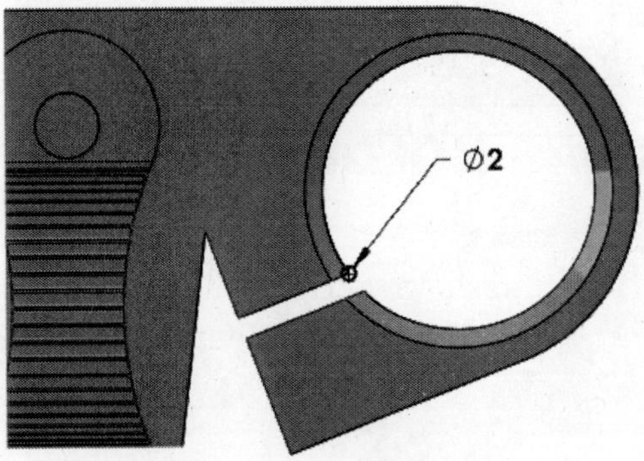

Figure 6-38 *Sketch of the cut feature*

Figure 6-39 *Model after creating the circular pattern*

7. Create the mirror feature of the previously created circular pattern feature by selecting the Right Plane as the mirroring plane. The model after mirroring the feature is shown in Figure 6-40.

8. After creating all the features of the model, you need to add fillet feature. Invoke the **Fillet PropertyManager** and select the required edges of the model to apply the fillet feature. The final model after applying the fillet feature is shown in Figure 6-41.

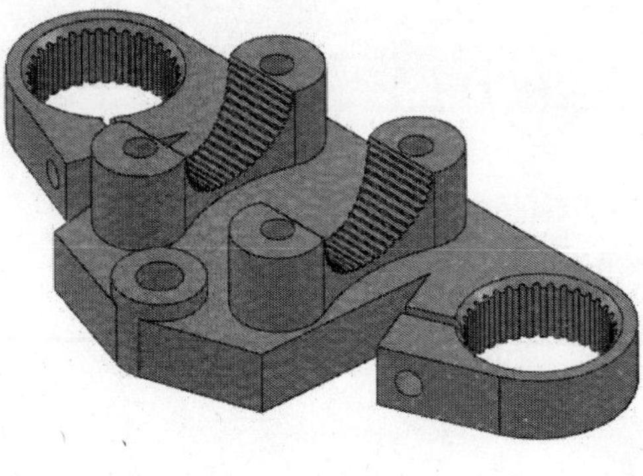

Figure 6-40 *Model after mirroring the feature*

Figure 6-41 *Final model after applying fillet*

Saving the Model

After creating the model, you need to save it in the *Motor Cycle Project* folder.

1. Invoke the **Save As** dialog box and browse to the *Motor Cycle Project* folder.

2. Enter the name of the model as Lower Handlebar Holder in the **File name** edit box and choose the **Save** button. The document will be saved in the *\Documents\Motor Cycle Project\Lower Handlebar Holder*.

3. Close document by choosing **File > Close** from the SOLIDWORKS menus.

CREATING THE UPPER HANDLEBAR HOLDER

Part Description

In this section, you will create the Upper Handlebar Holder, as shown in Figure 6-42. The views and dimensions of the model are given in Figure 6-43. In Figure 6-43, the hidden lines of the top and front views are removed for clarity.

Figure 6-42 *The Upper Handle Bar Holder of the Motor Cycle*

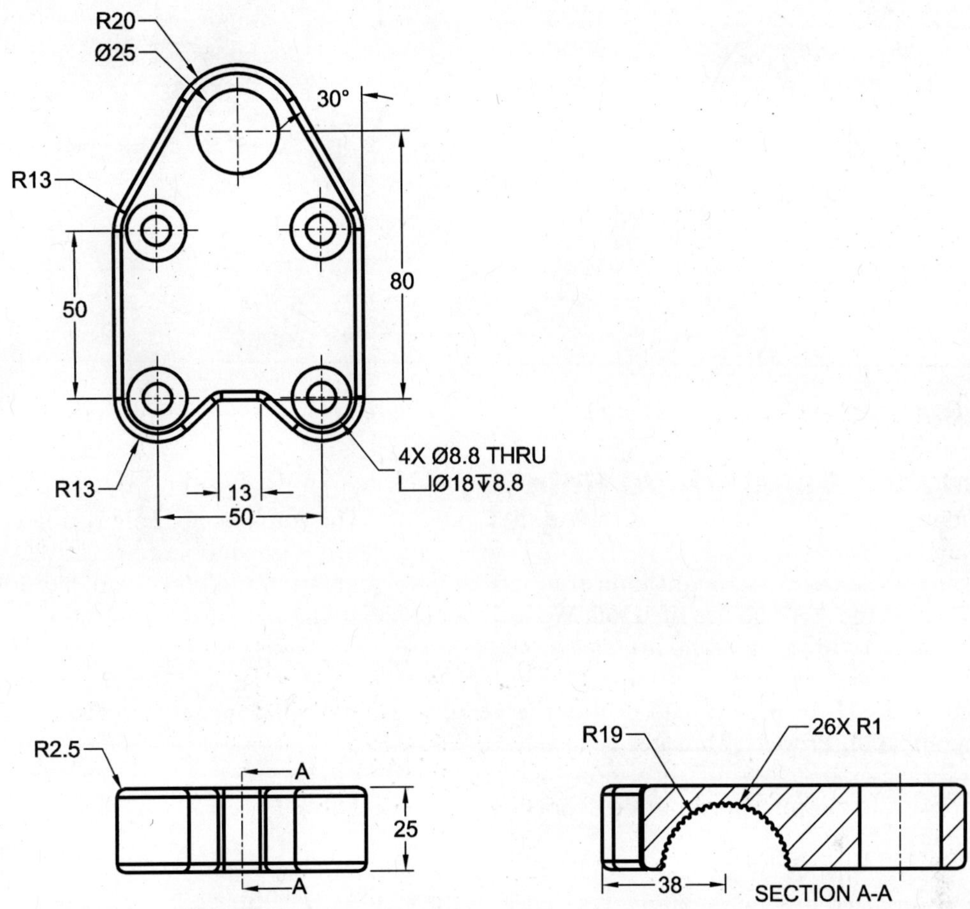

Figure 6-43 *Top, front, and side views of the model*

Starting a New Part Document

1. Start a new SOLIDWORKS part document using the **New SOLIDWORKS Document** dialog box. Next, modify the unit of the current session to millimeters, if not set by default.

   Once the new part document is invoked, you can create the base feature of the model.

Creating the Base Feature

The base feature of the Upper Handlebar Holder is an extruded feature.

1. Invoke the sketching environment by selecting the Top Plane as the sketching plane and draw the sketch, refer to Figure 6-44.

2. Exit the sketching environment and then extrude the sketch to the depth of 25 mm by using the **Extruded Boss/Base** tool. The model after creating the base feature is shown in Figure 6-45.

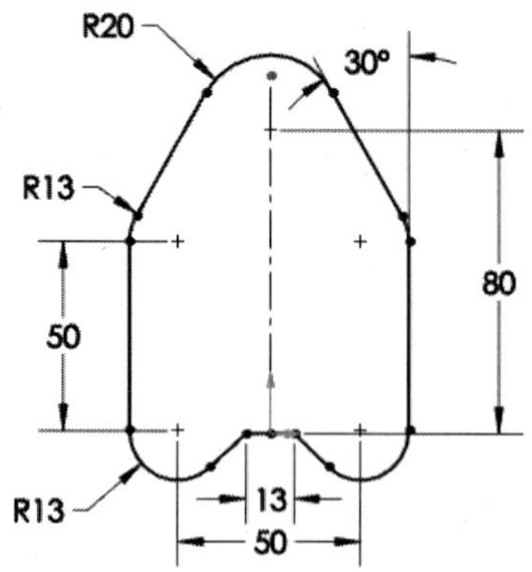

Figure 6-44 Sketch of the base feature

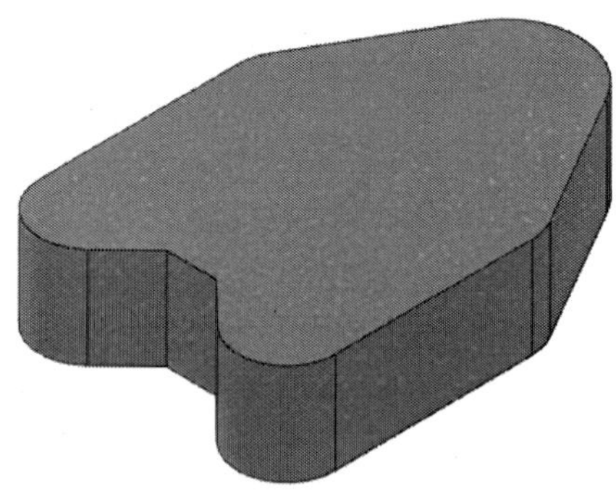

Figure 6-45 Base feature of the model

Adding the Counterbore Hole

The next feature of the model is the counterbore hole. The counterbore hole is created by using the **Hole Wizard** tool. As discussed earlier, the **Hole Wizard** tool of SOLIDWORKS is one of the largest standard industrial virtual hole generation methods available in any CAD package. You can use the **Hole Wizard** tool to create the standard holes to the model that can accommodate standard fasteners.

1. Choose the **Hole Wizard** button from the **Features CommandManager**; the **Hole Specification PropertyManager** is displayed.

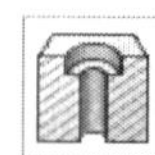

2. Choose the **Counterbore** button from the from the **Hole Type** rollout of the PropertyManager.

   Now, you need to set the parameters to define the Counterbore hole.

3. Select the **ANSI Metric** option from the **Standard** drop-down list of the **Hole Type** rollout in the PropertyManager.

4. Select the **Hex Bolt - ANSI B18.2.3.5M** option from the **Type** drop-down list of the **Hole Type** rollout.

5. Select the **M8** option from the **Size** drop-down list and the **Normal** option from the **Fit** drop-down list of the **Hole Specifications** rollout.

6. Select the **Show custom sizing** check box; the parameters of the counterbore hole are displayed in different spinners, as shown in Figure 6-46. You can use these spinners to create a user-defined counterbore hole.

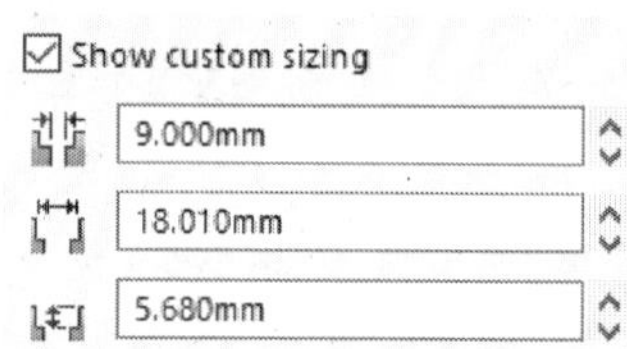

Figure 6-46 The parameters of the counterbore hole

The **Show custom sizing** check box of the **Hole Specification PropertyManager** is used to create a user-defined hole feature. If you change the default values of the parameters meant for the standard hole, the corresponding spinners will turn yellow. Also, the **Restore Default Values** button will be displayed in this area. You can choose this button to restore the default values of the standard holes.

It is evident from Figure 6-43, the through hole diameter of the model is 8.8 mm and the counterbore diameter is 18 mm. Therefore, you need to set the value of the spinners as per the requirement.

7. Set the value of the **Through Hole Diameter** spinner to **8.8 mm** and the **Counterbore Diameter** spinner to **18 mm**.

8. Select the **Through All** option from the **End Condition** drop-down list of the **End Condition** rollout.

   After specifying all the required parameters of the Counterbore hole, you need to define its placement.

9. Choose the **Positions** tab from the **Hole Specification PropertyManager**; you are prompted to use the dimensions and other sketching tools to position the hole. Also, the select cursor is replaced by the point cursor.

10. Move the point cursor towards the top planar face of the base feature and specify the point anywhere on it.

    Since, you have placed the point anywhere on the top planar face of the base feature, you need to add the required relations and dimensions to define the proper location of the placement point. Before doing that, you can change the model display from **Shaded With Edges** to **Hidden Lines Visible** for better visualization.

11. Right-click in the drawing area; the shortcut menu is displayed. Next, choose the **Select** option from the shortcut menu.

12. Choose the **Hidden Lines Visible** button from the **Display Style** flyout in the **View** (**Heads-up**) toolbar; the display style of the model is changed to hidden lines visible.

13. Right-click again in the drawing area; the shortcut menu is displayed. Next, choose the **Add Relation** option from the shortcut menu; the **Add Relations PropertyManager** is displayed at the left of the drawing area.

14. Select the placement point of the counterbore hole and then select the edge of the base feature, refer to Figure 6-47.

15. Choose the **Concentric** button from the **Add Relations** rollout of the PropertyManager; the concentric relation is applied between the selections. Next choose **OK**; the **Hole Position PropertyManager** is displayed.

16. Choose the **OK** button from the **Hole Position PropertyManager**; the counterbore hole is created. Next, change the display style of the model to **Shaded With Edges** style. The model after creating the counterbore hole with the shaded with edges display style is shown in Figure 6-48.

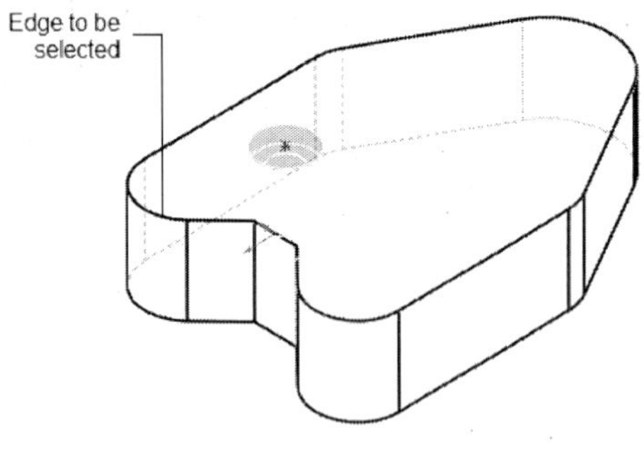

Figure 6-47 *Edge to be selected*

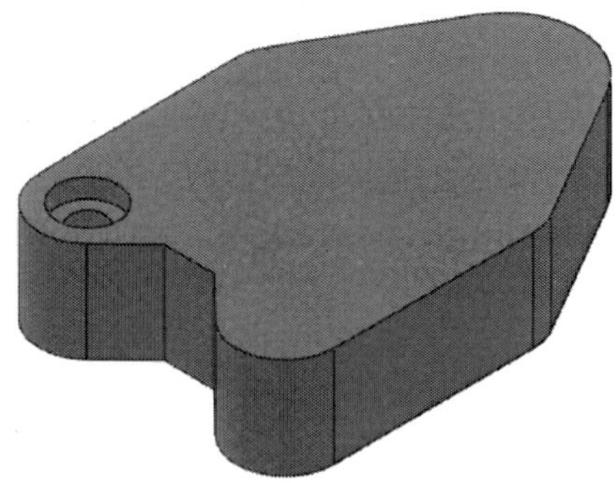

Figure 6-48 *Model after creating the counterbore hole*

Crating the Linear Pattern

After creating the counterbore hole, you will pattern it using the **Linear Pattern** tool.

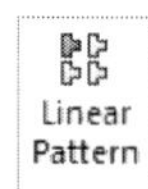

1. Select the counterbore hole and then choose the **Linear Pattern** button from the **Features CommandManager**; the **Linear Pattern PropertyManager** is displayed and you are prompted to select the directional reference.

2. Select the edge of the base feature as direction 1 reference, refer to Figure 6-49; the preview of the linear pattern is displayed in the drawing area along the selected direction. Also, the name of the selected edge is displayed in the **Pattern Direction** selection box of the **Direction 1** rollout.

3. Choose the **Reverse Direction** button from the **Direction 1** rollout of the PropertyManager to reverse the patterning direction, if required. Next, set the value of the **Spacing** spinner to **50** and **Number of Instances** spinner to **2** in the **Direction 1** rollout.

4. Select the edge of the base feature as direction 2 reference, refer to Figure 6-49; the preview of the linear pattern along the selected direction is displayed in the drawing area and the name of the selected edge is displayed in the **Pattern Direction** selection box of the **Direction 2** rollout.

5. Choose the **Reverse Direction** button from the **Direction 2** rollout of the PropertyManager to reverse the patterning direction, if required.

6. Set the value of the **Spacing spinner** to **50** and **Number of Instances** spinner to **2** in the **Direction 2** rollout of the PropertyManager. Next, choose the **OK** button from the PropertyManager. The model after patterning the counterbore hole is shown in Figure 6-50.

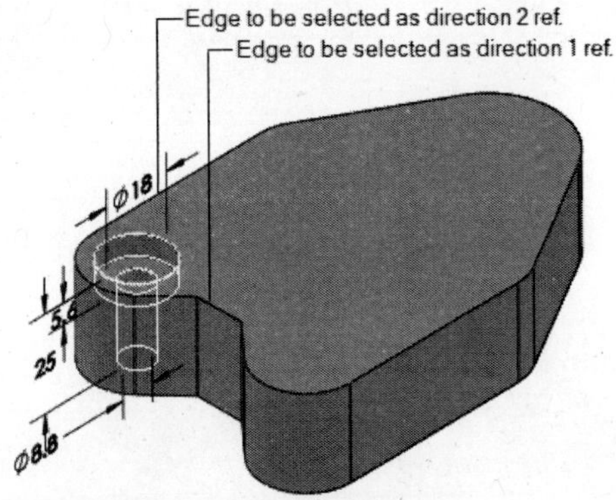

Figure 6-49 Edges to be selected

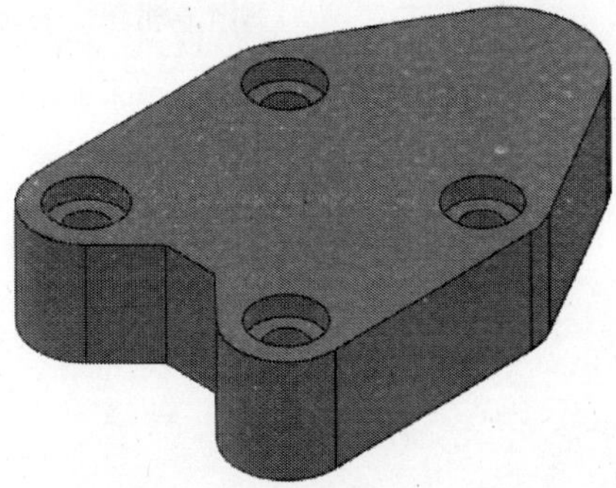

Figure 6-50 Model after patterning the feature

Crating the Cut Feature

Next feature of the model is a cut feature. The sketch of this extrude cut feature will be created on the top face of the base feature.

1. Invoke the sketching environment by selecting the top planar face of the model as the sketching plane and then draw the sketch of the cut feature, refer to Figure 6-51.

2. Exit the sketching environment and then extrude the sketch by using the **Extruded Cut** tool to the through all depth, as shown in Figure 6-52.

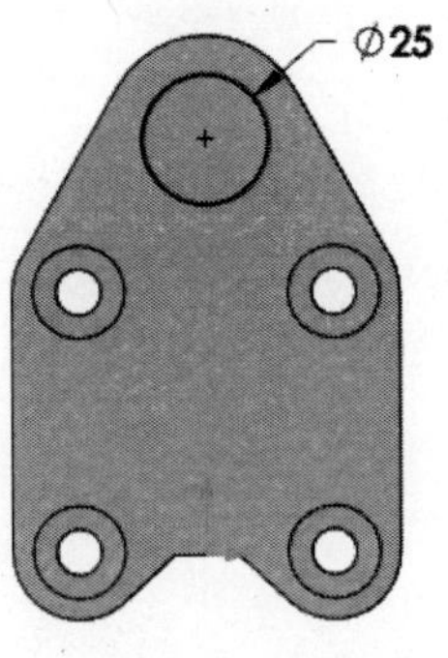

Figure 6-51 Sketch of the cut feature

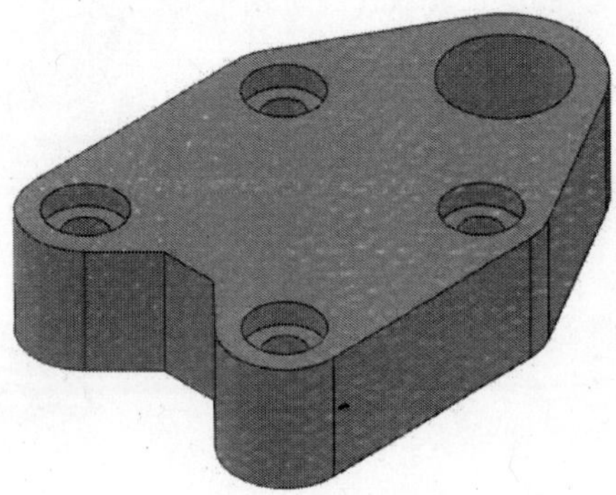

Figure 6-52 Model after creating the cut feature

Creating Remaining Features

The remaining features of the model are cut, circular pattern, and fillet features.

1. Create the semi-circular cut feature of radius 19 mm on the base feature of the model, as shown in Figure 6-53. For dimensions of this feature, refer to Figure 6-43.

2. Similarly, create the next cut feature of radius 1 mm on the right planar face of the model and then create the circular pattern it by specifying the number of instances to 26 and angle

of revolution to 180-degree by using the **Circular Pattern** tool. The model after creating this cut feature and patterning it in circular manner is shown in Figure 6-54.

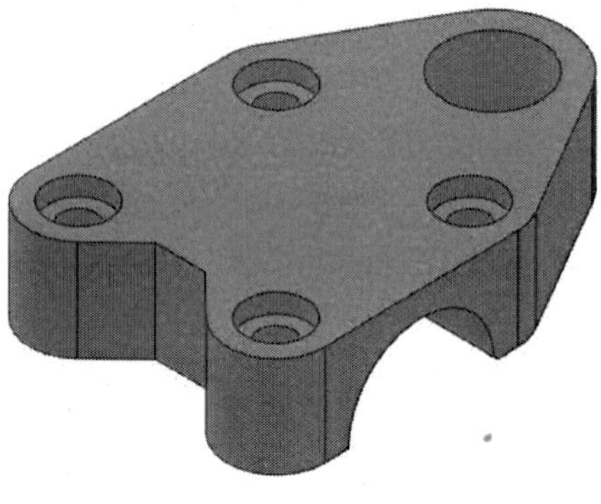

Figure 6-53 *Model after creating the cut feature*

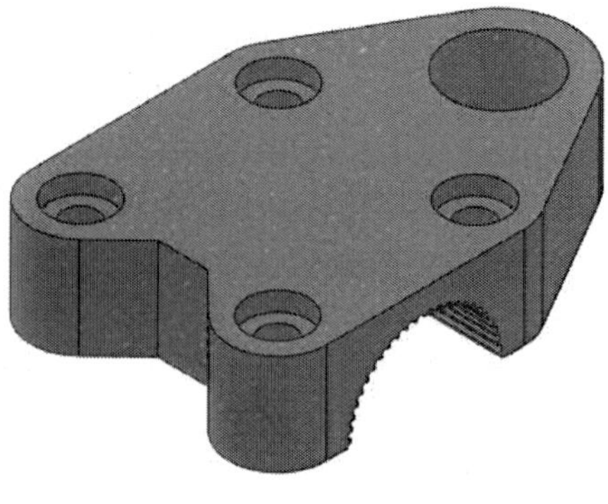

Figure 6-54 *Model after patterning the feature*

3. After creating all the features of the model, you need to apply the fillets of 2.5 radius on the required edges. The final model after creating all the features is shown in Figure 6-55.

4. Save the model.

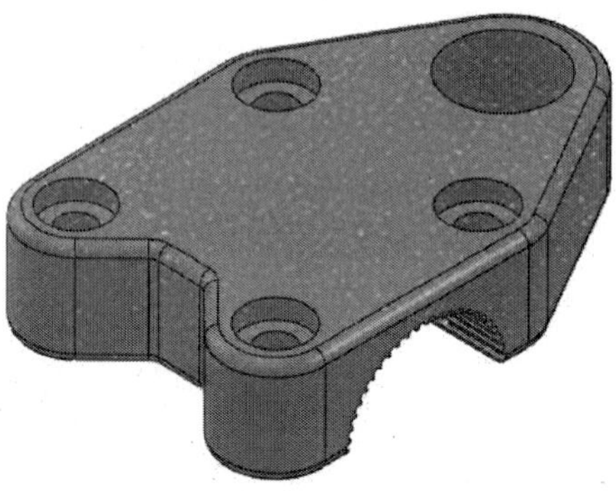

Figure 6-55 *Final model after creating all features*

Self-Evaluation Test

Answer the following questions and then compare them to those given at the end of this chapter:

1. The sweep feature is created by using the _________ tool.

2. A profile is a section for the feature and a path is the course taken by the profile while creating the _________ feature.

3. In the 3D sketching environment, you can toggle between the default planes by using the __________ key.

4. You can apply fillets in the sketching environment by using the __________ tool.

5. The __________ tool is used to creates a tangent arc at the intersection of two sketched entities. It __________ and __________ the entities to be filleted, depending on the geometry of the sketched entity.

6. The __________ drop-down list of the **From** rollout in the **Boss-Extrude PropertyManager** is used to specify the position from where the sketch will start to extrude.

7. The __________ check box of the **Hole Specification PropertyManager** is used to create a user-defined hole feature.

8. In SOLIDWORKS, you need a __________ and a __________ to create a sweep feature.

9. The contour selection method allows you to use partial sketches for creating the features. (T/F)

10. In SOLIDWORKS, the **Linear Sketch Pattern** tool is used to create the circular pattern of the sketched entities in the sketching environment. (T/F)

Review Questions

Answer the following questions:

1. In SOLIDWORKS, which one of the following tools is used to create a sweep feature?

   (a) **Sweep** (b) **Swept Boss/Base**
   (c) **Sweep Boss/Base** (d) None of these

2. Which one of the following tools is used to place point in the sketching environment?

   (a) **Point** (b) **Mark**
   (c) **Single Point** (d) None of these

3. Choose the __________ button from the **Features CommandManager** to invoke the **Sweep PropertyManager**.

4. Choose the __________ button from the Sketch flyout of the Sketch CommandManager to invoke the 3D sketching environment.

5. The __________ option of the __________ drop-down list is used to start the feature creation at an offset from the plane on which the sketch is drawn.

6. The __________ button of the **Hole Specification PropertyManager** is used to restore the default parameters of the standard holes.

7. In SOLIDWORKS, you can fillet two nonparallel lines by using the **Sketch Fillet** tool. (T/F)

8. On invoking the 3D sketching environment, some of the sketching tools are not activated in the **Sketch CommandManager**. (T/F)

9. The **Selected Contours** selection box of the **Selected Contours** rollout in the **Boss-Extrude PropertyManager** is used to display the name of the selected contour. (T/F)

10. The **Sweep Boss/Base** tool is used to extrude a open profile along an open or a closed path. (T/F)

Answers to Self-Evaluation Test

1. Swept Boss/Base, 2. sweep, **3.** TAB, **4. Sketch Fillet, 5. Sketch Fillet,** trims, and extends, **6. Start Condition, 7. Show custom sizing, 8.** profile, path, **9.** T, **10.** F.

Chapter 7

Creating Muffler and Swing Arm

Learning Objectives

After completing this chapter, you will be able to:

- *Create solid sweep feature*
- *Create loft feature*
- *Write text in the sketcher environment*
- *Wrap text on the model*
- *Assign material to the model*
- *Determine mass properties of the model*
- *Define the direction of extrusion*
- *Understand the FilletXpert PropertyManager*

CREATING THE MUFFLER

Part Description

In this section, you will create the Muffler, as shown in Figure 7-1. The base feature of the Muffler is a sweep feature. This sweep feature is created by sweeping a profile along a 3D path. The other features of the Muffler are loft, extrude, shell, and fillets. You will also write text and extrude it on the model, refer to Figure 7-1. After creating the model, you will apply the Alloy Steel (SS) material to the model. Also, determine the mass properties. The views and dimensions of the model are given in the Figures 7-2 and 7-3. The wall thickness of the model is 2.5 mm.

(Expected time: 45 min)

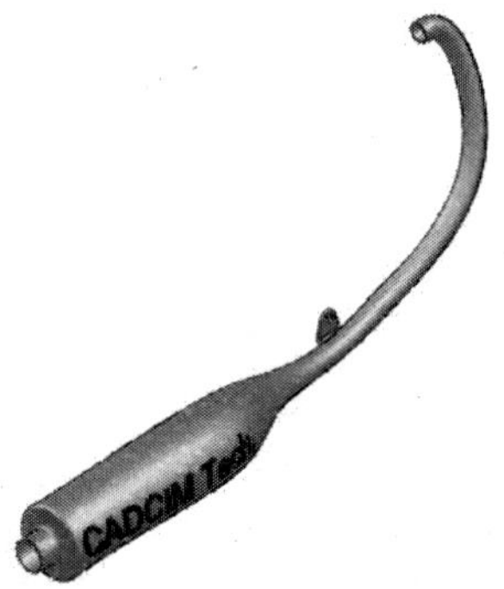

Figure 7-1 *The Muffler*

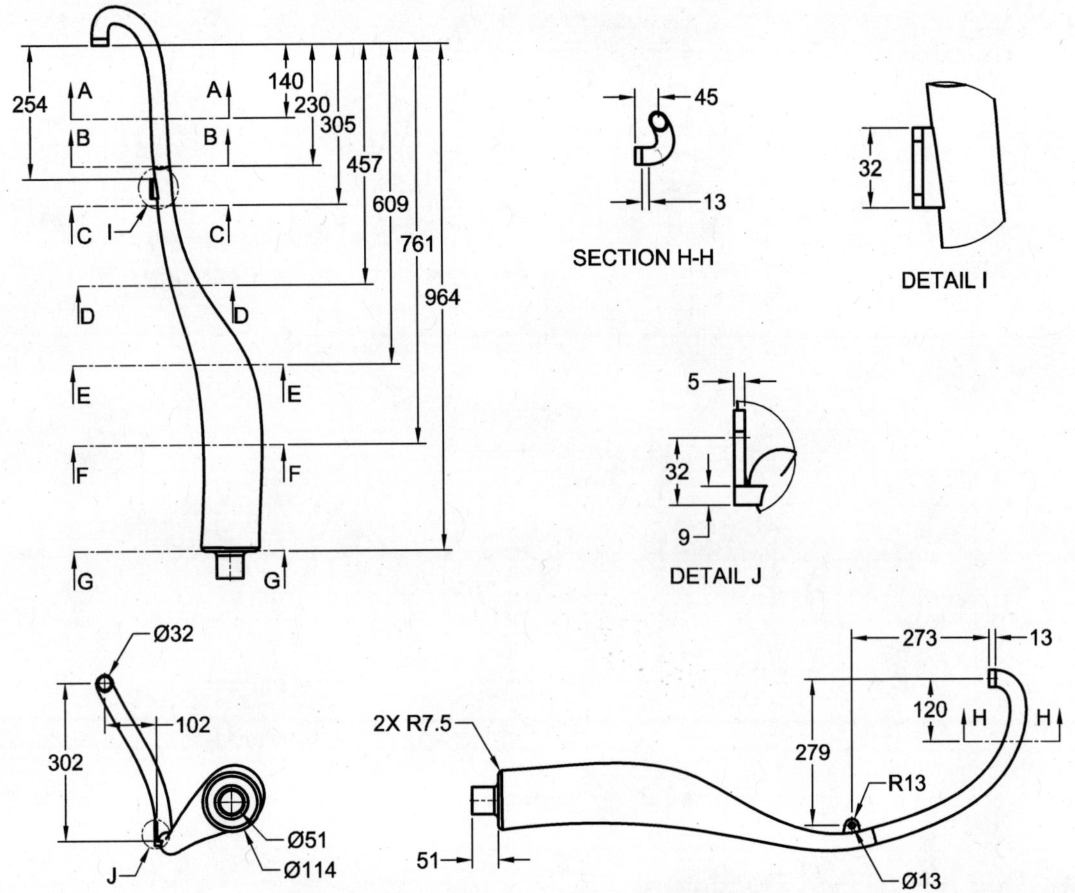

Figure 7-2 *Top, front, and side views of the model*

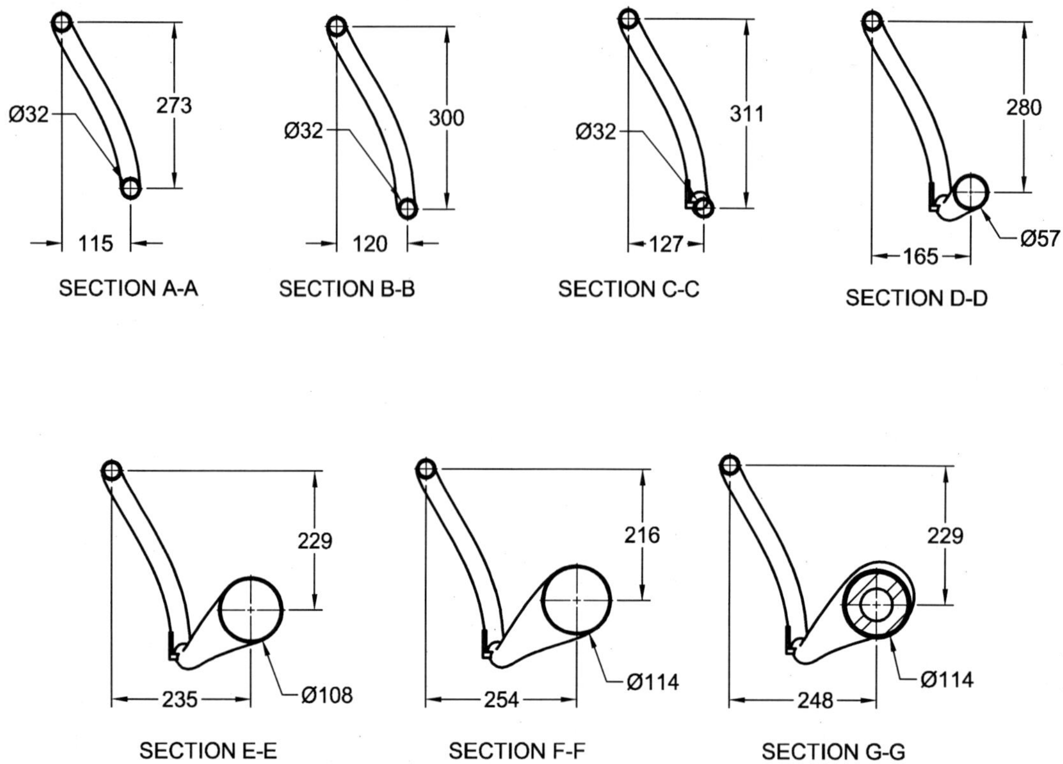

Figure 7-3 *Section views of the model*

Starting a New Part Document

1. Start a new SOLIDWORKS part document using the **New SOLIDWORKS Document** dialog box.

Creating the Base Feature

The base feature of the model is a sweep feature created by using **Swept Boss/Base** tool. As discussed earlier, to create a sweep feature, you need a profile and a path. A profile is a section for the sweep feature and a path is the course taken by the profile while creating the sweep feature. The profile has to be a 2D sketch, but the path can be a 2D sketch, 3D sketch, curve or an edge. In this section, it is evident from the Figure 7-2 that the base feature of the model is created by sweeping profile along a 3D path. To create 3D path, you first need to create reference planes at an offset distance from the Right Plane and then create points on them. These points will used to create the 3D path of the sweep feature.

Creating the Reference Planes

To create a reference plane, you need to invoke the **Plane PropertyManager**.

1. Create the reference planes at an offset distance of 65 mm, 115 mm, and 120 mm from the Right Plane using the **Plane** tool.

Creating the Points On the Reference Planes

After creating the reference planes, you need to create points on them. These points will be later used to create 3D path of the sweep feature.

1. Invoke the Sketcher environment by selecting the Right plane as the sketching plane.

2. Place two points using the **Point** tool and then apply required relations and dimensions to them, as shown in Figure 7-4. Next, exit from the sketcher environment.

3. Again, invoke the Sketcher environment by selecting the **Plane1** which is at 65 mm distance from the Right Plane.

4. Place a point using the **Point** tool and the apply the required dimensions, refer to Figure 7-5. Next, exit from the sketcher environment.

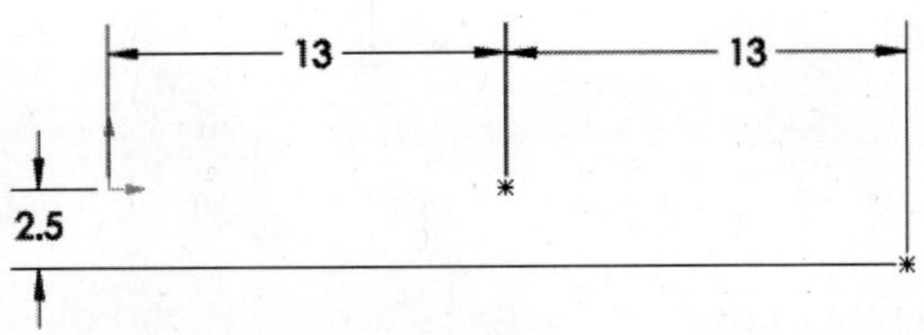

Figure 7-4 Points placed on Right Plane

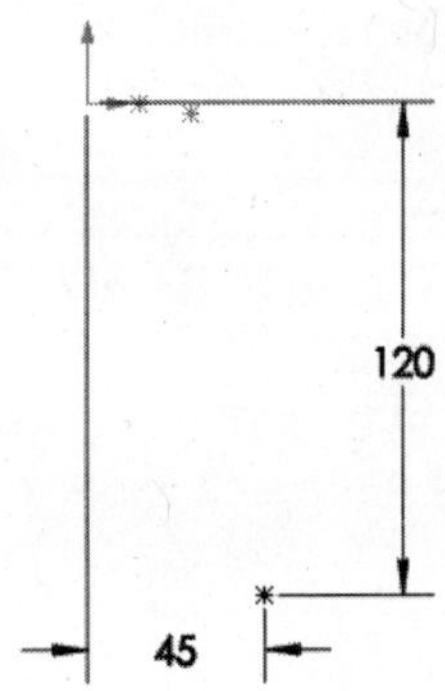

*Figure 7-5 Point placed on **Plane1***

5. Similarly, invoke the sketcher environment by selecting the **Plane2** as the sketching plane which is at 115 mm distance from the Right Plane and place a point, refer to Figure 7-6. Next, exit from the sketcher environment.

6. Again, invoke the Sketcher environment by selecting the **Plane3** as the sketching plane which is at 120 mm distance from the Right Plane. Next, place the point, as shown in Figure 7-7 and then exit from the sketcher environment.

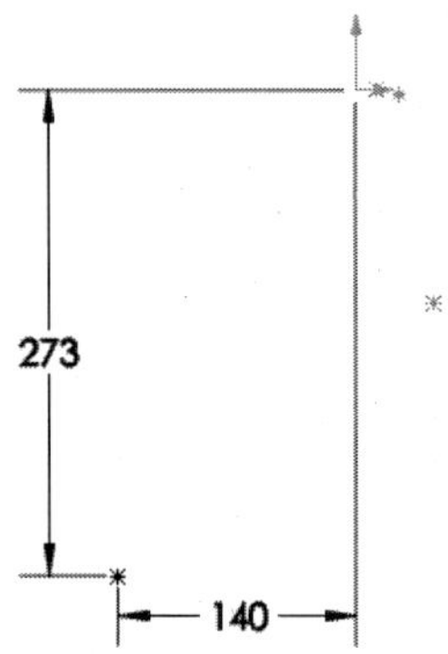

Figure 7-6 Point placed on ***Plane2***

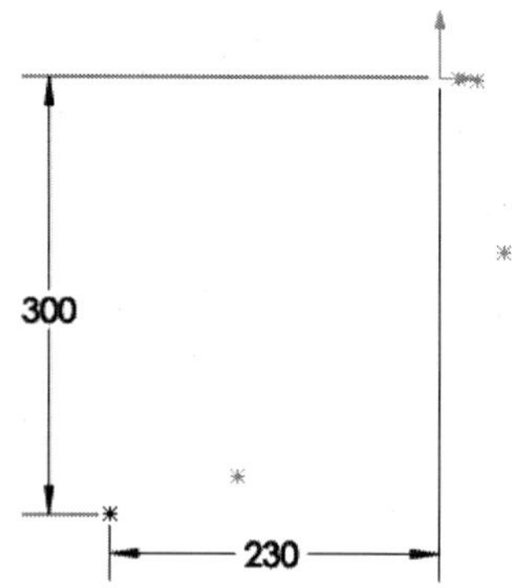

Figure 7-7 Point placed on ***Plane3***

Creating the 3D Path for the Sweep Feature

After creating the points, you need to invoke the 3D sketcher environment to create the 3D path for the sweep feature.

1. Choose the **3D Sketch** button from the **Sketch** flyout; the 3D sketcher environment is invoked and sketch origin is displayed in red color. You are also provided with the confirmation corner on the top right corner of the drawing area.

   As discussed earlier, on invoking the 3D sketcher environment, some of the sketching tools are activated in the **Sketch CommandManager**. These tools can be used to create a 3D sketch. Note that you do not need to select a sketching plane to draw the 3D sketch.

2. Invoke the **Line** tool and then move the cursor towards the origin. Next, specify the start point of the line when an orange dot is displayed at the origin.

3. Press the TAB key to toggle the plane such that ZX symbol display below the cursor. Next, move the cursor in the negative Z direction of the triad; a small triad with Z appears below the cursor indicating that you are drawing a line in the Z direction. Specify the end point of the line when a cursor snap to the point which is at 13 mm from the origin. Next, press the ESC key to exit from the **Line** tool.

4. Choose the **Spline** button from the **Sketch CommandManager**; the select cursor is replaced by the spline cursor. 

The **Spline** tool is used to draw a spline by specifying the points through which the spline will pass. The method of drawing splines is similar to that of drawing continuous lines.

5. Move the spline cursor to the end point of the line and specify the start point of the spline when an orange dot is displayed.

6. Move the cursor toward the second point placed on the Right Plane which is at 26 mm from the origin and specify the second point of the spline when a red dot is displayed.

7. Move the cursor toward the point placed in the **Plane1** and specify the third point of the spline when a red dot is displayed.

8. Similarly, specify the forth and fifth points of the spline using the points placed on **Plane2** and **Plane3**.

9. After specifying all the points of the spline, right-click in the drawing area to invoke the shortcut menu and then choose the **Select** option from it to exit from the **Spline** tool.

10. Exit from the 3D sketcher environment by clicking on the confirmation corner; the 3D path of the sweep feature is created. Next, hide the reference plane. The 3D path of the sweep feature after hiding the reference plane is shown in Figure 7-8.

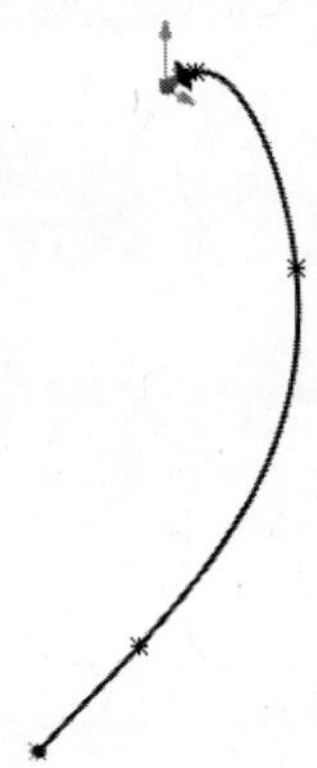

Figure 7-8 *The 3D path for the sweep feature*

Creating the profile of the Sweep Feature

After creating the path for the sweep feature, you need to create a profile. You can create profile of the sweep feature on the Front Plane, since it is normal to the line of the path.

1. Invoke the Sketcher environment by selecting the Front Plane as the sketching plane.

2. Draw a circle of diameter 32 mm with the center at origin, refer to Figure 7-9 and then exit from the sketcher environment.

Sweeping the Profile along the 3D Path

After creating the 3D path and the profile for the sweep feature, you need to sweep the profile along the path using the **Swept Boss/Base** tool. As discussed earlier, this tool is used to extrude a closed profile along an open or a closed path.

1. Choose the **Swept Boss/Base** tool from the **Features CommandManager**; the **Sweep PropertyManager** is displayed at the left of the drawing area and you are prompted to select the sweep profile.

2. Select the circle as the profile of the sweep feature; the name of the selected profile is displayed in the **Profile** selection box of the PropertyManager. Also, the selected sketch is highlighted and the profile callout is displayed in the drawing area. Now, you are prompted to select the path of the sweep feature.

You can also select the **Circular Profile** radio button from the **Profile and Path** rollout in the **Sweep PropertyManager** to create a sweep feature using the circular profile along a sketch line, edge, or curve directly on a model. Select the sketch or edge as the path along which circular profile is to be created from the drawing area and enter the diameter value in the **Diameter** spinner.

3. Select the 3D sketch as the path for the sweep feature; preview of the sweep feature is displayed in the drawing area and the name of the path is displayed in the **Path** selection box of the PropertyManager. Also, the path callout is displayed in the drawing area attached to the path of the sweep feature.

4. Choose the **OK** button to end the creation of the feature; the sweep feature is created. Next, hide all the points that are created for creating the 3D path. The sweep feature after hiding all the points is shown in Figure 7-10.

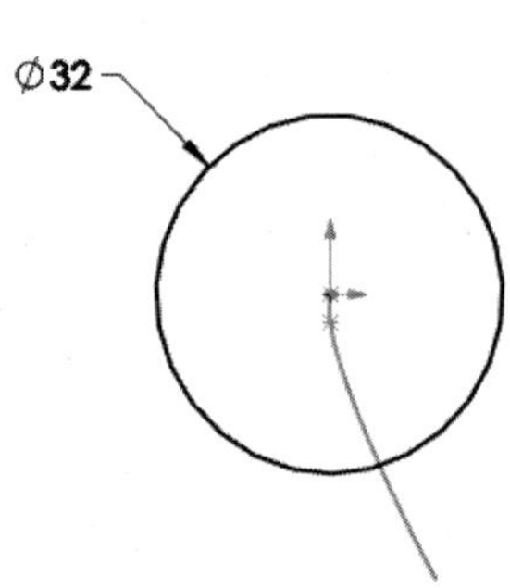

Figure 7-9 *Profile of the sweep feature*

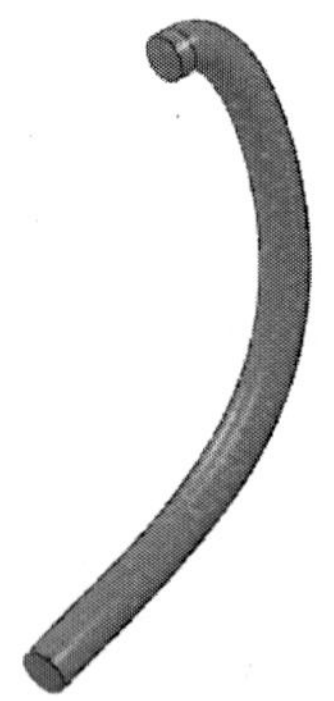

Figure 7-10 *Sweep feature of the model*

Creating the Loft Feature

The next feature of the model is a loft feature. The loft features are created by blending more than one similar or dissimilar sections together to get a free form shape. These similar or dissimilar sections may or may not be parallel to each other. In this section, you will create dissimilar sections nonparallel to each other to create the loft feature. To create these dissimilar sections, you need to first create there respective reference planes.

1. Create the reference planes at an offset distance of 305, 457, 609, 761, and 964 mm from the Front Plane by using the **Plane** tool.

   After creating all reference planes, you need to create profile of different sections of the loft feature.

2. Invoke the sketcher environment by selecting the **Plane4** which is at 305 mm from the Front Plane as the sketching plane and draw the circle of diameter 32 mm, refer to Figure 7-11. Next, exit from the sketcher environment.

3. Invoke the sketcher environment by selecting the **Plane5** which is at 457 mm from the Front Plane as the sketching plane and draw the circle of diameter 57 mm, refer to Figure 7-12. Next, exit from the sketch environment.

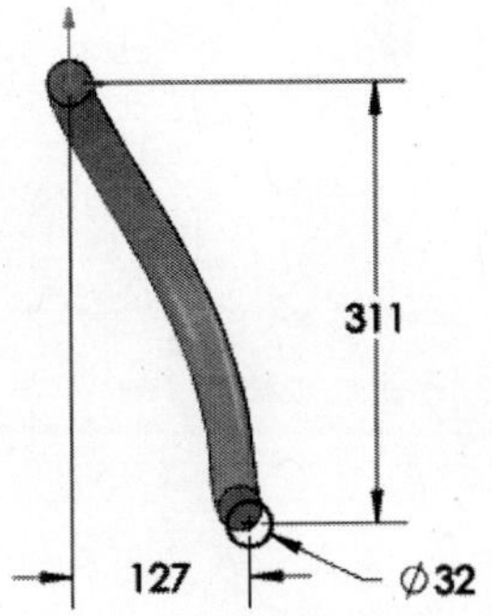

Figure 7-11 Sketch created on ***Plane4***

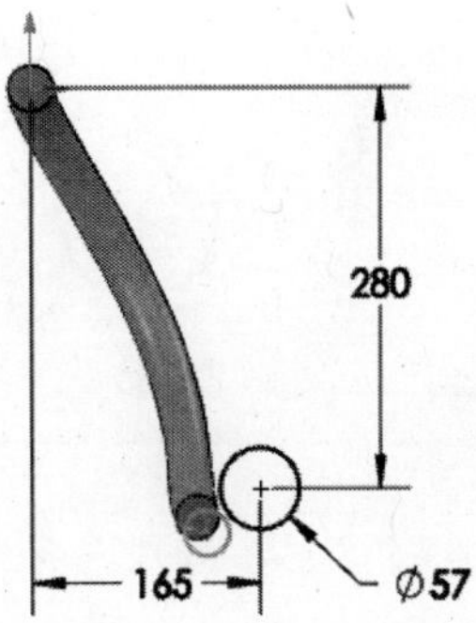

Figure 7-12 Sketch created on ***Plane5***

4. Invoke the sketcher environment by selecting the **Plane6** which is at 609 mm from the Front Plane as the sketching plane and draw a circle of diameter 108 mm, refer to Figure 7-13. Next, exit from the sketcher environment.

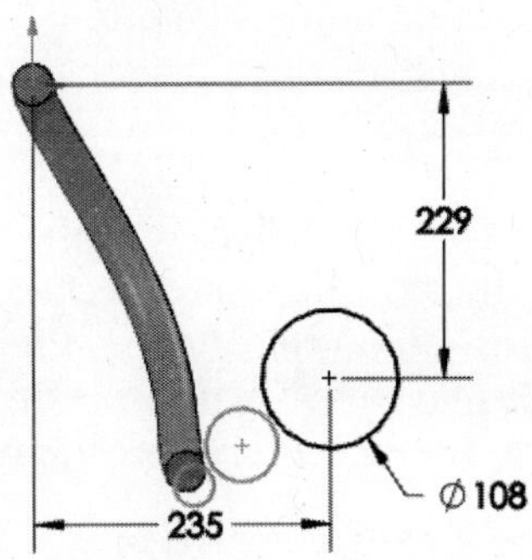

Figure 7-13 Sketch created on ***Plane6***

5. Similarly, draw the circle of diameter 114 mm on the **Plane7** that measures 761 mm and the **Plane8** that measures 964 mm from the Front Plane, refer to Figures 7-14 and 7-15.

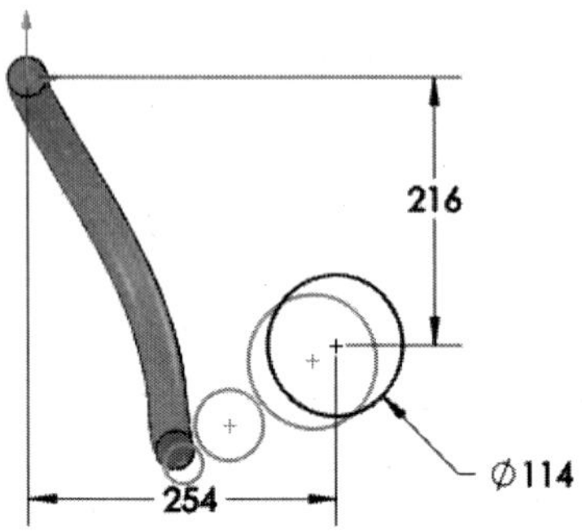

Figure 7-14 *Sketch created on* ***Plane7***

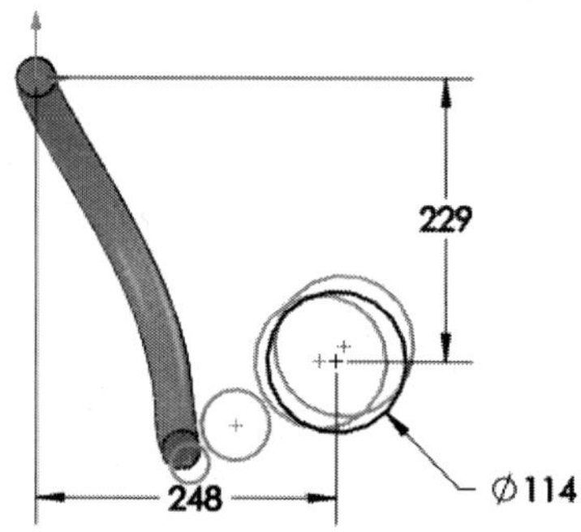

Figure 7-15 *Sketch created on* ***Plane8***

After creating all sections of the loft feature, you will invoke the **Loft PropertyManager** to create the loft feature.

6. Choose the **Lofted Boss/Base** button from the **Features CommandManager**; the **Loft PropertyManager** is displayed.

As discussed earlier, the **Lofted Boss/Base** tool is used to create loft features. In SOLIDWORKS, the loft features are created by blending more than one similar or dissimilar sections together to get a free form shape. These similar or dissimilar sections may or may not be parallel to each other.

7. Select the outer circular edge of the sweep feature as the first section of the loft feature, refer to Figure 7-16 and then from the drawing area, select the sketch of the second, third, forth, fifth, and sixth loft sections created on the **Plane4**, **Plane5**, **Plane6**, **Plane7**, and **Plane8**; preview of the loft feature is displayed in the drawing area with the connectors, as shown in Figure 7-17. Also, the names of the selections are displayed in the **Profile** selection box of the **Loft PropertyManager**.

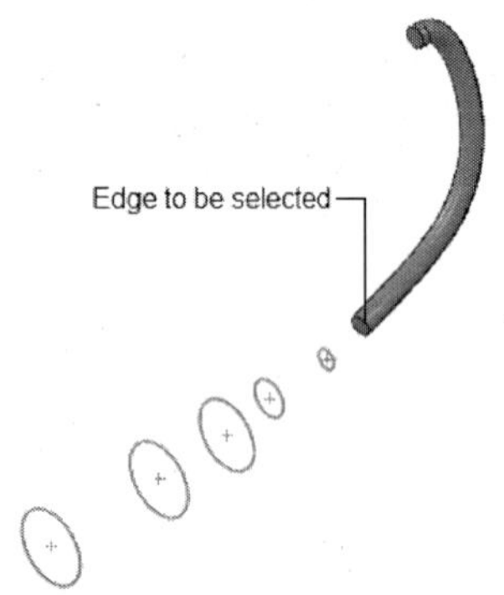

Figure 7-16 *Edge to be selected*

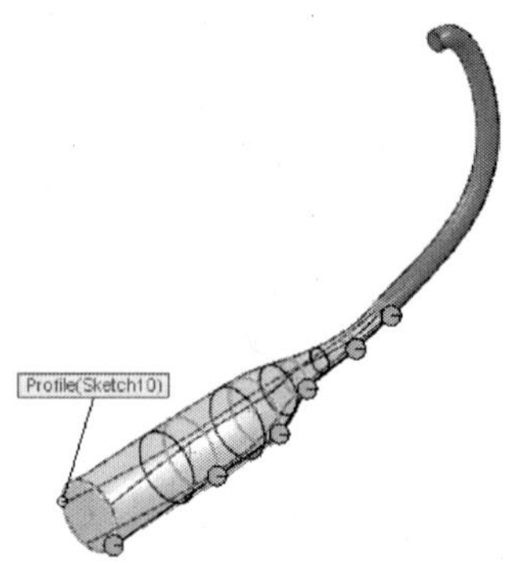

Figure 7-17 *Preview of the loft feature*

Note

All handles of the connector that appear as the filled circle in the preview should be in the same direction to avoid twisting. You can also reshape the loft feature by using these handles of the connector. To do so, press and hold the left mouse button on a handle, drag the cursor to specify a new location and release the left mouse button to place the connector on it. The process of controlling the loft shape using the connectors is known as Loft Synchronization.

Tip

Right-click in the drawing area and choose the ***Hide All Connectors*** *or* ***Show All Connectors*** *option from the shortcut menu to hide or show the connectors. Also, you can add more connectors to manipulate the loft feature. Connectors can be added to the straight profiles or the curved profiles. To add a connector, right-click in the sketch where a connector is to be added and choose the* ***Add Connector*** *option from the shortcut menu; a connector will be added to the loft feature.*

8. Expand the **Start/End Constraints** rollout of the **Loft PropertyManager** to define the tangency by clicking on the down arrow available on the right in the rollout.

In the **Start/End Constraints** rollout of the PropertyManager is used to define the constraints at the start and end sections of the loft feature. You can define the normal, tangency, or continuity constraints for the loft feature.

9. Select the **Tangency To Face** option from the **Start constraint** drop-down list in the **Start/End Constraints** rollout of the PropertyManager.

The **Tangency To Face** option is available only if the resulting loft feature will lie on an existing feature. If you select this option from the **Start constraint** or the **End constraint** drop-down list, the resulting loft feature will maintain the tangency along the adjacent curved faces. The face, along which the tangency is to be maintained, will be highlighted. You can also switch between the faces along which you need to maintain the tangency using the **Next Face** button. The spinners below the **Next Face** button can be used to specify the length of the start and end tangerines. You can also select the **Normal To Profile**, **Direction Vector** or **Curvature To Face** options from the **Start constraint** and the **End constraint** drop-down lists.

The **Normal To Profile** option is used to define the tangency normal to the profile. The **Direction Vector** is used to define the tangency at the start and end of the loft feature by defining a direction vector and the **Curvature To Face** option is used to maintain the curvature along the adjacent curved faces. This option will be available only if the resultant loft feature lies on an existing feature.

10. Select the **None** option from the **End constraint** drop-down list of the **Start/End Constraints** rollout, if not selected.

The **None** option implies that no constraint is applied to the loft feature.

11. Select the **OK** button from the **Loft PropertyManager**; the loft feature is created, as shown in Figure 7-18.

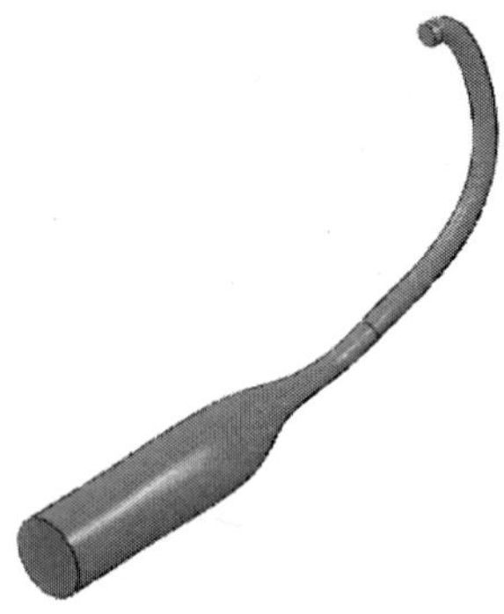

Figure 7-18 *Model after creating the loft feature*

Creating the Extrude Feature

The next feature of the model is a extrude feature.

1. Invoke the sketcher environment by selecting the front circular face of the loft feature as the sketching plane and draw a circle of diameter 51 mm, refer to Figure 7-19.

2. Exit from the sketcher environment and extrude the sketch to the distance of 51 mm by using the **Extruded Boss/Base** tool. The isometric view of the model after creating the extruded feature is shown in Figure 7-20.

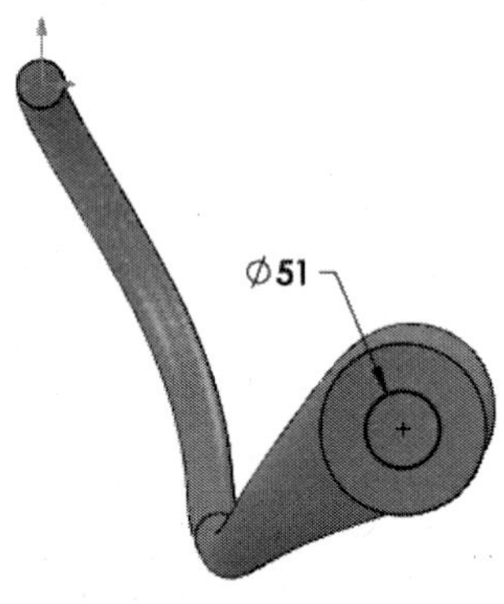

Figure 7-19 *Sketch of the extruded feature*

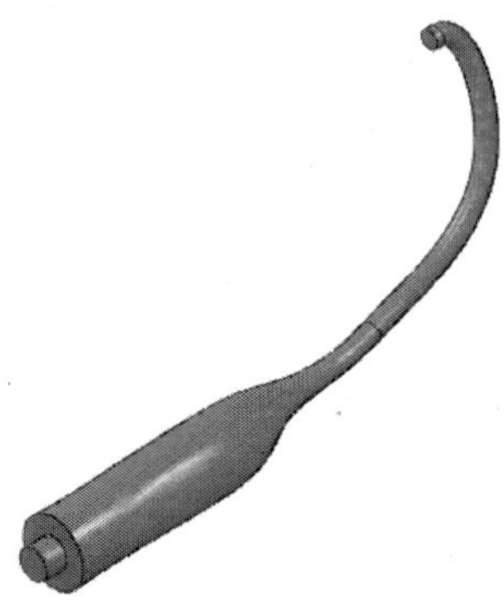

Figure 7-20 *Model after creating extruded feature*

Creating the Fillet Feature

Now, you will apply fillet to the model by using the **Fillet** tool.

1. Invoke the **Fillet PropertyManager** and you are prompted to select the edges, faces, features, or loops to fillet.

2. Select the face to be fillet, refer to Figure 7-21; preview of the fillet feature is displayed in the drawing area with the default radius value.

Note

When you select a face to add fillet feature, fillet will be added to all the connecting edges of the selected face.

3. Set the value of the **Radius** spinner to **7.5** in the **Fillet Parameters** rollout of the PropertyManager.

4. Choose the **OK** button from the PropertyManager; the fillet feature is created. The isometric view of the model after creating the fillet feature is shown in Figure 7-22.

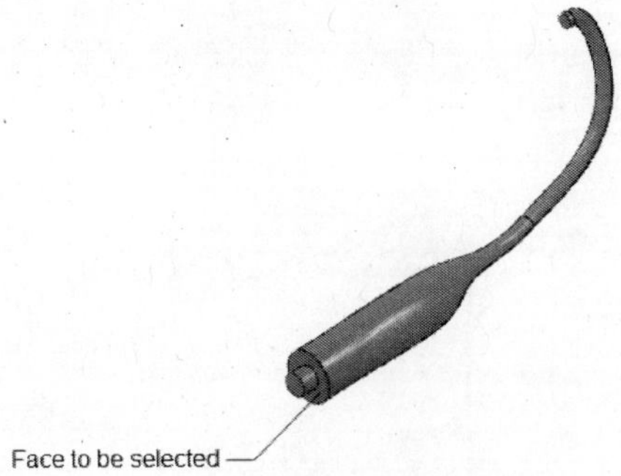

Figure 7-21 Face to be selected

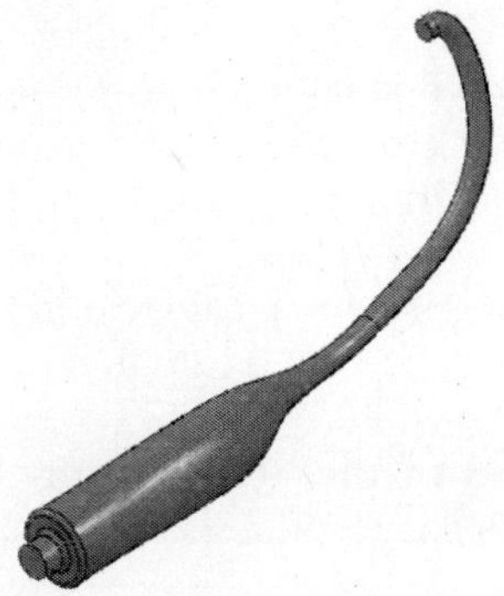

Figure 7-22 Model after adding fillet feature

Creating the Shell Feature

The next feature of the model is a shell feature.

1. Invoke the **Shell PropertyManager** and set the value of the **Thickness** spinner to **2.5** in the **Parameters** rollout of the PropertyManager.

2. Select the faces to be removed from the model, refer to Figure 7-23; the name of the selected faces are displayed in the **Faces to Remove** selection box of the PropertyManager.

3. Choose the **OK** button; the shell feature is created. The final model after shelling the model is shown in Figure 7-24.

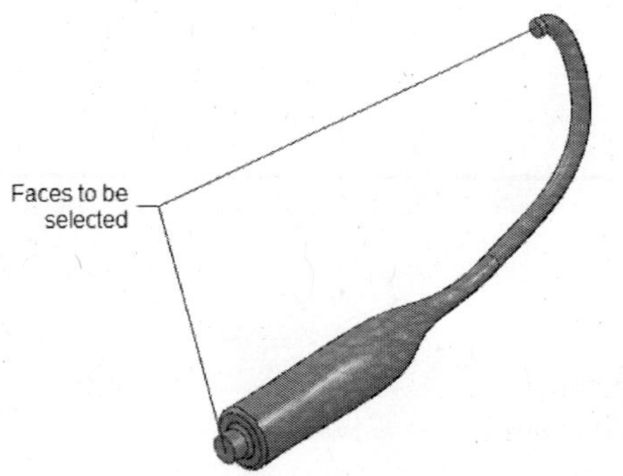

Figure 7-23 Faces to be selected

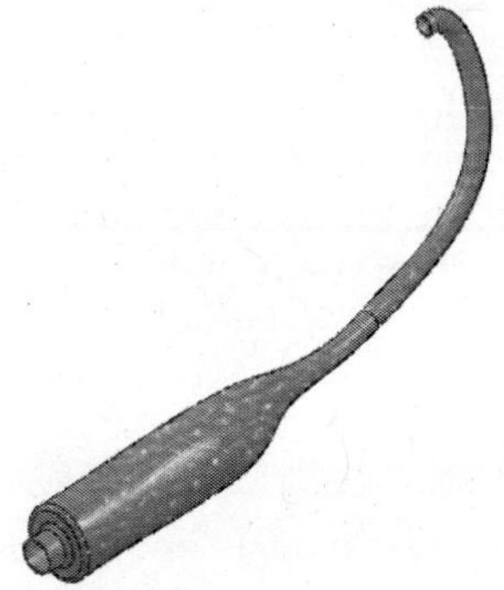

Figure 7-24 Model after creating the shell feature

Wrapping Text on the Model

Next, you need to write a text and extrude it using the **Emboss** option. This option is available in the **Wrap Type** rollout in the **Wrap PropertyManager**.

1. Create a reference plane at an offset distance of 356 mm from the Right Plane. Note that you can create a reference plane of different offset distance also, but it should be in the right side of the model.

2. Invoke the sketcher environment by selecting the newly created reference plane as the sketching plane.

3. Choose the **Text** button from the **Sketch CommandManager**; the **Sketch Text PropertyManager** is displayed on the left side of the drawing area, refer to Figure 7-25.

The **Text** tool is used to create text in the sketcher environment that can be later used to create join or cut features.

4. Enter text in the **Text** box in the **Text** rollout of the PropertyManager; the text will start from the origin.

5. After entering the text in the **Text** box of the **Text** rollout, clear the **Use document font** check box available at the bottom of the PropertyManager to choose the font other then the default one. As soon as, you will clear this check box, the **Font** button is enabled below the check box.

6. Choose the **Font** button from the PropertyManager; the **Choose Font** dialog box is displayed. Next, choose the required font, font style, and size for the text from the dialog box and then choose the **OK** button from it.

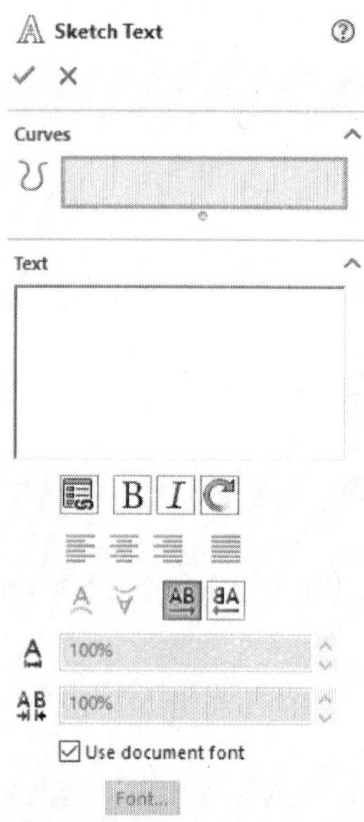

Figure 7-25** The **Sketch Text PropertyManager

7. Choose the **OK** button from the **Sketch Text PropertyManager**; the text is created and you will notice a dot at the start of the text on the origin.

8. After creating the text, you need to place it at the required location. To place the text at the required location, drag the dot that is at the start of the text and place it at the required location, refer to Figure 7-26. You can also drag the text itself to change its location.

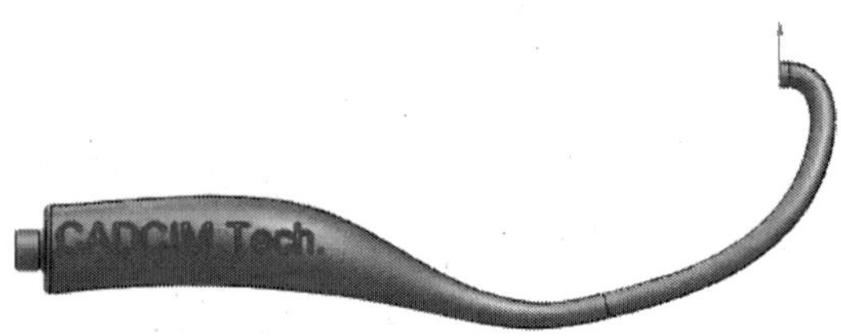

***Figure 7-26** Text is placed at required location*

9. Exit from the sketcher environment and then invoke the **Wrap** tool and select the text from the drawing area.

10. Select the **Emboss** option from the **Wrap Type** rollout in the **Wrap PropertyManager**.

The **Emboss** option is used to create an extrude feature on the selected face.

11. Select the outer face of the loft feature, refer to Figure 7-27. Next, make sure that the **Spline Surface** option is selected in the **Wrap Parameters** rollout of the PropertyManager and the value of the **Thickness** spinner is set to **2.1**.

12. Choose the **OK** button from the PropertyManager; the wrap feature is created. Next, the model after creating the wrap feature with black color assigned is shown in Figure 7-28.

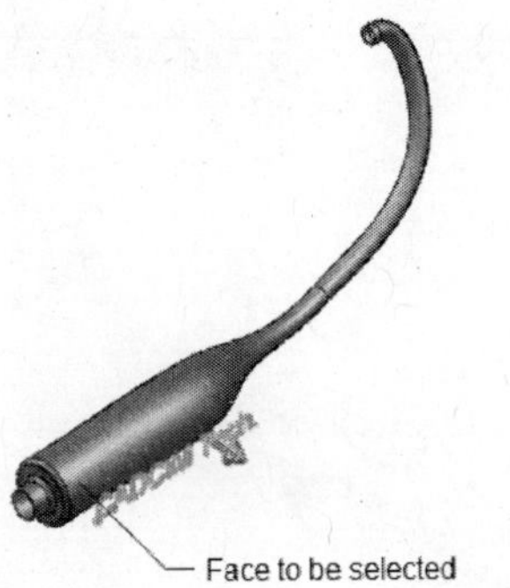

Figure 7-27 *Faces to be selected*

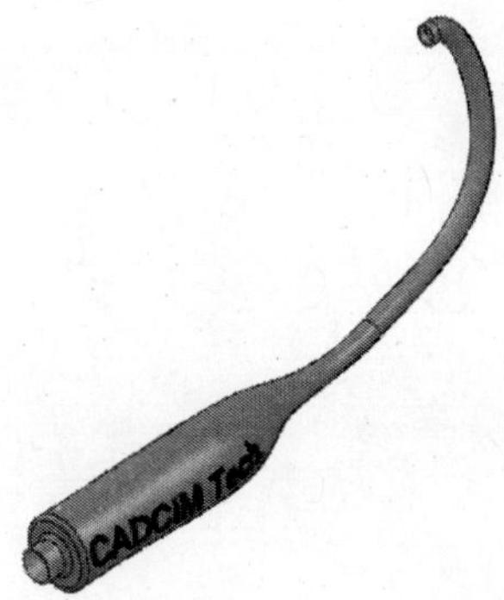

Figure 7-28 *The extruded feature is created*

Creating the Remaining Extruded Features

Next, you will create the remaining extruded features of the model.

1. Create the remaining extruded features of the model using the **Extruded Boss/Base** tool. For dimensions refer to Figure 7-2. The model after creating the remaining extruded features is shown in Figure 7-29.

Assigning Material to the Model

As mentioned in the part description, you will assign Alloy Steel (SS) material to the model.

1. Select the **Material <not specified>** option from the **FeatureManager design tree** and right-click to display a shortcut menu.

2. Choose the **Edit Material** option from the shortcut menu; the **Material** dialog box is displayed.

The **Material** dialog box is used to assigned material to the model. Whenever, you assign a material to a model, all the physical properties of the selected material are also assigned to the model. As a result, when you calculate the mass properties of the model, they will be based on the physical properties of the material applied.

Tip

*You can also invoke the **Material** dialog box by choosing the **Edit > Appearance > Material** from the SOLIDWORKS menus.*

3. Click on the > sign located on the left of the Steel option from the list of material available on the left area of the dialog box; the tree view expands and materials in this family are displayed.

4. Select the **Alloy Steel (SS)** option and choose the **Apply** button from the **Material** dialog box and then choose the **Close** button to exit. The model after assigning the material is shown in Figure 7-30.

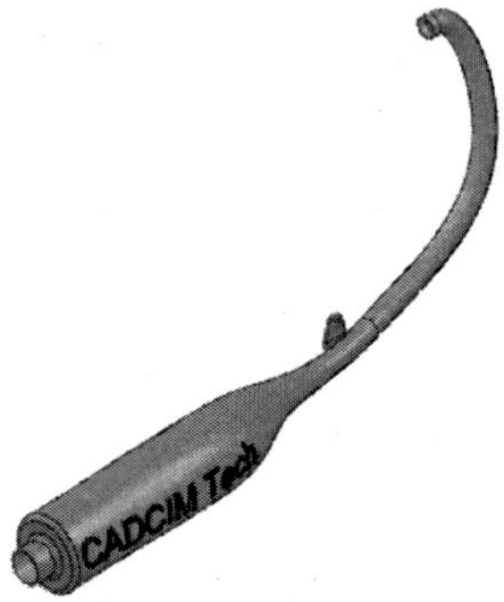

Figure 7-29 *Model after creating the extruded features*

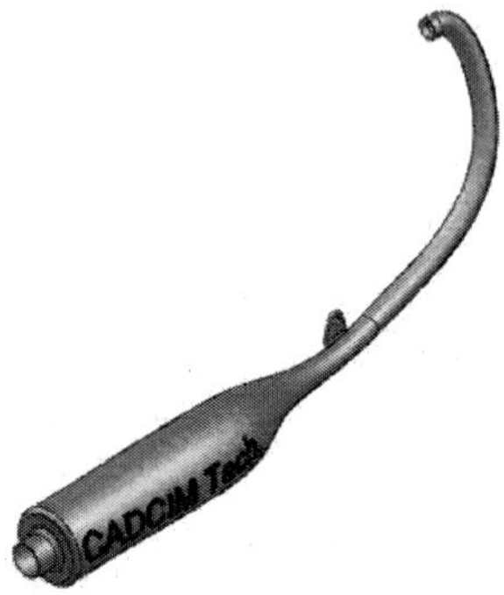

Figure 7-30 *Model after assigning the Alloy Steel (SS) material*

Determining the Mass Properties of the Model

As mentioned in the part description, you will determine the mass properties of the model. To determine the mass properties of the model, you need to invoke the **Mass Properties** dialog box.

1. Click on the **Evaluate** tab in the **CommandManagers** to invoke the **Evaluate CommandManager**.

2. Choose the **Mass Properties** button from the **Evaluate CommandManager**; the **Mass Properties** dialog box is displayed with the mass properties of the current model, as shown in Figure 7-31.

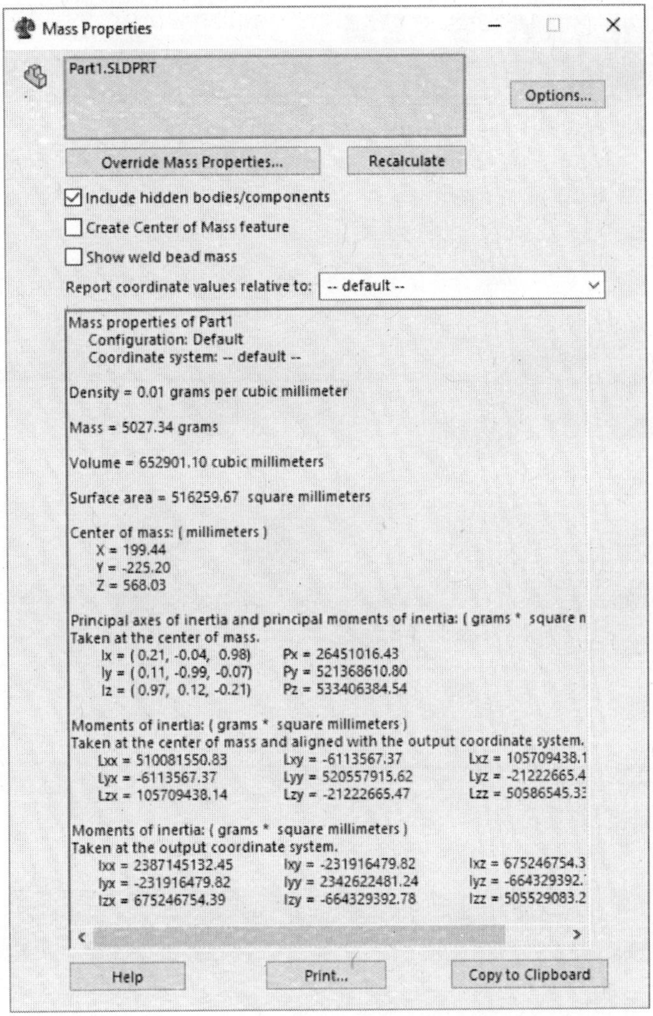

*Figure 7-31 The **Mass Properties** dialog box*

Saving the Model

After completing the model, you need to save it in the *Motor Cycle Project* folder.

1. Invoke the **Save As** dialog box and browse to the *Motor Cycle Project* folder.

2. Enter **Muffler** as the name of the model in the **File name** edit box and choose the **Save** button. The document will be saved in the *\Documents\Motor Cycle Project\Muffler*.

3. Close the document by choosing **File > Close** from the SOLIDWORKS menus.

CREATING THE SWING ARM

Part Description

In this section, you will create the Swing Arm, as shown in Figure 7-32. The views and dimensions of the Handle Bar are given in the Figure 7-33. **(Expected time: 25 min)**

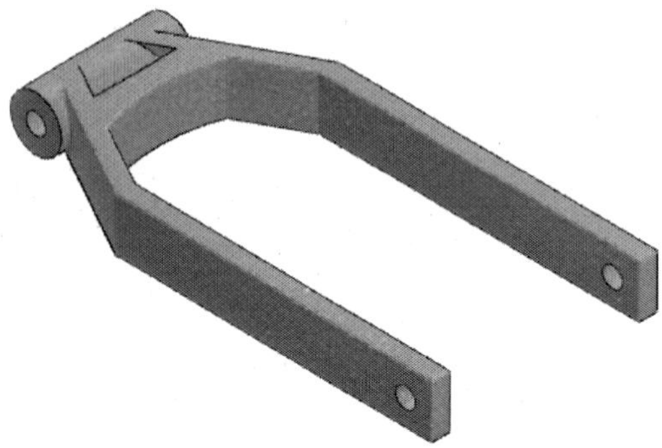

Figure 7-32 *The Swing Arm*

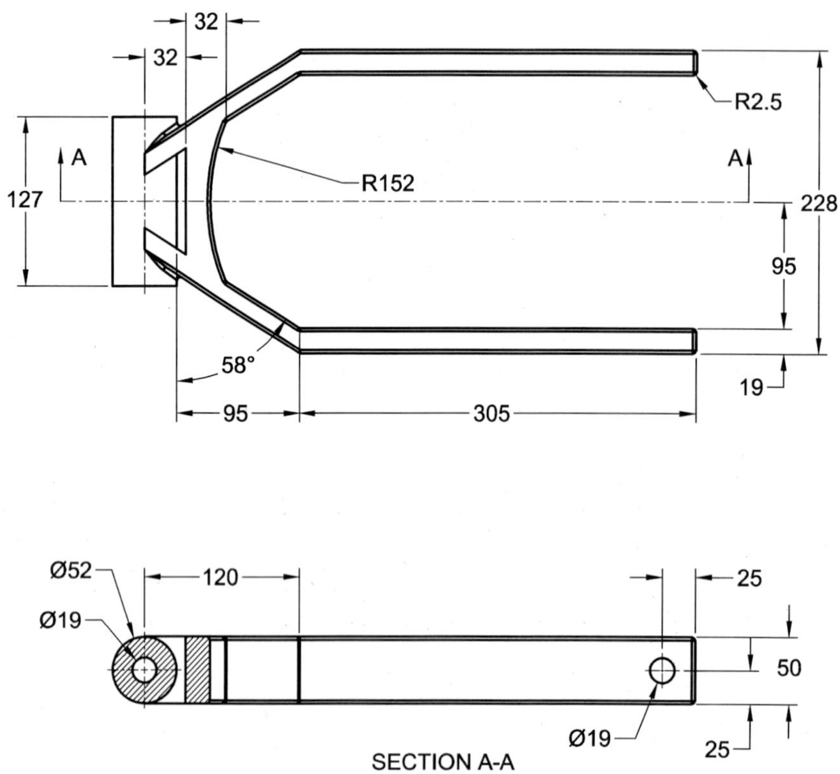

Figure 7-33 *The top and front views of the model*

Starting a New Part Document

1. Start a new SOLIDWORKS part document using the **New SOLIDWORKS Document** dialog box.

Creating the Base Feature

The base feature of the model is an extrude feature.

1. Invoke the **Extruded Boss/Base** tool and create the base feature of the model by selecting the Front Plane as the sketching plane. For dimensions of the base feature, refer to Figure 7-33. The model after creating the base feature is shown in Figure 7-34.

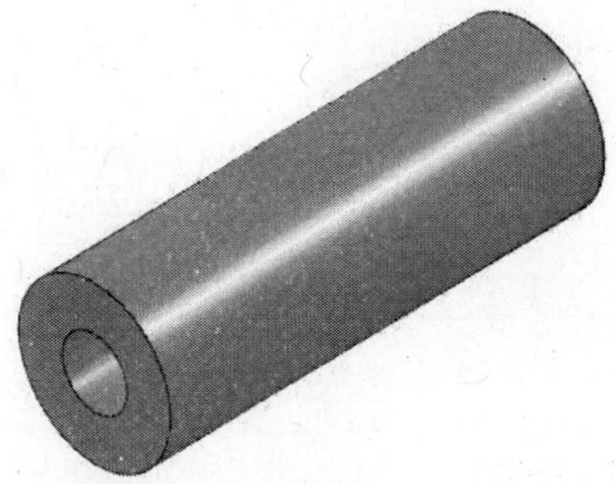

Figure 7-34 *Model after creating the base feature*

Note

*The base feature of this model is created by extruding the sketch using the **Mid Plane** option.*

Creating the Next Feature

The next feature of the model is an extrude feature. This extrude feature is extruded along a particular direction. Therefore, first you need to draw a sketch to define the direction of the extrusion and then sketch of the extrude feature on the reference plane. The reference plane will be created at an offset distance of 120 mm from the Right Plane.

1. Invoke the sketcher environment by selecting the Top Plane as the sketching plane and draw the sketch that will define the direction of the extrusion, refer to Figure 7-35 and then exit from the sketcher environment. Note that the dimensions shown in the Figure 7-35 are for your reference only.

   After drawing the sketch to define the direction of extrusion, you need to create a reference plane that will be used to draw the sketch of the extrude feature.

2. Invoke the **Plane PropertyManager** and create the reference plane at an offset distance of 120 mm from the Right Plane.

   After creating the reference plane, you need to draw the sketch of the extrude feature on it.

3. Invoke the **Extrude PropertyManager** and select the newly created plane as the sketching plane to invoke the sketcher environment.

4. Draw the sketch of the extrude feature, refer to Figure 7-36 and then exit from the sketcher environment; the **Boss-Extrude PropertyManager** is displayed. Change the current view to isometric view.

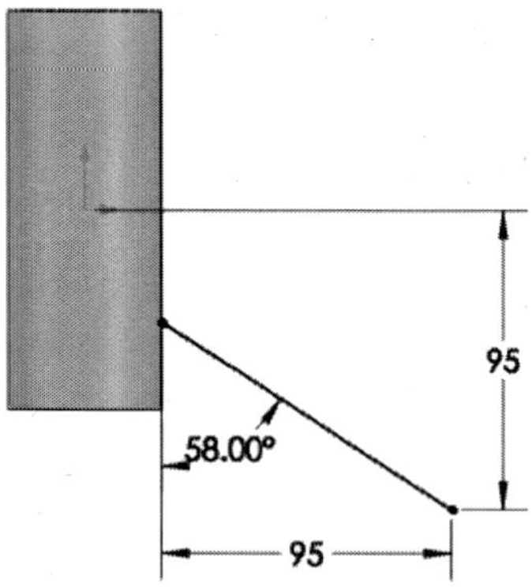

Figure 7-35 *Sketch for defining the direction of extrusion*

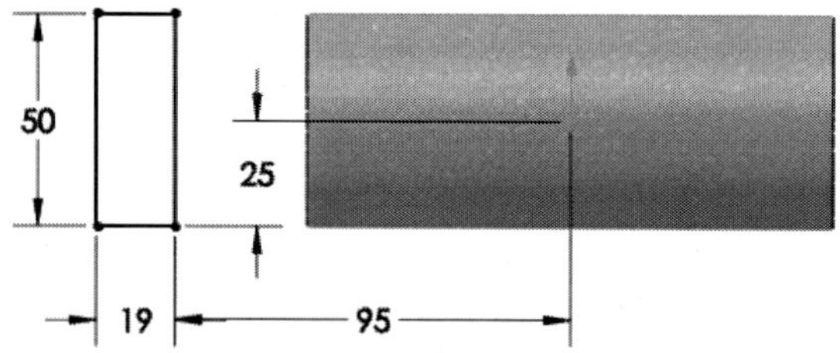

Figure 7-36 *Sketch of the extrude feature*

5. Choose the **Reverse Direction** button to reverse the direction of feature creation from the **Direction 1** rollout of the PropertyManager.

6. Click on the **Direction of Extrusion** selection box in the **Direction 1** rollout of PropertyManager to activate its selection mode.

In SOLIDWORKS, you can define the direction for extruding the sketches by using the **Direction of Extrusion** selection box. As mentioned in the pervious chapter, the direction of extrusion is generally normal to the sketching plane. You can also define the direction of extrusion using the sketched line, an edge, or a reference axis. Note that the entity you want to use for defining the direction of extrusion should not be drawn on the sketch plane parallel to the plane on which the sketch to be extruded is drawn.

7. Select the sketch from the drawing area that is created to define the direction of extrusion.

8. Select the **Up To Surface** option from the **End Condition** drop-down list of the PropertyManager; the **Face/Plane** selection area is displayed below the **Direction of Extrusion** selection area.

9. Select the cylindrical face of the base feature and then choose the **OK** button from the PropertyManager; the extrude feature is created. Next, hide the sketch and reference plane from the drawing area. The model after creating the extruded feature is shown in Figure 7-37.

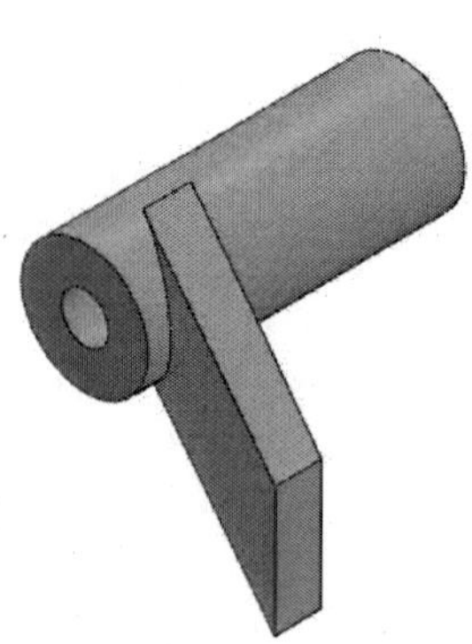

Figure 7-37 *Model after creating the extruded feature*

Creating the Extrude Feature

The next feature of the model is also a extrude feature.

1. Create the extrude feature, as shown in Figure 7-38. For dimensions of this extrude feature, refer to Figure 7-33.

Mirroring the Features

Now, you will create the mirror image of the last two extruded features by selecting Front Plane as the mirroring plane.

1. Invoke the **Mirror PropertyManager** and select the Front Plane as a mirroring plane.

2. Select the last two extruded feature as the mirroring features and choose the **OK** button from the PropertyManager. The model after mirroring the last two extruded feature is shown in Figure 7-39.

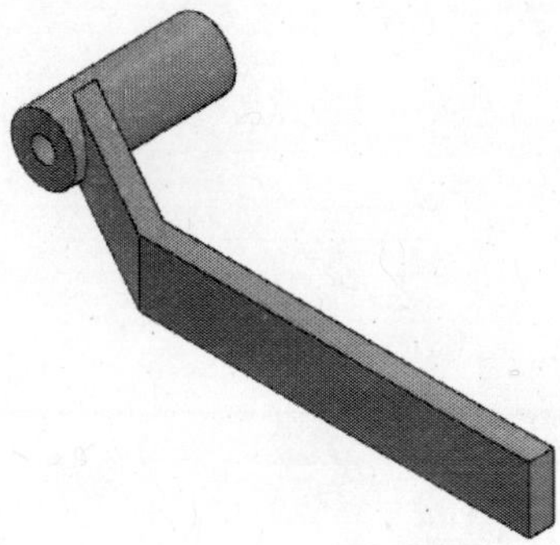

Figure 7-38 *Model after creating the extrude feature*

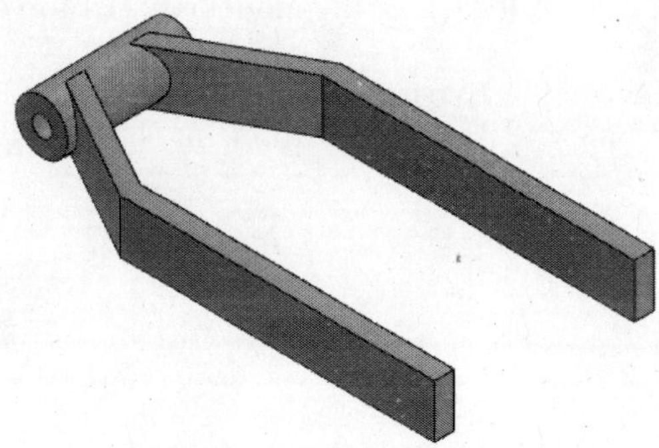

Figure 7-39 *Model after mirroring the features*

Creating the Next Feature

The next feature of the model is a extrude feature.

1. Invoke the sketcher environment by selecting the top planar face of the model as the sketching plane.

2. Draw the sketch of the extrude feature, refer to Figure 7-40. Next, exit from the sketcher environment.

3. Invoke the **Extruded Boss/Base** tool and extrude the newly created sketch by using the **Up To Surface** option and by selecting the bottom planar face of the model as the surface up to which you want to extrude the sketch. The model after creating the extrude feature is shown in Figure 7-41.

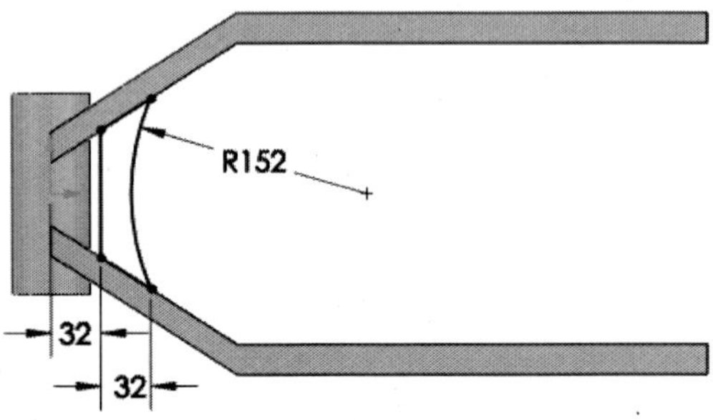

Figure 7-40 Sketch of the extrude feature

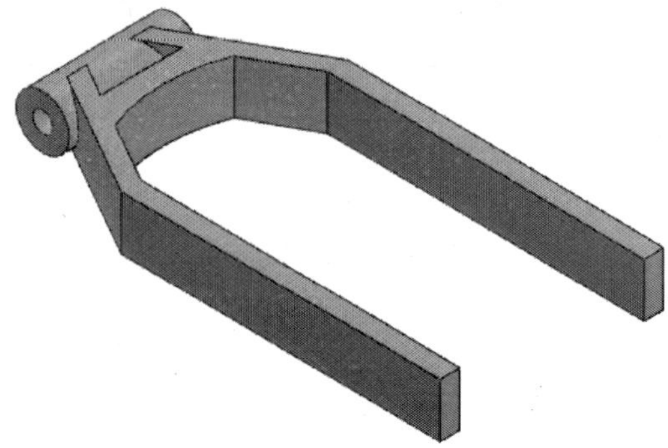

Figure 7-41 Model after creating the extrude feature

Creating the Extrude Cut Feature

The next feature of the model is a extrude cut feature.

1. Invoke the **Extruded Cut** tool and select the face, as shown Figure 7-42 as the sketching plane; the sketcher environment is invoked.

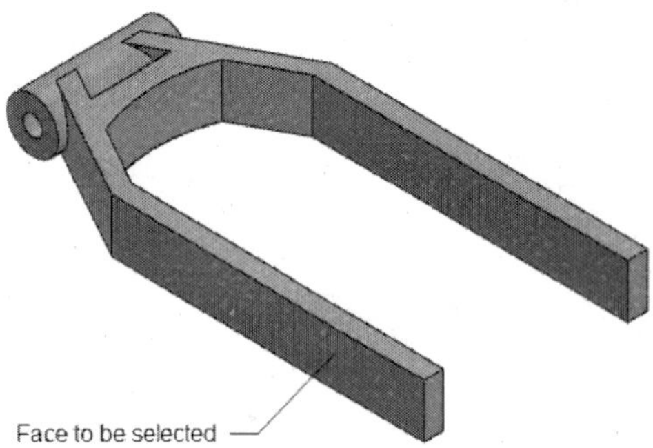

Figure 7-42 Face to be selected

2. Draw the sketch of the cut feature, as shown in Figure 7-43. Next, exit from the sketcher environment and extrude the sketch through all the model, refer to Figure 7-44.

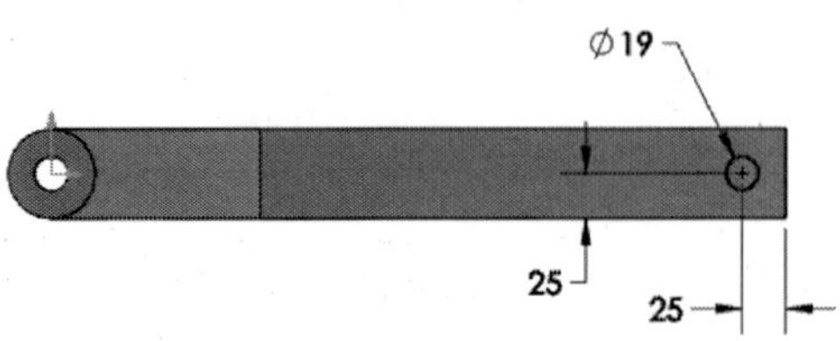

Figure 7-43 Sketch of the extrude cut feature

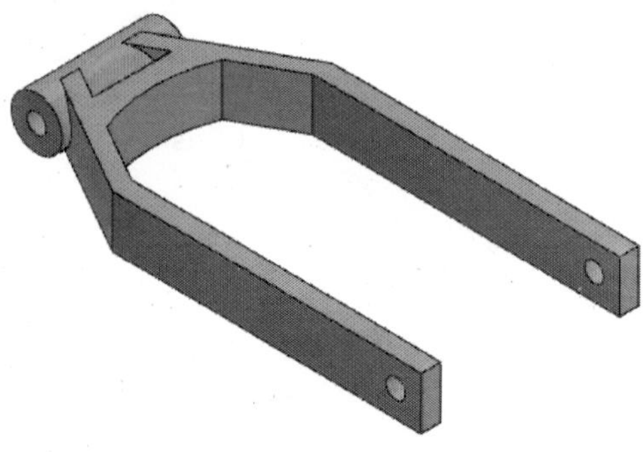

Figure 7-44 Model after creating the extrude cut feature

Applying the Fillet

After creating all the features of the model, you will apply fillet on the required edges of the model.

1. Invoke the **Fillet PropertyManager** and then choose the **FilletXpert** button from the PropertyManager. As soon as you choose the **FilletXpert** button, the **Fillet PropertyManager** will be changed to **FilletXpert PropertyManager**.

The **FilletXpert PropertyManager** allows you to create single or multiple fillets, change the existing fillet, and create fillets at corners.

2. Set the value of the **Radius** spinner to **2.5 mm** and then select the edge of the model, refer to Figure 7-45; a pop-up toolbar is displayed near the cursor. Also, the name of the selected edge is displayed in the **Edges, Faces, Features and Loops** selection box of the **Items To Fillet** rollout.

3. Choose the **Connected, 33 Edges** button from the pop-up toolbar; all the related edges are displayed in the **Edges, Faces, Features and Loops** selection box of the **Items To Fillet** rollout.

4. Choose the **Apply** button from the **Items To Fillet** rollout and then **OK** button from the **FilletXpert PropertyManager**. The final model after applying the fillet is shown in Figure 7-46.

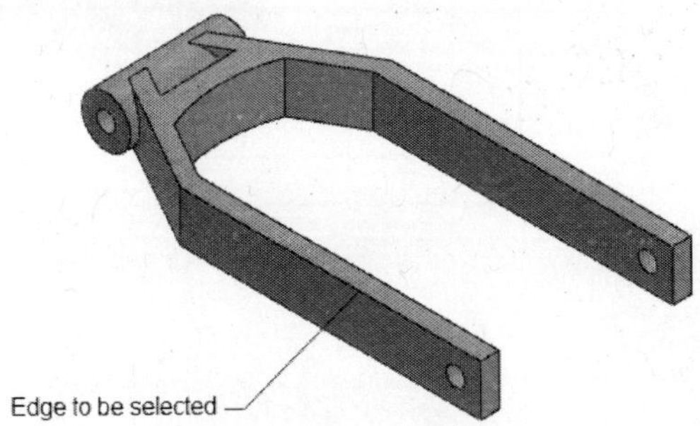

Figure 7-45 *Edge to be selected*

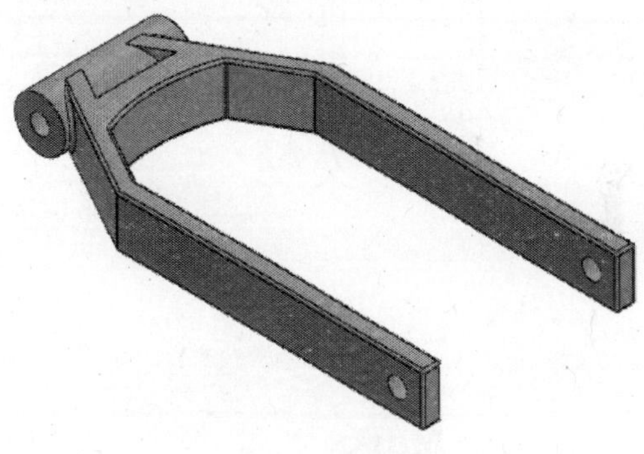

Figure 7-46 *Final model after applying fillet*

Saving the Model

After create the model, you need to save it in the *Motor Cycle Project* folder.

1. Invoke the **Save As** dialog box and browse to the location *Motor Cycle Project* folder.

2. Enter the name of the model as **Swing Arm** in the **File name** edit box and choose the **Save** button. The document will be saved in the *\Documents\Motor Cycle Project\Swing Arm*.

3. Close the document by choosing **File > Close** from the SOLIDWORKS menus.

CREATING THE CLAMP

In this section, you will create the Clamp, as shown in Figure 7-47. The views and dimensions of the Clamp are given in the Figure 7-48. **(Expected time: 15 min)**

Figure 7-47 *The Swing Arm*

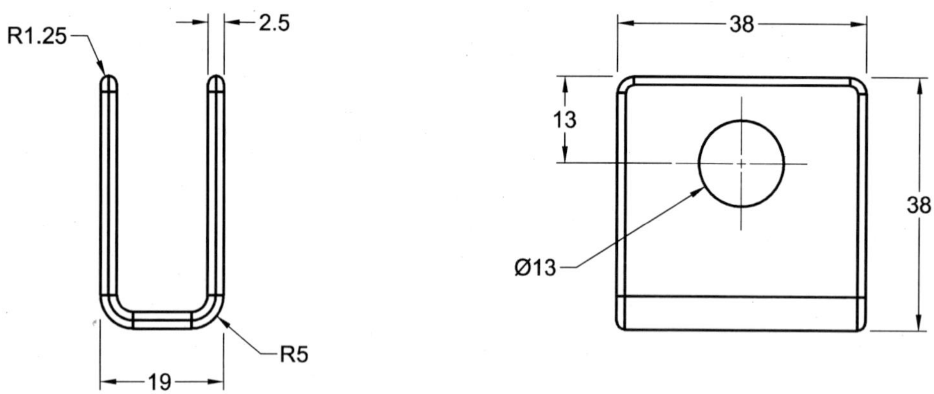

Figure 7-48 *The front and side views of the model*

Creating the Model

The base feature of the model is an extrude feature and the second feature of the model is a cut feature.

1. Start a new SOLIDWORKS Part document.

2. Create the base feature of the model, as shown in Figure 7-.49. Next, create the cut feature, as shown Figure 7-50. For dimensions of the base and cut features, refer to Figure 7-48.

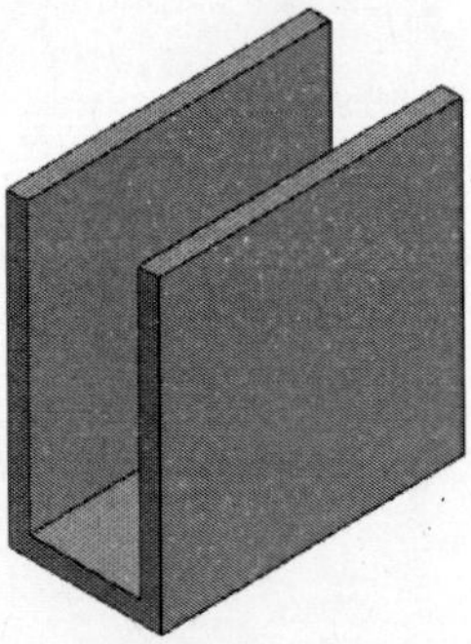

Figure 7-49 Edge to be selected

Figure 7-50 Final model after applying fillet

3. Apply fillets on the sharp edges of the model. For fillet radius refer to Figure 7-48. The final model after applying the fillet is shown in Figure 7-51.

Figure 7-51 Final model after applying fillets

Saving the Model

After creating the model, you need to save it in the *Motor Cycle Project* folder.

1. Save the model in the *Motor Cycle Project* folder by specifying it name as Clamp and then close the document.

EXERCISE

Exercise

In this exercise, you will create a Headlight Clamp, as shown in Figure 7-52. The views and dimensions of the model are given in the Figure 7-53. All the dimensions are in inches. After completing the model, save it at the location \Documents\Motor Cycle Project and name it *Headlight Clamp*.

(Expected time: 15 min)

Figure 7-52 The Headlight Clamp

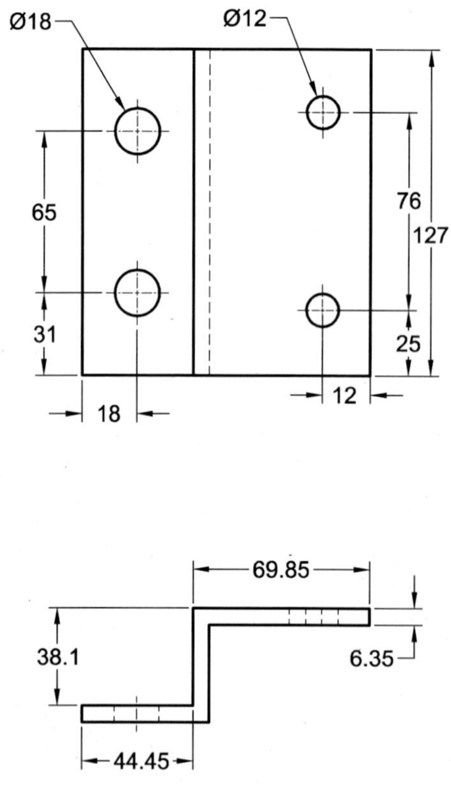

Figure 7-53 Top and front views of the model

Self-Evaluation Test

Answer the following questions and then compare them to those given at the end of this chapter:

1. Choose the __________ button from the Features CommandManager to create a loft feature.

2. __________ features are created by blending more than one similar or dissimilar sections together.

3. Choose the **Lofted Boss/Base** button from the Features CommandManager to invoke the __________ **PropertyManager**.

4. The __________ rollout of the **Loft PropertyManager** is used to define constraints at the start and end sections of the loft feature.

5. The __________ tool is used to create text in the sketcher environment.

6. The __________ dialog box is used to assign material to the model.

7. When you select a face to add fillet feature, fillet will be added to all the connecting edges of the selected face. (T/F)

8. The **None** option is used to implies that tangent constaint is applied to the loft feature. (T/F)

Review Questions

Answer the following questions:

1. The __________ **PropertyManager** allows you to create single or multiple fillets, change an existing fillet, and create fillets at corners.

2. The __________ selection area of the **Boss-Extrude PropertyManager** is used to define the user-defined direction of extrusion.

3. Whenever you assign a material to a model, all the physical properties of the selected material are also assigned to the model. (T/F)

4. The __________ option is used to start the extrude feature from a selected surface, face, or a plane, instead of the plane on which the sketch is drawn.

5. You can not reshape a loft feature. (T/F)

6. If you select the __________ option from the **Start constraint** or the **End constraint** drop-down list, the resulting loft feature will maintain tangency along the adjacent curved feces.

7. Which one of the following options is used to define tangency at the start and end of the loft feature by defining a direction vector?

(a) **Normal To Profile** (b) **Tangency To Face**
(c) **Direction Vector** (d) None of these

8. Which one of the following tools is used to calculate mass properties of a model?

(a) **Mass Properties** (b) **Mass**
(c) **Mass Pro** (d) None of these

9. You can clear the **Use document font** check box of the **Sketch Text PropertyManager** to choose the font other then the default one. (T/F)

10. If you select the _________ option from the **Start constraint** or the **End constraint** drop-down list, the resulting loft feature will maintain tangency normal to the profile.

Answers to Self-Evaluation Test

1. Lofted Boss/Base, 2. loft, **3. Loft, 4. Start/End Constraints, 5. Text, 6. Material, 7.** T, **8.** F

Chapter 8

Creating Shock Absorber and Engine Parts

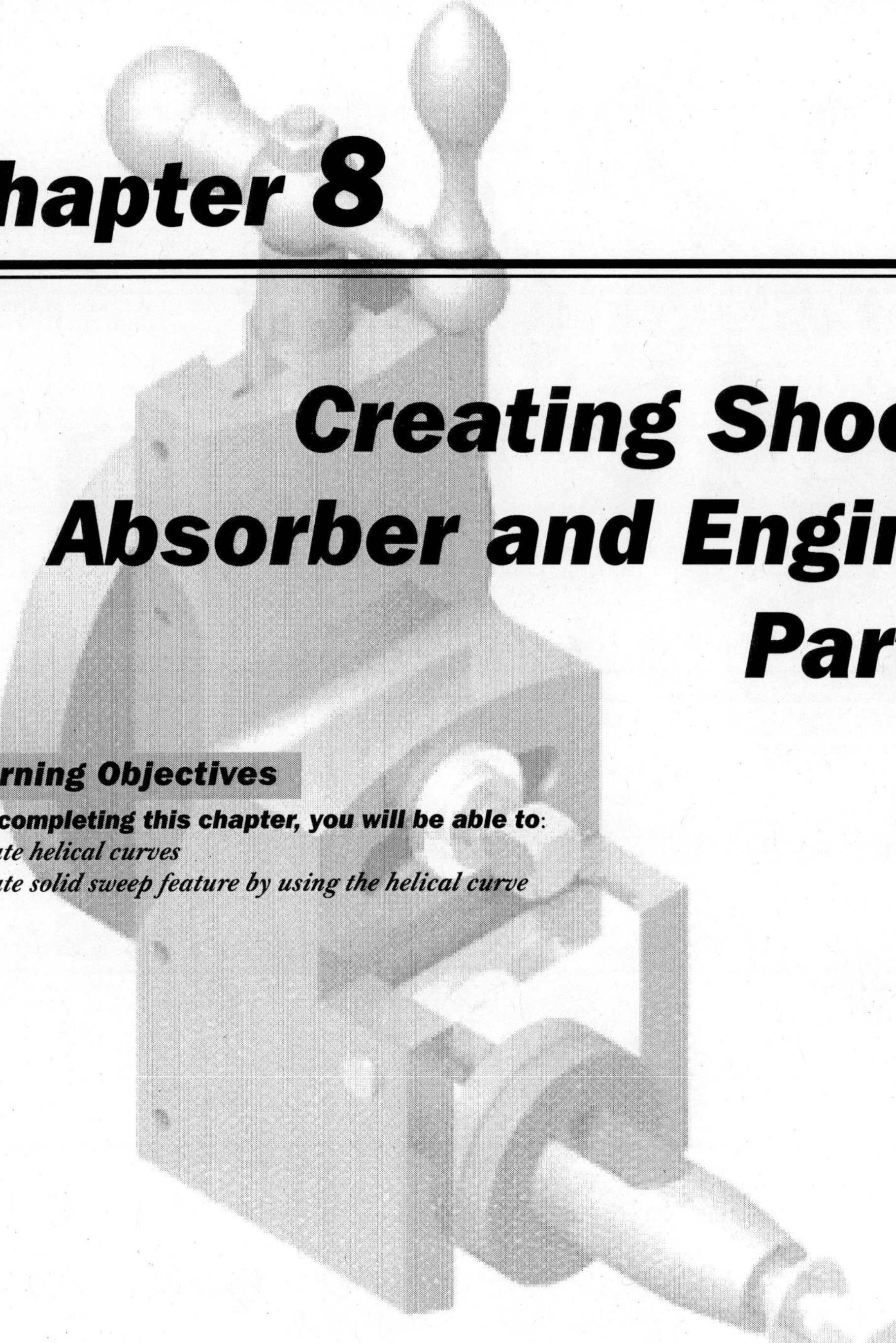

Learning Objectives

After completing this chapter, you will be able to:

- *Create helical curves*
- *Create solid sweep feature by using the helical curve*

CREATING THE SHOCK ABSORBER CYLINDER

Part Description

In this section, you will create the Shock Absorber Cylinder, as shown in Figure 8-1. The top and front views of the model with dimensions are given in the Figure 8-2. The wall thickness of the model is 2.5 mm. Also, apply fillets of radius 2.5 or 1.25 mm on the edges.

(Expected time: 55 min)

Figure 8-1 *The Shock Absorber Cylinder*

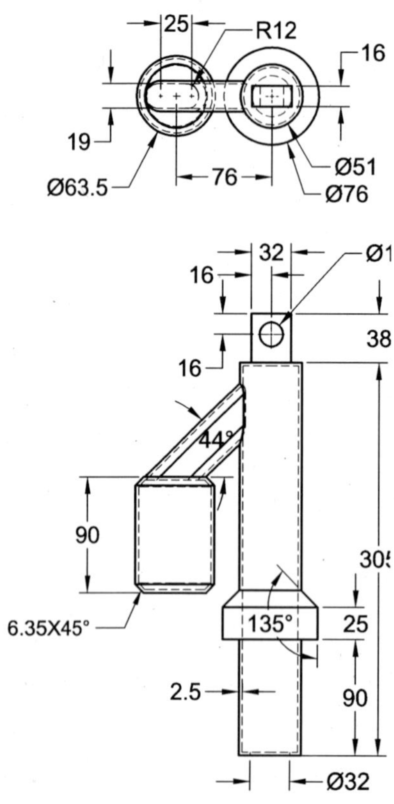

Figure 8-2 *Top and front views of the model*

Note

In Figure 8-2, the fillets and some of the hidden edges are removed for the clarity.

Starting a New Part Document

1. Start a new SOLIDWORKS part document using the **New SOLIDWORKS Document** dialog box.

   Once the new part document is invoked, you can create the base feature of the model.

Creating the Base Feature

The base feature of the model is an extrude feature, created on the Top Plane.

1. Invoke the sketching environment by selecting the Top Plane as the sketching plane and draw the sketch of the base feature, refer to Figure 8-3.

2. Exit the sketching environment and then extrude the sketch upto the distance of 305 mm in the upward direction, refer to Figure 8-4.

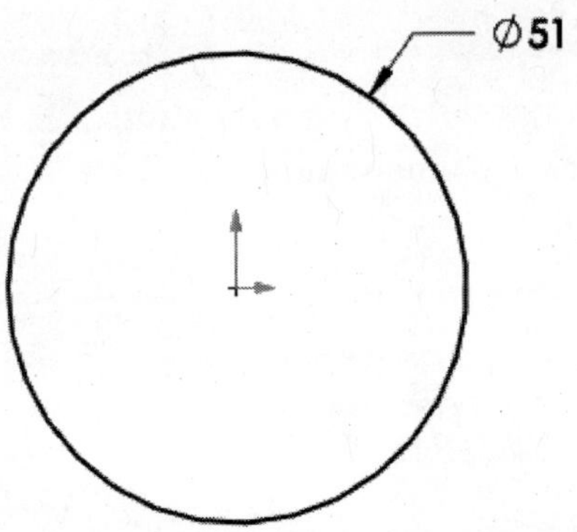

Figure 8-3 *Sketch of the base feature*

Figure 8-4 *Base feature of the model*

Creating the Second Feature

The second feature of the model is also an extrude feature. It is evident from Figure 8-2 that this extrude feature is created by extruding in the direction other than the default direction that is normal to the sketch. To create this feature, first you need to draw a sketch to define the direction of the extrusion on the Front Plane and then sketch of the extrude feature on the Top Plane.

1. Invoke the sketching environment by selecting the Front Plane as the sketching plane.

2. Draw the sketch that will define the direction of the extrusion, refer to Figure 8-5 and then exit the sketching environment.

   After having drawn the sketch to define the direction of extrusion, you need to draw the profile of extrusion.

3. Invoke the sketching environment by selecting the Top Plane as the sketching plane and draw the sketch of the extrude feature, refer to Figure 8-6.

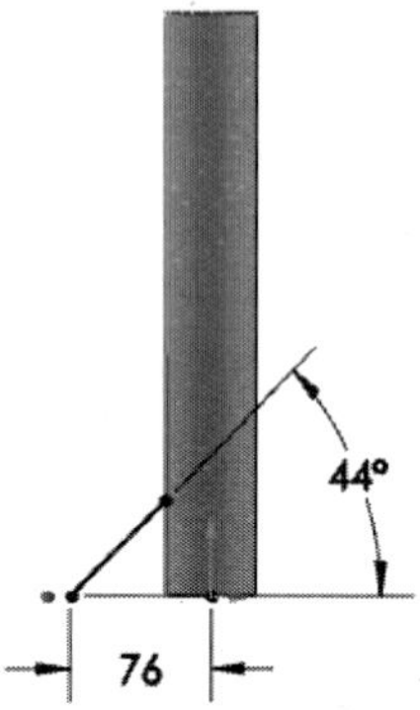

Figure 8-5 *Sketch to define the direction of extrusion*

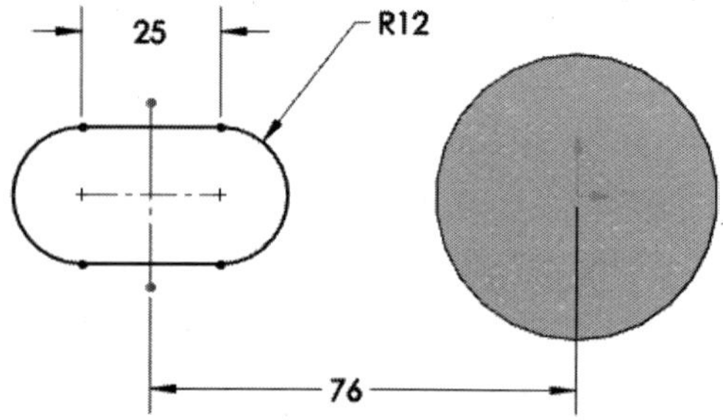

Figure 8-6 *Sketch of the extrude feature*

4. Exit the sketching environment and invoke the **Extruded Boss/Base** tool. Next, select the sketch of the extruded feature.

5. Select the **Offset** option from the **Start Condition** drop-drown in the **From** rollout of the **Boss-Extrude PropertyManager**. Next, set the value as 216 mm in the **Enter Offset Value** spinner of the **From** rollout.

Note

You can also create a reference plane at an offset distance of 216 mm from the Top Plane and select it as the sketching plane for creating the sketch of the second extruded feature, instead of creating the sketch in the Top Plane and then specifying the offset value from where the sketch will start extrusion.

6. Click in the **Direction of Extrusion** selection area in the **Direction 1** rollout of the PropertyManager to activate its selection mode. Next, select the sketch of line from the drawing area that is created to define the direction of extrusion; the preview of the feature is modified accordingly.

7. Select the **Up To Surface** option from the **End Condition** drop-down list of the **Direction 1** rollout in the PropertyManager and then select the circular face of the base feature. Next, choose the **OK** button from the PropertyManager; the second feature of the model is created. Hide the sketch created for defining the direction of extrusion from the drawing area. The model after hiding the sketch and creating the second feature is shown in Figure 8-7.

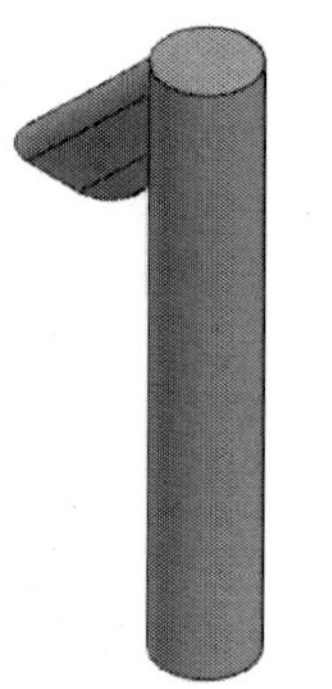

Figure 8-7 *Model after creating the extruded feature*

Creating the Third Feature

The third feature of the model is also an extrude feature.

1. Create the extrude feature, as shown in Figure 8-8. For dimensions, refer to Figure 8-3.

Creating the Chamfer

The next feature of the model is a chamfer feature. As discussed earlier, the chamfering is defined as a process in which the sharp edges are beveled in order to reduce the area of stress concentration.

1. Invoke the **Chamfer PropertyManager** by choosing the **Chamfer** button from the **Fillet** flyout.

2. Make sure that the **Angle distance** button is chosen in the **Chamfer Type** rollout of the PropertyManager. Next, select the sharp edges of the previously created extruded feature.

   The required values of the chamfer parameters are 6.35 mm and 45-degree. The value of the angle in the **Angle** spinner is set as 45-degree. Therefore, you do not need to modify this value. You need to set only the value of the distance in the **Distance** spinner.

3. Set the value of the distance in the **Distance** spinner to 6.35 mm and then choose the **OK** button. The model after creating the chamfer is shown in Figure 8-9.

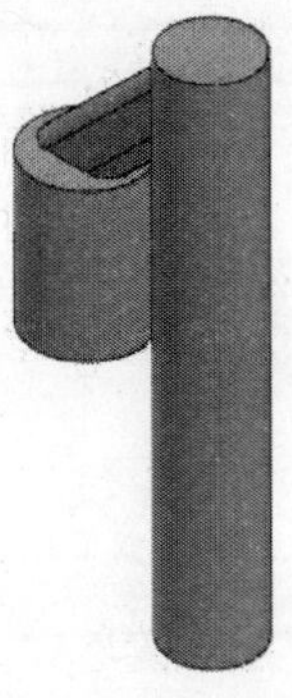

Figure 8-8 *Model after creating the third feature*

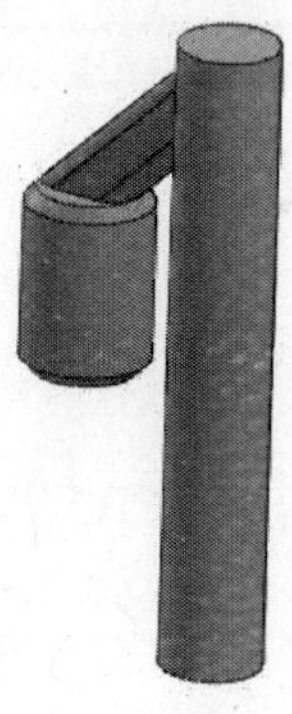

Figure 8-9 *Model after creating the chamfer*

Creating the Split Line

The next feature of the model is a split line feature created by using the **Split Line** tool. The **Split Line** tool is generally used to project a sketch on a planar or curved face, which in turn splits or divides the single face into two or more than two faces. In this section, you will project a sketched entity onto a bottom planar face of the base feature to create a split line on it. The split line splits the selected face on which the sketch is projected.

1. Invoke the sketching environment by selecting the bottom face of the base feature as the sketching plane.

2. Draw the circle of diameter 32 mm as the sketch of a split line, refer to Figure 8-10. Next, exit the sketching environment.

   After creating the sketch of the split line, you need to invoke the **Split Line PropertyManager** to create the split line feature.

3. Invoke **Split Line PropertyManager** by choosing the **Split Line** button from the **Curves** flyout in the **Features CommandManager**.

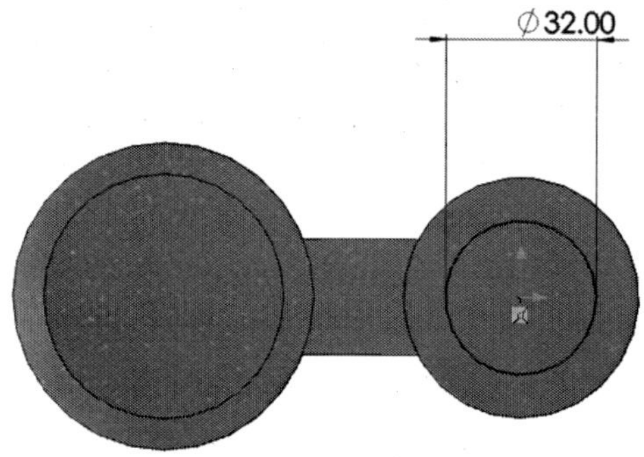

Figure 8-10 *Sketch created for splitting*

The **Split Line PropertyManager** is used to create three types of split lines, silhouette type, projection type, and intersection type. To create silhouette type split line, you need to select the **Silhouette** radio button from the **Type of Split** rollout of the PropertyManager. Similarly, you can create projection and intersection types split line by selecting their respective radio buttons. The silhouette type split line is used to split a curved face by creating a silhouette line at the intersection of the projection of direction entity and the curved face. The projection type split line is used to project a sketched entity onto a planar or curved face to create a split line on it and this split line splits the selected face on which the sketch is projected. The intersection type split line is used to split the selected bodies or faces using the tool bodies, faces, or planes.

4. Select the **Projection** radio button from the **Type of Split** rollout of the **Split Line PropertyManager**.

5. Select the sketch created as the splitting sketch; the selected sketch is highlighted in the drawing area and its name is displayed in the **Sketch to Project** selection area of the **Selections** rollout.

6. Select the bottom face of the base feature; the selected face is highlighted and its name is displayed in the **Faces to Split** selection area of the **Selections** rollout in the PropertyManager. To select the bottom face of the base feature, you need to rotate the model using the middle mouse button.

7. Choose the **OK** button; the split line feature is created. The rotated view of the model after creating the split line feature is shown in Figure 8-11.

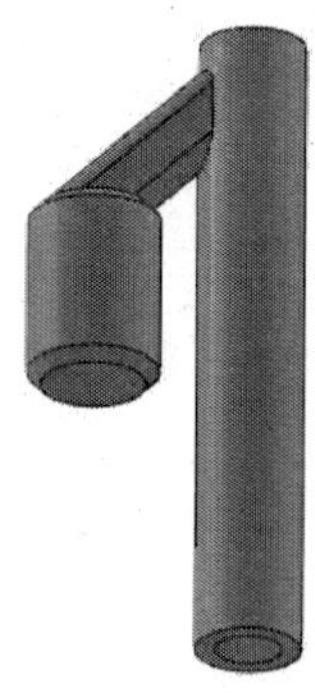

Figure 8-11 *Model after splitting*

Creating the Shell Feature

The next feature of the model is a shell feature.

1. Create the shell feature of thickness 2.5 mm by removing the face of the model created by splitting. Figure 8-12 shows the rotated view of the model and Figure 8-13 shows the section view of the model after creating the shell feature.

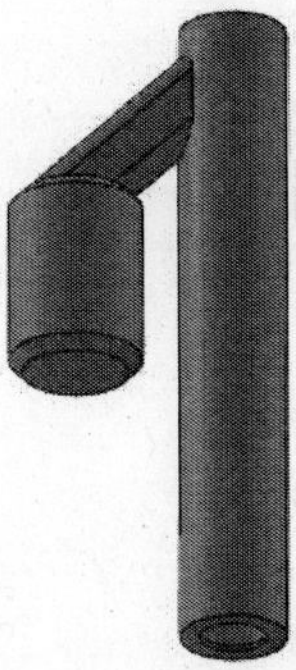

Figure 8-12 Model after creating the shell feature

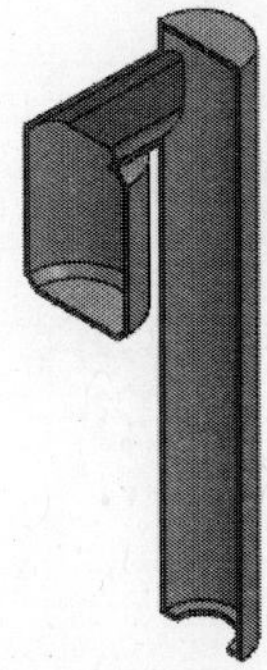

Figure 8-13 Section view of the model

Creating the Remaining Features

Next, create the remaining feature of the model.

1. Create the extrude feature on the top most planar face of the model, as shown in Figure 8-14. For dimensions, refer to Figure 8-3.
2. Create the cut feature on the previously created extruded feature, as shown in Figure 8-15.

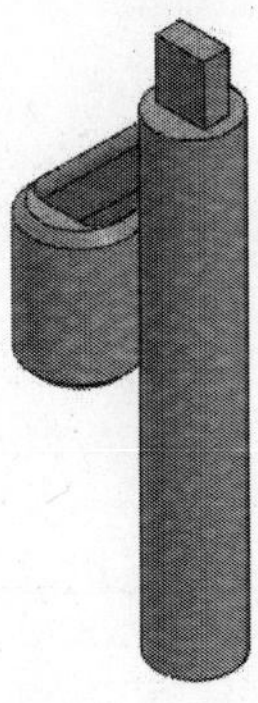

Figure 8-14 Model after creating the extrude feature

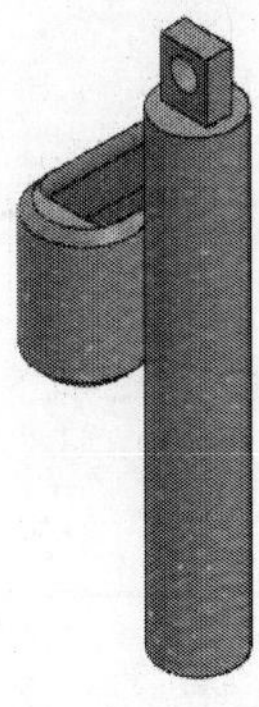

Figure 8-15 Model after creating the cut feature

3. Draw the sketch on the Front Plane, refer to Figure 8-16 and then revolve it using the **Revolve Boss/Base** tool around the center axis of the model. The model after creating the revolve feature is shown in Figure 8-17.

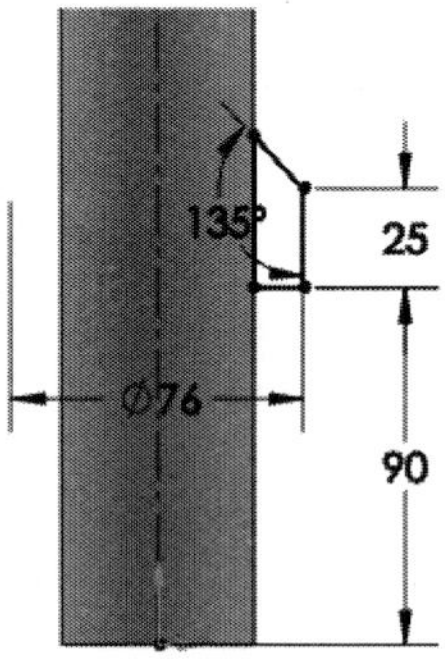

Figure 8-16 Sketch of the revolve feature

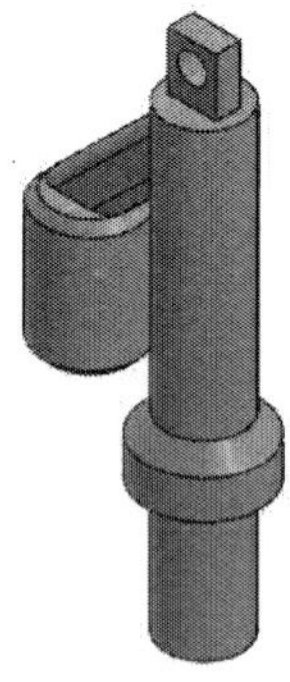

Figure 8-17 Model after creating the revolved feature

4. Apply fillets of radius 2.5 mm or radius 1.25 mm as per the requirement on the shape edges of the model. The final model after applying the fillets is shown in Figure 8-18.

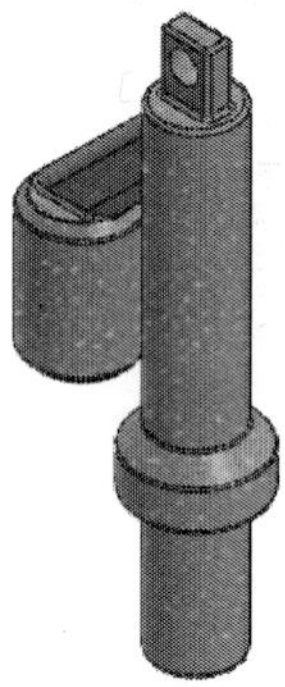

Figure 8-18 Final model after applying fillets

Saving the Model

After completing the model, you need to save it in the *Motor Cycle Project* folder.

1. Invoke the **Save As** dialog box and browse to the *Motor Cycle Project* folder.

2. Enter **Shock Absorber Cylinder** as the name of the model in the **File name** edit box and choose the **Save** button. The document will be saved in the *\Documents\Motor Cycle Project\Shock Absorber Cylinder*.

3. Close document by choosing **File > Close** from the SOLIDWORKS menus.

CREATING THE SHOCK ABSORBER SPRING

Part Description

In this section, you will create the Shock Absorber Spring, as shown in Figure 8-19. The diameter of the spring is 60 mm, height of the spring is 184 mm, and the pitch of the spring is 19 mm.

(Expected time: 15 min)

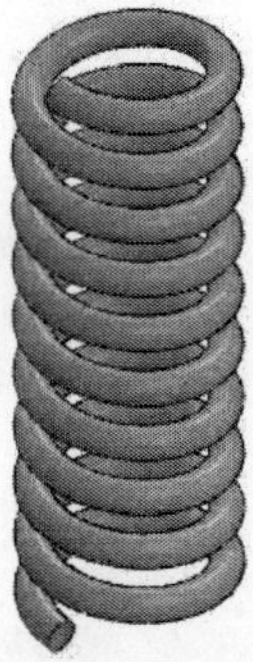

Figure 8-19 The Swing Arm

Creating the Helical Curve as the Path of the Sweep Feature

To create the helical curve, first you need to create the helical curve of the spring using the **Helix and Spiral** tool. This tool is used to create an helical curve or a spiral curve. This curve is generally used as the sweep path to create spring, threads, spiral coils, and so on.

1. Start a new SOLIDWORKS Part document.

2. Choose the **Helix and Spiral** button from the **Curves** flyout, refer to Figure 8-20; the **Helix/Spiral PropertyManager** is displayed and you are prompted to select a plane to create a sketch to define the helix cross-section.

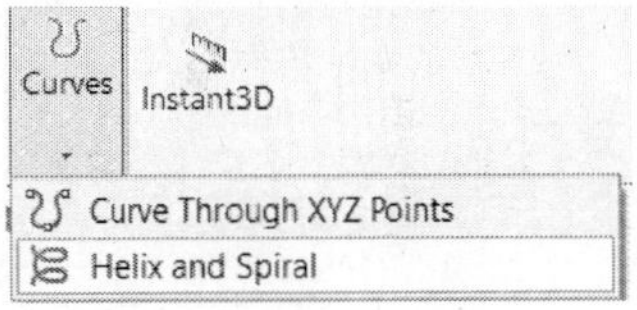

*Figure 8-20 The **Curves** flyout*

3. Select the **Top Plane** as the sketching plane to invoke the Sketching environment.

4. Draw a circle of diameter 60 mm. Next, exit from the sketching environment; the **Helix/Spiral PropertyManager** is displayed and the preview of the helical curve with the default values is displayed in the drawing area. Change the current view of the model to isometric view.

5. Select the **Height and Pitch** option from the **Type** drop-down list of the **Define By** rollout in the **Helix/Spiral PropertyManager**.

The **Type** drop-down list is used to define different methods for specifying the parameters of the helical curve. The **Height and Pitch** option of this drop-down list is used to define the parameters of the helix curve in terms of height and pitch of the helix. The **Pitch and Revolution** option of this drop-down list is used to specify the pitch of the helical curve and the number of revolutions. The **Height and Revolution** option of this drop-down list is used to define the parameters of the helix curve in the form of total helix height and the number of revolutions. The **Spiral** option of this drop-down list is used to create spiral coil.

6. Make sure that the **Constant Pitch** radio button is selected in the **Parameters** rollout of the PropertyManager. Next, set the value of the **Height** spinner to **184 mm** and the value of the **Pitch** spinner to **19 mm** in the **Parameters** rollout. You will observe that the preview of the helical curve is updated automatically when you modify the values in the spinners.

The **Constant Pitch** radio button is used to create a helical curve with constant pitch. You can also create a helical curve with variable pitch by selecting the **Variable Pitch** radio button from the **Parameters** rollout of the PropertyManager.

7. Make sure that the value of the **Start** angle spinner is set to **0** and the **Clockwise** radio button is selected. Next, choose the **OK** button; the helical curve is created, as shown in Figure 8-21.

The **Clockwise** and **Counterclockwise** radio buttons of the **Parameters** rollout are used to define the direction of rotation of the helix.

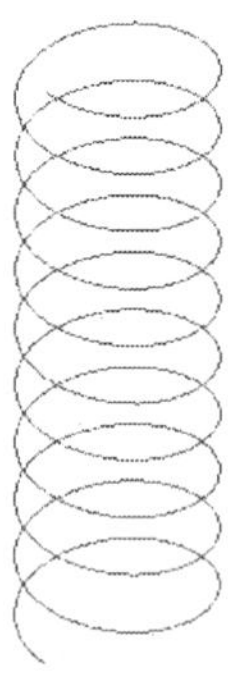

Figure 8-21 *The helical curve*

Creating the Profile of the Sweep Feature

Next, you need to create the profile of the sweep feature. The sketch of the profile will be drawn on a plane normal to the curve on the top endpoint.

1. Create a plane normal to the path and at the top endpoint. To do so, invoke the **Plane PropertyManager**. Next, select the helical curve as the first reference and then select its top endpoint as the second reference.

2. Invoke the Sketching environment by selecting the newly created plane as the sketching plane.

3. Next, draw a circle of diameter 10 mm and add the pierce relation between the center of the circle and the helical curve, refer to Figure 8-22. Next, exit the Sketching environment; the profile of the sweep feature is created normal to the helical curve.

Creating the Sweep Feature

After creating the profile and the path of the sweep feature, you will create a sweep feature to complete the creation of the spring.

1. Invoke the **Sweep PropertyManager** and select the circle of diameter 10 mm as the profile and then helical curve as the path; the preview of the sweep feature is displayed. Next, exit the PropertyManager; the spring is created, as shown in Figure 8-23.

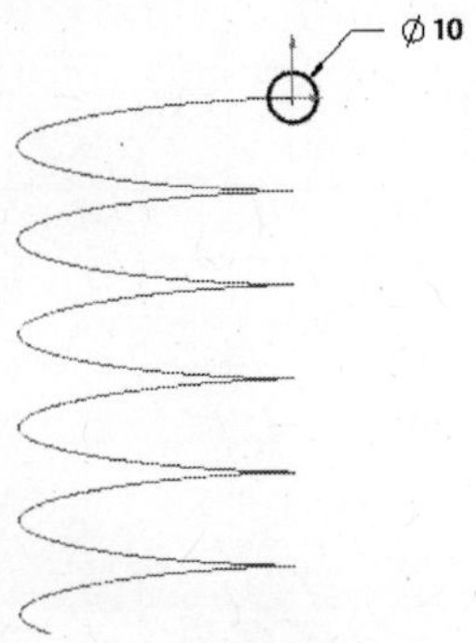

Figure 8-22 *Profile of the sweep feature*

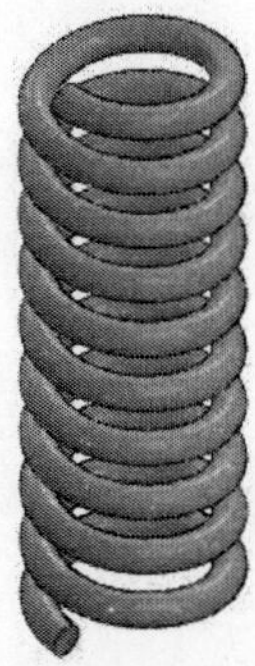

Figure 8-23 *The shock absorber spring*

Saving the Model

After creating the Shock Absorber Spring, you need to save it in the *Motor Cycle Project* folder.

1. Save the model with the name Shock Absorber Spring in the *Motor Cycle Project* folder.

2. Close document by choosing **File > Close** from the SOLIDWORKS menus.

CREATING THE SHOCK ABSORBER PISTON ROD

Part Description

In this section, you will create the Shock Absorber Piston Rod, as shown in Figure 8-24. The front and side views of the model with dimensions are given in the Figure 8-25. After creating all the features of the model, remove the sharp edges of the model by applying the fillets of radius 2.5 mm. **(Expected time: 25 min)**

Figure 8-24 *The Shock Absorber Piston Rod*

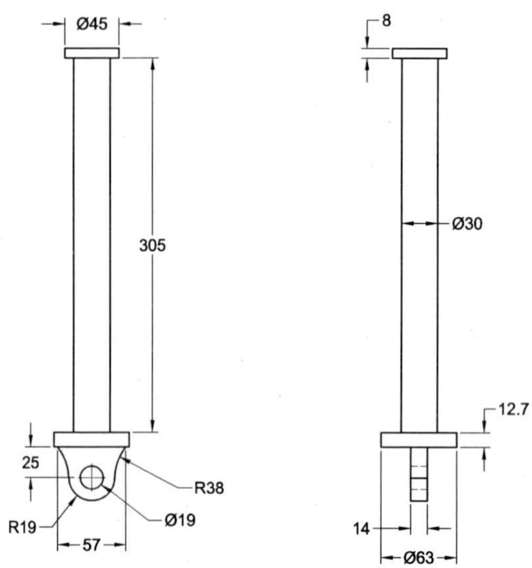

Figure 8-25 *The front and side views of the model*

Starting a New Part Document

1. Start a new SOLIDWORKS part document using the **New SOLIDWORKS Document** dialog box.

Creating the Shock Absorber Piston Rod

1. Create the base feature of the model, refer to Figure 8-26. For dimensions, refer to Figure 8-25.

2. Create the second feature of the model, refer to Figure 8-27. For dimensions, refer to Figure 8-25.

Figure 8-26 *Base feature of the model*

Figure 8-27 *Model after creating the second feature*

3. Create the third feature of the model, refer to Figure 8-28. For dimensions, refer to Figure 8-25.

4. Create the forth feature of the model, refer to Figure 8-29. For dimensions, refer to Figure 8-25.

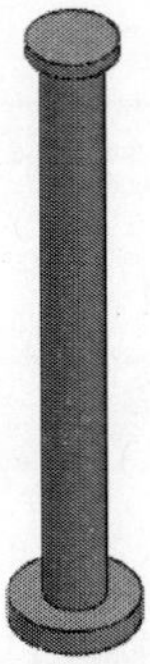

Figure 8-28 *Model after creating third feature*

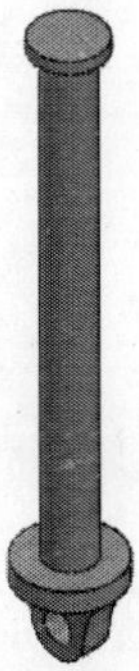

Figure 8-29 *Model after creating forth feature*

5. Apply fillets of radius 2.5 mm on the sharp edges of the model. The final model after applying the fillets is shown in Figure 8-30.

Saving the Model

After creating the Shock Absorber Piston Rod, you need to save it in the *Motor Cycle Project* folder.

1. Save the model with the name Shock Absorber Piston Rod in the *Motor Cycle Project* folder.

2. Close document by choosing **File > Close** from the SOLIDWORKS menus.

Figure 8-30 *Final model after applying fillets*

CREATING THE CYLINDER HEAD

Part Description

In this section, you will create the Cylinder Head, as shown in Figure 8-31. The top and front views of the model with dimensions are given in the Figure 8-32. **(Expected time: 50 min)**

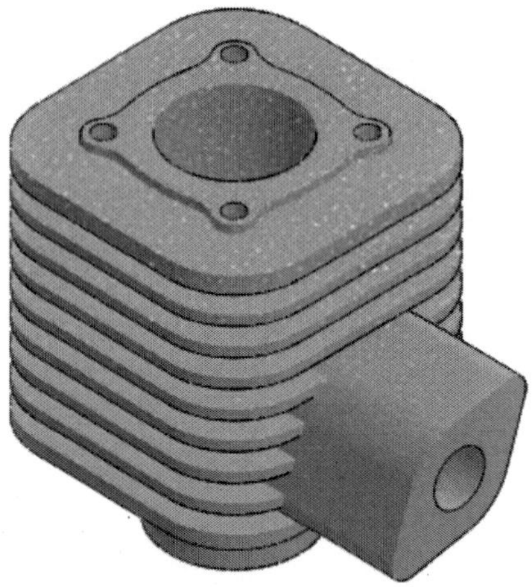

Figure 8-31 *The Cylinder head*

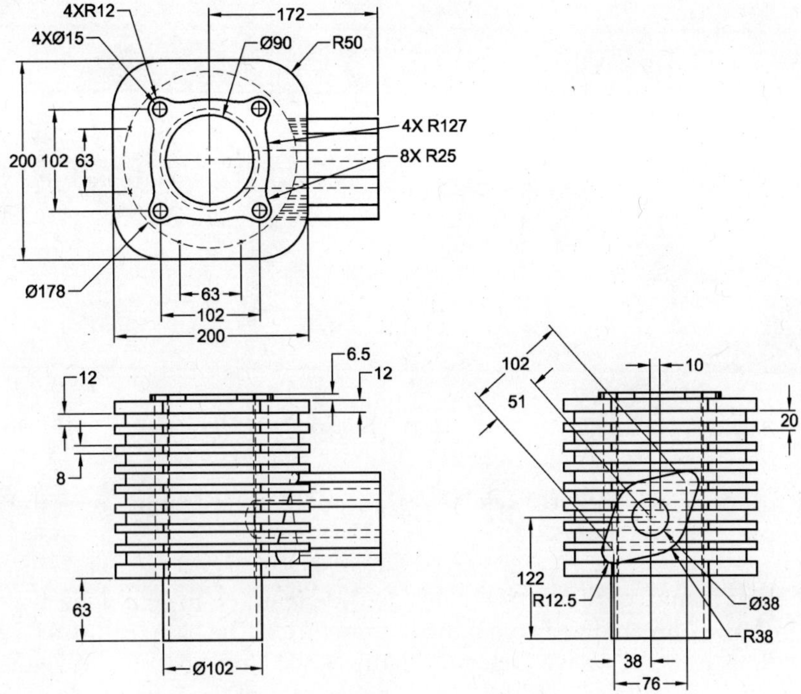

Figure 8-32 The views and dimensions of the model

Starting a New Part Document

1. Start a new SOLIDWORKS part document using the **New SOLIDWORKS Document** dialog box.

Creating the Cylinder Head

1. Invoke the sketching environment by selecting the Top Plane as the sketching plane and then draw the sketch of the base feature, as shown Figure 8-33.

2. Exit from the sketching environment and then extrude the sketch upto the depth of 114 mm in the direction 1 and 64 mm in direction 2 by using the **Extruded Boss/Base** tool. The base feature of the model is shown in Figure 8-34.

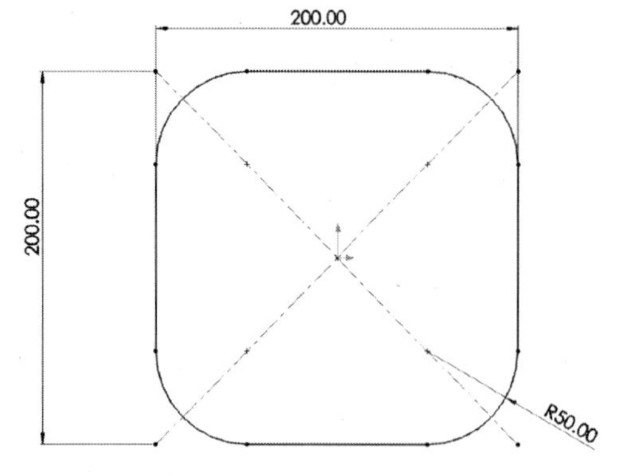

Figure 8-33 Sketch of the base feature

Figure 8-34 Base feature of the model

3. Create the second feature of the model that is through all cut feature, refer to Figure 8-35. For dimensions, refer to Figure 8-32.

4. Create the third feature of the model that is extrude feature. To create this feature, invoke the sketching environment by selecting the bottom face of the base feature as the sketching plane and then draw the sketch, refer to Figure 8-36. Note that in the Figure 8-36, the diameter of the outer circle is 102 mm and the diameter of the inner circle is coradial with the circular edge that measures diameter 90 mm. Next exit the sketching environment and extrude the sketch upto the depth of 63 mm The rotated view of the model after creating the third feature is shown in Figure 8-37.

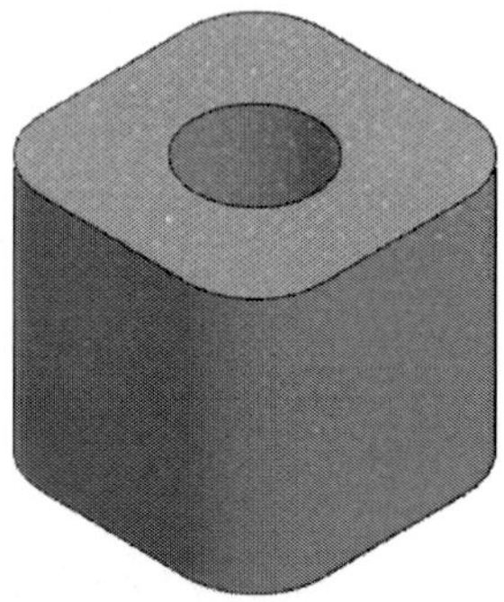

Figure 8-35 Model after creating the cut feature

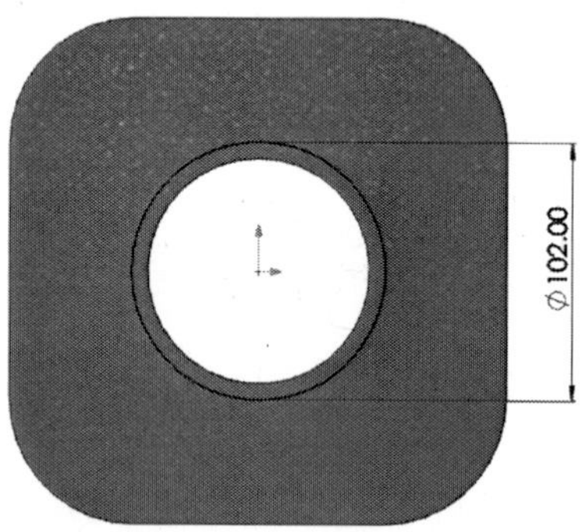

Figure 8-36 Sketch of the extrude feature

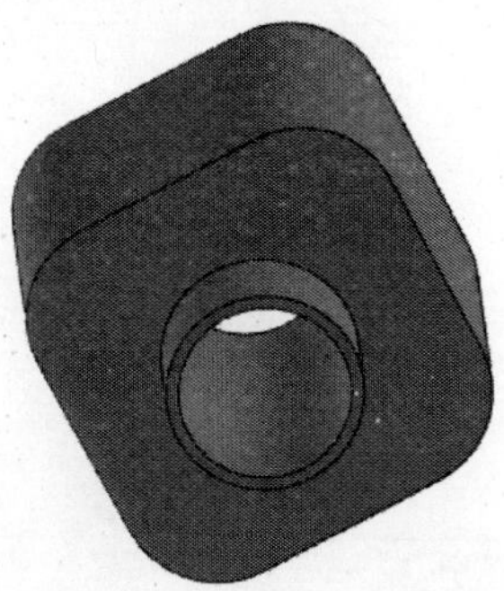

Figure 8-37 Model after creating the extrude feature

5. Create the fourth feature that is revolve cut feature. To create this feature, invoke the sketching environment by selecting the Front Plane as the sketching plane and draw the sketch, as shown in Figure 8-38. Next, exit the sketching environment and revolve the sketch around the centerline by using the **Revolved Cut** tool, refer to Figure 8-39.

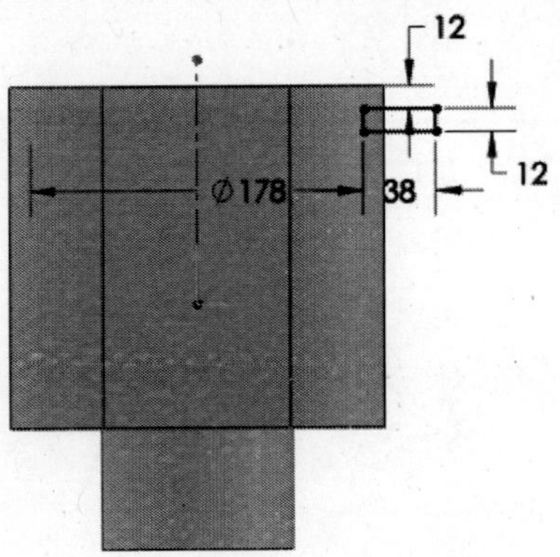

Figure 8-38 Sketch of the revolve cut feature

Figure 8-39 Model after creating the revolved cut feature

6. Create the linear pattern of the previously created revolved cut feature by using the **Linear Pattern** tool. For number of instances and the distance between instances, refer to Figure 8-32. The model after creating the linear pattern is shown in Figure 8-40.

7. The next feature of the model is an extrude feature. To create this extrude feature, invoke the Sketching environment by selecting the top planar face of the model as the sketching

plane and draw the sketch, refer to Figure 8-41. Next, exit the Sketching environment and extrude the sketch upto the depth of 6.5 mm, refer to Figure 8-42.

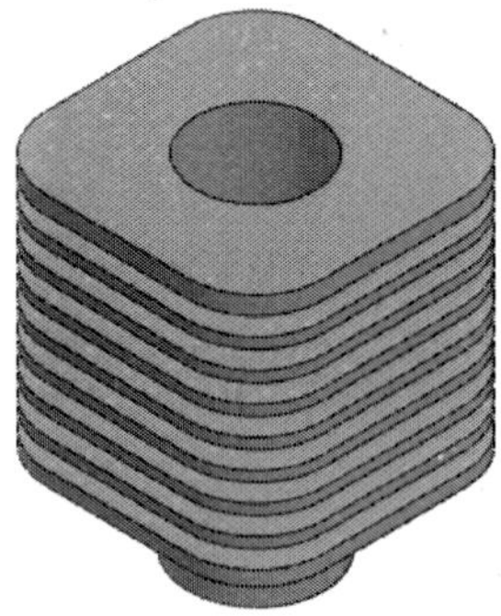

Figure 8-40 *Model after patterning the feature*

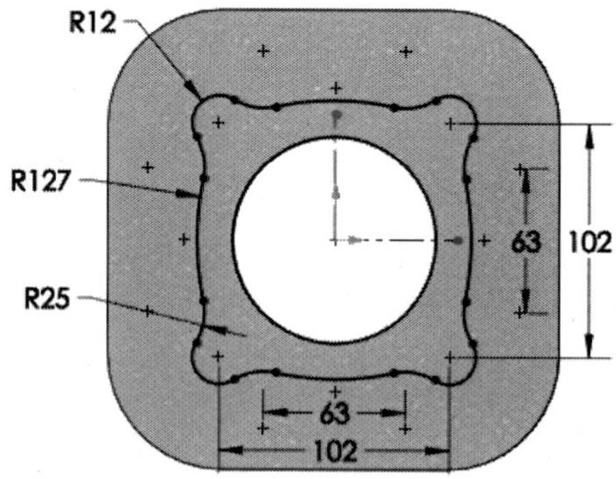

Figure 8-41 *Sketch of the extrude feature*

8. Create through holes as the extrude cut feature by using the **Extruded Cut** tool, as shown in Figure 8-43. For dimensions, refer to Figure 8-32. You can also create these holes by using the **Simple Hole** tool.

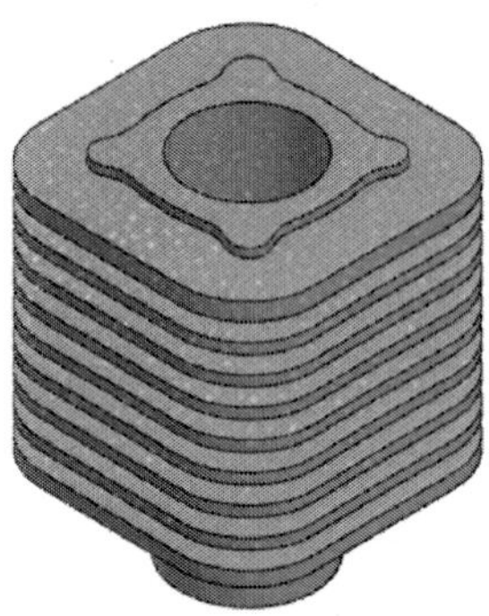

Figure 8-42 *Model after creating extruded feature*

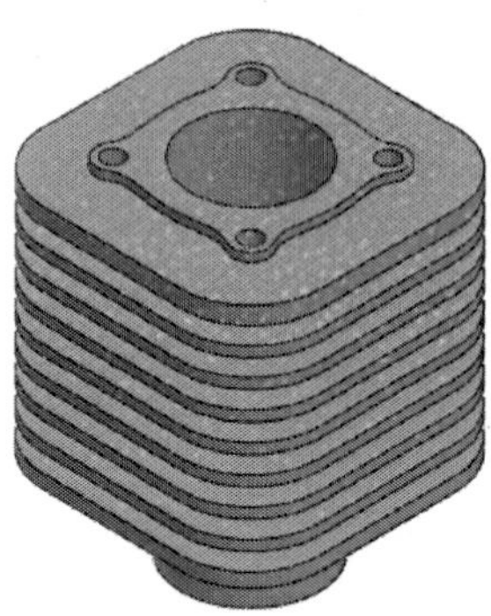

Figure 8-43 *Model after creating cut feature*

9. Create the reference plane at an offset distance of 172 mm from the Right Plane and then invoke the sketching environment by selecting it. Next, draw the sketch, as shown in Figure 8-44. After drawing the sketch, extrude it using the **Up to Next** option. The model after creating the extrude feature is shown in Figure 8-45.

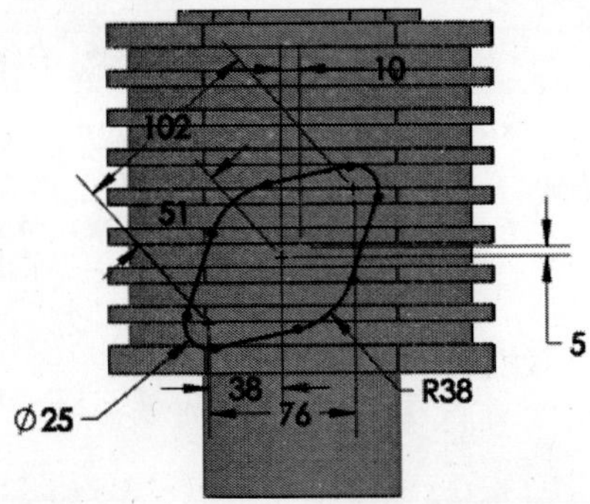

Figure 8-44 *Sketch of the extrude feature*

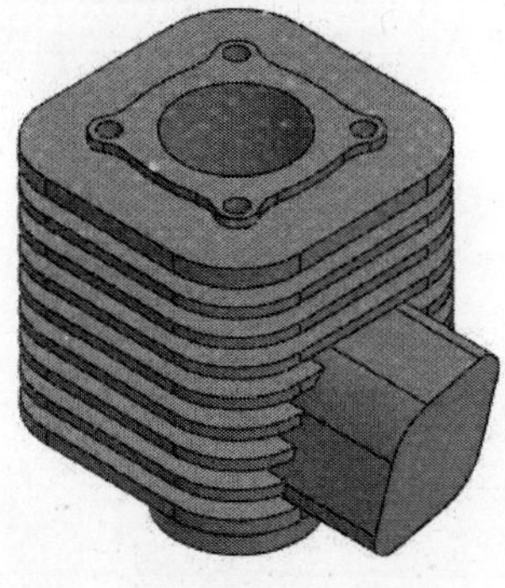

Figure 8-45 *Model after creating the extrude feature*

10. Create the cut feature up to the inner circular surface of the model, refer to Figure 8-46. For dimensions, refer to Figure 8-32.

11. Apply fillets of radius 0.5 mm on the sharp edges of the model. The final model after applying the fillets is shown in Figure 8-47.

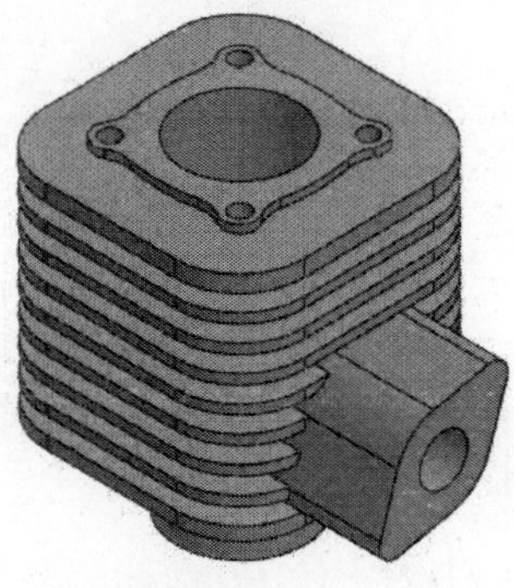

Figure 8-46 *Model after creating the cut feature*

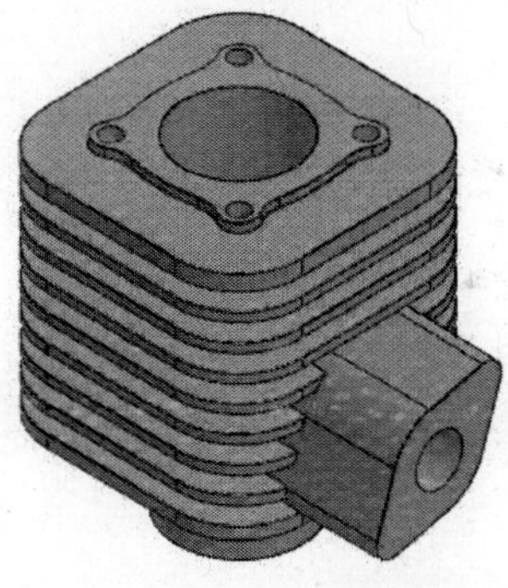

Figure 8-47 *Final model*

Saving the Model

After creating the model, you need to save it in the *Motor Cycle Project* folder.

1. Save the model with the name Cylinder Head in the *Motor Cycle Project* folder.

2. Close document by choosing **File > Close** from the SOLIDWORKS menus.

CREATING THE CYLINDER HEAD COVER

Part Description

In this section, you will create the Cylinder Head Cover, as shown in Figure 8-48. The top and front views of the model with dimensions are given in the Figure 8-49. Also, apply fillets of radius 2.5 mm on the sharp edges of the model. **(Expected time: 45 min)**

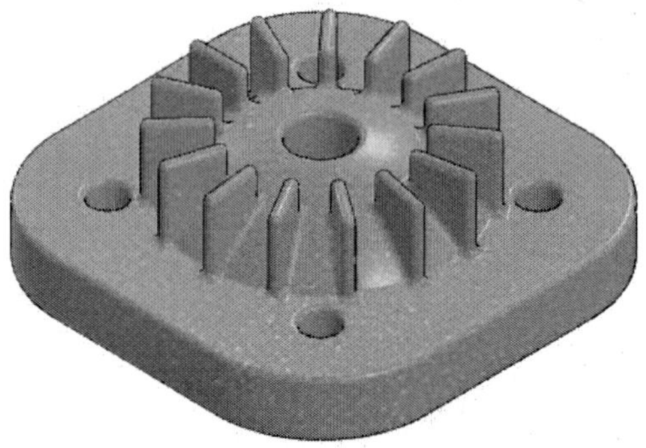

Figure 8-48 *The Cylinder Head Cover*

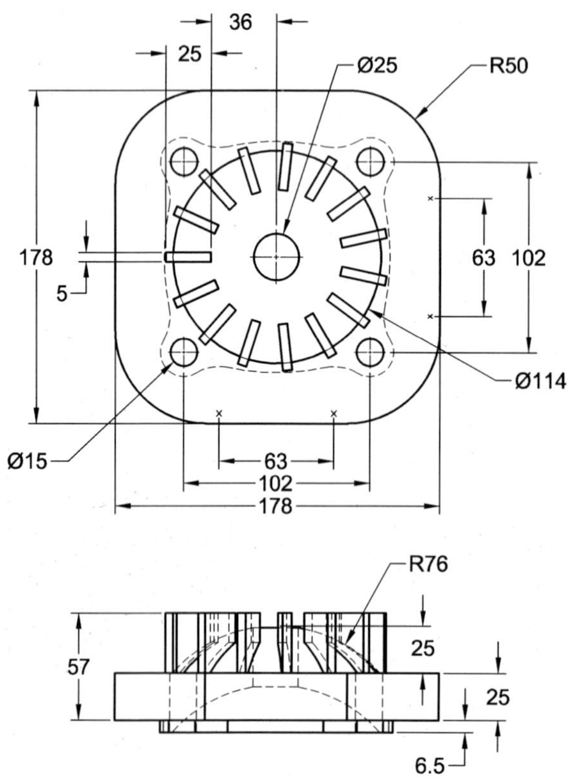

Figure 8-49 *Top and front views of the model*

Starting a New Part Document

1. Start a new SOLIDWORKS part document using the **New SOLIDWORKS Document** dialog box.

Creating the Cylinder Head Cover

1. Create the base feature of the model, as shown in Figure 8-50. For dimensions, refer to Figure 8-49.

2. Create the second feature of the model that is extrude feature on the bottom planar face of the base feature. For dimensions, refer to Figure 8-49. The rotated view of the model after creating the extruded feature is shown in Figure 8-51.

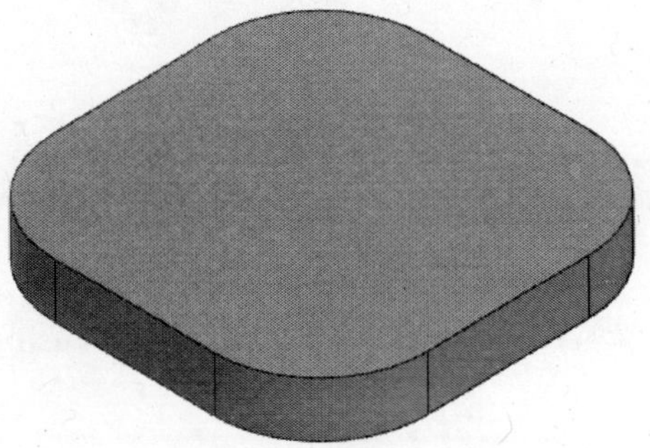

Figure 8-50 *Base feature of the model*

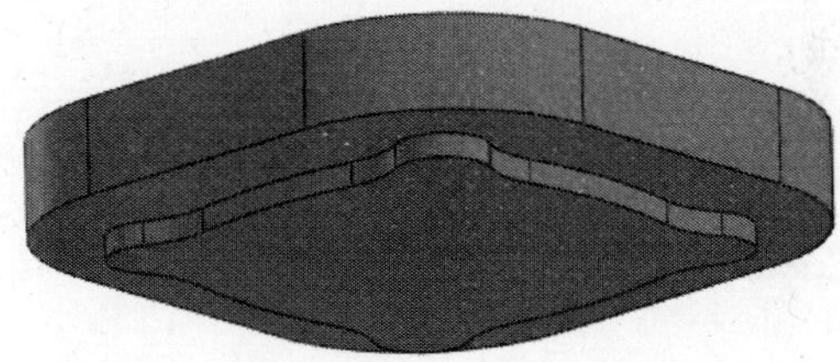

Figure 8-51 *Model after creating the second feature*

3. Invoke the sketching environment by selecting the Front Plane as the sketching plane and draw the sketch, refer to Figure 8-52. Next, exit from the sketching environment and revolve the sketch about the centerline of the sketch by using the **Revolved Boss/Base** tool, refer to Figure 8-53.

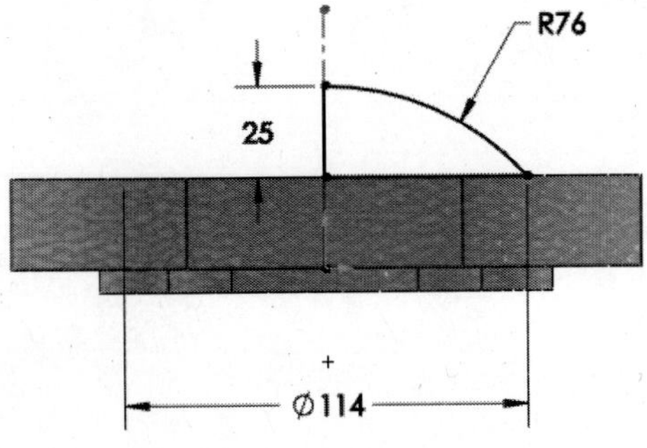

Figure 8-52 *Sketch of the revolve feature*

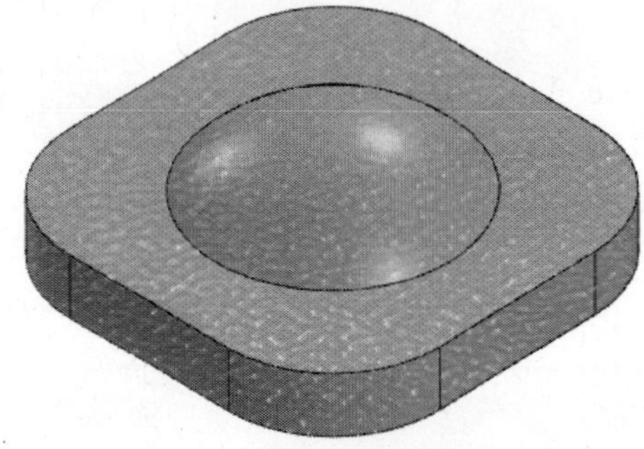

Figure 8-53 *Model after creating the revolved feature*

4. Invoke the sketching environment by selecting the Front Plane as the sketching plane and draw the sketch, refer to Figure 8-54. Next, exit from the sketching environment and revolve the sketch about the centerline of the sketch by using the **Revolved Cut** tool. The section view of the model after creating the revolve cut feature is shown in Figure 8-55.

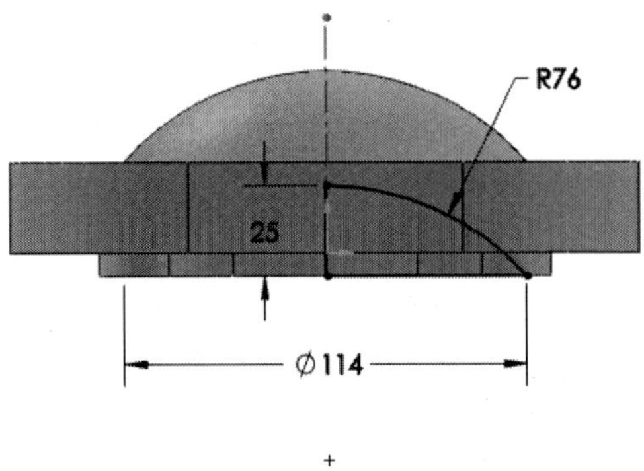

Figure 8-54 *Sketch of the revolve cut feature*

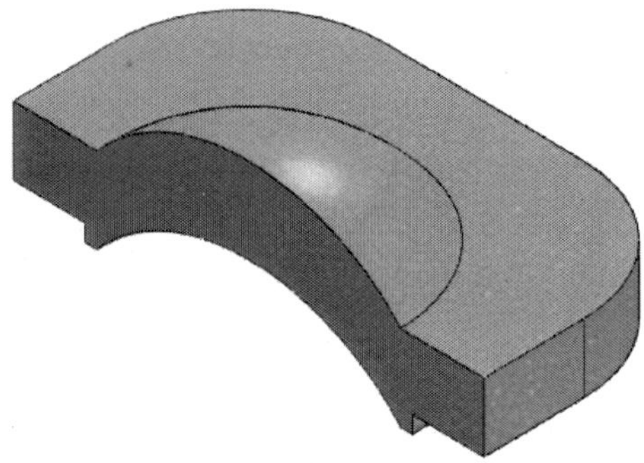

Figure 8-55 *Section view of the model after creating the revolved cut feature*

5. Create through holes as the extrude cut feature by using the **Extruded Cut** tool, as shown in Figure 8-56. For dimensions, refer to Figure 8-49. You can also create these holes by using the **Simple Hole** tool.

6. Create the extrude feature, as shown in Figure 8-57. For dimensions, refer to Figure 8-49. To create this feature, first create a reference plane at an offset distance of the 57 mm from the Top Plane and then invoke the sketching environment by selecting it. Next, draw the sketch of the extrude feature. After drawing the sketch, exit the sketching environment and extrude the sketch by using the **Up To Next** option.

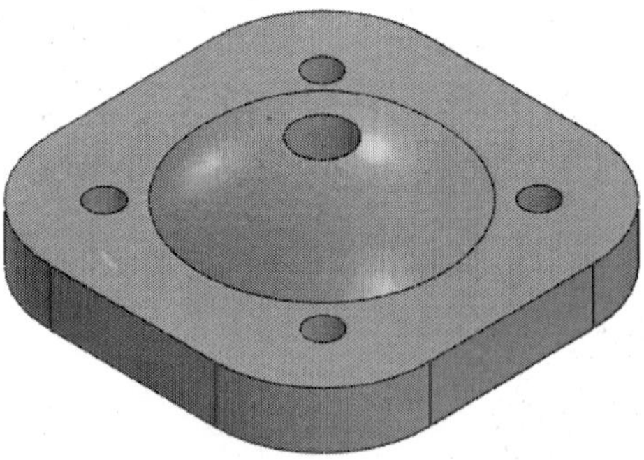

Figure 8-56 *Model after creating the holes*

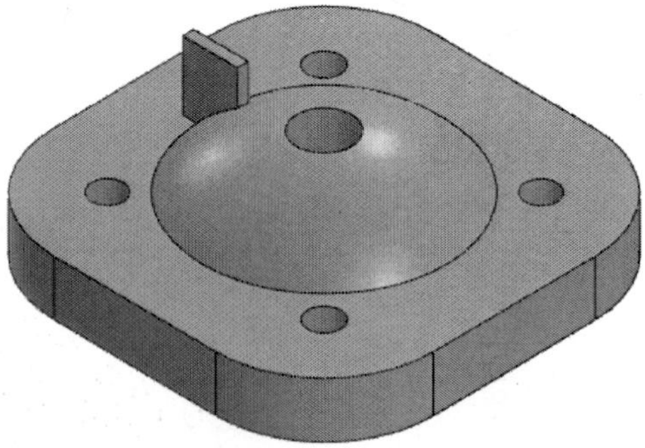

Figure 8-57 *Model after creating the extruded feature*

7. Create the circular pattern of the previously created extruded feature by specifying the number of instance as 15 and the circular face of the center hole as the axis of revolution.

The model after creating the circular pattern is shown in Figure 8-58.

8. Apply fillets of radius 2.5 mm on the sharp edges of the model by using the **FilletXpert PropertyManager**. The final model after applying the fillets is shown in Figure 8-59.

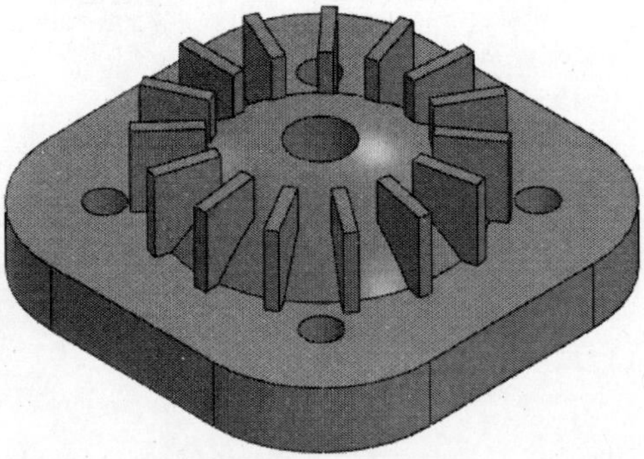

Figure 8-58 Model after creating the circular pattern

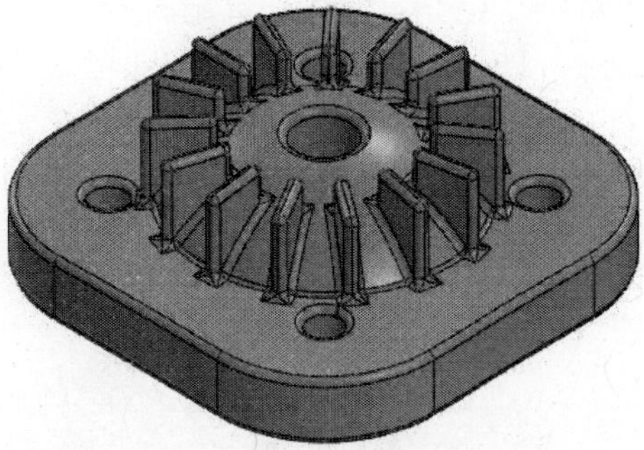

Figure 8-59 Final model after applying the fillets

Saving the Model

After creating the model, you need to save it in the *Motor Cycle Project* folder.

1. Save the model with the name Cylinder Head Cover in the *Motor Cycle Project* folder.

2. Close document by choosing **File > Close** from the SOLIDWORKS menus.

CREATING THE CRANKCASE COVER

Part Description

In this section, you will create the Crankcase Cover, as shown in Figure 8-60. The top and front views of the model with dimensions are given in the Figure 8-61. Apply fillets of radius 6.5 mm. Also, the wall thickness is 2.5 mm . **(Expected time: 30 min)**

Figure 8-60 The Crankcase Cover

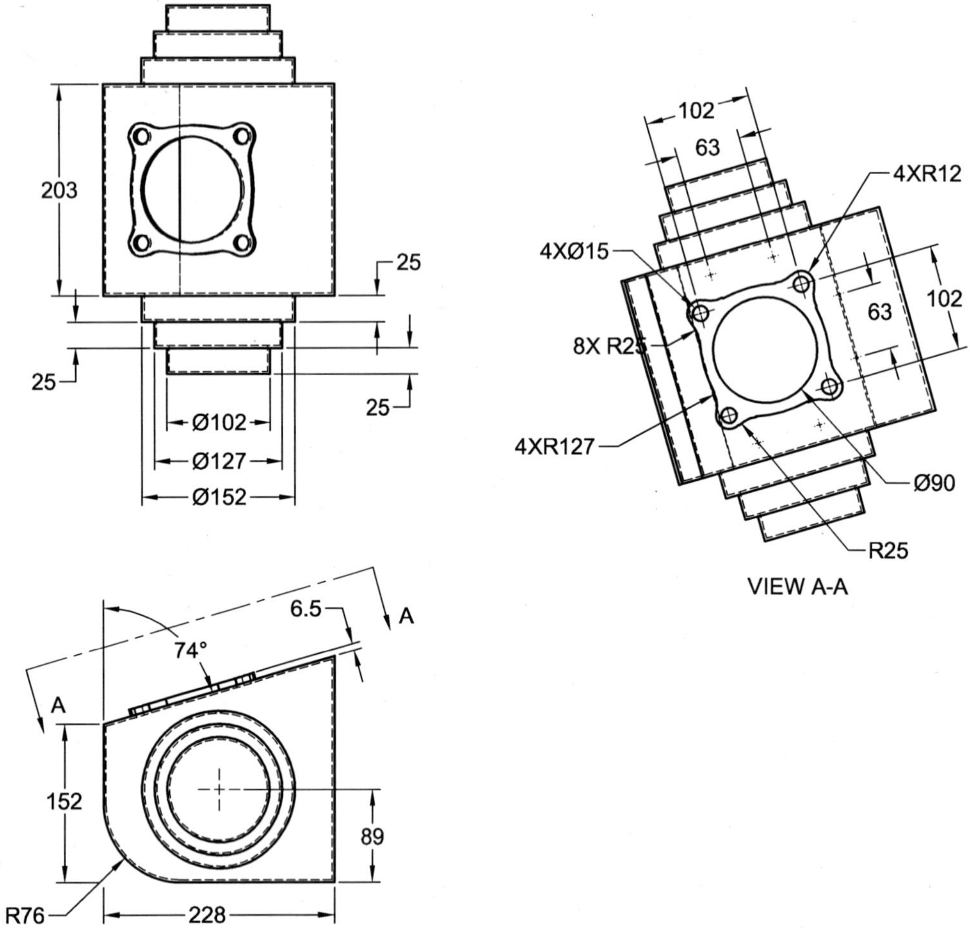

Figure 8-61 *The views and dimensions of the model*

Starting a New Part Document

1. Start a new SOLIDWORKS part document using the **New SOLIDWORKS Document** dialog box.

Creating the Cylinder Head Cover

1. Invoke the sketching environment by selecting the Front Plane as the sketching plane and draw the sketch of the base feature, as shown in Figure 8-62. Next, exit the sketching environment and extrude the sketch upto the depth of 203 mm using the **Mid Plane** option, refer to Figure 8-63.

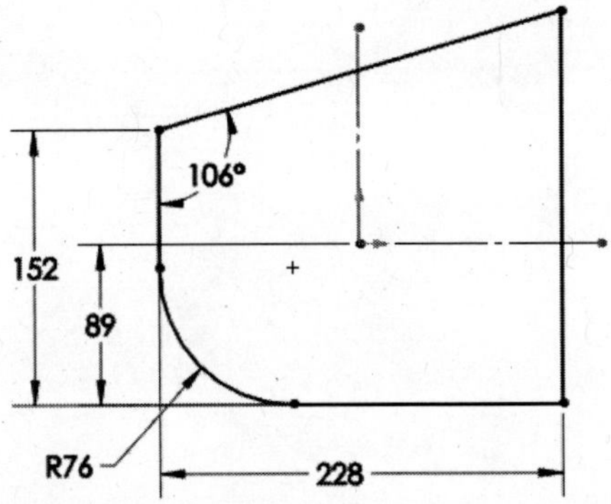

Figure 8-62 Sketch of the base feature

Figure 8-63 Base feature of the model

2. Create the second feature of the model that is extrude feature, refer to Figure 8-64. For dimensions, refer to Figure 8-61.

3. Create the third extrude feature of the model, refer to Figure 8-65. For dimensions, refer to Figure 8-61.

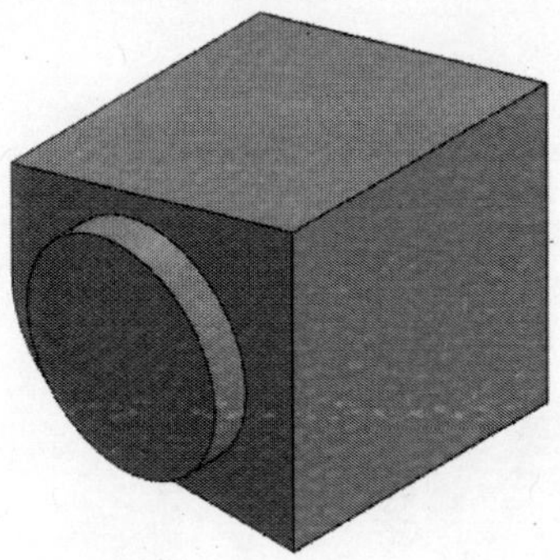

Figure 8-64 Model after creating second feature

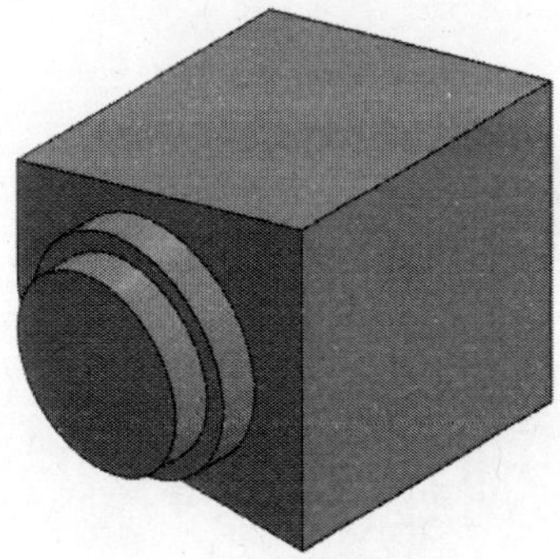

Figure 8-65 Model after creating the third feature

4. Create the forth extrude feature of the model, refer to Figure 8-66. For dimensions, refer to Figure 8-61.

5. Create the mirror feature of the second, third, and forth extruded features about the Front Plane. The model after mirroring the last three extruded features is shown in Figure 8-67.

Figure 8-66 Model after creating forth feature

Figure 8-67 Model after mirroring the last three features

6. Apply fillets of radius 6.5 mm on the sharp edges of the model, refer to Figure 8-68.

7. Create the shell feature by specifying the wall thickness 2.5 mm. The section view of the model after creating the shell feature is shown in Figure 8-69.

Figure 8-68 Model after applying the fillets

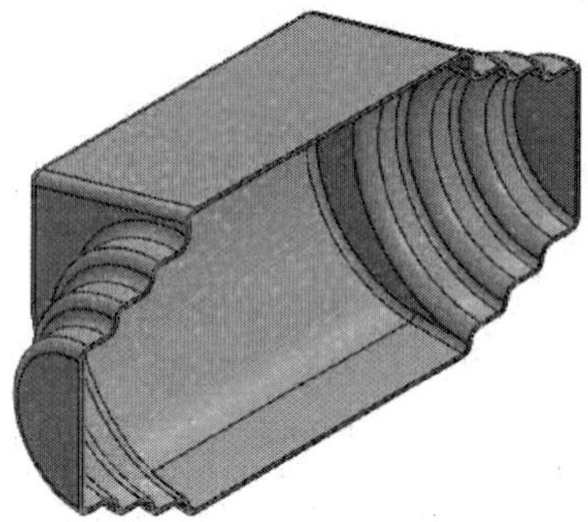

Figure 8-69 Section view of the model

8. Create the extrude feature on the top inclined face of the model, as shown in Figure 8-70. For dimensions, refer to Figure 8-61.

9. Create the extrude cut feature by using the **Up To Next** option of the **Extruded Cut** tool. The final model after creating all the features is shown in Figure 8-71.

Figure 8-70 *Model after creating the extrude feature*

Figure 8-71 *Final model*

Saving the Model

After creating the model, you need to save it in the *Motor Cycle Project* folder.

1. Save the model with the name Crankcase Cover in the *Motor Cycle Project* folder.
2. Close document by choosing **File > Close** from the SOLIDWORKS menus.

Self-Evaluation Test

Answer the following questions and then compare them to those given at the end of this chapter:

1. The **Split Line PropertyManager** is used to create three types of split lines, __________, projection, and __________ .
2. The __________ drop-down list of the **Helix/Spiral PropertyManager** is used to define methods for specifying the parameters of the helical curve.
3. The __________ option of the **Defined By** drop-down list is used to define the parameters of the helix curve in terms of height and pitch of the helix.
4. The __________ radio button of the **Helix/Spiral PropertyManager** is used to create a helical curve with constant pitch.
5. In SOLIDWORKS, you can not create variable pitch helix. (T/F)

Review Questions

Answer the following questions:

1. Which one of the following options of the **Type** drop-down list in the **Helix/Spiral PropertyManager** allows you to specify the pitch of the helical curve and the number of revolutions?

   (a) **Pitch Revolution** (b) **Pitch and Revolution**
   (c) **Revolution and Pitch** (d) None of these

2. Which one of the following options of the **Type** drop-down list in the **Helix/Spiral PropertyManager** allows you to define the parameters of the helix curve in the form of total helix height and number of revolutions?

   (a) **Height and Revolution** (b) **Height Revolution**
   (c) **Pitch and Revolution** (d) None of these

3. The __________ and __________ radio buttons of the **Parameters** rollout in the **Helix/Spiral PropertyManager** are used to define the direction of rotation of the helix.

4. The __________ option of the **End Condition** drop-down list of the PropertyManager is used to extrude the sketch upto the selected surface.

5. In SOLIDWORKS, you can create spiral coil by using the **Spiral** option from the **Type** drop-down list of the **Helix/Spiral PropertyManager**. (T/F)

Answers to Self-Evaluation Test

1. silhouette, intersection, **2. Defined By**, **3. Height and Pitch**, **4. Constant Pitch**, **5. F**

Chapter 9

Creating Mudguards, Fuel Tank, Headlight Mask, and Seat Cover

Learning Objectives

After completing this chapter, you will be able to:

- *Create Extruded surface*
- *Create sweep surface*
- *Trim a surface*
- *Thicken a surface*
- *Mirror a surface*

INTRODUCTION TO SURFACE MODELING

Surface modeling is a technique used to create planar or non planar geometry of zero thickness. A zero thickness geometry is known as surface. Surfaces are generally used to create models having complex shapes. You can easily convert a surface model into a solid. You can also extract a surface from the solid model by using the surface modeling tools. This chapter explains how to use the surface modeling tools of SolidWorks. Using these tools, you can create complex shapes as surfaces and then convert them into solid models, if required. Most of the real world components are created by using the solid modeling tools and techniques. But sometimes, you may need to create some complex features that can only be created by surface manipulation. Surface manipulation is done by using the surface modeling tools. After creating the required complex surface, you can convert it into a solid model. The reason why a surface model is converted for developing a solid model is that a surface is a zero thickness geometry and therefore has no mass and mass properties. But while designing real world models, you need mass and mass properties. The other reason for converting a surface model into a solid model is that you can only generate a section view of the solid model.

In SolidWorks, surface modeling is done in the **Part** environment and the tools used for creating surface models are available in the **Surfaces CommandManager**. The **Surfaces CommandManager** is not available by default. Therefore, you need to invoke this CommandManager by right-clicking on any CommandManager tabs and then choosing the **Surfaces** option from the shortcut menu displayed. The surface modeling tools can also be invoked by choosing **Insert > Surface** from the SolidWorks menus. You will notice that some of the tools available in the **Surfaces CommandManager** such as extrude, revolve, sweep, and loft are similar to those discussed in solid modeling.

CREATING THE FRONT MUDGUARD

Part Description

In this section, you will create the Front Mudguard, as shown in Figure 9-1. It will be created by using the surface modeling tools. These tools are available in the **Surfaces CommandManager**. After creating the surface model, you will convert it into a solid model by applying a thickness of 1.27 mm. The front and section views with the dimensions of the Front Mudguard are shown in Figure 9-2. The fillet radius of the model is 25.4 mm. **(Expected time: 55 min)**

Figure 9-1 *The Front Mudguard*

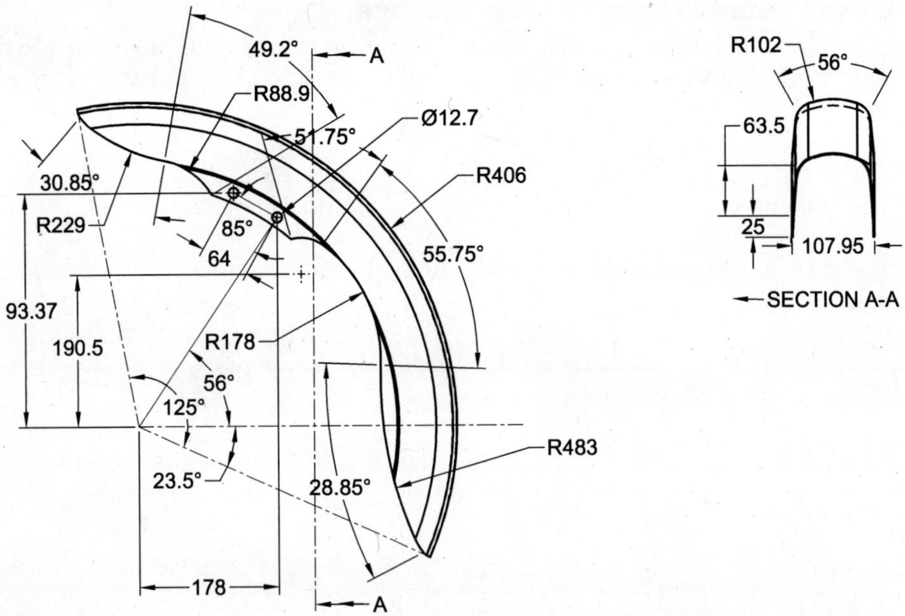

Figure 9-2 The views and dimensions of the model

To create this model, first you need to create the base surface. The base feature of this model is a sweep surface and is created by sweeping a profile along a path using the **Swept Surface** tool. The **Swept Surface** tool works similar to the **Swept Boss/Base** tool discussed in the earlier chapters.

Creating the Path for the Sweep Surface

As discussed earlier, the base feature of the model is a sweep surface. To create a sweep surface, first you need to create its path. This path will be created on the Front Plane.

1. Start the part document of SolidWorks by using the **New SolidWorks Document** dialog box. Modify the unit of the current session to mm, if it is not set by default.

2. Invoke the sketching environment by selecting the **Front Plane** as the sketching plane.

3. Draw the sketch of the path for the sweep feature, refer to Figure 9-3. Next, exit the sketcher environment.

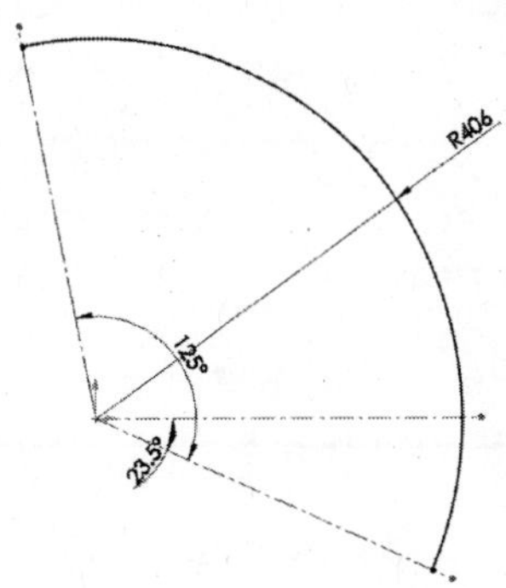

Figure 9-3 Path of the sweep feature

Creating the Profile for the Sweep Surface

After creating the path for the sweep surface, you will create its profile. To create the profile, first you need to create a reference plane normal to the path. This reference plane will be selected as a sketching plane for creating the profile for the sweep surface.

1. Change the current orientation of the model to isometric. Next, Invoke the **Plane PropertyManager** and create a plane normal to the path, refer to Figure 9-4.

   After creating the reference plane normal to the path, you need to create the profile for the sweep surface.

2. Invoke the sketcher environment by selecting the newly created plane as the sketching plane. Next, change the orientation, normal to the view.

3. Draw the open sketch as the profile of the sweep surface, refer to Figure 9-5. Next, exit from the sketcher environment.

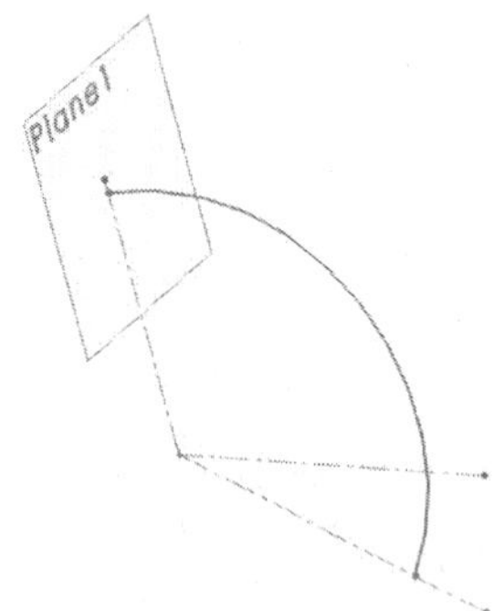

Figure 9-4 *Reference plane normal to the path*

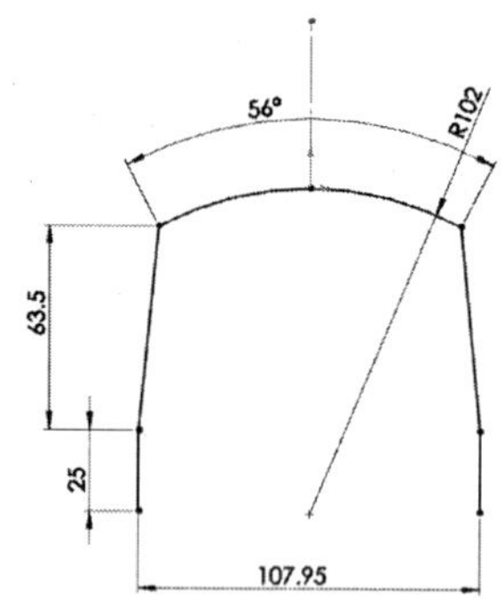

Figure 9-5 *Profile of the sweep feature*

Creating the Sweep Surface

After creating the path and profile, you will create the sweep surface using the **Swept Surface** tool.

1. Right-click on a **CommandManager** tabs to display a shortcut menu and then choose the **Surfaces** option; the **Surfaces** tab is displayed in the **CommandManager**.

2. Click on the **Surfaces** tab of the **CommandManager** to display the tools of the **Surfaces CommandManager**.

3. Choose the **Swept Surface** button from the **Surfaces CommandManager**; the **Surface-Sweep PropertyManager** is displayed, as shown in Figure 9-6. Also, you are prompted to select the sweep profile.

4. Select the profile of sweep surface from the drawing area; you are prompted to select the sweep path. Also, the name of the selected profile is displayed in the **Profile** selection area of the PropertyManager.

5. Select the path of the sweep surface from the drawing area; the preview of the sweep surface is displayed in the drawing area.

6. Choose the **OK** button from the PropertyManager; the sweep surface is created, as shown in Figure 9-7.

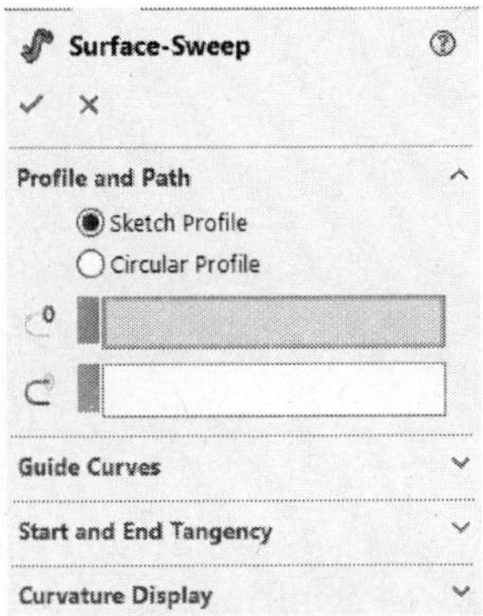

*Figure 9-6 The **Surface-Sweep PropertyManager***

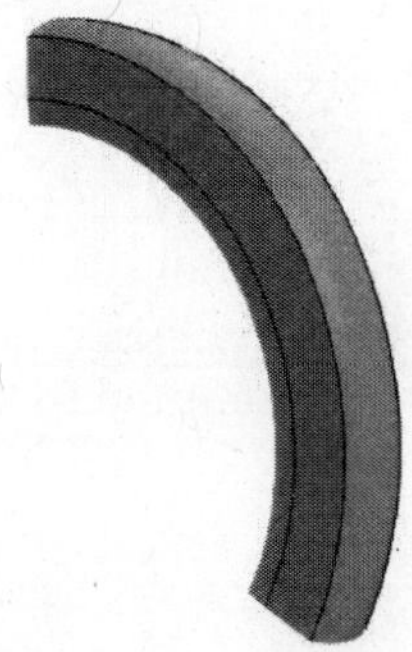

Figure 9-7 The base feature of the model

Trimming the Unwanted Surface

In the evidence from the Figures 9-1 and 9-2 that some of the portion of the sweep surface needs to be trimmed to get the desired shape of the surface model by using the **Trim Surface** tool. In SolidWorks, the **Trim Surface** tool is used to trim the unwanted surface using the trim tool. A trim tool can be a surface, a sketched entity, or an edge. In this section, you will trim the unwanted surface of the sweep surface using a sketched entity as trim tool.

1. Invoke the sketcher environment by selecting the Front Plane as the sketching plane and draw the sketch of the trim tool for trimming the sweep surface, refer to Figure 9-8.

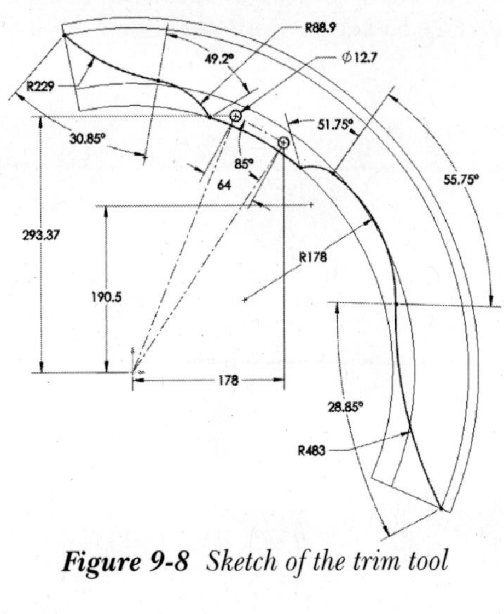

Figure 9-8 Sketch of the trim tool

2. Exit from the sketcher environment and click anywhere in the drawing area to exit from the current selection mode.

3. Choose the **Trim Surface** button from the **Surfaces CommandManager**; the **Trim Surface PropertyManager** is displayed.

As discussed earlier, the **Trim Surface** tool is used to trim the unwanted surface using the trim tool. A trim tool can be a surface, a sketched entity, or an edge.

4. Select the newly created sketch from the drawing area as the trim tool; the name of the selected sketch is displayed in the **Trim tool** selection area of the **Selections** rollout in the PropertyManager. Also, the selection mode of the **Pieces to Keep** selection area is activated and you are prompted to select pieces to keep.

Note

After selecting the trim tool, you will be prompted to select pieces to keep only if the ***Keep selections*** *radio button is selected by default in the* ***Selections*** *rollout of the* ***Trim Surface PropertyManager****.*

5. Ensure that the **Keep selections** radio button is selected in the **Selections** rollout of the PropertyManager. Next, move the cursor towards the upper portion of the sweep surface; the upper portion is highlighted in the drawing area.

The **Keep selections** radio button allows you to select the pieces that you want to keep in the surface model.

6. Click to select the upper portion of the sweep surface as a piece to keep; the name of the selected portion is displayed in the **Pieces to keep** selection area of the PropertyManager.

7. Choose the **OK** button from the **Trim Surface PropertyManager**; the surface of the model that is not selected as the surface to keep is removed from the surface model, as shown in Figure 9-9.

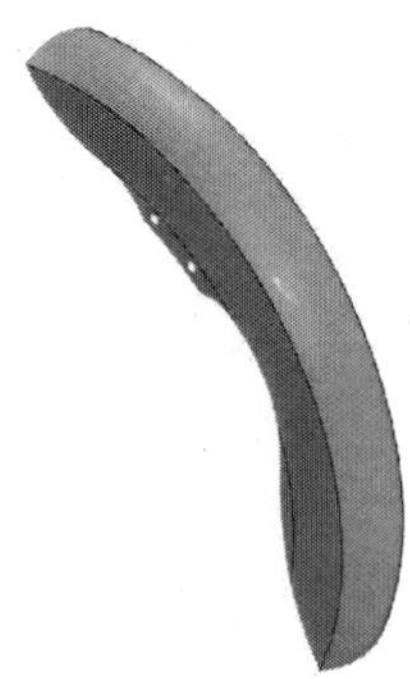

Figure 9-9 *Surface model after trimming the surface*

Applying the Fillet

Now, you need to apply fillet of radius 25.4 mm on the sharp edges of the surface model by using the **Fillet** tool.

1. Choose the **Fillet** button from the **Surfaces CommandManager**; the **Fillet PropertyManager** is displayed and you are prompted to select the edges, faces, features, or loops to fillet.

The options of the **Fillet** tool that are available in the **Surfaces CommandManager** are similar to the options which are discussed in the solid modeling.

2. Ensure that the **Constant Size Fillet** radio button is selected in the **Fillet Type** rollout of the PropertyManager and then set the value of the **Radius** spinner to **25**.4 mm in the **Fillet Parameters** rollout of the PropertyManager.

3. Select all the sharp edges of the model one by one; the preview of the fillet is displayed in the drawing area.

4. Choose the **OK** button from the **Fillet PropertyManager**; the fillet is added to the model, as shown in Figure 9-10.

Figure 9-10 *Model after applying the fillet*

Adding Thickness to the Surface Model

Now, you need to convert the surface model into a solid model by adding thickness of 1.27 mm.

1. Choose the **Thicken** button from the **Surfaces CommandManager**; the **Thicken PropertyManager** is displayed and you are prompted to select the surface to thicken.

The **Thicken** tool is used to add thickness to the surface bodies.

2. Select the surface model from the drawing area and then set the value of the **Thickness** spinner to **1.27** in the **Thickness** area of the PropertyManager.

3. Ensure that the **Thicken Side 1** button is chosen in the **Thickness** area of the PropertyManager.

In SolidWorks, you can specify the side on which you want to thicken the surface by using the buttons available in the **Thickness** area of the **Thicken PropertyManager**.

4. Choose the **OK** button from the PropertyManager; the thickness is added to the model, as shown in Figure 9-11.

Assign Color to the Model

Now, you will assign color to the model using the **Color PropertyManager**.

1. Choose **Edit > Appearance > Appearance** from the SolidWorks menu; the **Color PropertyManager** is displayed. Alternatively, select a face of the model; a Pop-up toolbar

is displayed. Now, from this toolbar, choose the **Appearances** button; a flyout is displayed with the name of the face, thicken, Body, and Part. Select the check box corresponding to the part to display the **Color PropertyManager**.

2. Select the required color that you want to assign to the model from the **Color PropertyManager**. Note that, if you have invoked the **Color PropertyManager** by choosing the **Appearance** from the SolidWorks menus then you need to select the model from the drawing area.

3. After selecting the required color, choose the **OK** button from the PropertyManager. The model after assigning the red color is shown in Figure 9-12.

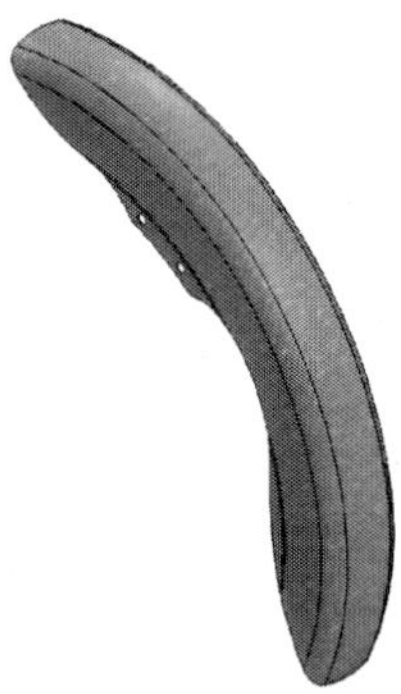

Figure 9-11 *Model adding the thickness*

Figure 9-12 *Model after assigning the red color*

Saving the Model

After creating the model, you need to save it in the *Motor Cycle Project* folder.

1. Save the model with the name Front Mudguard in the *Motor Cycle Project* folder.

2. Close document by choosing **File > Close** from the SolidWorks menus.

CREATING THE REAR MUDGUARD

Part Description

In this section, you will create the Rear Mudguard, as shown in Figure 9-13. It will be created by using the surface modeling tools. The different views and dimensions of the Rear Mudguard are given in the Figure 9-14. Assume the missing dimensions. **(Expected time: 55 min)**

Figure 9-13 The Rear Mudguard

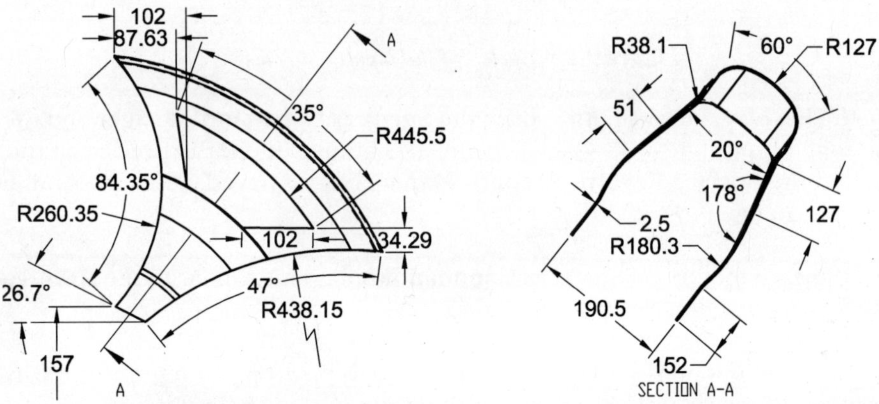

Figure 9-14 The views and dimensions of the model

Creating the Base Feature

The base feature of the model is a revolve surface, created by revolving a sketch along a centerline.

1. Start new SolidWorks part document using the **New SOLIDWORKS Document** dialog box. Modify the unit of the current session to mm, if it is not set by default.

2. Invoke the sketcher environment by selecting the Right Plane as the sketching plane and create the sketch of the revolve surface, refer to Figure 9-15. Next, exit from the sketcher environment.

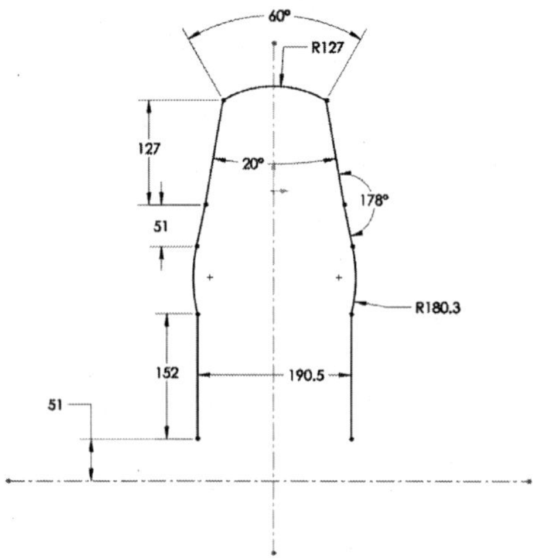

Figure 9-15 Sketch of the revolve surface

3. Choose the **Revolve Surface** button from the **Surfaces CommandManager** and then select the horizontal centerline of the sketch as the axis of revolution; the preview of the revolve surface and the **Surface-Revolve PropertyManager** is displayed. Also, the orientation of the sketch is changed to trimetric.

The **Revolve Surface** tool of the **Surfaces CommandManager** is similar to the **Revolved Boss/Base** tool that is discussed in the solid modeling.

4. Ensure the **Blind** option is selected in the **Revolve Type** drop-down list of the **Direction 1** rollout of the PropertyManager, Next, set the value of the **Angle** spinner to **65** and select the horizontal center line as axis.

5. Choose the **OK** button from the PropertyManager; the revolve surface is created, as shown in Figure 9-16.

Trimming the Unwanted Surfaces

Now, you will trim the unwanted surface of the revolve surface using a sketched entity as trim tool.

1. Invoke the sketcher environment by selecting the Front Plane as the sketching plane and draw the sketch of the trim tool for trimming the revolve surface, refer to Figure 9-17.

Figure 9-16 Base feature of the model

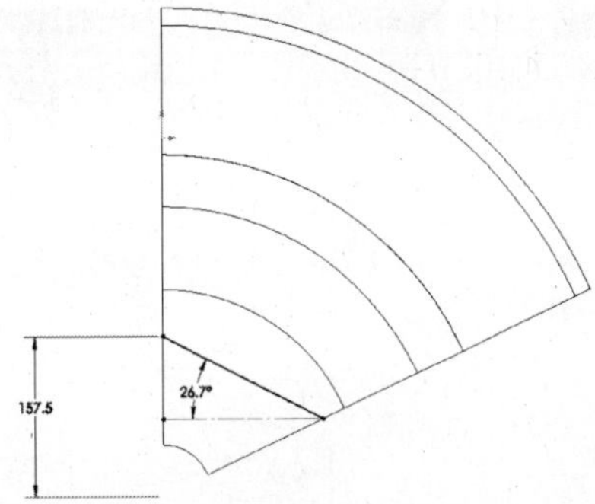

Figure 9-17 Sketch for trimming surface

2. Exit from the sketcher environment and click anywhere in the drawing area to exit from the current selection mode.

3. Choose the **Trim Surface** button from the **Surfaces CommandManager**; the **Trim Surface PropertyManager** is displayed and you are prompted to select trim tool.

4. Select the sketch from the drawing area as the trim tool and then select the **Remove selections** radio button from the **Selections** rollout of the PropertyManager.

The **Remove selections** radio button is allow you to select the pieces that you want to remove from the surface model.

5. Move the cursor toward a surface that is lies below the sketch; the surface is highlighted in the drawing area. Next, click to select it; the name of the selected surface is displayed in the **Pieces to Remove** selection area of the PropertyManager.

6. Similarly, select the other surface of the model that is lies below the sketch.

7. Choose the **OK** button from the **Trim Surface PropertyManager**; the selected surfaces are removed from the surface model, refer to Figure 9-18.

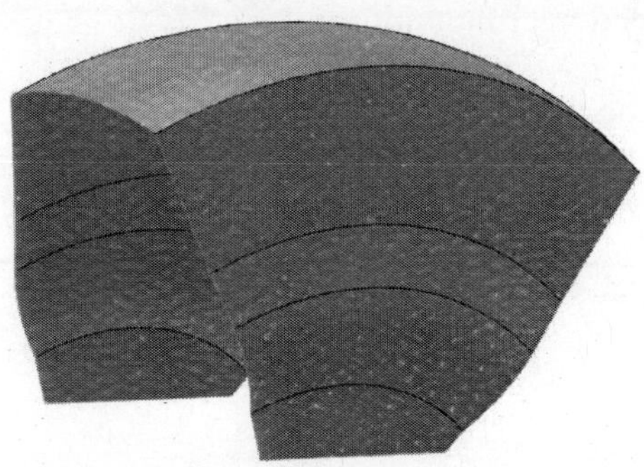

Figure 9-18 Model after removing the surfaces

Trimming the Remaining Unwanted Surfaces

Now, you will trim the remaining unwanted surfaces of the surface model using a sketched entity as trim tool.

1. Invoke the sketcher environment by selecting the Front Plane as the sketching plane and draw the sketch of the trim tool for trimming the remaining unwanted surfaces, refer to Figure 9-19.

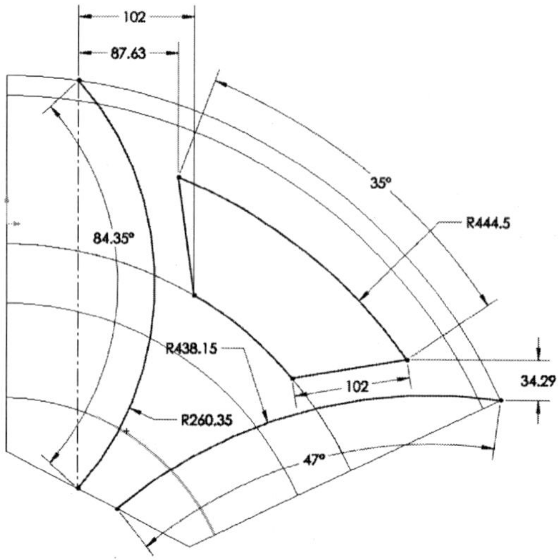

Figure 9-19 *Sketch for trimming surface*

2. Exit from the sketcher environment and click anywhere in the drawing area to exit from the current selection mode.

3. Choose the **Trim Surface** button from the **Surfaces CommandManager**; the **Trim Surface PropertyManager** is displayed and you are prompted to select trim tool.

4. Select the sketch from the drawing area as the trim tool and then select the **Keep selections** radio button from the **Selections** rollout of the PropertyManager.

5. Move the cursor toward the surface, refer to Figure 9-20. Next, click to select it. Next, choose the **OK** button from the PropertyManager. The surface model after trimming all the unwanted surfaces of the model is shown in Figure 9-21.

Figure 9-20 *Surface to be selected*

Figure 9-21 *Model after removing the unwanted surface*

Applying the Fillet

Now, you need to apply fillet of radius 38.1 mm on the sharp edges of the surface model by using the **Fillet** tool.

1. Choose the **Fillet** button from the **Surfaces CommandManager**; the **Fillet PropertyManager** is displayed and you are prompted to select the edges, faces, features, or loops to fillet.

2. Ensure that the **Constant Size Fillet** radio button is selected in the **Fillet Type** rollout of the PropertyManager and then set the value of the **Radius** spinner to **38.1 mm** in the **Items To Fillet** rollout of the PropertyManager.

3. Select all the sharp edges of the model one by one; the preview of the fillet is displayed in the drawing area.

4. Choose the **OK** button from the **Fillet PropertyManager**; the fillet is added to the model, as shown in Figure 9-22.

Adding Thickness to the Surface Model

Now, you need to convert the surface model into a solid model by adding thickness of 2.5 mm.

1. Choose the **Thicken** button from the **Surfaces CommandManager**; the **Thicken PropertyManager** is displayed and you are prompted to select the surface to thicken.

2. Select the surface model from the drawing area and then set the value of the **Thickness** spinner to **2.5** in the **Thickness** area of the PropertyManager.

3. Ensure that the **Thicken Side 2** button is chosen in the **Thickness** area of the PropertyManager.

4. Choose the **OK** button from the PropertyManager; the thickness is added to the model, as shown in Figure 9-23.

Figure 9-22 Model after applying fillet

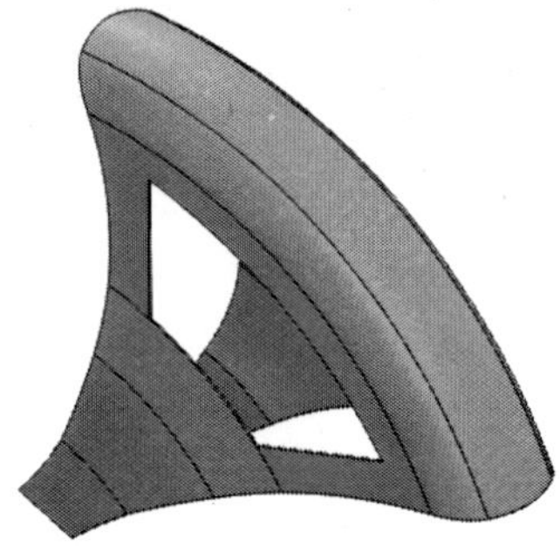

Figure 9-23 Model after adding the thickness

Assign Color to the Model

Now, you will assign color to the model using the **Color PropertyManager**.

1. Invoke the **Color PropertyManager** assign the color to the model as per your requirement. The final model after assigning the black color is shown in Figure 9-24.

Figure 9-24 Model after assigning black color

Saving the Model

After create the model, you need to save it in the *Motor Cycle Project* folder.

1. Save the model with the name Rear Mudguard in the *Motor Cycle Project* folder.

2. Close document by choosing **File > Close** from the SolidWorks menus.

CREATING THE FUEL TANK

Part Description

In this section, you will create the Fuel Tank, as shown in Figure 9-25. It will be created by using the surface modeling tools. The five sections to be used for creating the base feature are shown in Figures 9-26(a) and 9-26(b). The total spacing between Sections 1 and 2 is 102 mm, between Sections 2 and 3 is 102 mm, between sections 3 and 4 is 178 mm, and between sections 4 and 5 is 131 mm. The front and top views with dimensions of the Fuel Tank are shown in the Figure 9-27. Note that in this section, first you will create a half loft surface as the base feature and then mirror it. The fillet radius of the model is 25.4 mm. Assume the missing dimensions.

(Expected time: 55 min)

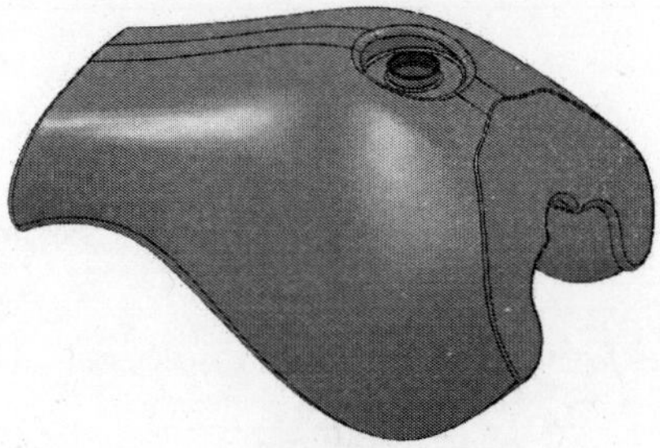

Figure 9-25 *The Fuel Tank*

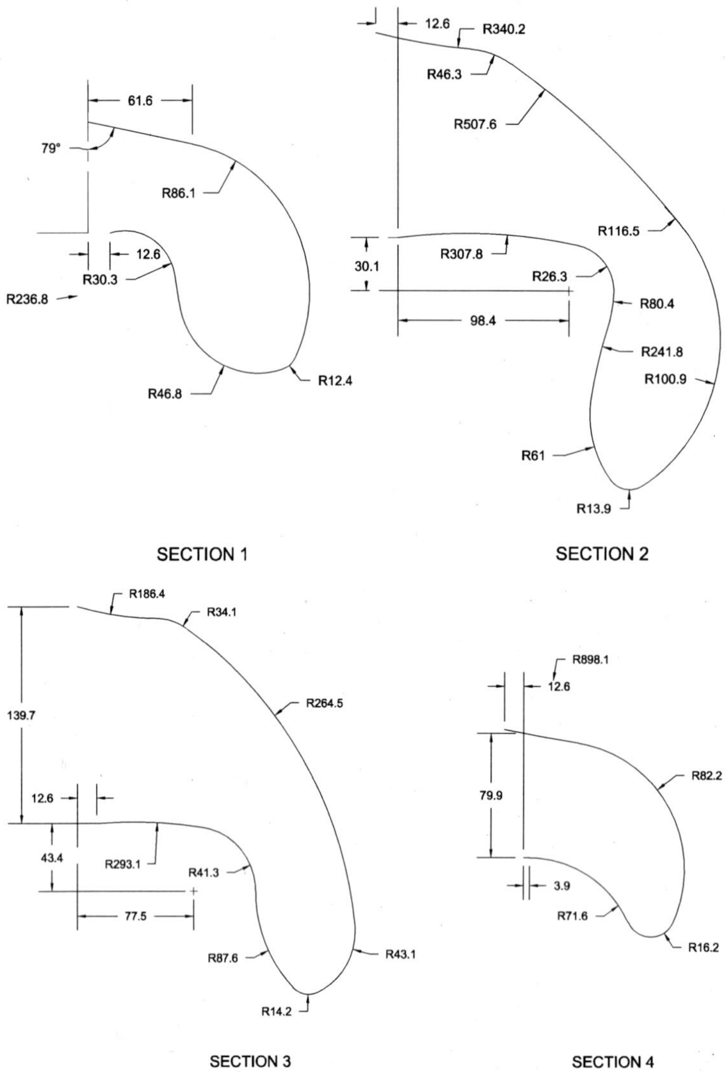

Figure 9-26 *Sections 1 to 4 for creating the loft surface*

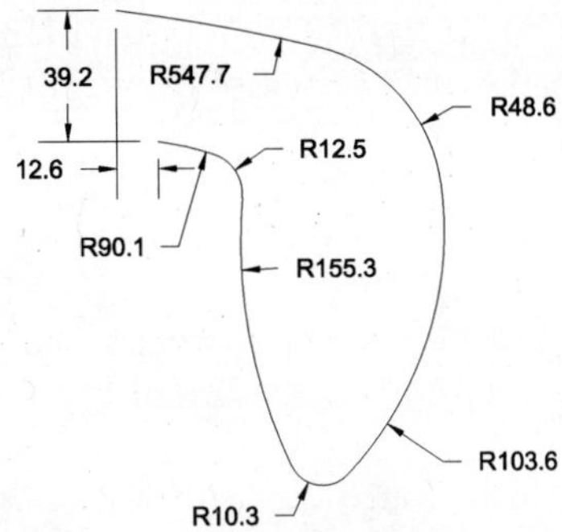

SECTION 5

Figure 9-26(b) Section 5 for creating the loft surface

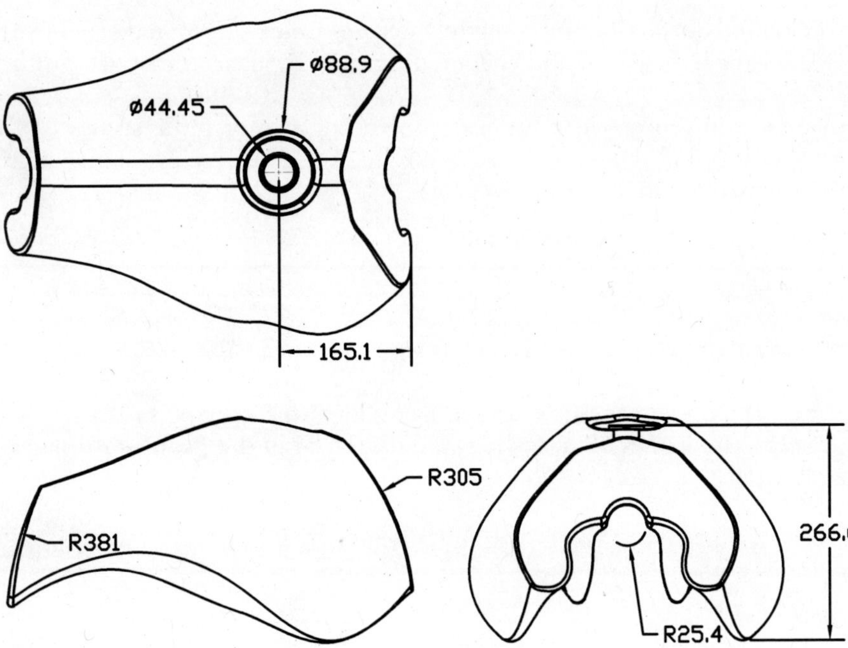

Figure 9-27 Different views of the model

Creating the Base Surface

As mentioned in the part description, the base surface of the model will be created by blending dissimilar sections. First you will create a half loft surface and then mirror it.

1. Start a new SolidWorks part document using the **New SolidWorks Document** dialog box.

2. Create four reference planes at the offset distance of 102, 204, 382 and 513 mm from the **Right Plane**. Note that while creating these reference planes, you need to select the **Flip** check box so that they are created at the back of the Right Plane, refer to Figure 9-28.

Next, you need to create sections to create a lofted surface.

3. Invoke the sketching environment by selecting the **Right Plane** as the sketching plane and then create the first section for the loft surface, refer to Figure 9-28. For dimensions, refer to Figure 9-26. Next, exit the sketching environment.

4. Similarly, create the second, third, fourth, and fifth sections for the loft surface on their respective planes, refer to Figure 9-28. For dimensions, refer to Figure 9-26. Apply tangent constraints to make the sketches fully-constrained.

After creating the sections of the lofted surface, you need to invoke the Lofted Surface tool.

5. Choose the **Lofted Surface** button from the **Surfaces CommandManager**; the **Surface-Loft PropertyManager** is displayed and you are prompted to select atleast two profiles.

   In SolidWorks, you can create a surface by blending two or more sections by using the Lofted Surface tool. All the options for creating a lofted surface are similar to those used for creating a solid lofted feature.

Note

If you want to create a loft surface with open section, all sections to be lofted must be open sections. Similarly, if you want to create a closed lofted surface, all sections must be closed sections. The combination of closed and opened sections is not possible in a lofted surface.

6. Select all sections one by one from the drawing area; the preview of the lofted surface is displayed. Also, the names of all sections are displayed in the **Profiles** display area of the PropertyManager.

7. Choose the **OK** button; the lofted surface is created, as shown in Figure 9-29.

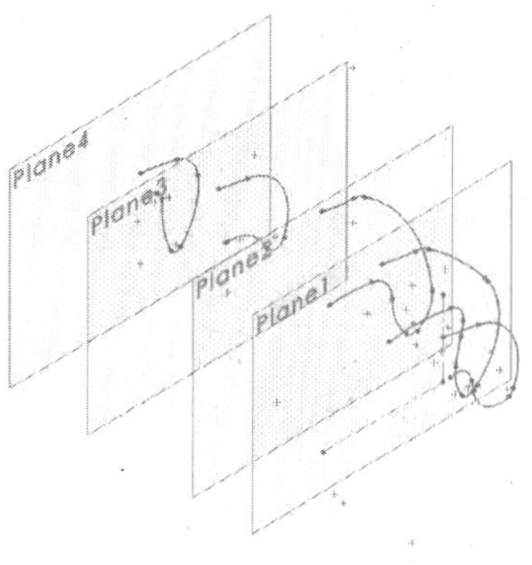

Figure 9-28 *Sections created for creating the loft surface*

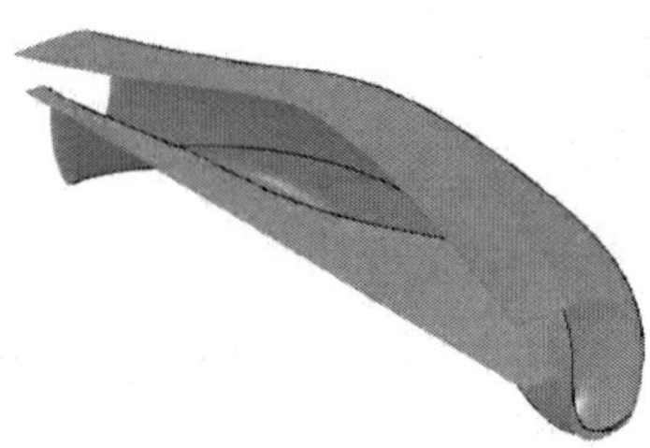

Figure 9-29 *The loft surface*

Creating the Mirror Surface

After creating the lofted surface, you need to mirror it using the **Front Plane** as a mirroring plane.

1. Choose **Insert > Pattern/Mirror > Mirror** from the Menu Bar; the **Mirror PropertyManager** is displayed.

2. Select the **Front Plane** as the mirroring plane from the **FeatureManager** design tree.

3. Expand the **Bodies to Mirror** rollout of the **Mirror PropertyManager**. Select the lofted surface as the body to mirror; the preview of the mirror surface is displayed.

4. Choose the **OK** button from the **Mirror PropertyManager**; the mirroring of the lofted surface is created, as shown in Figure 9-30.

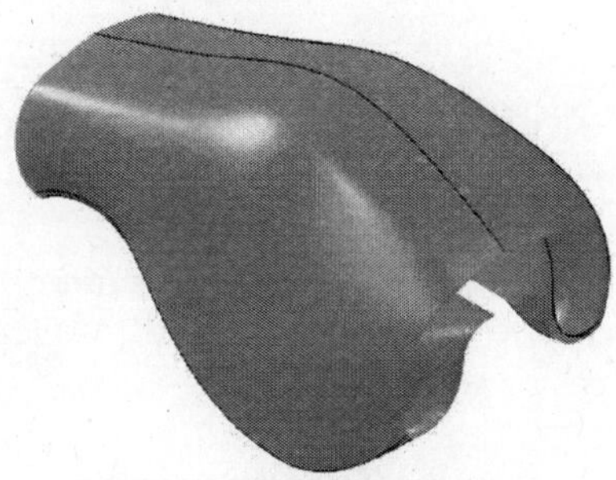

Figure 9-30 *The surface model after mirroring the loft surface*

Creating the Extruded Surface

Next, you will create the extruded surface by using the **Extruded Surface** tool.

1. Invoke the sketching environment by using the **Right Plane** as the sketching plane and then draw the sketch of the extrude surface, refer to Figure 9-31. Next, exit the sketching environment.

2. Choose the **Extruded Surface** button from the **Surfaces CommandManager** and then select the sketch from the drawing area; the preview of the extruded surface is displayed in the drawing area.

3. Choose the **Reverse Direction** button from the **Direction 1** rollout of the **PropertyManager** to reverse the direction of the surface creation.

4. Select the **Blind** option from the **End Condition** drop-down list of the **Direction 1** rollout of the **PropertyManager** and then enter **700** as the depth of extrusion in the **Depth** edit box.

5. Choose the **OK** button from the **PropertyManager**; the extrude surface is created, refer to Figure 9-32.

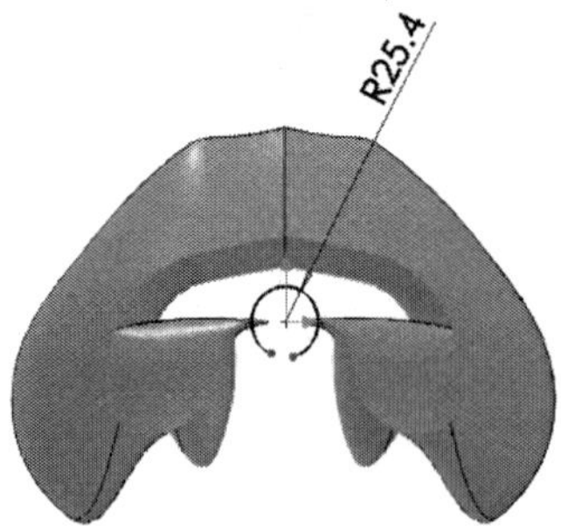

Figure 9-31 *The sketch for the extrude surface*

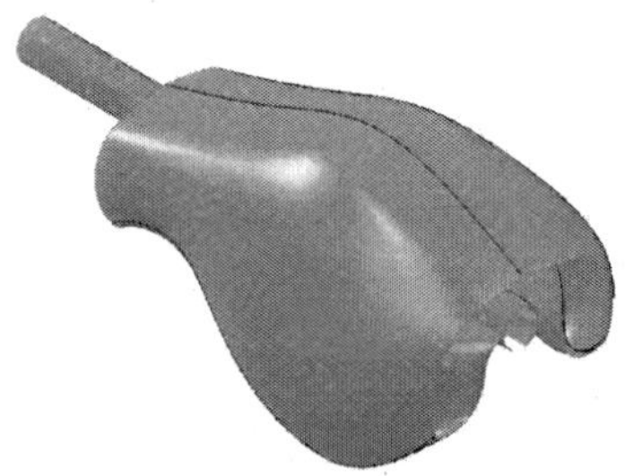

Figure 9-32 *The surface model after creating the extruded surface*

Trimming the Surfaces Using the Extruded Surface

Next, you need to trim the unwanted portions of the surfaces by using the Mutual option.

1. Choose the **Trim Surface** tool from the **Surfaces CommandManager**; the **Trim Surface PropertyManager** is displayed and you are prompted to select a trimming surface, plane, or sketch followed by the pieces to keep or remove.

2. Select the **Mutual** radio button from the **Trim Type** rollout of the PropertyManager.

   The **Mutual** radio button is used to select the surfaces to be trimmed and the surfaces to be kept or removed.

3. Select all surfaces from the drawing area as trimming surfaces and then select the **keep selections** radio button from the Selections rollout of the PropertyManager.

4. Click in the **Pieces to Keep** selection area to activate the selection mode and then select the surfaces as the pieces to keep, refer to Figure 9-33.

5. Choose the **OK** button from the **Trim Surfaces PropertyManager**. The isometric view of the model after trimming the unwanted portions of the surfaces is shown in Figure 9-34.

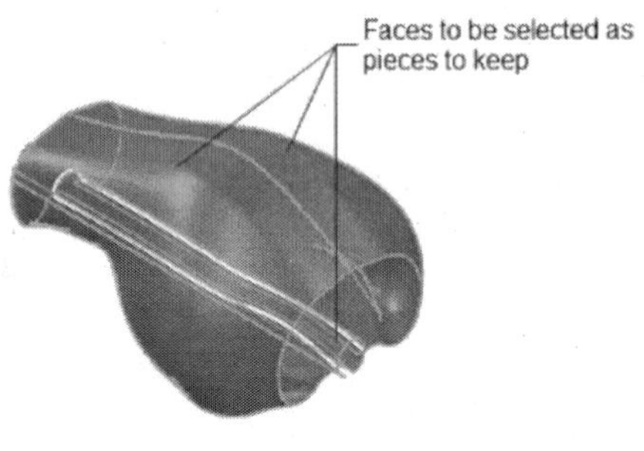

Figure 9-33 *Surfaces to be selected as the pieces to keep*

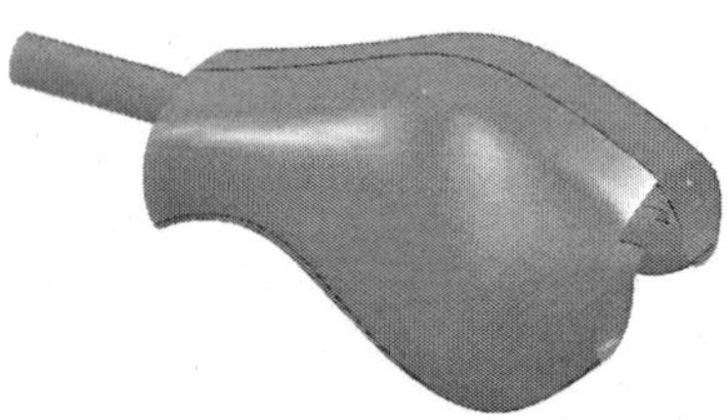

Figure 9-34 *Surface model after trimming the unwanted portions of the surfaces*

Creating the Second Extrude Surface

Next, you will create the extrude surface. This surface is created by extruding a sketch created on the **Front Plane**.

1. Invoke the sketching environment by selecting the **Front Plane** as the sketching plane and then change the orientation of the sketching plane normal to the view.

2. Draw the sketch of the extrude surface, refer to Figure 9-35. Note that the sketch should coincide with the surface both at top and bottom.

3. Choose the **Extruded Surface** button without exiting the sketching environment; the **Surface-Extrude PropertyManager** is displayed. Also, the preview of the extrude surface is displayed in the drawing area.

4. Right-click in the drawing area and then choose the **Mid Plane** option from the shortcut menu displayed.

5. Drag the handle displayed with the preview of the extruded surface in the drawing area in such a way that it passes through all the existing surfaces.

6. Choose the **OK** button from the PropertyManager; the extruded surface is created, refer to Figure 9-36.

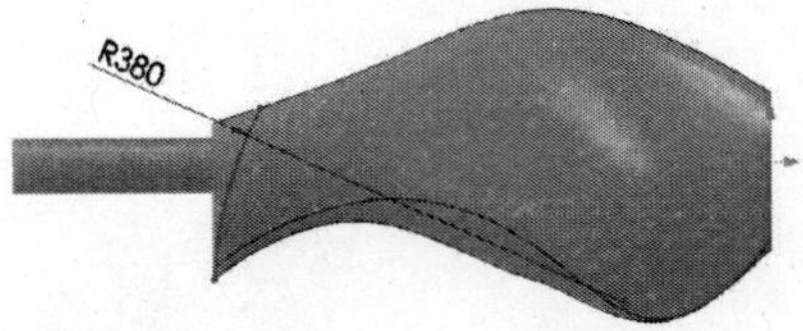

Figure 9-35 *Sketch for the extrude feature*

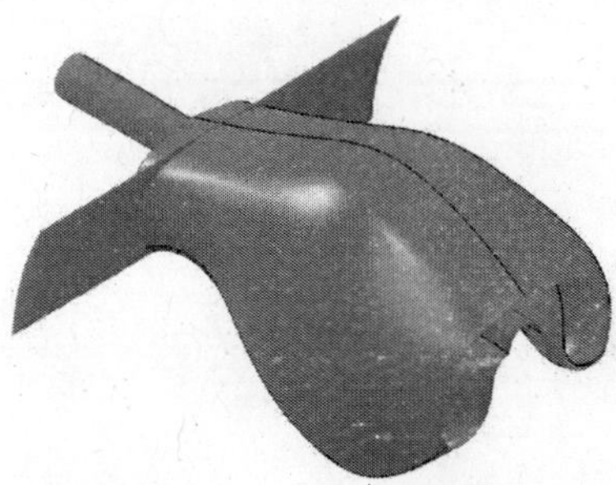

Figure 9-36 *Surface model after extruding the sketch*

Creating the Third Extrude Surface

In this section, you again need to create an extruded surface.

1. Invoke the sketching environment by selecting the **Front Plane** as the sketching plane and then change the orientation of the sketching plane normal to the view.

2. Draw the sketch for the extrude surface, refer to Figure 9-37, and then extrude it by using the **Mid Plane** option. Make sure that it passes through all the existing surfaces, refer to Figure 9-38.

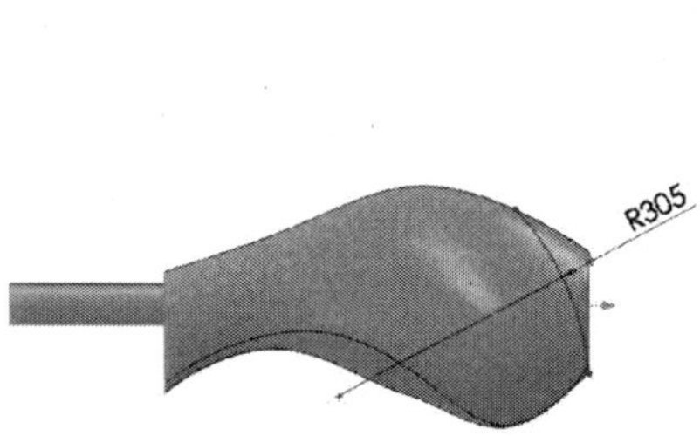

Figure 9-37 *Sketch for the extrude feature*

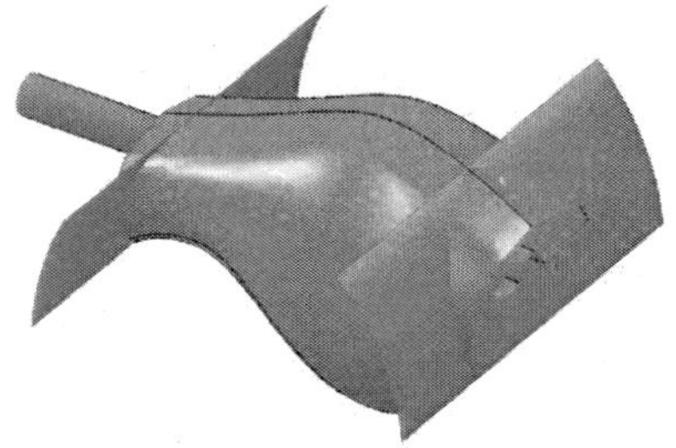

Figure 9-38 *Surface model after extruding the sketch*

Trimming the Unwanted Portions of the Surfaces

Next, you need to trim the unwanted portions of the surface by using the Mutual option.

1. Invoke the **Trim Surface PropertyManager** and select the **Mutual** radio button from the **Selections** rollout of this PropertyManager.

2. Select all the surfaces displayed in the drawing area as the trimming surfaces and then select the **keep selections** radio button from the **Selections** rollout of the PropertyManager.

3. Click in the **Pieces to Keep** selection area to activate the selection mode and then select the portions of the surfaces as the pieces to keep, refer to Figure 9-39.

4. Choose the **OK** button from the **Trim Surface PropertyManager**. The isometric view of the model after trimming the unwanted portions of the surfaces is shown in Figure 9-40.

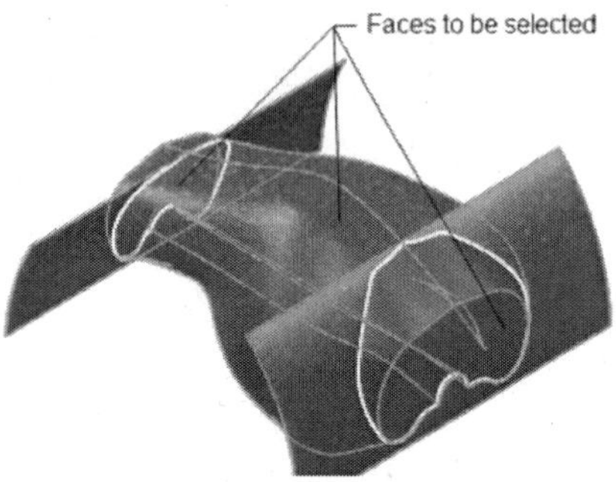

Figure 9-39 *Faces to be selected*

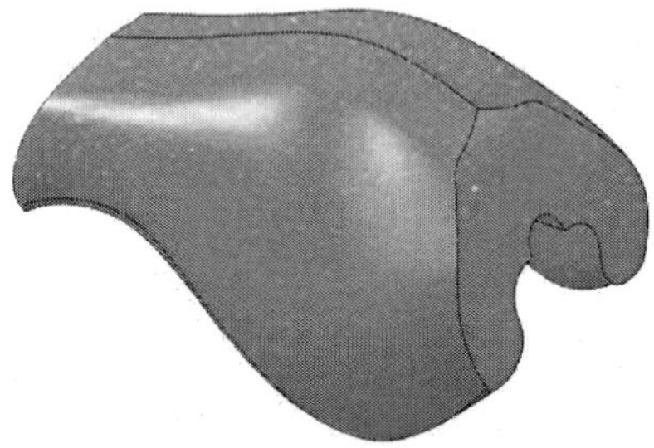

Figure 9-40 *Surface model after trimming the unwanted portions of the surfaces*

Creating the Fourth Extrude Surface

In this section, you need to create the fourth extruded surface.

1. Create a reference plane at an offset distance of 188 mm from the **Top Plane** and then invoke the sketching environment by selecting it as the sketching plane.

2. Draw the sketch for the extrude surface, refer to Figure 9-41, and then extrude it upto the distance of 76 mm by using the **Blind** option. The surface model after creating the extruded surface is shown in Figure 9-42.

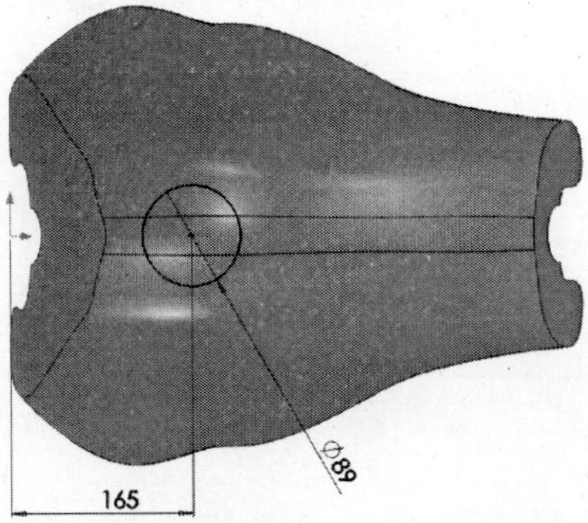

Figure 9-41 *Sketch for the extrude feature*

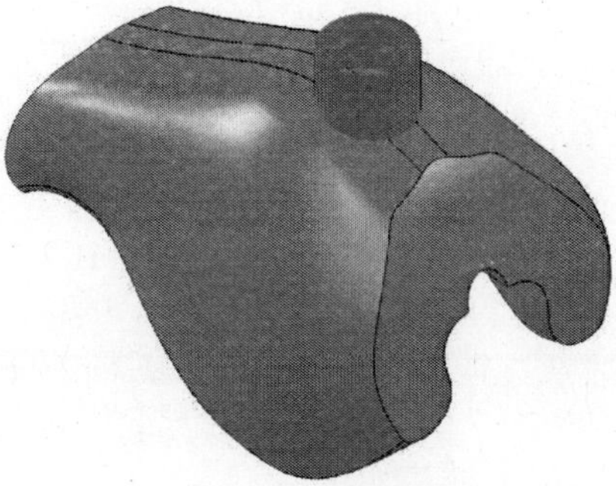

Figure 9-42 *Surface model after creating the extruded surface*

Trimming the Unwanted Portions of the Surface

Next, you need to trim the unwanted portions of the surface by using the **Standard** option.

1. Invoke the **Trim Surface PropertyManager** and select the **Standard** radio button in the **Selections** rollout of this PropertyManager.

2. Select the previously created extruded surface as the trim tool and then select the **Remove selections** radio button in the **Selections** rollout of the PropertyManager.

3. Click in the **Pieces to Remove** selection area to activate the selection mode and then select the portion lying inside the previously created extruded surface as the surface to be removed.

4. Choose the **OK** button from the **Trim Surfaces PropertyManager**, refer to Figure 9-43.

5. Similarly, invoke the **Trim Surface PropertyManager** and trim the upper extended portion of the previously created extruded surface, refer to Figure 9-44.

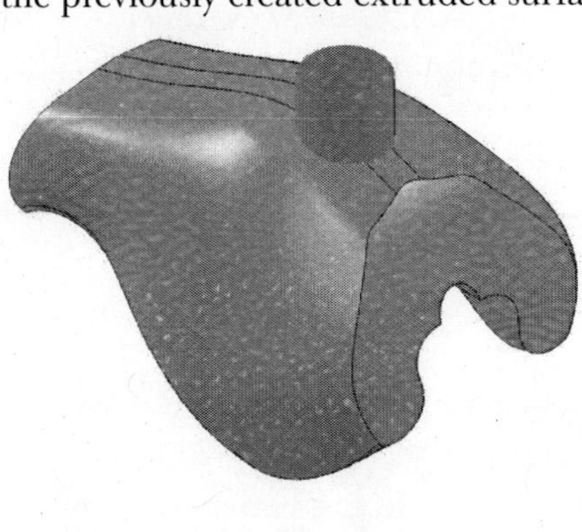

Figure 9-43 *Surface model after trimming the surface lying inside the extruded surface*

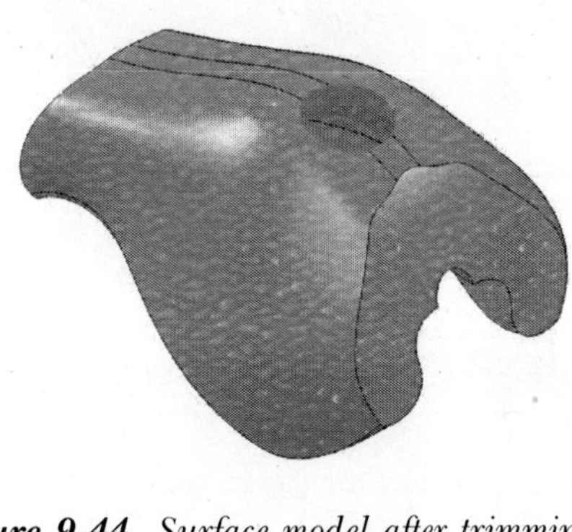

Figure 9-44 *Surface model after trimming the upper portion of the previously created extruded surface*

Creating the Planar Surface

Next, you need to create the planar surface by using the **Planar Surface** tool.

1. Choose the **Planar Surface** button from the **Surfaces CommandManager**; the **Planar Surface PropertyManager** is displayed.

The Planar Surface tool is used to fill gaps between surfaces by using a planar patch.

2. Select the circular edge of the surface model, refer to Figure 9-45; the preview of the planar surface is displayed. Next, choose the **OK** button from the PropertyManager; the planar surface is created, refer to Figure 9-46.

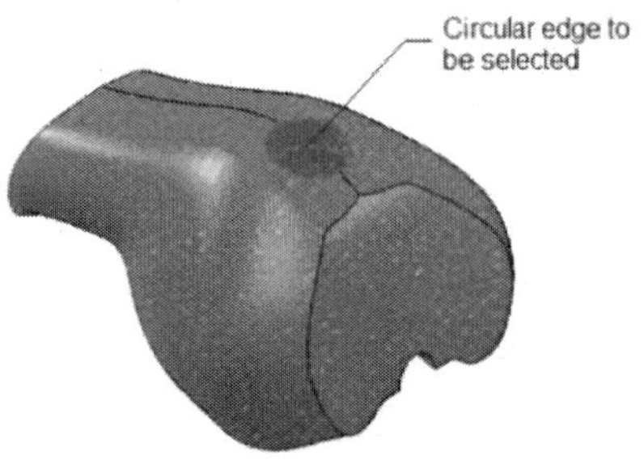

Figure 9-45 *Circular edge to be selected*

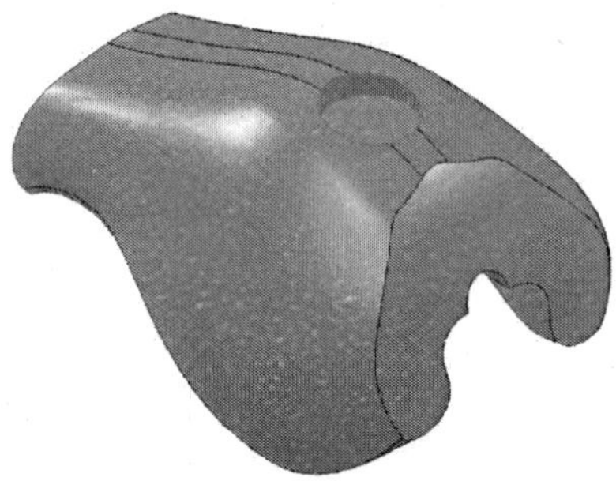

Figure 9-46 *Surface model after creating the planar surface*

Creating the Fifth Extrude Surface

Next, you need to create another extrude surface and then trim the surface lying inside it.

1. Invoke the sketching environment by selecting the previously created planar surface as the sketching plane and draw the sketch for the extrude surface, refer to Figure 9-47. Next, extrude the sketch upto the distance of **11.5** mm in the upward direction, refer to Figure 9-48.

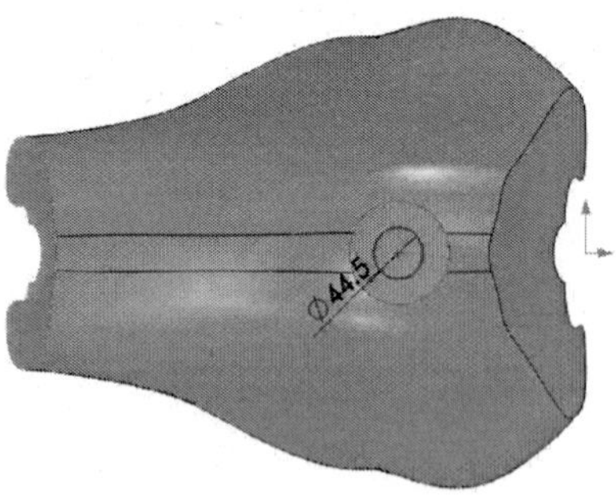

Figure 9-47 *Sketch for the extrude surface*

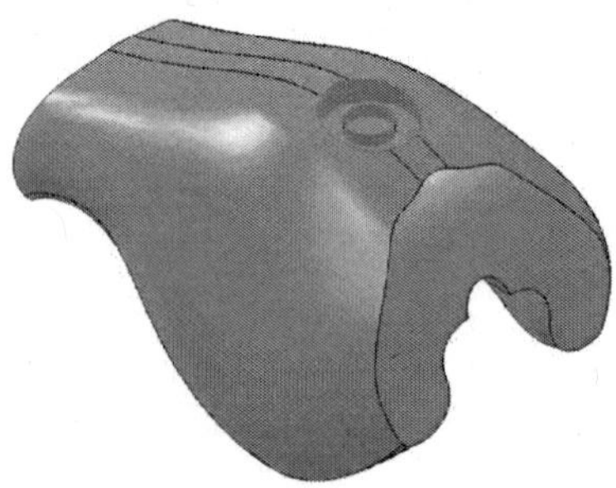

Figure 9-48 *Surface model after creating the extruded surface*

2. Trim the portion lying inside the previously created circular extruded surface, refer to Figure 9-49.

Knitting all Surfaces

After creating all the surfaces, you need to knit them together by using the **Knit Surface** tool.

1. Choose the **Knit Surface** button from the **Surfaces CommandManager**; the **Knit Surface PropertyManager** is displayed and you are prompted to select the surfaces to knit.

   The **Knit Surface** tool is used to knit multiple surfaces together to create a single surface.

2. Select all surfaces from the drawing area one by one and then choose the **OK** button from the PropertyManager

Applying the Fillet

After creating all the surfaces of the model, you need to add the fillet using the **Fillet PropertyManager**.

1. Invoke the **Fillet PropertyManager** and set **3.8 mm** in the **Radius** spinner of the **Items To Fillet** rollout.

2. Select all sharp edges of the surface model to apply fillet and then choose the **OK** button; the fillet is created. The isometric view of the model after applying the fillet is shown in Figure 9-50.

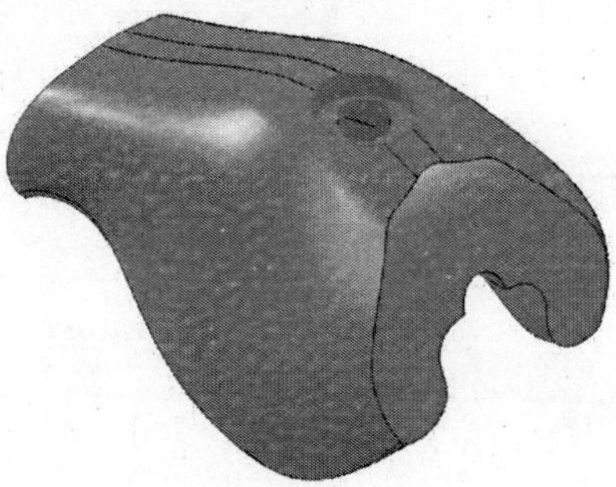

Figure 9-49 *Surface model after trimming the surface*

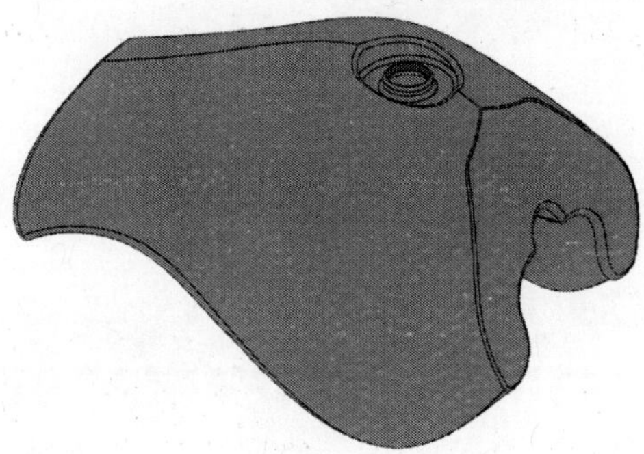

Figure 9-50 *Surface model after applying the fillet*

Adding Thickness to the Surface Model

Next, you need to add thickness to the surface model.

1. Choose the **Thicken** button from the **Surfaces CommandManager**; the **Thicken PropertyManager** is displayed.

2. Select the surface model from the drawing area and then set the value of the **Thickness** spinner to **2.54 mm**. Next, choose the **Thicken Side 2** button to specify the thickness of the surface.

3. Choose the **OK** button from the PropertyManager. The section view of the model after thickening the surface is shown in Figure 9-51.

Applying Color to the Model

Next, you need to assign a color to the model.

1. Assign a color of your choice to the model by using the **color PropertyManager**. The final model, after assigning the red color to it is shown in Figure 9-52.

Saving the Model

After creating the model, you need to save it in the *Motor Cycle Project* folder.

1. Save the model with the name *Fuel Tank* in the *Motor Cycle Project* folder.

2. Close the document by choosing **File > Close** from the SolidWorks menus.

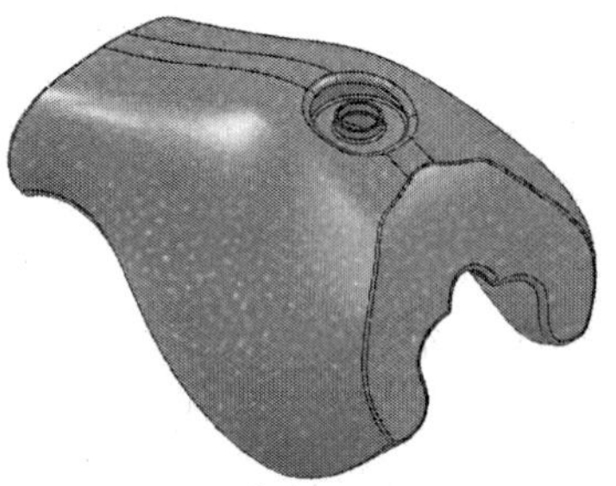

Figure 9-51 *Model after adding thickness*

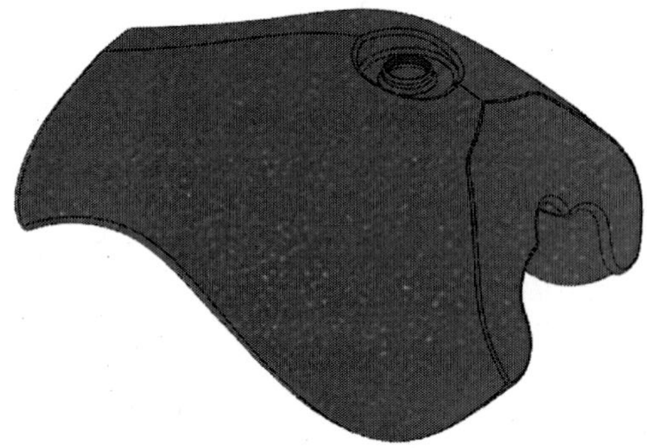

Figure 9-52 *Model after assigning color*

CREATING THE HEADLIGHT MASK

Part Description

In this section, you will create the Headlight Mask, as shown in Figure 9-53. The base feature of the model will be created by blending four dissimilar sections along a guide curve. The four sections to be used for creating the base feature are shown in Figure 9-54(a). The spacing between Sections 1 and 2 is 102 mm, between Sections 2 and 3 is 115 mm, and between Sections 3 and 4 is 115 mm. This model will be created by using the surface modeling tools. The dimensions of guide curve are shown in Figure 9-54(b). The different views and dimensions of the Headlight Mask are shown in Figure 9-54(c). Assume the missing dimensions.

(Expected time: 50 min)

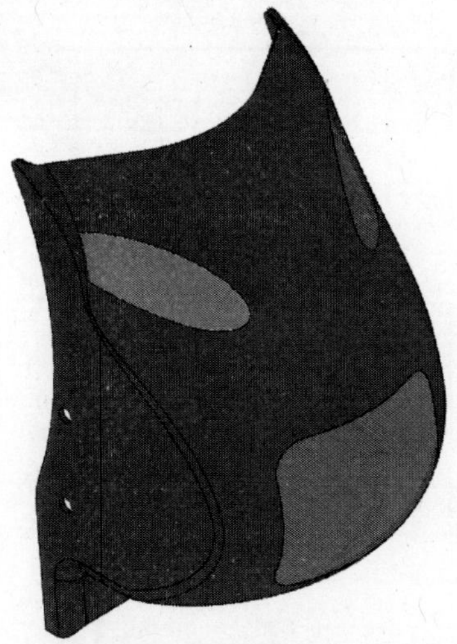

Figure 9-53 Headlight Mask

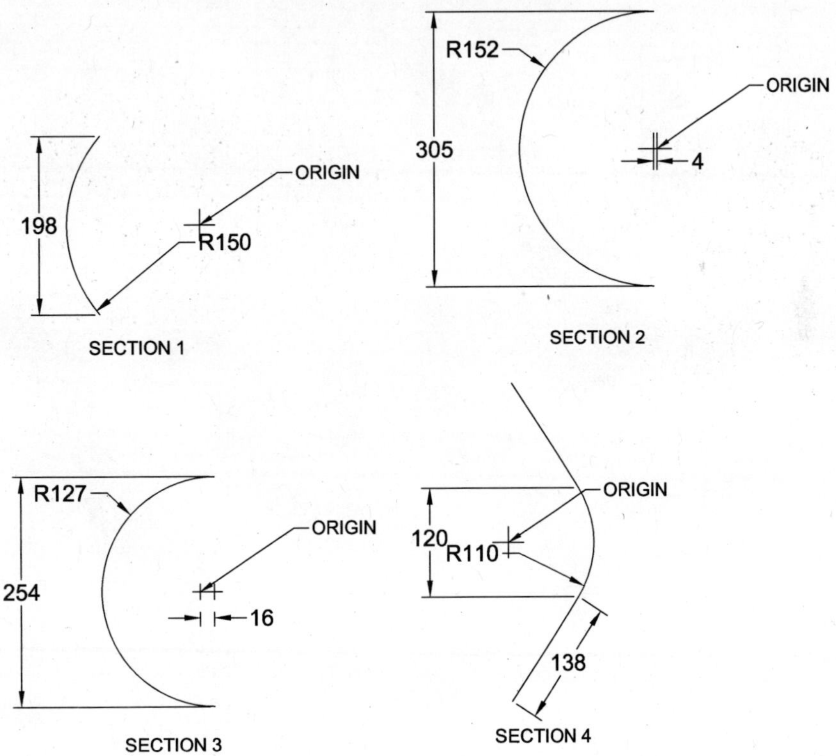

Figure 9-54(a) *The four sections to create the base feature*

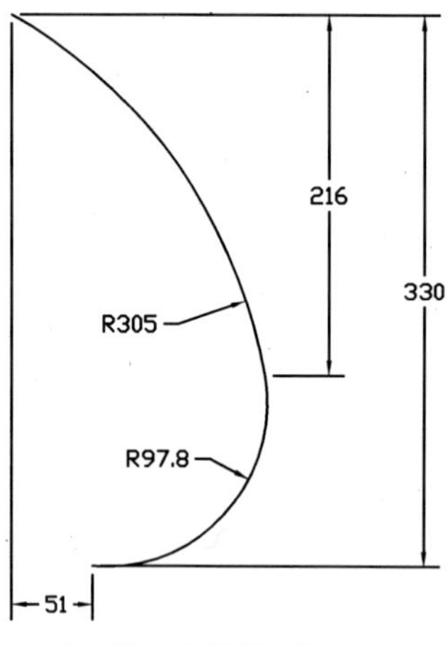

Figure 9-54(b) *The dimensions of the guide curve*

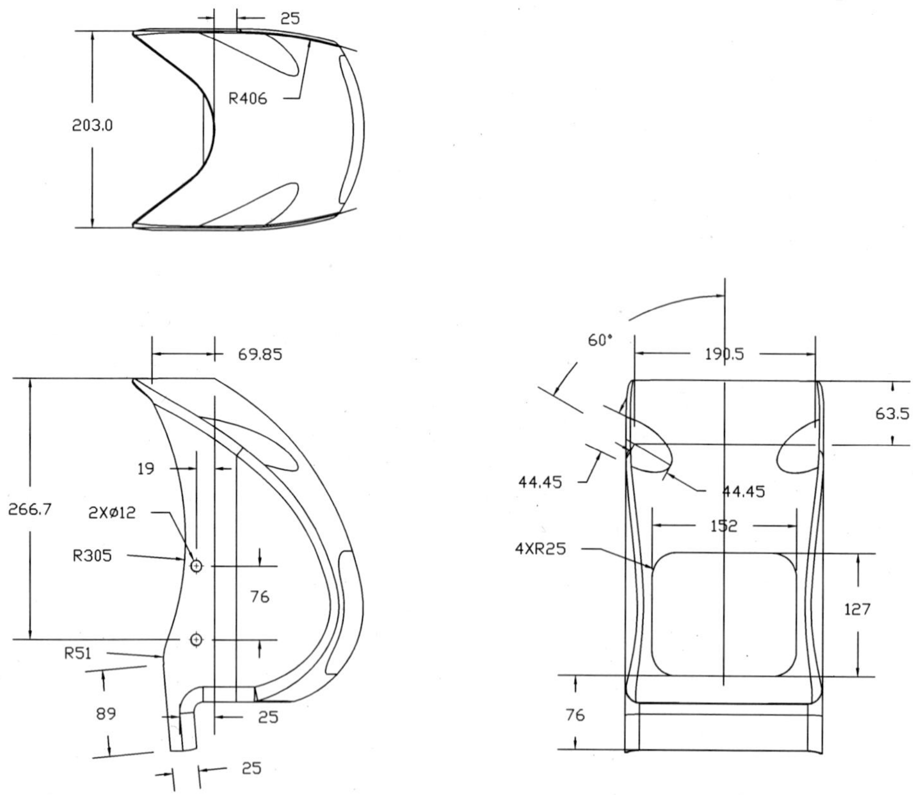

Figure 9-54(c) *The views and dimensions of the model*

Creating the Base Feature

The base surface of this model will be created by blending the sections along the guide curves. The sections will be created on different planes. So, first you need to create three planes at some offset distance from the Top Plane.

1. Start a SolidWork part document by using the **New SolidWorks Document** dialog box.

2. Create three reference planes at the offset distance of 102, 216 and 330 mm from the **Top Plane**.

Next, you need to create sections and guide curves for creating a lofted surface.

3. Invoke the sketching environment by selecting the **Top Plane** as the sketching plane and create the first section for the loft surface, refer to Figure 9-55. Next, exit the sketching environment.

4. Similarly, create the second, third, and fourth sections for the loft surface on their respective planes, refer to Figure 9-56. For dimensions, refer to Figure 9-54. Make the sketches symmetric about the horizontal centerlines.

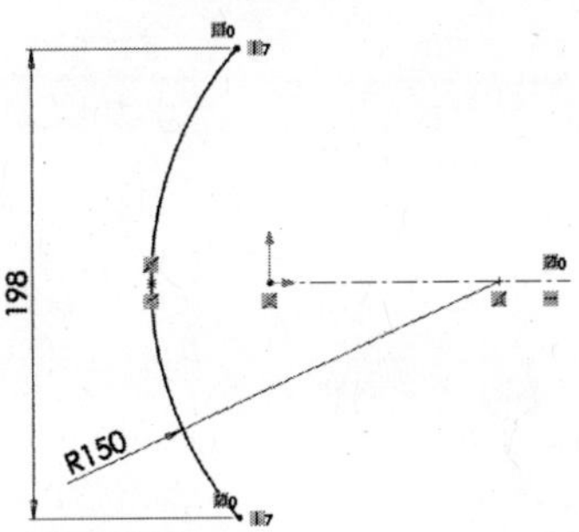

Figure 9-55 Sketch of the first section of the loft surface

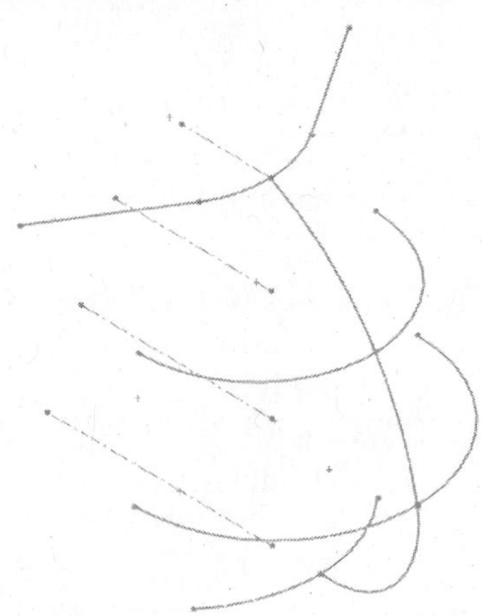

Figure 9-56 Sections for the loft surface

5. Invoke the sketching environment by selecting the **Front Plane** as the sketching plane and then create the guide curve, refer to Figure 9-57. Note that you need to apply the pierce or coincident relation between the sections and the guide curve. Also, the guide curve is created using three arcs, refer to Figure 9-57. Next, exit the sketching environment.

6. Invoke the **Surface-Loft PropertyManager** by choosing the **Lofted Surface** button from the **Surfaces CommandManager**.

7. Select all sections one by one from the drawing area; the names of the sections are displayed in the display area of the **Profiles** rollout. Also, the preview of the lofted surface is displayed.

8. Click once in the selection area of the **Guide Curves** rollout in the PropertyManager to activate its selection mode. Next, select the guide curve from the drawing area; the name of the guide curve is displayed in the selection area of the **Guide Curves** rollout of the PropertyManager. Also, the preview of the loft surface is modified according to the guide curve.

9. Choose the **OK** button from the Su**rface-Loft PropertyManager**. The isometric view of the surface model after creating the loft surface is shown in Figure 9-58.

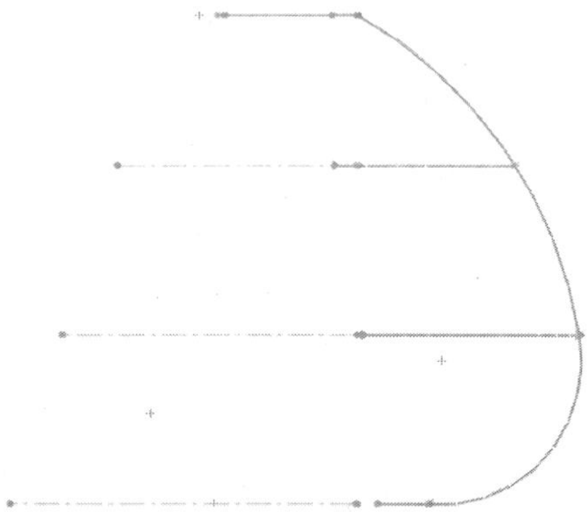

Figure 9-57 *Sketch for the guide curve*

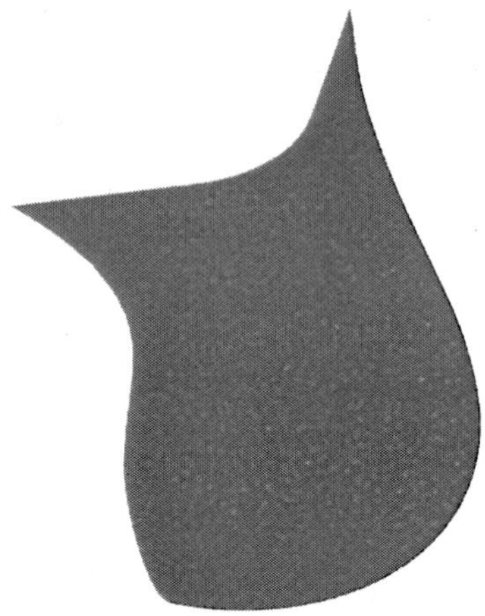

Figure 9-58 *The loft surface*

Creating the Extrude Surface

Next, you will create the extrude surface. This surface will be created by extruding the sketch created on the **Front Plane**.

1. Invoke the sketching environment by selecting the **Front Plane** as the sketching plane and then draw the sketch of the extrude surface, refer to Figure 9-59. Next, exit the sketching environment.

2. Choose the **Extruded Surface** button and then choose the newly created sketch; the preview of the extrude surface is displayed in the drawing area.

3. Right-click in the drawing area and choose the **Mid Plane** option from the shortcut menu.

4. Extrude the surface such that it passes through all the existing surfaces by dragging the handle displayed in the drawing area. Next, choose the **OK** button; the extrude surface is created, refer to Figure 9-60.

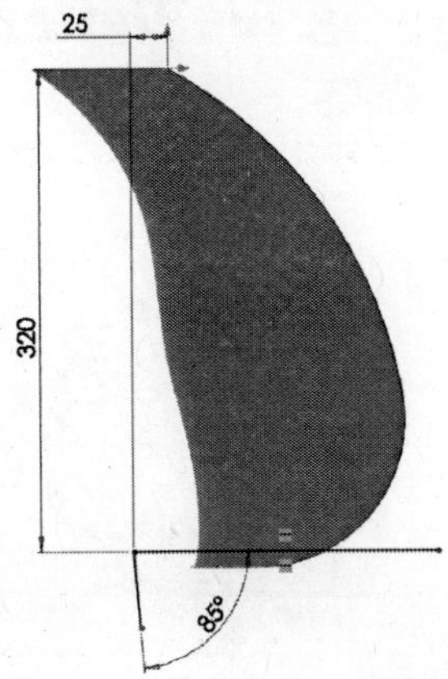

Figure 9-59 Sketch for the extrude surface

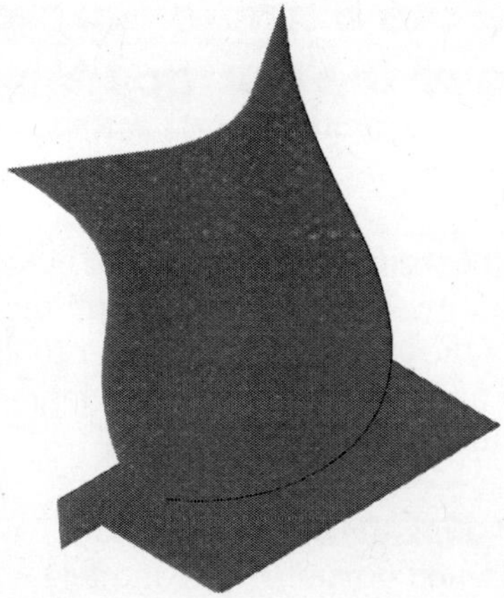

Figure 9-60 Surface model after creating the extruded surface

Trimming the Model Using the Extruded Surface

Next, you need to trim the unwanted portions of the surface model by using the last created extruded surface.

1. Invoke the **Trim Surface PropertyManager** and select the **Mutual** radio button from the **Trim Type** rollout of the PropertyManager.

2. Select both the lofted and extruded surfaces as trimming surfaces. Next, make sure that the **Keep selections** radio button is selected in the PropertyManager.

3. Click in the **Pieces to Keep** selection area to activate the selection mode and then select the portion of the surface to be kept, refer to Figure 9-61.

4. Choose the **OK** button. The rotated view of the model after trimming the surfaces is shown in Figure 9-62.

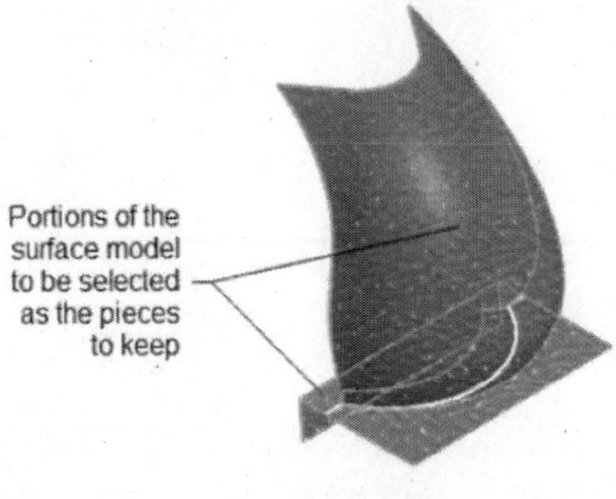

Figure 9-61 Sketch for the extrude surface

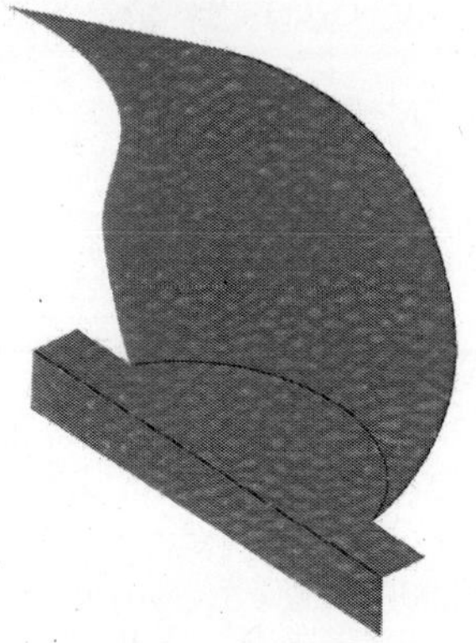

Figure 9-62 Surface model after trimming the extruded surface

Creating the Extrude Surface and Trimming the Unwanted Portions of the Surface Model

Next, you will create an extrude surface on the Plane 3 and then trim the surface model by using this surface.

1. Invoke the sketching environment by selecting the **Plane 3** as the sketching plane and then draw the sketch of the extrude surface, refer to Figure 9-63. Next, extrude the sketch upto the depth of 381 mm toward the downward direction.

   After creating the extruded surface, you will trim the unwanted portion of the model.

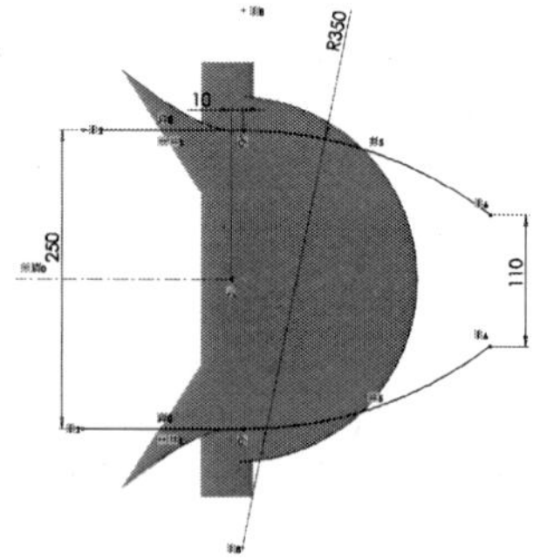

Figure 9-63 Sketch of the extrude surface

2. Invoke the **Trim Surface PropertyManager** and select the **Mutual** radio button from the **Trim Type** rollout.

3. Select all surfaces of the surface model as trimming surfaces. Next, make sure that the **Keep selections** radio button is selected.

4. Click in the **Pieces to Keep** selection area to activate the selection mode and then select the portion of the surfaces to be kept, refer to Figure 9-64. Next, choose the **OK** button. The isometric view of the model after trimming the surface model is shown in Figure 9-65.

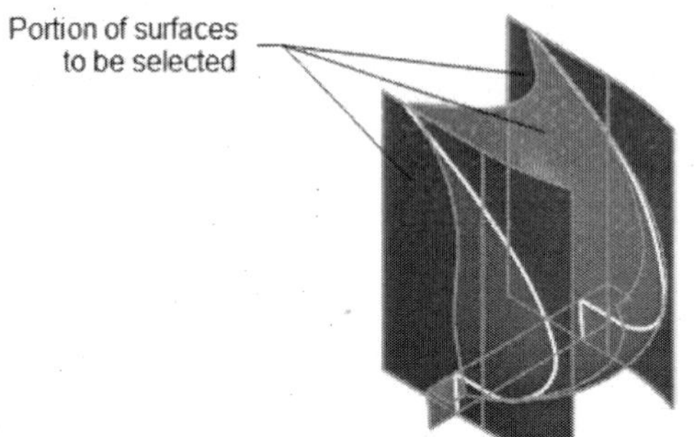

Figure 9-64 Portion of the surfaces to be selected

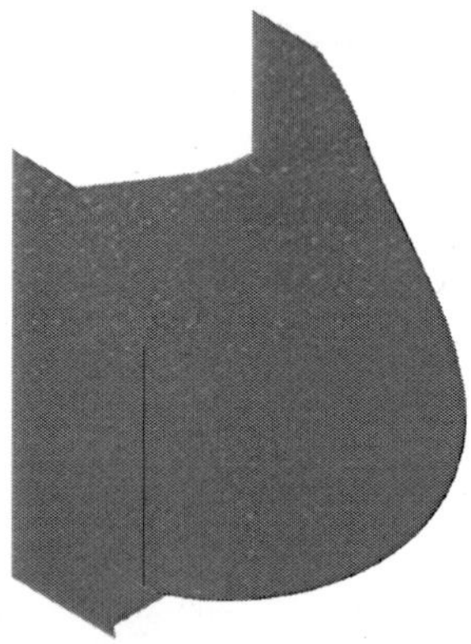

Figure 9-65 Surface model after trimming the surfaces

Drawing the Sketch and Trimming the Model

Next, you will draw the sketch on the **Front Plane** and then trim the model using it.

1. Invoke the sketching environment by selecting the **Front Plane** as the sketching plane and then draw the sketch, refer to Figure 9-66. Next, trim the surface model using the sketch, refer to Figure 9-67.

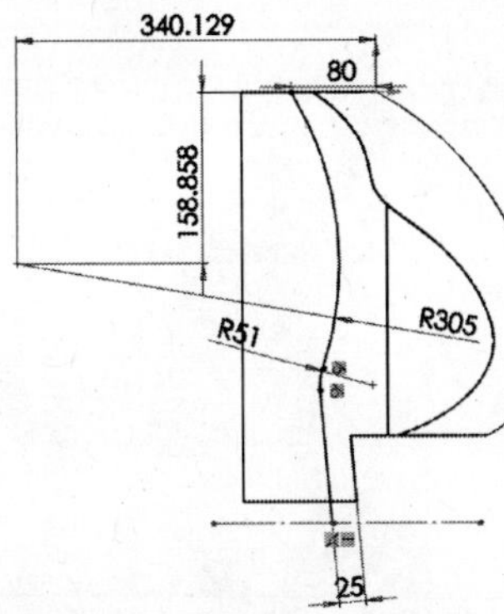

Figure 9-66 Sketch for trimming the surfaces

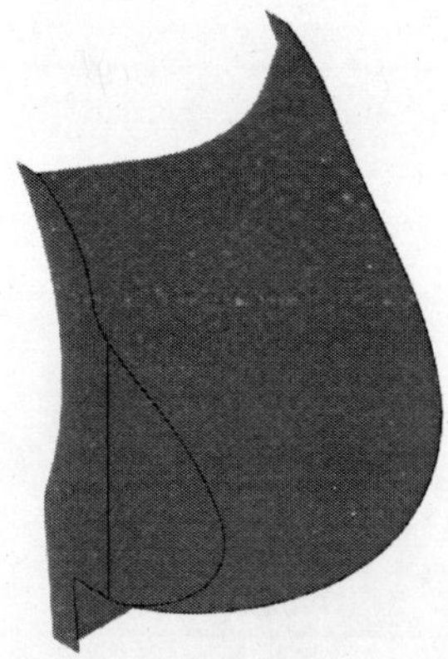

Figure 9-67 Surface model after trimming the surfaces

Applying Fillets

After creating all surfaces of the model, you need to fillet them using the Fillet PropertyManager.

1. Invoke the **Fillet PropertyManager** and set the value of the **Radius** spinner to 12.7 mm in the **Items To Fillet** rollout.

2. Select all sharp edges of the surface model from the drawing area by using the cross window selection method. Next, choose the **OK** button. The isometric view of the model after applying the fillets is shown in Figure 9-68.

Adding Thickness to the Surface Model

Next, you need to add thickness to the surface model.

1. Choose the Thicken button from the **Surfaces CommandManager**; the **Thicken PropertyManager** is displayed.

2. Select the surface model and then set the value of the **Thickness** spinner to **2.54** mm in the **Thickness** area of the PropertyManager. Next, choose the **Thicken Side 2** button to add the thickness outside the surface.

3. Choose the **OK** button. The section view of the model after thickening the surface model is shown in Figure 9-69.

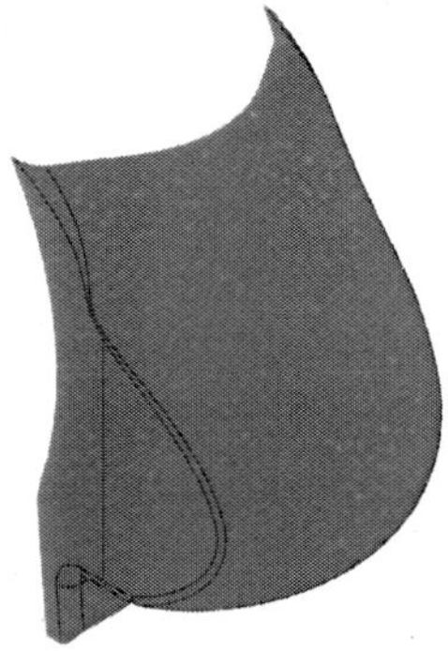

Figure 9-68 *Surface model after filleting it*

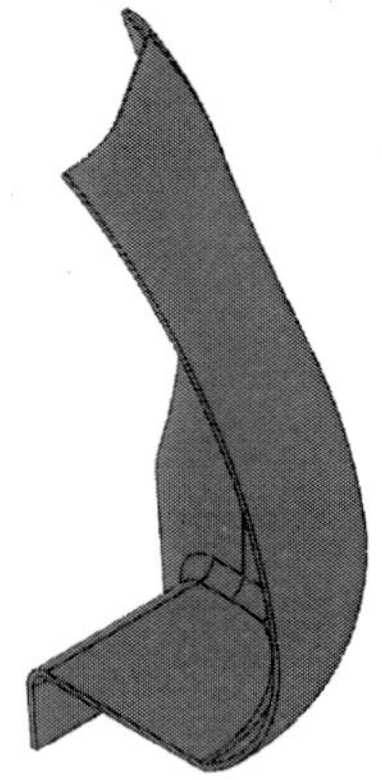

Figure 9-69 *Section view of the model after adding the thickness*

Creating the Extrude Cut Feature

Next, you need to create an extrude cut feature using the **Extruded Cut** tool.

1. Create the extruded cut feature by using the **Extruded Cut** tool, refer to Figure 9-70. For dimensions refer to Figure 9-54.

Splitting the Front Face of the Model

Next, you will split the front face of the model using the **Split Line** tool in order to represent the Headlights. As the sketch of the split line will be created on the reference plane, first you need to create a reference plane.

1. Invoke the **Plane PropertyManager** and then create a reference plane at any offset distance using the **Right Plane** as the reference entity. Note that the reference plane should be on the front side of the reference entity and should not intersect the model.

2. Invoke the sketching environment by selecting the newly created plane as the sketching plane and then draw the sketch, refer to Figure 9-71. Next, exit the sketching environment.

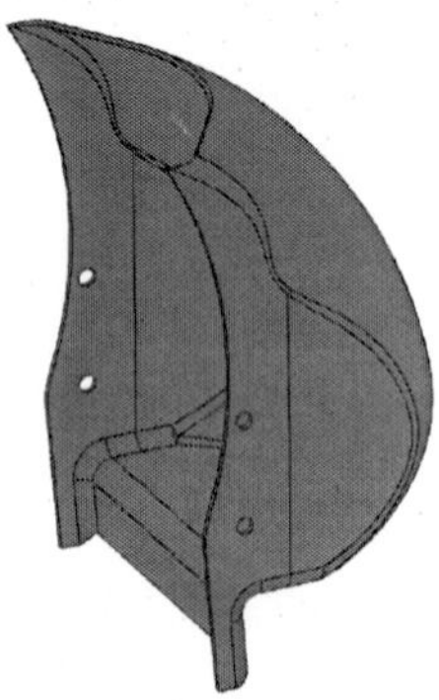

Figure 9-70 *Model after creating the cut feature*

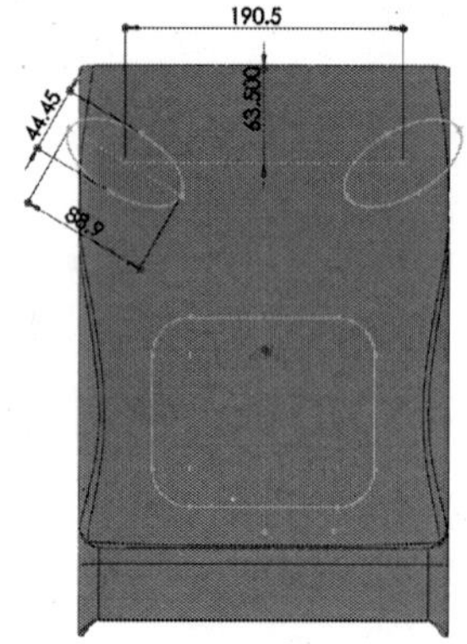

Figure 9-71 *Sketch of the split line*

After creating the sketch of the split line, you need invoke the Split Line PropertyManager to create the split line feature.

3. Choose **Curves** > **Split Line** from the **Surfaces CommandManager**; the **Split Line PropertyManager** is displayed.

4. Select the **Projection** radio button from the **Type of Split** rollout of the **Split Line PropertyManager**. Next, select the sketch from the drawing area.

5. Select the front curved face of the model; the selected face is highlighted and its name is displayed in the **Faces to Split** selection area of the **Selections** rollout in the PropertyManager.

6. Choose the **OK** button; the split line feature is created, refer to Figure 9-72.

Applying Color to the Model

Next, you will assign the color to the model by using the color **PropertyManager**.

1. Select a face of the model; a pop-up toolbar is displayed. Choose the **Appearances** button from the pop-up toolbar; a flyout is displayed with the name of the Face, Split Line, Body, and Part. Select the part name check box corresponding to the color; the **color PropertyManager** is displayed. Next, assign the required color to the model using the PropertyManager.

2. Similarly, apply a color to the faces that are divided by using the split line. The final model after applying the red color to the model and the white color to the portion lying inside the split lines is shown in Figure 9-73.

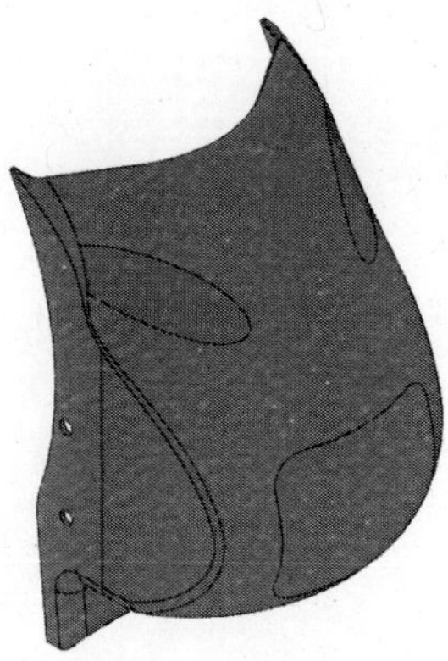

Figure 9-72 *Model after splitting the surface*

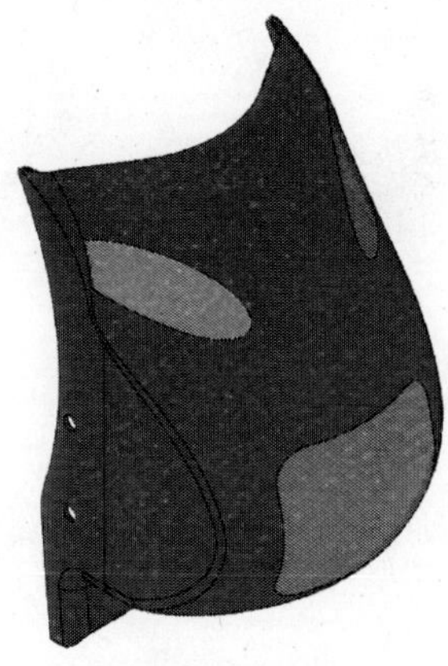

Figure 9-73 *Model after assigning the color*

Saving the Model

1. Save the model with the name Headlight Mask in the Motor Cycle Project folder.

2. Close the document by choosing **File > Close** from the SolidWorks menus.

CREATING THE SEAT COVER

Part Description

In this section, you will create the Seat Cover, as shown in Figure 9-74(a). The dimensions of profile and path is shown in Figure 9-74(b). The views and dimensions of seat cover is shown in Figure 9-74(c). It will be created by using the surface modeling tools. Assume missing dimensions.

(Expected time: 45 min)

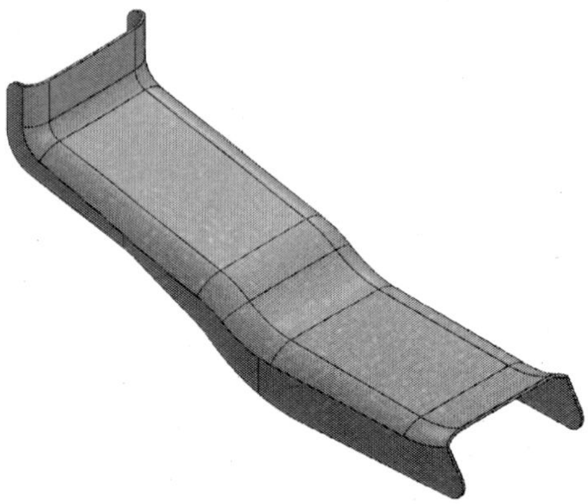

Figure 9-74(a) *Seat Cover*

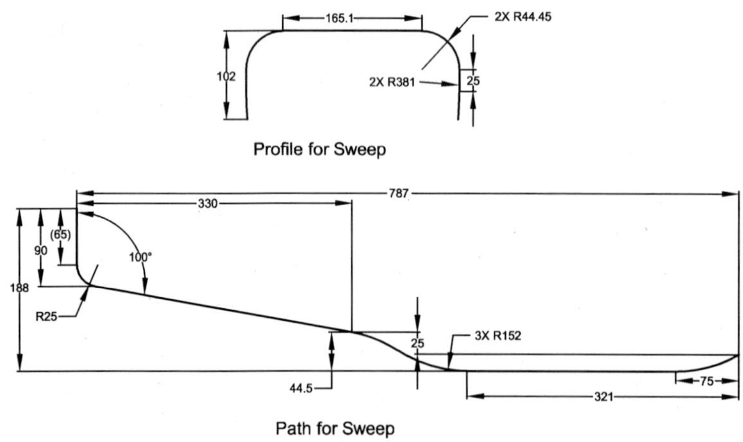

Figure 9-74(b) *The dimension of profile and path for seat cover*

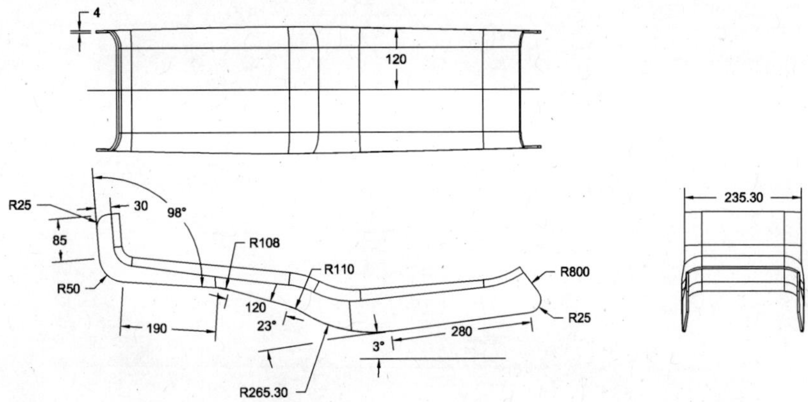

Figure 9-74(c) *The views and dimensions of the model*

Creating the Base Feature

The base surface of the surface model will be created by sweeping a profile along a path using the **Swept Surface** tool. Therefore, first you need to create a profile and a path.

Creating the Path for the Sweep Surface

As discussed earlier, the base feature of the model is a sweep surface. To create the sweep surface, first you need to create its path. This path will be created on the Front Plane.

1. Start a SolidWorks part document using the **New SolidWorks Document** dialog box.

2. Invoke the sketching environment by using the **Front Plane** as the sketching plane.

3. Draw the sketch of the path for the sweep surface, as shown in Figure 9-75. Apply tangent relation to fully-constrain the sketch. Next, exit from the sketcher environment.

Creating the Profile for the Sweep Surface

After creating the path for the sweep surface, you will create its profile. To create the profile, first you need to create a reference plane normal to the path. This reference plane will be selected as a sketching plane for creating the profile of the sweep surface.

1. Invoke the **Plane PropertyManager** and then create a plane normal to the path for the sweep surface.

   After creating the reference plane normal to the path, you need to create the profile for the sweep surface.

2. Invoke the sketching environment by selecting the newly created plane as the sketching plane. Next, draw the open sketch as the profile for the sweep surface, refer to Figure 9-76, and then exit the sketching environment.

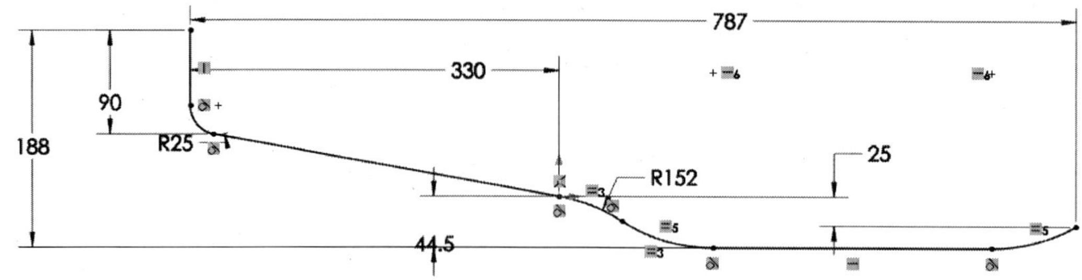

Figure 9-75 Sketch of the path for the sweep surface

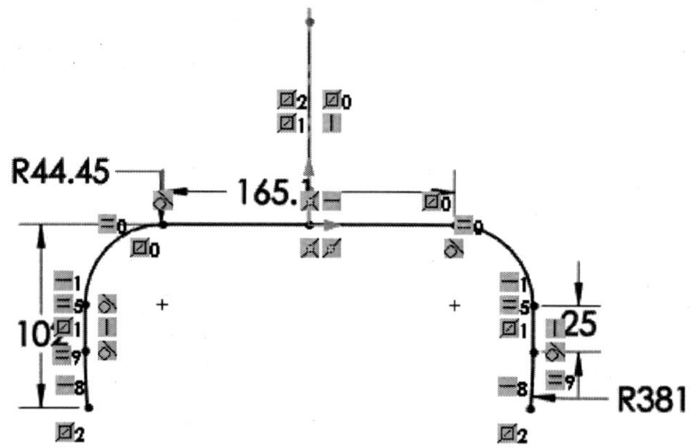

Figure 9-76 Sketch of the profile

Creating the Sweep Surface

After creating the path and the profile, you will create the sweep surface using the **Swept Surface** tool.

1. Choose the Swept Surface button from the **Surface CommandManager**; the **Surface-Sweep PropertyManager** is displayed and you are prompted to select the sweep profile.

2. Select the sweep profile from the drawing area; you are prompted to select a sweep path.

3. Select the path drawn for the sweep surface; the preview of the sweep surface is displayed in the drawing area. Next, choose the **OK** button; the sweep surface is created, as shown in Figure 9-77.

Creating the Extrude Surface

Next, you need to create the extrude surface. This surface will be created by extruding the sketch created on the **Top Plane**.

1. Invoke the sketching environment by selecting the **Top Plane** as the sketching plane and then draw the sketch of the extrude surface, refer to Figure 9-78. Next, exit the sketching environment.

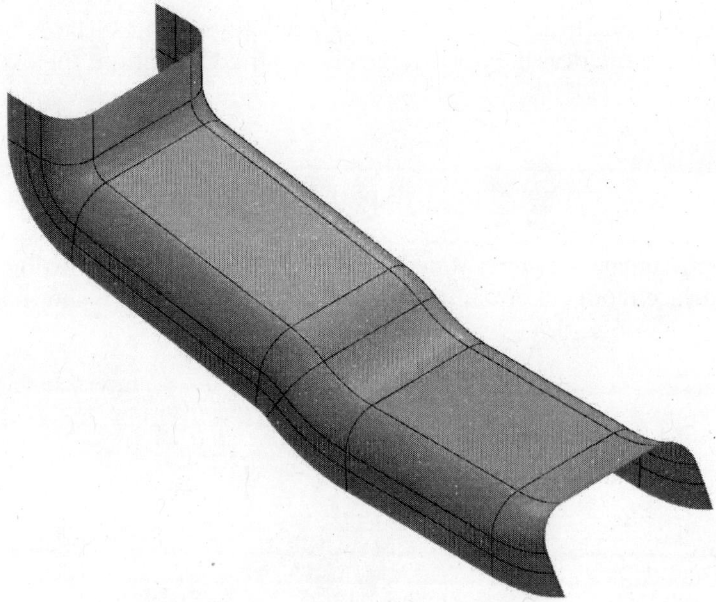

Figure 9-77 The sweep surface

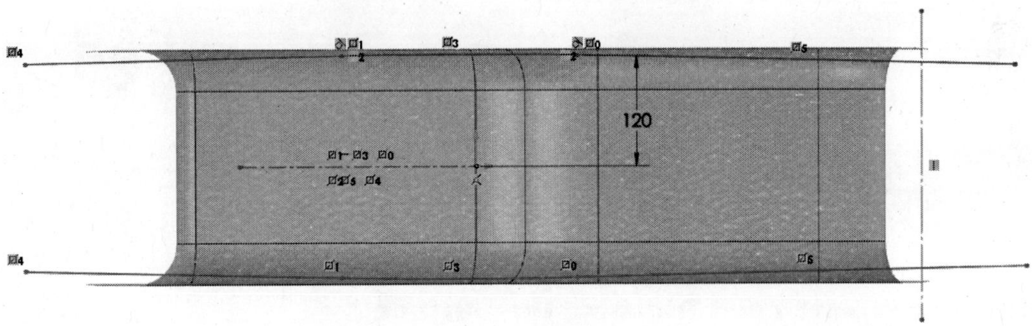

Figure 9-78 Sketch of the profile

2. Choose the **Extruded Surface** button and select the newly created sketch; the preview of the extrude surface is displayed in the drawing area.

3. Right-click in the drawing area and then choose the **Mid Plane** option from the shortcut menu displayed.

4. Extrude the surface such that it passes through all the existing surfaces by dragging the handle displayed in the drawing area. Next, choose the **OK** button; the extrude surface is created, refer to Figure 9-79.

Trimming the Surface

Next, you need to trim the unwanted portions of the surface model.

1. Invoke the **Trim Surface PropertyManager** and trim the unwanted portions of the surface model. The surface model after trimming the unwanted portions is shown in Figure 9-80.

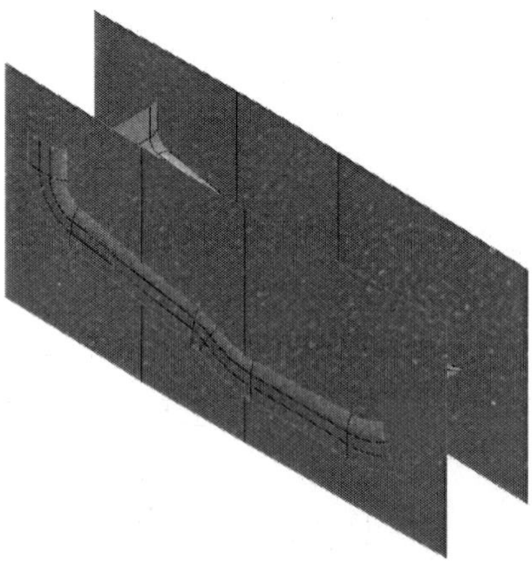

Figure 9-79 *The extruded surface created*

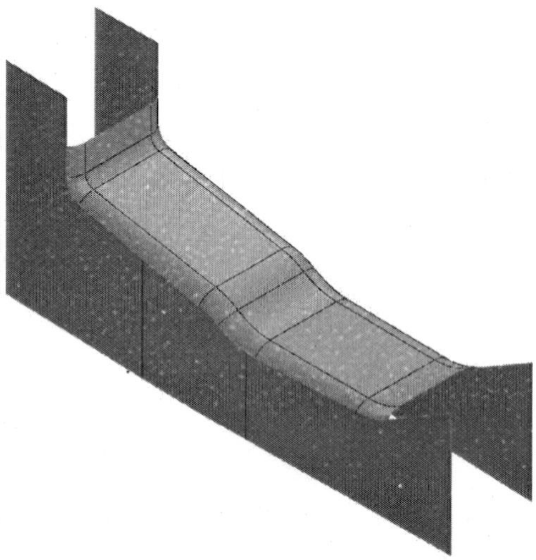

Figure 9-80 *Surface model after trimming the unwanted portions*

Drawing the Sketch and Trimming the Surface

Next, you need to draw the sketch on the Front Plane and then trim the model using it.

1. Invoke the sketching environment by selecting the **Front Plane** as the sketching plane and then draw the sketch shown in Figure 9-81. Next, trim the surface model using the sketch. The final model after trimming is shown in Figure 9-82.

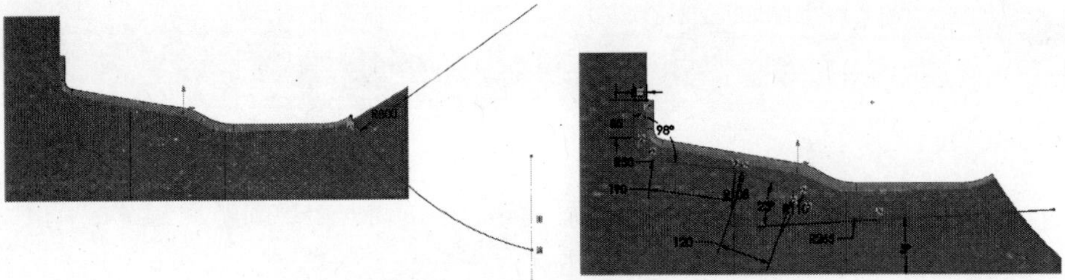

Figure 9-81 *Sketch for trimming surface*

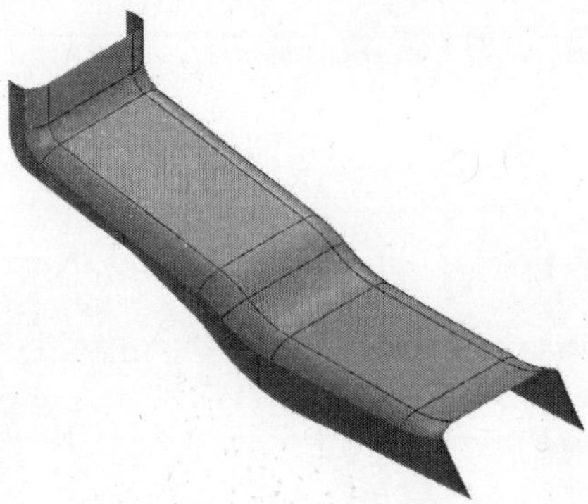

Figure 9-82 *Surface model after trimming the unwanted portions*

Knitting all Surfaces

After creating all the surfaces, you need to knit them together by using the Knit Surface tool.

1. Choose the Knit Surface button from the **Surfaces CommandManager**; the Knit **Surface PropertyManager** is displayed and you are prompted to select the surfaces to knit.

2. Select all surfaces from the drawing area one by one and then choose the **OK** button from the PropertyManager.

Adding Thickness to the Surface Model

Next, you need to add thickness to the surface model.

1. Invoke the **Thicken PropertyManager** and then add thickness of 2 mm using thicken both side button, refer to Figure 9-83.

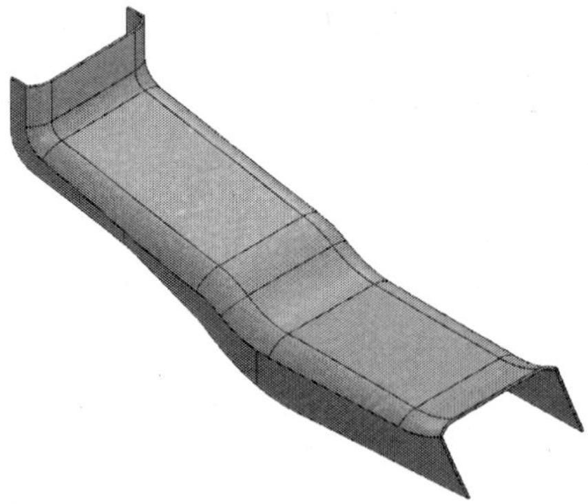

Figure 9-83 Surface model after adding thickness

Adding Fillets

After thickening the surface, you need to fillet the remaining sharp edges.

1. Remove all sharp edges of the model by applying the fillet of required radius by using the **Fillet PropertyManager,** refer to Figure 9-74(c). The isometric view of the model after adding the fillets is shown in Figure 9-84.

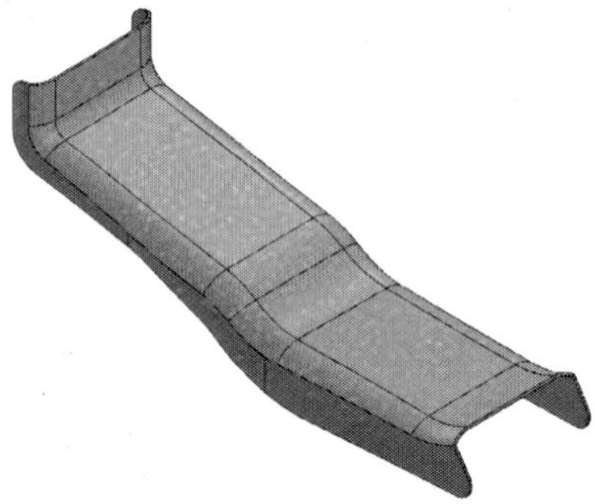

Figure 9-84 Isometric view of the model

Saving the Model

1. Save the model with the name Seat Cover in the Motor Cycle Project folder.

2. Close the document by choosing **File > C**lose from the SolidWorks menus.

Self-Evaluation Test

Answer the following questions and then compare them to those given at the end of this chapter:

1. Which of the following PropertyManagers is used to create a fillet surface?

(a) **Fill Surface** (b) **Surface Fill**
(c) **Fillet** (d) None of these

2. The surface modeling tools are available in the ____________ **CommandManager**.

3. The __________ tool is used to create the extrude surface of a closed or open sketch.

4. The __________ **PropertyManager** is used to create a lofted surface.

5. The __________ **PropertyManager** is used to add thickness to a surface body.

6. When you choose the __________ button from the **Thicken PropertyManager**, thickness is added on the inner surface.

7. The _______________ tool is used to fill gaps between surfaces using a planar patch.

8. In SolidWorks, surface modeling is done in the Part environment. (T/F)

9. You can knit multiple surfaces together to create a single surface. (T/F)

Review Questions

Answer the following questions:

1. The __________ **PropertyManager** is used to create a revolved surface.

2. On selecting the __________ radio button in the **Trim Surface PropertyManager**, you can select the pieces to keep from the surface while trimming.

3. Choose the _____________ button from the **Surfaces CommandManager** to create a planar surface.

4. The ______________ tool is used to knit multiple surfaces together to create a single surface.

5. You cannot create a loft surface with the combination of closed and open sections. (T/F)

6. You can loft one or more sections along guide curves by using the **Lofted Surface** tool. (T/F)

7. By default, the **Surfaces CommandManager** is not displayed; you need to customize to add it to the CommandManager. (T/F)

Answers to Self-Evaluation Test

1. (c) Fillet, 2. Surfaces, 3. Extruded Surface, 4. Lofted Surface, 5. Thicken, 6. Thicken Side1, 7. Planar Surface, 8. T , 9. T

Chapter 10

Weldment Structural Frames

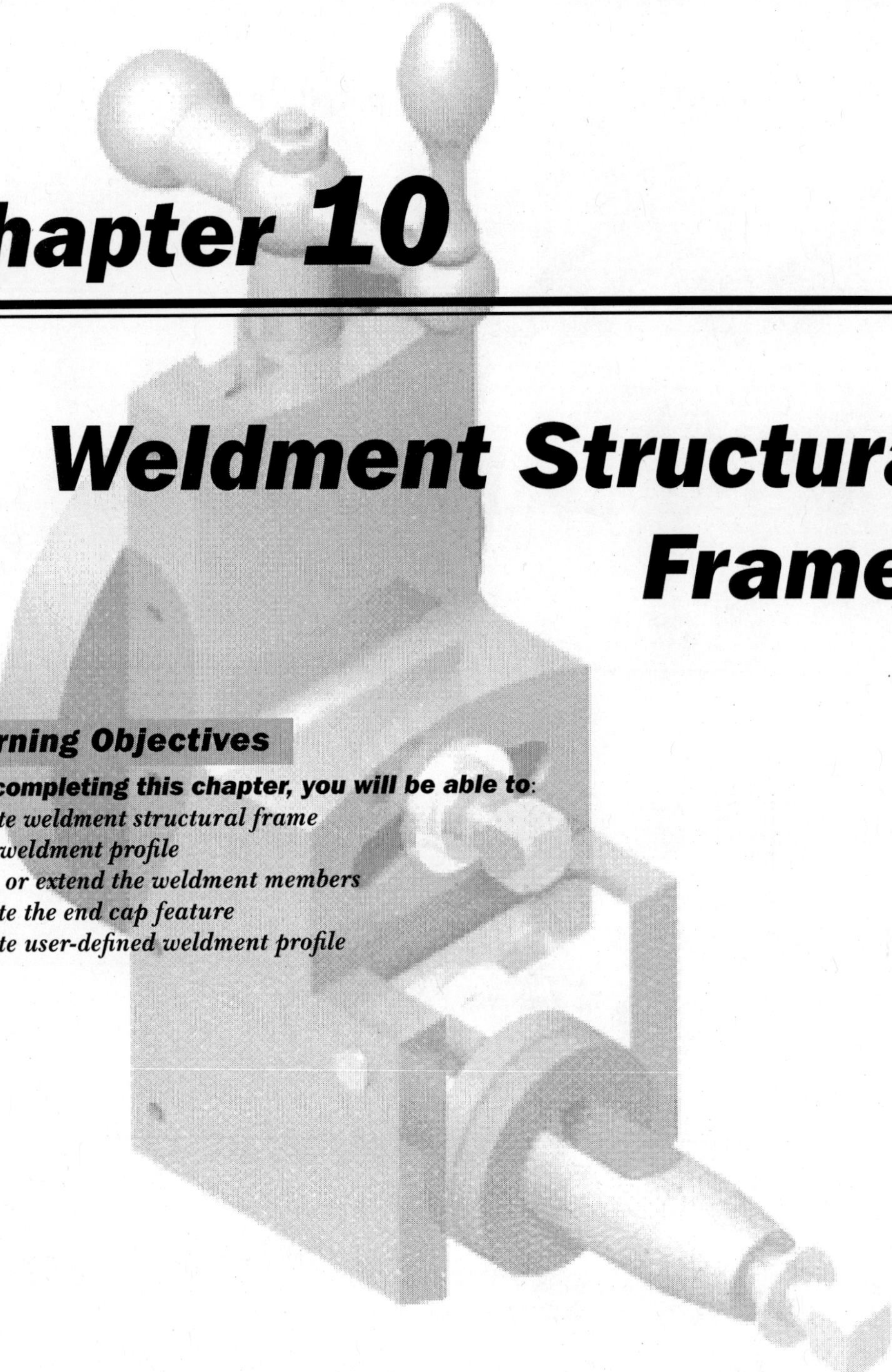

Learning Objectives

After completing this chapter, you will be able to:

- *Create weldment structural frame*
- *Edit weldment profile*
- *Trim or extend the weldment members*
- *Create the end cap feature*
- *Create user-defined weldment profile*

CREATING WELDMENT STRUCTURAL FRAME

Part Description

In this session, you will create the Weldment structural frame, as shown in Figure 10-1. It is created in the Part environment by using the tools available in the **Weldments CommandManager**. The views and the dimensions of the frame are shown in Figures 10-2 and 10-3 respectively. Assume the missing dimensions. **(Expected time: 55 min)**

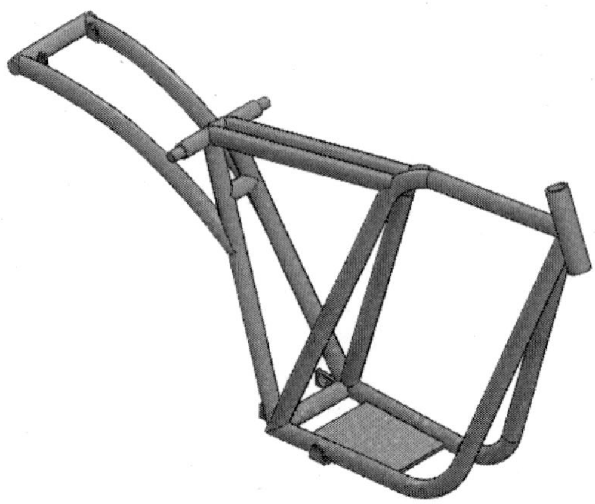

Figure 10-1 *Weldment structural frame*

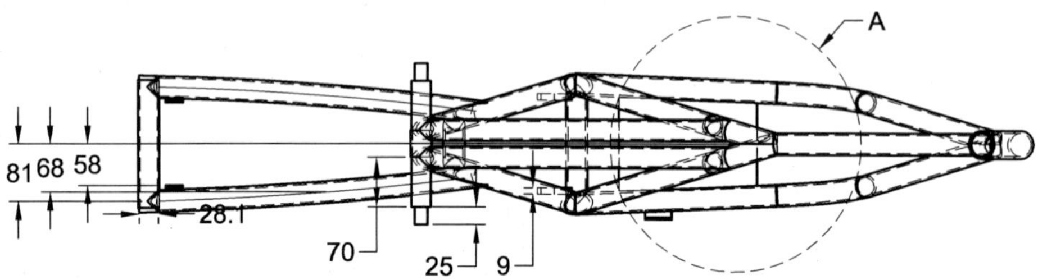

Figure 10-2 *Top view of the model*

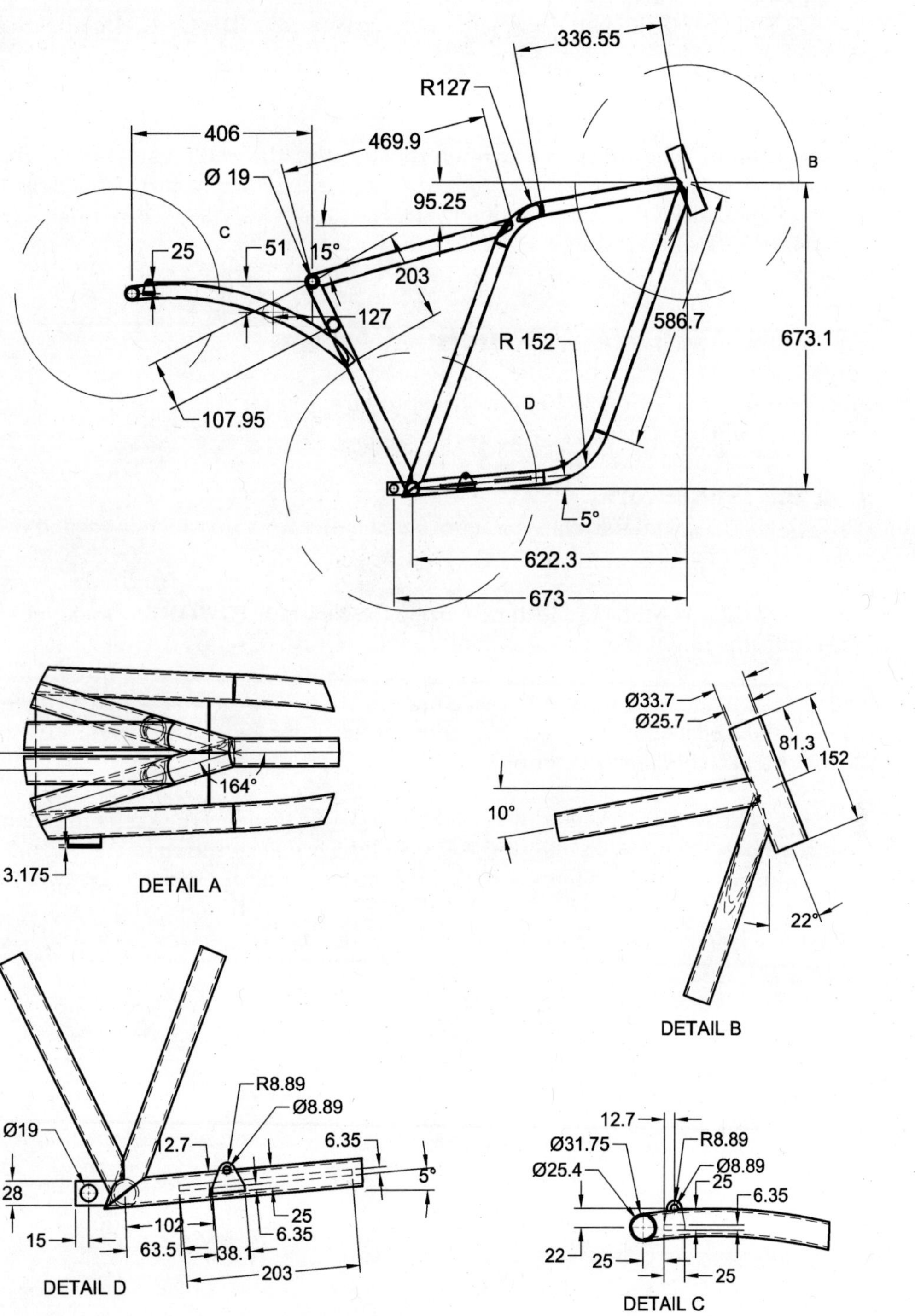

Figure 10-3 *Front and detail views of the model*

Starting a New Part Document

Start a new SOLIDWORKS part document using the **New SOLIDWORKS Document** dialog box.

Introduction to Weldments

SOLIDWORKS provides you with the options of creating the weldment structure in which the members of the weldment structure are grouped together to form complex shaped structure. In SOLIDWORKS, the weldment structures are created in the Weldments mode. You can use the 2D and 3D sketches to define the basic framework for creating the weldment structure.

Creating the Weldment Structural Frame

As discussed in the introduction, the weldment structure is created in Weldments mode of SOLIDWORKS. To create a weldment structure, first you need to create a framework by using the 2D and 3D sketches.

Creating the Framework

In this section, you need to create framework of a basic structure which is created by using the 2D and 3D sketches.

1. Start a new SOLIDWORKS part document using the **New SOLIDWORKS Document** dialog box. Modify the unit of the current session to mm, if it is not set by default.

2. Invoke the sketcher environment by selecting the Front Plane as the sketching plane and then draw the sketch of the first sketch member of the frame, as shown in Figure 10-4. Next, exit from the sketcher environment.

3. Invoke the sketcher environment by selecting the Front Plane as the sketching plane and then draw the sketch of the second sketch entity of the frame, as shown in Figure 10-5. Note that the vertical construction line created at the end point of this sketch entity will be used for creating a reference plane for third sketch member of the frame in the next step. Next, exit from the sketcher environment.

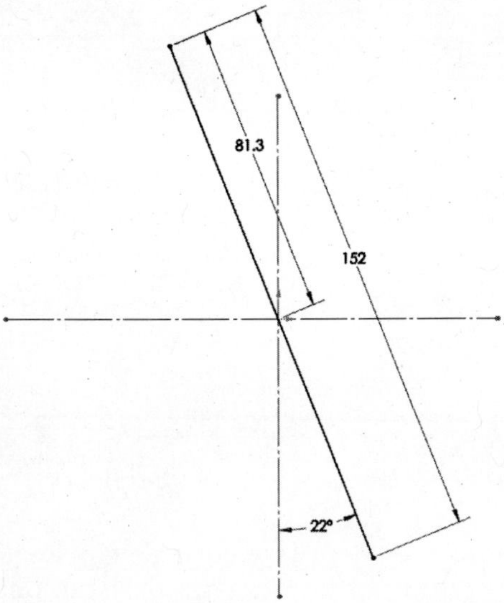

Figure 10-4 *First sketch member of the frame*

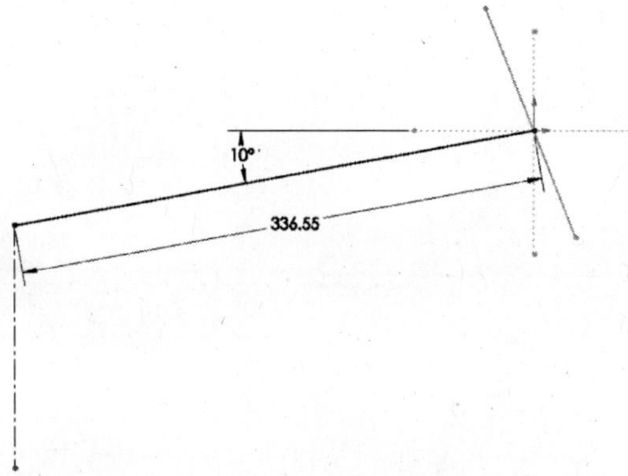

Figure 10-5 *Second sketch member of the frame*

To create the third sketch entity of the frame, first you need to create a reference plane by using the vertical construction line which was created while creating the second sketch entity of the frame. You can also create a vertical construction line as a separate sketch entity instead of creating it in the second sketch entity.

4. Invoke the **Plane PropertyManager** and then select the vertical construction line created in the second sketch entity as the first reference and then select the Front Plane as the second reference.

5. Choose the **At angle** button from the **Second Reference** rollout of the **Plane PropertyManager**; the **Angle** spinner in front of the **At angle** button is enabled. Next, set the value of the **Angle** spinner to **163.6** and then choose the **OK** button from the PropertyManager; the reference plane is created, refer to Figure 10-6.

6. Invoke the sketcher environment by selecting the newly created plane as the sketching plane and draw the sketch of the third member of the frame, as shown in Figure 10-7. Next, exit from the sketcher environment.

7. Invoke the sketcher environment by selecting the newly created plane as the sketching plane and draw the sketch of the third entity of the frame, as shown in Figure 10-7.

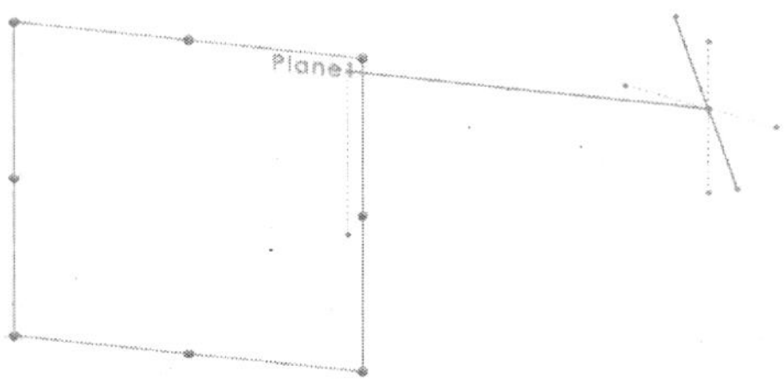

Figure 10-6 Reference plane created

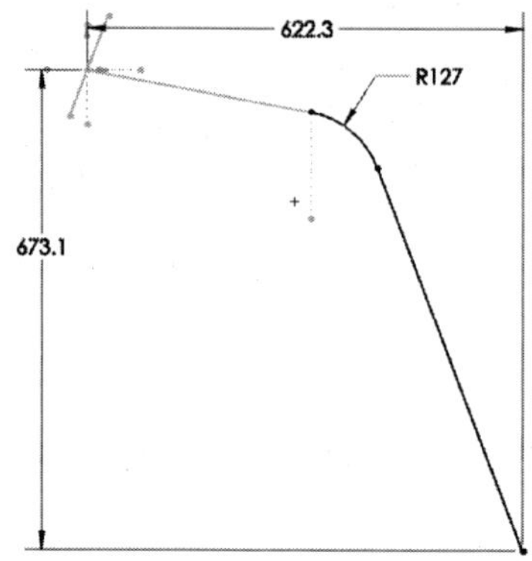

Figure 10-7 Third sketch member of the frame

8. Similarly, create the fourth sketch of the frame on the reference plane created at an angle of 196.4 degree. This plane is created by using the vertical construction line of the second sketch entity as the first reference and the Front Plane as the second reference, refer to Figure 10-8. The isometric view of the frame after creating its fourth sketch member of the frame is shown in Figure 10-9.

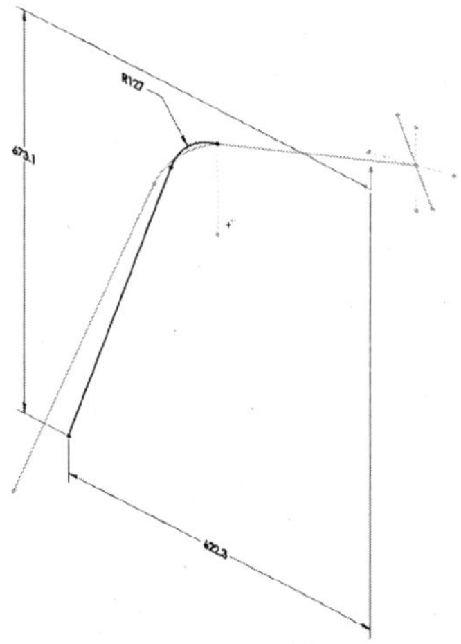

Figure 10-8 *Fourth sketch of the frame*

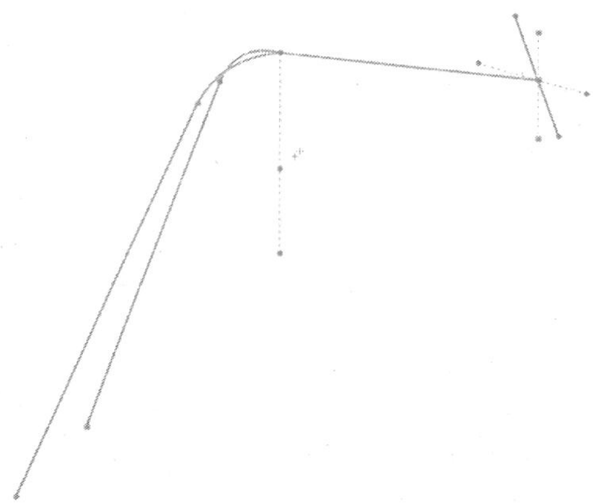

Figure 10-9 *Isometric view after creating the fourth sketch*

9. Create the reference plane by using the first, second, and third references points, as shown in Figure 10-10. Next, invoke the sketcher environment by selecting it as the sketching plane and draw the sketch of fifth member, as shown in Figure 10-11. Exit from the sketcher environment.

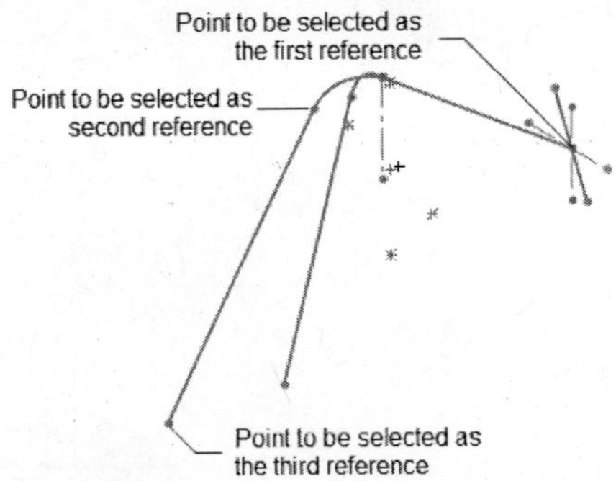

***Figure 10-10** Points to be selected*

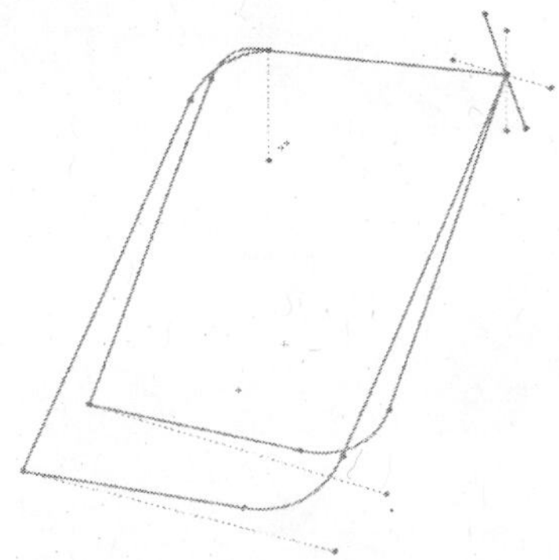

***Figure 10-11** Sketch of the fifth member*

10. Similarly, create the sixth sketch member of the frame, refer to Figure 10-12. Hide all the reference planes from the drawing area.

11. Create a reference plane at an offset distance of 19.558 mm from the Front Plane. Next, invoke the sketcher environment by selecting it as the sketching plane and draw the sketch of the seventh member of the frame, as shown in Figure 10-13. Next, exit from the sketcher environment.

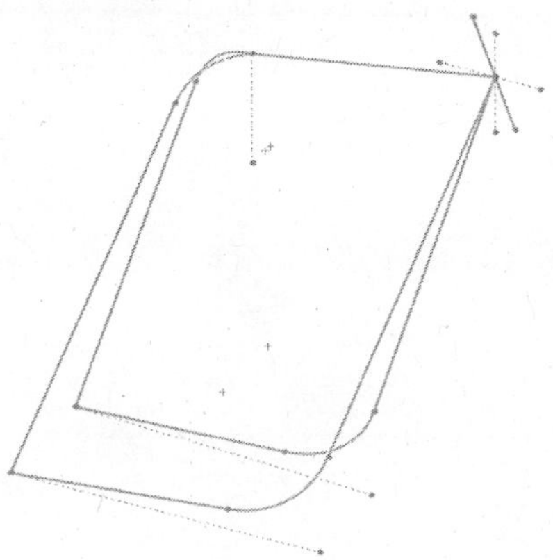

***Figure 10-12** Frame after creating the sixth sketch member*

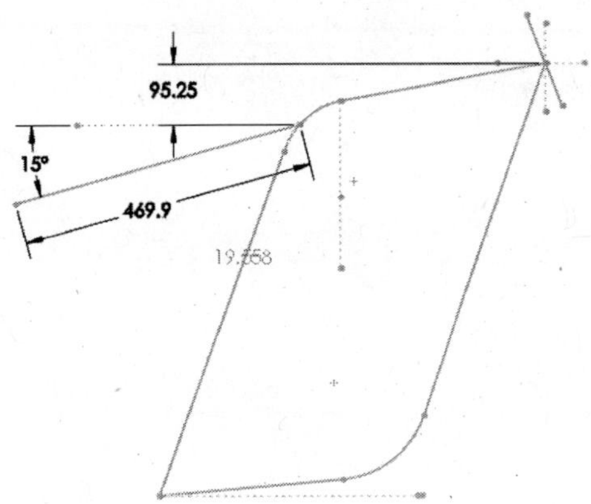

***Figure 10-13** Sketch of the seventh member*

12. Similarly, create the eighth sketch member of the frame. The isometric view of the frame after creating the eighth sketch member and hiding the reference planes is shown in Figure 10-14.

13. Invoke the 3D sketcher environment by choosing the **3D Sketch** button from the **Sketch** flyout of the **Sketch CommandManager**. Next, draw the sketch of the ninth member of the frame by using the **Line** tool, refer to Figure 10-15. Next, exit from the sketcher environment.

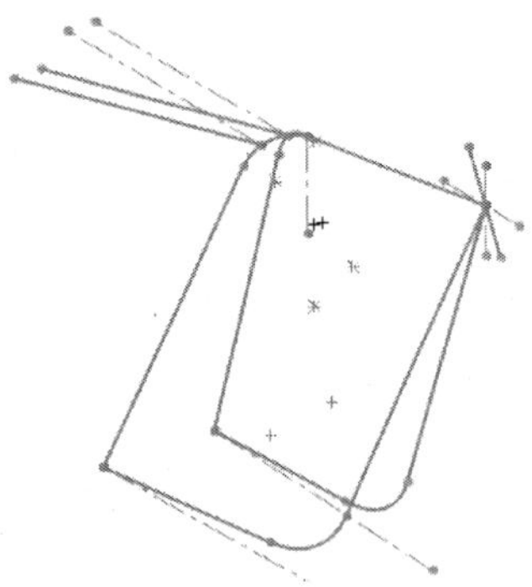

Figure 10-14 *Frame after creating the eighth sketch member of the frame*

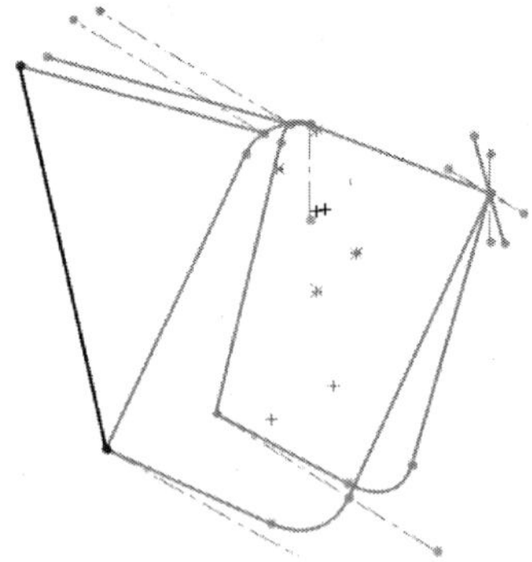

Figure 10-15 *Sketch of the ninth sketch member*

14. Similarly, create the tenth, eleventh, and twelfth sketch members of the frame in the separate 3D sketcher environment by using the **Line** tool, refer to Figure 10-16.

15. Create a reference plane at an offset distance of 82.55 mm from the Front Plane and then invoke the sketcher environment by selecting it as the sketching plane. Next, place a point, refer to Figure 10-17. Exit from the sketcher environment.

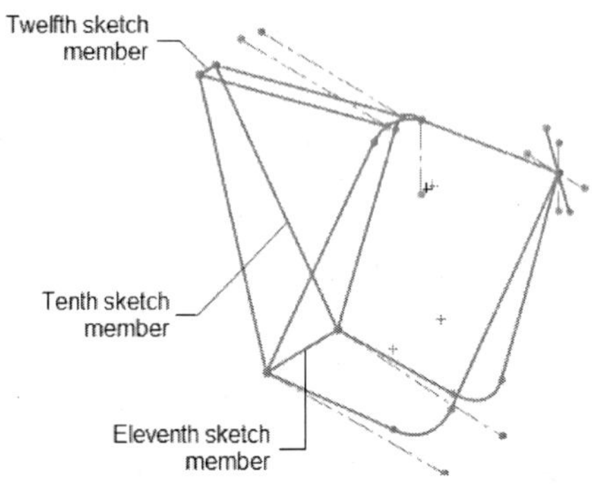

Figure 10-16 *Frame after creating the tenth, eleventh, and twelfth sketch members*

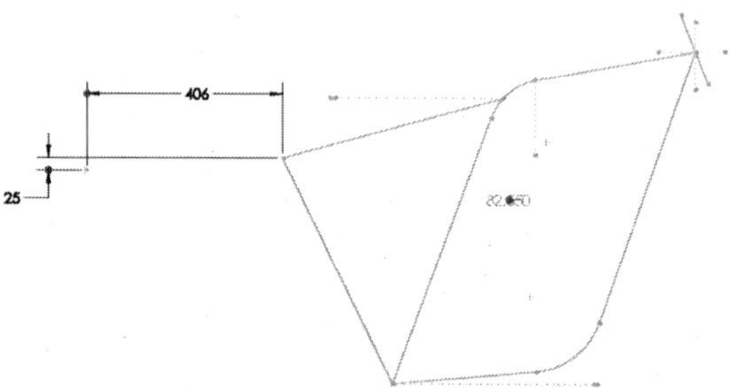

Figure 10-17 *Point on the reference plane*

16. Create a reference plane at an offset distance of 68.58 mm from the Front Plane and then invoke the sketcher environment by selecting it as the sketching plane. Next, place the point, refer to Figure 10-18. Exit from the sketcher environment.

17. Invoke the 3D sketcher environment and draw the sketch of the thirteenth member of the

frame by using the points created on the reference planes that measure 82.55 and 68.58 mm from the Front Plane, refer to Figure 10-19. Next, exit from the 3D sketcher environment.

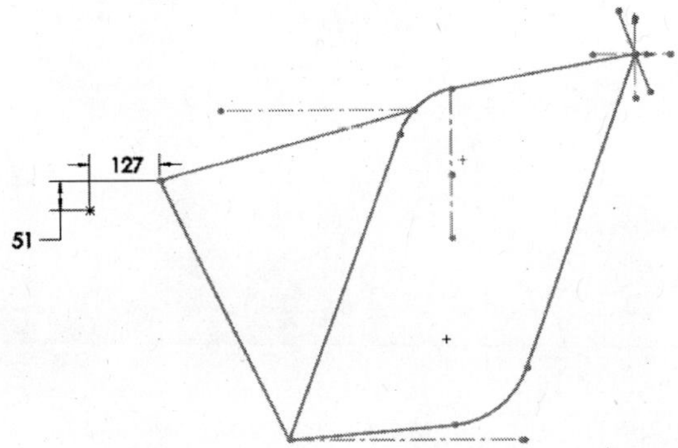

Figure 10-18 *Point on the reference plane*

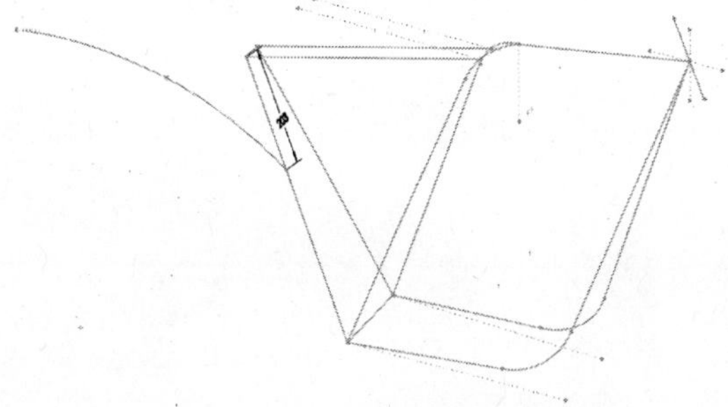

Figure 10-19 *Sketch of the thirteenth member*

18. Similarly, create the fourteenth sketch member of the frame on the other side of the Front Plane, refer to Figure 10-20.

19. Invoke the 3D sketch environment and create the fifteenth sketch member of the frame by joining the end points of the last two members, refer to Figure 10-21.

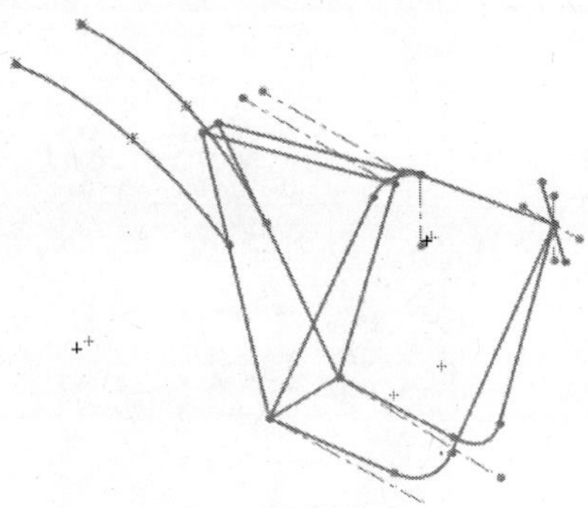

Figure 10-20 *Frame after creating the fourteenth sketch member*

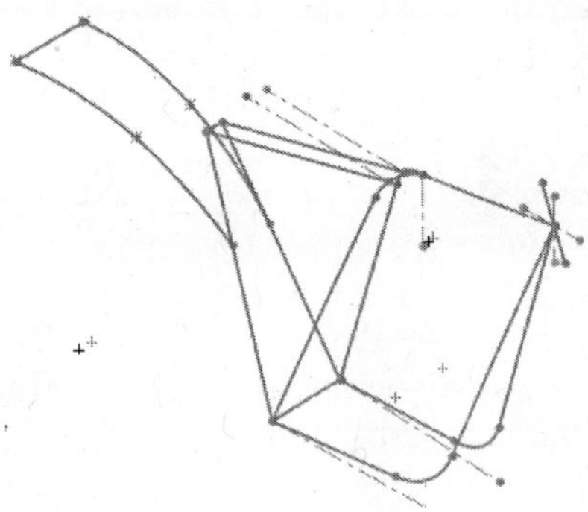

Figure 10-21 *Frame after creating the fifteenth sketch member*

20. Invoke the 3D sketch environment and create the last sketch member of the frame, as shown in Figure 10-22. The final structural frame after creating all its members is shown in Figure 10-23.

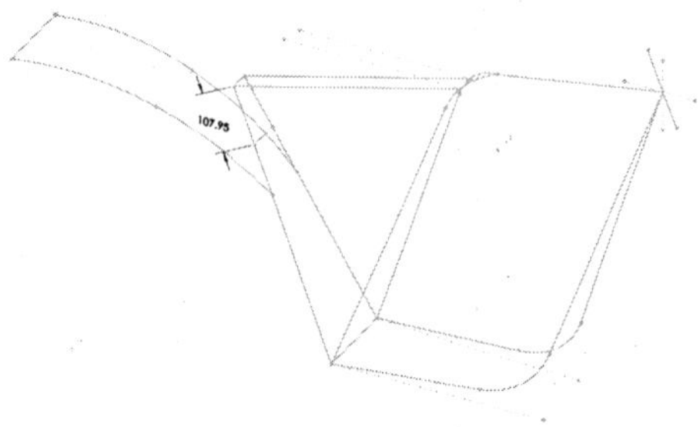

Figure 10-22 Last sketch member

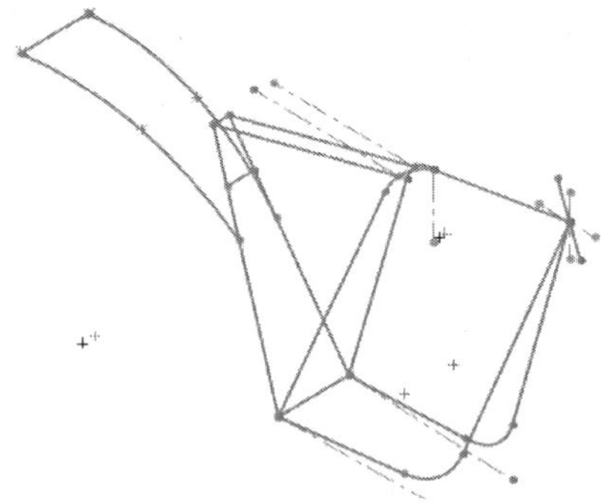

Figure 10-23 Frame after creating all sketch members

Creating the Structure

After creating the framework, you will use the **Structural Member** tool of the **Weldments CommandManager** to create the weldment structure.

1. Right-click on the **CommandManager** tab to display a shortcut menu and then choose the **Weldments** option; the **Weldments** tab is added in the **CommandManager**.

2. Choose the **Weldments** tab in the **CommandManager** to display the tools of the **Weldments CommandManager**.

3. Choose the **Structural Member** button from the **Weldments CommandManager**; the **Structural Member PropertyManager** is displayed, as shown in Figure 10-24. Also, you are prompted to select the sweep profile.

The **Structural Member** tool is used to create a structural member feature by sweeping the pre-defined profile along the user-defined path.

4. Select the **iso** option from the **Standard** drop-down list, the **pipe** option from the **Type** drop-down list, and the **33.7 x 4.0** option from the **Size** drop-down list of the **Selections** rollout in the **Structural Member Property-Manager**.

The options in the **Standard** drop-down list are used to define the weldment standard, the options in the **Type** drop-down list are used to define the type of the weldment profile, and the options in the **Size** drop-down list are used to define the size of the weldment profile.

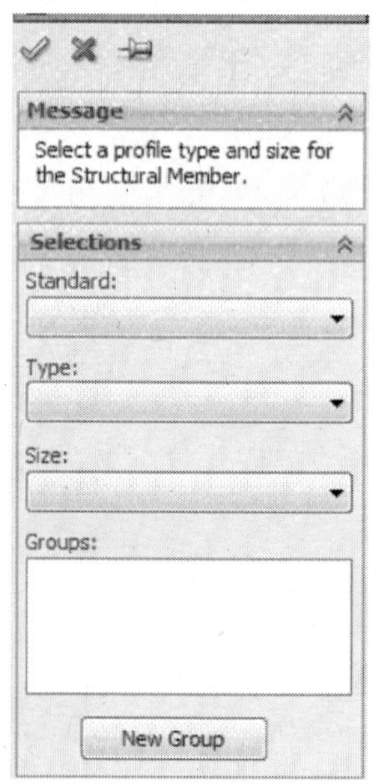

Figure 10-24** The **Structural Member PropertyManager

5. Click in the **Groups** selection area of the PropertyManager to activate it and select the sketch created as the first member of the frame from the drawing area; the preview of the structural feature is displayed in the drawing area. Next, choose the **OK** button from the PropertyManager. The first structural member feature is created, as shown in Figure 10-25. Also, the weldment feature is added in the **FeatureManager design tree**.

The **Groups** selection area is used to select sketch segments to define the path for the structural member.

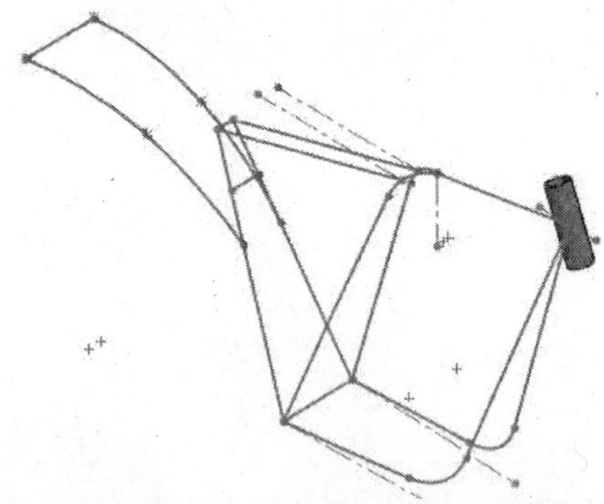

Figure 10-25 *First structural member feature*

6. After creating the structural member feature, you can edit its profile. To do so, expand **Structural Member** node provided in the **FeatureManager design tree** and then select the sketch of the structural member; a pop-up toolbar is displayed. Choose the **Edit Sketch** button from pop-up toolbar; the sketcher environment is invoked. Edit the sketch of the structural member such that its inner diameter changes to 25 and outer diameter changes to 33. Exit from the sketcher environment.

7. Again, choose the **Structural Member** button from the **Weldments CommandManager**; the **Structural Member PropertyManager** is displayed.

8. Select the **iso** option from the **Standard** drop-down list, the **pipe** option from the **Type** drop-down list, and the **21.3 x 2.3** option from the **Size** drop-down list of the **Selections** rollout in the **Structural Member PropertyManager**.

9. Click in the **Groups** selection area of the PropertyManager to activate it and select the sketched segments 2, 3, 4, 5, 6, and 7 one by one from the drawing area, refer to Figure 10-26; the preview of the structural members is displayed in the drawing area, refer to Figure 10-27. Note that the **Group1** is displayed in the **Groups** selection area of the PropertyManager, indicateing that all the selected segments are in group 1. Also, the name of the selected segments is displayed in the **Path segments** selection area of the **Settings** rollout in the PropertyManager.

Note

In SOLIDWORKS, you can create a weldment structure that contains one or more groups, which can be treated as a single unit. You can select parallel or contiguous segments in a group. Also, the weldment profile of all the groups within a structural member feature is same.

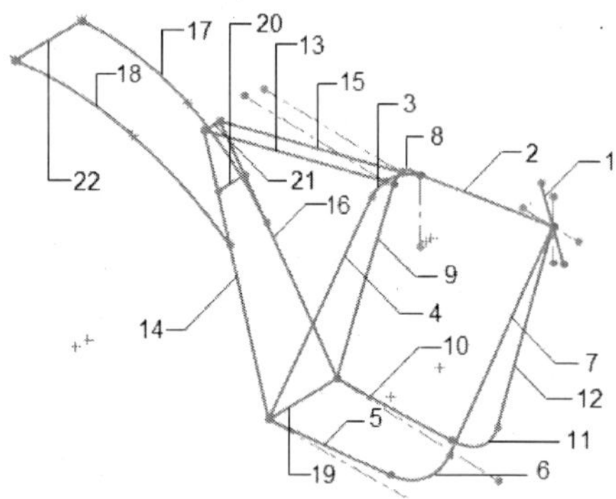

Figure 10-26 Sketch members with annotation

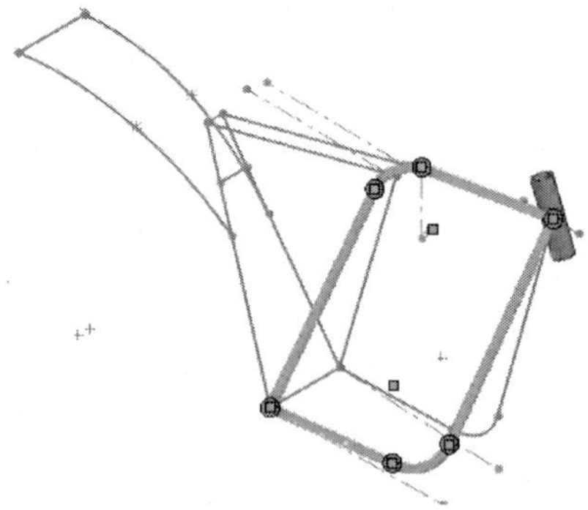

Figure 10-27 Preview of the structural members

10. Make sure that the **Apply corner treatment** check box is selected. Next, choose the **End Miter** button from the buttons provided below the **Apply corner treatment** check box. Set the value of the **Gap between Connected Segments in Same Group** spinner to 0.

The buttons provided below the **Apply corner treatment** check box are used to define the method of trimming the segments when they intersect at corners. The **Gap between Connected Segments in Same Group** is used to specify the weld gap at the corners of the same group segments.

11. Choose the **New Group** button from the PropertyManager; the **Group2** is added in the **Groups** selection area of the PropertyManager. Now, you can select the segments for group 2.

The **New Group** button of the PropertyManager is used to create a new group in the weldment structure. You can select a set of segments that can be parallel or contiguous in a group.

12. Select the sketched entities 8, 9, 10, 11, and 12 from the drawing area, refer to Figure 10-26; the preview of the structural members is displayed in the drawing area.

13. After defining the members of group 2, choose the **New Group** button from the PropertyManager; the **Group3** is added in the **Groups** selection area of the PropertyManager. Now, you can select the segments for group 3.

14. Select the sketched entities 19, 20, 21 and 22 from the drawing area, refer to Figure 10-26; the preview of the structural members is displayed in the drawing area.

15. Choose the **New Group** button from the PropertyManager; the **Group4** is added in the **Groups** selection area of the PropertyManager. Next, select the sketched entities 13 and 14 from the drawing area, refer to Figure 10-26; the preview of the structural members is displayed.

16. Choose the **New Group** button from the PropertyManager; the **Group5** is added in the **Groups** selection area of the PropertyManager. Next, select the sketched entities 15 and 16 from the drawing area, refer to Figure 10-26; the preview of the structural members is displayed.

17. Choose the **New Group** button from the PropertyManager; the **Group6** is added in the **Groups** selection area of the PropertyManager. Next, select the sketched entity 17, refer to Figure 10-26; the preview of the structural member is displayed.

18. Choose the **New Group** button from the PropertyManager; the **Group7** is added in the **Groups** selection area. Next, select the sketched entity 18, refer to Figure 10-26; the preview of the structural member is displayed.

19. Choose the **OK** button from the **Structural Member PropertyManager**; the weldment structure is created. The isometric view of the weldment structure after hiding all the sketch entities and reference planes is shown in Figure 10-28.

20. Expand **Structural Member2** node provided in the **FeatureManager design tree** and then select the sketch of the structural member; a pop-up toolbar is displayed. Choose the **Edit Sketch** button from pop-up toolbar; the sketcher environment is invoked. Next, edit the sketch of the structural member such that its inner diameter changest to 25.50 and outer diameter changest to 31.50 and then exit from the sketcher environment. The weldment structure after modifying the profile of the structural member is shown in Figure 10-29.

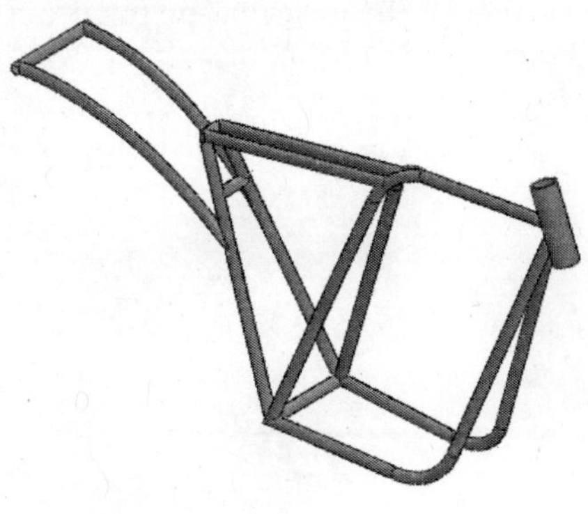

***Figure 10-28** Weldment structure*

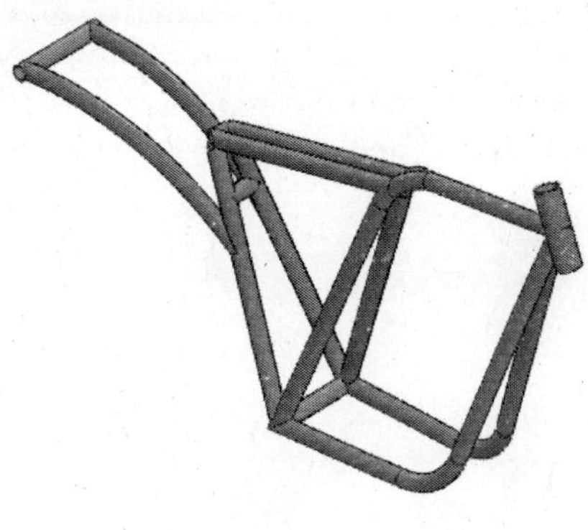

***Figure 10-29** Weldment structure after modifying the profile*

Trimming or Extending the Weldment Members

After creating the weldment structure, you need to trim or extend its members to get the desired shape.

1. Choose the **Trim/Extend** button from the **Weldments CommandManager**; the **Trim/Extend PropertyManager** is displayed.

The **Trim/Extend** tool is used to trim or extend one or more structural members at a corner where they intersect or trim or extend one or more segments with another solid body.

2. Make sure that the **End Trim** button is chosen in the **Corner Type** rollout of the **Trim/ Extend PropertyManager**.

The buttons in the **Corner Type** rollout are used to define the type of trimming or extending the members when they are intersect at corners.

3. Click in the **Bodies to be Trimmed** selection area of the **Bodies to be Trimmed** rollout and then select the members from the drawing area to be trimmed, refer to Figure 10-30; the selected members are highlighted in the drawing area and their names are displayed in the **Bodies to be Trimmed** selection area.

The **Bodies to be Trimmed** selection area allow you to select the body to be trimmed.

4. Make sure that the **Bodies** radio button is selected in the **Trimming Boundary** rollout of the PropertyManager. Next, click in the **Face/Bodies** selection area of the **Trimming Boundary** rollout.

The **Bodies** radio button in the **Trimming Boundary** rollout is used to select a body as a trimming boundary. Whereas, the **Face /Plane** radio button is used to select a planar face as a trimming boundary.

5. Select the member from the drawing area, refer to Figure 10-30, as the trimming boundary; the preview after trimming the members is displayed in the drawing area. Also, the callouts are attached with the members of the weldment structure with the information that whether the selected member or the part of selected member will be kept or discarded from the weldment structure, refer to Figure 10-31. You can also use these callouts to keep or discard the members of the weldment structure.

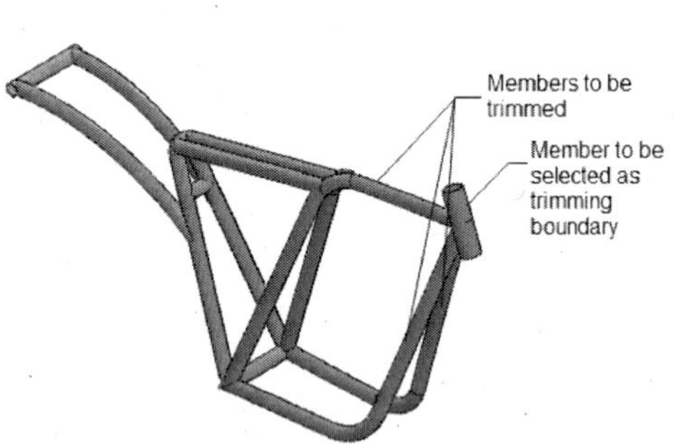

Figure 10-30 *Members to be selected*

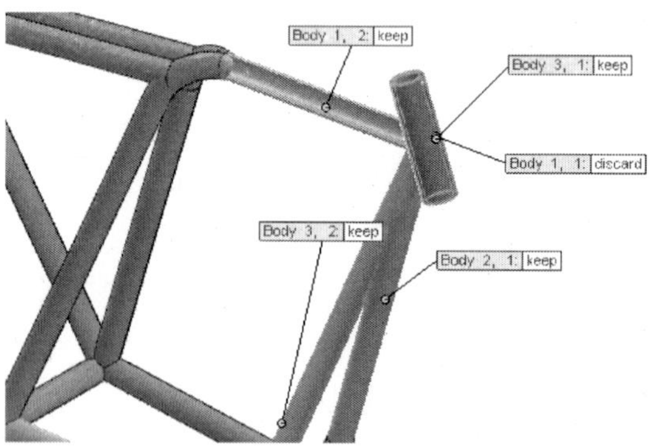

Figure 10-31 *Preview of the structural members*

6. Click on the **keep** area of the **Body 3, 1** callout in the drawing area; **keep** is changed to **discard**. Note that the name of the callout can be different in your case.

7. Choose the **Simple cut between bodies** button from the **Trimming Bodies** rollout of the PropertyManager. Next, choose the **OK** button from the PropertyManager; the members are trimmed, refer to Figure 10-32.

The **Simple cut between bodies** button is used to trim the member such that it flush with the planar contact of the member selected as the trimming boundary.

8. Similarly, invoke the **Trim/Extend** tool and select the members to be trimmed and members as the trimming boundary, refer to Figure 10-33.

9. Similarly, invoke the **Trim/Extend** tool and select the members to be trimmed and members as the trimming boundary, refer to Figure 10-33. Next, exit from the tool.

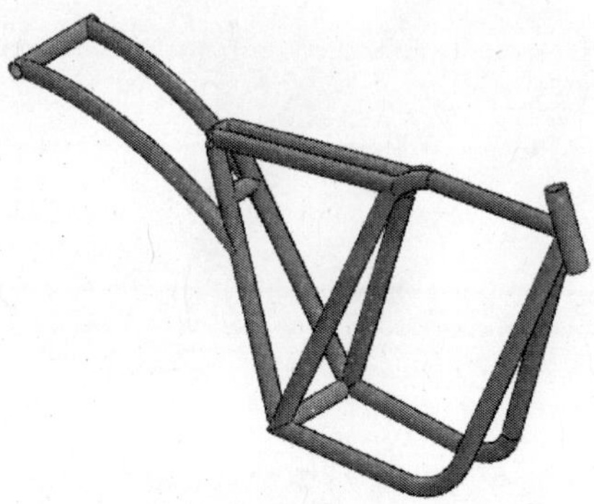

Figure 10-32 Weldment structure after trimming the unwanted portion of the members

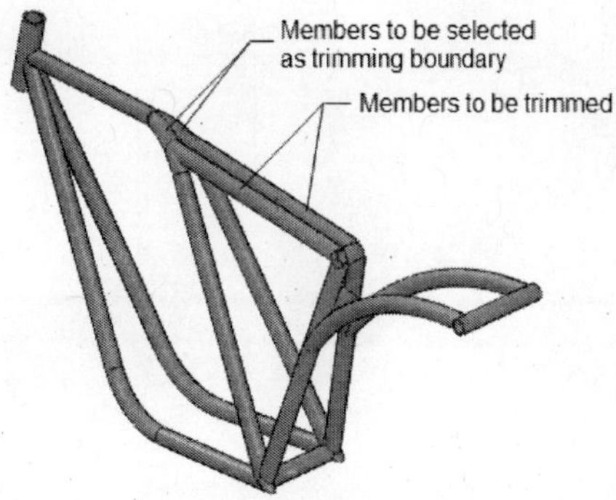

Figure 10-33 Members to be selected

Creating the End Cap Feature

After creating the weldment structure, you need to close the opening of the structural members by using the **End Cap** tool.

1. Choose the **End Cap** button from the **Weldments CommandManager**; the **End Cap PropertyManager** is displayed.

The **End Cap** tool is used to add end caps on the open structural members in order to close their opening.

2. Select the circular planar faces of member 1, refer to Figure 10-34; the preview of the end caps on the selected faces is displayed in the drawing area. Also, the name of the selected faces is displayed in the **Face** selection area of the **Parameters** rollout in the PropertyManager.

3. Choose the **Inward** button from the **Thickness direction** area of the **Parameters** rollout in the PropertyManager; the preview of the end caps is modified accordingly.

The **Thickness direction** area is provided with two buttons, **Outwards** and **Inwards**. These buttons are used to define the direction of end caps, outwards or inwards, respectively.

4. Set the value of the **Thickness** spinner to **6.35 mm** in the **Parameters** rollout. Next, choose the **OK** button from the PropertyManager; the end caps are added to the selected faces of member 1. The partial view of the weldment structure after adding the end caps on member 1 is shown in Figure 10-35.

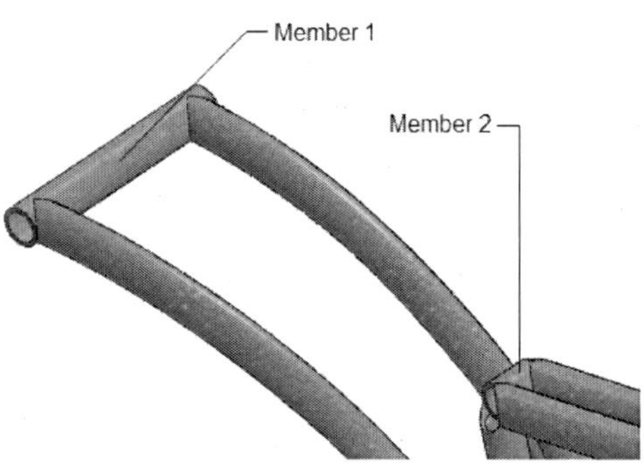

Figure 10-34 *End caps to be added on the members*

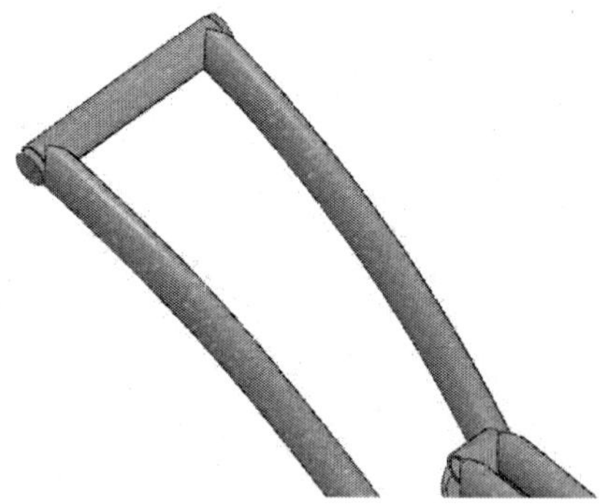

Figure 10-35 *Partial view after adding end caps*

5. Similarly, add the end caps on the circular planar faces of the member 2 shown in Figure 10-34 in the outward direction by specifying **71.12 mm** thickness. The weldment structure after adding the end caps is shown in Figure 10-36.

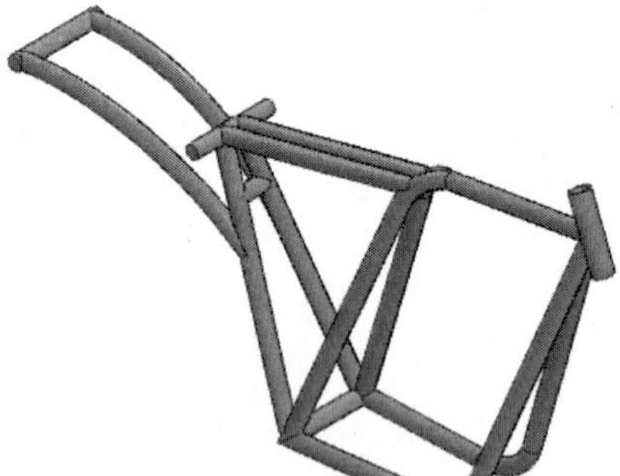

Figure 10-36 *Structure after adding end caps*

Creating the Extrude and Cut Features

Now, you need to create the extrude and cut features of the weldment structure.

1. Invoke the sketcher environment by selecting the Front Plane as the sketching plane and then draw the sketch of the extrude feature, as shown in Figure 10-37. Next, exit from the sketcher environment.

2. Invoke the **Extruded Boss/Base** tool and extrude the sketch in direction 1 and direction 2 by using the **Up To Next** option. The weldment structure after creating the extruded feature is shown in Figure 10-38.

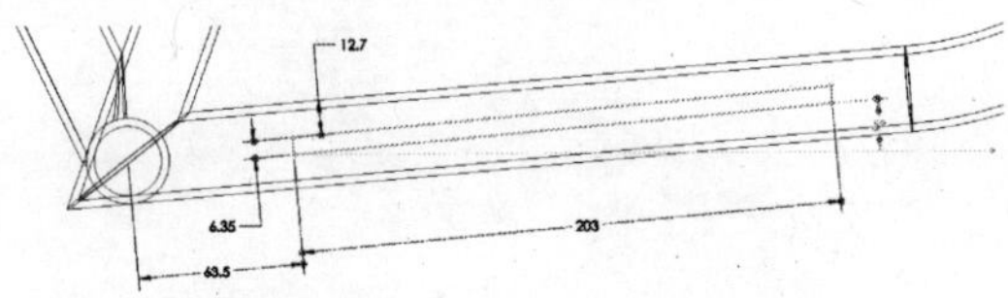

Figure 10-37 *Sketch of the extrude feature*

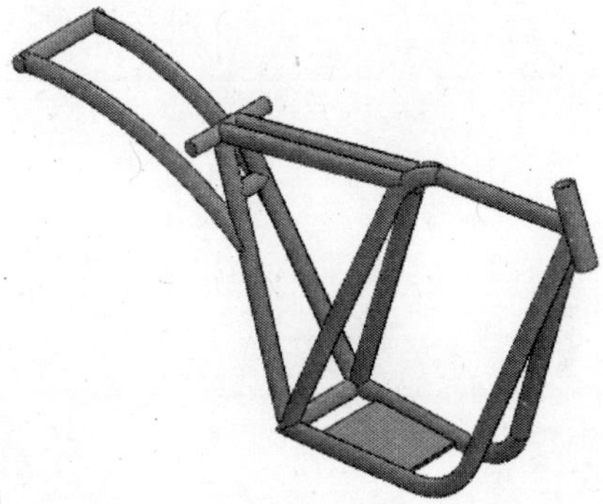

Figure 10-38 *Weldment structure after creating the extruded feature*

3. Create a reference plane at an offset distance of 108.585 mm from the Front Plane and then invoke the sketcher environment by selecting it as the sketching plane. Draw the sketch, refer to Figure 10-39. Note that the sketch shown in Figure 10-39 has two closed contours. Next, extrude both the contours of the sketch one by one by using the contour selection method. First extrude the rectangular shaped contour of the sketch by using the **Up To Next** option of the **Extruded Boss/Base** tool and then extrude the other contours of the sketch upto the depth of 3.1 in the inwards direction by using the **Extruded Boss/Base** tool. Make sure that while extruding the sketch the **Merge result** check box is selected in the **Boss-Extrude PropertyManager**. The partial view of the model after extruding both the contours of the sketch is shown in Figure 10-40.

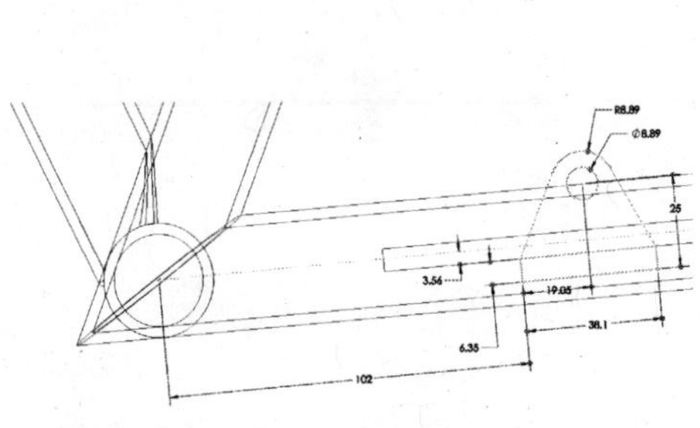

Figure 10-39 *Sketch with contours*

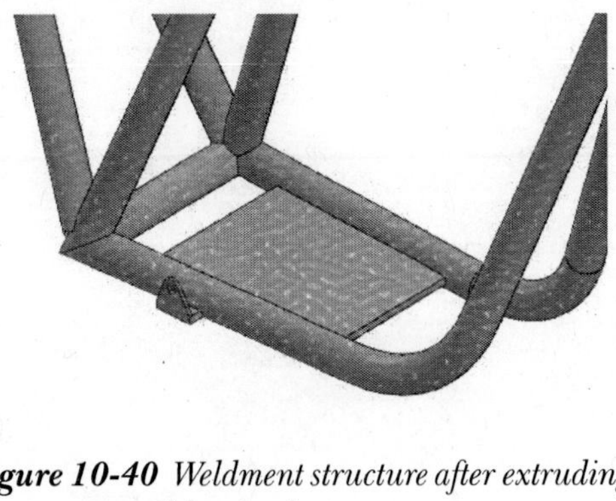

Figure 10-40 *Weldment structure after extruding the contours of the sketch*

4. Create a reference plane at an offset distance of 680.72 mm from the Right Plane and then invoke the sketcher environment by selecting it as the sketching plane. Draw the sketch of the extrude feature, refer to Figure 10-41. Next, exit from the sketcher environment and then extrude the sketch by using the **Up To Next** option of the **Extruded Boss/Base** tool, as shown in Figure 10-42.

Note

In Figure 10-40, the visibility of the temporary axes is turned ON. To do so, choose the ***View Temporary Axes*** *button from the* ***Hide/Show Items*** *flyout of the* ***(Heads-up) View*** *toolbar.*

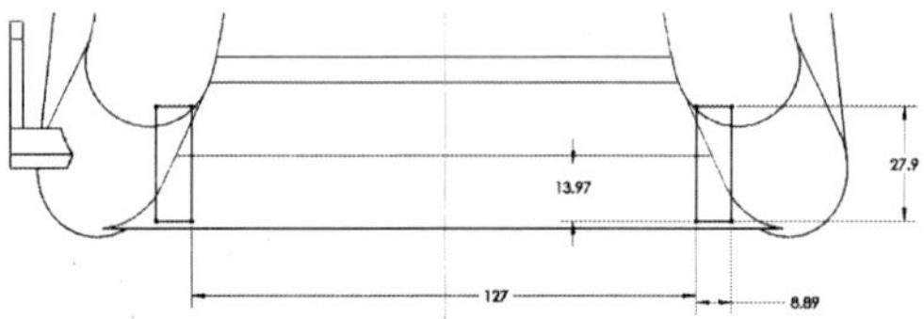

Figure 10-41 *Sketch of the extrude feature*

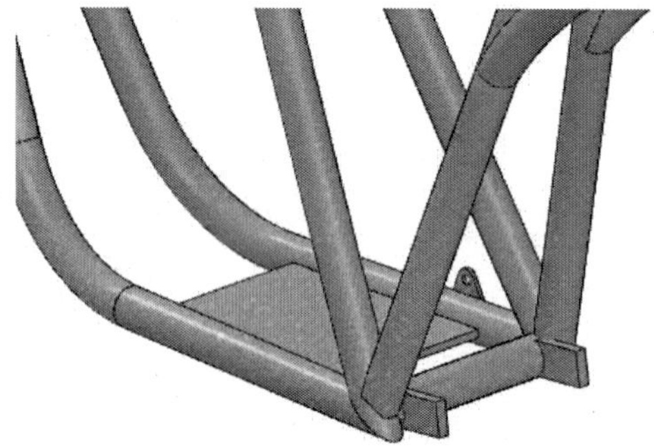

Figure 10-42 *Partial view of the weldment structure after extruding the sketch*

5. Create a circular cut feature on the planar face of the previously created extruded feature, refer to Figure 10-43.

6. Create the extrude feature, as shown in Figure 10-44.

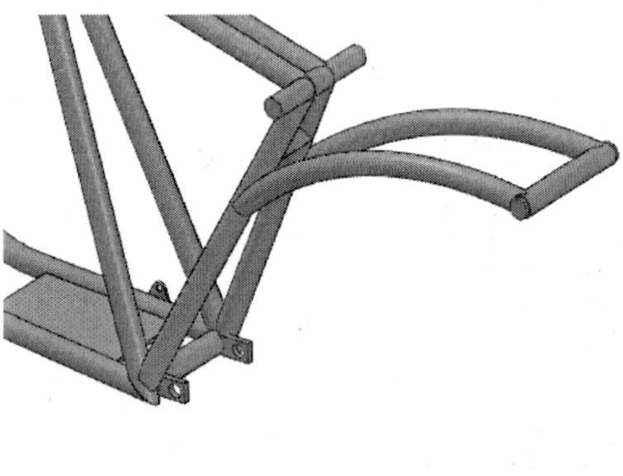

Figure 10-43 *Sketch of the extrude feature*

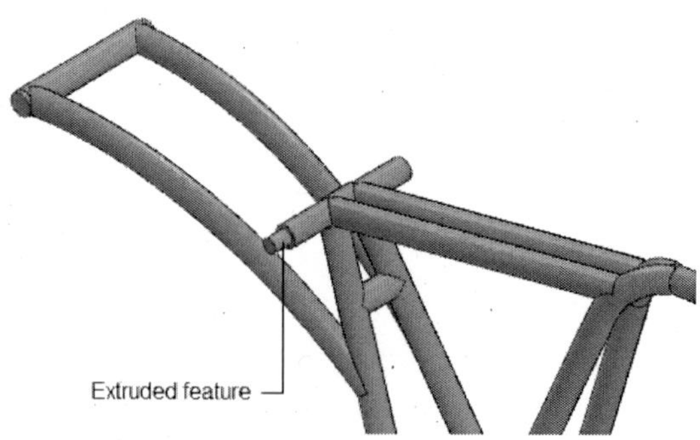

Figure 10-44 *Partial view of the weldment structure after creating the extruded feature*

7. Create a reference plane at an offset distance of 59.69 mm from the Front Plane and then invoke the sketcher environment by selecting it as the sketching plane. Draw the sketch of the extrude feature, refer to Figure 10-45. Note that the sketch shown in Figure 10-45 has two closed contours. Exit from the sketcher environment and then extrude both the contours of the sketch one by one by using the contour selection method, refer to Figure 10-46.

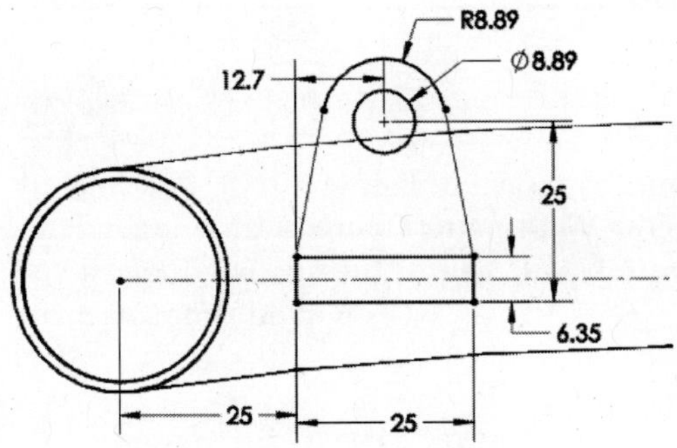

Figure 10-45 *Sketch with contours*

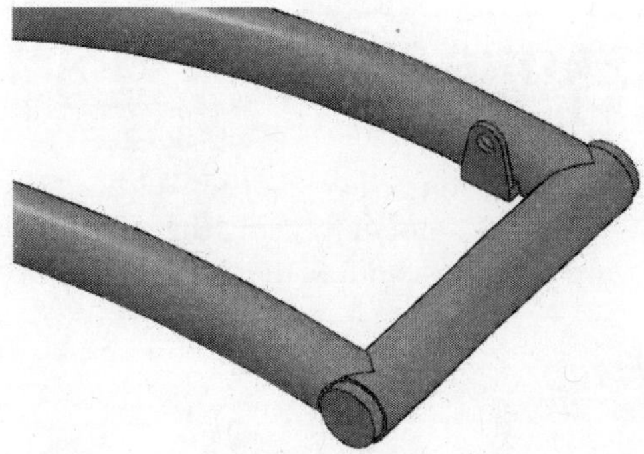

Figure 10-46 *Partial view of the weldment structure after extruding the contours of the sketch*

8. Similarly, create the remaining extrude features. Hide all the sketches and the reference planes. The final weldment structural frame after creating all features is shown in Figure 10-47.

Figure 10-47 *The final weldment structural frame*

Saving the Model

After creating the model, you need to save it in the *Motor Cycle Project* folder.

1. Save the model with the name *Weldment Structural Frame* in the *Motor Cycle Project* folder.

2. Close the document by choosing **File > Close** from the SOLIDWORKS menus.

CREATING THE SEAT FRAME

Part Description

In this session, you will create the Weldment seat frame, as shown in Figure 10-48. It is created in the Part environment by using the tools available in the **Weldments CommandManager**. The views and the dimensions of the frame are shown in Figure 10-49. Assume the missing dimensions.

(Expected time: 20 min)

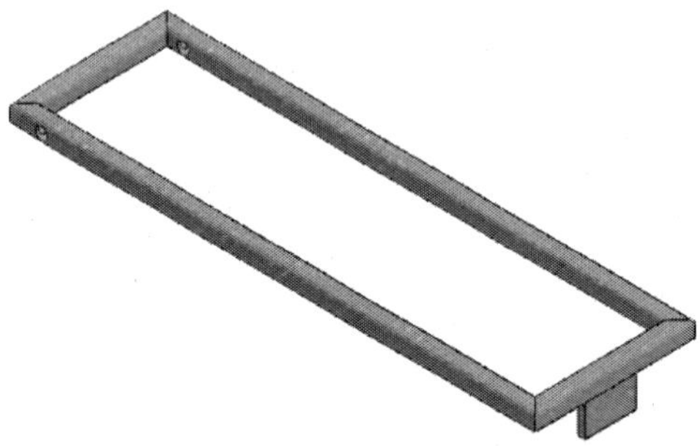

Figure 10-48 *Weldment seat frame*

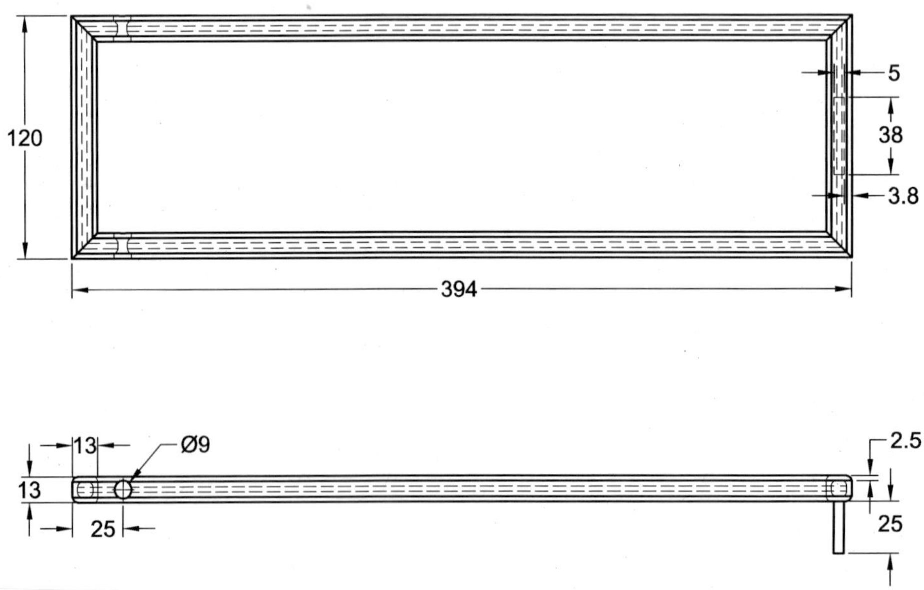

Figure 10-49 *Top and Front views of the model*

Creating the Seat Frame

As discussed earlier, you can select the pre-defined weldment profile from the **Selections** rollout of the **Structural Member PropertyManager** for creating the structural members. In this section, you will create your own weldment profile and save it as a library part feature and then you will use it for creating the structure.

1. Start a new SOLIDWORKS part document using the **New SOLIDWORKS Document** dialog box. Modify the unit of the current session to mm, if it is not set by default.

2. Invoke the sketcher environment by selecting the Right Plane as the sketching plane and then draw the sketch of the profile, as shown in Figure 10-50.

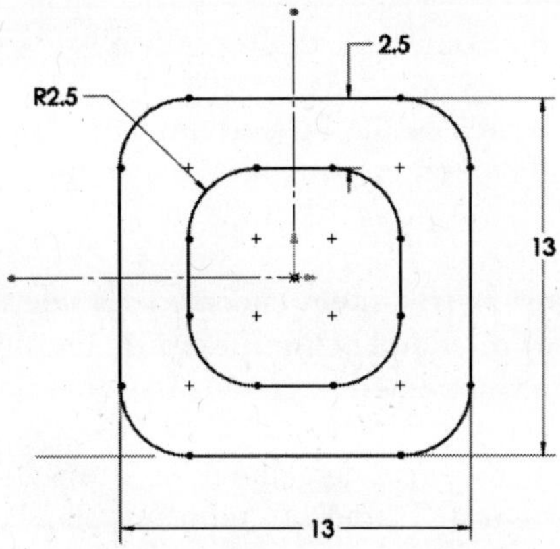

Figure 10-50 Sketch of the weldment profile

3. Exit from the sketcher environment and then choose the **File > Save As** from the SOLIDWORKS menu; the **Save As** dialog box is displayed.

4. Browse to *installation directory > data > weldments* and then select the **Lib Feat Part (*.sldlfp)** from the **Save as type** drop-down list of the dialog box.

5. Enter **13 x 13 x 2.5** in the **File name** edit box of the dialog box. Next, choose the **Save** button. Note that you will be able to save the profile in the above mentioned location only if you have run the program as an administrator.

6. Choose **File > Close** from the SOLIDWORKS menus to close the document.

7. Start a new part document and then modify the current unit to millimeters, if it is not set b default.

8. Invoke the sketcher environment by selecting the Top Plane as the sketching plane and then draw the sketch of the structure, as shown in Figure 10-51. Next, exit from the sketcher environment. Change the current orientation to isometric.

9. Choose the **Structural Member** button from the **Weldments CommandManager**; the **Structural Member PropertyManager** is displayed.

10. Select the **ansi inch** option from the **Standard** drop-down list, the **square tube** option from the **Type** drop-down list of the **Selections** rollout in the **Structural Member PropertyManager**. Note that the name **13 x 13 x 2.5** of the weldment profile that you have saved in the earlier steps now appears in the **Size** drop-down list of the PropertyManager.

11. Select the **13 x 13 x 2.5** option from the **Size** drop-down list of the PropertyManager.

12. Click in the **Groups** selection area of the PropertyManager to activate its selection mode and then select all the sketched members one by one from the drawing area; the preview of the structural members is displayed in the drawing area.

13. Make sure that the **Apply corner treatment** check box is selected. Next, choose the **End Miter** button from the buttons provided below the **Apply corner treatment** check box. Set the value of the **Gap between Connected Segments in Same Group** spinner to **0**.

14. Choose the **OK** button from the PropertyManager; the weldment structural frame is created. The weldment structural frame after hiding the sketch entities is shown in Figure 10-52.

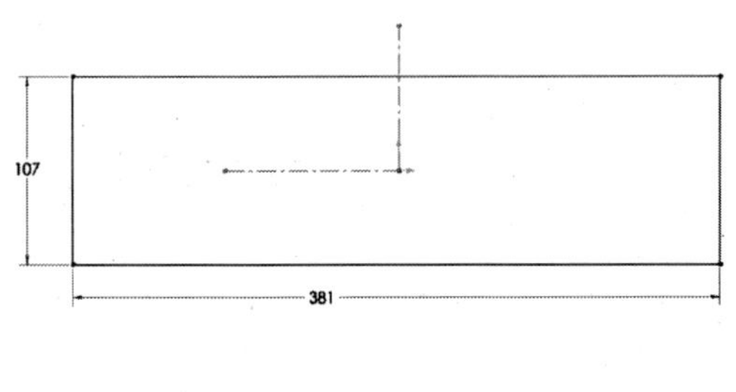

Figure 10-51 *Sketch of the structure*

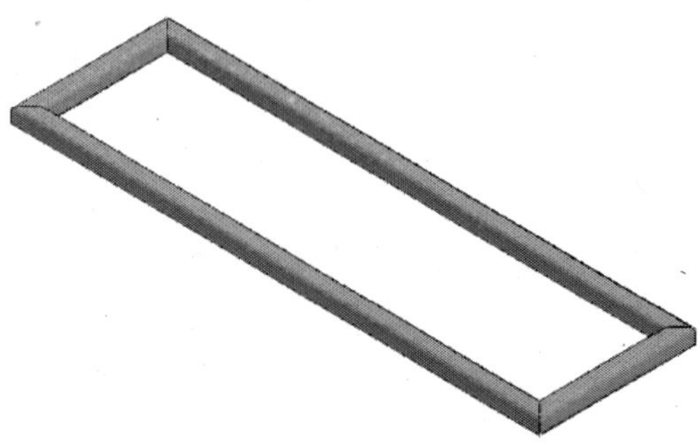

Figure 10-52 *Weldment structural frame*

Creating the Cut and Extrude Features

After creating the weldment structural frame, you need to create the cut and extrude features.

1. Create the cut feature, refer to Figure 10-53.

2. Create the extrude feature, refer to Figure 10-54.

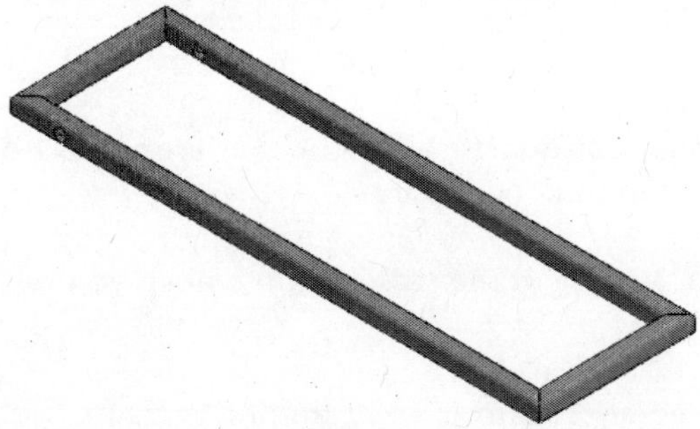

Figure 10-53 Model after creating the cut feature

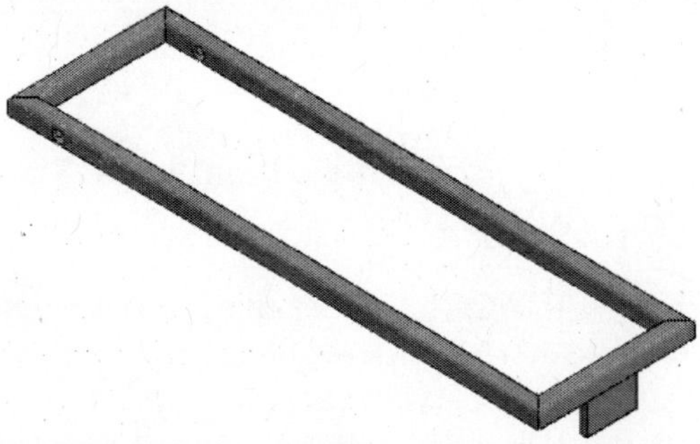

Figure 10-54 Final model after creating the extruded feature

Saving the Model

After creating the model, you need to save it in the *Motor Cycle Project* folder.

1. Save the model with the name *Weldment Seat Frame* in the *Motor Cycle Project* folder.

2. Close the document by choosing **File > Close** from the SOLIDWORKS menus.

Self-Evaluation Test

Answer the following questions and then compare them to those given at the end of this chapter:

1. The __________ tool is used to create a structural member feature by sweeping the pre-defined profile along the user-defined path.

2. The options in the __________ drop-down list of the **Structural Member PropertyManager** are used to define the size of the weldment profile.

3. The __________ selection area of the **Structural Member PropertyManager** is used to select the sketch segments to define the path of the structural member.

4. The __________ button of the **Structural Member PropertyManager** is used to create a new group of segments in the weldment structure.

5. The __________ tool is used to trim or extend one or more structural members at the corner where they intersect.

6. In SOLIDWORKS, the weldment profile of all the groups within a structural member feature is same. (T/F)

7. In SOLIDWORKS, the weldment structures are created in the Weldments mode. (T/F)

8. The _________ radio button in the **Trimming Boundary** rollout of the **Trim/Extend PropertyManager** is used to select a body as a trimming boundary.

9. In SOLIDWORKS, other than the pre-defined profiles of the structural member, you can also create your own profile. (T/F)

10. In SOLIDWORKS, after creating a structural member feature, you cannot edit its profile. (T/F)

Review Questions

Answer the following questions:

1. The _________ and _________ buttons in the **Thickness direction** area of the **End Cap PropertyManager** is used to define the outward and inward directions of the end caps.

2. To display the **End Cap PropertyManager**, choose the _________ button from the **Weldments CommandManager**.

3. The _________ button of the **Trim/Extend PropertyManager** is used to trim a member such that it flush with the planar contact of a member selected as the trimming boundary.

4. The options in the _________ drop-down list of the **Structural Member PropertyManager** are used to define the type of weldment profile.

5. The _________ tool is used to add end caps on the opened structural members in order to close their opening.

6. The **Face / Plane** radio button in the **Trim/Extend PropertyManager** allows you to select a body as a trimming boundary. (T/F)

7. The _________ selection area of the **Trim/Extend PropertyManager** allows you to select a body to be trimmed.

8. On choosing which of the following buttons, the **Structural Member PropertyManager** is displayed?
   (a) **Trim/Extend** (b) **Structural Members**
   (c) **Structural Member** (d) None of these

9. On choosing which of the following buttons, the **Trim/Extend PropertyManager** is displayed?

    (a) **Trim/Extend**
    (b) **Trim Extend**
    (c) **Structural Member**
    (d) None of these

10. In SOLIDWORKS, you can create a weldment structure that contains one or more groups. (T/F)

Answers to Self-Evaluation Test

1. Structural Member, **2.** Size, **3.** Groups, **4.** New Group, **5.** Trim/Extend, **6.** T, **7.** T, **8.** Bodies, **9.** T, **10.** F

Chapter 11

Creating Motor Cycle Assembly

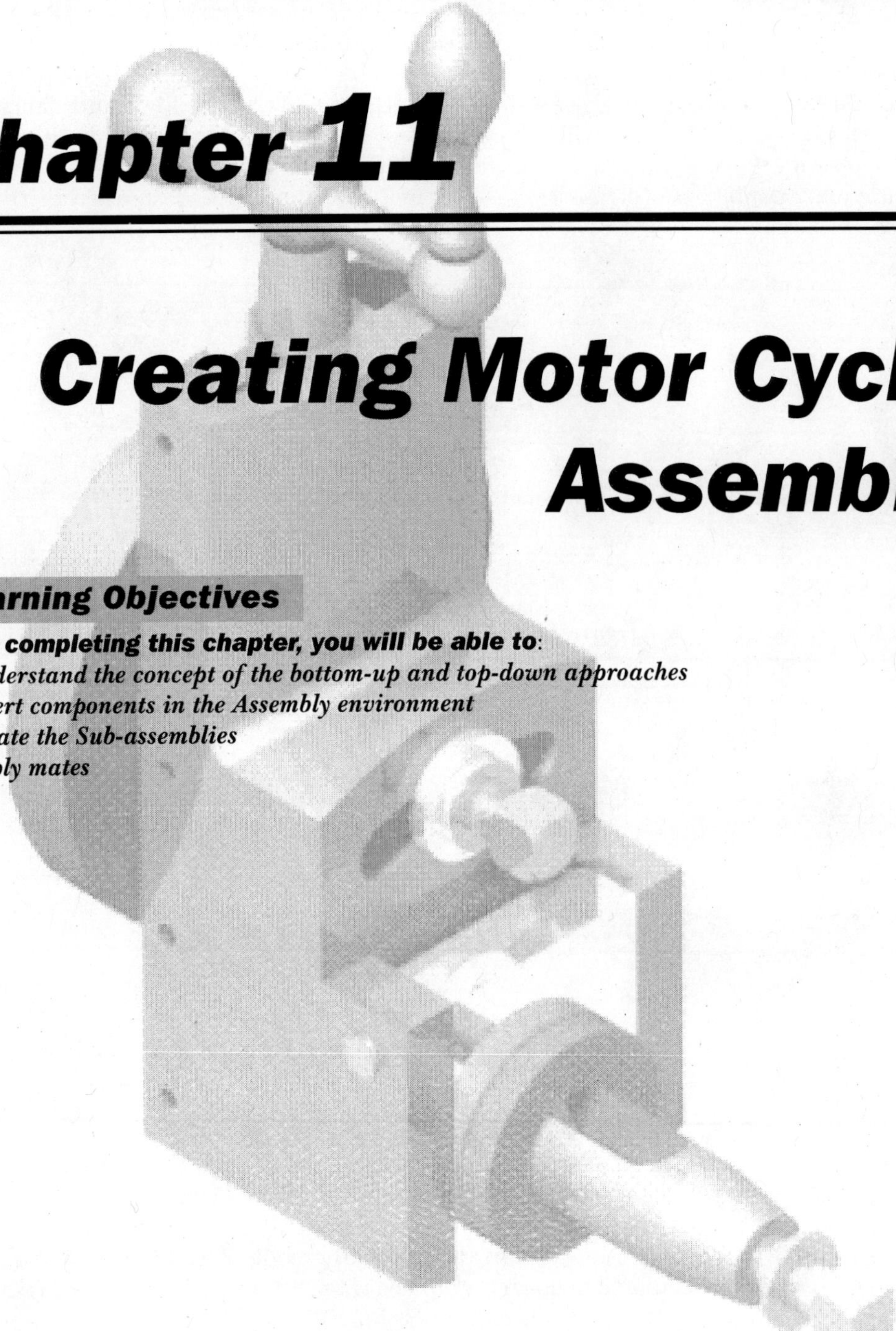

Learning Objectives

After completing this chapter, you will be able to:

- *Understand the concept of the bottom-up and top-down approaches*
- *Insert components in the Assembly environment*
- *Create the Sub-assemblies*
- *Apply mates*

CREATING THE MOTOR CYCLE ASSEMBLY

Part Description

In this section, you will create the Motor Cycle assembly shown in Figure 11-1. This assembly will be created in three parts: two sub-assemblies; Brake sub-subassembly and the Shock Absorber sub-assembly, as shown in Figures 11-2 and 11-3 and the main assembly, refer to Figure 11-1. You will use the parts of the motor cycle created in the earlier chapters to create the sub-assemblies and the main assembly of the motor cycle in the Assembly mode. In the Brake sub-assembly, you will restrict the linear motion of the Caliper Piston between 0 to 5.

Figure 11-1 *Motor Cycle assembly*

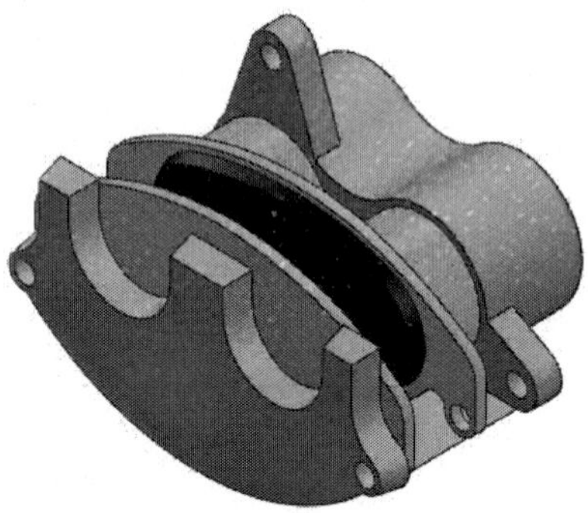

Figure 11-2 *Brake sub-assembly*

Figure 11-3 *Shock Absorber sub-assembly*

Introduction to Assembly Mode

An assembly design consists of two or more components assembled together at their respective work positions by using parametric relations. In SolidWorks, these relations are called mates. These mates allow you to constrain the degrees of freedom of the components at their respective work positions. To start the **Assembly** mode of SolidWorks, invoke the **New SOLIDWORKS Document** dialog box and then choose the **Assembly** button, as shown in Figure 11-4 and then **OK** button to start a new SolidWorks document in the Assembly mode.

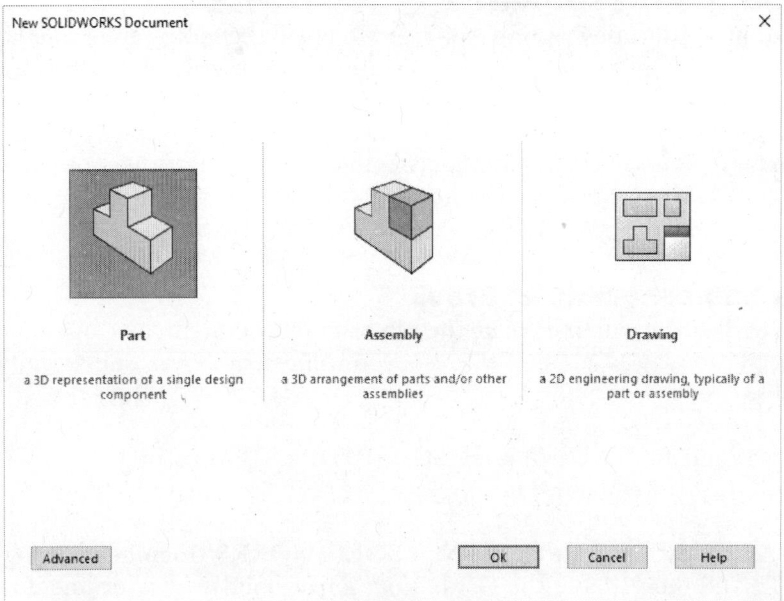

Figure 11-4 *The* ***New SolidWorks Document*** *dialog box*

In SolidWorks, assemblies are created by using two types of design approaches: bottom-up approach and top-down approach. The bottom-up assembly design approach is the traditional and the most widely preferred approach of assembly design. In this assembly design approach, all components are created as separate part documents, and then they are placed and referenced in the assembly as external components. In this type of approach, components are created in the **Part** mode and saved as the *.sldprt* documents. After creating and saving all components of the assembly, start a new assembly document (*.sldasm*) and insert the components in it using the tools provided in the **Assembly** mode. After inserting the components, assemble them using the assembly mates. The main advantage of this assembly design approach is that the view of the part is not restricted because there is only a single part in the current file. Therefore, this approach allows you to concentrate on the complex individual features. This approach is preferred while handling large assemblies or assemblies with complex parts.

In the top-down assembly design approach, the components are created in the same assembly document, but they are saved as separate part files. Therefore, the top-down assembly design approach is entirely different from the bottom-up design approach. In this approach, you will start your work in the assembly document and the geometry of one part will help in defining the geometry of the other.

Note

You can also create an assembly with the combination of both the bottom-up and top-down assembly approaches.

Creating the Sub-assemblies

As mentioned in the part description, you need to break the motor cycle assembly in three steps because it is a large assembly. One will be the sub-assembly of the Break, second will be the sub-assembly of the Shock Absorber, and the third will be the main assembly. First, you will create the sub-assembly of Break consisting of Caliper Body, Caliper Piston, and Caliper Pad. Next, you will create the sub-assembly of Shock Absorber consisting of Shock Absorber Cylinder, Shock Absorber Piston Rod, and Shock Absorber Spring. After creating the both the sub-assemblies, you need to create the main assembly.

Creating the Sub-assembly of Break

As discussed earlier, you will first create the sub-assembly of the Break consisting of Caliper Body, Caliper Piston, and Caliper Pad. Also, you will assemble this sub-assembly with the main assembly later.

1. Start SolidWorks and then invoke the **New SOLIDWORKS Document** dialog box by choosing the **New** button from the Menu Bar.

2. Choose the **Assembly** button from the **New SOLIDWORKS Document** dialog box, refer to Figure 11-4 and then choose the **OK** button; a new SolidWorks document is started in the Assembly mode and the **Begin Assembly PropertyManager** is invoked, as shown in Figure 11-5. Also, the **Open** dialog box is displayed; choose the **Cancel** button to close this dialog box.

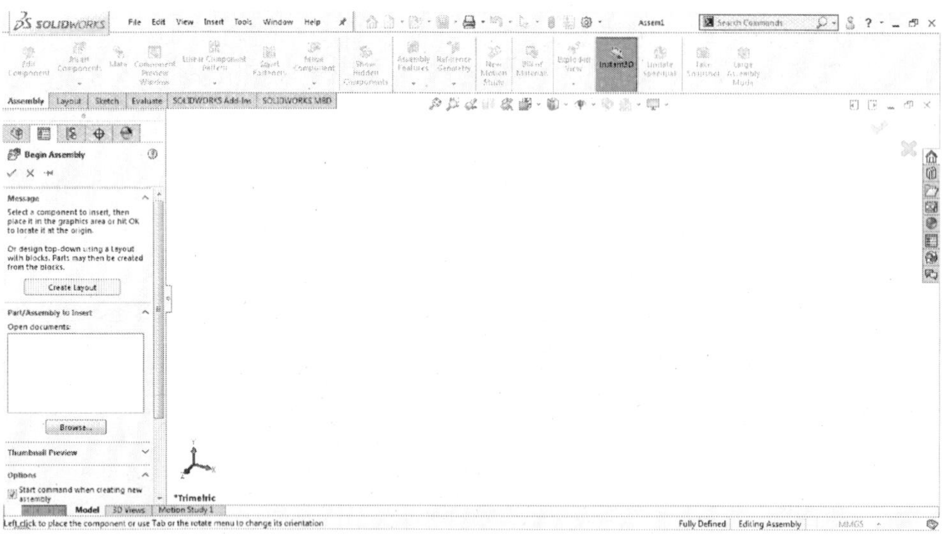

Figure 11-5** The Assembly mode with the **Begin Assembly PropertyManager

When you start a new SolidWorks document in the Assembly mode, the **Begin Assembly PropertyManager** will be displayed, refer to Figure 11-5. Note that this PropertyManager will be displayed only when you start a new assembly document. The **Message** rollout in the **Begin Assembly PropertyManager** prompts you to select a part or an assembly and then place the component in the graphics area.

The **Start command when creating new assembly** check box in the **Options** rollout of the **Begin Assembly PropertyManager** is selected by default. So, the **Begin Assembly PropertyManager** is invoked automatically when you start a new SolidWorks assembly document. The **Graphics preview** check box in the **Options** rollout is also selected by default and is used to display the graphic preview of the component selected to be inserted.

3. Choose the **Browse** button from the **Part/Assembly to Insert** rollout of the **Begin Assembly PropertyManager**; the **Open** dialog box is displayed.

4. Browse to the *Motor Cycle Project* folder, where you have saved all the components of the Motor Cycle and then select the Caliper Body.

5. Choose the **Open** button; the cursor will be replaced by the component cursor and the graphic preview of the component is displayed. Also, the name of the selected component is displayed in the **Open documents** selection area of the **Part/Assembly to Insert** rollout.

The **Open documents** selection area of the **Part/Assembly to Insert** rollout, display the name of the selected component and the components that are already opened in the current session of the SolidWorks.

6. Choose the **OK** button from the PropertyManager; the origin of the selected component is align with the assembly origin, as shown in Figure 11-6. It is recommended to align the origin of the first component with the assembly origin. Also, the name of the inserted component is added in the FeatureManager design tree.

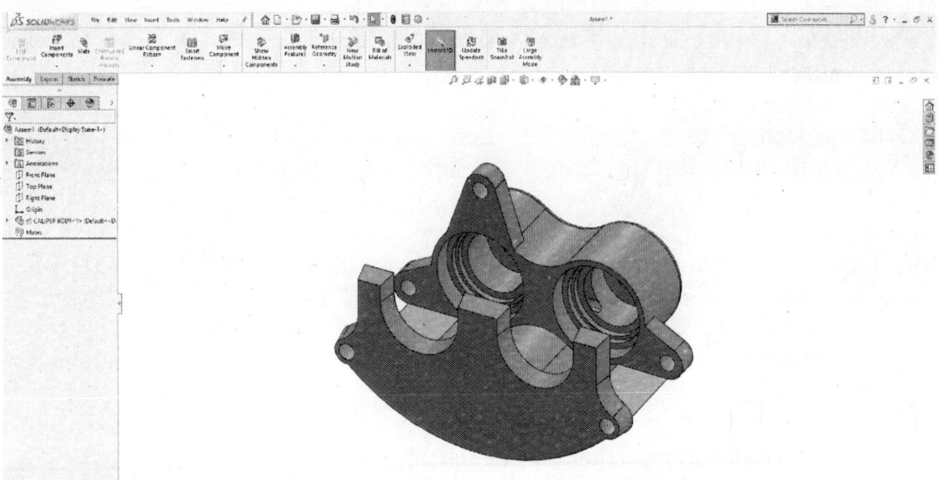

Figure 11-6 *The Assembly mode after inserting the Caliper Body*

> **Tip**
> *When you insert a component in the assembly, it will be displayed in the* ***FeatureManager design tree****. The naming convention the first component is* ***(f) Name of Component <1>****. In this convention, (f) indicates that the component is fixed. You cannot move a fixed component. Next, the name of the component will be displayed. The* ***<1>*** *symbol denotes the serial number of the same component in the entire assembly. The* ***(-)*** *symbol before the name of the component implies that the component is floating and under-defined. You need to apply the required mates to the component to fully define it. You will learn more about assembly mates later in this chapter. The* ***(+)*** *symbol implies that the component is over-defined. If no symbol appears before the name of the component, then the component will be fully defined.*

After inserting the Caliper Body in the Assembly environment, you need to insert the Caliper Piston.

7. Choose the **Insert Components** button from the **Assembly CommandManager**; the **Insert Component PropertyManager** is displayed along with the **Open** dialog box. Close the **Open** dialog box.

The **Insert Components** tool of the **Assembly CommandManager** is used to insert components in the **Assembly** environment. As discussed earlier, the **Begin Assembly PropertyManager** will be displayed only when you start a new assembly document. Therefore, to insert the other components of the assembly, you need to use the **Insert Components** tool.

8. Choose the **Browse** button from the **Part/Assembly to Insert** rollout of the **Insert Component PropertyManager**; the **Open** dialog box is displayed.

9. Browse to the *Motor Cycle Project* folder, where you have saved all the components of the Motor Cycle and then select the Caliper Piston.

10. Choose the **Open** button; the cursor will be replaced by the component cursor and the graphic preview of the component is displayed. Also, the name of the selected component is displayed in the **Open documents** selection area of the **Part/Assembly to Insert** rollout.

It is evident from the Figure 11-2 that you need to insert two instances of the Caliper Piston in the Assembly envrionment.

11. Choose the **Keep Visible** button that is provided at the top of the **Insert Component PropertyManager** and then click the left mouse button anywhere in the graphic area of the Assembly environment to place the first instance of the Caliper Piston. Make sure that the instance of the Caliper Piston should not intersect with the Caliper Body. As soon as, you placed the first instance of the Caliper Piston, the graphic preview of the second instance of the Caliper Piston is displayed.

The **Keep Visible** button of the **Insert Component PropertyManager** is used to place multiple components or multiple instances of the same components in the Assembly environment.

12. Move the cursor in the graphic area and click the left mouse button to place the second instance of the Caliper Piston, refer to Figure 11-7. Make sure that you place components in the Assembly environment without any intersection. After placing the second instance of the Component, the preview of one more instance is displayed attached with the cursor, indicating that you can place multiple instances of the selected component.

13. Choose the **OK** button from the **Insert Component PropertyManager**. The Figure 11-7 shows the Assembly environment after inserting the two instances of the Caliper Piston.

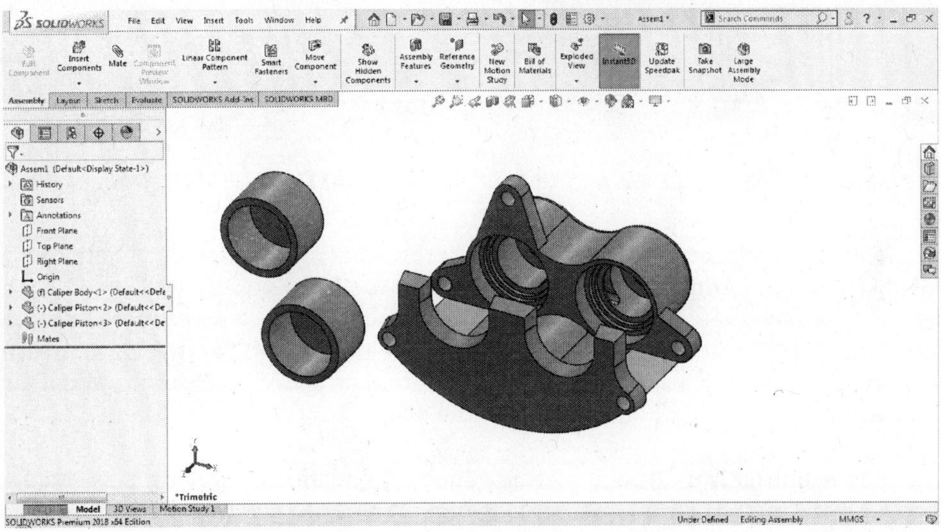

Figure 11-7 *The Assembly environment after inserting two instances of the Caliper Piston*

After inserting the two instances of the Caliper Piston, you need to apply the required mates to assemble them with the Caliper Body by using the **Mate** tool.

14. Choose the **Mate** button from the **Assembly CommandManager**; the **Mate PropertyManager** is displayed.

The **Mate PropertyManager** allow you to apply the required mates to the components in order to constrain their degrees of freedom at their respective work positions. Mates help you to precisely place and position the component with respect to the other components and the surroundings in the assembly. You can also define the linear and rotatory movements of the component with respect to the other components. Additionally, you can create a dynamic mechanism and check its stability by precisely defining the combination of mates.

15. Select the outer circular face of a Caliper Piston, refer to Figure 11-8 and then select the circular face of the Caliper Body, refer to Figure 11-8; the selected faces is highlighted in the graphic window and their names are displayed in the **Entities to Mate** selection area of the **Mate Selections** rollout in the PropertyManager. Also, the **Mate** pop-up toolbar is invoked, refer to Figure 11-9 and the most suitable mates can be applied to the current selections set are displayed in the **Mate** pop-up toolbar. Also, the most appropriate mate is selected, by default, in this pop-up toolbar as well as in the **Standard Mates** rollout of the

Mate PropertyManager. Also, note that preview of the assembly using the most appropriate mate is displayed in the graphic window.

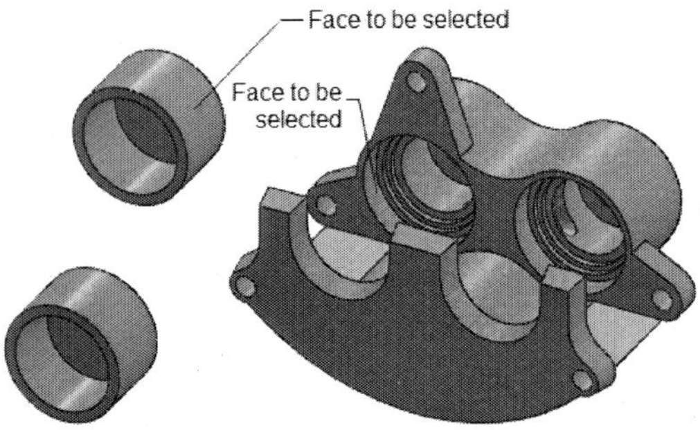

Figure 11-8 Faces to be selected

*Figure 11-9 The **Mate** pop-up toolbar*

By default, the **Concentric** button is chosen in the **Mate** pop-up toolbar. Therefore, you can directly choose the **Add/Finish Mate** button from the **Mate** pop-up toolbar.

16. Choose the **Add/Finish Mate** button from the **Mate** pop-up toolbar; the concentric relation is applied between the selected set of faces. Note that the **Mate PropertyManager** is still displayed and you can add other mates to the assembly.

The **Concentric** button is used to apply the concentric relation between the selected circular faces. In this relation, the central axis of one component is aligned with that of the other.

17. Select the back planar face of the same Caliper Piston and then select the planar face of the Caliper Body, refer to Figure 11-10. You need to rotate and zoom the graphic area for these selections. The selected faces is highlighted in the graphic window and their names are displayed in the **Entities to Mate** selection area of the **Mate Selections** rollout in the PropertyManager. The **Mate** pop-up toolbar is displayed in the graphic window with the **Coincident** button chosen in it, by default. Also the preview of the assembly using the coincident relation is displayed.

The **Coincident** button is used to make two planar faces coplanar. However, you can apply this mate to other entities as well.

18. Expand the **Advance Mates** rollout of the PropertyManager by click on the down arrows provided on the right of the **Advance Mates** rollout title bar.

19. Choose the **Distance** button from the **Advance Mates** rollout of the PropertyManager; the **Distance**, **Maximum Value**, and the **Minimum Value** spinners are enabled, refer to Figure 11-11. 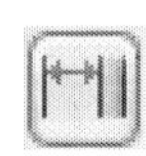

The **Distance** button of the **Advance Mates** rollout is used to create a to and fro motion between the components.

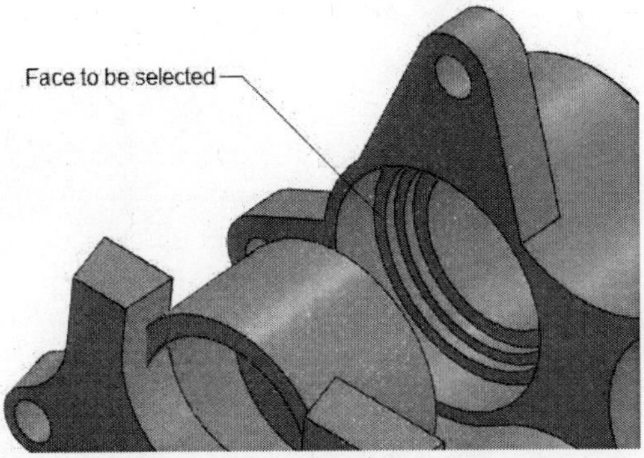

Figure 11-10 Face to be selected

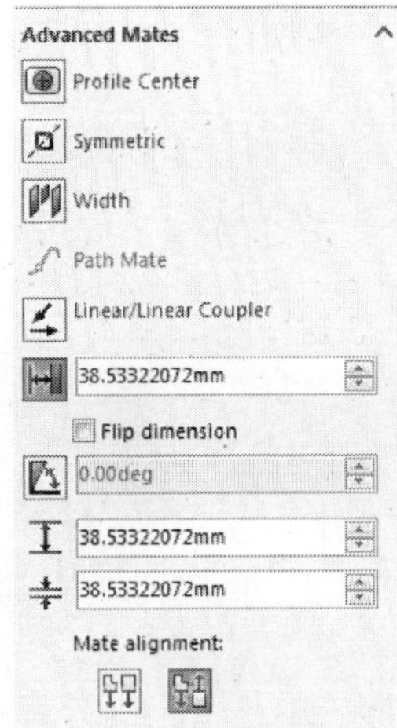

*Figure 11-11 The **Advanced Mates** rollout*

20. Set the value of the **Distance** spinner to 5 and press ENTER. As soon as you set the value of the **Distance** spinner, the value of the **Maximum Value** spinner and the **Minimum Value** spinner is automatically set to 5.

The maximum distance by which the two selected faces can be moved apart is specified in the **Distance** spinner; this value will be displayed in both the **Maximum Value** and the **Minimum Value** spinners. However, if you want the selected faces to be moved in a to and fro motion, specify the minimum distance in the **Minimum Value** spinner.

21. Set the value of the **Minimum Value** spinner to **0** and press ENTER. Next, choose the **OK** button once from the PropertyManager. Now, you can drag the Caliper Piston to check its linear motion that is restricted between 0 to 5. Note that, the **Mate PropertyManager** is still displaced.

22. Choose the **Parallel** button from the **Standard Mates** rollout of the **Mate PropertyManager**.

The **Parallel** button is used to apply the parallel mate between two components.

23. Expand the **FeatureManager design tree** that is now displayed in the graphic window by clicking on the ▸ sign. Next, expand the same Caliper Piston node.

24. Select the Right Plane of the Caliper Piston 1 and then select the Right Plane of the Caliper Body to apply the parallel relation between them; the **Mate** pop-up toolbar is displayed. Next, choose the **Add/Finish Mate** button from the **Mate** pop-up toolbar.

25. Similarly, apply the distance, concentric and parallel relations between the faces or planes of the other instance of the Caliper Piston and the Caliper Body. Also, apply, the coincident relation between the planar faces of both the instances of the Caliper Piston. The assembly after assembling the two instances of the Caliper Piston and the Caliper Body is shown in Figure 11-12. Next, exit from the **Mate PropertyManager** by choosing the **OK** button.

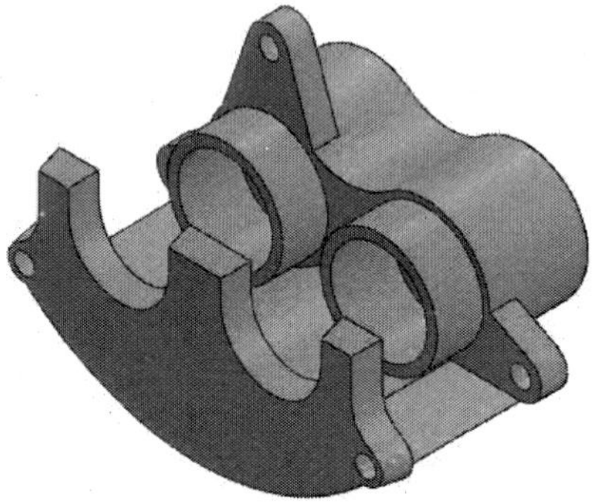

Figure 11-12 *Assembly after assembling the two instances of the Caliper Piston and the Caliper Body*

Since, you have applied coincident relation between the planar faces of both the instances of the Caliper Piston, if you move any one of the instances between its limit, the other instance of the Caliper Piston will also move accordingly.

After assembling the two instances of the Caliper Piston, you need to assemble the two instances of the Caliper Pad.

26. Choose the **Insert Components** button from the **Assembly CommandManager**; the **Insert Component PropertyManager** is displayed.

27. Choose the **Browse** button from the **Part/Assembly to Insert** rollout of the **Insert Component PropertyManager**; the **Open** dialog box is displayed.

28. Browse to the *Motor Cycle Project* folder, where you have saved all the components of the Motor Cycle and then select the Caliper Pad.

29. Choose the **Open** button; the cursor will be replaced by the component cursor and the graphic preview of the component is displayed. Also, the name of the selected component is displayed in the **Open documents** selection area of the **Part/Assembly to Insert** rollout.

It is evident from the Figure 11-2 that you need to insert two instances of the Caliper Pad in the Assembly environment.

30. Choose the **Keep Visible** button of the **Insert Component PropertyManager** and then click the left mouse button anywhere in the graphic area of the Assembly environment to place the first instance of the Caliper Pad. Make sure that the instance of the Caliper Pad should not intersect with any other parts of the assembly. As soon as, you placed the first instance of the Caliper Pad, the graphic preview of the second instance of the Caliper Pad is displayed.

31. Move the cursor in the graphic area and click the left mouse button to place the second instance of the Caliper Pad, refer to Figure 11-13.

32. Choose the **OK** button from the **Insert Component PropertyManager**. The Figure 11-13 shows the Assembly environment after inserting the two instances of the Caliper Pad.

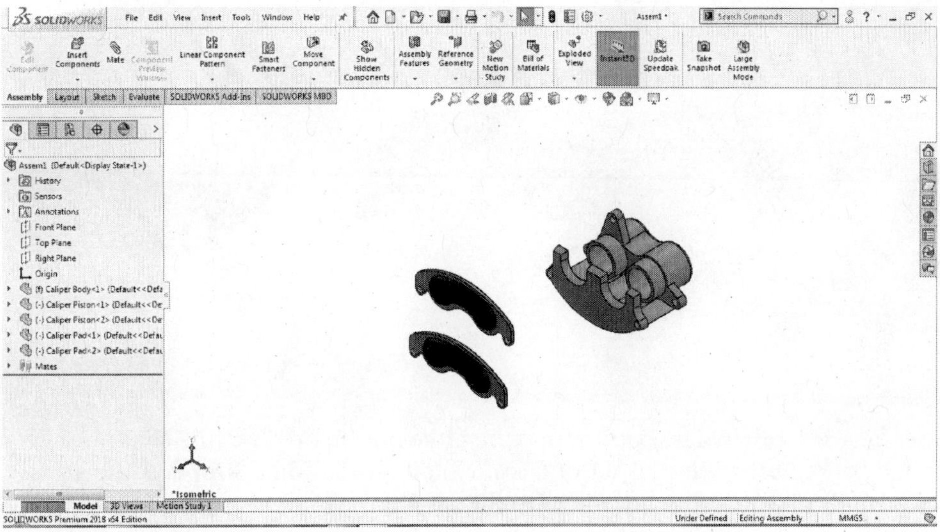

***Figure 11-13** The Assembly mode after inserting two instances of the Caliper Pad*

After inserting the two instances of the Caliper Piston, you need to apply the required mates to assemble them with the Caliper Body by using the **Mate** tool.

33. Choose the **Mate** button from the **Assembly CommandManager**; the **Mate PropertyManager** is displayed.

34. Select the circular face of a Caliper Pad, refer to Figure 11-14 and then select the circular face of the Caliper Body, refer to Figure 11-14; the **Mate** pop-up toolbar is displayed with the **Concentric** button chosen, by default. Also, the preview of the assembly with the concentric relation applied is displayed in the graphic window.

By default, the **Concentric** button is chosen in the **Mate** pop-up toolbar. Therefore, you can directly choose the **Add/Finish Mate** button from the **Mate** pop-up toolbar.

35. Choose the **Add/Finish Mate** button from the **Mate** pop-up toolbar; the concentric relation is applied between the selected set of faces. Note that the **Mate PropertyManager** is still displayed and you can add other mates to the assembly.

36. Select the circular face of a Caliper Pad, refer to Figure 11-15 and then select the circular face of the Caliper Body, refer to Figure 11-15; the **Mate** pop-up toolbar is displayed with the **Concentric** button chosen, by default. Also, the preview of the assembly with the concentric relation applied is displayed in the graphic window.

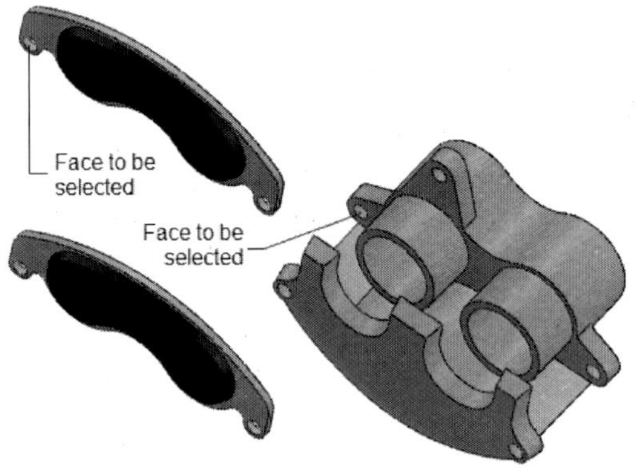

Figure 11-14 *Faces to be selected*

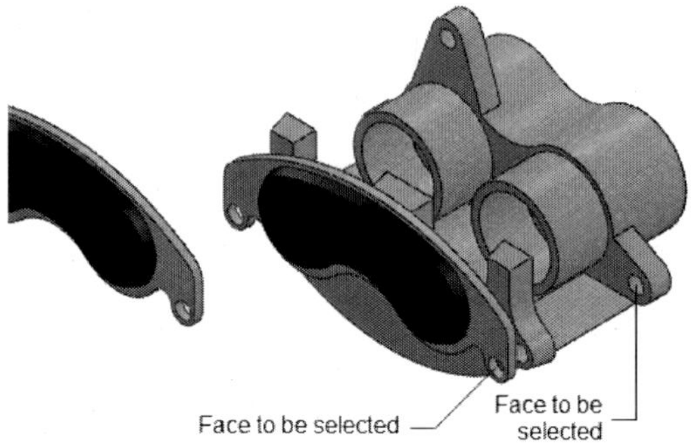

Figure 11-15 *Faces to be selected*

37. Choose the **Add/Finish Mate** button from the **Mate** pop-up toolbar; the concentric relation is applied between the selected set of faces. Note that the **Mate PropertyManager** is still displayed and you can add other mates to the assembly.

38. Select the back planar face of the Caliper Pad and select the front planar face of a Caliper Piston; the **Mate** pop-up toolbar is displayed with the **Coincident** button chosen, by default. Also, the preview of the assembly with the coincident relation applied is displayed in the graphic window. Next, choose the **Add/Finish Mate** button from the pop-up toolbar. Exit from the **Mate PropertyManager** by choosing the **OK** button.

39. Choose the **Rotate Component** button from the **Move Component** flyout in the **Assembly CommandManager**; the **Rotate Component PropertyManager** is displayed. Refer to Figure 11-16 for selection of tool.

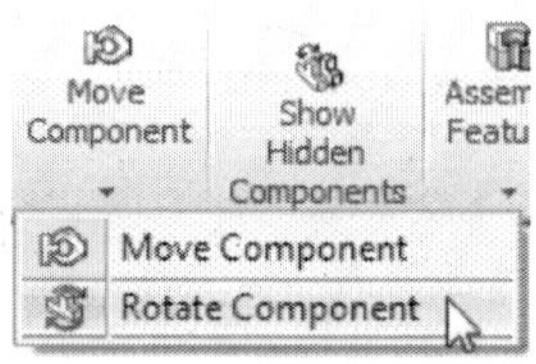

Figure 11-16 ***Move Component*** *flyout*

The **Rotate Component** tool is used to rotate an individual component in the Assembly environment. You can also rotate a component by selecting it and then pressing and holding the right mouse button and then dragging the cursor.

40. Select the instance of the Caliper Pad that is not assembled and then drag the left mouse button to rotate the selected component such that its tapper planar face move towards the tapper planar face of the other instance of the Caliper Pad. Next, choose the **OK** button from the PropertyManager.

41. Invoke the **Mate PropertyManager** by choosing the **Mate** button from the **Assembly CommandManager**.

42. Select the left circular face of the Caliper Pad and then select the circular face of the Caliper Body, refer to Figure 11-17 and apply the concentric relation.

43. Select the right circular face of the Caliper Pad and then select the circular face of the Caliper Body, refer to Figure 11-18 and apply the concentric relation.

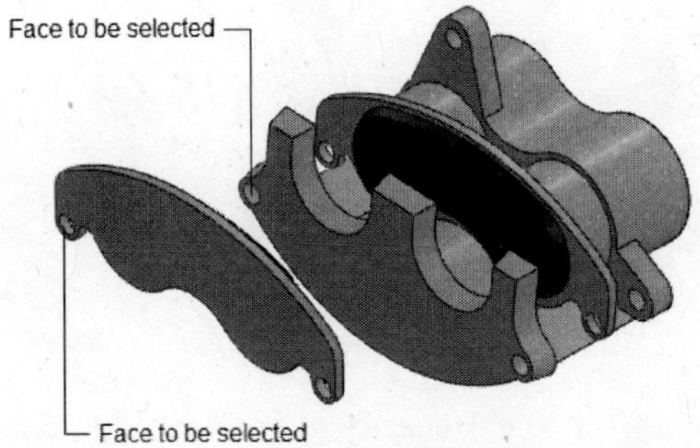

Figure 11-17 *Faces to be selected*

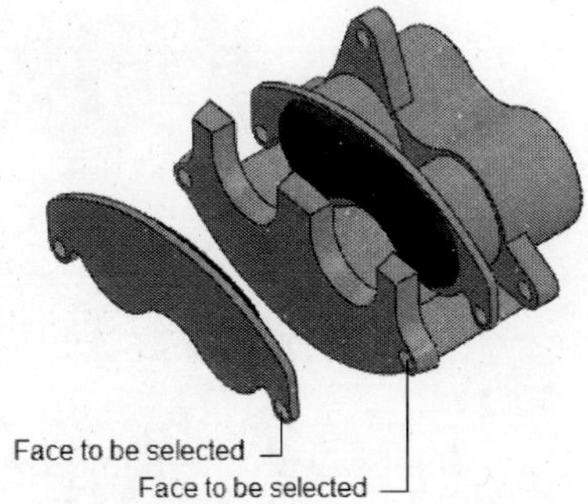

Figure 11-18 *Faces to be selected*

44. Select the planar face of the Caliper Pad, refer to Figure 11-19 and then select the planar face of the Caliper Body, refer to Figure 11-20 and apply the coincident relation. Next, exit from the **Mate PropertyManager** by choosing the **OK** button. The final assembly after applying all the required relations is shown in Figure 11-21.

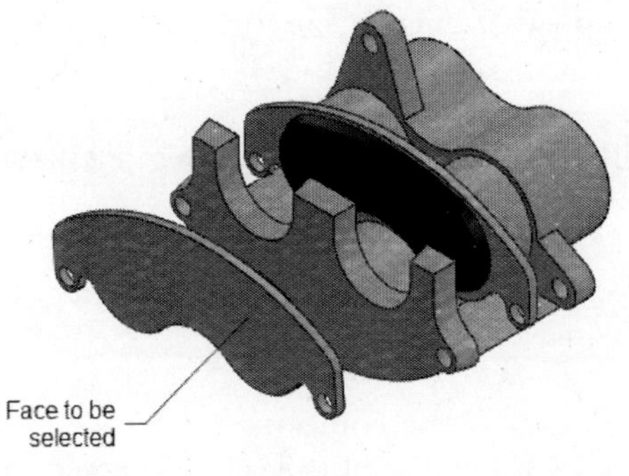

Figure 11-19 *Faces to be selected*

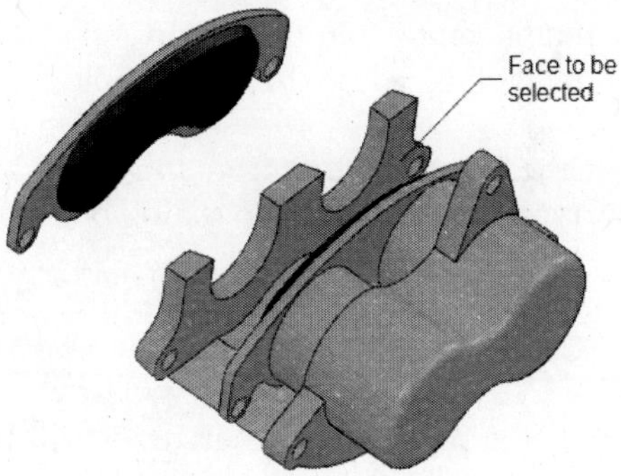

Figure 11-20 *Faces to be selected*

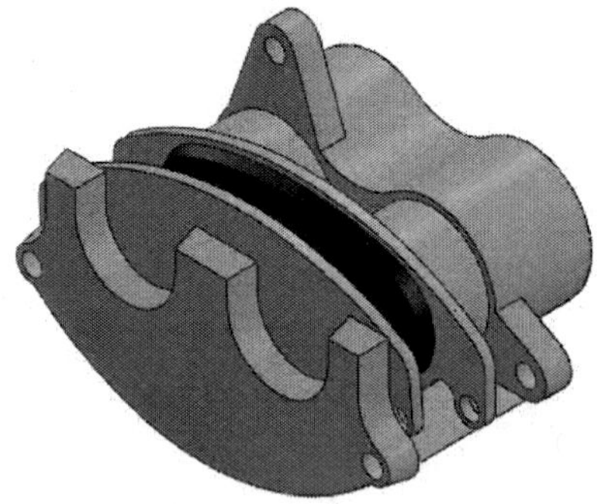

Figure 11-21 Final assembly of the Brake

45. Save the assembly with the name *Brake sub assembly* in the *Motor Cycle Project* folder. Next, close the document by choosing **File > Close** from the SolidWorks menus

Creating the Sub-assembly of Shock Absorber

After creating the sub-assembly of the Brake, you will create the sub-assembly of the Shock Absorber consisting of Shock Absorber Cylinder, Shock Absorber Pistion Rod, and Shock Absorber Spring.

1. Invoke the **New SOLIDWORKS Document** dialog box and then choose the **Assembly** button from the it. Next, choose the **OK** button; a new SolidWorks document is started in the Assembly mode and the **Begin Assembly PropertyManager** is invoked along with the **Open** dialog box. Close the **Open** dialog box.

2. Choose the **Browse** button from the **Part/Assembly to Insert** rollout of the **Begin Assembly PropertyManager**; the **Open** dialog box is displayed.

3. Browse to the *Motor Cycle Project* folder, where you have saved all the components of the Motor Cycle and then select the *Shock Absorber Cylinder*.

4. Choose the **Open** button; the cursor will be replaced by the component cursor and the graphic preview of the component is displayed. Also, the name of the selected component is displayed in the **Open documents** selection area of the **Part/Assembly to Insert** rollout.

5. Click anywhere in the graphic window; the origin of the selected component is align with the assembly origin, as shown in Figure 11-22. Also, the name of the inserted component is added in the **FeatureManager Design Tree** and the PropertyManager is closed.

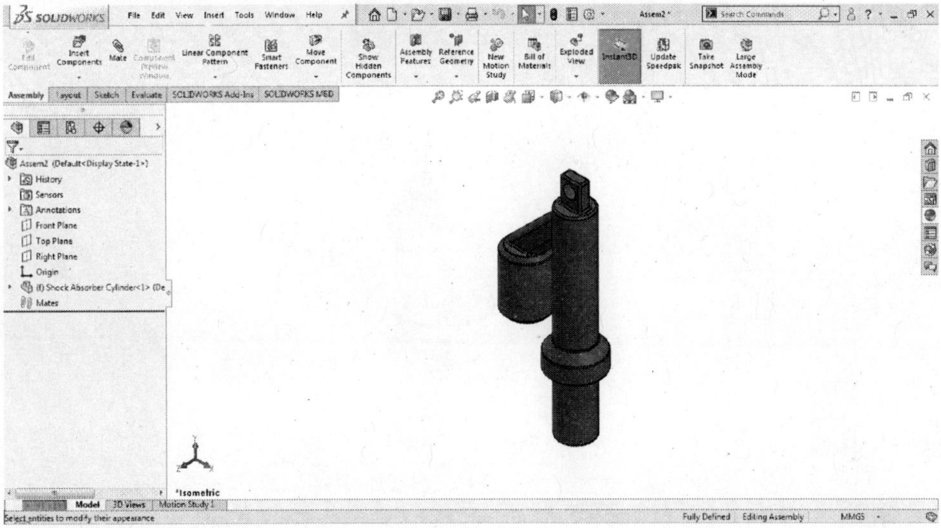

Figure 11-22 The Assembly mode after inserting the Shock Absorber Cylinder

After inserting the Shock Absorber Cylinder in the Assembly environment, you need to insert the Shock Absorber Piston Rod.

6. Choose the **Insert Components** button from the **Assembly CommandManager**; the **Insert Component PropertyManager** is displayed.

7. Browse to the *Motor Cycle Project* folder by using the **Browse** button of the PropertyManager and then double-click on the Shock Absorber Piston Rod; the cursor will be replaced by the component cursor and the graphic preview of the component is displayed.

8. Move the cursor in the graphic area and click the left mouse button to place the component, refer to Figure 11-23.

9. Choose the **OK** button from the **Insert Component PropertyManager**. The Figure 11-23 shows the Assembly environment after inserting the Shock Absorber Piston Rod.

   After inserting the Shock Absorber Piston Rod, you need to apply the required mates to components of the assemble using the **Mate** tool.

10. Choose the **Mate** button from the **Assembly CommandManager**; the **Mate PropertyManager** is displayed.

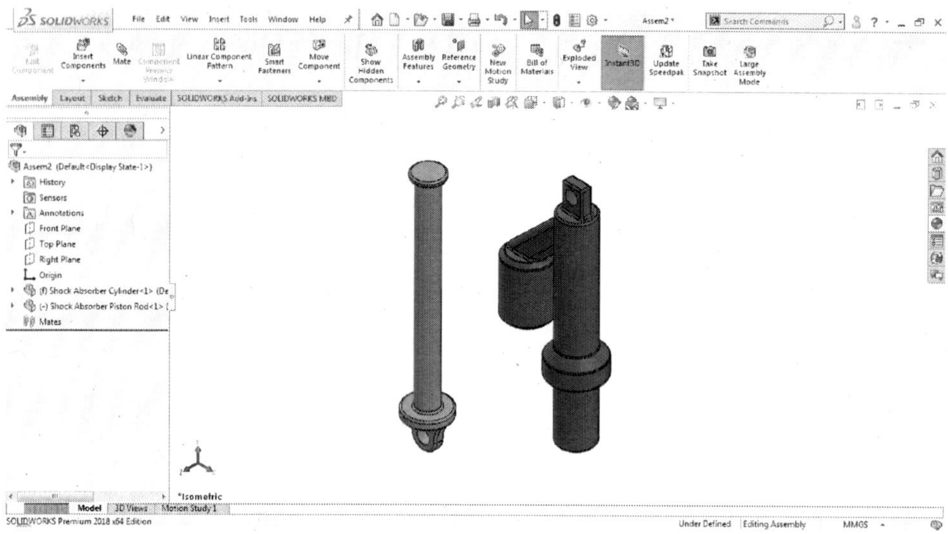

Figure 11-23 The Assembly environment after inserting the Shock Absorber Piston Rod

11. Select the circular face of a Shock Absorber Piston Rod, refer to Figure 11-24 and then select the circular face of the Shock Absorber Cylinder, refer to Figure 11-24; the **Mate** pop-up toolbar is displayed with the **Concentric** button chosen, by default. Also, the preview of the assembly with the concentric relation applied is displayed in the graphic window.

12. Accept the default selected mate and choose the **Add/Finish Mate** button from the **Mate** pop-up toolbar; the concentric relation is applied between the selected set of faces. Note that the **Mate PropertyManager** is still displayed and you can add other mates to the assembly.

13. Expand the **FeatureManager design tree** that is now displayed in the graphic window by clicking on the ▸ sign. Next, expand the same Shock Absorber Piston Rod node.

14. Select the Front Plane of the Shock Absorber Piston Rod and then select the Front Plane of the Shock Absorber Cylinder; the **Mate** pop-up toolbar is displayed with the **Coincident** button chosen, by default. Also, the preview of the assembly with the coincident relation applied is displayed in the graphic window. Next, choose the **Add/Finish Mate** button from the **Mate** pop-up toolbar.

    After applying the concentric and coincident relations, you can only move the Shock Absorber Piston Rod in the linear direction by selecting it and dragging the left mouse button. It indicating that all the degree of freedoms of the Shock Absorber Piston Rod are fixed except its linear motion. In this sub-assembly, you will not restrict this linear motion of the Shock Absorber Piston Rod by applying the mates.

15. Select the Shock Absorber Piston Rod and then drag the left mouse button in such a way that the Shock Absorber Piston Rod and the Shock Absorber Cylinder look like similar to one shown in Figure 11-25. Exit form the PropertyManager.

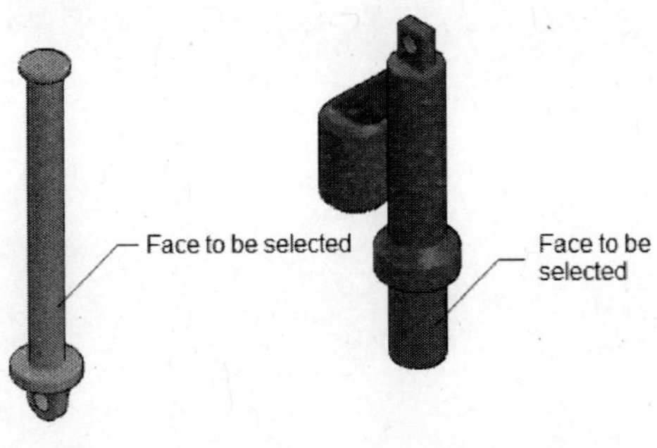

Figure 11-24 *Faces to be selected*

Figure 11-25 *Assembly after assembling the Shock Absorber Piston Rod and Shock Absorber Cylinder*

Now, you will insert the Shock Absorber Spring in the Assembly environment and then apply the required relations to assemble it with the other components of the assembly.

16. Insert the Shock Absorber Spring in the Assembly environment by using the **Insert Components** tool.

17. Invoke the **Mate PropertyManager** by choosing the **Mate** button from the **Assembly CommandManager**.

18. Select the Front Plane of the Shock Absorber Spring and the Front Plane of the Shock Absorber Piston Rod and apply the coincident relation.

19. Similarly, apply the coincident relation between the Right Plane of the Shock Absorber Spring and the Right Plane of the Shock Absorber Piston Rod.

20. Select the Top Plane of the Shock Absorber Spring and then select the planar face of the Shock Absorber Piston Rod, refer to Figure 11-26; the **Mate** pop-up toolbar is displayed with the **Coincident** button chosen, by default. Also, the preview of the assembly with the coincident relation applied is displayed in the graphic window.

21. Choose the **Distance** button from the **Mate** pop-up toolbar; the **Distance** spinner is displayed in the pop-up toolbar and the **Standard Mates** rollout of the PropertyManager.

The **Distance** button of the **Mate** pop-up toolbar is used to apply the distance mate between the two components.

22. Enter **5** in the **Distance** spinner of the **Mate** pop-up toolbar and then choose the **Add/Finish Mate** button from the **Mate** pop-up toolbar. Next, exit from the **Mate PropertyManager** by choosing the **OK** button.

23. Select the Shock Absorber Piston Rod and then drag the left mouse button in such a way that the assembly is look like similar to one shown in Figure 11-27.

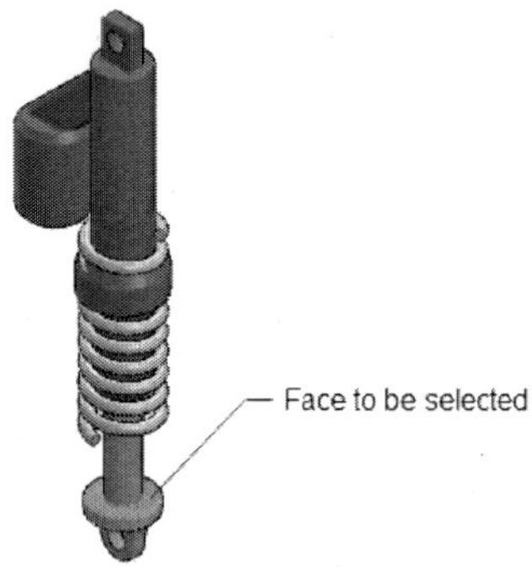

Figure 11-26 *Face to be selected*

Figure 11-27 *Final sub-assembly of the Shock Absorber*

24. Save the assembly with the name *Shock Absorber sub assembly* in the *Motor Cycle Project* folder. Next, close the document by choosing **File > Close** from the SolidWorks menus.

Creating the Main Assembly

After creating the Brake and Shock Absorber sub-assemblies, you will create the main assembly of the motor cycle and then assemble the sub-assemblies with it.

1. Invoke the **New SolidWorks Document** dialog box and then choose the **Assembly** button from the it. Next, choose the **OK** button; a new SolidWorks document is started in the Assembly mode and the **Begin Assembly PropertyManager** is invoked.

2. Browse to the *Motor Cycle Project* folder by using the **Browse** button of the PropertyManager and then double-click on the Rim; the cursor will be replaced by the component cursor and the graphic preview of the component is displayed.

3. Click anywhere in the graphic window; the origin of the selected component is align with the assembly origin, as shown in Figure 11-28. Also, the name of the inserted component is added in the **FeatureManager design tree** and the PropertyManager is closed.

   After inserting the Rim in the Assembly environment, you need to insert the Front Tire.

4. Choose the **Insert Components** button from the **Assembly CommandManager**; the **Insert Component PropertyManager** is displayed.

5. Browse to the *Motor Cycle Project* folder by choosing the **Browse** button from the PropertyManager and then double-click on the Front Tire; the cursor will be replaced by the component cursor and the graphic preview of the component is displayed.

6. Move the cursor in the graphic area and click the left mouse button to place the component, refer to Figure 11-29.

***Figure 11-28** The Assembly mode after inserting the Rim*

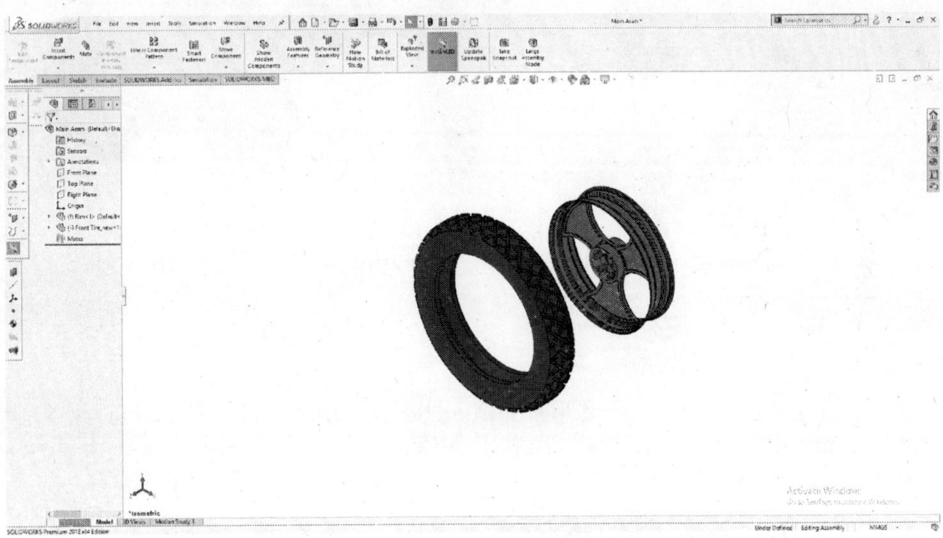

***Figure 11-29** The Assembly mode after inserting the Front Tire*

Note

*In the figures of this chapter, the tangent edges of the components are removed for the clarity. To do so, choose the **Options** button from the Menu Bar; the **System Options** dialog box is displayed. Next, select the **Display/Selection** option from the area that is available on the left of the dialog* *box to display the options related to display and selection. By default, the* ***As visible*** *radio button is selected in the* ***Part/Assembly tangent edge display*** *area. Select the* ***Removed*** *radio button form this area of the dialog box. Next, choose the* ***OK*** *button.*

7. Choose the **OK** button from the **Insert Component PropertyManager**. The Figure 11-29 shows the Assembly environment after inserting the Front Tire.

   After inserting the Front Tire, you need to apply the required mates to the components of the assemble using the **Mate** tool.

8. Choose the **Mate** button from the **Assembly CommandManager**; the **Mate PropertyManager** is displayed.

9. Zoom the graphic area and then select the circular face of a Front Tire, refer to Figure 11-30. Next, select the circular face of the Rim, refer to Figure 11-31; the **Mate** pop-up toolbar is displayed with the **Concentric** button chosen, by default. Also, the preview of the assembly with the concentric relation applied is displayed in the graphic window.

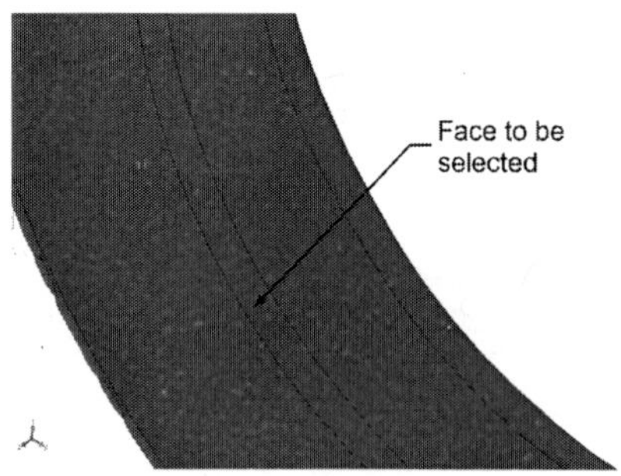

Figure 11-30 *Face to be selected*

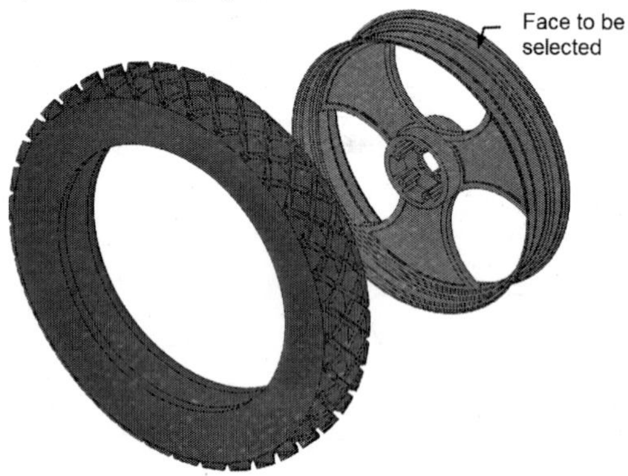

Figure 11-31 *Face to be selected*

10. Accept the default selected mate and choose the **Add/Finish Mate** button from the **Mate** pop-up toolbar; the concentric relation is applied between the selected set of faces. Note that the **Mate PropertyManager** is still displayed and you can add other mates to the assembly.

11. Expand the **FeatureManager design tree** that is now displayed in the graphic window by clicking on the ▸ sign. Next, expand the same Front Tire node.

12. Select the Front Plane of the Front Tire and then select the Front Plane of the Rim; the **Mate** pop-up toolbar is displayed with the **Coincident** button chosen, by default. Also, the preview of the assembly with the coincident relation applied is displayed in the graphic window. Next, choose the **Add/Finish Mate** button from the **Mate** pop-up toolbar. The

Figure 11-32 shows the assembly after assembling the Front Tire with the Rim by using the required mates. Next, exit from the **Mate PropertyManager** by choosing the **OK** button.

Figure 11-32 *Assembly after assembling the Front Tire and the Rim*

Now, you will insert the two instances of the Fork Bodies in the Assembly environment by using the **Insert Components** tool.

13. Insert the two instances of the Fork Bodies in the Assembly environment by using the **Insert Components** tool.

    The Fork Bodies component has two configuration; Right Fork Body and Left Fort Body. But in the Assembly environment, both the instances of the Fork Bodies are displayed with same configuration. Therefore, you need to modify the configuration of any one of the instances of the Fork Bodies.

14. Select a Fork Bodies component from the graphic window and then right-click to display a shortcut menu. Next, choose the **Configure Component** option from the shortcut menu; the **Modify Configurations** dialog box is displayed. Note that the name of the current configuration of the component is selected in the drop-down list provided in the **Configuration** column of the dialog box.

15. By default, if the **Right Fork Body** configuration is selected in the drop-down list of the **Configuration** column, select the **Left Fork Body** configuration or vise-versa. Next, choose the **OK** button from the dialog box; the selected component is modified according to the configuration selected in the dialog box.

16. Rotate the component of Right Fork Body configuration by using the **Rotate Component** tool and arrange it similar to one shown in Figure 11-33.

17. Invoke the **Mate PropertyManager**. Next, select the circular face of the Right Fork Body

configuration component, refer to Figure 11-34 and then select the inner most circular face of the Rim and apply the concentric relation. Next, exit from the PropertyManager.

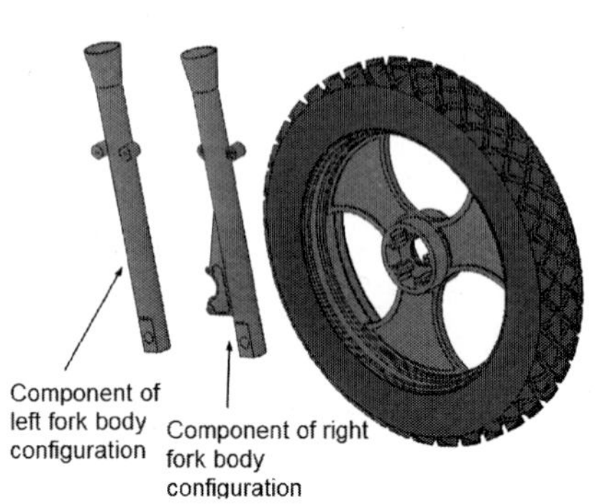

Figure 11-33 *After rotating the Right Fork Body configuration component*

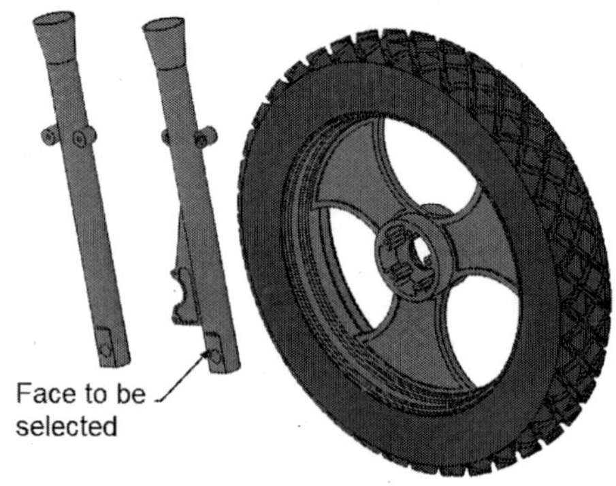

Figure 11-34 *Face to be selected*

18. Rotate the component of Left Fork Body configuration by using the **Rotate Component** tool and arrange it similar to one shown in Figure 11-35.

19. Invoke the **Mate PropertyManager**. Next, select the circular face of the Left Fork Body configuration component, refer to Figure 11-35 and then select the inner most circular face of the Rim and apply the concentric relation. Exit from the PropertyManager.

20. Choose the **Move Component** button from the **Assembly CommandManager**; the **Move Component PropertyManager** is displayed. Next, select the Left Fork Body configuration component and drag it to the right side of the graphic window, refer to Figure 11-36. Next, exit from the PropertyManager.

The **Move Component** tool is used to move an individual component in the Assembly environment. You can also press and hold the left mouse button on the component and drag the cursor to move it.

Figure 11-35 *Face to be selected*

Figure 11-36 *After moving the Left Fork Body configuration component*

Now, you will insert the Front Axle in the Assembly environment and then apply the required relations to assemble it with the other components of the assembly.

21. Insert the Front Axle in the Assembly environment by using the **Insert Components** tool.

22. Invoke the **Mate PropertyManager** by choosing the **Mate** button from the **Assembly CommandManager**.

23. Select the circular face of the Front Axle and then select the circular face of the Right Fork Body configuration component, refer to Figure 11-37 and apply the concentric relation.

24. Select the Planar face of the Right Fork Body configuration component, refer to Figure 11-37 and then select the planar face of the Front Axle, refer to Figure 11-38. Next, apply the coincident relation between the selected faces.

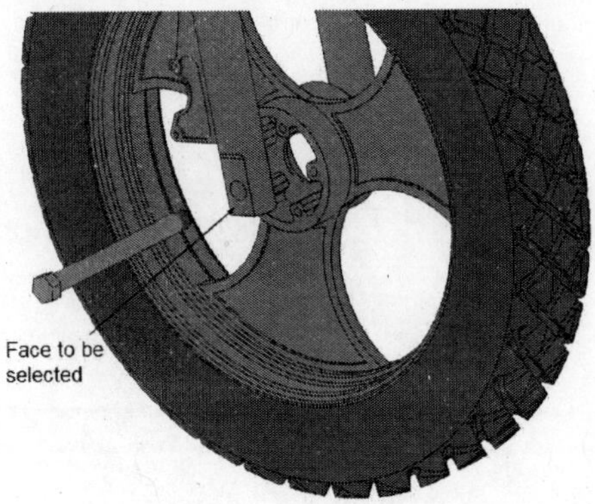

Figure 11-37 *Face to be selected*

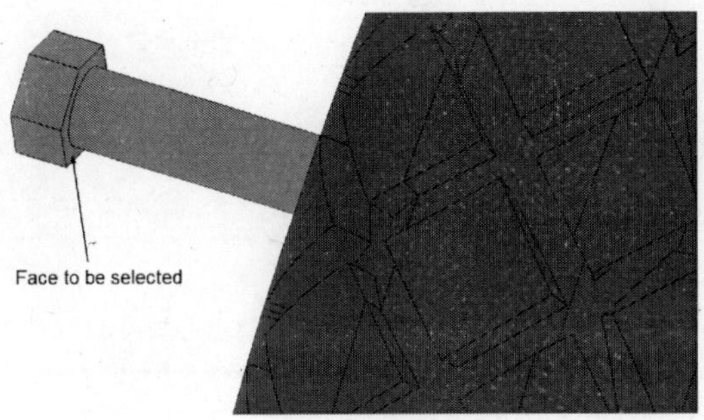

Figure 11-38 *Face to be selected*

25. Select the Front Plane of the Front Axle and the Front Plane of the Rim; the **Mate** pop-up toolbar is displayed with the **Coincident** button chosen, by default.

26. Choose the **Distance** button from the **Mate** pop-up toolbar; the **Distance** spinner is displayed in the pop-up toolbar and the **Standard Mates** rollout of the PropertyManager.

27. Enter **0** in the **Distance** spinner of the **Mate** pop-up toolbar and then Press ENTER; the preview of the component is modified accordingly.

28. Choose the **Flip Dimension** button from the **Mate** pop-up toolbar or clear the **Flip dimension** check box of the **Standard Mates** rollout in the PropertyManager to flip the dimension value. Next, choose the **Add/Finish Mate** button from the **Mate** pop-up toolbar; the distance relation is applied, refer to Figure 11-39. Next, choose the **OK** button from the **Mate PropertyManager**.

Now, you will insert the Fork Tube in the Assembly environment and then apply the required relations to assemble it with the other components of the assembly.

29. Insert the Fork Tube in the Assembly environment by using the **Insert Components** tool.

30. Invoke the **Mate PropertyManager** by choosing the **Mate** button from the **Assembly CommandManager**.

31. Select the outer circular face of the Fork Tube and then select the outer circular face of the Right Fork Body configuration component and apply the concentric relation.

32. Press and hold the left mouse button on the Fork Tube and then drag to move it outside the Right Fork Body configuration component, as shown in Figure 11-40. Next, release the left mouse button.

Figure 11-39 *Assembly after assembling the Front Axle*

Figure 11-40 *Position of the Fork Tube after moving*

33. Select the bottom planar face of the Fork Tube and then select the inner planar face of the Right Fork Body configuration component, refer to Figure 11-41; the **Mate** pop-up toolbar is displayed with the **Coincident** button chosen, by default.
34. Choose the **Distance** button from the **Mate** pop-up toolbar; the **Distance** spinner is displayed in the pop-up toolbar and the **Standard Mates** rollout of the PropertyManager.

35. Enter **240** in the **Distance** spinner of the **Mate** pop-up toolbar and then choose the **Add/Finish Mate** button from the pop-up toolbar. Next, choose the **OK** button from the **Mate PropertyManager**. The Figure 11-42 shows the assembly after assembling the Fork Tube.

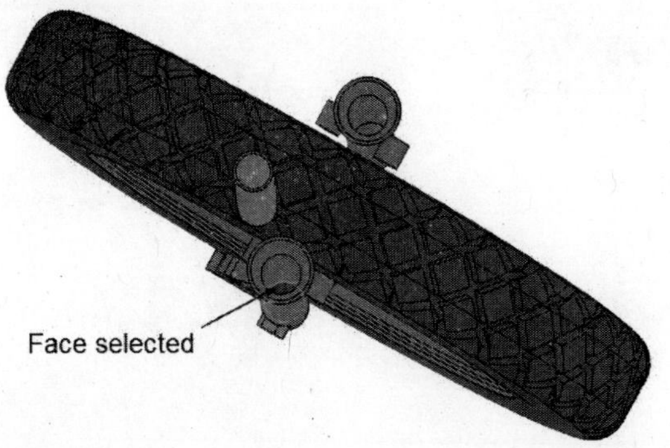

Figure 11-41 *Face to be selected*

Figure 11-42 *Assembly after assembling the Fork Tube*

36. Press and hold the CTRL key and then press and hold the left mouse button on the Fork Tube. Next, drag the cursor; the preview of the other instance of the Fork Tube is attached with the cursor. Now, release the left mouse button to the location where you want to position attached Fork Tube.

37. Invoke the **Mate PropertyManager** and then assemble this Fork Tube with the Left Fork Body configuration component in the same manner as you have assembled the Fork Tube with the Right Fork Body configuration component. The Figure 11-43 shows the assembly after assembling the other instance of the Fork Tube with the Left Fork Body configuration component. Next, exit from the PropertyManager.

    Now, you will insert the Fork Holder in the Assembly environment and then apply the required relations to assemble it with the other components of the assembly.

38. Insert the Fork Holder in the Assembly environment by using the **Insert Components** tool.

39. Invoke the **Mate PropertyManager** by choosing the **Mate** button from the **Assembly CommandManager**.

40. Select a left circular cut face of the Fork Holder and the circular face of the left Fork Tube, refer to Figure 11-44 and apply the concentric relation. The assembly after applying the concentric relation between the selected set of faces is shown in Figure 11-45.

41. Similarly, apply the concentric relation between a right circular cut face of the Fork Holder and the circular face of the right Fork Tube, refer to Figure 11-46. Next, press the ESC key.

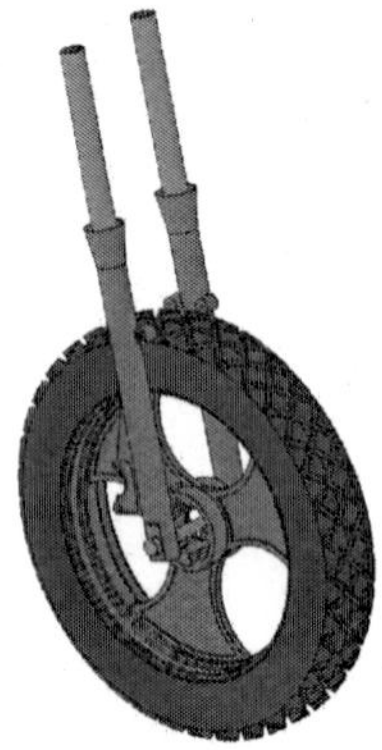

Figure 11-43 *Assembly after assembling the second instance of the Fork Tube*

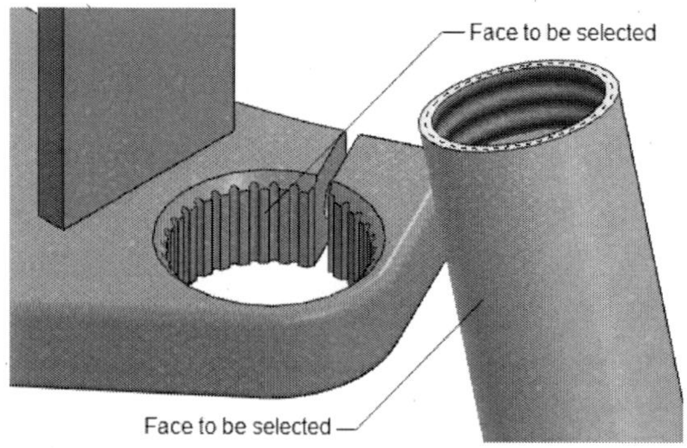

Figure 11-44 *Faces to be selected*

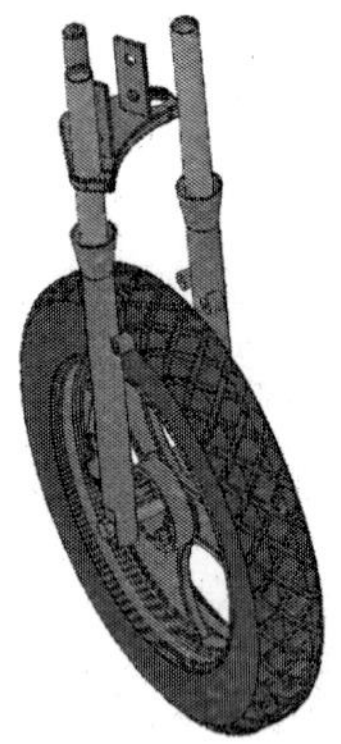

Figure 11-45 *The concentric relation is applied*

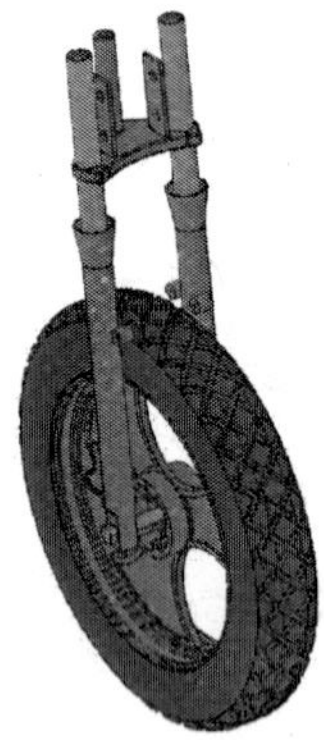

Figure 11-46 *Assembly after assembling the Fork Holder*

Now, you will insert the Weldment Structure Frame in the Assembly environment and then apply the required relations to assemble it with the other components of the assembly.

42. Insert the Weldment Structure Frame in the Assembly environment by using the **Insert Components** tool.

43. Invoke the **Mate PropertyManager** by choosing the **Mate** button from the **Assembly CommandManager**.

44. Select the circular face of the Weldment Structure Frame and then circular face of the Fork Holder, refer to Figure 11-47, and apply the concentric relation.

45. Select the Front Plane of the Weldment Structure Frame and the Right Plane of the Fork Holder and then apply the coincident relation.

46. Select the planar face of the Weldment Structure Frame, refer to Figure 11-48 and then select

the planar face of the Fork Holder, refer to Figure 11-49. Next, apply the coincident relation. The assembly after assembling the Weldment Structure Frame is shown in Figure 11-50. Next, choose the **OK** button from the **Mate PropertyManager**.

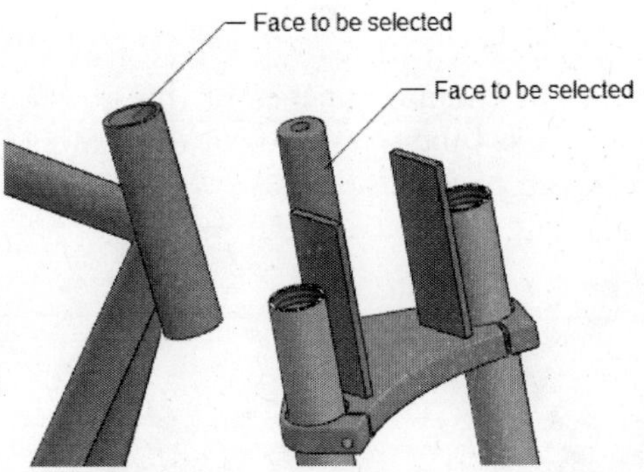

Figure 11-47 *Faces to be selected*

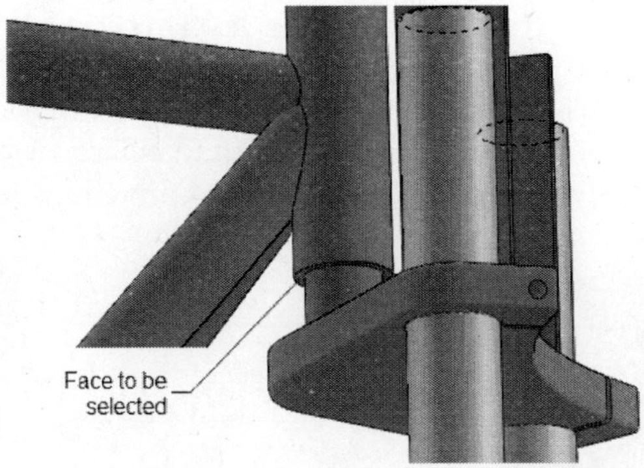

Figure 11-48 *Face to be selected*

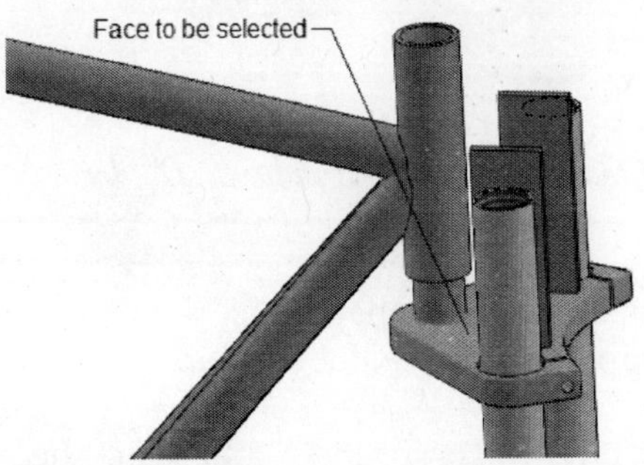

Figure 11-49 *Face to be selected*

Figure 11-50 *Assembly after assembling the Weldment Structure Frame*

Now, you will insert the Lower Handlebar Holder in the Assembly environment and then apply the required relations to assemble it with the other components of the assembly.

47. Insert the Lower Handlebar Holder in the Assembly environment by using the **Insert Components** tool.

48. Invoke the **Mate PropertyManager** by choosing the **Mate** button from the **Assembly CommandManager**.

49. Select a left circular cut face of the Lower Handlebar Holder, refer to Figure 11-51 and then select the circular face of the left Fork Tube and apply the concentric relation.

50. Similarly, apply the concentric relation between the right circular cut face of the Lower Handlebar Holder and the circular face of the right Fork Tube. Next, move the Lower Handlebar Holder in the upward direction, refer to Figure 11-52.

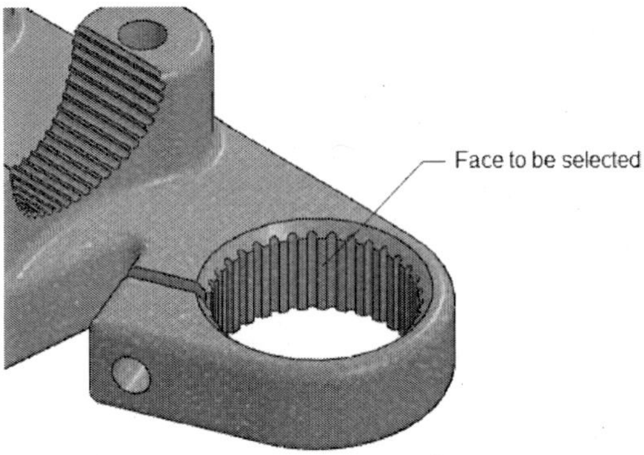

Figure 11-51 *Face to be selected*

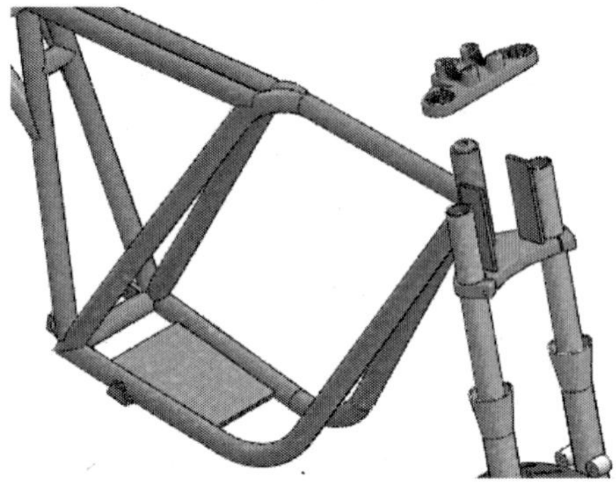

Figure 11-52 *The Lower Handlebar Holder*

51. Select the bottom planar face of the Lower Handlebar Holder and then select the planar face of the Fork Holder, refer to Figure 11-53. Next, apply the coincident relation.

52. Select the planar face of the Lower Handlebar Holder, refer to Figure 11-54 and select the top planar face of the Fork Tube and then apply the coincident relation. The assembly after assembling the Lower Handlebar Holder is shown in Figure 11-55. Press the ESC key.

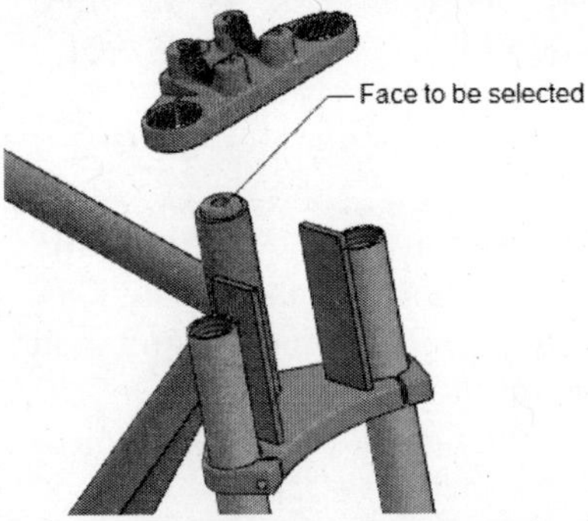

Figure 11-53 *Face to be selected*

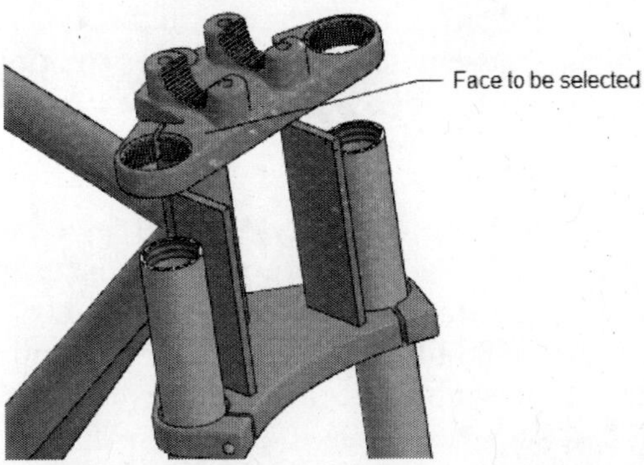

Figure 11-54 *Face to be selected*

Figure 11-55 *Assembly after assembling the Lower Handlebar Holder*

Now, you will insert the Rim in the Assembly environment and then apply the required relations to assemble it with the other components of the assembly.

53. Insert the second instance of the Rim in the Assembly environment by using the **Insert Components** tool.

54. Invoke the **Mate PropertyManager** by choosing the **Mate** button from the **Assembly CommandManager**.

55. Apply the coincident relation between the Front Plane of the second instance of the Rim and the Front Plane of the First instance of the Rim. Next, again apply the coincident relation between the Top Plane of the second instance of the Rim and the Top Plane of the First instance of the Rim. Press the ESC key. Next, move the second instance of the Rim in the position similar to the one shown in Figure 11-56 by pressing and dragging the left mouse button.

Now, you will insert the Rear Tire in the Assembly environment and then apply the required relations to assemble it with the other components of the assembly.

56. Insert the Rear Tire in the Assembly environment by using the **Insert Components** tool.

57. Invoke the **Mate PropertyManager** by choosing the **Mate** button from the **Assembly CommandManager**. Next, apply the concentric relation between a circular face of the Rear Tire and a circular face of the second instance of the Rim. Next, apply the coincident relation between the Front Plane of the Rear Tire and the Front Plane of the second instance of the Rim. The assembly after assembling the Rear Tire is shown in the Figure 11-57. Next, press the ESC key to exit from the PropertyManager.

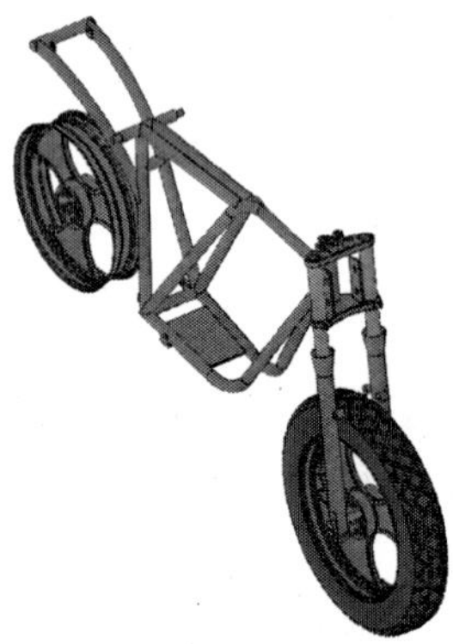

Figure 11-56 *Position of the second instance of the Rim*

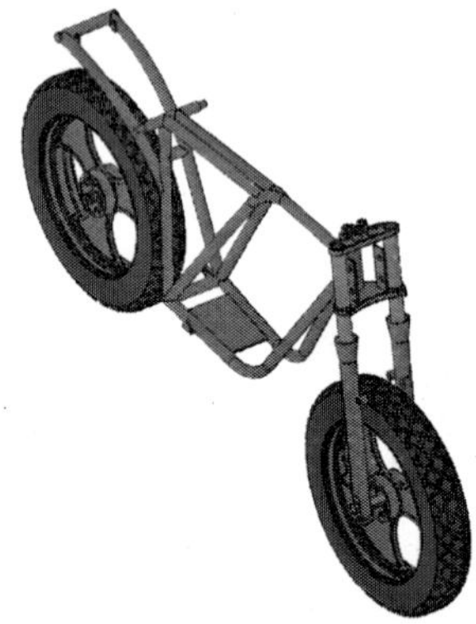

Figure 11-57 *Assembly after assembling the Rear Tire*

Now, you will insert the Swing Arm in the Assembly environment and then apply the required relations to assemble it with the other components of the assembly.

58. Insert the Swing Arm in the Assembly environment by using the **Insert Components** tool. Next, rotate and move the Swing Arm such that its orientation and position looks similar to one shown in Figure 11-58.

59. Invoke the **Mate PropertyManager** by choosing the **Mate** button from the **Assembly CommandManager**.

60. Apply the concentric relation between the circular faces of the Swing Arm and the Weldment Structure Frame, refer to Figure 11-59. Next, apply the coincident relation between the planar faces of the Swing Arm, refer to Figure 11-60 and Weldment Structure Frame, refer to Figure 11-61. Next, apply the concentric relation between the circular faces of the Swing Arm and second instance of the Rim, refer to Figure 11-62.

61. Apply the parallel relation between the top planar face of the Swing Arm and Top Plane of the first instance of the Rim. Next, press the ESC key to exit from the **Mate PropertyManager**. The assembly after assembling the Swing Arm is shown in Figure 11-63.

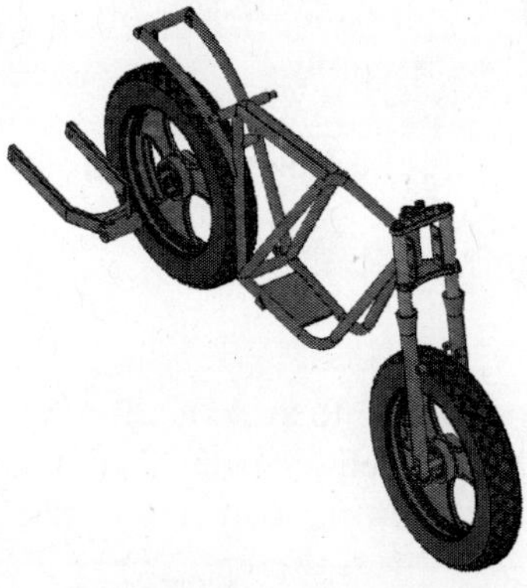

Figure 11-58 *Position and orientation of the Swing Arm*

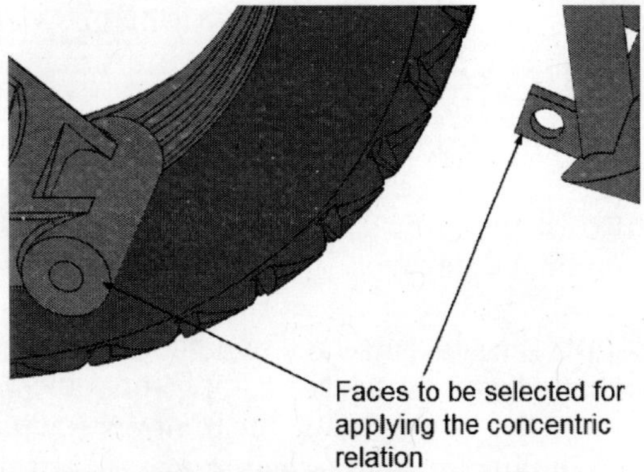

Figure 11-59 *Faces to be selected for applying the concentric relation*

Figure 11-60 *Planar face of the Swing Arm to be selected*

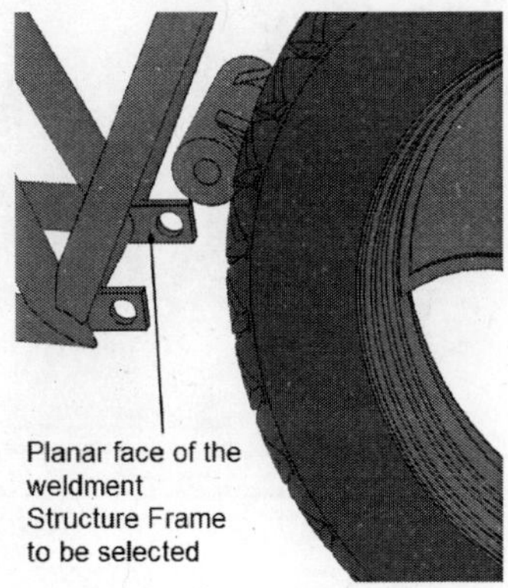

Figure 11-61 *Planar face of the Weldment Structure Frame to be selected*

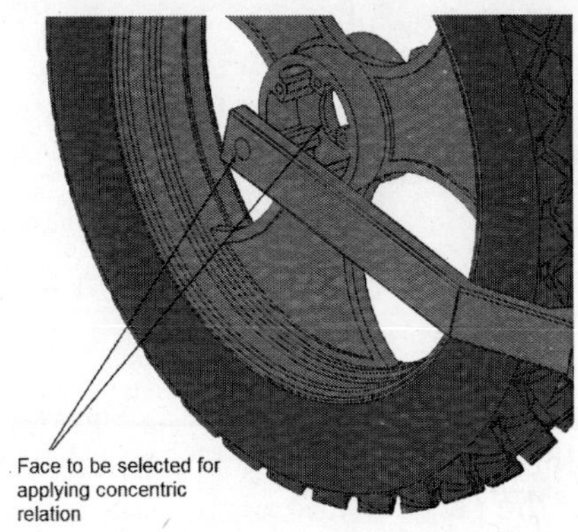

Figure 11-62 *Faces to be selected for applying the concentric relation*

Figure 11-63 *Assembly after assembling the Swing Arm*

Now, you will insert the Rear Axle in the Assembly environment and then apply the required relations to assemble it with the other components of the assembly.

62. Insert the Rear Axle in the Assembly environment by using the **Insert Components** tool.

63. Invoke the **Mate PropertyManager** by choosing the **Mate** button from the **Assembly CommandManager**.

64. Apply the concentric relation between the circular faces of the Rear Axle and Swing Arm, refer to Figure 11-64. Next, apply the coincident relation between the back hexagonal planar face of the Rear Axle and the front vertical planar face of the Swing Arm. The assembly after assembling the Rear Axle is shown in Figure 11-65. Next, press the ESC key.

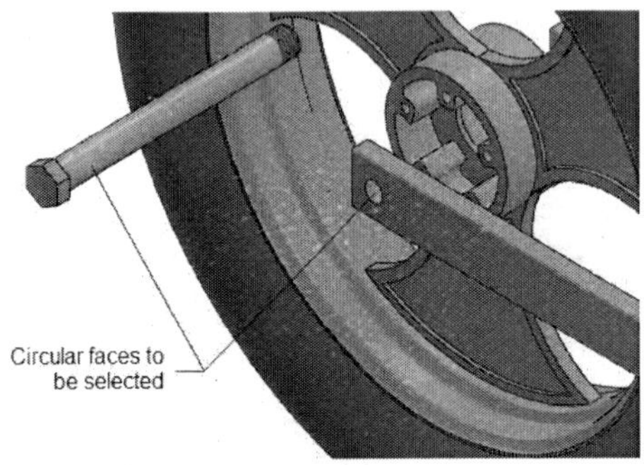

Figure 11-64 *Circular faces to be selected*

Figure 11-65 *Assembly after assembling the Rear Axle*

Now, you will insert the Handlebar in the Assembly environment and then apply the required relations to assemble it with the other components of the assembly.

65. Insert the Handlebar in the Assembly environment by using the **Insert Components** tool. Next, rotate and move the Handlebar such that its orientation and position looks similar to one shown in Figure 11-66.

66. Invoke the **Mate PropertyManager** by choosing the **Mate** button from the **Assembly CommandManager**.

67. Apply the concentric relation between the circular face of the Handlebar, refer to Figure 11-67 and the circular cut face of the Lower Handlebar Holder, refer to Figure 11-68. Next, apply the coincident relation between the Right Plane of the Handlebar and the Right Plane of the Lower Handlebar Holder.

Figure 11-66 The Handlebar in the Assembly environment

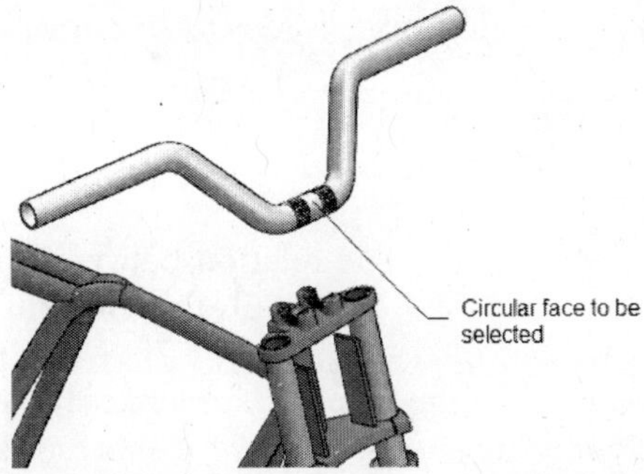

Figure 11-67 Circular face of the Handlebar to be selected

68. Select the Front Plane of the Handlebar and the Right Plane of the first instance of the Rim; the **Mate** pop-up toolbar is displayed.

69. Choose the **Angle** button from the **Mate** pop-up toolbar; the **Angle** spinner is displayed in the pop-up toolbar. 

The **Angle** button is used to apply the angle relation between two components. This mate is used to specify the angular position between the selected planes, planar faces, or edges of the two components.

70. Enter **150** in the **Angle** spinner of the **Mate** pop-up toolbar and then Press ENTER; the preview of the component is modified. Next, choose the **Add/Finish Mate** button from the **Mate** pop-up toolbar; the angle relation is applied, refer to Figure 11-69. Next, choose the **OK** button from the **Mate PropertyManager**.

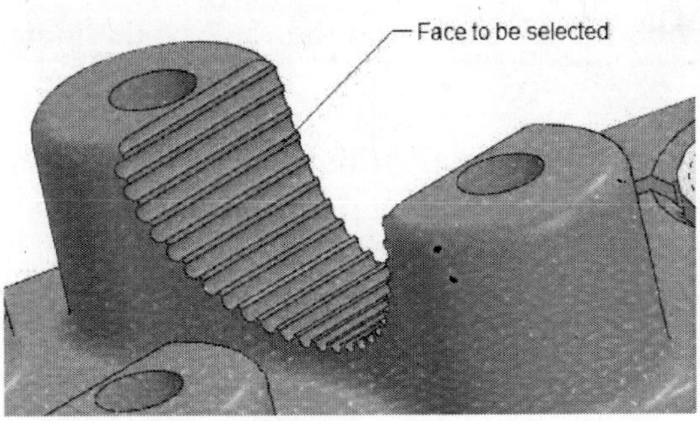

Figure 11-68 Face to be selected

Figure 11-69 Assembly after assembling the Handlebar

Now, you will insert the Upper Handlebar Holder in the Assembly environment and then apply the required relations to assemble it with the other components of the assembly.

71. Insert the Upper Handlebar Holder in the Assembly environment and then invoke the **Mate PropertyManager**.

72. Apply the concentric relation between the circular faces of the first set of holes, refer to Figure 11-70. Similarly, apply the concentric relation between the circular faces of the second set of holes, refer to Figure 11-70. Next, apply the coincident relation between the bottom planar face of the Upper Handlebar Holder and the top planar face of the Lower Handlebar Holder, refer to Figure 11-71. Next, press the ESC key. The assembly after assembling the Upper Handlebar Holder is shown in Figure 11-72.

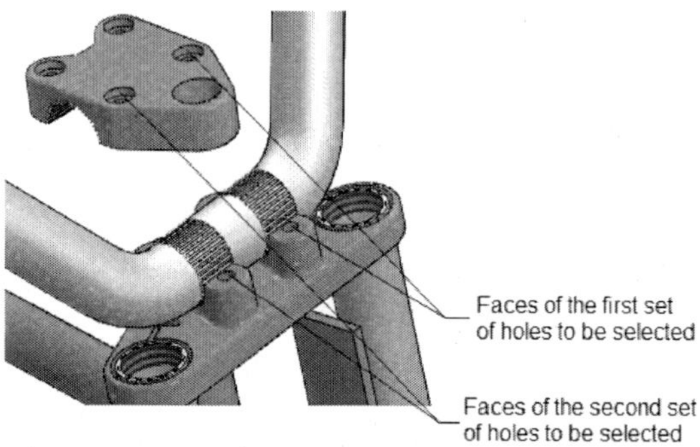

Figure 11-70 *Faces to be selected*

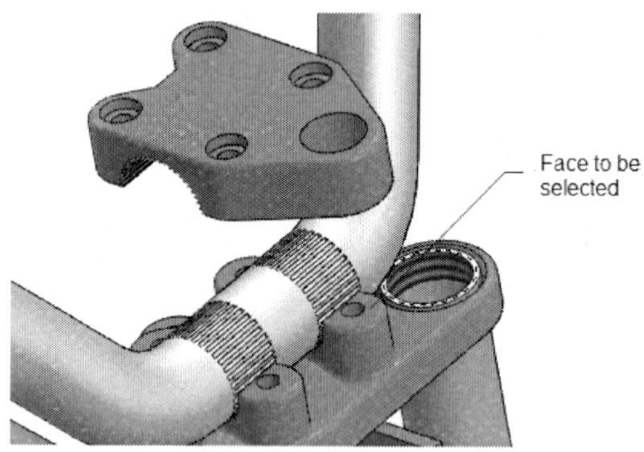

Figure 11-71 *Face of the Lower Handlebar Holder to be selected*

Now, you will insert the Weldment Seat Frame in the Assembly environment and then apply the required relations to assemble it with the other components of the assembly.

73. Insert the Weldment Seat Frame in the Assembly environment and then invoke the **Mate PropertyManager**.

74. Apply the concentric relation between the circular faces of the Weldment Seat Frame and Weldment Structure Frame, refer to Figure 11-73.

Figure 11-72 Assembly after assembling the Upper Handlebar Holder

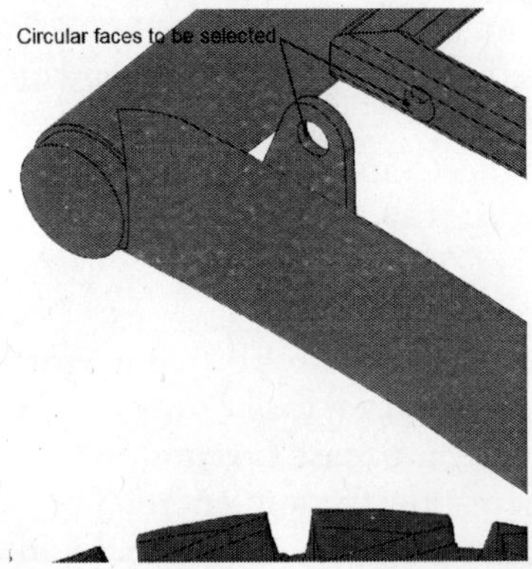

Figure 11-73 Faces to be selected for applying the concentric relation

75. Similarly, apply the coincident relation between the planar face of the Weldment Seat Frame, refer to Figure 11-74 and the planar face of the Weldment Structure Frame, refer to Figure 11-75. Next, apply the tangent relation between the faces of the Weldment Seat Frame and Weldment Structure Frame, refer to Figure 11-76. Next, press the ESC Key. The assembly after assembling the Weldment Seat Frame is shown in Figure 11-77.

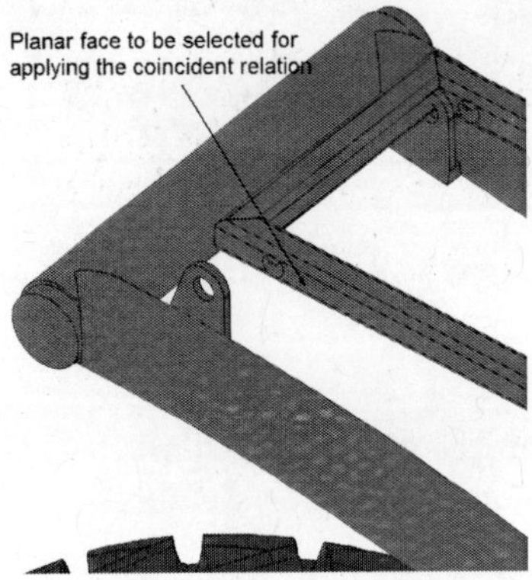

Figure 11-74 Planar face to be selected for applying the coincident relation

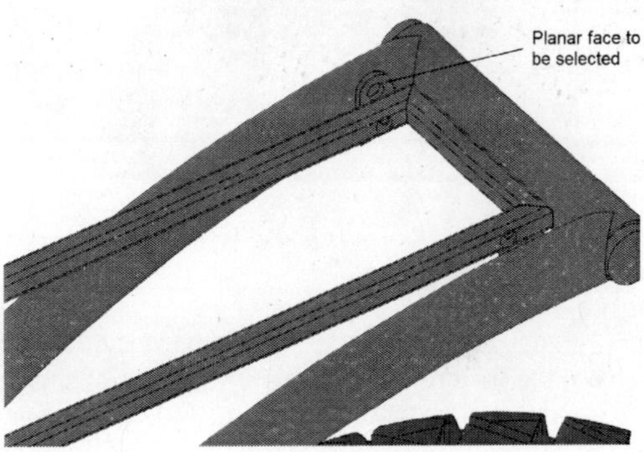

Figure 11-75 Planar face to be selected for applying the coincident relation

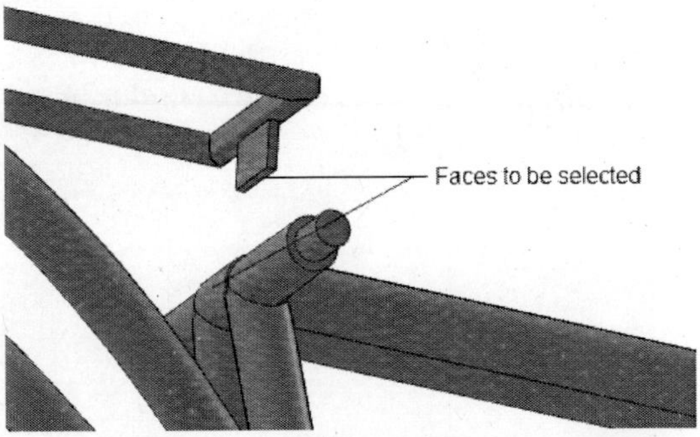

Figure 11-76 Faces to be selected for applying the tangent relation

Figure 11-77 Assembly after assembling the Weldment Seat Frame

Now, you will insert the Crankcase Cover in the Assembly environment and then apply the required relations to assemble it with the other components of the assembly.

76. Insert the Crankcase Cover in the Assembly environment. Next, rotate and move the Crankcase Cover such that its orientation and position looks similar to one shown in Figure 11-78.

77. Invoke the **Mate PropertyManager** and apply the coincident relation between the Front Plane of the Crankcase Cover and the Front Plane of the Weldment Structure Frame. Next, move the Crankcase Cover at the top of the planar sheet of the Weldment Structure Frame and then apply the tangent relation between the bottom planar face of the Crankcase Cover and the circular face of the Weldment Structure Frame, refer to Figure 11-79. Press the ESC key.

Figure 11-78 *The Crankcase Cover in the Assembly environment*

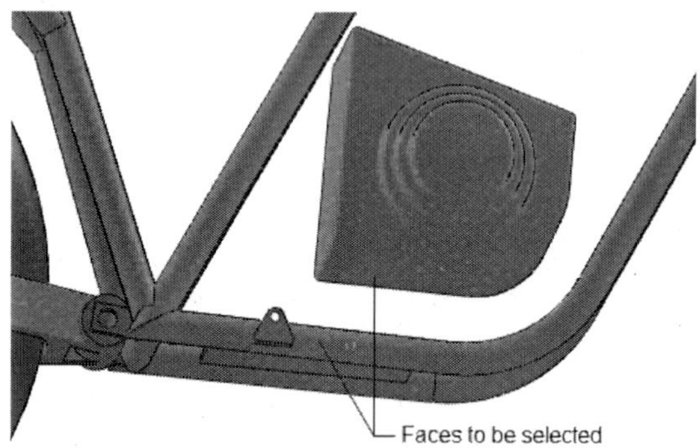

Figure 11-79 *Faces of the Crankcase Cover and Weldment Structure Frame to be selected*

Now, you will insert the Cylinder Head in the Assembly environment and then apply the required relations to assemble it with the other components of the assembly.

78. Insert the Cylinder Head in the Assembly environment and then invoke the **Mate PropertyManager**.

79. Apply the concentric relation between the circular faces of the Cylinder Head and Crankcase Cover, refer to Figure 11-80. Next, apply the coincident relation between the planar faces of the Cylinder Head and Crankcase Cover, refer to Figure 11-80. Press the ESC key. The assembly after applying the concentric and coincident relations between the Cylinder Head and Crankcase Cover looks similar to one shown in Figure 11-81.

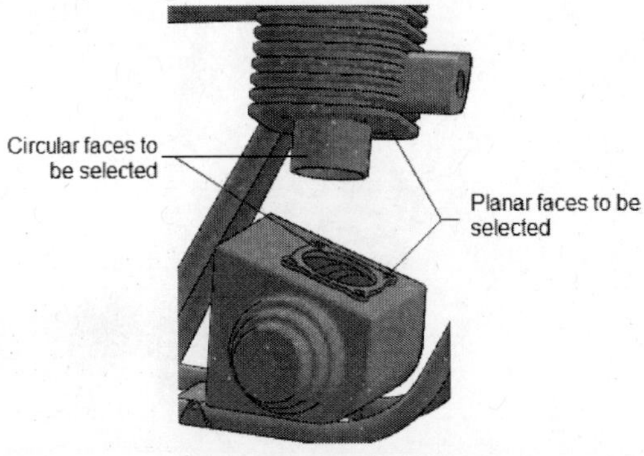

Figure 11-80 Faces to be selected

Figure 11-81 Assembly after assembling the Cylinder Head

Now, you will insert the Muffler in the Assembly environment and then apply the required relations to assemble it with the other components of the assembly.

80. Insert the Muffler in the Assembly environment. Next, rotate and move the Muffler such that its orientation and position looks similar to one shown in Figure 11-82.

81. Invoke the **Mate PropertyManager** and apply the concentric relation between the circular faces of the Muffler and Weldment Structure Frame, refer to Figure 11-83.

Figure 11-82 The Muffler in the Assembly environment

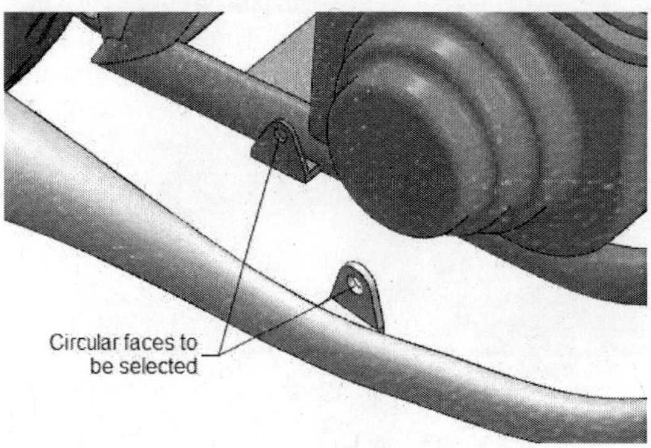

Figure 11-83 Circular faces to be selected

82. Apply the concentric relation between the circular faces of the Muffler and Cylinder Head, refer to Figure 11-84. Next, exit from the **Mate PropertyManager** by pressing the ESC key or choosing **OK** button. The assembly after assembling the Muffler is shown in Figure 11-85.

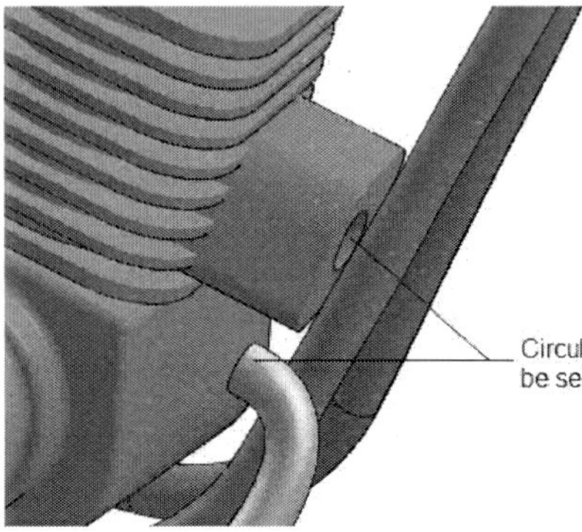

Figure 11-84 *Faces to be selected*

Figure 11-85 *Assembly after assembling the Muffler*

Now, you will insert the Cylinder Head Cover in the Assembly environment and then apply the required relations to assemble it with the other components of the assembly.

83. Insert the Cylinder Head Cover in the Assembly environment and then assemble it with the Cylinder Head by using the **Mate PropertyManager**. The assembly after assembling the Cylinder Head Cover is shown in Figure 11-86.

84. Insert the Clamp in the Assembly environment and then apply the coincident relation between its bottom face and the top planar face of the Swing Arm. Also, apply the coincident relation between the front vertical planar face of the Swing Arm and the right vertical planar face of the Clamp. Next, apply the distance relation by maintaining the distance 45 between the end or left planar faces of the Swing Arm and Clamp. The rotated view of the assembly after assembling the Clamp is shown in Figure 11-87.

Figure 11-86 *Assembly after assembling the Cylinder Head Cover*

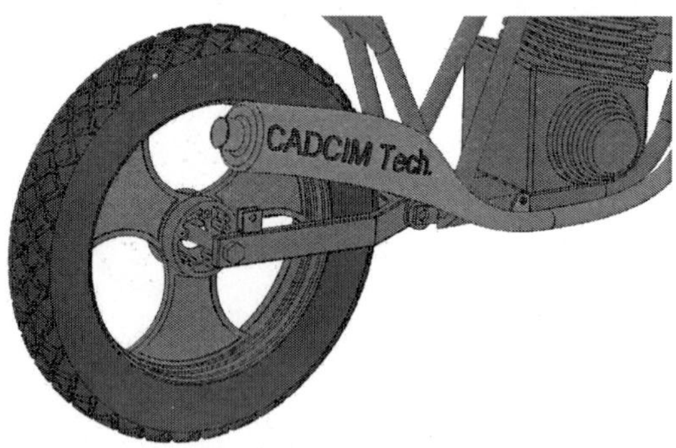

Figure 11-87 *Assembly after assembling the Clamp*

85. Similarly, insert the one more instance of the Clamp in the Assembly environment and then assemble them on the other side of the Swing Arm, as shown in Figure 11-88.

Figure 11-88 *Assembly after assembling second instance of the Clamp*

Now, you will insert two instances of the Fork Cap in the Assembly environment.

86. Insert two instances of the Fork Cap in the Assembly environment and then assemble them with fork tubes by using the **Mate PropertyManager**, refer to Figure 11-89.

Now, you will insert the Front Mudguard in the Assembly environment.

87. Insert the Front Mudguard in the Assembly environment. Next, rotate and move it such that its orientation and position looks similar to one shown in Figure 11-90.

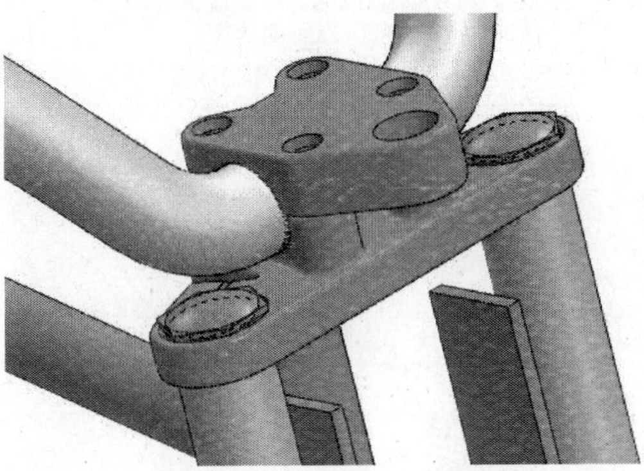

Figure 11-89 *Partial view of the assembly after assembling two instances of the Fork Cap*

Figure 11-90 *The Front Mudguard*

88. Assemble the Front Mudguard with Forks Bodies by applying the required relations, refer to Figure 11-91. After applying the relations, make sure that all the degrees of freedom of the Front Mudguard are fixed and it can not move or rotate in any direction.

Now, you will insert the Rear Mudguard in the Assembly environment.

89. Insert the Rear Mudguard in the Assembly environment. Next, rotate and move it such that its orientation and position looks similar to one shown in Figure 11-92.

Figure 11-91 *Assembly after assembling the Front Mudguard*

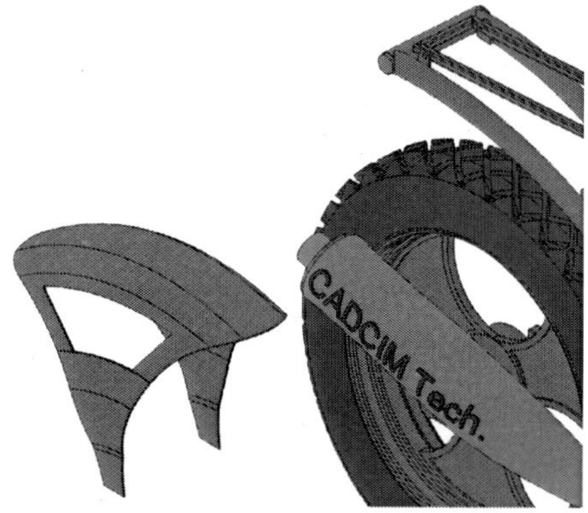

Figure 11-92 *The Rear Mudguard*

90. Invoke the **Mate PropertyManager** and then apply the coincident relation between the bottom planar face of the Rear Mudguard and the top planar face of the Swing Arm. Next, apply the coincident relation between the Front Plane of the Rear Mudguard and the Front Plane of the rear Rim.

91. Select the horizontal edge of the Rear Mudguard, refer to Figure 11-93 and then select the end planar face of the Swing Arm, refer to Figure 11-93; the **Mate** pop-up toolbar is displayed with the **Coincident** button chosen, by default.

92. Choose **Distance** button and then enter **5** in the **Distance** spinner. Next, choose the **Add/ Finish Mate** button from the **Mate** pop-up toolbar and the **OK** button from the **Mate PropertyManager**. The rotated view of the assembly after assembling the Rear Mudguard is shown in Figure 11-94.

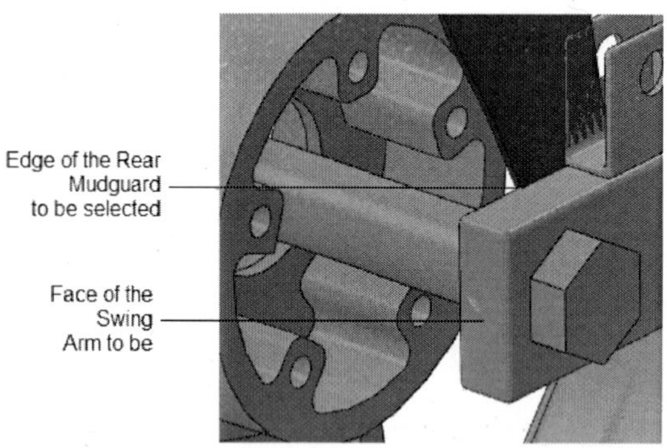

Figure 11-93 *Assembly after assembling the Front Mudguard*

Figure 11-94 *The Rear Mudguard*

As discussed earlier, you can also edit the existing parts or create new parts in the Assembly environment. In this session, you will edit the Fork Holder of the assembly in the Assembly environment and create two holes of diameter 18 in its rectangular flanges. These holes will used to assemble the Headlight Clamp and later the Headlight Clamp will use to assemble the Headlight Mask in the Assembly environment.

93. Select the Fork Holder from the drawing area or the **FeatureManager design tree**; a pop-up toolbar is displayed.

94. Choose the **Edit Part** button from the pop-up toolbar or **Edit Component** button from the **Assembly CommandManager**; the part modeling environment is invoked and the entire assemably, except the component selected to be edited, is turn transparent, refer to Figure 11-95.

The **Edit Component** or **Edit Part** tool is used to edit the parts in the Assembly environment. You can edit features, sketches, and sketch planes.

95. Choose the **Extruded Cut** button from the **Features CommandManager**; the **Extrude PropertyManager** is displayed. Next, select the planar face of the rectangular flange in the Fork Holder as the sketching plane, refer to Figure 11-96; the sketcher environment is invoked.

Figure 11-95 *Entire assembly, except the Fork Holder, is turn transparent*

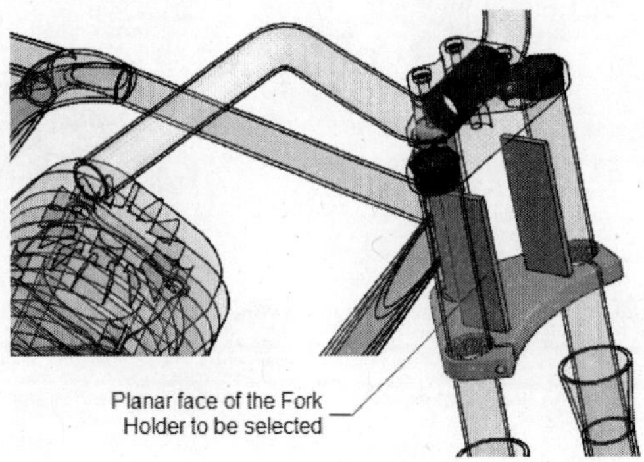

Figure 11-96 *The planar face of the Fork Holder to be selected*

96. Change the current orientation normal to the screen and then draw the sketch, as shown in Figure 11-97. Next, exit from the sketcher environment; the **Cut-Extrude PropertyManager** and the preview of the cut feature are displayed.

97. Select the **Through All** option from the **End Condition** drop-down list of the PropertyManager; the preview of the cut feature is extend from the sketching plane through all geometric entities of the Fork Holder. Next, choose the **OK** button from the PropertyManager and then choose the **Edit Component** button from the **Sketch CommandManager**; the holes are created on both the flanges of the Fork Holder, refer to Figure 11-98. Also, the Assembly environment is invoked.

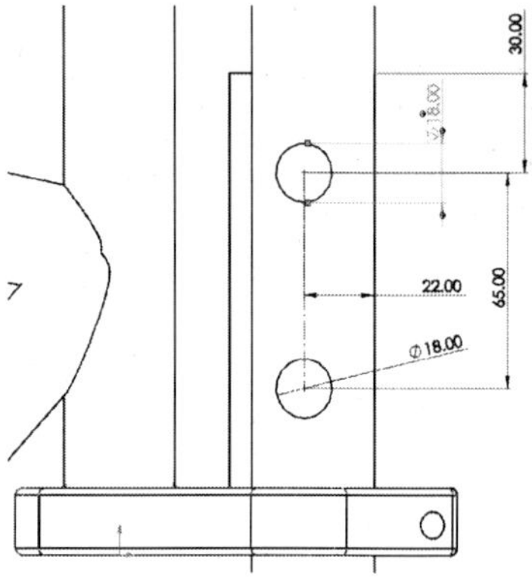

Figure 11-97 Sketch of the cut feature

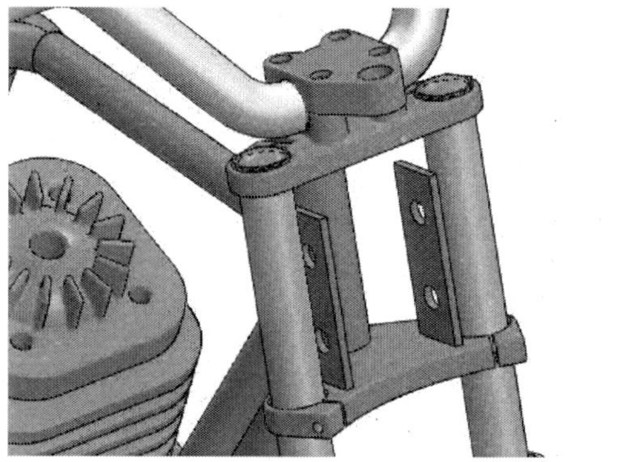

Figure 11-98 Partial view of the assembly after editing the Fork Holder

Note

As discussed earlier, because of the bidirectional associativity between all the modes of the SolidWorks, if any modification made in the model in any one of the modes of SolidWorks is automatically reflected in the other mode.

Tip

You can also open individual part of the assembly in the Part environment and make the necessary modification. To do so, select a part from the drawing area or from the ***FeatureManager design tree*** *to display a pop-up toolbar. Next, choose the* ***Open Part*** *button from the pop-up toolbar.*

After editing the Fork Holder, now, you will insert two instances of the Headlight Clamp in the Assembly environment that is created in the exercise of chapter 7.

98. Insert two instances of the Headlight Clamp in the Assembly environment and then assemble them with the Fork Holder, refer to Figure 11-99. To assemble a Headlight Clamp with the Fork Holder, apply concentric relations between the holes of both the components that measures 18 diameter. Also, you need to apply the coincident relation between planar faces.

Now, you will insert the Headlight Mask in the Assembly environment and assemble it.

99. Insert Headlight Mask in the Assembly environment and then assemble it with the Headlight Clamp, refer to Figure 11-100. To assemble a Headlight Mask with the Headlight Clamp, apply concentric relations between the holes of both the components that measures 12 diameter. Also, maintain the distance of 20 between inner planar face of the Headlight Mask and the outer planar face of the Headlight Clamp by applying the distance relation.

Figure 11-99 Assembling after assembling the two instances of the Headlight Clamp

Figure 11-100 Assembling after assembling the Headlight Mask

Now, you will insert the Fuel Tank in the Assembly environment and assemble it.

100. Insert the Fuel Tank in the Assembly environment. Next, apply the concentric and tangent relations between the set of circular faces of the Fuel Tank and Weldment Structure Frame, refer to Figure 11-101. Next, apply the coincident relation between the Front Plane of the Fuel Tank and the Front Plane of the Weldment Structure Frame. The assembly after assembling the Fuel Tank is shown in Figure 11-102.

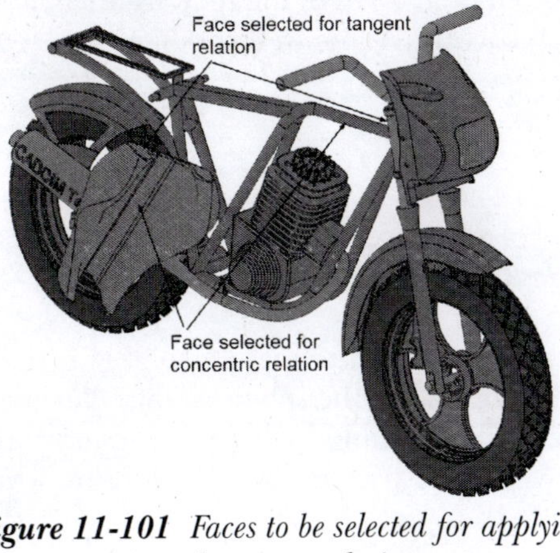

Figure 11-101 Faces to be selected for applying the concentric and tangent relations

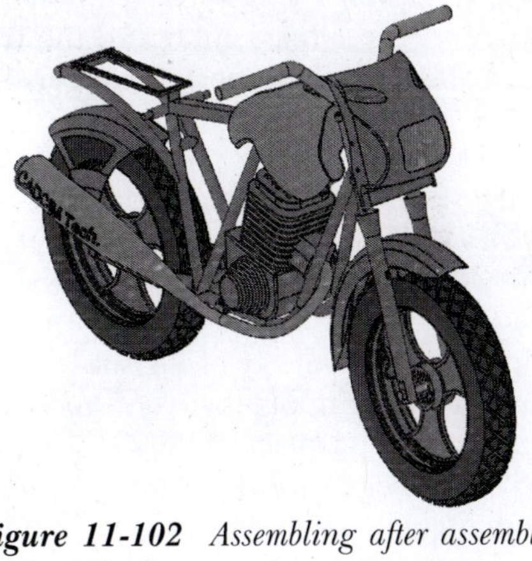

Figure 11-102 Assembling after assembling the Fuel Tank

Now, you will insert two instances of the Shock Absorber sub-assembly created earlier in this chapter.

101. You need to insert two instances of the Shock Absorber sub-assembly in the **Assembly** environment. To do so, choose the Insert Components button from the **Assembly CommandManager**; the **Insert Component PropertyManager** is displayed.

102. Choose the Browse button from the **Part/Assembly to Insert** rollout of the **Insert Component PropertyManager**; the **Open** dialog box is displayed.

103. Browse to the Motor Cycle Project folder and then select the **Assembly (*.asm;*.sldasm)** option from the SolidWorks files drop-down list; all assemblies or sub-assemblies are displayed in the **Open** dialog box.

104. Double-click on the Shock Absorber sub-assembly; the cursor is replaced by the component cursor and the graphic preview of the component is displayed.

105. Choose the **Keep Visible** button in the **Insert Component PropertyManager** and the place two instances of the Shock Absorber sub assembly.

106. Choose the **OK** button from the **Insert Component PropertyManager**.

107. Choose Apply the concentric relation between the circular faces of the first instance of the Shock Absorber sub-assembly and the Weldment Structure Frame, refer to Figure 11-103. Next, exit the **Mate PropertyManager**.

Note

When you insert a sub-assembly or an assembly in the Assembly environment, it acts as a single part by default. It means that you cannot move the components of the sub-assembly even if their movements are not restricted by applying the relations while assembling them.

By default, the property of the sub-assembly when inserted in the main assembly is rigid. Therefore, you cannot move the Shock Absorber Piston Rod of the sub-assembly. Next, you will change the property of the sub-assembly from rigid to flexible so that you can move the Shock Absorber Piston Rod linearly, since you have not restricted its linear motion while assembling it.

108. Select the first instance of the Shock Absorber sub-assembly from the **FeatureManager design tree**; a pop-up toolbar is displayed. Choose the **Component Properties** button from the pop-up toolbar; the **Component Properties** dialog box is displayed.

109. Select the **Flexible** radio button in the Solve as area of the dialog box. Next, choose the **OK** button to exit the dialog box. Note that you can now move the Shock AbsorberPiston Rod component of the sub-assembly in the linear direction, as its linear motion is not restricted. Also, the symbol that is on the left of the component name in the **FeatureManager design tree** is also changed.

110. Now, apply the concentric relation between the circular faces of the first instance of the Shock Absorber sub-assembly and the Clamp, refer to Figure 11-104.

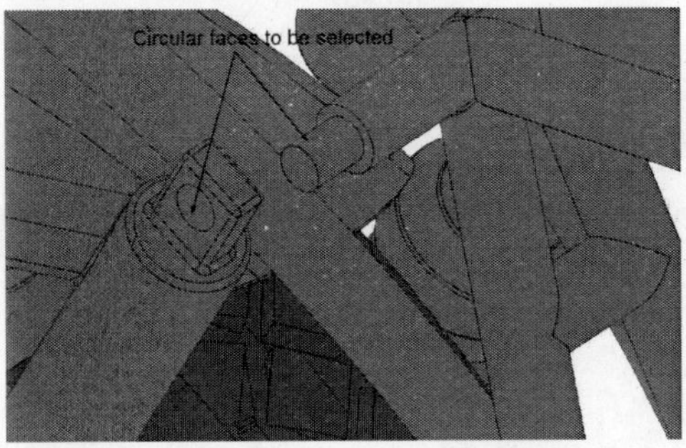

Figure 11-103 *Faces of the Shock Absorber and Weldment Structure to be selected*

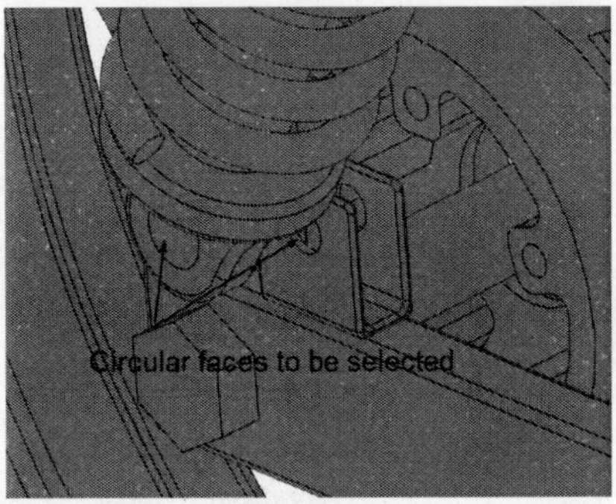

Figure 11-104 *Faces to be selected*

111. Apply the coincident relation between the planar face of the Shock Absorber sub-assembly, refer to Figure 11-105, and the back face of the Clamp, refer to Figure 11-106. Note that in Figure 11-106, the model is rotated so as to select the back face of the clamp. The assembly after assembling the first instance of the Shock Absorber sub-assembly is shown in Figure 11-107.

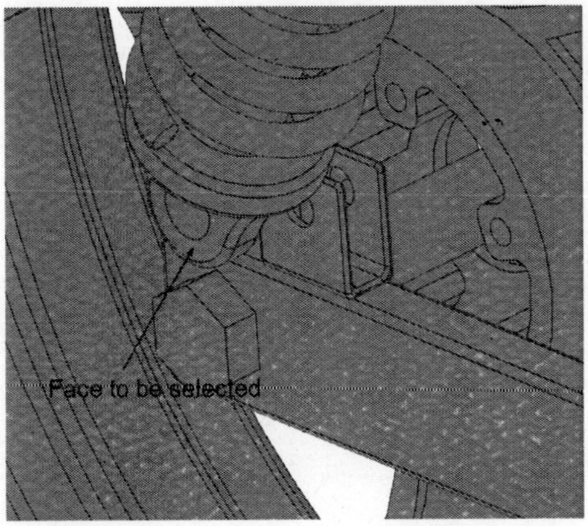

Figure 11-105 *Face to be selected from the Shock Absorber*

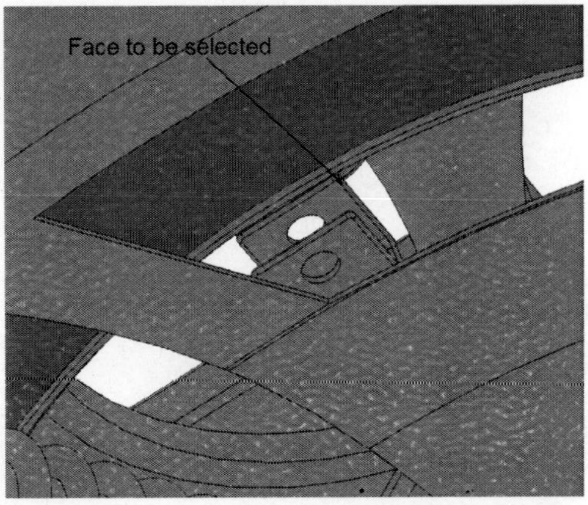

Figure 11-106 *Face to be selected from the Clamp*

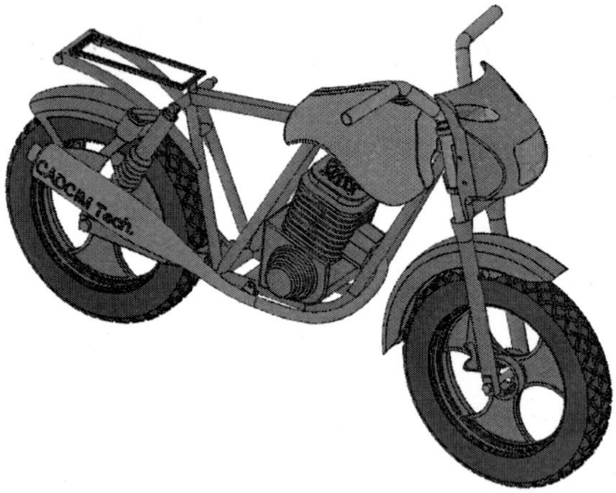

Figure 11-107 *Assembly after assembling first instance of Shock Absorber sub-assembly*

112. Similarly, assemble the second instance of the Shock Absorber sub-assembly, refer to Figure 11-108.

Figure 11-108 *Assembly after assembling both instances of the Shock Absorber sub-assembly*

Next, you will insert the Seat Cover in the Assembly environment.

113. Insert the Seat Cover in the Assembly environment and then apply the coincident relation between the Front Planes of the Seat Cover and the Weldment Structure Frame.

Next, maintain a distance of 2 mm between the bottom planar face of the Seat Cover, refer to Figure 11-109, and the top planar face of the Seat Frame by applying the distance relation. Note that you may need to flip the dimension.

114. Apply the tangent relation between the curved faces of the Seat Cover and the Fuel Tank, refer to Figure 11-110. The assembly after assembling the Seat Cover is shown in Figure 11-111.

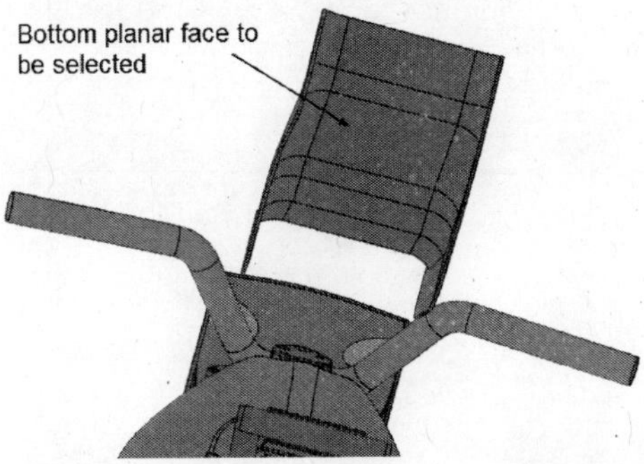

Figure 11-109 *Face of the Seat Cover to be selected*

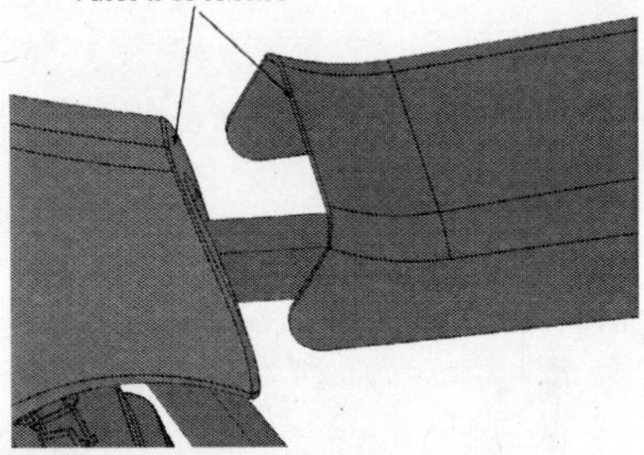

Figure 11-110 *Faces to be selected from Seat Cover and Fuel Tank*

115. Insert the Disc Plate in the Assembly environment and then assemble it with the front Rim of the assembly, refer to Figure 11-112.

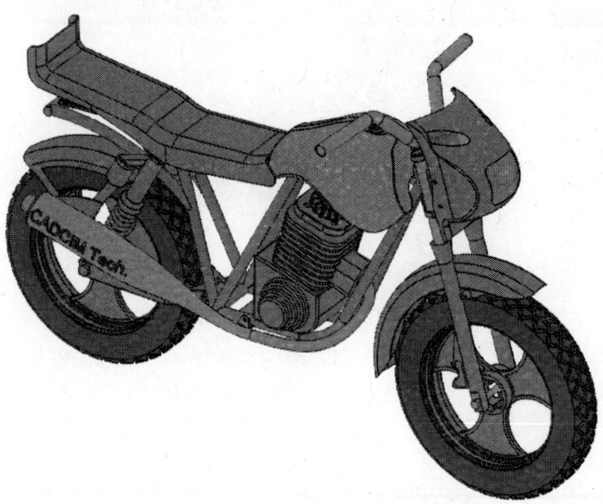

Figure 11-111 *Assembly after assembling the Seat Cover*

Figure 11-112 *Assembly after assembling the Disc Plate*

Next, you will insert the Brake sub-assembly created earlier in this chapter.

116. Insert the Brake sub-assembly in the **Assembly** environment and then apply the concentric relations between the faces shown in Figure 11-113. Next, apply the coincident relation between the planar face of the Brake sub-assembly, refer to Figure 11-114, and the

planar face of the Right Fork Body, refer to Figure 11-115. Note that you may need to flip the direction of coincident relation. The partial view of the assembly after assembling the Brake sub-assembly is shown in Figure 11-116.

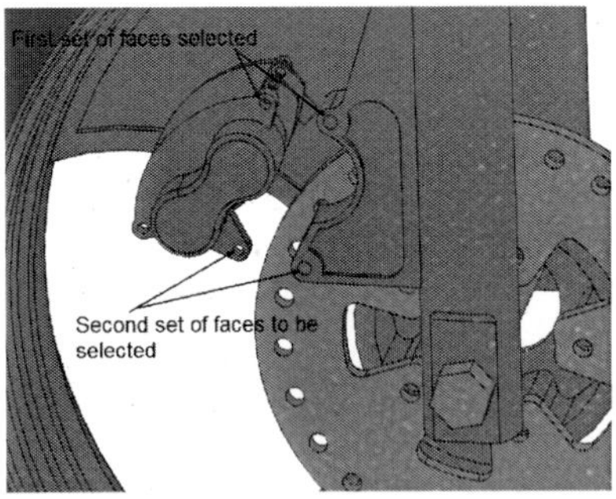

Figure 11-113 *Faces to be selected from the Brake sub-assembly and Right Fork Body*

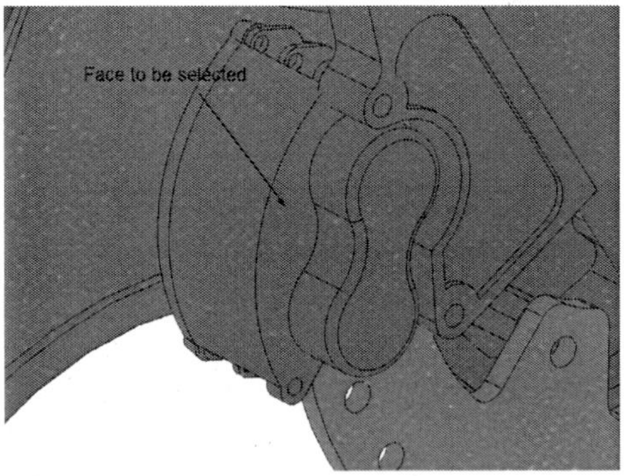

Figure 11-114 *Planar face of the Brake sub-assembly to be selected*

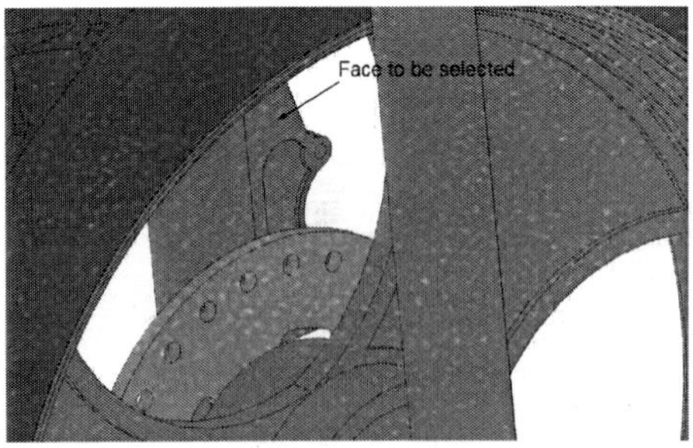

Figure 11-115 *Face of the Right Fork Body to be selected*

Figure 11-116 *Assembly after assembling the Brake sub-assembly*

117. Next, insert two instances of the Handlebar Grip in the **Assembly** environment and then assemble them. The final assembly after assembling all parts or sub-assemblies together in the Assembly environment is shown in Figure 11-117.

118. After assembling all the components and sub-assemblies of the main assembly, you can assign different colors to different components. To do so, select a component to display a pop-up toolbar. Next, choose the **Appearances** button from the pop-up toolbar to display the flyout. Next, select the **Edit color** check box in front of the name of the component to display the **color PropertyManager**. Next, using this PropertyManager, you can assign the color to the selected component. The final assembly after assigning colors to some of the components of the main assembly is shown in Figure 11-118.

Figure 11-117 Final assembly of the Motor Cycle

Figure 11-118 Final assembly of the Motor Cycle after assigning colors

Saving the Model

After assembling all components and sub-assemblies, you need to save the assembly in the Motor Cycle Project folder.

1. Save the assembly with the name Motor Cycle in the Motor Cycle Project folder.

2. Close the document by choosing **File > Close** from the SolidWorks menus.

Self-Evaluation Test

Answer the following questions and then compare them to those given at the end of this chapter:

1. In SolidWorks, assemblies are created by using two types of design approach: _________ and _________.

2. When you start a new SolidWorks document in the **Assembly** mode, the _________ **PropertyManager** is displayed.

3. The _________ tool of the **Assembly CommandManager** is used to insert components in the **Assembly** environment.

4. The _________ button of the **Insert Component PropertyManager** is used to place multiple components or multiple instances of the same components in the **Assembly** environment.

5. The _________ tool is used to apply mates to the components in order to constrain their degrees of freedom at their respective work positions.

6. In SolidWorks, the _________ button in the **New SOLIDWORKS Document** dialog box is used to open an assembly document.

7. The _________ relation forces the central axis of one component to align with the other.

8. The _________ tool is used to rotate an individual component in the **Assembly** environment.

9. In SolidWorks, when you insert a sub-assembly in the **Assembly** environment, its property becomes rigid. (T/F) .

10. In SolidWorks, you can edit the existing parts or create new parts in the **Assembly** environment. (T/F)

Review Questions

Answer the following questions:

1. The _________ relation is used to specify the angular position between the selected planes, planar faces, or edges of two components.

2. The _________ button in the **Mate** pop-up toolbar is used to flip the dimension value.

3. The _________ tool is used to move an individual component in the **Assembly** environment.

4. The _________ relation is used to apply the distance mate between two components.

5. The _________ button of the **Advanced Mates** rollout is used to create a to and fro motion between the components.

6. The _________ tool is used to edit the parts in the **Assembly** environment.

7. In SolidWorks, you can open an individual part of an assembly in the **Part** environment and make the necessary modification. (T/F)

Answers to Self-Evaluation Test

1. bottom-up approach, top-down approach, 2. **Begin Assembly**, 3. **Insert Components**, 4. **Keep Visible**, 5. **Mate**, 6. **Assembly**, 7. concentric, 8. **Rotate Component**, 9. T, 10. T

Chapter 12

Generating Drawing Views

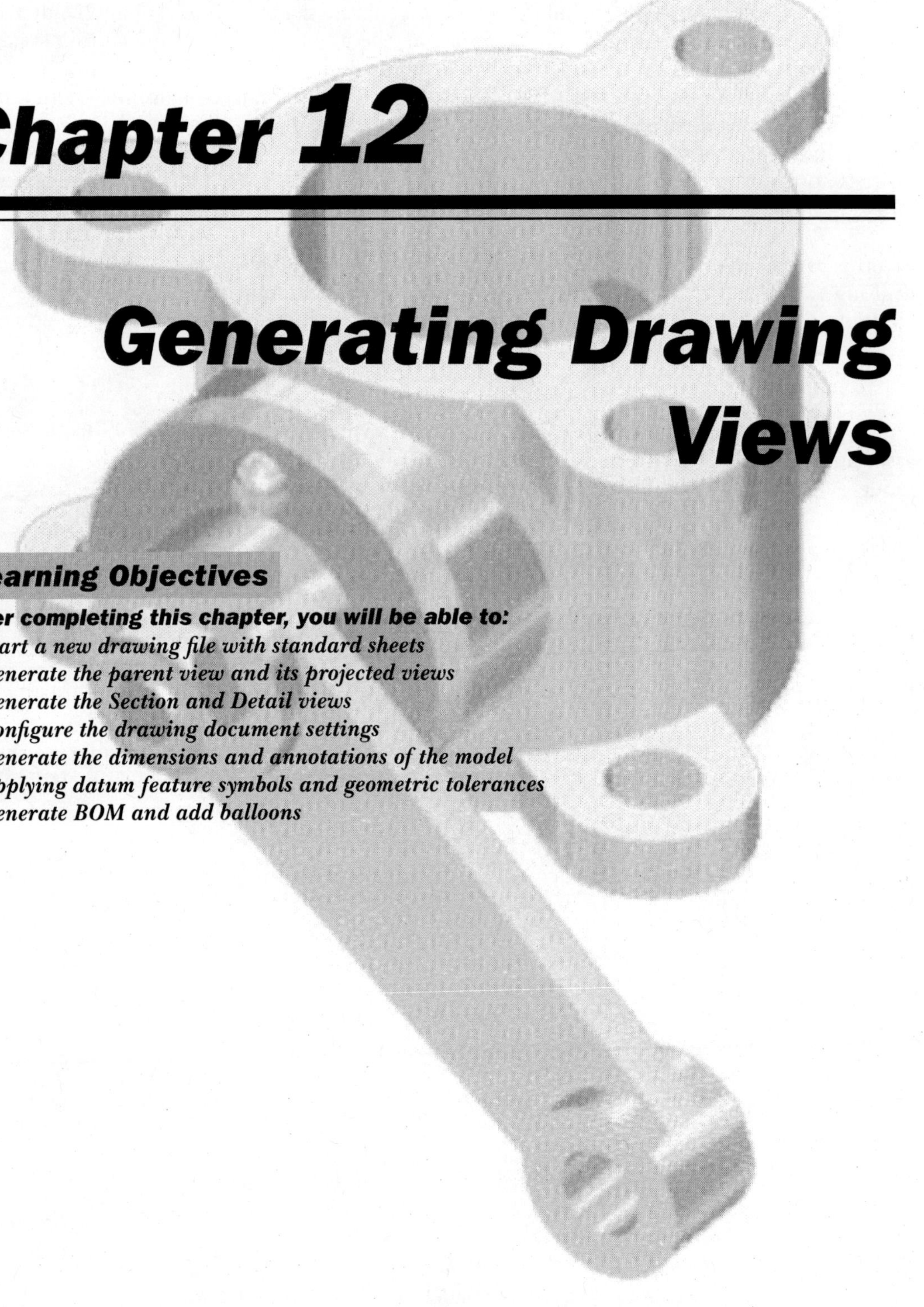

Learning Objectives

After completing this chapter, you will be able to:

- *Start a new drawing file with standard sheets*
- *Generate the parent view and its projected views*
- *Generate the Section and Detail views*
- *Configure the drawing document settings*
- *Generate the dimensions and annotations of the model*
- *Applying datum feature symbols and geometric tolerances*
- *Generate BOM and add balloons*

INTRODUCTION

After creating solid models or assemblies, you can generate the two-dimensional (2D) drawing views of the models or assemblies. These views are the lifeline for all manufacturing systems because the machinist at the shop floor or the machine floor mostly needs the 2D drawing of a model or assembly for manufacturing. SolidWorks provides a specialized environment, known as the **Drawing** mode, which has all tools required for generating and modifying the drawing views, and adding dimensions and annotations to them. In other words, you can get the final drawing for the shop floor by using this mode of SolidWorks. You can also sketch the 2D drawings in the **Drawing** mode of SolidWorks by using the sketching tools provided in this mode.

In other words, there are two type of drafting methods available in SolidWorks: Generative drafting and Interactive drafting. Generative drafting is a technique of generating the drawing views of a solid model or an assembly. Interactive drafting is a technique of sketching a drawing view by using the sketching tools available in the **Drawing** mode. In this chapter, you will learn about generating the drawing views of parts or assemblies.

One of the major advantages of using SolidWorks is that this software has bidirectionally associative property. This property ensures that the modifications made in a model in the **Part** mode reflect in the **Assembly** and **Drawing** modes, and vice-versa.

WORKING WITH DRAWING VIEWS-I

Part Description

In this section, you will generate the front view, top view, section view, detail view, and isometric view of the Rim created in Chapter 3. Also, you will generate dimensions, add annotations, and change the display style of the drawing views. You will use the Standard A4 Landscape sheet format for generating the views. **(Expected time: 40 min)**

Starting a New Drawing Document

To generate the drawing views, you need to start a new drawing document. To start a new drawing document, you need to invoke the New SolidWorks Document dialog box.

1. Invoke the **New SOLIDWORKS Document** dialog box and choose the **Drawing** button, as shown in Figure 12-1. Next, choose the **OK** button; a new drawing document starts and the **Sheet Format/Size** dialog box is displayed. Figure 12-2 shows the initial screen of the drawing document with the **Sheet Format/Size** dialog box.

2. Select the **A4(ANSI) Landscape** sheet from the list box of the **Sheet Format/Size** dialog box and choose the **OK** button; the new drawing document starts with the standard A4 sheet. Also, the **Model View PropertyManager** is displayed and you are prompted to select a part or an assembly to generate the drawing view, refer to Figure 12-3.

Note

*If you choose the **Cancel** button from the **Sheet Format/Size** dialog box, a blank custom sheet of size 431.80 mm x 279.40 mm will be inserted into the drawing document.*

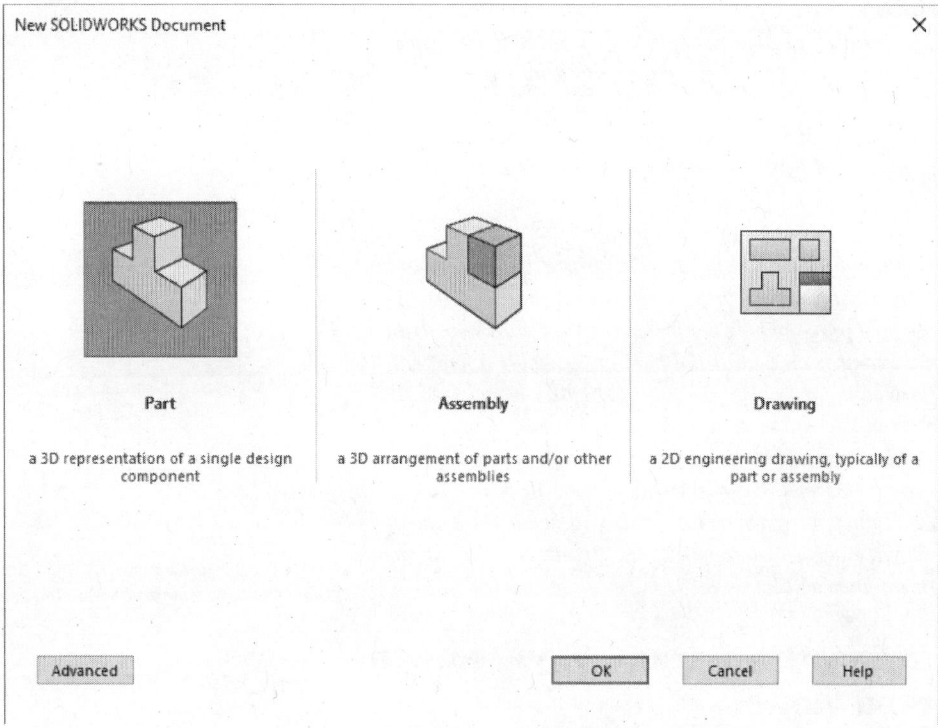

Figure 12-1 *The New* ***SOLIDWORKS Document*** *dialog box*

The **Model View PropertyManager** is used to generate the base view of the model in the drawing sheet. You can also invoke this PropertyManager by choosing the **Model View** button from the **View Layout CommandManager**, if it is not invoked by default.

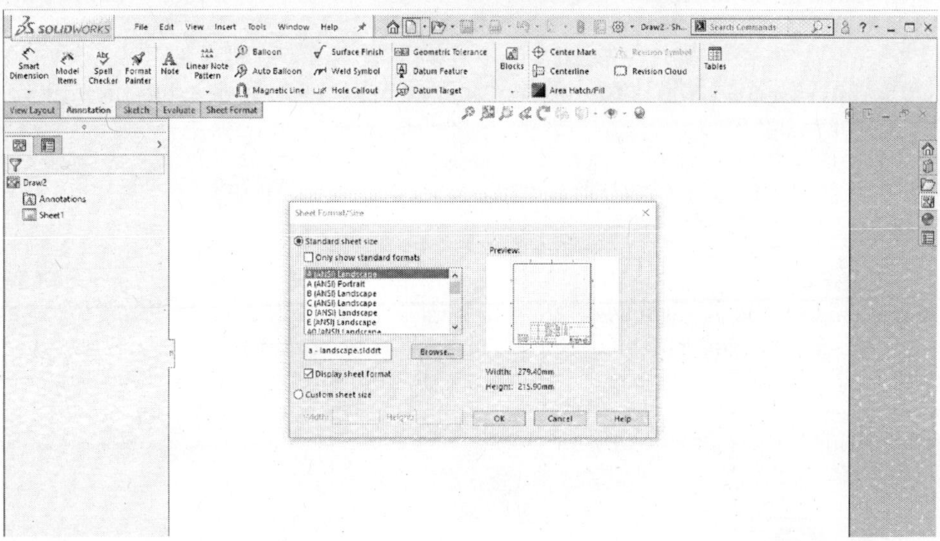

Figure 12-2 *Initial screen with the* ***Sheet Format/Size*** *dialog box*

Note

*The **Model View PropertyManager** will be displayed when you start a new drawing document. Also, its appearance will depend on whether any part or assembly document is opened or not. If any part or assembly document is opened, it will be displayed in the **Open documents** selection box of the **Part/Assembly to Insert** rollout of the PropertyManager. You can preview the part or assembly document by expanding the **Thumbnail Preview** rollout. You can also invoke the drawing environment directly from the part or assembly document. If you start a new drawing document from within the part or assembly document, the part or the assembly will automatically be selected and it will enable you to place the desired views using the **View Palette** that will be displayed on the right side of the drawing sheet. This method of starting a new drawing document is recommended when the part or assembly document for which you want to generate the drawing views is opened in another window.*

***Figure 12-3** The **Model View** PropertyManager*

Generating the Parent View and the Projected Views

Before you generate the drawing views, you need to confirm whether the projection type for the current sheet is set to the third angle.

1. Close the **Model View PropertyManager** by choosing the **Cancel** button. Select **Sheet1** from the FeatureManager design tree and then right-click on it to display a shortcut menu. Next, choose the **Properties** option from the shortcut menu; the **Sheet Properties** dialog box is displayed.

2. Select the **Third angle** radio button from the **Type of projection** area and then choose the **Apply Changes** button.

3. Invoke the **Model View PropertyManager** by choosing the **Model View** button from the **View Layout CommandManager**.

4. Choose the **Browse** button from the **Part/Assembly** to **Insert** rollout of the PropertyManager; the **Open** dialog box is displayed. Next, browse to the Motor Cycle Project folder and then double-click on the Rim created in Chapter 3; the **Model View PropertyManager** is modified and the options related to generating the standard views are displayed in it, refer to Figure 12-4. Also, the cursor is changed into the view cursor and a rectangular shape empty drawing view is attached to the cursor.

5. Make sure the **Front** button is chosen in the **Orientation** rollout, the **Auto-start projected** view check box is selected in the **Options** rollout, and the **Hidden Lines Removed** button is chosen in the **Display Style** rollout of the PropertyManager.

   The buttons in the **Orientation** rollout of the PropertyManager are used to specify the orientation of the drawing view. You can select the additional orientations by selecting the check box corresponding to the required orientation in the More views list box area.

   If the **Auto-start projected view** check box in the **Options** rollout is selected, the **Projected View PropertyManager** will be invoked immediately after generating the front view. This PropertyManager is used to generate the projected views of the model.

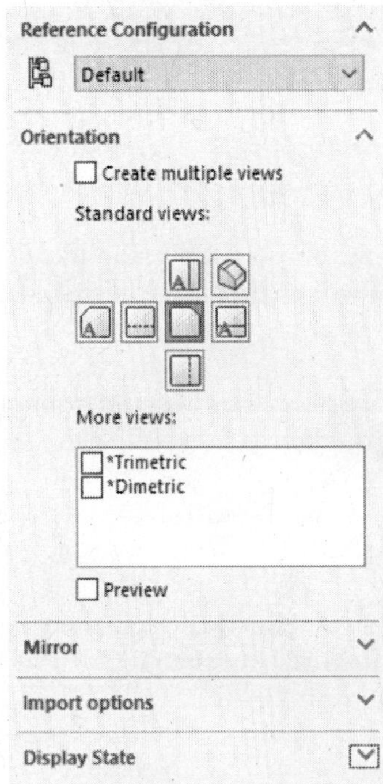

*Figure 12-4 Partial view of the **Model View PropertyManager** displayed on selecting the model to generate the drawing views*

> **Note**
> *You can change the orientation of the model view even after placing it. To do so, double-click on the required view; the **Drawing View PropertyManager** will be displayed. Select the required view from the **Orientation** rollout; the orientation of the view will be modified automatically.*

6. Select the **Preview** check box from the **Orientation** rollout of the PropertyManager to preview the drawing view before it is placed. Next, select the **Use Custom Scale** radio button in the **Scale** rollout of the PropertyManager and select the **1:10** option from the drop-down.

> **Note**
> *The **Use sheet scale** radio button is selected by default in the **Scale** rollout. Therefore, when you select a template to start a new drawing sheet, a default scale is automatically defined to generate the drawing views. To define a custom scale for a model view, select the **Use custom scale** radio button and select the scale factor from the drop-down list below this radio button. If you select the **User Defined** option from this drop-down list, then an edit box will be displayed below the drop-down list enabling you to specify the required scale factor.*

7. Move the view cursor horizontally toward the left of the title block of the drawing sheet and specify the placement point of the view by clicking the left mouse button, refer to Figure 12-5; the front view of the model is generated and placed at this location. Note that since you have selected the option to start the projected views immediately after generating the front view, the **Projected View PropertyManager** is invoked and the preview of the projected view is attached to the cursor. This view is being generated by referencing the front view as the parent view.

8. Move the cursor above the front view and click at a point to place the top view, refer to Figure 12-5. On doing so, the top view of the model is generated and the preview of another projected view with the front view as the base view is attached to the cursor.

9. Move the cursor diagonally upward; the preview of the isometric view is displayed. Specify a point to place the isometric view. Next, exit the **Projected View PropertyManager**.

   You can also change the location of the drawing views after placing them. In this section, you will change the current location of the isometric view close to the top right corner of the drawing sheet.

10. Move the cursor over the isometric view; the bounding box of the view is displayed in orange. Next, click to select the view.

11. Move the cursor on one of the borderlines of the view; the cursor is replaced by the move cursor.

12. Press and hold the left mouse button and drag the view close to the upper right corner of the drawing sheet. The drawing sheet after generating and moving the drawing view is shown in Figure 12-5.

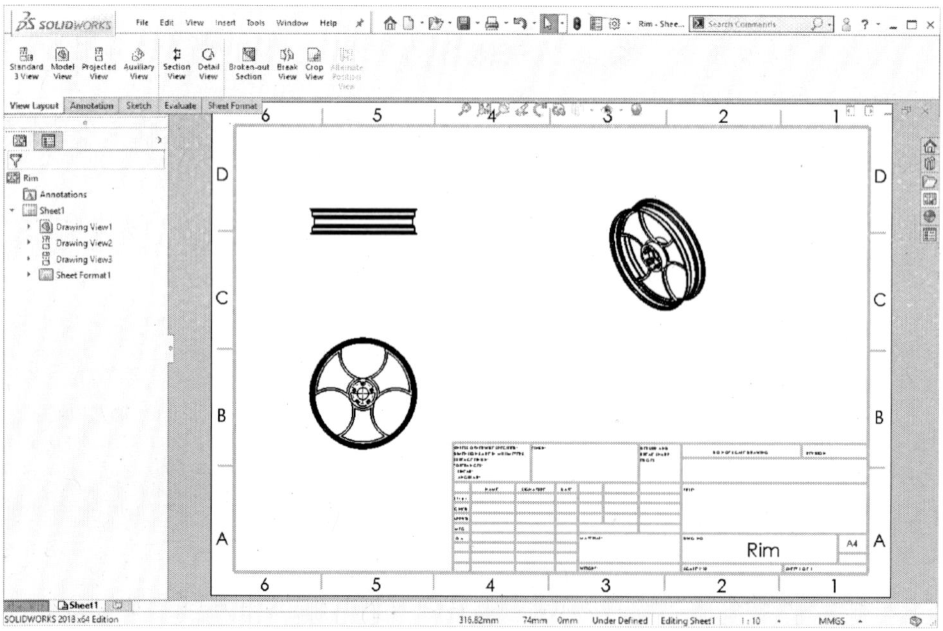

Figure 12-5 The drawing sheet after generating the front, top, and isometric views

Note

*The tangent edges of the drawing views shown in Figure 12-5 have been removed for clarity. To remove the tangent edges from the drawing view, select the view and right-click to display the shortcut menu. Next, choose the **Tangent Edge > Tangent Edges Removed** from the shortcut menu.*

Tip

*In SolidWorks, you can also generate three default orthographic views of the specified part or assembly by using the **Standard 3 View** tool. To create the standard views automatically, choose the **Standard 3 View** button from the **View Layout CommandManager**; the **Standard 3 View PropertyManager** will be displayed. If any part or assembly document is opened in the current session of SolidWorks, it will be displayed in the Open documents list box of the **Part/Assembly to Insert** rollout.*

*You can select the document from this list box or choose the **Browse** button to select the part or assembly document, if no documents are opened. As soon as you select a document, three standard views will be generated based on the default scale set for the current sheet.*

Generating the Section Views

Section views are generated by chopping a portion of the existing view using a cutting plane (defined by the sketched lines) so that the parent view can be viewed from a direction normal to the cutting plane.

1. Choose the **Section View** button from the **View Layout CommandManager**; the **Section View PropertyManage**r is displayed and you are prompted to sketch a line to continue the creation of the view.

   In SolidWorks, you can use the **Section View** tool to create a full section view or a half section view. A full section view is defined by using a single line segment, whereas a half section view is defined by using three line segments. Note that the section plane for a full section view can be defined after invoking the **Section View** tool. But to generate a half section view, you need to draw the line segments to define the section plane before invoking the **Section View** tool. In this section, you will create the full section view.

2. Move the cursor closer to the center of the front view and then move it vertically upward; a doted line is displayed. Next, click the left mouse button to specify the start point of the section line when the cursor crosses all the entities of the front view. After specifying the start point of the section line, move the cursor vertically downward and specify the endpoint of the section line, refer to Figure 12-6. Choose the **OK** button from the **Section View PropertyManager**; the preview of the section view is attached to the cursor. Also, some other options are displayed in the **Section View PropertyManager**.

3. Move the cursor horizontally toward the right and specify a point on the drawing sheet to place the section view; the name of the section view is displayed below it, refer to Figure 12-6. Next, click anywhere in the drawing sheet to exit the PropertyManager. Now, you can zoom in the drawing sheet to view the hatch pattern in the section view.

Note

The default hatch pattern in the section view depends upon the material assigned to the model. Sometimes, you may need to increase or decrease the spacing of the hatch pattern, if it is not correct. To change the spacing of the hatch pattern, double-click on the hatch pattern in the section view; the ***Area Hatch/Fill PropertyManager*** *is displayed with the* ***Material crosshatch*** *check box selected but the other options are not available. If you want to make the other options also available, clear the* ***Material crosshatch*** *check box. Next, specify the required type of hatch pattern using these options.*

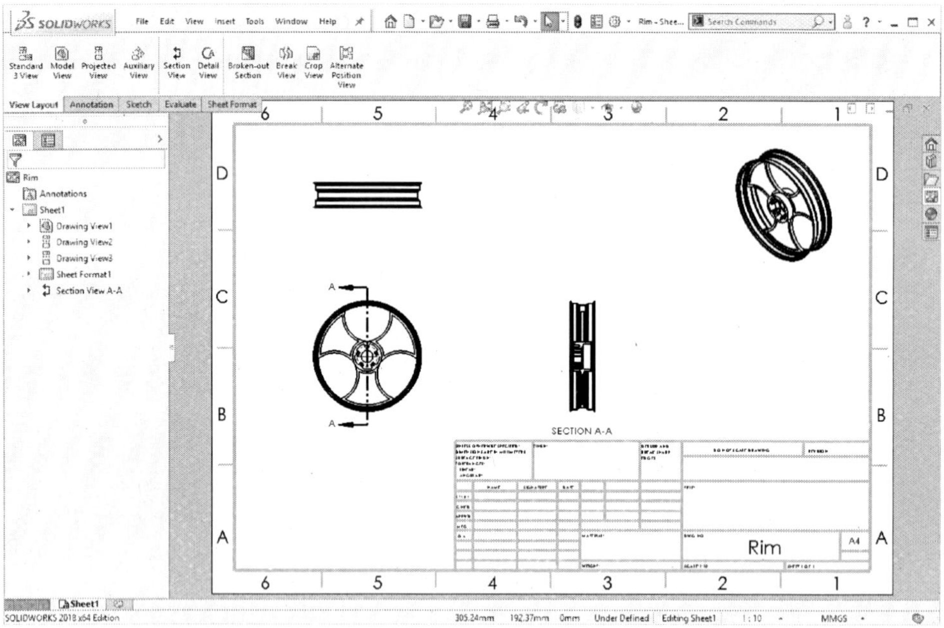

Figure 12-6 *The drawing sheet after generating the section view*

Generating the Detail View

Next, you need to generate the detail view of the inner circular feature of the model. Before doing so, you need to activate the view from which you will derive the detail view.

1. Activate the Front view and then choose the **Detail View** button from the **View Layout CommandManager**; the **Detail View PropertyManager** is displayed and you are prompted to sketch a circle to continue creating the view. Also, the cursor is replaced by the circle cursor.

   The **Detail View** tool is used to display the details of a portion of an existing view. You can select the portion whose detailing has to be shown in the parent view. On doing so, the selected portion will be magnified and placed as a separate view. You can control the magnification of the detail view.

2. Draw a small circle around the inner circular feature of the model in the front view, refer to Figure 12-7. As you draw the circle, the detail view is attached to the cursor.

3. Place the detail view on the right of the drawing sheet and above the title block, refer to Figure 12-7.

4. Select the **Use custom scale** radio button in the **Scale** rollout of the PropertyManager. Then, select the **User Defined** option from the drop-down list below the **Use custom scale** radio button; the edit box is enabled below the drop-down list.

   Note that you may need to move the detail view and its label so that the view does not overlap the title block, refer to Figure 12-7.

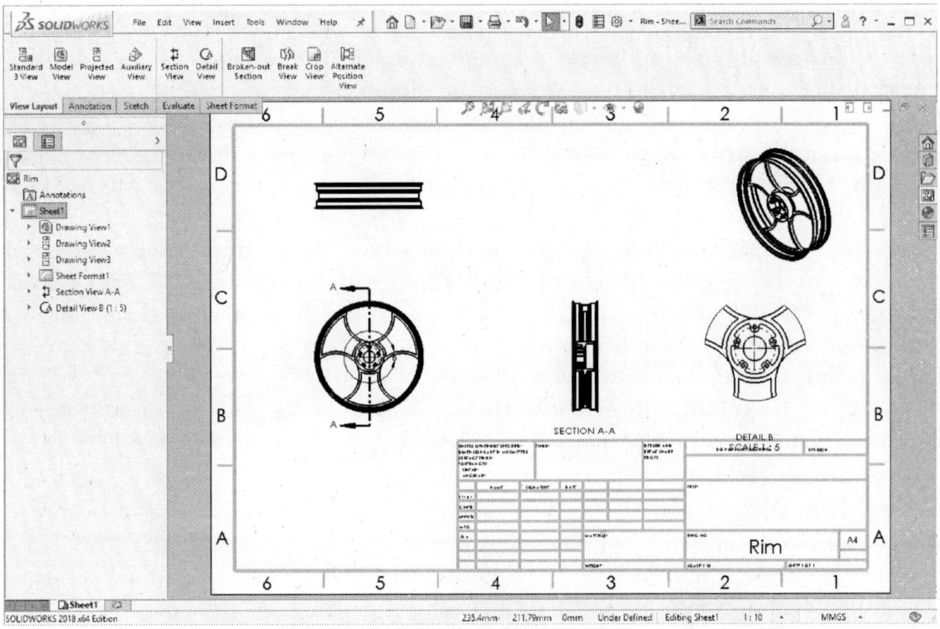

Figure 12-7 The drawing sheet after generating the detail view

5. Set **1.4** as the value of the scale factor of the detail view and choose the **OK** button from the **Detail View PropertyManager**; the detail view is placed with its name and scale value.

   After generating all the required views of the model, you will generate their dimensions and add annotations to them. Also, you will change the display style of the top view to hidden lines visible and the isometric view to the shaded mode.

Applying the Document Settings

Before generating the dimensions of the model, you need to configure the document settings. After specifying these settings, you can view the dimensions and other annotations in the current sheet properly.

1. Invoke the **Document Properties - Drafting Standard** dialog box by choosing the **Options** button from the Menu Bar; the **System Options - General dialog** box is displayed. Next, choose the **Document Properties** tab.

2. Choose **Annotations > Notes** from the area on the left of the **Document Properties - Drafting Standard** dialog box.

3. Choose the **Font** button from the **Text** area of the dialog box; the **Choose Font** dialog box is displayed.

4. Select the **Points** radio button from the **Height** area and set **14** as the value of the font size in the list box.

5. Choose the **OK** button from the **Choose Fon**t dialog box.

6. Choose the **Dimension** option from the area on the left; the related options are displayed on the right. Also, set **14** as the font size for the dimensions.

7. Make sure the units are set to mm, and then set the height, width, and length of the arrows as **1.25 mm**, **4 mm**, and **6** mm respectively in their respective edit boxes in the **Arrows** area.

8. Choose **View > Section** from the left of the dialog box; the related options are displayed on the right. Set the height, width, and length of the section arrows as **2.5 mm**, **6 mm**, and **12.5 mm** respectively in their respective edit boxes in the **Section/view size** area. Also, set **14** as the font size of the Section View.

9. Similarly, select the **Detail** option under the **View** head and set **14** as the font size. Next, choose the **OK** button from the dialog box to exit it.

Generating the Dimensions

Next, you need to generate dimensions using the **Model Items** tool. If you do not select any view while generating the dimensions using the **Model Items** tool, all dimensions will be displayed in all views. Sometimes, the dimensions may overlap each other. Therefore, you will select the view in which you need to generate the dimension and then you will invoke the **Model Items** tool.

1. Select the detail view and choose the **Model Items** button from the **Annotation CommandManager**; the **Model Items PropertyManager** is displayed and the name of the selected view is displayed in the **Source/Destination** rollout.

   The **Model Items** tool is used to generate the annotations or dimensions that were added to the model while creating it in the **Part** mode.

2. Select the **Entire model** option from the **Source** drop-down list and choose the **OK** button from the **Model Items PropertyManager**; the dimensions of the model that can be displayed in the selected view are generated.

   Note that the dimensions generated are scattered arbitrarily on the drawing sheet. Therefore, you need to arrange the dimensions by moving them to appropriate locations. Also, you need to delete the dimensions of the inner portion of the front view as these dimensions can be shown in the detail view.

3. Delete all dimensions of the inner portion of the front view one by one by selecting them and pressing the DELETE key. Also, delete the dimensions whose values are **8.5 mm** and **2.5 mm**. Next, arrange the remaining dimensions of the front view one by one by selecting

and dragging them to the desired locations. The drawing view after deleting the unwanted dimensions and arranging the remaining dimensions is shown in Figure 12-8.

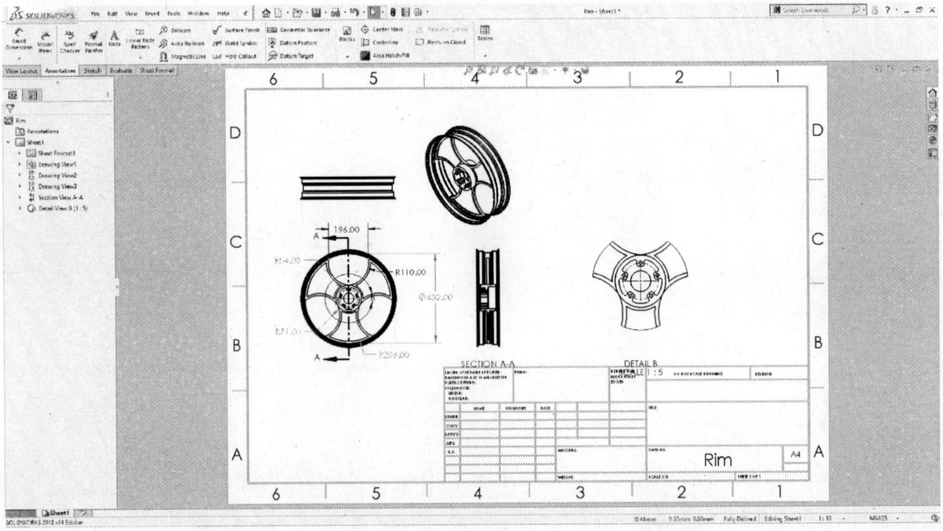

***Figure 12-8** The drawing sheet after generating the dimensions on the front view*

Note

*You can also use the **Smart Dimension** tool to add reference dimensions to the drawing views in the Drawing mode of SolidWorks. Adding dimensions to the drawing views by using the **Smart Dimension** tool is similar to applying dimensions to a sketch in the sketching environment. To invoke this tool, choose the **Smart Dimension** button from the **Annotation CommandManager**.*

Applying the Datum Feature Symbol to the Drawing View

After generating the dimensions, you need to add the datum feature symbol to the drawing view. The datum feature symbols are used as the datum reference for adding the geometric tolerance to the drawing views.

1. Select the outermost circular edge from the front view and then choose the **Datum Feature** button from the **Annotation CommandManager**; the **Datum Feature PropertyManager** is displayed and a datum callout is attached to the cursor.

2. Place the datum symbol at an appropriate location, refer to Figure 12-9. Next, choose the **OK** button from the **Datum Feature PropertyManager**.

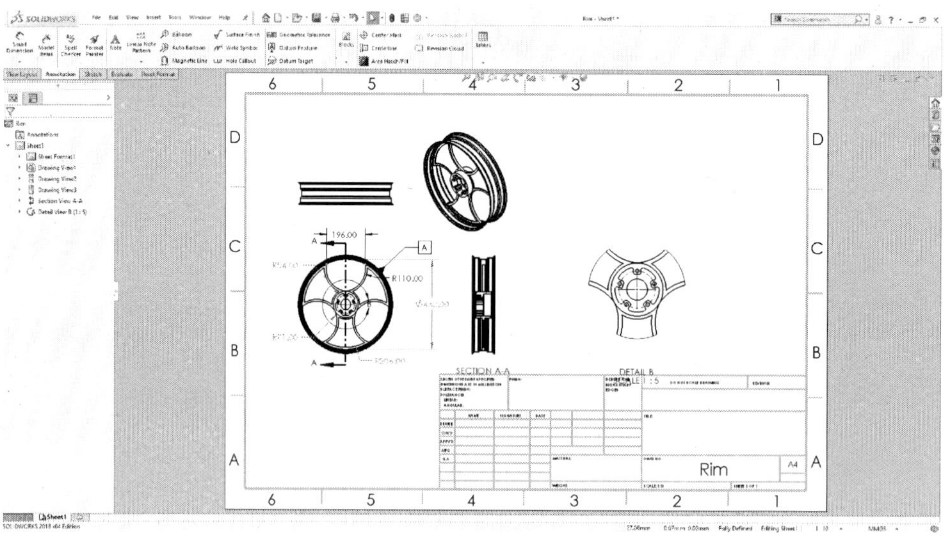

Figure 12-9 The drawing sheet after adding the datum feature symbol

Applying the Geometric Tolerance to the Drawing View

After defining the datum feature symbol, you will add the geometric tolerance to the drawing view.

1. Select the circular edge that has a diameter of 432 mm from the front view and choose the **Geometric Tolerance** button from the **Annotation CommandManager**; the Properties dialog box is displayed. This dialog box is used to specify the parameters of the geometric tolerance.

2. Click on the arrow in drop-down list of the first row; the **Symbols** flyout is displayed. Next, choose the **Concentricity** option from this flyout.

3. Enter **0.002** in the **Tolerance 1** edit box. Next, enter **A** in the **Primary** edit box to define the primary datum reference.

4. Choose the **OK** button from the **Properties** dialog box; the geometric tolerance is attached to the selected circular edge. You may need to move the geometric tolerance, if it overlaps the dimensions. Figure 12-10 shows the drawing view after adding and rearranging the geometric tolerance.

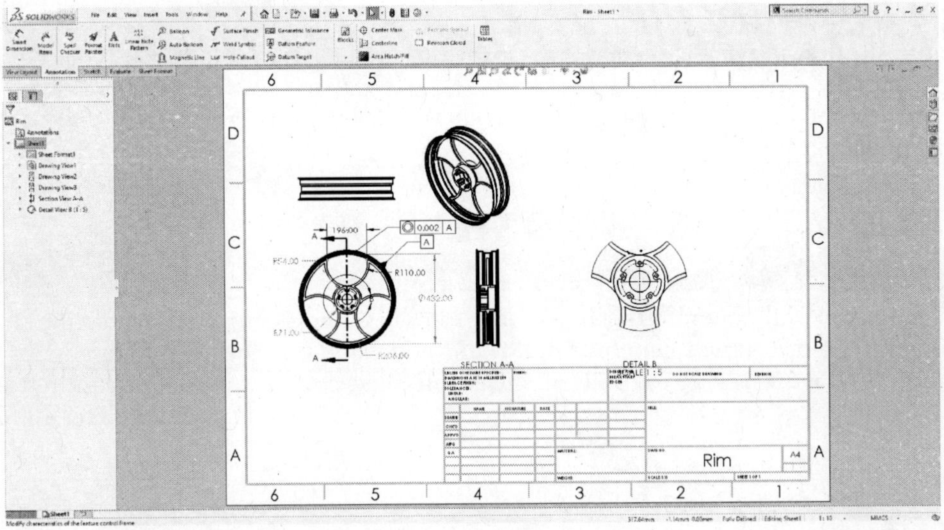

Figure 12-10 *The drawing sheet after adding the geometric tolerance to the drawing view*

Changing the View Display Style

After adding all annotations to the drawing views, you need to change the display setting of the drawing views.

1. Select the top view from the drawing sheet; the **Drawing View PropertyManager** is displayed. Next, choose the **Hidden Lines Visible** button from the **Display Style** rollout of the PropertyManager; the hidden lines are displayed in the selected drawing views.

2. Select the isometric view from the drawing sheet and then choose the **Shaded With Edges** button from the **Display Style** rollout of the PropertyManager. Next, click anywhere in the drawing area to exit the PropertyManager. Figure 12-11 shows the final drawing sheet after changing the display view settings.

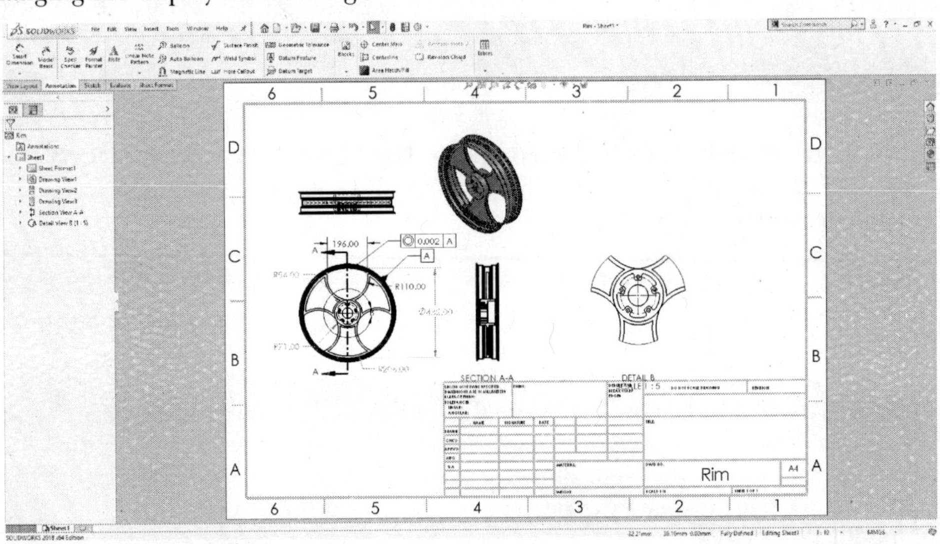

Figure 12-11 *The final drawing sheet after changing the display style of the drawing view*

Saving the Document

After creating the drawing views, you need to save the document in the Motor Cycle Project folder.

1. Save the document with the name Rim.slddrw in the Motor Cycle Project folder. Next, close the document.

WORKING WITH DRAWING VIEWS-II

Part Description

In this section, you will generate the front view, top view, and isometric view of the Motor Cycle Assembly. Also, you will generate BOM and add balloons to the components of the assembly, refer to Figure 12-12. You will use the empty sheet format for generating the views.

(Expected time: 40 min)

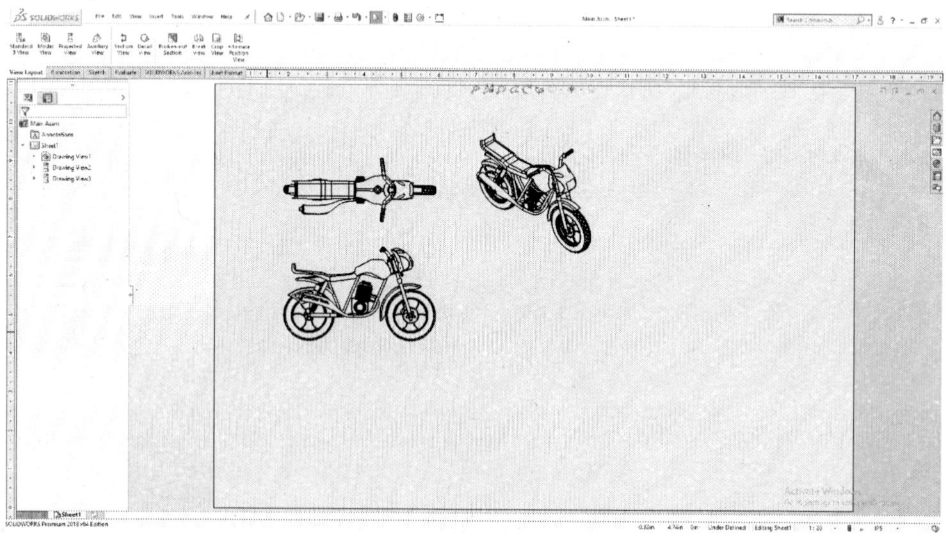

Figure 12-12 *The drawing sheet*

Starting a New Drawing Document from the Assembly Document

You will open the Motor Cycle Assembly in the Assembly environment and then invoke the drawing document from it.

1. Open Motor Cycle Assembly in the **Assembly** environment and then choose **File > Make Drawing from Assembly** from the SolidWorks menus; a new drawing document starts and the **Sheet Format/Size** dialog box is displayed.

2. Select the **A4(ANSI) Landscape** sheet from the list box in the **Sheet Format/Size** dialog box and choose the **Cancel** button; a new blank drawing document starts and the **View Palette** task pane is displayed on the right of the drawing window, as shown in Figure 12-13. The **View Palette** task pane displays the preview of all views of the assembly.

*Figure 12-13 A new drawing document with the **View Palette***

Starting the Parent View and the Projected Views

Before you generate the drawing views, you need to confirm whether the projection type for the current sheet is set to the third angle.

1. Click anywhere on the sheet to close the **View Palette** task pane. Select **Sheet1** from the **FeatureManager Design Tree** and then right-click on it. Next, choose the **Properties** option from the shortcut menu displayed; the **Sheet Properties** dialog box is displayed.

2. In this dialog box, select the **Third angle** radio button from the **Type of projection** area and choose the **Apply Changes** button.

3. Next, open the task pane, choose the **View Palette** taskpane.

4. Select the **Front** view from the **View Palette** task pane and drag it to the lower left corner of the drawing sheet. Drop the view at this location to place the front view, refer to Figure 12-12. As soon as you specify the placement point, the **Projected View PropertyManager** is invoked and the preview of the projected view is attached to the cursor. This view is generated by referencing the front view as the parent view.

5. Move the cursor above the front view and specify a point to place the top view, refer to Figure 12-12. The top view of the model is generated and the preview of another projected view with the front view as the base view gets attached to the cursor.

6. Move the cursor diagonally upward; the preview of the isometric view is displayed. Specify a point to place the isometric view. Next, exit the **Projected View PropertyManager**.

7. Move the cursor over the isometric view; the bounding box of the view is displayed in orange. Next, click to select the view.

8. Move the cursor on one of the borderlines of the view; the cursor is replaced by the move cursor.

9. Press and hold the left mouse button and drag the view to the new location, refer to Figure 12-12.

Generating the BOM

Next, you need to generate the BOM. The BOM generated in SolidWorks is parametric. If a component is deleted or added in the assembly, the change is automatically reflected in the BOM. However, before generating the BOM, you need to set its text parameters.

1. Invoke the **Document Properties - Drafting Standard** dialog box and choose **Annotations > Notes** from the area on the left of the dialog box.

2. Choose the **Font** button from the **Text** area of the dialog box; the **Choose Font** dialog box is invoked. Select the **Points** radio button from the **Height** area and set **14** as the value of the font size from the list box.

3. Choose the **OK** button from the **Choose Font** dialog box. Similarly, change the text height of balloons to **14** points. Next, close the dialog box.

4. Select the isometric view and choose **Tables > Bill of Materials** from the **Annotation CommandManager**; the **Bill of Materials PropertyManager** is displayed.

5. Choose the **OK** button from the **Bill of Materials PropertyManager**; the BOM is generated and attached to the cursor.

6. Place the BOM at the upper right corner of the drawing sheet by clicking the left mouse button, refer to Figure 12-14.

   You will notice that the **Description** column is also displayed in the BOM. As this column is not required, you need to delete it.

7. Move the cursor over the **Description** heading and right-click when a down arrow is displayed. Choose **Delete > Column** from the shortcut menu displayed; the **Description** column is deleted. Next, move the BOM and adjust it in the drawing sheet such that its upper right corner is attached with the upper right corner of the drawing sheet. The drawing sheet after generating the BOM and deleting the **Description** column is shown in Figure 12-15.

Note

If the color of the BOM is gray and it is not clearly visible, then to make it visible, invoke the ***System Options - Colors*** *dialog box. Then, select* ***Annotations, Imported*** *from the* ***Color scheme settings*** *list box and change its color to black.*

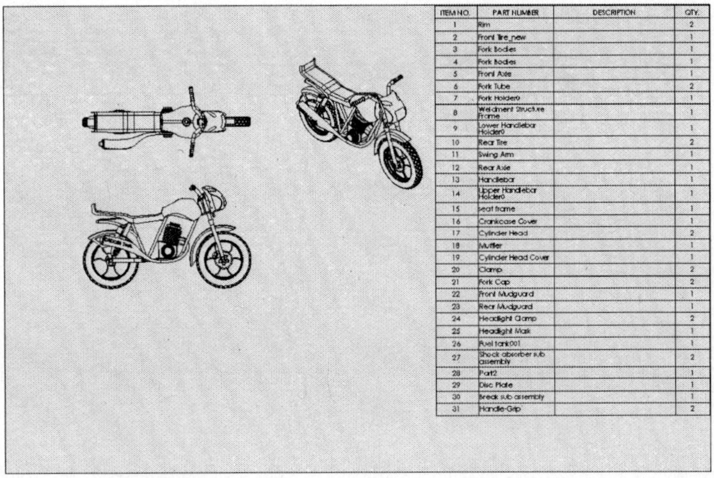

Figure 12-14 BOM generated at drawing sheet

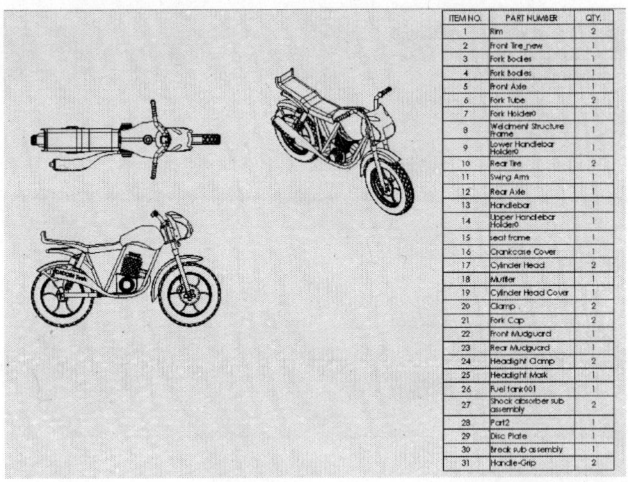

*Figure 12-15 BOM generated after deleting the **Description** column*

Adding Balloons to the Components

After generating the BOM, you need to add balloons to the components. Before proceeding further, make sure that you have changed the font height of balloons to 14 points as discussed in the previous section.

1. Select the isometric view and choose the **Auto Balloon** button from the **Annotation CommandManager**; balloons are automatically added to all components in the isometric view and the **Auto Balloon PropertyManager** is also displayed.

2. Choose the Layout Balloons to Square button from the **Balloon Layout** rollout of the PropertyManager. Make sure that the **Ignore multiple instances** check box is selected in the **Balloon Layout** rollout so that the multiple instances of any component are ignored.

3. Select **2 Characters** from the **Size** drop-down list in the **Balloon Settings** rollout. Next, choose **OK** to close this PropertyManager. Figure 12-16 shows the final drawing sheet after adding balloons to components.

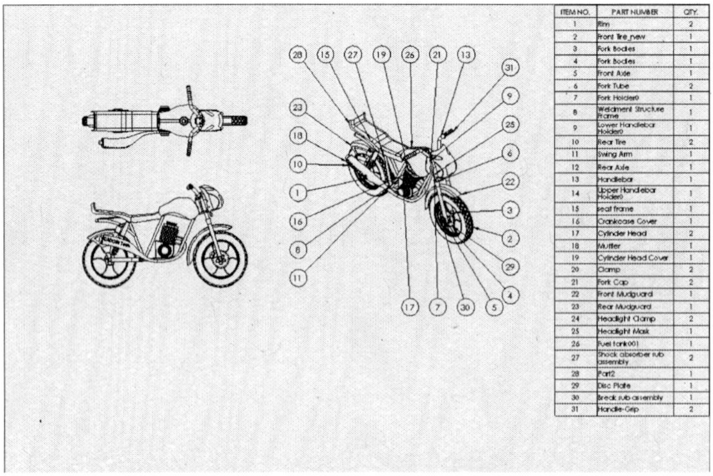

Figure 12-16 *Drawing sheet after adding balloons*

Note

The balloons of the components should not overlap the drawing views. If any balloons intersects any drawing views, then drag and place the corresponding balloon at a new location.

Saving the Document

Now, you will save the document in the **Motor Cycle Project** folder.

1. Save the document in the **Motor Cycle Project** folder with the name Motor Cycle Assembly.slddrw. Next, close the document.

Self-Evaluation Test

Answer the following questions and then compare them to those given at the end of this chapter:

1. Which of the following tools is used to generate the default orthographic views of the model automatically?

   (a) **Standard 3 View** (b) **Projecting View**
   (c) **Auxiliary View** (d) **Model View**

2. To start a new drawing document from the part document, choose the __________ option from the Menu Bar.

3. The ________________ **PropertyManager** is used to generate the base view of a model.

4. On selecting the ___________ check box, the projected views start immediately after generating the front view.

5. The _______________ view displays the details of a portion of an existing view.

6. You can create automatic balloons by using the _____________ tool.

7. In the **Drawing** mode of SolidWorks, you can generate drawing views from a model as well as draw them using the sketching tools. (T/F)

Review Questions

Answer the following questions:

1. Which of the following PropertyManagers is invoked to add automatic balloons to the selected drawing view?

   (a) **AutoBalloon** (b) **Balloon**
   (c) **Properties** (d) **CenterMark**

2. In which of the following shapes is the detail view boundary displayed by default?

   (a) Circle (b) Ellipse
   (c) Rectangular (d) None of these

3. In technical terms, creating a 2D drawing in a drawing document is known as ___________.

4. To change the scale of a drawing view, first select the drawing view and then select the _________ radio button from the **Scale** rollout.

5. You can change the model display setting from the hidden lines removed to the hidden lines visible, wireframe, or shaded by using the options available in the __________ toolbar.

6. You cannot add annotations to a part while creating it in SolidWorks. (T/F)

7. The **Standard sheet** size radio button is selected by default in the **Sheet Format/Size** dialog box. (T/F)

Answers to Self-Evaluation Test

1. (a), 2. **Make Drawing from Part**, 3. **Model View**, 4. **Auto-start projected view**, 5. **Detail**, 6. **AutoBalloon** , 7. T

Index

CAD/CAM/CIM/GIS/ANIMATION/CIVIL BOOKS

by **Prof. Sham Tickoo** (Purdue University, USA and Autodesk Authorised Author)

Autocad 2019
Problem Solving Approach
Basic and Intermediate
ISBN 978-93-8817-628-6
Price: ₹ 1499/-

AutoCAD MEP 2018
for Designers
ISBN 978-93-8655-161-0
Price: ₹ 749/-

AutoCAD Plant 3D 2018
for Designers
ISBN 978-93-8655-171-9
Price: ₹ 799/-

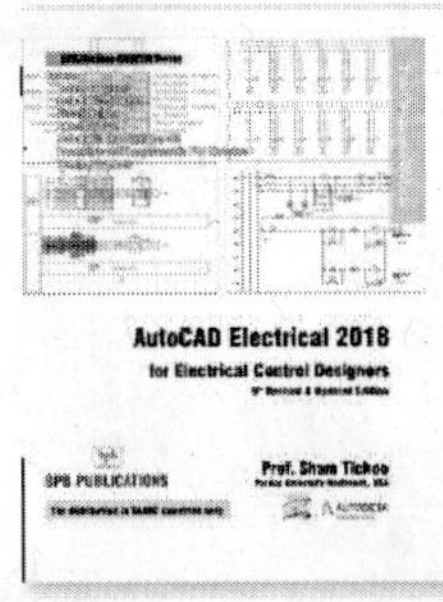

AutoCAD Electrical 2018
for Electrical Control Designers
ISBN 978-93-8655-162-7
Price: ₹ 1099/-

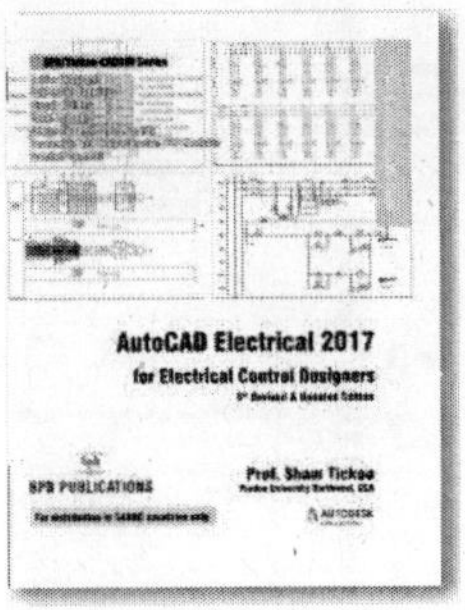

AutoCAD Electrical 2017
for Electrical Control Designers
ISBN 978-93-8655-123-8
Price: ₹ 1099/-

CATIA V5-6R 2017
for Designers
ISBN 978-93-8728-404-3
Price: ₹ 1099/-

CATIA V5-6R 2016
for Designers
ISBN 978-93-8655-119-1
Price: ₹ 1099/-

AutoCAD LT 2017
For Designers
ISBN 978-93-8655-125-2
Price: ₹ 1299/-

MAXON CINEMA
4D R19 Studio
A Tutorial Approach
ISBN 978-93-8728-405-0
Price: ₹ 799/-

MAXON CINEMA
4D R18 Studio
A Tutorial Approach
ISBN 978-93-8655-111-5
Price: ₹ 799/-

Creo Parametric 4.0
for Designers
ISBN 978-93-8655-165-8
Price: ₹ 1099/-

Creo Parametric 5.0
for Designers
ISBN 978-93-8817-630-9
Price: ₹ 1299/-

Available on **www.bpbonline.com** and all leading book stores.

bpb PUBLICATIONS | #1 Publisher of Computer Books | 62 Years of Excellence | OVER 90 Million Books Sold Worldwide